Sabri Boubaker • Duc Khuong Nguyen
Editors

Corporate Governance in Emerging Markets

Theories, Practices and Cases

Springer

Editors
Sabri Boubaker
Department of Accounting and Finance
Champagne School of Management
(Groupe ESC Troyes en Champagne)
Troyes
France

Duc Khuong Nguyen
IPAG Research Lab
IPAG Business School
Paris
France

ISSN 2196-7075
ISSN 2196-7083 (electronic)
ISBN 978-3-642-44954-3
ISBN 978-3-642-44955-0 (eBook)
DOI 10.1007/978-3-642-44955-0
Springer Heidelberg New York Dordrecht London

Library of Congress Control Number: 2014934665

Printed on acid-free paper

Springer is part of Springer Science+Business Media (www.springer.com)

Foreword

Corporate governance has long been recognized as an important area of scholarship in many fields that include economics, finance, law, and management. Corporate governance practices vary from one country to another due to differing legal and institutional settings, economic conditions, and cultural disparities around the world. As such, there is a significant need for corporate governance scholars to understand the institutional context. Those that are interested in emerging markets naturally need specialized knowledge of such markets. Said differently, solutions to corporate governance problems are not merely adoptable from one country to the next, given the differences in legal, institutional, economic, and cultural conditions.

China represents a classic case in point. China has had the fastest growing economy for many years in a row, yet corporate governance is vastly different in China than in western contexts. Corporate governance legal rules are not adopted in China in a way that corresponds to western style legal settings. Rather, informal institutions appear to be extremely important in the context of China, as explained in the widely referenced study of Allen et al. (2005). Similar evidence is found in India (Allen et al. 2006).

Given the importance of context in corporate governance scholarship, it is extremely useful to have a book dedicated to corporate governance in emerging markets. This volume edited by leading scholars Sabri Boubaker and Duc Khuong Nguyen is an excellent source on topic. This book comprises 25 chapters on corporate governance in emerging markets. There are a total of 59 coauthors representing 22 countries (Australia, Bangladesh, Brazil, China, Estonia, France, Germany, Hong Kong, India, Indonesia, Italy, Japan, Morocco, the Philippines, Poland, Russia, Spain, Switzerland, Thailand, the United Kingdom, Ukraine, and the United States). The authors are among the top scholars in the field of corporate governance and have specialized expertise in emerging markets. Overall, this book represents a significant contribution to the literature on corporate governance in emerging markets, and as such, it is an invaluable reference for academics, practitioners, and policymakers alike.

There are five parts to this book. Part I addresses issues pertaining to Corporate Governance and Firm Performance, which represents the first four chapters. Data are presented from India (Chaps. 1, 3, and 4), China (Chaps. 2 and 4), and Hong Kong, Indonesia, the Philippines, and Thailand (Chap. 2). The authors present analyses of shareholder rights (Chaps. 1 and 2), product market competition (Chap. 3), and boards (Chap. 4). The authors show how firm value is affected by governance in these specific contexts.

Part II (Chaps. 5, 6, 7, 8 and 9) covers topics on Corporate Governance and Firm Behavior. Data are presented from Bangladesh (Chap. 5), China (Chap. 6), Russia (Chap. 7), and multi-country samples (Chaps. 8 and 9). Topics covered include family firms and board structure (Chap. 5), earnings management (Chap. 6), organizational behavior (Chap. 7), accounting conservatism (Chap. 8), and privatization (Chap. 9). The authors explain how corporate governance has a pronounced impact in each of these specific contexts.

Part III (Chaps. 10, 11, 12, 13, 14, 15 and 16) examines Corporate Governance Practices in Emerging Markets. Data are presented from the Ukraine (Chap. 10), Estonia (Chap. 11), Poland (Chap. 12), Eastern Europe (Chap. 13), the Philippines and Switzerland (Chap. 14), Nigeria (Chap. 15), and Bangladesh (Chap. 16). Topics covered include the evolution of corporate governance standards (Chaps. 10, 11, 14, 15, and 16), audit committees and supervisory boards (Chap. 12), and multinational companies (Chap. 13). The authors provide useful analyses of differences in governance practices and standards across countries and over time.

Part IV (Chaps. 17, 18, 19, 20, and 21) studies practical issues surrounding corporate governance laws and reforms. Data are presented from Bangladesh (Chap. 18), Brazil (Chaps. 19 and 20), and a multitude of countries (Chaps. 17 and 21). Topics covered include corruption (Chap. 17), regulatory and legal reforms (Chap. 18 and 19), pension funds (Chap. 20), and banks (Chap. 21). The authors show that legal reforms are not easily transferrable across countries and governance provided by pension funds and banks is likewise not implemented in the same way and does not have the same effects across countries.

Part V (Chaps. 22, 23, 24 and 25) provides lessons from practitioners that corporate governance matters. The authors discuss data and cases from the MENA region (Chap. 22), Morocco (Chap. 24), and a multitude of countries (Chaps. 23 and 25). The authors review topics that include shareholder activism and investment behavior (Chap. 22), microfinance institutions (Chap. 23), non-listed companies (Chap. 24), and the international corporate governance best practices (Chap. 25). Among other things, the authors provide many practical insights associated with implementing corporate governance in these contexts.

In sum, this book is very well organized and provides in-depth analyses of corporate governance in many interesting and unique contexts in emerging markets. It will serve as an excellent resource for scholars for years to come.

Toronto, Canada
26 September 2013

Douglas Cumming
Schulich School of Business
York University

References

Allen, F., Qian, J., & Qian, M., (2005). Law, finance, and economic growth in China. *Journal of Financial Economics*, *77*(1), 57–116.

Allen, F., Chakrabarti, R., De, S., Qian, J., & Qian, M. (2006). Financing firms in India. *Journal of Financial Intermediation*, *21*(3), 409–445.

Preface

Emerging markets are commonly known as financial markets of rapid growth economies that have, over the recent decades, undertaken a wide range of social, political, and economic reforms to put their economies on a more sustainable footing. In general, the expression of emerging markets also refers to emerging economies. With increasing integration of trade and finance flows in the context of globalization, emerging markets now play an important role for global economy growth and portfolio diversification. Altogether, they reached about 54 % of the world GDP measured at purchasing power parity, and they accounted for three-quarters of global real GDP growth over the past decade (*The Economist*, print edition in August 2011). While developed countries experienced severe economic slowdown in the aftermath of the US subprime crisis, economic growth across emerging countries is still projected to grow at a steady rate through the next decade. Thus, the differences in growth potential between emerging and developed countries lead necessarily to changes in the way investors worldwide allocate their available funds and value their investments in emerging countries.

Despite their high potential of growth, emerging markets investments are not without risk. They are commonly known as risky investments due to a number of market imperfections including particularly the lack of transparency, sound regulations, stringent accounting and reporting standards, and minority investor protection. Then, all potential investors should enter these markets with a clear-eyed view of corporate governance laws, rules, and practices. In particular, they should be able to grasp the underlying realities of the business environment and to adapt global corporate governance standards to local market specificities. In the meantime, research on corporate governance in emerging markets remains scanty and sparse and requires additional studies at both country and firm levels.

This edited volume is intended to provide the readers with an in-depth understanding of governance mechanisms, practices, and cases in emerging markets. This book is an invaluable resource not only for academic researchers and graduate students in law, economics, management, and finance but also for people practicing governance such as lawmakers, policymakers, and international organizations promoting best governance practices in emerging countries. Investors benefit from this book to make judicious decisions regarding their future projects in emerging economies.

This book is broadly divided into three parts. The first part focuses on the legal framework and codes of best practices of corporate governance. The second part presents some country experiences in the field of corporate governance. The last part addresses the topical issues of corporate social responsibility.

Troyes, France Sabri Boubaker
Paris, France Duc Khuong Nguyen

About the Editors

Sabri Boubaker is an Associate Professor of Finance at Champagne School of Management (Groupe ESC Troyes en Champagne, France) and research fellow at the Institut de Recherche en Gestion (University of Paris Est). He holds a Ph.D. in Finance from University of Paris Est (2006) and an HDR degree (Habilitation for Supervising Doctoral Research) in 2010 from the same university. He is a Visiting Professor at IESEG School of Management (France) and IAE Paris Gustave Eiffel (France). He was a member of the team that drafted the *Tunisian Code of Best Practice of Corporate Governance* and the *Guidelines for Annual Reports of Tunisian Listed Companies*. He has recently published several academic papers in international refereed journals including *Journal of Banking and Finance*, *Review of Accounting and Finance*, *Multinational Finance Journal*, *Global Finance Journal*, *International Journal of Business*, and *Journal of International Financial Markets, Institutions and Money*. Dr. Boubaker has also edited several books on corporate governance and corporate social responsibility issues.

Duc Khuong Nguyen is a Professor of Finance and Deputy Director for Research at IPAG Business School (France). He holds a Ph.D. in Finance from the University of Grenoble II (France) and an HDR (Habilitation for Supervising Scientific Research) degree from University of Cergy-Pontoise (France). His research articles are published in various refereed journals such as *Journal of Banking and Finance*, *Journal of International Money and Finance*, *Journal of International Financial Markets, Institutions and Money*, *Quarterly Review of Economics and Finance*, and *Review of Accounting and Finance*. Dr. Nguyen has also edited several books on corporate governance and corporate social responsibility issues.

Acknowledgments

We would like to thank Christian Rauscher and Barbara Bethke (Springer Berlin/Heidelberg, Germany) for their helpful comments and editorial assistance. We are grateful to Professor Douglas Cummings who kindly agreed to write the foreword to this edited volume. Our sincere thanks also go to all the contributing authors. Their intellectual contribution is greatly appreciated.

All expressed views in the chapters remain the sole responsibility of the authors.

Sabri Boubaker
Duc Khuong Nguyen

Contents

List of Contributors

Ruth Alas is the Vice-Rector for Scientific Affairs and Head of Management Department at Estonian Business School (Estonia). Her research focuses on change and innovation management, crisis management, organizational culture, leadership, business ethics and corporate governance, and social responsibility. Ruth Alas is a Chairman of EIASM workshops' series on "Organizational Development and Change," which has been held since 2006. She has supervised several research projects at the Estonian Business School that link corporate governance to change management and risk management.

Nadia Albu is an Associate Professor of Accounting at the Bucharest University of Economic Studies (Romania). She obtained her Ph.D. in 2005 from the same university. Her research focuses on transformations in accounting in emerging economies, including IFRS application, management accounting, corporate governance, and changes in the accounting profession. Nadia's research has recently been published in *Critical Perspectives on Accounting*, the *Journal of International Financial Management and Accounting*, *Australian Accounting Review*, *Accounting in Europe*, and the *Journal of Accounting in Emerging Economies*.

Carlos Almeida graduated from Fluminense Federal University and has an MBA Degree in Organizational Management and a Master's Degree in Economics and Finance at Getulio Vargas Foundation. Currently, he is an Executive Director at TELOS (a large pension fund in Brazil) and has vast experience in auditing acquired at KPMG, where he was an auditing manager and whose main clients were banks and national and foreign investment funds. He was a statutory audit committee member of Brasil Telecom Participações S.A. (telecom industry) and PAME S/C – Planos de Assistência Médica (health insurance industry).

Francesca Battaglia is a Senior Lecturer of Financial Markets and Institutions at the University of Naples "Parthenope" (Italy). Her main research interests focus on cooperative banks, securitization, governance of financial intermediaries, and systemic risk. She is the author of several publications on financial institutions, including several chapters in Palgrave book editions (i.e., Asset pricing, real estate and public finance over the crisis; New issues in financial and credit markets; Bank performance, risk and securitization; Advances in risk management), and articles in journals such as *Applied Financial Economics* and *International Review of Financial Analysis*.

Igor Belikov holds a Ph.D. from Voronezh State University. He is the founder and CEO of the Russian Institute of Directors, an NGO set up in 2001. He is also a member of the Expert Council on Corporate Governance of the Federal Service for Financial Markets and is also a coauthor of the Russian Code of Corporate Governance (2002) and of a number of books in English and Russian. He is the author of over 150 articles on various aspects of corporate governance in Russia published in Russia and abroad. He has served on boards of a number of Russian companies, among which are Acron, Lukoil, North-West Telecom, Sibirtelecom, Southern Telecom, Uralsvyazinvest, and State Mortgage Agency (AIZhK). In 2006–2007, he worked as a member of international team of experts to evaluate corporate governance practices in the Middle East (a part of the MENA Corporate Governance Project by the IFC). He has led a number of consulting projects on corporate governance by the RID.

Lamia El Bouanani is the Executive Director of the Moroccan Institute (IMA) of Directors since January 2012. She joined the Caisse de Dépôt et de Gestion (one of the largest institutional investors in Morocco and sponsor of IMA) in May 2009 as a project manager. She graduated from Sciences Po Paris (France) in international affairs in 2001 and earned in 2002 a postgraduate degree in applied economics from the same university. She started her career at the Microfinance Program of the Global Environment Facility in Rabat in 2003 and managed projects in legal education at the American Bar Association in Morocco. She also worked as a consultant in 2007–2008, with MENA Members of Parliaments, to improve governance of IFIs (international financial institutions), for the Paris-based association: the Parliamentary Network on the World Bank. Lamia is the recipient of the International Corporate Governance Network scholarship, since June 2013.

Hua Bu is a Professor of the School of Management, China University of Mining and Technology (China). His research interests are in corporate finance and quality of accounting information. His works have been published in prestigious Chinese journals such as *China Accounting Monthly Journal*, *China Commercial Accounting Journal*, and *China Mining Journal*.

Andre Carvalhal is an Associate Professor of Finance at Pontifical Catholic University of Rio de Janeiro (Brazil). He was a postdoctorate fellow in Finance at University of California at Los Angeles (UCLA) and holds a Ph.D. from the Federal

University of Rio de Janeiro (Brazil). He has worked at the Brazilian Development Bank, the Central Bank of Brazil, and several investment banks and consulting firms. He has written ten books and several papers in top finance journals such as *Journal of Corporate Finance*, *Quantitative Finance*, *Corporate Governance: An International Review*, *Emerging Markets Finance and Trade*, and *Latin American Business Review*.

Yan-Leung Cheung is the President and Chair Professor of Public Policy at the Hong Kong Institute of Education. He was previously the Dean of the School of Business at Hong Kong Baptist University. He was the Chairman of Core Group on Corporate Governance, Pacific Economic Cooperation Council, and has provided consultancy services to the Asian Development Bank, United Nations ESCAP, Securities and Futures Commission of Hong Kong, Financial Services Bureau, and Stock Exchange of Hong Kong. In 2007, he was appointed as Justice of the Peace by the HKSAR government.

Saima Ferdous Chowdhury is an Assistant Professor in the Department of International Business, Faculty of Business Studies, University of Dhaka (Bangladesh). She was awarded her Ph.D. from Birmingham Business School, University of Birmingham (United Kingdom). She has published articles on corporate governance issues, work-life balance, and human resource practices.

Richard Chung received his Ph.D. from Ohio State University (United States). He taught at Concordia University (Canada) and The Hong Kong Polytechnic University (Hong Kong). He joined Griffith University (Australia) as an Associate Professor in 2011. His research interests include corporate governance, Real Estate Investment Trusts (REITs), and investment.

Gian Piero Cigna is a Senior Counselor at European Bank for Reconstruction and Development (EBRD). Gian Piero, who is an Italian-qualified attorney, is the corporate governance and securities markets specialist in the Legal Transition and Knowledge Management Team. Prior to joining the EBRD, he worked on corporate governance and capital markets at the European Commission and at the Italian Ministry of Economy. He practiced law in an international law firm in Italy, Albania, and Romania and acted as a consultant to international organizations and various state institutions and ministries in Eastern Europe. He graduated in law in Italy and attended postgraduate studies in the Netherlands and the United States focusing on European and International business law. His publications include several essays on corporate governance, capital markets, and banking law, most recently with a focus on emerging markets in Eastern Europe and central Asia.

J.Thomas Connelly is a faculty member at the Faculty of Commerce and Accountancy, Chulalongkorn University (Thailand). He has extensive experience in the private sector and has provided consulting services to the Asian Development Bank Institute and the Thai Institute of Directors Association.

Gloria Cuevas-Rodríguez is an Associate Professor at the Management Department of Pablo de Olavide University (Seville, Spain). Her research interests include corporate governance, privatization, organizational design, and innovation. She has published journals such as the *Journal of Management Studies*, *Corporate Governance: An International Review*, *British Journal of Management*, *Human Relations*, and *Business History*.

Angela Donaggio is Professor of Corporate Law of GVlaw (FGV) and FECAP. She is researcher at the Center for Business Law of the Getulio Vargas Foundation (FGV-SP). She is a Ph.D. candidate at University of Sao Paulo (USP), holds a master´s degree in Business Law and Social and Political Development from the Getulio Vargas Foundation (FGV) and is a bachelor in law from the Pontifical Catholic University of Sao Paulo. She was fellow researcher of the FGV Law School between 2009 and 2011, receiving, twice, the Scholarship Mario Henrique Simonsen awarded for exceptional academic performance. Donaggio has published several papers on corporate governance and corporate law and is author of the book *Corporate Governance and Novo Mercado: Investor protection and Flaws of Regulation and Self-Regulation* (Saraiva, 2012). She is coauthor of the books: *Corporate Governance and Initial Public Offerings in Brazil* (Direito GV, 2013); *State and Business: An Imbricated Relationship* (Direito GV, 2013); *Family Business: Corporate Governance, Family Governance and Legal Governance* (Saraiva, 2010); and *Corporate Law: Legal Strategies and Succession Planning* (Saraiva, 2009).

Tiit Elenurm is a Chairman of the Entrepreneurship Department at the Estonian Business School (Estonia) and author of more than 110 research publications. He acquired entrepreneurial experience in the 1990s as the main owner of EM International, a training and consulting company. The vision of Tiit Elenurm is to develop synergy between knowledge management, corporate governance, and entrepreneurship training, consulting, and research activities in entrepreneurship. His expert knowledge has been applied by the OECD team, when checking Estonian compliance with OECD corporate governance principles. His research principally concerns knowledge management, change management, corporate governance, international transfer of knowledge management, and cross-cultural impacts of SMEs on economic growth.

Jesus P. Estanislao is the Chairman of the Philippines Institute of Corporate Directors. He has had an illustrious career in government serving in various posts, such as the Secretary of Finance, the Republic's chief economic officer. He was also the founding Dean of the Asian Development Bank Institute in Tokyo. In

2011, he was awarded the prestigious "Outstanding Filipino" Award by the JCI Senate Philippines.

Michael Firth started his career as an accountant with Poulsom and Co, a firm of chartered accountants. Subsequently, he worked as an auditor for Whinney Murray (Ernst and Young) and as an investment analyst at Phillips and Drew (UBS Phillips and Drew). He has professional qualifications in accounting and finance and earned his Ph.D. at Bradford University. Professor Firth's first academic post was at the University of Stirling (United Kingdom). His subsequent professional appointments were at Victoria University of Wellington (New Zealand), the University of Colorado (United States), Lingnan University (Hong Kong), and the Hong Kong Polytechnic University (Hong Kong). He rejoined Lingnan University as Chair Professor of Finance in 2007. He has held visiting positions at University of British Columbia, University of California at Los Angeles, China-Europe Management Institute (Beijing), China-Europe International Business School (Shanghai), Norges Handelshoyskole, Helsinki School of Economics, and Nanyang Technological University. Professor Firth's research interests cover issues in accounting, auditing, economics, and finance.

Angela Gallo is a Senior Lecturer of Financial Markets and Institutions at the University of Salerno (Italy) and faculty member of LUISS Business School (Italy). Her main research interests focus on regulation, supervision, and governance of banks and pension funds. She is the author of several publications in journals such as *Applied Financial Economics* and *International Review of Financial Analysis.*

Chinmoy Ghosh has been a faculty member at the Department of Finance of the University of Connecticut since 1986, the year he graduated from the Pennsylvania University with a Ph.D. in Finance with minors in Economics and Quantitative Analysis. He has published over 50 articles in top academic journals in Finance, including the *Journal of Financial Economics*, *Journal of Banking and Finance*, *Financial Management*, *Journal of International Money and Finance*, *Journal of Financial Research*, and *Journal of Financial Services Research*. Prof. Ghosh has presented his research papers at academic conferences in the United States, Canada, Europe, Australia, South America, and Asia; he has organized and attended multiple open houses and business forums. His research has been recognized with 2012 Best Paper Award by the International Business Finance Conference, ICFAI Business School, India, 2002 and 2006 Ackerman Scholar Award by University of Connecticut School of Business, 1990 SBA/SNET Best Article Award, and 1998 Best Paper Award in International Finance by the Financial Management Association. Prof. Ghosh has also served as an independent consultant to major corporations in the United States. Prof. Ghosh is also an active consultant in the seminar circuit of the AICPA and AIMR CFA Program. He set up and is currently the Director and Chairman of the Board of Advisers for the Student Managed

Investment Fund at UConn, a $1 m fund managed entirely by UConn UG and MBA students. He serves as a member of the Board of Directors at the UConn Coop.

Anna Elvira Graziano is a Ph.D. candidate in Banking and Finance at the University of Rome Tor Vergata (Italy). She is currently developing a research project on the role of media in disseminating announcements of spin-off deals. Her main research fields include behavioral finance, performance drivers, and governance of financial intermediaries.

Jaime Guerrero-Villegas is an Assistant Professor in Human Resource Management at the Management Department of Pablo de Olavide University (Seville, Spain). His current work focuses on research in corporate governance, boards of directors, and privatization. He teaches human resource management courses to undergraduate students.

Stephan Hartenstein holds a Master's Degree in Economics from Johann-Wolfgang-von-Goethe-University, Frankfurt (Germany). From 1999 until 2008, he worked in Frankfurt at a US-based Asset Management company as a Risk Manager and COO. From 2008 to 2010, he worked at a large Germany-based MFI as the global head of operational risk management. In his position, he designed and implemented new systems and processes in the areas of operational risk management, fraud prevention, information security, and business contingency, and, on a one-year interim basis, for market risk management and anti-money laundering. In 2011, Mr. Hartenstein founded NomoRisk GmbH, a consulting firm specialized on providing risk management and corporate governance consultancy services plus corresponding training programs, mainly to smaller and medium-sized financial institutions. In his capacity as a consultant, he also works for the International Finance Cooperation (IFC).

Ichiro Iwasaki is a Professor of Economics at the Institute of Economic Research, Hitotsubashi University (Japan). He received his doctoral degree in Economics from the same university in 2001. His research interests are focused upon transition economies, comparative economic systems, and financial and organizational economics. He is the author and editor of numerous books including the following: *Organization and Development of Russian Business: A Firm-Level Analysis* (coedited with Tatiana G. Dolgopyatova and Andrei A. Yakovlev), published in 2009 from Palgrave Macmillan (Basingstoke, UK), and *Economic Transformation and Industrial Restructuring: The Hungarian Experience* (coauthored with Csaba Makó and others), published in 2012 from Maruzen Publishing Co. (Tokyo, Japan). Moreover, his recent articles have appeared in *Comparative Economics Studies*, *European Journal of Political Economy*, *International Economic Journal*, *Journal of Comparative Economics*, *Journal of Corporate Finance*, *Journal of Economic Surveys*, *Transnational Corporations*, and many other international journals.

Arifur Khan is a Lecturer in Accounting at Deakin University (Australia). He received his Ph.D. from Monash University (Australia). He has published a wide range of journals including *Corporate Governance: An International Review*, *Journal of Business Ethics*, and *Australian Journal of Management*. Dr. Khan's current research interests include corporate governance, audit pricing, and corporate social responsibility disclosure.

Jeong-Bon Kim is a Chair Professor and Head of the Department of Accountancy, City University of Hong Kong. He is also the Honored Professor at the School of Management, Fudan University, Shanghai, and Vice-President of the *International Association of Accounting Education and Research*. He obtained BBA and M.Sc. degrees from Seoul National University, and a Ph.D. from Temple University (United States). Prior to joining City University of Hong Kong, Professor Kim served as the Canada Research Chair (Tier 1) at Concordia University. He also taught for many years at the Hong Kong Polytechnic University and Syracuse University. He is currently the editor in chief of the *China Journal of Accounting Research* and editor of the *Asian Pacific Journal of Accounting and Economics*. Professor Kim has published more than 70 papers in leading scholarly journals, including *The Accounting Review, Journal of Financial Economics, Contemporary Accounting Research, Review of Accounting Studies,* and *Journal of International Business Studies*. His current research focuses on financial reporting, corporate governance, and audit quality.

Izabela Koladkiewicz is an Assistant Professor of Corporate Governance at Kozminski University in Warsaw (Poland). Her current research interests include corporate governance, corporate social responsibility, and family business. She involves in several research projects (as Project Head as well as research team member) and is the author of several books and papers concerning corporate governance, published in *Corporate Governance: An International Review*, *Social Responsibility Journal*, and *International Journal of Banking Accounting and Finance*. She is the coeditor of the first textbook on corporate governance in Poland.

Alissa Amico Koldertsova is responsible for managing the OECD's work on improving corporate governance in the Middle East and North Africa region. Since joining the OECD in 2005, Ms. Amico has been working with both government and private sector representatives in the region on advancing national and regional corporate governance priorities though capacity building activities, research, and policy roundtables. She has provided technical expertise to a number of governments in the region in the design of regulatory initiatives and institution building. Ms. Amico has authored and coauthored a number of publications including *Private Sector Development in the Middle East and North Africa (2008), Policy Brief on Corporate Governance of Banks in the Middle East and North Africa (2009), The Role of MENA Stock Exchanges in Corporate Governance (2012), and Towards*

Better Arrangements for State Ownership (2012) as well as articles in regional and international magazines and media. Ms. Amico holds a Bachelor's Degree in Business Administration from York University (Canada) and a Master's Degree in Political Economy from the London School of Economics (United Kingdom). She is a member of the French Institute of Directors (IFA) and has in 2011 been named one of the Top 100 Leaders in Europe and the Middle East by the Centre for Sustainability and Excellence. She is a regular contributor to regional conferences and discussions on corporate governance, capital market development, and state-owned enterprises.

Alexander Kostyuk is a Professor in Corporate Governance at the Ukrainian Academy of Banking and Chairman of the *International Center for Banking and Corporate Governance*. He holds a Ph.D. in corporate governance (Ukraine, 2001) and a DBA (Switzerland, 2007). As the editor of six books since 2002, he managed establishing the groups of more than 280 corporate governance experts from more than 50 countries around the world. Under the initiative and participation of Alex, several corporate governance international conferences have been successfully organized in Taiwan (2008), Ukraine (2011, 2012), France (Tours, 2011), Finland (Helsinki, 2012), Italy (Pisa, 2012), and Paris (2013). Two more conferences will be administered by him in Italy (Rome, 2013, and Milan, 2014). Prof. Alexander Kostyuk is also a Visiting Professor at Hanken School of Economics (since 2011).

Dimitrios N. Koufopoulos is a Senior Lecturer at the Brunel Business School (United Kingdom). He has published research articles in various journals such as *Long Range Planning Journal*, *Journal of Strategic Change*, *Journal of Financial Services Marketing*, *Corporate Ownership and Control*, *Corporate Board*, *International Journal of Corporate Governance and Ethics*, and *Journal of Business Ethics*. He is the founder and Scientific Director of the Hellenic Observatory of Corporate Governance (www.hocg.eu). His research interests cover strategic planning systems, top management teams, corporate governance, board of directors, and corporate strategies.

Yuliya Lapina is a Ph.D. researcher at the Ukrainian Academy of Banking of the National Bank of Ukraine. In 2011, she received her Master's Degree with honors in International Economics from the Ukrainian Academy of Banking of the National Bank of Ukraine. Since 2010, Yuliya is a member of the *International Center for Banking and Corporate Governance*. Her research work covers the fields of corporate governance and investment banking.

Piman Limpaphayom is the Director of the Master in International Management Program at Portland State University and a board member of the CFA Society of Portland. While at Sasin GIBA of Chulalongkorn University, he worked with the Thai IOD and McKinsey & Company to develop the first corporate governance scorecard in Asia. He has provided consulting services to the Asian Development Bank, the World Bank, and the Court of Justice.

Ioana Lupu is an Assistant Professor in Management Control at the Rouen Business School (France). She obtained her Ph.D. in 2011 from the Conservatoire National des Arts et Métiers in Paris (France). Her main research interests are identity construction in professional services firms, business school rankings as devices of control, and legitimacy practices of MNCs in transitional economies. Ioana's work has received several awards from the *Academy of Management*, *AFC*, and *FNEGE*. Her work was published in *Critical Perspectives on Accounting*, and her doctoral dissertation is forthcoming at the Editions *Vuibert*, Paris.

Tong Lu is the Chairperson of the Institute of Director in East Asia Network (IDEANet) and a member of the Shanghai Stock Exchange Corporate Governance Advisory Committee. She is the founder of the Chinese Center for Corporate Governance (CCCG). She also holds an academic post as a Professor of economics in the Institute of World Economics and Politics at the Chinese Academy of Social Sciences.

Christine Mallin is a Professor in Corporate Governance at Norwich Business School, University of East Anglia (United Kingdom). She was the editor of *Corporate Governance: An International Review* for 7 years. She has published widely corporate governance issues in journals including the *Journal of Business Ethics*, *Corporate Governance: An International Review*, and the *European Journal of Finance*. Her book "*Corporate Governance*", published by Oxford University Press, is in its fourth edition.

Mohammad Badrul Muttakin is a Lecturer in Accounting at Deakin University (Australia). He received his Ph.D. from the same university. He has published many articles in different journals, including *Journal of Business Ethics* and *Journal of Accounting in Emerging Economies*. Dr. Muttakin's research interests are corporate governance and corporate social responsibility disclosure.

Ekaterina Nikitchanova is a Deputy Director of the Russian Institute of Directors and Head of the RID Expert Center. She is the author of many articles on corporate governance in Russian. She has led a number of consulting projects on corporate governance by the RID and surveys on corporate governance in Russian companies. She has served on boards of several medium Russian companies.

Chris Ogbechie is a Senior Lecturer at Lagos Business School and a Visiting Lecturer at Strathmore University, Kenya. His research works have appeared in a number of peer-reviewed journals such as the *International Journal of Business*

Governance and Ethics, *Journal of Corporate Citizenship*, *Management Research Review*, and *International Journal of Critical Accounting*. He is currently the Director of the Etisalat Corporate Social Responsibility Centre, Lagos Business School. Dr. Ogbechie is also a Director/fellow at the Society for Corporate Governance Nigeria. His research interests include corporate strategy, sustainability, and corporate governance.

Kean Ow-Yong is a Lecturer in Finance at the University of Birmingham Business School (United Kingdom). Prior to his current appointment, he held a similar academic post at Nottingham Trent University (United Kingdom). He has published a number of refereed journals including the *European Journal of Finance* and *Corporate Governance: An International Review*.

Lei Pang received her Ph.D. in Finance from the Hong Kong Polytechnic University in 2010 and her B.A. degree in Finance from Nankai University, China, in 2006. She is currently a Research Assistant Professor in the Department of Finance & Decision Sciences, School of Business, Hong Kong Baptist University. She previously taught at City University of Hong Kong for one and a half years. Her research interests include corporate investment, capital market, and corporate governance.

Milena Petrova has a Master's Degree in Business Administration from the Helsinki School of Economics (Finland), a Master's Degree in Finance from Hofstra University (Unites States), and a Ph.D. in Finance, with a focus on Corporate Finance and Real Estate from the University of Florida. She has published top academic and practitioner finance journals including *Financial Management*, *Journal of International Money and Finance*, *Journal of Applied Finance*, *Real Estate Economics*, and *Journal of Real Estate Finance and Economics*. Dr. Petrova has won several awards for her research and teaching. She was awarded the 2012 Best Paper Award by the International Business Finance Conference, ICFAI Business School, India; the CoStar Best Paper Award in 2010 and 2007; the Oberwager Award in 2009 for outstanding faculty, and the Gerald R. Brown 2003 Award for best paper on "Real Estate and Finance" from the Asian Real Estate Society; and was a finalist for the 2010 Financial Management Association Best Paper in "Investments." Dr. Petrova has been part of the Department of Finance at Whitman School of Business, Syracuse University, since 2006. Prior to taking an academic position, Dr. Petrova worked as a consultant for Booz Allen Hamilton and as a project finance analyst for Finnvera, Finland's Export Credit Agency.

Marie dela Rama is an Associate Lecturer at the Management Discipline Group of the UTS Business School in Sydney (Australia) and is a core research member of the UTS Centre for Corporate Governance. She holds a Ph.D. in Corporate Governance from the University of Technology, Sydney, and received an Australian

Government Endeavour Research Fellowship for her doctoral work with the results published in the *Journal of Business Ethics*. Her other publications include the three-volume edited series *Corporate Governance and Globalization* and four-volume edited series *Fundamentals of Corporate Governance* (both with Professor Thomas Clarke, published by SAGE in London).

Dmitriy Riabichenko is a Ph.D. researcher at the Ukrainian Academy of Banking of the National Bank of Ukraine. In 2012, he received his Master's Degree with honors in Banking from the Ukrainian Academy of Banking of the National Bank of Ukraine. Since 2012, Dmitriy is a member of the *International Center for Banking and Corporate Governance*. His research areas include corporate governance and risk management. He has published several articles in refereed journals.

David Risser is a Manager at Nestor Advisors Ltd., a London-based boutique firm founded in 2003 and a global leader in corporate governance advisory services. David, an economist, is primarily responsible for the director development program, research, internal audit, and risk management activities of Nestor Advisors. He has executed numerous research projects, governance assessments, and audit missions for financial institutions and nonfinancial companies. He also contributed to *Governing Banks – A Primer on Governance, Banking and Risk Management*, a training toolkit for bank directors published by the Global Corporate Governance Forum of the World Bank's International Finance Corporation. He is the main author of the bank assessment and scoring methodology developed for the EBRD. Prior to joining Nestor Advisors in 2003, David was a Ph.D. candidate at University of Lyon 2 (France) and an Assistant Professor at EM Lyon (France). He holds a post-graduate diploma in Banking, Finance, and International Economics, with Honors, Magna cum Laude, from the University Lumière of Lyon (France). David lectures for the London Stock Exchange Academy and various Institutes of Directors.

Hind Sami is an Associate Professor of Finance at Lumière Lyon 2 University (France) since September 2009. In December 2005, Hind Sami received her Ph.D. in Finance from the University of Lyon 2 (France). From 2002 to 2004, she spent 2 years at the Wharton School, University of Pennsylvania (United States), as a visiting researcher. Her work is published in the *Quarterly Review of Economics and Finance*, *Economic Modelling*, and the *Review of Accounting and Finance*, among others.

Raluca Sandu is an Assistant Professor in Finance and Accounting at SKEMA Business School (France). She obtained her Ph.D. in 2013 from the University of Orléans (France). Her research focuses on emergence of practices in transitional economies, corporate social responsibility – reporting and disclosures, history of accounting, accounting education, and innovation.

Ekta Selarka is an Assistant Professor at Madras School of Economics. She holds a Ph.D. in Economics from Indira Gandhi Institute of Development Research, Mumbai (India) and an Engineering degree from the Bhilai Institute of Technology (India). She has published articles in *Journal of Corporate Finance* and *Journal of Emerging Market Trade and Finance*. Her main research interests include corporate governance, board diversity, and corporate social responsibility. She is a winner of a research grant from British Council under UK-US-India Trilateral Research Collaboration and Indian Council of Social Science Research to pursue research on comparative corporate governance and corporate social responsibility issues in Indian firms.

Javed Siddiqui is a Lecturer of Accounting at the Manchester Business School, University of Manchester (United Kingdom). Javed is primarily interested in studying international regulatory developments in the area of auditing, corporate governance, and CSR, especially in the context of developing economies. In addition, Javed has a long-standing interest in the development of auditing regulations in the United Kingdom and European Union.

Markus Stiglbauer is a Professor and Head of the Department of Corporate Governance at the School of Business and Economics, University of Erlangen-Nürnberg (FAU), Germany. His research interests cover the fields of corporate governance, corporate social responsibility, and organizational behavior.

Nava Subramaniam is a Professor of Accounting at Deakin University (Australia). She has published extensively academic and professional journals including the *Accounting, Auditing and Accountability, Journal of Accounting and Public Policy, International Journal of Accounting, Accounting and Finance*, and *Australian Accounting Review*. Professor Subramaniam's research interests are in the areas of corporate governance, accounting education, management control systems, and auditing.

Konari Uchida is an Associate Professor of the Faculty of Economics, Kyushu University (Japan). His research interests are in corporate finance and governance. His works have been published in reputable journals such as *Accounting and Finance, International Review of Economics and Finance, Pacific-Basin Finance Journal,* and *Review of Quantitative Finance and Accounting*.

Sidharta Utama is the Chairman of the Indonesian Institute for Corporate Directorship and a Professor in the Department of Economics at the University of Indonesia, where he was also the Vice-Dean. He has served as a member of the Tax Oversight Committee, Ministry of Finance, the National Management Board of the Indonesian Institute of Accountants, and the Indonesian Accounting Standard Board. He is also a Chartered Financial Analyst (CFA).

Ramón Valle-Cabrera is a full Professor in Human Resource Management at the Management Department, Pablo de Olavide University (Seville, Spain). His teaching and research interests focus on strategic human resource management and innovation. He is heading up several research projects on innovation, organizational capital, and employment relationships, and he has coauthored several HRM textbooks and papers in international journals.

Patrick Velte is an Associate Professor and Chair of Financial Accounting and Auditing at the School of Business, Economics and Social Sciences, University of Hamburg in Germany. His research interests focus on national and international accounting and corporate governance.

Vladimir Verbitsky is the first Deputy Director of the Russian Institute of Directors. He graduated from the Stockholm School of Economics (MBA) and is the author of about 20 articles on corporate governance in Russian. He is a member of the Expert Council of the Federal Agency for State Property Management. He also served on boards of a number of Russian companies, among which are Globalstroiengeneering, Sibirtelecom, Energomera, Interdentos, Supermetal, Technonikol, and led a number of consulting projects on corporate governance by the RID.

Christophe Volonté is a postdoc research fellow and teaching associate at the Department of Financial Management, Faculty of Business and Economics, University of Basel (Switzerland). He has been a visiting researcher at Simon Fraser University (United States), University of Technology, Sydney (Australia), as well as the Manchester Business School (United Kingdom). He completed his Ph.D. in 2011 at the University of Basel with the dissertation entitled "*Corporate Governance in Switzerland*". His research interests cover the areas of corporate governance, corporate finance, and law and economics.

Duane Windsor is Lynette S. Autrey Professor of Management in the Jesse H. Jones Graduate School of Business at Rice University (United States). He holds a Ph.D. in Political Economy and Government from Harvard University. He is the editor (since 2007) of the quarterly journal *Business & Society*, founded 1960 and sponsored by the International Association for Business and Society (IABS). He served as an elected program chair and Head of IABS and of the Social Issues in Management (SIM) Division of Academy of Management. He received the Sumner Marcus Award for Outstanding Service from the SIM Division (2009). Professor Windsor has published several books or monographs. His recent work focuses on corporate social responsibility and stakeholder theory. His articles have appeared in *Business & Society*, *Business Ethics Quarterly*, *Cornell International Law Journal*, *Journal of Business Ethics*, *Journal of Business Research*, *Journal of Corporate Citizenship*, *Journal of International Management*, *Journal of Management Studies*, *Journal of Public Affairs*, and *Public Administration Review*.

Simon Zaby is a postdoc research fellow and Associate Lecturer at the Department of Financial Management, Faculty of Business and Economics, University of Basel (Switzerland). After studying Business Administration at the Ingolstadt School of Management, Catholic University of Eichstaett-Ingolstadt (Germany), and International Relations at the Graduate School of International Studies, Sogang University, Seoul (Korea), he serves as a research assistant at the Department of Bank Management and Controlling, Faculty of Business and Economics, University of Basel. In 2009, Simon Zaby was awarded a Doctorate of Political Science at the University of Basel. Currently, his research focus lies in the field of venture capital.

Yuyang Zhang is a Ph.D. student at Kyushu University (Japan). His research interests are in corporate finance, governance, and earnings management. His works have been published in peer-reviewed journals such as *Emerging Markets Review*.

Part I
Corporate Governance and Firm Performance

Security Voting Structure and Firm Value: Synthesis and New Insights from Emerging Markets

Chinmoy Ghosh and Milena Petrova

Abstract The value of vote hypothesis states that the value of differential voting rights reflects the value of private benefits of control enjoyed by controlling shareholders with superior voting rights at the expense of minority shareholders with lower voting rights. Although the extant evidence is generally consistent with this hypothesis, it is inconclusive, and based mainly on studies in developed economies. We first synthesize the evidence on this issue in the emerging economies. Next, we provide new insight on this subject with description and analysis of a proposed regulatory change for removal of the 10 % voting cap in the banking sector in India in 2005. We hypothesize that removal of the voting cap would increase the probability of a takeover and induce positive value gain for banks that the proposal relates to. Consistent with our prediction, we observe significant abnormal returns of 7.8 % for private Indian banks over the 2-day interval surrounding the announcement. Cross-sectional analyses further reveal that the valuation gain is inversely proportional to the bank's foreign and insider ownership. This study makes important contributions to the growing literature on the valuation impact and efficiency gains of liberalization of foreign ownership restrictions in emerging markets.

C. Ghosh (✉)
Department of Finance, School of Business, University of Connecticut, Storrs, USA
e-mail: Chinmoy.ghosh@business.uconn.edu

M. Petrova
Department of Finance and SDA School of Management, Bocconi University, Milan, Italy
e-mail: milena.petrova@unibocconi.it

S. Boubaker and D.K. Nguyen (eds.), *Corporate Governance in Emerging Markets*, CSR, Sustainability, Ethics & Governance, DOI 10.1007/978-3-642-44955-0_1,

1 Introduction

The "one share-one vote" rule which prescribes that there be no wedge between shareholders' cash flow and voting rights is the natural specification to ensure that no shareholder has excess voting power to influence the outcome on a decision requiring shareholder vote. However, deviations from the "one share-one vote" rule are common in numerous countries across the world. In comprehensive reviews of the theoretical and empirical evidence on the issue, Burkart and Lee (2008) and Adams and Ferreira (2008) discuss the implications of frequent violations of this cardinal rule. While disproportional voting power can arise in various ways, including multiple share classes with differential voting rights, voting agreements, pyramidal control structures, cross-ownership, voting rules and caps, the most prevalent are the dual-class shares and pyramidal structures. Quoting from a recent survey of 464 firms in 16 European countries, Adams and Ferreira (2008) note that 44 % of the companies have some control-enhancing mechanisms, including 27 % pyramids and 24 % dual-class share structures.

A priori, it would seem that ownership concentration through differential voting structure would hurt the interest of minority shareholders. However, while the majority of papers that examine this issue have come to the conclusion that the dual-class and other differential voting structures have adverse impact on the value of firms, the consensus on this issue remains illusive. The proponents of unequal cash flow and voting rights argue that in an environment of widely dispersed share-ownership, the atomistic shareholder has no incentive to monitor managers because of the classic "free rider problem". The consequent lack of discipline allows entrenched managers to divert corporate resources to their own benefit to the detriment of minority shareholders' interest; whereas, shareholders with concentrated voting control can act as custodians of the minority shareholders by wielding their power to monitor and discipline self-interested managers and directors. Conversely, the common argument against skewed voting control is that it introduces agency conflicts between controlling and non-controlling shareholders. Specifically, controlling shareholders can use their disproportionate voting power to pressure management into deals that directly benefit them in control contests.

In this chapter, we synthesize the extant evidence on the benefits and disadvantages of differential voting rights and examine the impact of differential voting rights on performance and valuation, with special emphasis on emerging nations. The unique regulatory and institutional environments in these countries provide us with a rare opportunity to observe how shareholders' voting rights evolve as each country goes through economic reforms. We further focus on a type of control-enhancing mechanisms that is relatively infrequent compared to the more prevalent pyramid and dual-class structures. Specifically, we study the implications of voting ceilings or voting caps. Burkart and Lee (2008) observe that a voting cap or ceiling specifies that a shareholder cannot cast votes in excess of a certain number (often expressed as a percentage of the total number of shares outstanding) regardless of the number of shares owned by him/her. Although this provision does not technically violate the proportionality principle between cash flow and voting rights, it effectively prevents dissident shareholders from accumulating sufficient voting power to initiate a potent takeover threat. As such, in a situation where incumbent management and the board are inclined to act in ways to enhance their own welfare at the expense of minority shareholders, a cap or ceiling on voting power can induce significant loss of shareholder wealth by shutting off dissident voices. Interestingly, published research on this topic is scarce. An exhaustive search of the web yielded only a handful of articles including several that have been cited by Burkart and Lee (2008). A major reason for the paucity of interest and research on this topic must be the relative infrequency of use of this mechanism to insulate managers from hostile takeover threats.[1]

In our analysis of voting caps we present a recent case study from the Indian banking sector. The banking industry in India is especially interesting as it has gone through phenomenal growth, accompanied with liberalization and sweeping regulatory transition in the last 20 years. Until the 1990s, foreign ownership was not allowed in Indian banks as policy makers maintained that foreign intervention in the banking industry of a developing economy hurts growth by denying access to easy credit to the small entrepreneurs in rural areas. We examine the regulatory changes in the Indian banking sector that started in the early 2000s and allowed foreign ownership up to 74 % in 2004. These changes failed to have a discernible impact on the ownership of private Indian banks by foreign banks, due to the existence of the Indian Banking Regulation Act of 1949, which stipulated that each shareholder was allowed only a maximum of 10 % voting control, regardless of the size of the ownership stake. In 2005 a bill was introduced to lift this cap. We analyze the reaction of Indian banking stocks to the introduction of the bill to amend the Banking Regulation Act. Our results provide empirical evidence on the impact of voting ceilings and caps on the firm value and suggest the market perception that a voting cap can stunt the growth of the market for corporate control.

The rest of the chapter proceeds as follows. In the next section, we briefly discuss the theoretical foundation for the "one share-one vote" rule. The empirical evidence, focused mainly on the creation and reunification of dual-class shares, is also reviewed. We further examine the relation between voting and ownership structures and firm value and the determinants of voting premiums. In addition, Sect. 2 includes an overview of the literature on voting ceilings and caps. In Sect. 3, we review the use of multiple class shares and the empirical evidence on the impact of differential voting structures on value in the emerging countries. In Sect. 4, we present a case study on the rapidly changing landscape of regulatory and institutional environment in India. We summarize the bank liberalization developments during 2002–2005. Since the oft-stated rationale for voting cap in India is to protect the strategic banking sector from foreign intervention, we review the extant

[1] However, as we note later in the paper, voting caps and ceilings exits in several European countries.

literature on the impact of foreign bank presence on access to credit and domestic banks' performance. Finally, we examine the reaction of bank stocks to the proposed removal of voting caps in India. Section 5 offers our concluding remarks.

2 Voting Rights, Corporate Governance and Value

2.1 "One Share-One Vote" Rule: Theoretical Foundation and Empirical Evidence

Burkart and Lee (2008) and Adams and Ferreira (2008) have presented comprehensive reviews of the theoretical model and the extensive empirical evidence on the implications of "one share-one vote" rule, and deviations thereof. As such, in the interest of brevity, we will briefly note the main findings of the voluminous research on this topic. In doing so, we will focus especially on the evidence from the emerging economies.

The "one share-one vote" rule is the norm to ensure equality between cash flow and voting rights. Grossman and Hart (1988) and subsequently Hart (1995) describe the circumstances under which deviation from the "one share-one vote" rule is sub-optimal and can destroy value by transferring control to an inferior management team in a control contest. Assuming two management groups, the incumbent and a rival attempting to wrest control, Hart shows that if only the rival group has private benefits of control, it will offer a premium to buy the superior voting shares so long as the private benefits exceed the premium and the superior voting shareholders tender. Conversely, a dual-class voting structure will enable an inefficient incumbent controlling group to fend off a superior rival team by offering a premium to buyout the high voting shareholders. However, if both incumbent and rival groups have private benefits of control such that they compete for control of the firm, a dual-class voting structure may be conducive to maximization of firm value in a control contest. In a similar vein, Gilson (1987) argues that although a dual-class structure may be optimal when a firm is issuing new shares through IPO because the value of the shares will reflect any potential coercion of minority shareholders, it is detrimental to shareholder interest if a superior voting class of shares is created by a seasoned firm to insulate incumbent management from hostile suitors.

In Europe, the use of dual-class structure consisting of voting and non-voting shares has been common in firms in Italy, Germany, Switzerland and northern Europe (Faccio and Lang 2002). In this case, shareholders giving up their voting rights typically do so in exchange of preferred dividends. Because voting rights are worth little to a transferee who is a minority shareholder of the firm, or a transferor who already has a controlling position, the evidence implies that companies implementing a dual-class ownership structure are characterized by high concentration of shares controlled by the management group (Arruñada and Paz-Ares

1995). By issuing nonvoting shares insiders can retain or consolidate their control (Ibid.).

The agency costs associated with insulation of incumbent management from hostile threats and proxy fights is the major concern of the critics of dual-class shares. The separation of cash flow and voting rights can potentially create a situation where as the fraction of cash flow rights decreases, the shareholders in control of greater voting power bear very little of the costs of inefficient decisions, but enjoy larger private benefits. This behavior will have an adverse effect on the long-term value of the firm.

To examine the impact of dual-class structures on firm value a number of studies have focused on the change in share prices surrounding the announcement of dual-class recapitalizations. Partch (1987) found no significant reaction to adoption of dual-class shares. In contrast, Jarrell and Poulsen (1988) find significantly negative abnormal stock returns surrounding the announcement of dual class recapitalizations. The authors interpret the evidence as consistent with the entrenchment hypothesis that management use dual-class recapitalizations to shield themselves from hostile acquirers. However, a series of subsequent papers have failed to find any significant reaction to dual-class recapitalizations. For instance, Dimitrov and Jain (2006) conclude that the stock market, on average, views dual-class recapitalizations to be mildly positive in that firms adopting dual class structures significantly outperform a matching portfolio over a 4-year period following the adoption. Overall, the results from the event study analyses yield no conclusive evidence for the potentially detrimental effects of dual-class recapitalizations on shareholder wealth.[2]

Recent research documents the trend of share class unification in several countries. Amoako-Adu and Smith (2001) focus on recapitalization to single class of dual-class firms in Canada. Dittman and Ulbricht (2008) examine the wealth effects of German dual class unifications and report that firm value increases by about 4 % on the announcement day. Similar results are observed by Ehrhardt et al. (2008) who find significant positive announcement stock price effect for both voting and non-voting shares. Bigelli et al. (2011) examine dual-class share unifications in Italy and record an overall effect on firm market capitalization of 0.6 % in the 3 day window [−1,1] around the announcement. However, while cumulative abnormal returns (CARs) for the non-voting shares over this window were 11.3 %, voting shares sustained significant negative announcement returns of −1.5 %. Therefore, the unification represented a wealth transfer from voting to non-voting shareholders, but interestingly approximately in half of the sample firms the controlling shareholder owned non-voting shares. Based on this observation, the authors

[2] Khanna and Yafeh (2007) argue that in underdeveloped countries, concentrated control by business groups may be more efficient for poorly-managed economic institutions. Some control by management may also prevent expropriation by other control groups, and control can also motivate monitoring. Adams and Ferreira (2008) present a detailed review of this literature.

concluded that unifications in Italy generally increase firm value, but also induce wealth transfer from the minority to the majority shareholders of the firm.

In share unifications or removal of voting restrictions voting shareholders are often compensated for the dilution of their voting rights, which has been used to measure the value of voting premium. Hauser and Lauterbach (2004) examine 84 dual-class unifications from Tel Aviv Stock Exchange and conclude that the price of vote is a direct function of the vote loss by majority shareholders. Ang and Megginson (1989) record an extraordinary dividend of 12.3 % of the voting share stock price as compensation for dilution of voting rights in 45 out of 49 stock unifications in the UK. Voting premiums can also be associated to the value of the option to participate in future premiums paid to the voting/high-vote shares in the event of a takeover (Cox and Roden 2002). For example, DeAngelo and DeAngelo (1985) observed that premiums to high-vote shares during 1960–1980 ranged from 83.3 % to 200 %.

Another stream of literature attempts to directly measure the premium at which superior voting shares (SVS) should sell over the reduced voting shares (RVS). In Zingales' (1995) model, the value of vote derives from the probability that a control contest can be successfully initiated and executed. During a control contest, the value of the superior voting privilege is determined by the magnitude of private benefits of control, and the proportion of shares owned by the majority with SVS. Nenova (2003) asserts that if variable cash flow rights of SVS and RVS are equal, the market value of a marginal vote equals the expected discounted equilibrium value of a vote at the time of a control contest. Tests of the model based on dual-class firms in the U.S. confirm that the voting premium is a positive function of the relative size of the private benefits of control. Smith and Amoako-Adu (1995) corroborate the result with dual-class recapitalization of Canadian firms. These studies imply a change in the value of vote in response to the announcement of a major and unexpected change in the ownership distribution that influences the takeover probability of a firm.

2.2 Voting Caps and Voting Ceilings

Compared to dual-class shares, voting caps and voting ceilings are relatively infrequent. There are two main types of voting right ceilings. The most prevalent variety caps the use of voting rights beyond a given proportion of all outstanding voting rights. The second type of ceiling caps the use of voting rights beyond a given proportion of all votes actually cast at a general meeting, which limits the voting power of shareholders even more. Deminor (2005) presents a comparative analysis of the capital structure of European companies aimed at identifying how many follow the "one share-one vote" principle. The study covers all European companies included in the FTSE Eurofirst 300 index and is based on an examination of their annual reports, articles of association and other published information. The author reports that the three most frequent deviations from the "one share-one vote" principle is Europe are voting right ceilings, multiple voting rights, and ownership ceilings, and that voting right ceilings are in force in 10 % of all companies analyzed. Some companies combine the two types of ceiling. Except for Belgium and the Netherlands, all countries feature companies with a voting right ceiling. In Spain, Denmark, Czechoslovakia, and Switzerland the voting right ceiling is the most important exception to the 'one share – one vote' principle. These voting right ceilings prohibit shareholders from voting above a certain threshold irrespective of the number of shares they hold. The percentage of companies that have voting right ceilings are highest in Spain (41 %), and Czechoslovakia (35 %), and lowest in Denmark (3 %) and United Kingdom (3 %). The threshold of voting ceilings range from 15–30 % in United Kingdom to 2–5 % in Czechoslovakia.

Burkart and Lee (2008) argue that by limiting the percentage of shares that can be voted, voting caps diminish the influence of large shareholders and render takeover attempts nearly impossible to execute. In addition, reduced voting power may jeopardize large shareholders' ability and incentive to monitor and discipline incumbent management. As such, by protecting entrenched management, voting caps may adversely impact value. On the other hand, the rationale often cited by the proponents of voting caps is that they protect minority shareholders from raiders that are interested in control of the firm for their own private benefits. In addition, voting caps may protect strategic industries from hostile intervention by parties who are interested only in profit or value maximization, with little tolerance for potential social programs and benefits.[3]

Especially pertinent to the issue at hand is a series of papers that focus on the impact of foreign ownership restrictions on share value in emerging economies. Bailey and Jagtiani (1994) study the effects of segmenting local and foreign trading of securities that have reached foreign ownership limits at the Stock Exchange of Thailand. The authors find that cross-sectional differences between local and foreign prices are correlated with proxies that include the severity of foreign ownership limits. Domowitz et al. (1997) report that in the equity market in Mexico, unrestricted shares sell at a significant premium over those where foreign ownership is restricted and that the premium is an increasing function of favorable exchange rate, and market capitalization of the firm, consistent with notion that foreign investors prefer larger companies. Bailey et al. (1999) observe that many countries impose legal limits on the percentage of shares that foreigners can own in local

[3] India imposes a 10 % cap (26 % cap since January 2013) on the voting rights of foreign investors in private banks which, according to many market observers, is acting as a major barrier to foreign banks taking large ownership positions in Indian banks despite a 74 % ownership limit. As a result, there is increasing pressure on the Government and the RBI to relax the voting cap and allow proportional voting rights. However, supporters of the voting cap maintain that as a sector of "strategic importance", the banking sector is the channel not just for monetary policy but also for many preferential policy directives. For example, they highlight the thrust on "financial inclusion" and "micro finance" in the Indian context. It is a natural anxiety for many of these market participants that foreign banks will not have the necessary commitment to developmental priorities of the host country (Dr. Rupa Rege Nitsure, *Chief Economist, Bank of Baroda, December 2006).*

companies. In these countries, foreigners keen on diversification are willing to pay high premiums for these shares. For evidence, when separate classes of shares are created for local and foreign investors, shares for the foreigners sell at a significant premium. Ødegaard (2007) present an interesting case in Norway where prior to 1995, foreigners were allowed to own 33 % of voting shares. Due to demand by foreigners, non-voting shares sold at a higher price than voting shares, creating a negative premium. However, after the ownership restriction was lifted in 1995, the voting shares started to sell at a premium. Ødegaard (2007) concludes that in the presence of ownership restrictions, market segmentation pushes the value of restricted shares higher; conversely, when there are no ownership restrictions, voting shares sell at a premium.

Finally, a theoretical rationale for foreign ownership restriction has been advanced by Stulz and Wasserfallen (1995) who argue that a voting ceiling on foreign ownership may enable a firm to charge a premium to foreign investors interested in a large position. In their model, foreign investors face deadweight costs in their home country so that they value the payoffs of domestic shares more than domestic investors. So, foreign investors are willing to pay a premium for domestic shares and the premium is an increasing function of ownership restrictions. It follows that the value of the restricted shares will fall when these restrictions are removed. Stulz and Wasserfallen (1995) provide evidence consistent with this prediction with Swiss data.

3 Differential Voting Rights in the Emerging Markets Countries

3.1 Use of Multiple Class Shares

While multiple-class share (MCS) structures are relatively common for developed countries, their use varies significantly by country. For example in a study of 5,232 corporations in 13 developed European countries Faccio and Lang (2002) show that the use of dual class shares varies from 66 % in Switzerland to 0.16 % in Spain and none in Belgium, and Portugal. We observe similar variation in the adoption of multiple classes share structures in the developing countries. In Table 1 we present summary statistics for the current percentage of firms with outstanding multiple share classes by number and market capitalization. We note that in Asia, with the exception of China, MCSs are rather uncommon. Eastern European countries also exhibit mixed patterns with firms with MCS structures' share varying between 0 % and 37 %, based on market capitalization. Interestingly, Latin American countries exhibit consistently high share of MCSs, especially in terms of market capitalization, which implies that firms with MCS structures tend to be larger.

Table 1 Firms with outstanding multiple-class shares in the emerging markets

Country (region)	Number of firms	Firms with MCS	Percent firms with MCS	Total market capitalization	Market capitalization MCS	Percent firms with MCS (based on market cap)
China	6,922	3,135	45.3	51,600	46,000	89.1
India	5,426	10	0.2	66,160	1,800	2.7
Malaysia	1,379	0	0.0	1,620	0	0.0
South Korea	3,168	0	0.0	1,256,970	0	0.0
Taiwan	2,738	0	0.0	24,900	0	0.0
Asia Pacific emerging	***21,094***	***3,231***	***15.3***			
Czech Republic	391	19	4.9	686.06	68.61	10.0
Hungary	485	7	1.4	4,580	1,710	37.3
Poland	2,917	378	13.0	554.47	45.09	8.1
Russia	4,398	25	0.6	57,070	38.41	0.1
Turkey	740	23	3.1	833.72	147.65	17.7
Eastern Europe	***20,623***	***518***	***2.5***			
Argentina	674	115	17.1	269.87	115.73	42.9
Brazil	2,475	577	23.3	8,440	6,710	79.5
Chile	440	42	9.5	186,730	54,050	28.9
Colombia	215	26	12.1	535,130	204,140	38.1
Mexico	1,002	66	6.6	11,130	5,240	47.1
Latin America and Caribbean	***7,073***	***1,021***	***14.4***			
Israel	1,587	14	0.9	928	4.81	0.5
Saudi Arabia	182	0	0.0	1,450	0	0.0
South Africa	1,559	37	2.4	5,580	636.63	11.4
U.A.E. – Dubai	216	0	0.0	451.03	0	0.0
Middle-East/ Africa	***6,515***	***95***	***1.5***			

This table presents summary statistics for the number of, market capitalization and share of firms with multiple-class shares in the developing countries, as reported by Bloomberg. All market capitalization values are in local currencies based on prices of actively traded securities on April 15, 2013. Number of firms is based on the reported number by Bloomberg of active, inactive, unlisted and private companies by country or geo-political region. We present statistics for the major 19 developing countries as well as all countries in the Asia Pacific Emerging Market, Eastern Europe, Latin American & Caribbean, and Middle East/Africa

3.2 Impact of Differential Voting Structures on Firm Value

The literature on the impact of differential voting structures on emerging firms' value is limited. Chung and Kim (1999) suggest that controlling shareholders in emerging capital markets enjoy greater power that controlling shareholders in the U.S. However, there is little empirical evidence on the economic value of these private benefits of control. Chung and Kim (Ibid.) present evidence that the voting premium in the Korean market is significantly positively related to the control value of block shares held by minority shareholders. In addition, the authors estimate the value of voting premium in Korea to be approximately worth 10 % of the value of the firm's equity.

Using a sample of over 1,000 publicly traded firms in Hong Kong, Indonesia, Korea, Malaysia, the Philippines, Singapore, Taiwan and Thailand, Claessens et al. (2002) find that firm value is a decreasing function of the wedge between control rights of the largest shareholder and its cash flow ownership. The negative effect is particularly severe for large deviations between control and ownership rights. The authors attribute these findings to family controlled firms with concentrated ownership, which dominate the sample (908 observations), unlike in the US.

Similarly, Lemmon and Lins (2003) examine 800 firms from the same eight Asian emerging markets, but analyze the impact of ownership structure on value during the Asian financial crisis (July 1, 1997–August 1, 1998). The authors found that the negative effect of the crisis was more pronounced by 10–20 %age points for firms where managers had higher divergence of cash flow and voting rights. Mitton (2002) observes similar results for a sample of 398 firms in five Asian developing countries, Indonesia, South Korea, Malaysia, the Philippines and Thailand during the same period. Baek et al. (2004) investigate the relationship between governance and firm value during the Asian financial crisis and find that firms with larger divergence between voting rights and cash flow rights of controlling shareholders had lower returns during the period examined.

Finally, Lins (2003) examines a sample of 1,433 firms from 18 developing countries during 1995–1997 and establishes that when a management group's control rights exceed its cash flow rights, firm values are lower, with the effect being significantly more pronounced in countries with low shareholder protection.

Overall, although the literature examining the relationship between differential voting rights and firm value is limited for emerging markets when compared to the studies of developed countries, the evidence shows a consistent and strong negative effect of cash flow/voting rights divergence and firm value.

4 A Case-Study on the Indian Banking Sector

4.1 Background of Liberalization in India

As previously noted, our choice of India as the appropriate setting to study the effect of voting caps on shareholder value is largely dictated by the surprising lack of sufficient detail on this control-enhancing mechanism in other parts of the world. While voting caps and ceilings are prevalent in many European countries, academicians have paid little attention to this voting structure. In addition, the gradual evolution of the regulation in India over a 10-year period allows us to examine the effect on stock prices at various stages of the development.

Private banks in India were first allowed to sell shares to foreign investors in January 1993, with the amount limited to only 20 % of total capital. However, the fast expanding economy in India soon created a situation where domestic banks were unable to supply sufficient capital to support the growth and the Indian government was forced to create conditions to attract international capital. To operate in India, foreign banks must apply to the Reserve Bank of India (RBI) and go through a lengthy approval process. However, even with RBI approval, the opportunity for expansion and growth by opening more branches is restricted by India's commitment to World Trade Organization's guidelines, which limit the number of branches a foreign bank can open in a given year to 12. As such, for foreign banks aspiring for a presence in the growing Indian banking market, growth through acquisition of domestic banks is an appealing option.

In response to pressure from Indian business community and foreign banks eager to participate in the growth in India, the RBI announced in February 2002 that foreign direct investors (FDIs) were allowed to own up to 49 % of capital in private banks. Market participants believed that, in conjunction with the ownership by foreign institutional investors (FIIs), foreign investors could finally assume majority control of private Indian banks. Ghosh et al. (2008) report that private banks, on average, gained over 20 % market value around the announcement, and the value gain by individual banks was an increasing function of the probability of takeover as indicated by traditional proxies. The authors concluded that the regulatory change signaled a potential increase in the probability of takeover and improvement of managerial efficiency.

Unfortunately, the 2002 liberalization had no discernible impact on the threat and incidence of hostile takeovers by foreign banks in the Indian banking sector. Three factors contributed to this phenomenon. One, significant concern remained that the final passage of the proposed liberalization could be threatened by the ensuing debate in the parliament and the political uncertainty in India. Further, it was unclear if the ownership cap was cumulative or not, majority ownership would be impossible if the ownership cap was cumulative.[4] This barrier was removed in March 2004 when an amendment allowed 74 % ownership of capital by foreign direct investors. Two, the Security and Exchange Board of India (SEBI)'s Substantial Acquisition of Shares and Takeovers Regulation Act, 1997, prohibits an acquirer from accumulating more than 15 % of outstanding shares/voting rights without making a public announcement. As a consequence, it is virtually impossible for an acquirer to attempt a takeover without the participation and support of the current management or promoter.

[4] Ghosh et al. (2008) note that predominantly FIIs owned stocks in Indian banks, which implies that foreign investors were more interested in short-term gains with no long-term commitment.

4.2 Voting Cap in Indian Banks for Foreign Investors

The most potent deterrent to a hostile takeover attempt is the main focus of this study. In accordance with the Indian Banking Regulation Act of 1949, each shareholder was allowed only 10 % voting control (until January 2013 when this restriction was relaxed to 26 %), regardless of the size of holding.[5] The rationale for the cap was to prevent owner-managers from abuse through credit concentration and credit diversion.[6] Under the cap, if an entity holds 90 % of the outstanding shares, it has only 50 % voting power. Given that 74 % is the maximum ownership allowed to foreign shareholders, any single foreign entity can control a maximum of only 28 % of votes, making a hostile takeover impossible. Because of the cap on voting rights, foreign investors that were interested in the direct benefits of control avoided investing in Indian banks because the voting cap prevented the accumulation of sufficient votes to influence decision making and ultimately takeover. As a consequence, foreign ownership was concentrated in FIIs that invest primarily for performance with no interest in control. To our knowledge, there is no other evidence in the extant literature where a specific voting cap has been the main deterrent to foreign investors assuming controlling ownership positions in domestic businesses.

Despite public outcry and pressure from foreign investors, the voting cap continued although on several occasions, the RBI and the central government contemplated specific action facilitating its removal, but no consensus could be reached because of strong resistance from certain sectors of the political landscape. Over the next 3 years, there were several occasions when public debate brought intense pressure on the central government to act on this issue.[7] Finally, on May 5, 2005, the Union Cabinet introduced a bill in the Parliament to amend the Banking Regulation Act, 1949 and lift the 10 % voting rights cap in Indian banks, and make voting rights commensurate with ownership. The bill was referred to a standing committee by the members. On December 13, 2005, The Parliamentary Standing

---

[5] Section 12(2) of the 1949 Banking Regulation Act states that, "No person holding shares in a banking company shall, in respect of any shares held by him, exercise voting rights on poll in excess of ten per cent of the total voting rights of all the shareholders of the banking company." The only exceptions were the Government of India which was the majority owner in nationalized banks, and the RBI.

[6] Questioned on the reasons for placing a restriction of 10 % on voting rights as presently applicable under the Act, the Ministry, in a written reply inter alia informed: "The reasons for placing restrictions on voting rights arose primarily from the concern that permitting proportionate voting rights to the promoters may result in abuse by them such as problems of credit concentration and credit diversion that had beset the banking sector in the past, prior to nationalization."

[7] Ghosh et al. (2012) discuss this period in detail. Throughout this period, the foreign investment community pressured the Indian Government for further liberalization of the capital market. For example, On March 20, 2004, K.N. Memani, the Chairman of the American Chamber of Commerce in India, expressed disappointment that US-based investors are not enthusiastic about investing in Indian private sector banks despite the Government hiking the foreign direct investment cap to 74 % because the voting cap prevented foreign investor from having any effective control on the decision-taking process.

Committee gave its approval to remove the 10 % voting cap on shareholders of Indian banks, signaling a further boost towards liberalization.

In broad terms, the proposed policy deregulations 2002–2004 (allow ownership up to 74 %) and 2005 (remove 10 % voting cap) are similar forms of liberalization in that both were intended to facilitate the acquisition of domestic banks in India by foreign entities. However, it is the occurrence of these two regulatory changes that make the Indian case unique. Indeed, it is the failure of the 2002 liberalization (which increased the ownership cap of foreign entities in private Indian banks to 49 %, and later in 2004 to 74 %) to induce foreign banks to take ownership positions in Indian banks that focused attention on the voting cap. It became clear that foreign investors with control motives had little incentive to acquire ownership stakes in Indian banks because of the potentially large gap between cash flow and voting rights. Of course, there was good reason to expect that the removal of the voting cap was imminent because of repeated complaints from social and political commentators and most importantly, foreign investors. However, it is difficult to discern from the results in Ghosh et al. (2008) if and to what extent the valuation gain is attributable to the anticipations of removal of the voting cap and the consequent mitigation of agency costs. In conjunction, these two deregulations highlight one interesting fact about the role of foreign investors in emerging economies. Foreign institutions are less excited about investing in emerging countries unless they can monitor and influence performance and efficiency through control mechanisms.

4.3 *The Role of Foreign Banks in Banking*

The rationale for the 10 % voting cap is to protect the strategic banking sector from intervention and competition from the strictly profit-motivated foreign banks. Whether foreign banks should be allowed to participate in the economic development of an emerging nation, and the appropriate role for them is an issue of great interest to academicians and policy-makers alike. Claessens and Van Horen (2012) provide a comprehensive review of the academic literature on this topic. Overall, the extant research indicates that the impact of foreign banks has been favorable – foreign presence leads to lower cost of financial intermediation, and lower profitability, and lower loan-loss provision. Foreign banks are not an unmixed blessing, however. In several studies, there is credible evidence that by "cherry-picking" borrowers, foreign banks undermine the availability of banking services, and squeeze the credit pool, resulting in lower financial growth. Lensink et al. (2008) document a negative effect of foreign banks on the efficiency of domestic banks, although the effect is less pronounced in countries with better governance and regulatory environment.[8]

[8] A long list of studies have explored these issues. We do not review these studies individually in the interest of brevity. Interested readers are urged to look at Claessens and Van Horen (2012) for more details on these studies.

4.3.1 Foreign Bank Presence in India

Until early 1990s, Indian banks were closely held with majority ownership by the central government; foreign ownership was not allowed. The rationale was to keep business segments with strategic national interest inaccessible to foreign investors to minimize potential deviations from government's policy of credit access to the disadvantaged sections of the population, and the threat of takeover. The liberalization in January 1993 first allowed new private banks to sell shares to foreign investors, but only up to 20 % of total capital. The rule distinguished between FIIs and FDIs. By definition, FDIs participated in new issues and had control motives; FIIs bought shares from the secondary market and were interested only in performance and investment potential with no control objectives.

Several recent studies have focused on the effect of foreign bank entry in the Indian banking sector. Kumbhakar and Sarkar (2003) investigate the effect of deregulation in the Indian banking sector, and relate it to the ownership structure of banks. Their data reveal no significant growth in total factor productivity following deregulation, although growth is marginally higher for private sector banks than public sector banks. The authors contend that the dominance of public sector banks insulates them against any potential impact of deregulation. Bhaumik and Dimova (2004) corroborate that private sector and foreign banks performed better than public sector banks, but the difference has disappeared since the late 1990s. Bhaumik and Piesse (2008) conclude that increasing presence of foreign banks induce steady improvement in the performance of domestic banks. Ataullah and Le (2006) document a negative relationship between presence of foreign banks and efficiency of domestic banks. Conceivably, competitive pressure from foreign banks in the early stages of development increases costs.

Finally, Gormley (2010) focuses on the effect of foreign bank entry on domestic credit access. His analysis reveals that foreign bank presence is associated with reduced credit access for domestic firms, particularly firms that are smaller, have lower tangible assets, and are linked to business groups. The resulting reallocation of loans benefits more profitable and larger firms at the cost of less profitable, smaller firms. The author interprets the evidence as consistent with the notion that due to less access to "soft" information, foreign banks avoid informationally opaque firms, resulting in "cream-skimming" and a segmented market for bank loans.

4.4 Reaction of Bank Stocks to the Proposed Removal of Voting Cap

We analyze the reaction of Indian banking stocks to the introduction of the bill to amend the Banking Regulation Act to lift the 10 % voting rights cap. The results presented below are discussed in detail in a companion working paper with two

Table 2 Ownership composition of individual Indian banks during 2003–2005

	2003			2004			2005		
Ownership groups	IP	FDI	FII	IP	FDI	FII	IP	FDI	FII
Government banks (N = 18)	65.40	0.00	2.26	64.25	0.00	6.45	62.61	0.00	9.45
New private banks (N = 6)	31.96	NMF	17.67	23.17	NMF	22.36	20.91	NMF	22.71
Old private banks (N = 9)	11.81	NMF	1.12	12.20	NMF	6.68	11.32	NMF	7.59

This table presents summary statistics for the ownership composition by ownership group of Indian banks by year during 2003–2005. The observations are as of the end of the fiscal year (March 31). Numbers represent the ownership of common stock by respective types of shareholders as a percentage of number of shares outstanding. IP, FDI & FII denote Indian Promoter, Foreign Direct Investor and Foreign Institutional Investor, respectively. Data are obtained directly from the annual statements of individual banks from the website of the bank and the RBI

other collaborators.[9] Our sample includes 33 banks, of which 18 are majority owned by the government of India, and 15 banks are privately owned, 9 of which were formed under the old rules in the 1940s to extend banking services to underserved areas, and the remaining 6 have been formed under the new rules following the liberalization of the banking sector pursuant to the January 1993 RBI guidelines regarding the formation and functioning of private banks.

In Table 2, we report the aggregate foreign ownership of Indian banks including both direct owners (promoters) who purchased primary shares at the offering (FDI) and foreign institutions (FII) who acquired the shares in the secondary market.[10] In aggregate, for each group, the data reveal an increasing trend in foreign ownership over the period. However, nearly all of the activity is by foreign institutions. For government banks, foreign institutional investment increased from 2.26 % in 2003 to 9.45 % in 2005. For the new privates, ownership by foreign institutions increased from 16.67 % to 22.71 % over the same period. For old privates, foreign institutional ownership increased from 1.01 % to 6.86 %. Overall, this is convincing evidence that while foreign institutions increased their holding in Indian banks, foreign direct investors remained passive.

Clearly, despite the liberalization, which allowed foreign direct investment up to 74 % of outstanding shares, foreign banks avoided equity positions in Indian banks. This is consistent the conjecture and press reports that FDIs were possibly

[9] Interested readers are referred to Ghosh et al. (2013) for a detailed discussion of the institutional and political developments that forced the central Indian government to send the bill for debate at the parliament as well as empirical analysis of the determinants of the observed positive stock reaction around the announcement of the introduction of the bill to amend the Banking Regulation Act.

[10] A promoter is a person or entity who exercises substantial control over the company or a person who undertakes all necessary steps in the floatation of the company. The relationship between a promoter and a company which he has floated must be deemed to be a fiduciary relationship from the day the work of floating the company started. Control shall include the right to appoint the majority of the directors or to control the management or policy decisions exercisable by a person or persons acting individually or in concert, directly or indirectly, including by virtue of their shareholding or management rights or shareholding agreements or voting agreements or in any other manner.

Table 3 Descriptive statistics of variables used in the analysis of the cumulative abnormal returns and their determinants around the announcement of the proposal to remove the 10 % voting cap for Indian private banks

Variable	Min	1st quartile	Mean	Median	3rd quartile	Max
CAR(−1,0)	−5.68	−0.17	4.27	2.40	7.44	18.31
CAR(0,+1)	−9.47	−1.07	2.37	1.71	5.76	13.50
Old private bank	0.00	0.00	0.27	0.00	1.00	1.00
New private bank	0.00	0.00	0.18	0.00	0.00	1.00
Ln(Total assets)	3.28	5.04	5.67	5.79	6.29	8.43
ROA	−0.82	0.54	0.84	0.94	1.28	1.59
NPL/TA	0.20	1.29	1.97	1.81	2.64	5.23
Leverage	6.98	13.24	16.12	16.29	19.52	24.54
Insider ownership	0.00	31.30	46.26	57.17	66.83	76.77
Foreign ownership	0.00	2.00	11.35	10.82	18.04	43.64

This table presents descriptive statistics of the CARs and variables used in the analysis of the determinants of the valuation effect around the announcement of the proposal to remove the 10 % voting cap for Indian private banks. CAR(−1,0) and CAR(0,+1) represent the CARs for the [−1,0] and [0,1] windows surrounding the announcement in percentage. CARs are calculated using standard event study methodology following Mikkelson and Partch (1988). The market proxy is the Bombay Stock Exchange (BSE) value-weighted portfolio. Daily returns from days −120 to −20 are used for estimation of the market model; days −20 to +20 represent the event period. All other variables are measured as of the end of the previous fiscal year (ending March 31). Old private bank is a dummy variable, indicating that the bank was created in the 1940s to extend banking services to underserved areas. New private bank is a dummy variable, indicating that the bank was created, pursuant to the January 1993 RBI guidelines for the formation and functioning of private sector banks. ROA is the bank's return on assets. NPL/TA is the ratio of non-performing loans to total assets. Leverage is the ratio of debt to debt plus equity and reserves in percentage. Insider and foreign ownership represent the fractional holdings of insiders and foreigners, respectively, in Indian banks

discouraged by the voting cap. Finally, Ghosh et al. (2012) report that in 2004 and 2005, aggregate ownership by FIIs exceeded the voting cap of 10 % for several banks. All Indian banks are required to report to SEBI large ownership stakes (in excess of 1 % of outstanding shares) and disclose it in annual statements. Ghosh et al. (2012) found no large ownerships by blockholders or individual institutions during the period under study. This trend implies that for the majority of Indian banks, the voting cap was non-binding, and removal of the cap would not alter the distribution of voting rights.[11]

Table 3 presents the descriptive statistics of the CARs and variables, used in the multivariate analysis, determining the valuation effect of the announcement of the bill. The summary statistics for the CARs show that the distributions are right skewed. For most other continuous variables the mean is very close to the median. Insider and foreign ownership are fractions and therefore limited between 0 and 1. The summary stats for insider ownership show that its distribution is right

[11] In 2003, only three private banks had holdings by foreign promoters (or, direct investors). One of these ownership positions was divested by 2005.

skewed. Based on the summary statistics, we conclude that there are no outliers in the data. Next, in Table 4 we present the Spearman (Panel A) and Pearson (Panel B) correlation coefficients. We observe several significant correlations between the independent variables. Size is negatively correlated with old private banks, as is ROA and insider ownership, while NPL/TA is positively correlated with old private banks. This leads us to the conclusion that old private banks are smaller and poor performers, and tend to have higher insider ownership. On the other hand, newer banks tend to have lower leverage. Size is positively correlated with insider and foreign ownership. In addition, foreign ownership is positively correlated with new banks, and associated with lower NPL/TA and lower leverage. These correlations imply that new banks are associated with higher foreign ownership by institutions, which invest in larger, better performing banks, with lower leverage. Since, multiple of the correlations are significant we conduct VIF analysis to test for multicollinearity issues in the regression models. Mean VIF values are presented for each model in Table 6 where we discuss the multivariate results.

Table 5 presents CARs for [−1,0] and [0,1] windows by bank ownership. CARs are calculated using standard event study methodology following Mikkelson and Partch (1988). The market proxy is the Bombay Stock Exchange (BSE) value-weighted portfolio. Daily returns from days −120 to −20 are used for estimation of the market model; days −20 to +20 represent the event period. We observe that the sample of 33 banks posted a highly significant gain of 4.3 % during the 2-day window [−1,0] around the announcement. The portfolio of private banks gained over 7.5 % over the same interval, the gains over the [0,1] window surrounding the event date are equally strong. Overall, these results are consistent with the notion that the market expects that the removal of the voting cap will induce foreign banks to hold ownership stakes and monitor the performance of domestic banks, which will enhance their efficiency and increase their share values.

Table 6 develops cross-sectional models to examine if the factors that are generally associated with a probability of a takeover influence value gains by individual banks. In Model 1 we only include old and new private banks as independent variables. The results show that the valuation impact is stronger and significantly positive for old private banks, which is consistent with the idea that old private banks are easier targets because they are smaller, and perform poorer than the new private banks. Next, in Model 2 we control for bank size, profitability, leverage, insider and foreign ownership. The coefficient of insider ownership is negative and significant, which suggests that firms where insiders and managers have greater control are less vulnerable to takeover threats. Furthermore, the proportion of total shares owned by foreign investors has also a significantly negative coefficient. As already noted, foreign ownership of Indian banks was concentrated in institutions with no foreign direct investment. Given that such institutions are unlikely to hold large ownership stakes, this result suggests that the takeover probability is inversely related to ownership, not subject to the voting cap. Since the old private bank variable is significantly correlated with ln(total assets) and ROA, with Pearson correlation coefficients of −62 % and −44 %, while the new private bank variable has Pearson correlation coefficients with leverage and

Table 4 Spearman and Pearson correlation coefficients between the variables used in the regression analyses determining CARs around the announcement of the proposal to remove the 10 % voting cap for Indian private banks

	CAR (0,+1)	Old private bank	New private bank	Ln (Total assets)	ROA	NPL/TA	Leverage	Insider ownership	Foreign ownership
Panel A: Spearman correlation coefficients									
CAR(0,+1)	1.00								
Old private bank	0.54*	1.00							
	0.00								
New private bank	0.00	−0.29	1.00						
	1.00	*0.10*							
Ln(total assets)	−0.47*	−0.64*	−0.08	1.00					
	0.01	*0.00*	*0.65*						
ROA	−0.22	−0.31*	0.25	0.13	1.00				
	0.22	*0.07*	*0.16*	*0.48*					
NPL/TA	0.31*	0.38*	−0.17	−0.29	−0.55*	1.00			
	0.08	*0.03*	*0.33*	*0.10*	*0.00*				
Leverage	−0.02	0.08	−0.49*	0.05	−0.58*	0.48*	1.00		
	0.91	*0.66*	*0.00*	*0.76*	*0.00*	*0.01*			
Insider ownership	−0.55*	−0.62*	−0.36*	0.50*	−0.01	−0.24	0.35*	1.00	
	0.00	*0.00*	*0.04*	*0.00*	*0.94*	*0.19*	*0.04*		
Foreign ownership	−0.17	−0.25	0.45*	0.37*	0.29	−0.56*	−0.56*	−0.12	1.00
	0.34	*0.16*	*0.01*	*0.03*	*0.11*	*0.00*	*0.00*	*0.52*	
Panel B: Pearson correlation coefficients									
CAR(0,+1)	1.00								
Old private bank	0.61*	1.00							
	0.00								
New private bank	−0.04	−0.29	1.00						
	0.82	*0.10*							
Ln(total assets)	−0.47*	−0.62*	−0.10	1.00					
	0.01	*0.00*	*0.59*						

ROA	−0.31*	−0.44*	0.23	0.30*	1.00				
	0.08	*0.01*	*0.20*	*0.09*					
NPL/TA	0.31*	0.34*	−0.21	−0.30*	−0.62*	1.00			
	0.08	*0.05*	*0.24*	*0.09*	*0.00*				
Leverage	−0.03	0.10	−0.51*	0.09	−0.52*	0.46*	1.00		
	0.87	*0.59*	*0.00*	*0.62*	*0.00*	*0.01*			
Insider ownership	−0.60*	−0.59*	−0.35*	0.49*	0.03	−0.25	0.37*	1.00	
	0.00	*0.00*	*0.04*	*0.00*	*0.86*	*0.16*	*0.03*		
Foreign ownership	−0.20	−0.23	0.54*	0.39*	0.29*	−0.49*	−0.56*	−0.15	1.00
	0.26	*0.19*	*0.00*	*0.02*	*0.10*	*0.00*	*0.00*	*0.39*	

Panels A and B present the Spearman and Person correlation coefficients, respectively. Significance levels are presented in italics. "*" indicates that the correlation coefficient is significant at the 10 % level or lower

Table 5 Cumulative abnormal returns by bank type on the announcement that the introduction of a bill lifting the 10 % voting rights cap in India was approved

	All banks	Government banks	Private banks
	(n = 33) (%)	(n = 18) (%)	(n = 15) (%)
CAR(−1,0)	4.27**	1.37	7.75**
CAR(0,+1)	2.37**	0.00	5.20**

This table presents CARs for [−1,0] and [0,1] windows by bank ownership. CARs are calculated using standard event study methodology following Mikkelson and Partch (1988). The market proxy is the Bombay Stock Exchange (BSE) value-weighted portfolio. Daily returns from days −120 to −20 are used for estimation of the market model; days −20 to +20 represent the event period

"**" indicates significantly different from zero at 5 % level of confidence

foreign ownership of −51 % and 54 %, respectively, including these two variables in the model specification may introduce multicollinearity issues. Therefore, in Model 3 we drop old and new private bank variables from the estimation. We note that ROA is significantly negatively associated with value, while both insider and foreign ownership increase their level of significance to 5 % or better. The mean VIFs in each model suggest that multicollinearity is not a concern in the multivariate analyses as the VIF values are lower than 10. Overall, the empirical analysis reveals that the valuation gain around the proposed lifting of 10 % voting cap is significantly positive for private banks, the group that the proposed change relates to. Further, the abnormal returns for private banks are significantly related to the factors that influence the takeover probability of individual banks. The large majority of banks had no ownership by foreign direct investors who are expected to provide monitoring with the prospect of ultimate takeover. Ownership was concentrated in institutions. For these banks, there is no direct change in distribution of voting power at the redistribution. The valuation effect derives entirely from the investors' anticipation of ownership and control by FDIs after the cap is lifted.

5 Conclusion

Deviations from the "one share-one vote" rule are common in many countries of the world. The main consequence of disproportionate voting rights is to concentrate voting control in the hands of some privileged shareholders. If these shareholders use their voting power to divert corporate resources to their personal benefits, the value of shares will be adversely affected to the detriment of minority shareholders' interest. We summarize the evidence in the extant literature on the impact of security voting structure on firm value and the value of a vote in developed vs. emerging markets. We also examine the use of multiple class shares in the two markets and find no significant differences. Overall, results based on event study analyses for developed countries yield no conclusive evidence for the potentially detrimental effects of dual-class recapitalizations on shareholder wealth. The

Table 6 Regression analysis of cumulative abnormal returns around the announcement of the proposal to remove the 10 % voting cap for Indian private banks

	Model 1	Model 2	Model 3
Old private bank	7.3756***	1.3436	
	(3.64)	(0.35)	
New private bank	1.9210	−0.8037	
	(1.55)	(−0.30)	
Ln(Total assets)		0.4779	0.4524
		(0.54)	(0.52)
ROA		−3.3218	−3.8868**
		(−1.42)	(−2.11)
NPL/TA		−0.9528	−1.1570
		(−1.01)	(−1.58)
Leverage		−0.1252	−0.0935
		(−0.53)	(−0.41)
Insider ownership		−0.1238*	−0.1379***
		(−1.94)	(−3.62)
Foreign ownership		−0.1811*	−0.2116**
		(−1.91)	(−2.14)
Const	0.0042	13.9043*	15.6336***
	(0.00)	(1.84)	(3.07)
Observations	**33**	**33**	**33**
R-squared	**0.39**	**0.54**	**0.53**
Mean VIF	**1.09**	**2.58**	**3.83**

This table presents cross-section regression models of the determinants of CARs in a 2-day window [0,+1] surrounding the May 5, 2005 announcement of the proposal to remove the 10 % voting cap for Indian private banks. The dependent variable is CAR(0, +1). Old private bank is a dummy variable, indicating that the bank was created in the 1940s to extend banking services to underserved areas. New private bank is a dummy variable, indicating that the bank was created, pursuant to the January 1993 RBI guidelines for the formation and functioning of private sector banks. ROA is the bank's return on assets. Leverage is the ratio of debt to debt plus equity and reserves in percentage. NPL/TA is the ratio of non-performing loans to total assets. Insider and foreign ownership represent the fractional holdings of insiders and foreigners, respectively, in Indian banks. All explanatory variables are measured as of the end of the previous fiscal year "*", "**", and "***" indicate significantly different from zero at 10 %, 5 % and 1 % level of confidence, respectively

empirical evidence for this issue, while limited in the case of developing countries, establishes a strong and consistent negative impact of differential voting rights on firm value.

We further examine a special form of control-enhancing mechanism – voting caps and ceilings. Although not as prevalent as dual class shares, voting cap and ceiling exist in most European countries. Indeed, in several of these countries, voting cap or ceiling is the most widely used control mechanism. However, the implications of voting caps have received little attention from academics. Our objective is to present some evidence on the impact of voting caps on share value from a natural experiment in one of the leading emerging economies. Specifically, we provide new insights with a proposed regulatory change in the voting cap in the banking sector in India. We analyze the reaction of Indian banking stocks to the introduction of a bill to amend the Banking Regulation Act to lift the 10 % voting rights cap. We observe a significant positive valuation gain around the announcement window, which is driven by the positive wealth effect for private banks. Our cross-sectional analyses, presented in Table 6, reveal that the valuation effect is significantly related to the ownership structure of banks. Specifically, CARs around the announcement of the introduction of the bill are significantly negatively related to both, the bank's insider and foreign ownership. The negative and significant coefficient of insider ownership suggests that firms where insiders and managers have greater control are more immune to takeover threats. Similarly, the negative and significant coefficient of foreign ownership implies that foreign ownership, which is dominated by foreign institutions, is negatively related to a bank's takeover probability and hence to the bill's announcement valuation effects. Against the backdrop of limited empirical evidence on the impact of voting ceilings and caps on firm value, this chapter makes a significant contribution to the literature by documenting the received evidence, and more importantly, highlighting the need for research on this topic.

References

Adams, R., & Ferreira, D. (2008). One share-one vote: The empirical evidence. *Review of Finance, 12*(1), 51–91.

Amoako-Adu, B., & Smith, B. F. (2001). Dual class firms: Capitalization, ownership structure and recapitalization back into single class. *Journal of Banking and Finance, 25*(6), 1083–1111.

Ang, J. S., & Megginson, W. L. (1989). Restricted voting rights, ownership structure, and the market value of dual class firms. *Journal of Financial Research, 12*(4), 301–318.

Arruñada, B., & Paz-Ares, C. (1995). The conversion of ordinary shares into nonvoting shares. *International Review of Law and Economics, 15*(4), 351–372.

Ataullah, A., & Le, H. (2006). Economic reforms and bank efficiency in developing countries: The case of the Indian banking industry. *Applied Financial Economics, 16*(9), 653–663.

Baek, J.-S., Kang, J.-K., & Park, K. S. (2004). Corporate governance and firm value: Evidence from the Korean financial crisis. *Journal of Financial Economics, 71*(2), 265–313.

Bailey, W., & Jagtiani, J. (1994). Foreign ownership restrictions and stock market prices in the Thai capital market. *Journal of Financial Economics, 36*(1), 57–87.

Bailey, W., Chung, P., & Kang, J. K. (1999). Foreign ownership restrictions and equity price premiums: What drives the demand for cross-border investments? *Journal of Financial and Quantitative Analysis, 34*(4), 489–511.

Bhaumik, S. K., & Dimova, R. (2004). How important is ownership in a market with level playing field? The Indian banking sector revisited. *Journal of Comparative Economics, 32* (1), 165–180.

Bhaumik, S. K., & Piesse, J. (2008). Does lending behaviour of banks in emerging economies vary by ownership? Evidence from the Indian banking sector. *Economic Systems, 32*(2), 177–196.

Bigelli, M., Mehrotra, V., & Rau, P. R. (2011). Why are shareholders not paid to give up their voting privileges? Unique evidence from Italy. *Journal of Corporate Finance, 17*(5), 1619–1635.

Burkart, M., & Lee, S. (2008). One share - one vote: The theory. *Review of Finance, 12*(1), 1–49.

Chung, K. H., & Kim, J.-K. (1999). Corporate ownership and the value of a vote in an emerging market. *Journal of Corporate Finance, 5*(1), 35–54.

Claessens, S., & Van Horen, N. (2012). *Foreign banks: Trends, impact and financial stability*. IMF Working Paper WP/12/10.

Claessens, S., Djankov, S., Fan, J. P. H., & Lang, L. H. P. (2002). Disentangling the incentive and entrenchment effects of large shareholdings. *Journal of Finance, 57*(6), 2741–2771.

Cox, S. R., & Roden, D. M. (2002). The source of value of voting rights and related dividend promises. *Journal of Corporate Finance, 8*(4), 337–351.

DeAngelo, H., & DeAngelo, L. (1985). Managerial ownership of voting rights: A study of public corporations with dual-classes of common stock. *Journal of Financial Economics, 14*(1), 33–69.

Deminor Rating (2005). *Application of the one share – one vote principle in Europe*. Commissioned by the Association of British Insurers.

Dimitrov, V., & Jain, P. C. (2006). Recapitalization of one class of common stock into dual-class: Growth and long-run returns. *Journal of Corporate Finance, 12*(2), 342–366.

Dittman, I., & Ulbricht, N. (2008). Timing and wealth effects of German dual class stock unifications. *European Financial Management, 14*(1), 163–196.

Domowitz, L., Glen, J., & Madhavan, A. (1997). Market segmentation and stock prices: Evidence from an emerging market. *Journal of Finance, 52*(3), 1059–1085.

Ehrhardt, O., Kuklinski, J., Nowak, E. (2008). *Unifications of dual-class shares in Germany: First empirical evidence on liquidity effects of share class unifications*. Swiss Finance Institute Working Paper.

Faccio, M., & Lang, L. H. P. (2002). The ultimate ownership of Western European corporations. *Journal of Financial Economics, 65*(3), 365–395.

Ghosh, C., Harding, J., & Phani, B. V. (2008). Does liberalization reduce agency costs? Evidence from the Indian banking sector. *Journal of Banking and Finance, 32*(3), 405–419.

Ghosh, C., Hilliard, J., Petrova, M., Phani, B. V. (2013). *Exogenous change in distribution of voting rights and firm value: An analysis of voting cap in Indian banks*. University of Connecticut Working Paper.

Gilson, R. (1987). Evaluating dual class common stock: The relevance of substitutes. *Virginia Law Review, 73*(5), 807–844.

Gormley, T. A. (2010). The impact of foreign bank entry in emerging markets: Evidence from India. *Journal of Financial Intermediation, 19*(1), 26–51.

Grossman, S. J., & Hart, O. D. (1988). One share-one vote and the market for corporate control. *Journal of Financial Economics, 20*(1/2), 175–202.

Hart, O. (1995). *Firms contracts and financial structure*. Oxford: Clarendon Press.

Hauser, S., & Lauterbach, B. (2004). The value of voting rights to majority shareholders: Evidence from dual-class stock unifications. *Review of Financial Studies, 17*(4), 1167–1184.

Jarrell, G. A., & Poulsen, A. B. (1988). Dual-class recapitalization as antitakeover mechanisms. *Journal of Financial Economics, 20*(1/2), 129–152.

Khanna, T., & Yafeh, Y. (2007). Business groups in emerging markets: Paragons or parasites? *Journal of Economic Literature, 45*(2), 331–372.

Kumbhakar, S. C., & Sarkar, S. (2003). Deregulation, ownership, and productivity growth: Evidence from Indian banks. *Journal of Money, Credit, and Banking, 35*(3), 403–424.

Lemmon, M., & Lins, K. V. (2003). Ownership structure, corporate governance, and firm value: Evidence from the East Asian financial crisis. *The Journal of Finance, 58*(4), 1445–1468.

Lensink, R., Meesters, A., & Naaborg, I. (2008). Bank efficiency and foreign ownership: Do good institutions matter? *Journal of Banking and Finance, 32*(5), 834–844.

Lins, K. V. (2003). Equity ownership and firm value in emerging markets. *Journal of Financial and Quantitative Analysis, 38*(1), 159–184.
Mikkelson, W. H., & Partch, M. M. (1988). Withdrawn security offerings. *Journal of Financial and Quantitative Analysis, 23*(2), 119–134.
Mitton, T. (2002). A cross-firm analysis of the impact of corporate governance on the East Asian financial crisis. *Journal of Financial Economics, 64*(2), 215–241.
Nenova, T. (2003). The value of corporate voting rights and control: A cross-country analysis. *Journal of Financial Economics, 68*(3), 325–351.
Ødegaard, B. A. (2007). Price differences between equity classes. Corporate control, foreign ownership or liquidity? *Journal of Banking and Finance, 31*(12), 3621–3645.
Partch, M. (1987). The creation of a class of limited voting common stock and shareholders' wealth. *Journal of Financial Economics, 18*(2), 313–339.
Smith, B. F., & Amoako-Adu, B. (1995). Relative prices of dual class shares. *Journal of Financial and Quantitative Analysis, 30*(2), 223–239.
Stulz, R., & Wasserfallen, W. (1995). Foreign equity investment restrictions, capital flight, and shareholder wealth maximization: Theory and evidence. *Review of Financial Studies, 8*(4), 1019–1057.
Zingales, L. (1995). What determines the value of corporate votes. *Quarterly Journal of Economics, 110*(4), 1047–1073.

Corporate Governance and Firm Valuation in Asian Emerging Markets

Yan-Leung Cheung, J. Thomas Connelly, Jesus P. Estanislao, Piman Limpaphayom, Tong Lu, and Sidharta Utama

Abstract One of the most contentious issues in the corporate governance debate is the presumed benefits of adopting internationally accepted corporate governance practices. This study investigates the relation between the quality of corporate governance practices and market valuation for listed firms in five Asian economies: China, Hong Kong, Indonesia, the Philippines, and Thailand. Based on the OECD Corporate Governance Principles (Organization of Economic Co-operation and Development, 1999), we use a survey instrument to assess the quality of corporate governance practices of listed companies in these Asian emerging markets. The new instrument represents an improvement over existing instruments as it is more comprehensive, covering five aspects of corporate governance (rights of shareholders, treatment of shareholders, roles of stakeholders, disclosure and transparency, and board responsibilities). The survey instrument also captures variation in the quality of governance practices across firms. The empirical results show there is a positive relation between the quality of corporate governance practices and firm value in each of the five nations.

Y.-L. Cheung
The Hong Kong Institute of Education, New Territories, Hong Kong

J.T. Connelly
Faculty of Commerce and Accountancy, Chulalongkorn University, Bangkok, Thailand

J.P. Estanislao
Philippines Institute of Corporate Directors, Makati City, Philippines

P. Limpaphayom (✉)
Portland State University and Sasin GIBA of Chulalongkorn University, Bangkok, Thailand
e-mail: piman@pdx.edu

T. Lu
Chinese Academy of Social Sciences, Beijing, China

S. Utama
Indonesian Institute for Corporate Directorship and University of Indonesia, Depok City, Indonesia

S. Boubaker and D.K. Nguyen (eds.), *Corporate Governance in Emerging Markets*, CSR, Sustainability, Ethics & Governance, DOI 10.1007/978-3-642-44955-0_2,

1 Introduction

Since the late 1990s, corporate governance began to receive earnest attention from regulators and investors in the Asia-Pacific region. The reason for the scrutiny is that corporate governance was identified as one of the key factors believed to have caused the Asian Financial Crisis in 1997. Zhuang et al. (2000) contend that poor corporate governance practices led to poor investment and financing decisions among firms in East Asia. As a result of the heightened awareness of firms' corporate governance practices, considerable effort has been devoted to improving the quality of corporate governance practices among firms in East Asia.

Capital market regulators have been pushing for major corporate governance reforms throughout the region. However, efforts to reform or enhance corporate governance practices in East Asia have been met with resistance and indifference on two fronts. Many managers and company owners argue that the costs of adopting good corporate governance practices outweigh the resulting benefits. In addition, costly improvements in governance may not be appreciated or valued by investors. There is a widespread perception that many investors across East Asia are less sophisticated. These investors may not be able to discern the governance improvements implemented by managers. In addition, investors may also be unable to differentiate among firms the quality of corporate governance practices. Investors are thus unable to reward firms that do improve their governance practices.

To further cloud the issue, regulators face challenges if they use the empirical evidence gathered from US firms to guide their efforts to improve governance practices in Asia. One challenge arises because there is inconclusive empirical evidence surrounding the benefits of good governance for US firms. For example, there are a number of empirical studies examining the relation between board composition and firm valuation among US firms (see for example Agrawal and Knoeber 1996; Hermalin and Weisbach 2003). However, these two studies show conflicting results. A second challenge comes about because some governance practices may not be easily extended to Asia. For example, two frequently cited studies each use a takeover code to develop a corporate governance index as a proxy of the quality of governance practices (Gompers et al. 2003; Bebchuk et al. 2009). The authors then find a positive relation between improved governance practices, based on takeover codes, and market valuation. However, since takeovers are exceedingly rare in Asia, this finding may be of limited use.

The third challenge centers on the proxies used to assess corporate governance practices. The studies by Agrawal and Knoeber (1996) and Hermalin and Weisbach (2003) use board composition as the only measure of corporate governance. However, the number of independent directors on the board represents only one aspect of corporate governance. Similarly, the governance indexes in studies by Gompers et al. (2003) and Bebchuck et al. (2009) use only the protection of shareholder rights related to corporate takeovers as the proxy for governance. The measures of corporate governance employed in these US studies fail to provide a holistic view of corporate governance practices.

A new set of problems may arise when regulators attempt to measure governance practices. Different aspects of corporate governance could be complementary. The breadth of the governance proxy thus becomes more important. In addition, it is vital to assess the quality of practices when examining the effect of governance on firm performance. The studies mentioned earlier note the presence or absence of a specific governance-related measure. With the measures these studies employ, it is not a straightforward task to distinguish between firms based solely on the overall quality of observed corporate governance practices. The key to examining the relation between governance practices and firm performance is a proper measure of corporate governance. The measure should be applicable across a wide range of institutional settings, incorporate sufficient breadth, and offer ways to discern the quality of practices between firms.

The objective of this study is to examine the relation between the corporate governance practices and firm valuation in five Asian equity markets: China, Hong Kong, Indonesia, the Philippines, and Thailand. Using annual, publicly available information from publicly traded firms, we rate the corporate governance practices of the major companies in each market.

This study makes three contributions to the literature. First, a comprehensive survey of corporate governance practices is used to assess the quality of corporate governance practices of firms in these five East Asian countries. The questions in the survey are based on the OECD Principles of Corporate Governance Principles (OECD 1999). These five principles are: (A) Rights of Shareholders, (B) Equitable Treatment of Shareholders, (C) Role of Stakeholders, (D) Disclosure and Transparency, and (E) Board Responsibilities. In each country, the survey was completed several times during 2002–2008. The survey quantifies the quality of the corporate governance practices in use. The results of the survey yield a Corporate Governance Index (CGI) value for each company. There is some variation in the surveys used in the five markets because of differences in the regulatory frameworks. While each market has a unique version of the corporate governance survey instrument, there are 81 criteria common to all five markets. To make a cross-country comparison, the CGI scores are standardized based on the common 81 criteria compiled from each market.

The second contribution concerns the procedure used to measure corporate governance practices. In many prior studies, researchers calculate the governance measure by searching for specific items of information in firms' annual reports and financial statements. Each firm receives one point for the presence of an item and zero points if an item is missing. The procedure in this study represents a major improvement from the methods commonly found in previous work. This study adds a qualitative element to the assessment of governance practices. We evaluate the amount and quality of information for many of the criteria in the governance survey. Consequently, the final CGI scores are more comprehensive, and the scores are more representative of the quality of the corporate governance practices, after taking into account the quantity of the reported practices.

For the final contribution, this study examines the relation between corporate governance and firm valuation in emerging markets in the Asia-Pacific region. We hypothesize a positive relation between the CGI and firm valuation. The reason is that a nation's corporate governance framework exists to encourage the efficient use of resources and to require accountability for the stewardship of the resources. As stated by Sir Adrian Cadbury: "Corporate governance is concerned with holding the balance between economic and social goals and between individual and communal goals.... The aim is to align as closely as possible the interests of individuals, corporations and society" (Iskander and Chamlou 2000, p. vi). Therefore, good corporate governance makes corporations more transparent and makes monitoring easier for shareholders and outsiders. Improved monitoring and transparency should improve the accountability of the managers, leading to better or more efficient investment decisions and eventually to higher shareholder value. An understanding of the relation between the quality of corporate governance practices and firm valuation has policy implications for capital market development. The results could also provide incentives for managers and founding families to adopt good corporate governance practices.

Previous studies have largely focused on developed markets such as the US and European markets; comparably few studies have been completed for Asian markets. Asia has been demonstrating rapid economic growth since the 1980s. As a result, investment interest has been rising, particularly investments targeting China and India. International fund management companies have launched a range of investment vehicles, some dedicated solely to Asia and some with explicit policies to invest a fixed portion of the portfolio in the region. Apart from the growth potential of the region, fund managers may seek to diversify away the risk inherent in developed markets, such as the US and Europe.

Asian equity markets are, however, quite different from those of western countries. Firms comprising the Asian business community are characterized by high family ownership and a lack of transparency. The 1997 Asian Financial Crisis was the key event spawning awareness of the need for corporate governance reform in the Asia-Pacific region. The traditional agency problem of managers versus shareholders is rarely applicable in Asia because there is seldom a separation of management and ownership. For example, it is common to find that the chairman of the board is also the chief executive officer in Asian listed companies. Top management teams are frequently peppered with family members who are also shareholders. In addition, market disciplinary mechanisms, such as hostile takeovers, cannot function properly in Asia because of the concentrated or family ownership. This could explain why corporate governance has had a slow start in Asia.

As another complication, the enforcement mechanisms in many Asian economies are relatively weaker than in the US. In most cases, the regulators in Asian countries do not have the kind of legal or regulatory power enjoyed by their US counterparts. In addition, investors in Asia are fragmented and often lack the legal powers that US investors possess. For example, class action lawsuits are not available in most countries in Asia. Consequently, it is possible that the lack of enforcement and legal power makes the quality of corporate governance more important for firms in Asian markets.

Our empirical results show that the corporate governance practices of the listed firms in these five markets fluctuated during the sample period. More importantly, the empirical findings offer compelling evidence that good corporate governance practices matter in these five markets and that the market rewards firms with superior corporate governance practices. We observe a positive and statistically significant relation between firm valuation and the quality of corporate governance practices, as measured by the corporate governance index (CGI), even after the addition of variables to control for differences in firm characteristics. To check the robustness of our findings, we employ a simultaneous equations estimation technique to take into account the possibility that well-performing firms also tend to improve the quality of their corporate governance practices. Even after controlling for endogeneity, the results from the two-stage least squares (2SLS) regression analyses confirm the positive relation between the quality of corporate governance practices and firm valuation.

The remainder of this chapter is organized as follows. We provide a brief literature review in the next section, followed by overviews of the institutional backgrounds for each of the five nations we study. The data and empirical methodology are described in Section 4. Section 5 contains a discussion of the empirical results, followed by the conclusion in Section 6.

2 Literature Review

A growing body of literature studies the relation between corporate governance and stock market valuation or firm performance in both developed and emerging markets. In the past, the empirical approach has been to examine specific aspects of corporate governance such as ownership concentration (e.g., Himmelberg et al. 1999; Morck et al. 1988; Barontini and Caprio 2006), board composition (e.g., Agrawal and Knoeber 1996; Hermalin and Weisbach 2003), or executive compensation (e.g., Abowd and Kaplan 1999; Bebchuk et al. 2002). However, these empirical studies provide contradictory or inconclusive evidence of the presumed benefits of adopting good corporate governance practices.

Several recent studies have utilized a different approach by constructing an overall governance index and then examining the effect of overall corporate governance practices on firm value (Black 2001; Gompers et al. 2003; Klapper and Love 2003; Bebchuk et al. 2009; Durnev and Kim 2005; Black et al. 2006; Cheung et al. 2007). The logic behind this approach is that corporate governance mechanisms may be substitutes for one another. Consequently, one must consider the overall quality of corporate governance when examining the impact on firm performance.

In one of the most widely cited studies on corporate governance, Gompers et al. (2003) construct a "Governance Index" (G-Index) to proxy for the level of shareholder rights at approximately 1,500 large U.S. firms during the 1990s. The G-Index consists of 24 provisions related to takeover defenses and shareholder rights. They find that firms with stronger shareholder rights have higher firm value, higher profits, higher sales growth, and lower capital expenditures. Firms with stronger shareholder rights also make fewer corporate acquisitions. They also document a statistically significant positive relationship between G-Index scores and stock returns over the sample period. They posit that weak shareholder rights create agency conflicts which, in turn, lead to low firm value in the long run. Because of this influential study, the G-Index has become one widely-cited benchmark for measuring the corporate governance quality of U.S. companies.

Bebchuk et al. (2009) also put forward a governance measure based around shareholder rights. The authors construct an entrenchment index based on six provisions: four "constitutional" provisions that prevent a majority of shareholders from having their way (staggered boards, limits to shareholder bylaw amendments, supermajority requirements for mergers, and supermajority requirements for charter amendments), plus two "takeover readiness" provisions that boards put in place to defend against hostile takeovers (poison pills and golden parachutes). These six provisions are selected from a total of 24 governance provisions developed by the Investor Responsibility Research Center (IRRC). Bebchuk et al. (2009) examine the relation between market valuation and performance of US firms during 1990–2003. They find a negative relation between the index scores and firm valuation, as measured by Tobin's q. They conclude the entrenchment provisions lead to low market valuations among US firms. The two corporate governance indexes mentioned above make important contributions to the literature on takeover defenses in the US. However, the studies are of limited relevance to markets where hostile takeovers are rare.

Compared to research in developed markets, recent research on the relation between corporate governance and firm performance in emerging markets generates results more demonstrative of the benefits of good governance practices. Black et al. (2006) construct a corporate governance index for 515 Korean companies using a survey conducted by the Korea Stock Exchange. They also document a positive relation between the quality of corporate governance practices and market valuation, as measured by Tobin's q and the market-to-book ratio. In addition, the two-stage and three-stage least squares analyses confirm their ordinary least squares regression results. Black et al. (2006) conclude that an overall corporate governance index is an important factor, and likely a causal factor, in explaining the market value of Korean public companies. For Russian firms, Black (2001) constructs a corporate governance risk measure and finds a positive relation between corporate governance practices and market valuation among a small sample of 21 Russian firms.

Cheung et al. (2007) examine the relation between corporate governance and firm value using a single year of data from major companies listed on the Hong Kong Stock Exchange. Their corporate governance index is based on the OECD Principles of Corporate Governance (1999). Unlike measures used in other studies, their index reflects not only the presence of good corporate governance practices but also the variation in the quality of corporate governance practices. The authors show that company market valuation is positively related to the overall composite measure of corporate governance practices. In summary, their study provides cross-sectional evidence supporting the notion that, in Hong Kong, good corporate governance practices are consistent with value maximization.

Studies of Chinese firms show empirical evidence supporting the benefits of adopting good corporate governance practices. However, the results befit an evolving economy, in contrast with prior research in developing markets. For instance, Cheung et al. (2008) find no contemporaneous relation between corporate governance and firm valuation when examining the relation between the quality of corporate governance practices and firm valuation. However, using more recent data, Cheung et al. (2009) show results in support of the notion that good corporate governance relates to market valuation in China. The finding that corporate governance matters in China is quite striking. In both studies, most of the firms in the samples are state-owned enterprises. Investors appear to take into account the quality of corporate governance practices of a firm when making their investment decisions.

There is another stream of research which compares the relation between the overall quality of corporate governance and firm performance among different markets. Durnev and Kim (2005) use an aggregate approach to assess whether corporate governance predicts firm market value. They employ the Credit Lyonnais Securities Asia (CLSA) aggregate governance index and the S&P disclosure score (Patel and Dallas, 2002) to measure corporate governance practices for a sample of 859 large firms in 27 countries. Durnev and Kim (2005) conclude that firms with higher scores are valued higher in their respective stock markets. In a separate study, Klapper and Love (2003) also use the CLSA aggregate governance index to examine the relation between corporate governance and firm performance for 374 firms in 14 countries. They find positive correlations between corporate governance and two performance measures: market valuation and return on assets. Doidge et al. (2007) show that country characteristics, such as the legal protection of minority shareholders and the level of a nation's economic and financial development, affect firms' costs and benefits when implementing measures to improve corporate governance and transparency.

3 Institutional Background

The push for corporate governance reform in Asia originated at the onset of the 1997 Asian Financial Crisis, which exposed structural weaknesses inherent in many Asian economies. Since then, a wide range of regulatory changes and structural reforms have been implemented throughout the region. The following nation-by-nation overviews highlight the key elements in the corporate governance reform efforts in the five countries included in this study.

3.1 China

Two institutional features drive the governance framework in China. The first is the fact that the majority of listed companies are majority-owned by the government. The second feature is that the stock market is heavily regulated by the government, an approach to governance called "administrative governance" by Pistor and Xu (2005). The guiding pieces of legislation for the stock markets in China are the Company Law (1993) and the Securities Law (1998). Another important law, the 1985 Accounting Law, was revised in 1999. Cheung et al. (2008) note that the "administrative governance" actions may have stymied efforts to create an effective governance system in China. The authors also note that Chinese stock markets have "concentrated ownership by the state, ... a weak legal system, inadequate financial disclosure, [and] expropriation of minority shareholders by controlling shareholders (p. 466)" as well as short-run speculative behavior by investors. These problems are serious challenges to the improvement of corporate governance practices in China.

A Code of Corporate Governance of Listed Companies was released in 2002. The Code was jointly released by the China Securities Regulatory Commission and the National Economic and Trade Commission. The Code was based on the OECD Principles, and spelled out the foundations of a corporate governance system. In an effort to establish a corporate governance framework in China, both the Company Law and the Securities Law were revised in 2006. The revisions updated many aspects of governance, including improved shareholder protection, outlining the duties and responsibilities of directors, and improved disclosure requirements. Despite the recent improvements, the Chinese regulators continue to make a concerted effort to improve the quality of corporate governance practices among Chinese listed companies.

3.2 Hong Kong

Hong Kong has been recognized as having governance practices approaching international standards. The Securities and Futures Commission, which was established in 1989, oversees the capital market in Hong Kong. Hong Kong Stock Exchange has had, as part of its listing rules, a Code of Best Practices since 1993. In addition to the Code, the regulatory authorities have made significant efforts to improve corporate governance practices after the Asian Financial Crisis (World Bank 2003). Proof of these efforts came with the passage of the Securities and Futures Ordinance in 2003. The Ordinance was promulgated to improve governance practices and offer greater protection to shareholders. Amendments to the Companies Ordinance, effective in 2004, improved the protection of shareholders' rights and expanded the requirements and expectations for directors.

Not content to rest on its good reputation, the Hong Kong Stock Exchange continues to update the requirements it sets for public companies. Recently, the Exchange announced new requirements, effective in 2012. The new requirements will bring Hong Kong firms closer to international best practices. For example, boards of directors must now have independent directors comprise one-third of the board, and boards must have a remuneration committee. The new requirements stress improved disclosure and transparency, and clarify and expand the obligations and requirements for directors. Through all the activity going into improving governance practices at listed firms, Hong Kong is striving to maintain its status as the financial center of Asia.

3.3 Indonesia

Indonesia has made drastic advancements in governance since the Asian Financial Crisis (World Bank 2004, 2010). Indonesia established a National Committee on Corporate Governance in 1999. The National Committee created and adopted the Code of Good Corporate Governance in 1999. The Code was then amended in 2006. A new Company Law was introduced in 2006. The revised Company Law listed the duties expected of board members. The revised Company Law also includes provisions for shareholders to seek compensation for violations of their rights. The capital market regulator (Bapepam-LK) is responsible for implementing the Company Law (1995) and the Capital Market Law (1995). Bapepam-LK issued updated regulations in 2008 and 2009 covering related party transactions, and increasing the level of disclosure required of firms. For example, the updated regulations now require independent shareholders to approve certain related party transactions that are deemed to be conflicts of interest.

Some weaknesses remain in the corporate governance system in Indonesia. For example, major shareholdings are required to be reported, but beneficial or ultimate share ownership is not. Ownership remains highly concentrated. Concentrated ownership and the lack of disclosure affect the ability of minority shareholders to influence the selection or appointments of directors. In the wake of the reform efforts, financial disclosure by firms has improved markedly. However, shareholders often face difficulty getting access to other company information, such as compensation for and the qualifications of board members. Corporate governance statements are voluntary. While many companies have statements, the statements that do exist often have limited content. In addition, listed companies are not required to "comply or explain" with the Code of Good Corporate Governance. As a result, compliance with the Code has slipped in recent years. In addition, awareness of the code by the general public has eroded somewhat. Nevertheless, the Indonesian regulators are still moving forward with new rules and regulations, working closely with listed firms to improve the quality of corporate governance practices in Indonesia.

3.4 Philippines

Corporate governance reform efforts in the Philippines began in earnest in 2000 when the Securities Regulation Code was passed (World Bank 2006). The Code gave new powers to the capital market regulator, established other important safeguards to protect minority shareholders, and made significant changes to enhance other regulatory agencies. For example, the Securities Regulation Code and the Code of Corporate Governance mandate that firms have at least two independent directors, or enough independent directors to comprise 20 % of the board. The Code of Corporate Governance also mandated that each firm have an audit committee, comprised of at least three board members. At least two members of the audit committee should be independent directors, with one independent director serving as chairman of the committee. In 2002, the Securities Exchange Commission (SEC), the capital market regulator, issued a Code of Corporate Governance. All listed companies were expected to observe the Code, and make available to shareholders a Manual of Corporate Governance. By 2005, the SEC required all companies to submit a self-assessment questionnaire. The objective of the survey was to get firms to evaluate their observance of corporate governance principles.

Corporate governance practices have been strengthened through the creation of a number of institutions and organizations, such as the Institute for Corporate Directors and the Corporate Governance Institute of the Philippines. IFRS reporting standards were implemented in 2005, improving the level of disclosure, the quality of financial reporting, and boosting disclosure and transparency. Provisions in the Corporation Code and the Securities Regulation Code help protect shareholder rights. The SEC now requires firms to provide a list of all shareholders. In addition, the Securities Regulation Code requires firms to disclose beneficial ownership and managerial ownership above certain thresholds. This requirement is especially valuable to shareholders, as public companies in the Philippines are largely family owned. Pyramidal shareholding structures are common. Despite the existence of many laws, rules, and regulation, there remains a notable divergence between observed practices at firms and the enforcement of the laws and regulations. The regulators in the Philippines continue to focus on improving legal enforcements and the quality of corporate governance practices in the Republic.

3.5 Thailand

The underlying legal and regulatory frameworks in Thailand are the Securities and Exchange Act (1992) and the Public Company Act (1992). The Securities and Exchange Act or SEA is enforced by the Securities and Exchange Commission, established in 1992 with the passage of the SEA. Although the stock market was growing at a very fast pace during the 1990s, corporate governance rarely received attention from the regulators, firms, or investors. Poor governance practices led to excessive investments and aggressive financing, which, in turn, led to the Asian Financial Crisis in 1997.

Governance reform efforts began in Thailand in 1998, immediately after the start of the Asian Financial Crisis (World Bank 2005). Several institutions were created in the wake of the reform efforts, such as the Thai Institute of Directors Association in 1999. That year also brought the release of a Code of Best Practices for directors, written by the Stock Exchange of Thailand, and a new law requiring improved disclosure. Another landmark governance reform event came in 2001 when the Stock Exchange of Thailand (SET) released a wide-ranging report on governance. The report created governance principles and guidelines for listed companies. The guidelines spanned board practices, disclosure standards, and many other areas. New SET regulations promulgated in 2001 forced boards of Thai public companies to establish an audit committee, staffed with at least three independent directors. In the financial services sector, the Bank of Thailand introduced new regulations, aimed at tightening disclosure standards and forcing financial services companies to have an internal audit function. The National Corporate Governance committee was formed in 2002. The Committee included representatives from government ministries, industry associations, and regulatory bodies. That same year, the SET issued its 15 Principles of Good Corporate Governance. Newly listed companies were required to "comply or explain" with the Principles.

Since the flurry of activity immediately after the Asian Financial Crisis, governance reform efforts have continued. The SET has introduced measures to improve the exercise of minority shareholders' rights at annual meetings and improve disclosure standards for executive and director remuneration. The SET recently introduced a measure to require public company boards to have independent directors comprise one-third of the board. In spite of the progress over the past decade and a half, the Thai government is still determined to improve the state of corporate governance in the Kingdom.

4 Data and Methodology

The sample consists of a select group of the largest public companies in five Asian nations: China, Hong Kong, Indonesia, the Philippines, and Thailand. The sample size varies depending on the number of firms included in the governance survey in a particular country in each year. Due to budgetary and logistical constraints, the surveys were not conducted in the same years in all the countries. In the end, there are total of 356 firm-year observations for China, 502 for Hong Kong, 514 for Indonesia, 330 for the Philippines, and 985 for Thailand. The descriptive statistics in Table 1 show the number of firms surveyed in each year for each nation.

The centerpiece of this study is an index constructed to measure the quality of corporate governance practices. Adapted from the OECD Principles of Corporate Governance (1999), we establish a set of criteria to measure corporate governance. The classification scheme for the criteria mirrors the five subsections of the OECD

Table 1 Descriptive statistics of Corporate Governance Index by country and survey year

	Year	CGI	Section A	Section B	Section C	Section D	Section E	Number of firms
China								
Mean	2003	54.63	39.79	71.53	15.31	73.18	46.76	80
	2004	53.39	32.42	72.45	33.04	75.44	45.21	84
	2005	58.72	57.73	71.84	23.81	80.40	46.31	96
	2006	50.78	57.33	60.94	26.76	67.43	42.95	96
Std Dev	2003	4.84	8.56	8.34	13.70	6.88	10.41	
	2004	5.32	9.03	12.09	17.64	8.36	9.04	
	2005	5.96	10.40	7.81	14.39	11.26	7.62	
	2006	7.21	12.79	12.47	15.25	15.75	10.05	
Hong Kong								
Mean	2002	57.12	53.56	76.04	54.35	62.21	46.11	161
	2004	57.28	56.37	65.83	39.09	80.37	48.87	167
	2005	68.73	64.64	67.88	44.41	84.30	68.79	174
Std Dev	2002	6.80	10.36	7.69	19.48	7.83	12.69	
	2004	11.72	10.88	8.51	20.39	8.20	18.79	
	2005	9.20	10.06	8.80	19.33	7.97	14.47	
Indonesia								
Mean	2005	51.21	18.74	82.76	54.31	62.22	45.27	58
	2006	40.22	26.80	74.80	39.18	60.39	28.62	297
	2008	46.86	25.87	81.26	48.20	58.35	40.55	159
Std Dev	2005	12.56	7.69	6.22	29.39	17.86	19.49	
	2006	10.34	6.21	11.09	23.30	13.86	16.21	
	2008	11.72	7.15	7.06	21.12	18.79	17.11	
Philippines								
Mean	2005	52.32	34.07	82.67	42.50	71.54	33.43	45
	2006	53.62	45.80	75.28	42.36	67.59	37.17	54
	2007	62.20	64.81	82.71	57.51	77.00	44.92	107
	2008	72.41	77.08	87.10	66.09	78.05	59.11	124
Std Dev	2005	8.45	12.12	13.88	29.60	12.23	12.16	
	2006	10.91	18.04	15.55	29.88	15.00	13.13	
	2007	13.00	19.13	13.19	25.86	14.27	16.05	
	2008	14.21	18.98	11.09	24.31	17.27	19.04	
Thailand								
Mean	2002	57.61	72.45	69.32	43.06	55.54	49.26	294
	2004	61.30	63.68	72.52	61.80	74.05	50.09	327
	2005	61.79	64.40	74.85	64.04	73.09	50.84	364
Std Dev	2002	7.76	10.71	6.61	18.94	10.26	11.45	
	2004	9.37	13.03	7.61	20.07	7.68	13.30	
	2005	10.82	14.54	7.92	19.70	10.01	14.91	

This table presents the descriptive statistics of the corporate governance index (*CGI*) and the five sub-indices based on the OECD Corporate Governance Principles (1999). The CGI ranges from 0 to 100. The sample is drawn from publicly-traded firms in China, Hong Kong, Indonesia, the Philippines, and Thailand. The surveys were completed during 2002–2008 but not for every country in every year. The five subsections in the corporate governance indices are: rights of shareholders (Section A); equitable treatment of shareholders (Section B); role of stakeholders (Section C); disclosure and transparency (Section D); and board responsibilities (Section E)

Corporate Governance Principles: (A) Rights of Shareholders; (B) Equitable Treatment of Shareholders; (C) Role of Stakeholders; (D) Disclosure and Transparency; and (E) Board Responsibilities. In each nation, a small number of unique survey items apply only to that particular country. To enable insightful comparisons across firms and across different survey years, the core version of the survey, with the original 81 criteria, is used to build the CGI scores. The measurement instrument is attached in the Appendix. A brief discussion of each of the OECD Principles follows.

The first section of the survey covers the protection of shareholders' rights through the corporate governance structure. The corporate governance structure should also make it easy for shareholders to exercise their rights. Basic shareholder rights include secure methods to register ownership and transfer shares, regular and timely provision of company information, the ability to participate and vote in general shareholder meetings, elect and remove members of the board, and obtain a share of the profits. A total of 15 measures are included in this section of the survey, designed to capture the actual rights of shareholders.

The next section assesses the equitable treatment of shareholders. In East Asia, it is common for majority shareholders to have an advantage over outside, minority shareholders (Claessens et al. 2002). Thus, the equitable treatment of shareholders is critical. All shareholders should be treated similarly whether they are a dominant owner, a minority owner, or a foreign shareholder. For example, equitable treatment would include the processes and procedures employed at shareholder meetings. Equitable treatment means that all types of shareholders can vote easily and inexpensively. There are 10 items used to evaluate the equitable treatment of shareholders.

The third section of the survey evaluates the roles of stakeholders in corporate governance, specifically the interactions of the firm with stakeholder groups such as employees, creditors, suppliers, shareholders, and the environment. The corporate governance framework should recognize the rights of stakeholders established by law or through mutual agreements, and encourage active cooperation between corporations and stakeholders in creating financially sound enterprises. This section assesses whether stakeholders can participate in the corporate governance process or have access to relevant and reliable information on a timely and regular basis. There are four survey items in this section.

The fourth section covers disclosure and transparency, the cornerstones of good governance. The firm should ensure timely and accurate disclosure of matters that are important to investors and regulators. Examples include the firm's financial situation, performance, and ownership. This section gauges whether the information was prepared and disclosed in accordance with acceptable corporate standards of accounting, as well as the standards for financial and non-financial disclosure. Further, it assesses whether the channels for disseminating information provide for equal, timely, and cost-efficient access to the relevant information by all users. Twenty-nine items in the survey assess disclosure practices.

The final section of the survey evaluates board responsibilities, an area that has generated extensive research. The OECD Principles assert that the board plays an important role ensuring strategic guidance and effective monitoring of the managers. The board is accountable to the company and the shareholders. In total, there are 29 survey items used to assess board responsibilities.

From the standpoint of good corporate governance practices, the main concern in most Asian emerging markets is the well-being of outside/minority shareholders. Consequently, in this study it is more appropriate to assess the quality of corporate governance practices from the perspective of outside shareholders (i.e., assessments based on publicly available information obtainable when making investment decisions). Our data sources include annual reports, articles of association, memorandums of association, notices to call shareholders' meetings, annual general meeting minutes, company websites, analyst reports, and other sources available to the general public.

We rate each company on each criterion in the survey. The overall corporate governance index (*CGI*) for each company is the equally weighted score of the 81 criteria that are common to the surveys used in each country. We also create scores for five sub-indexes by using the equally weighted average score of all criteria contained in each section. All indexes, including the overall *CGI* and the five sub-indexes, are transformed so that the scores range from 0 to 100. We calculate a total corporate governance rating for each company, and this score ranges from 0 to 100. High *CGI* scores indicate good corporate governance practices whereas low scores indicate poor corporate governance practices. The *CGI* scores allow us to quantify the quality of corporate governance practices and investigate the effect of corporate governance practices, as measured by the *CGI*, on firm valuation.

Other financial data are obtained from Datastream. All data are matched according to the fiscal year of each sample firm. In the analysis, Tobin's q is used as the measure of firm valuation. Tobin's q is defined as the sum of the market value of equity plus the book value of total (all interest-bearing) debt divided by the sum of the book value of equity plus the book value of total debt. The values for Tobin's q have been winsorized to offset extreme values, which may have an undue influence in the regression analyses. To make sure that the results are not driven by firm heterogeneity, control variables are included in the regression model. The control variables used are: firm size (natural logarithm of the book value of total assets in local currency at the end of the fiscal year); leverage (measured as the debt-equity ratio or total interest-bearing divided by the total assets); liquidity (measured as cash holdings scaled by total assets); and the level of investment (measured as capital expenditures scaled by total assets). Variables to indicate the survey year are also included in the regression as a year fixed effect.

For each of the five nations, we conduct a regression analysis shown in Eq. 1 using all observations across all the years that data are available. We estimate the following model:

$$q_i = \beta_0 + \beta_1 CGI_i + \beta_2 Size_i + \beta_3 Leverage_i + \beta_4 Liquidity_i + \beta_5 Investments_i + \beta_t Year + \varepsilon_i \quad (1)$$

We hypothesize there is a positive relation between the quality of corporate governance practices, as measured by *CGI*, and firm valuation, as measured by Tobin's *q*. The regression coefficients for *CGI* will show the relation between the quality of corporate governance practices and firm valuation.

There is also a possibility that well-performing companies have incentives to improve the quality of their corporate governance practices. Therefore, the observed relation between *CGI* and Tobin's *q* may be a result of endogeneity in the relationship. To check the robustness of the results, we also perform the following two-stage least squares regression analysis, for each nation:

$$q_i = \beta_0 + \beta_1 CGI_i + \beta_2 Size_i + \beta_3 Leverage_i + \beta_4 Liquidity_i + \beta_5 Investments_i + \beta_t Year + \varepsilon_i \quad (2)$$

$$CGI_i = \beta_0 + \beta_1 q_i + \beta_2 Size_i + \beta_3 Leverage_i + \beta_t Year + \varepsilon_i \quad (3)$$

A positive and statistically significant coefficient for *CGI* in Eq. 2 will be supporting evidence of the positive relation between the quality of corporate governance practices and firm valuation in the five Asian nations in the study. This should confirm that the relationship is robust. We shall also observe the regression coefficient for Tobin's *q* in Eq. 3. If the coefficient for Tobin's *q* in Eq. 3 is statistically significant, it implies that there is a relation between firm valuation and the quality of corporate governance.

5 Empirical Results

5.1 Descriptive Statistics

Descriptive statistics for the *CGI* are contained in Table 1. For each nation, graphs of the overall *CGI* score and the scores for five survey subsections are shown in Fig. 1. The results are presented for each of the five countries in the sample, for each survey year.

For the firms surveyed in China, the yearly average *CGI* score does not exhibit a clear pattern. From an average value of 54.63 on the initial survey in 2003, the score falls slightly to 53.39, then rises to 58.72 in 2005 but falls to 50.78 in 2006. The scores on the individual subsections also do not show a clear pattern. The average scores for Section A, Protection of Shareholder Rights, rise from 39.79 in 2003 to 57.33 in 2006, but do not exhibit a consistent pattern of rises. The yearly averages for Section C, Rights of Stakeholders, also show the same pattern. In contrast, the average value for Section B, Equitable Treatment of Shareholders, is around 71 for

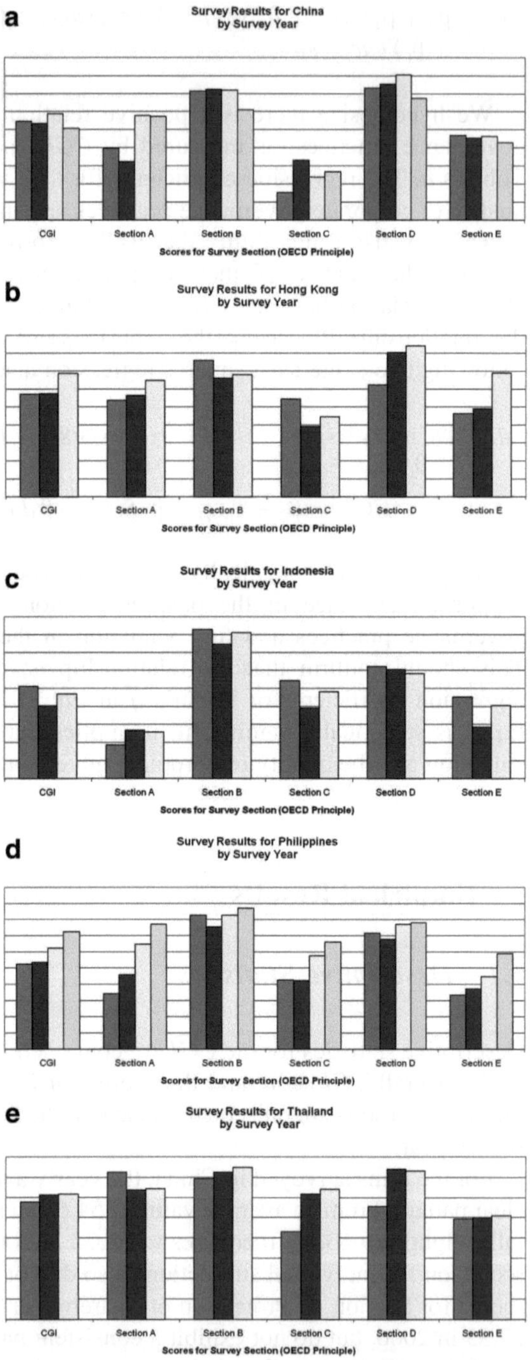

Fig. 1 Average CGI scores by country. The following figures show the average scores of the Corporate Governance index (CGI) for each of the five nations surveyed: (**a**) China (2003–2006); (**b**) Hong Kong (2002, 2004, and 2005); (**c**) Indonesia (2005, 2006, and 2008); (**d**) the Philippines (2005–2008); and (**e**) Thailand (2002, 2004, and 2005). The data are taken from the years in which a corporate governance survey was conducted. The five subsections in the corporate governance survey are: Section A, Rights of Shareholders; Section B, Equitable Treatment of Shareholders; Section C, Role of Stakeholders; Section D, Disclosure and Transparency; and Section E, Board Responsibilities.

the first three years of the survey, but then the average falls sharply, dropping below 61 in 2006. This pattern is repeated for Section D, Disclosure and Transparency, and for Section E, Board Responsibilities. Overall, the descriptive statistics are consistent with the situation in China. Awareness of corporate governance is gradually gaining momentum. However, the adoption of improved governance practices by firms is still in the early stages.

Looking next at the survey results for Hong Kong, the *CGI* rises steadily across the three survey years, from an average of 57.12 in 2002 to 68.73 in 2005. This is consistent with the notion that the Hong Kong market has made continuous improvements and is moving to the forefront of the corporate governance movement in Asia. The subsection results for Sections A, D, and E show similar, steady improvements. However, the average values for Sections B and C do not show consistent improvement. The average for Section B is 76.04 in 2002 but then it falls to 65.83 and rises slightly to 67.88 during the two subsequent survey years. Likewise, the average value for Section C is the highest in the first survey year, then it tumbles and recovers in the two following years. This is the reason that the regulators in Hong Kong are still pushing new reform measures to protect minority investors and other stakeholders.

The results for Indonesian firms show an uneven pattern, as the *CGI* score rises from an average of 51.21 in 2005, then falls to 40.22 before rising to 46.86 in the most recent survey conducted in 2008. The patterns across the subsections are inconsistent. For Sections B, C, D, and E, the average values drop in the second survey year, but then rise in the last survey year. Section A shows a different pattern. The average value for Section A rises in the second year but then falls slightly in the final survey year. It is noteworthy that the values for Section A are by far the lowest of the five sections. It is possible that the uneven patterns may be the result of the large changes in the sample sizes for the three survey years. The first survey year covered only the 58 largest companies. The sample in the second year zoomed to 297 firms but only 159 companies were included in the third survey. The greater numbers of smaller firms included in the surveys could explain the observed drops in the *CGI* and subsection scores. Smaller companies often have governance practices that lag practices at larger firms.

Firms surveyed in the Philippines showed a steady improvement across the four survey years, as gauged by the *CGI*. The average value was 52.32 in the first survey year and the average rose steadily to 72.41 by 2008. This pattern was largely consistent across Sections A, C, and E. Sections B and D each recorded a slight decrease in the second survey year, but then the section averages increased steadily for the following two years. These results are noteworthy as the sample size more than doubled, rising from 54 firms in the second survey year to 107 firms and 124 companies in the third and fourth surveys. The results provide support to the notion that the reform effort by the regulators and related parties is gaining ground in the Philippines.

Lastly, the survey results overall show a steady improvement in corporate governance among Thai firms. The sample of Thai companies was the largest of the five countries included in this survey. The average *CGI* value rose consistently from 57.61 in the first survey year to 61.79 in the final year. Sections B, C, and E showed a similar pattern of steady improvement. The average for Section A exhibited a marked deterioration in the second survey year, with a slight improvement in the final year. However, the value had not returned to the level recorded in the first year. Section D showed a large improvement from the first year to the second, followed by a slight decrease in the last survey year. Interestingly, the scores on board responsibilities are always the lowest among Thai firms. The regulators in Thailand are still working to improve the quality and practices of boards of directors among listed firms in the Stock Exchange of Thailand.

Descriptive statistics for the firms in the sample are presented in Table 2, again separated by country. The values of Tobin's q show a wide range across the five countries in the sample. Chinese firms have the highest value of Tobin's q, with an average of 2.09 across four sample years. At the other end of the spectrum, the average Tobin's q value is lowest for Thai firms, with an average value of 1.28 across the three survey years. Within a country, this performance measure exhibits a large amount of variation, as shown by the wide range of annual values. For example, for the sample of Chinese firms, Tobin's q ranged from a low yearly average value of 1.48 in 2004 to a high of 3.06 in 2006.

The other company characteristics selected as control variables did not show as much year-to-year variation with a country. The values of leverage, as measured by the book value of total interest-bearing debt divided by total assets, were not excessive. Thai firms showed the highest values of leverage, with an average ratio of 25 % across the three survey years. The average values for the cash to total assets ratio (*Liquidity*) ranged from 10 % to 16 % across the five countries, while the average ratio of capital expenditures to total assets (*Investments*) spanned a low of 4 % in the Philippines to a high of 8 % in China. In summary, the financial variables show some notable differences when compared across countries. However, the ratios *within* a country seemed relatively consistent over time.

5.2 *Quality of Corporate Governance (CGI) and Firm Valuation*

Table 3 reports the results of multivariate regressions of Tobin's q on the corporate governance index and other explanatory variables, as shown in Eq. 1. The regressions are pooled regressions, incorporating all firm-year observations for single country in one regression. The regressions include year fixed effects. Table 3 shows that all regressions are statistically significant at the 1 % level or better.

With *CGI* as the independent variable, all five markets show a positive relation between the level of corporate governance score and firm valuation as measured by Tobin's q. All five coefficients are statistically significant at conventional levels. The regressions control for firm size, leverage, cash holdings, and capital expenditures. The positive relation between the quality of corporate governance practices

Table 2 Descriptive statistics

	Year	Tobin's *q*	Market value (millions)	Size	Leverage	Liquidity	Investments	Sample size
China								
Mean	2003	1.82	34.52	16.53	0.23	0.15	0.08	80
	2004	1.48	30.90	16.71	0.24	0.14	0.09	84
	2005	1.89	37.48	16.70	0.20	0.16	0.08	96
	2006	3.06	94.94	17.05	0.23	0.15	0.08	96
All years		**2.09**	**50.75**	**16.76**	**0.22**	**0.15**	**0.08**	**356**
Std Dev	2003	0.72	103.57	1.39	0.16	0.10	0.07	
	2004	0.68	94.15	1.41	0.16	0.10	0.07	
	2005	1.00	128.07	1.58	0.16	0.15	0.07	
	2006	2.40	276.26	1.70	0.17	0.14	0.07	
All years		**1.55**	**173.21**	**1.54**	**0.16**	**0.13**	**0.07**	
Hong Kong								
Mean	2002	1.36	24.18	16.20	0.18	0.16	0.04	161
	2004	1.76	43.90	16.60	0.18	0.16	0.05	167
	2005	1.75	51.42	16.89	0.19	0.15	0.06	174
All years		**1.63**	**40.18**	**16.57**	**0.19**	**0.16**	**0.05**	**502**
Std Dev	2002	1.13	77.50	1.65	0.14	0.15	0.05	
	2004	1.19	140.90	1.57	0.15	0.15	0.07	
	2005	1.40	155.09	1.54	0.16	0.14	0.07	
All years		**1.26**	**130.13**	**1.61**	**0.15**	**0.14**	**0.06**	
Indonesia								
Mean	2005	1.80	11,118.85	22.53	0.22	0.14	0.06	58
	2006	1.39	4,042.38	20.59	0.23	0.10	0.05	297
	2008	1.27	4,645.40	21.14	0.22	0.13	0.06	159
All years		**1.40**	**5,027.43**	**20.98**	**0.23**	**0.11**	**0.05**	**514**
Std Dev	2005	1.30	18,675.01	1.59	0.19	0.12	0.07	
	2006	1.09	15,113.72	1.86	0.20	0.12	0.08	
	2008	1.06	15,029.21	1.97	0.21	0.16	0.09	
All years		**1.12**	**15,649.98**	**1.96**	**0.20**	**0.13**	**0.08**	
Philippines								
Mean	2005	1.36	37.90	17.74	0.24	0.11	0.04	45
	2006	1.73	51.25	17.40	0.20	0.14	0.04	54
	2007	2.05	31.73	15.80	0.15	0.14	0.03	107
	2008	1.29	16.37	15.91	0.17	0.14	0.05	124
All years		**1.62**	**29.99**	**16.37**	**0.18**	**0.14**	**0.04**	**330**
Std Dev	2005	0.78	60.12	1.35	0.19	0.13	0.05	
	2006	1.16	81.58	1.56	0.16	0.14	0.04	
	2007	2.06	74.65	2.05	0.16	0.14	0.04	
	2008	1.51	43.70	2.05	0.16	0.14	0.07	
All years		**1.62**	**64.95**	**2.05**	**0.17**	**0.14**	**0.05**	
Thailand								
Mean	2002	1.14	5.48	14.90	0.25	0.10	0.05	294
	2004	1.41	11.39	15.08	0.25	0.10	0.06	327
	2005	1.29	11.92	15.10	0.25	0.10	0.07	364
All years		**1.28**	**9.82**	**15.04**	**0.25**	**0.10**	**0.06**	**985**

(continued)

Table 2 (continued)

	Year	Tobin's *q*	Market value (millions)	Size	Leverage	Liquidity	Investments	Sample size
Std Dev	2002	0.68	16.01	1.53	0.24	0.13	0.07	
	2004	0.98	41.03	1.56	0.22	0.11	0.09	
	2005	0.79	47.24	1.58	0.21	0.12	0.07	
All years		**0.84**	**38.28**	**1.56**	**0.22**	**0.12**	**0.08**	

This table shows the descriptive statistics of the listed companies included in our sample. The sample is drawn from publicly-traded firms in China, Hong Kong, Indonesia, the Philippines, and Thailand. The data are taken from the years in which a corporate governance survey was conducted. *Tobin's q* is the ratio of the sum of the market value of equity at fiscal year end plus total (all interest-bearing) debt divided by the sum of the book value of equity plus total debt. Market value is the market value of shareholders' equity, in millions, in local currency. *Size* is the log of total assets. *Leverage* denotes the debt ratio (total interest-bearing debt divided by total assets). *Liquidity* is represented by the cash to assets ratio, defined as the balance sheet value of cash and equivalents divided by total assets. *Investments* is defined as the ratio of capital expenditures divided by total assets. The sample was winsorized to eliminate extreme values.

Table 3 Regression results for market valuation and *CGI*

	China	Hong Kong	Indonesia	Philippines	Thailand
CG index (*CGI*)	0.015[a]	0.030***	0.012**	0.013*	0.012***
	(1.28)	(5.37)	(2.19)	(1.67)	(3.68)
Size	−0.273***	−0.139***	0.044[a]	−0.245***	0.030[a]
	(−5.71)	(−3.66)	(1.31)	(−4.68)	(1.53)
Leverage	−2.616***	−2.329***	−0.535**	0.042	−0.190[a]
	(−5.78)	(−6.45)	(−2.16)	(0.08)	(−1.50)
Liquidity	1.293**	1.436***	0.187	1.937***	1.423***
	(2.08)	(3.57)	(0.50)	(3.14)	(6.18)
Investments	0.395	3.021***	2.803***	0.420	1.605***
	(0.38)	(3.59)	(4.57)	(0.26)	(5.00)
Intercept	5.879***	1.924***	0.097	4.806***	−0.168
	(5.97)	(3.13)	(0.15)	(5.68)	(−0.66)
Year fixed effects	Yes	Yes	Yes	Yes	Yes
Adjusted R-squared	0.325	0.233	0.083	0.128	0.110
F-statistic	22.38***	22.85***	7.62***	7.02***	18.40***
No. of observations	356	502	514	330	985

This table presents ordinary least squares regression results with *Tobin's q* as the dependent variable. The sample is drawn from publicly-traded firms in China, Hong Kong, Indonesia, the Philippines, and Thailand. The data are taken from the years in which a corporate governance survey was conducted. *Tobin's q* is the ratio of the sum of the market value of equity at fiscal year-end plus total (all interest-bearing) debt divided by the sum of the book value of equity plus total debt. Market value of equity is the market value of shareholders' equity, in millions, in local currency. The corporate governance index (*CGI*) is based on the OECD Corporate Governance Principles (1999). *Size* is the log of total assets. *Leverage* denotes the debt ratio (total interest-bearing debt divided by total assets). *Liquidity* is represented by the cash to assets ratio, defined as the balance sheet value of cash and equivalents divided by total assets. *Investments* is defined as the ratio of capital expenditures divided by total assets. Year fixed effects are included in the regressions but the coefficients are not reported. t-statistics are reported in parentheses. *, **, and *** denote statistical significance at the 10 %, 5 %, and 1 % level (two-tailed) respectively.
[a]Denotes statistical significance at the 10 % level (one-tailed).

and firm valuation is strongest among listed firms in Hong Kong, Thailand, and Indonesia. The coefficient for size is negative and significant for three out of the five countries. This result indicates that smaller firms have higher values of Tobin's q in these three nations. The coefficient for leverage is negative and significant for four out of five countries, indicating that as leverage rises, Tobin's q decreases. The coefficient for liquidity, as measured by the ratio of cash holdings to total assets, is positively related to Tobin's q. Lastly, the level of investment, as measured by the ratio of capital expenditures to total assets, is positively related to Tobin's q for three out of five countries.

Table 4 shows the results for the two-stage least squares regression analyses. Overall, the results confirm that the relation between the quality of corporate governance practices and firm valuation still holds even after controlling for the influence of firm performance on the quality of corporate governance practices. Interestingly, the regression coefficients for Tobin's q in Eq. 3 are statistically significant in Hong Kong, Indonesia, the Philippines and Thailand. We interpret this finding as evidence of a feedback loop in the relation between the quality of corporate governance practices and firm valuation. Nevertheless, the main hypothesis – a positive relation between *CGI* and firm performance – receives strong empirical support from the two-stage least squares regression analyses.

6 Conclusion

The benefits of good corporate governance practices on firm value remain one of the more contentious issues in corporate finance. Despite the large body of research investigating this question, there remains scant evidence of the benefits among Asian emerging markets. This study provides empirical evidence to support the notion that good corporate governance has a positive association with firm performance in Asian emerging markets. The study utilizes a comprehensive corporate governance index to measure the levels of corporate governance in China, Hong Kong, Indonesia, the Philippines, and Thailand. Furthermore, this study is the first to use an international standard, the OECD Principles of Corporate Governance (1999), as a benchmark to assess the progress of these five markets in terms of corporate governance reform.

The findings show governance practices have improved across these five markets. The improvements can be taken as evidence that East Asian listed companies have been making progress in their efforts to adopt internationally accepted corporate governance practices. The improvements in the quality of corporate governance practices are quite important because the improvements enable listed firms in East Asian markets to participate more effectively in the international capital market. Having firms that employ internationally accepted corporate governance practices could encourage the international investment community to invest in listed East Asian firms.

Table 4 Two-stage least squares regression results for market valuation and *CGI*

	China	China	Hong Kong	Hong Kong	Indonesia	Indonesia	Philippines	Philippines	Thailand	Thailand
Dependent variable	*CGI*	*q*	*CGI*	*q*	*CGI*	*q*	*CGI*	*q*	*CGI*	*q*
CG index (*CGI*)		0.309*		0.155***		0.067*		0.108[a]		0.068***
		(1.73)		(3.08)		(1.67)		(1.33)		(2.89)
q	0.510		1.942**		4.746***		4.449***		4.890***	
	(0.70)		(2.47)		(2.85)		(2.95)		(4.29)	
Size	1.080***	−0.465***	2.467***	−0.529***	3.375***	−0.181	4.015***	−0.379***	3.098***	−0.169**
	(3.98)	(−3.19)	(9.34)	(−3.27)	(12.15)	(−1.09)	(8.28)	(−2.58)	(16.16)	(−1.99)
Leverage	2.292	−2.279***	0.348	−1.989***	−3.921*	−0.199	1.699	0.249	−1.852[a]	−0.028
	(0.82)	(−2.69)	(0.11)	(−3.43)	(−1.78)	(−0.55)	(0.39)	(0.33)	(−1.33)	(−0.17)
Liquidity		2.793*		0.141		−0.226		1.017		0.989***
		(1.93)		(0.18)		(−0.46)		(0.87)		(3.01)
Investments		1.812		1.435		2.183***		−2.700		1.375***
		(0.87)		(1.00)		(2.72)		(−0.80)		(3.60)
Intercept	35.241***	−7.265	14.101***	0.934	−31.564***	2.442[a]	−25.092***	0.998	5.772**	−0.580*
	(5.88)	(−0.90)	(2.78)	(0.88)	(−5.99)	(1.36)	(−2.50)	(0.33)	(2.14)	(−1.70)
Year fixed effects	Yes	Yes	Yes	Yes	Yes	Yes	Yes	Yes	Yes	Yes
Adj. R-squared	0.237	0.120	0.366	0.101	0.429	0.066	0.389	0.060	0.305	0.082
F-statistic	19.36***	7.04***	58.96***	9.05***	78.13***	6.16***	35.96***	3.64***	86.43***	13.51***
No. of observations	356	356	502	502	514	514	330	330	985	985

This table presents two-stage least squares regression results for each of the five countries in the sample. In the first model, the dependent variable is the corporate governance index (*CGI*). In the second model, the dependent variable is *Tobin's q*. The sample is drawn from publicly-traded firms in China, Hong Kong, Indonesia, the Philippines, and Thailand. The data are taken from the years in which a corporate governance survey was conducted. The corporate governance index (*CGI*) is based on the OECD Corporate Governance Principles (1999). *Tobin's q* is the ratio of the sum of the market value of equity at fiscal year end plus total (all interest-bearing) debt divided by the sum of the book value of equity plus total debt. Market value of equity is the market value of shareholders' equity, in millions, in local currency. *Size* is the log of total assets. *Leverage* denotes the debt ratio (total interest-bearing debt divided by total assets). *Liquidity* is represented by the cash to assets ratio, defined as the balance sheet value of cash and equivalents divided by total assets. *Investments* is defined as the ratio of capital expenditures divided by total assets. Instruments used in the regressions include the ratio of plant, property, and equipment to sales, return on equity as a measure of firm profitability, and an industry dummy variable for financial services firms (except for the Philippines). Year fixed effects are included in the regressions but the coefficients are not reported. t-statistics are reported in parentheses. *, **, and *** denote statistical significance at the 10 %, 5 %, and 1 % level (two-tailed) respectively.

[a]Denotes statistical significance at the 10 % level (one-tailed).

The second part of the paper examines the relation between the *CGI* and the market valuation of the major East Asian listed firms. The key research question is: Are internationally accepted corporate governance practices beneficial to East Asian listed firms? Conventional wisdom suggests that good corporate governance should lead to better performance and, in turn, higher firm valuation. The reason is that good corporate governance helps ensure that managers will act on behalf of shareholders and make decisions that maximize firm value.

The empirical results show a positive relation between firm valuation and corporate governance practices among the major listed firms in five Asian emerging markets. The paper provides empirical evidence that firms in select Asian emerging markets have made strides toward adopting more internationally recognized corporate governance practices. This finding is also significant from the viewpoint of the regulators in emerging markets. Regulatory authorities and government agencies have pushed for changes in each of the five markets we study. Managers and investors are not always convinced of the benefits which can accrue when firms improve governance practices. The regulatory changes have continued despite occasionally facing skeptical managers and apathetic investors. The pace of change may be slow at times, and the regulators face a challenge as they try to prevent backsliding by firms. However, the results from this study show the reward for the regulators' efforts: in Asian emerging markets, firms benefit from adopting good governance practices. Market valuations are higher for firms with better quality corporate governance practices.

Acknowledgements The authors are indebted to the late Charnchai Charuvastr, the former Chairman of the Thai Institute of Directors Association (IOD), for the permission to use the original scorecard developed by the Thai IOD. His pioneering efforts made it possible to share the corporate governance survey through the Institutes of Directors in East Asia Network (IDEANet). We also thank Ping Jiang, James Simanjuntak, and Pornkanok Wipusanawan for technical assistance. Earlier versions of the material in this chapter benefited from comments by participants at the OECD Asian Corporate Governance Roundtable held in Manila in September, 2009 and the American Accounting Association Meeting in 2010. The usual disclaimers apply.

Appendix: Corporate Governance Survey Instrument

Question number	Criteria
Section A	**Rights of shareholders**
A.01	Does the company offer other ownership rights beyond voting?
A.02	Is the decision on the remuneration of board members or executives approved by the shareholders annually?
A.03	How is the remuneration of the board presented?
A.04	Quality of notice to call a shareholders meeting in the past one year
	(i) Appointment of directors, providing their names and background

(continued)

Question number	Criteria
	(ii) Appointment of auditors, providing their names and fees
	(iii) Dividend policy, providing the amount and explanation
A.05	Did the chairman of the board attend at least one AGM in the past two years?
A.06	(i) Did the CEO/managing director attend at least one AGM in the past two years?
	(ii) Is a name list of board attendance available?
A.07	Do AGM minutes record that there was an opportunity for shareholders to ask questions/raise issues in the past one year?
	(i) Is there a record of answers and questions?
	(ii) Is any resolution being resolved?
A.08	Does the company have anti-takeover defenses?
	(i) Cross shareholding
	(ii) Pyramid holding
	(iii) Board members hold more than 25 % of shares outstanding
Section B	**Equitable treatment of shareholders**
B.01	Does the company offer one-share, one-vote?
B.02	Is there any mechanism to allow minority shareholders to influence board composition?
B.03	Have there been any cases of insider trading involving company directors and management in the past two years?
B.04	Does the company provide rationales/explanations for related-party transactions affecting the corporation?
B.05	Is the company part of an economic group where the parent/controlling shareholder also controls key suppliers, customers, and/or similar businesses?
B.06	Have there been any non-compliance cases regarding related-party transactions in the past one year?
B.07	Does the company facilitate voting by proxy?
B.08	(i) Does the notice to shareholders specify the documents required to give proxy?
	(ii) Is there any requirement for a proxy appointment to be notarized?
B.09	How many days in advance does the company send out the notice of general shareholder meetings?
Section C	**Role of stakeholders**
C.01	Does the company explicitly mention the safety and welfare of its employees?
C.02	Does the company explicitly mention the role of key stakeholders such as customers or the community at large (or creditors or suppliers)?
C.03	Does the company explicitly mention environmental issues in its public communications?
C.04	Does the company provide an ESOP (employee share option program), or other long-term employee incentive plan linked to shareholder value creation, to employees?
Section D	**Disclosure and transparency**
D.01	Does the company have a transparent ownership structure?
	(i) Breakdown of shareholdings
	(ii) Is it easy to identify beneficial ownership?
	(iii) Are director shareholdings disclosed?
	(iv) Is management shareholding disclosed?
D.02	Does the company have a dispersed ownership structure?
D.03	Is the company's actual ownership structure obscured by cross-shareholdings?

(continued)

Question number	Criteria
D.04	Assess the quality of the annual report, in particular, the following: (i) Financial performance (ii) Business operations and competitive position (iii) Board member background (iv) Basis of the board remuneration (v) Operating risks
D.05	Is there any statement requesting the directors to report their transactions of company stock?
D.06	Does the company use an internationally recognized accounting standard?
D.07	(i) Does the company have an internal audit operation established as a separate unit in the company? (ii) To whom does the internal audit function report?
D.08	Does the company perform an annual audit using independent and reputable auditors?
D.09	Are there any accounting qualifications in the audited financial statements apart from the qualification on uncertainty of situation?
D.10	Does the company offer multiple channels of access to information? (i) Annual report (ii) Company website (iii) Analyst briefing (iv) Press conference/press briefing
D.11	Is the financial report disclosed in a timely manner?
D.12	Does the company have a website, disclosing up-to-date information? (i) Business operations (ii) Financial statements (iii) Press releases (iv) Shareholding structure (v) Organizational structure (vi) Corporate group structure (vii) Annual report downloadable (viii) Provided in two languages (local language plus English)
Section E	**Role of the board of directors**
E.01.1	Does the company have its own written corporate governance rules?
E.01.2	Does the board of directors provide a code of ethics or statement of business conduct for all directors and employees?
E.01.3	Does the company have a corporate vision/mission?
E.02	Does the regulatory agency have any evidence of the firm's non-compliance with rules and regulations over the last three years?
E.03	Assess the quality and content of the audit committee report in the annual report (i) Attendance (ii) Internal control (iii) Management control (iv) Proposed auditors (v) Financial report review (vi) Legal compliance (vii) Conclusions or opinions

(continued)

Question number	Criteria
E.04	Have board members participated in training on corporate governance?
E.05	How many board meetings are held per year?
E.06	(i) Is the chairman an independent director?
	(ii) Is the chairman also the CEO?
E.07	Does the company have an option scheme with incentives for top management?
	(i) Did the company have an option (and/or other performance incentive) scheme in the past which is still in effect?
	(ii) Does the company currently have option (and/or other performance incentive) schemes?
E.08	Does the board appoint independent committees with independent members to carry out various critical responsibilities such as: audit, compensation and director nomination?
	(i) Audit
	(ii) Compensation
	(iii) Director nomination committee
E.09	What is the size of the board?
E.10	How many board members are non-executive directors?
E.11	Does the company state in its annual report the definition of 'independence'?
E.12	Among directors, how many are independent directors?
E.13	Does the company provide contact details for a specific investor relations person?
E.14	Does the company have a board of director's report?
E.15	Does the company disclose how much they paid the independent non-executive directors?
E.16	Does the company provide training to directors (including executive and nonexecutive directors)?

References

Abowd, J. M., & Kaplan, D. S. (1999). Executive compensation: Six questions that need answering. *Journal of Economic Perspectives, 13*, 145–168.

Agrawal, A., & Knoeber, C. R. (1996). Firm performance and mechanisms to control agency problems between managers and shareholders. *Journal of Financial and Quantitative Analysis, 31*, 377–397.

Barontini, R., & Caprio, L. (2006). The effect of family control on firm value and performance: Evidence from continental Europe. *European Financial Management, 12*(5), 689–723.

Bebchuk, L. A., Fried, J. M., & Walker, D. I. (2002). Managerial power and rent extraction in the design of executive compensation. *The University of Chicago Law Review, 69*, 751–846.

Bebchuk, L., Cohen, A., & Ferrell, A. (2009). What matters in corporate governance? *Review of Financial Studies, 22*(2), 783–827.

Black, B. (2001). The corporate governance behavior and market value of Russian firms. *Emerging Markets Review, 2*, 89–108.

Black, B., Jang, H., & Kim, W. (2006). Does corporate governance predict firms' market values? Evidence from Korea. *Journal of Law, Economics, and Organization, 22*, 366–413.

Cheung, Y. L., Connelly, J. T., Limpaphayom, P., & Zhou, L. (2007). Do investors really value corporate governance? Evidence from the Hong Kong market. *Journal of International Financial Management and Accounting, 18*, 86–122.
Cheung, Y. L., Jiang, P., Limpaphayom, P., & Lu, T. (2008). Does corporate governance matter in China? *China Economic Review, 19*(3), 460–479.
Cheung, Y. L., Jiang, P., Limpaphayom, P., & Lu, T. (2009). Corporate governance in China: A step forward. *European Financial Management, 16*(1), 94–123.
Claessens, S., Djankov, S., Fan, J., & Lang, L. (2002). Disentangling the incentive and entrenchment effects of large shareholdings. *Journal of Finance, 57*, 2741–2771.
Doidge, C., Karolyi, A., & Stulz, R. (2007). Why do countries matter so much for corporate governance? *Journal of Financial Economics, 86*, 1–39.
Durnev, A., & Kim, E. H. (2005). To steal or not to steal: Firm attributes, legal environment, and valuation. *Journal of Finance, 60*, 1461–1493.
Gompers, P., Ishii, J., & Metrick, A. (2003). Corporate governance and equity prices. *Quarterly Journal of Economics, 118*, 107–155.
Hermalin, B. E., & Weisbach, M. S. (2003). Boards of directors as an endogenously determined institution: A survey of the economic literature. *Economic Policy Review, 9*, 7–26.
Himmelberg, C. P., Hubbard, R. G., & Palia, D. (1999). Understanding the determinants of managerial ownership and the link between ownership and performance. *Journal of Financial Economics, 53*, 353–384.
Iskander, M. R., & Chamlou, N. (2000). *Corporate governance: A framework for implementation.* Washington, DC: World Bank Group.
Klapper, F., & Love, I. (2003). Corporate governance, investor protection, and performance in emerging markets. *Journal of Corporate Finance, 195*, 1–26.
Morck, R., Shleifer, A., & Vishny, R. W. (1988). Management ownership and market valuation: An empirical analysis. *Journal of Financial Economics, 20*, 293–315.
Organization of Economic Co-operation and Development (OECD). (1999). *Principles of corporate governance*. Paris: Organization of Economic Co-operation and Development.
Patel, S., & Dallas, G. (2002). *Transparency and disclosure: Overview of methodology and study results—United States*. Working paper, Standard & Poor's.
Pistor, K., & Xu, C. (2005). Governing emerging stock markets: Legal vs. administrative governance. *Corporate Governance: An International Review, 13*, 5–10.
World Bank. (2003). *People's Republic of China–Hong Kong special administrative region: Financial system stability assessment*. Washington, DC: World Bank Group.
World Bank. (2004). *Indonesia – Report on the Observance of Standards and Codes (ROSC): Corporate governance*. Washington, DC: World Bank Group.
World Bank. (2005). *Thailand – Report on the Observance of Standards and Codes (ROSC): Corporate governance*. Washington, DC: World Bank Group.
World Bank. (2006). *Philippines – Report on the Observance of Standards and Codes (ROSC): Corporate governance*. Washington, DC: World Bank Group.
World Bank. (2010). *Indonesia – Report on the Observance of Standards and Codes (ROSC): Corporate governance*. Washington, DC: World Bank Group.
Zhuang, J., Edwards, D., Webb, D., & Capulong, M. (2000). *Corporate governance and finance in East Asia. A study of Indonesia, Republic of Korea, Malaysia, Philippines, and Thailand* (Vol. 1). Manila: Asian Development Bank.

Corporate Governance, Product Market Competition and Firm Performance: Evidence from India

Ekta Selarka

Abstract On one hand product market competition acts as an ultimate solution to align interests of managers and shareholders, and on the other hand, competition alone may not be sufficient because it may not prevent managers from expropriating the competitive return after the capital is sunk. These hypotheses motivate us to investigate the interaction between corporate governance and product market competition in India where predominance of owner-managers might cause corporate governance reforms to have a slow impact. Using a sample of 1,330 listed firms at the end of 2005 we attempt to capture various attributes of corporate governance by constructing an index of corporate governance based on board structure, audit quality and investor information disclosure. The index is then used along with traditional measures of competition to analyze the question of whether corporate governance and competition are complements or substitutes. In general the empirical analysis shows the weak substitution effects of product market competition which further suggests that relying on product market competition to improve corporate governance of firms may not be appropriate in the Indian setting and therefore, direct corporate governance reforms seem to be necessary and are likely to be effective.

1 Introduction

The fundamental objective of corporate governance is to ensure efficient use of resources by managers, thereby ensuring good economic performance of the firm and its ability to access low cost and long term external finance. Corporate finance research in the last three decades has analyzed the importance of corporate governance mechanisms to overcome agency conflicts between management and

E. Selarka (✉)
Madras School of Economics, Behind Government Data Center, Chennai 600025, India
e-mail: ekta@mse.ac.in

S. Boubaker and D.K. Nguyen (eds.), *Corporate Governance in Emerging Markets*, CSR, Sustainability, Ethics & Governance, DOI 10.1007/978-3-642-44955-0_3,

shareholders. While evidence on effectiveness of these mechanisms is widely accepted, we observe that corporations even do well in markets where many of these mechanisms are not in place at firm level neither at the country level. For example, Gomes (2000) shows that firms are adhering to protecting the rights to shareholders even in environments where there is little legal protection and very few governance mechanisms to align incentives of management and shareholders. This is being pointed out by researchers across developed and developing markets. For example, Allen and Gale (2000) point to the success of foreign car maker Toyota in the US markets, despite the lack of similar internal governance mechanisms or takeover threats to align incentives employed by the US corporations. Also, Khanna and Palepu (2004) have shown that in the case of the software firm of India – Infosys – exposure to global product markets, seems to have primarily driven some adoption of shareholder-style corporate governance in India. In contrast to the stance taken by the existing literature on the convergence of corporate governance, the authors do not find much of a role for capital markets as drivers of this process. These findings support the widely held view among economists that the product market competition mitigates agency costs – managerial or expropriation – at the firm level by driving persistently inefficient firms, whether manager controlled or family controlled, out of the market acting as an ultimate discipline (Alchian 1950, Stigler 1958). If product market competition acts as an ultimate disciplinary mechanism, should one be too much concerned with corporate governance? Or if competition in product market causes a firm to follow good governance practices acting as a complementary external mechanism?

In this study, we explore if product market competition acts as a substitute to corporate governance, or in the very least, acts as a complement to good governance. This question acquires importance in the context of emerging countries like India, where corporate governance mechanisms might take longer time to change because of predominance of concentration of ownership in hands of families and group corporations. Family firms in India controlled by founding business families often replace the need of formal external finance Khanna and Palepu (2000) and capital market discipline may play a limited role. In such a scenario, greater competition in product markets would force managers to use resources efficiently and constraint private benefits of control. On the regulatory front, along with corporate governance reforms, India has undertaken a series of structural reforms to increase domestic and international competition among companies. It would be therefore interesting to investigate the interaction between corporate governance and product market competition – to see if the two act as substitutes or complements in the Indian context.

Utilizing a sample of listed firms in 2005 we study the effects of corporate governance on firm value and efficiency, given a level of competition in firm's product market. Consistent with previous studies, we find that firms in less competitive industries are less efficient than firms in more competitive industries. The results are robust after controlling for industry sectors, size, and firm age. Instead of relying on a particular governance mechanism such as ownership concentration or managerial incentives, we construct a corporate governance index (CGI) based on the board, disclosure and audit. Thus, construction of an overall index of corporate governance using scoring methodology also becomes an important contribution of this chapter. We find that our corporate governance index is positively related to firm value and is robust to different measures of firm performance.[1] We further explore whether the effectiveness of good and bad corporate governance at the firm level differs across competitive and concentrated industries. We find that product market competition complements the good governance mechanisms.

The remaining of the chapter is organized as follows. The next section discusses the related literature to build hypotheses. Section 3 describes the data, variables and empirical model. Section 4 describes the construction of corporate governance index, section 5 reports the results and Section 6 concludes.

2 Background Literature and Development of Hypotheses

Economists have generally agreed that product market competition is an *ultimate* solution to disciplining entrenched managers. This is reflected in the writings of Adam Smith (1976) who stated – monopoly is a great enemy to good management – and early research (Alchian 1950, Stigler 1958). Product market competition is pivotal in influencing firm profitability and strategy (Porter 1990), improves corporate performance (Nickell 1996), and leads to insolvency if management waste resources (Schmidt 1997). In addition to the direct effect on performance, scholars have shown the channels through which product market competition plays a role in mitigating agency costs through reducing managerial slack (Hart (1983) reducing information asymmetry and by exerting financial pressure Nalebuff and Stiglitz 1983; Aghion and Dewatripoint 1999).

Alchain (1950), Friedman (1953) and Stigler (1958) argue that regardless of the Berle and Means' (1932) separation of ownership and control, competitive selection process in the product markets would ensure that managers are obliged to maximize profits. According to their view, one should not worry about corporate governance because in the long run managerial slack cannot exist, or survive, in competitive industries. However, the real state of the world is characterized by imperfect competition, barriers to entry and/or economies of scales and under these conditions the managers of corporations would not need to maximize profits in order to survive (Winter 1964). In fact, the product market competition can only limit the amount available to expropriate and therefore, corporate governance mechanisms are essential to prevent the expropriation of competitive rents by managers once the capital is sunk by investors (Shleifer and Vishny 1997). Berglof

[1] Other studies on corporate governance index for Indian companies include Mohanty (2002) who constructed a CG index based on questionnaire to institutional investors and Black and Khanna (2007) constructed a CG index based on survey of 370 companies. Other than these academic research, corporate governance rating for large Indian firms are developed by rating agencies like ICRA and S&P which are not publicly available.

and Thadden (1999) conjecture that competition in factor and output markets may mitigate the agency problem, but in itself competition is insufficient because market signals are generated after corporate funds and resources have been committed. The role of corporate governance is therefore to ensure that the signals and other relevant information are actually translated into investment decisions. Therefore, insufficient role of product market competition is overcome by existing corporate governance system in a country. These studies form a basis for the interaction between competition in firm's product market and governance mechanisms in place.

Lack of product market competition and poor corporate governance at individual firm level are identified as two main reasons for poor firm performance in continental European countries (Baily and Gersbach 1995). Nickell et al. (1997) were the first direct study on interaction between CG, debt and product market competition. They find that product market competition and financial pressure can substitute for shareholder control. Januszewski et al. (2000) find that in the German firms, competition weakly compensates for the negative influence of dominant owners. Grodfeld and Tressel (2001) find that product market competition complements good corporate governance for Polish firms. In another research comparing UK and German firms, Koke and Renneboog (2008) find that positive impact of bank debt complements the positive effect of competition in poorly performing and distressed firms. Whereas in UK insider control discipline firms subjected to weak product market competition (in other words the two act as substitutes). All these studies consider shareholder control and ownership concentration as corporate governance variable. Regarding other governance mechanisms, Bozec (2005) finds positive impact of board composition when Canadian firms are operating in a competitive environment. On the other hand, Randy and Jenssen (2004) find that board independence enhance performance of Swedish firms when these firms operate in less competitive industries. The authors find that corporate governance works best through family leadership and ownership when firms operate in weakly competitive markets. More recently, Cremers et al. (2006) shows that weak corporate governance is associated with poor performance only in more concentrated industries. This raises important question that stringent governance mechanisms may not *always* result in increased performance when agency costs are alleviated through competitive markets.

A recent analysis based on management practices of manufacturing firms in UK, France, Germany and US shows that poor management practices are prevalent not only when product market competition is weak but also when governance is weakly effective (Bloom and Reenen 2006). Using European Union Single Market Programme as an instrument for product market competition, Griffith (2001) finds that competition increased efficiency of firms with principal-agent set up but not in firms where manager-owner separation was relatively less. Also, in a recent cross-country research, Guadalupe and Pérez-González (2006) find that product market competition constrain private benefits of control. Recently, Karuna (2007), Ammann et al. (2010) and Giroud and Mueller (2010) document that firms benefit relatively less from good internal corporate governance in competitive industries, whereas better internal corporate governance exerts positive and significant effects on firm value in non-competitive industries, thereby implying that these two corporate governance mechanisms are substitutes. These studies have focused on the incentive role of good governance when comparing with the competition. For example, Giroud and Mueller (2011) argue that the need to provide managers with incentives through good governance – and thus the benefits of good governance – should be smaller for firms in competitive industries. In contrast, firms in noncompetitive industries, where lack of competitive pressure fails to enforce discipline on managers, should benefit relatively more from good governance.

Product markets have become more competitive in India after liberalization as entry and trade barriers being lifted (Glen et al. 1999, 2000). In addition to structural reforms in the industrial sector, transparent and fair practices were instituted to reduce information asymmetry in capital market. Corporate governance reforms are such that the country is moving towards Anglo-American type model of corporate governance while the existence of strong family and insider control still dominate the corporate landscape. Survey of literature highlights that for firms that are already operating with good corporate governance practices, competition may act either as complement strengthening corporate governance or might not at all have any differential effect. Thus India provides a good case study for analyzing the interplay between competition and corporate governance.

We conjecture that if the firm level corporate governance is very good then product market competition may not have any differential impact on firm performance. Similarly, when the corporate governance is very bad, product market competition may act as a discipline for such firms. The substitution or complement hypotheses may work in the middle range of corporate governance – moderately good or moderately bad.

H1: The effect of product market competition will have substitution effect on firms with moderately good CG and complementary effect on firms with moderately bad CG

3 Data, Variables and Methodology

3.1 Data

We begin with all manufacturing firms which are publicly traded on Bombay Stock Exchange (BSE) as on March 31, 2005. The corporate governance data is hand collected from the corporate governance reports of the companies and therefore we selected 2005 when most of the formal governance rules were implemented. Financial and stock price information is obtained from Prowess which is maintained by Center for Monitoring Indian Economy (CMIE). Prowess is similar to Compustat database for US companies. It maintains information for over 8,000 companies (publicly traded and private companies) operating across various industries. As a first step of sample selection public utilities, government controlled and financial firms are excluded from the sample but are included when competition is measured. Of this initial sample of 2,907 companies, we begin collecting data on ownership structure, balance sheet variables and corporate governance reports. Information on cross-listing is taken from JP Morgan and Citibank websites. Ownership structure for sample firms is supplemented by hand collection of the names and equity holdings of shareholders with more than 1 % holding from BSE website.[2] Our final sample consists for 1,330 companies. We further augmented our dataset by going through each company's website and corporate governance reports to quantify indicators on investor information availability at company's website and presence of a remuneration committee made of independent directors.[3]

3.2 Firm Performance

We use profitability and efficiency measures in our regressions. Firm profitability is measured using accounting as well as stock price data. Table 1 describes the performance and other firm specific variables used in empirical analysis. A proxy for Tobin's q (QRATIO) is used as a stock market valuation of firms. Stock market valuation measures reflect firm's attempt in shareholder value maximization and therefore one could understand QRATIO as market assessment of firm's equity listed in a stock exchange. Stock price variation is affected by the confidence of the investors in a firm and hence QRATIO can be interpreted as the capital market assessment of the firm. Firm profitability measure calculated from balance sheet data is Return on Assets (ROA). Product market competition force monopoly rents in the product market to dissipate and therefore, intense competition would reduce firm's profits by reducing the market power. Therefore, one can observe a decline in profitability in competitive industries especially for a country in transition like India. All the performance variables are ratio and therefore likely to take extreme values if scaling variable takes too small or high values. To mitigate the effect of outliers in our empirical results, we drop 1 % of observations at tails of performance variables.

3.3 Product Market Competition

Our measure of product market competition is based on Herfindahl-Hirschman index (HHI) which is rather a reflective of concentration in the industry (Giroud

[2] Promoters are defined under SAST section 5(h) as those individuals or corporations who directly or indirectly control a company. PACs are individuals/companies or any other legal entities through which promoters exert indirect control. Most recently SEBI has amended the two as combined and reported under promoters. See amendments in definition of Promoters and PACs at http://www.sebi.gov.in/Index.jsp?contentDisp=Section&sec_id=1

[3] We also observed that for every sample firm, audit committee was set up meeting the mandatory requirement of Clause 49 of listing agreement.

Table 1 Definitions of variables

Variable	Definition
Qratio	Proxy for Tobin's q in emerging market where replacement cost of assets cannot be computed. Measured as (Market value of total equity + book value of debt)/book value of assets
Size	Natural logarithm of total assets
Roa	Ratio of profit before depreciation, interest and tax to total assets
Leverage	Book value of debt/book value of equity
Age	Natural logarithm of 2005-incorporation year
R&D intensity	Ratio of R&D expenditure to sales
Advertising intensity	Ratio of advertising expense to sales
Export intensity	Ratio of export revenue to sales
Depreciation intensity	Ratio of depreciation to sales
CR4	Four firm concentration ratio, which is computed as total sales of largest four firms in firm's four digit industry
HHI	Herfindahl-Hirschman index, computed as sum of square of market shares of all firms in same four-digit industry
HHI(low)/HHI (high)	Dummy variables that equal one if HHI lies below and above median of its empirical distribution
Block	Ownership by blockholders is the percentage of blocks of at least 5 % of the firm's common shares which are not directly owned by promoter group
Insider	Ownership by promoters and persons acting in concert with the promoters that are declared as controlling owners following the listing agreement
Institutional	Ownership by institutional investors who own more than 5 % of total ownership
Foreign	Ownership by foreign investors who own more than 5 % of total ownership
Wedge	Divergence of control and cash flow rights computed as difference of equity holdings by promoters and persons acting in concert from share ownership by promoters holding more than 1 %
Group	Dummy variable that equals one if firm belongs to large business houses founded by family group

and Mueller 2011).[4] HHI is a widely used measure of industry concentration defined as sum of squared market shares of all firms in the respective three digit industry as $HHI = \sum_{i=1}^{i=n} {s_i}^2$ where s_i = market share of firm i and n = total number

[4] Manufactured products are grouped according to first four digits of product code in the database. Advantage of this approach is that it will consider all the firms having shares in the product group. For every product category we calculate the market share of each firm. For example, firm A produces items in product group P1 (60 %) and product group P2 (40 %). Firm A's main activity is defined as product group p1 but the concentration ratio for both the product groups will have firm A's respective market shares.

of firms in the industry.[5] Market shares are computed from PROWESS using all manufacturing firms' sales in their respective industry.[6] For robustness checks, we run all our regressions using four firm concentration ratio (CR4) as a sum of market shares of four firms in the industry with highest market shares.

3.4 Methodology

Our methodology follows to see the effect of corporate governance on firm performance after controlling for firm-specific variables. Specifically, we estimate:

$$\mathrm{P_i} = \beta_0 + \beta_1 CGI_i + \sum_{k=2}^{n} \beta_k X_i + \varepsilon_i \tag{1}$$

where $\mathrm{P_i}$ proxies for firm performance. $\mathrm{CGI_i}$ equals the firm-level corporate governance index and $\mathrm{X_i}$ includes firm specific control variables. In this context, we also study if firm characteristics such as – firms belonging to business groups, and firms with net worth more than 250 Million Rupees – would differently affect the relationship between corporate governance given the level of industry competition in firm's product market.

Second, we test whether the effect of governance varies depending on the industry-level product market competition. Equation 1 is augmented in the following way:

$$\mathrm{P_i} = \beta_0 + \beta_1 CGI_i + \beta_2 CINDEX_i + \beta_3 CGI_i * CINDEX_i + \sum_{k=4}^{n} \beta_k X_i + \varepsilon_i \tag{2}$$

,where CINDEX is 1-HHI The total effect of corporate governance on firm value can be computed as β_1+ β_3*CINDEX. The coefficient β_1 measures the direct effect of corporate governance on firm performance and the coefficient β_3 measures the indirect effect that varies with product market competition. The coefficient β_2 measures the direct effect of product market competition on firm performance. The interaction term captures whether the corporate governance affects firm performance differently depending on how competitive the firm's industry is.

Finally, we extend our hypotheses of differential effect of corporate governance depending on the level of industry competition across firms belonging to business

[5] Research papers in industrial organization widely use HHI and four firm concentration ratio as proxies for inverse measure of product market competition. For example see Curry and George (1983); Nickell et al. (1997). Chari and Gupta (2008) and Veermani (2001) are studies using Prowess database to compute market concentration.

[6] Ideally we would like to add sales of all plants in the industry but it is not possible to obtain plant level data and hence we use total sales of all firms in the industry as a denominator. This is common practice is empirical research (for example see Giroud and Mueller (2010)).

groups. These firms are a dominant feature of emerging economies which leads to agency costs through tunneling due to higher control over company's resources by controlling shareholders (Johnson et al. 2000). The phenomenon of expropriation is more likely in companies where controlling shareholders hold control through cross- holdings among corporations controlled by founding family. In such an ownership structure, the sub-optimal performance due to misuse of resources is allocated to small investors which leads to lower firm value (Bertrand and Mullainathan 2002).

All the equations are estimated using OLS methodology after removing the influential observations falling in extremes of 1 and 99 percentile of dependent variable.[7] We report the p- value corresponding to the Chi Square statistic corresponding to the specification test for heteroskedasticity because the sample is a cross section of companies that differ significantly in size. The specification test is done following the methodology suggested by White (1980).[8]

Our empirical analysis is based on cross sectional sample and treats corporate governance index as an exogenous variable affecting firm performance. Since we do not have a time variation in our sample, we cannot address the issue of causality from corporate governance to performance directly. In the context of our study, following many studies employing a cross sectional data, to ensure that our empirical results could not be spuriously caused by firm specific variables, we include firm specific control variables to control for size, capital structure, age, capital intensity, tangibility of assets, entry barriers and international competition. This is common approach in cross-sectional studies to control for possible causes of endogeneity (see for example Klapper and Love 2002).

Table 1 describes variables used in the empirical analysis. Summary statistics on performance and control variables is reported in the Table 2. Around 41 % of firms belong to business groups in our sample.

4 Corporate Governance Index

We construct three sub-indices using 12 corporate governance elements: Board structure (5 elements); entrenchment (1 element); disclosure and transparency (5 elements) and audit quality (2 elements). Existing research methodologies that have developed the corporate governance index rely on the binary valuation based on the widely accepted argument that the quality of corporate governance lacks due to non-compliance. Corporate governance index studies that are most cited in the literature include Gomperset al. (2003) – constructed shareholder rights index using

---

[7] We also checked for Cook's D statistic and results are robust after removing the influential observations where Cook's D statistic is greater than 2.

[8] A joint Null hypothesis is developed by White (1980, p 823), which maintains that model's specification of the first and the second moments of the dependent variable is correct. Not rejecting null thus indicates not only that the errors are homoskedastic; independent of the regressors but also that the model specification is correct.

Table 2 CGI description

1. The board sub-index is based on the ability of board of directors to monitor the executive management. The index is based on following components:
Board size: In principle, role of the board is to monitor the actions of management and advise on strategic decisions in a firm. Existing empirical evidence is mixed (e.g. Yermack 1996; Eisenberg et al. 1998; Hermalin and Weisbach (2003) for smaller boards and Dalton and Kesner (1987); Pearce and Zahra 1992 for larger boards). Optimal size is recommended between 5 and 12 (e.g. Jensen 1986). Contemporaneous working papers based on the advising role of board support larger boards (e.g. Boone et al. (2007); Linck et al. (2006) and Lehn et al. 2004).[a] On one hand, smaller boards are good in co-ordination among directors whereas, on the other hand, as firms expand and become complex larger board size is evident to bring in more expertise Coles et al. (2008). Therefore, board size should not be too small or too large. In the Indian context the company law requires minimum of 3 directors and the most recent recommendation on minimum board size is given by the most recent CG committee as 7.[b] We allot scores as follows: −1 if board size is less than 3 (Company law requirement); 2 if a board size is between 3 and 7 (just meeting the NCC recommendation), 4 if board size is between 8–12 and 3 if board size exceeds 12 directors[c]
Composition of board: The objective of having Non-Executive Directors (NEDs) on board is to bring two principle components: monitoring executive activity and contributing to the development of strategy (Higgs 2003). However, actual effectiveness of these directors depends upon the flow of information on company specific knowledge from Executive Directors (EDs) and therefore majority of outsiders might be better than super majority. Following this logic, firms with proportion of NEDs more than 75 % are allotted a lower score compared to firms with majority of NEDs. We set scores of−1, 4 and 2 if proportion of NEDs is less than 50 %, more than 50 % but less than 75 % and exceeds 75 %[d]
Board activity: The company law requires that board should meet at least four times in a year to discuss the quarterly results before the results are published for shareholders. If the board is meeting less than four times a year, we set a score −1. We allot a firm score of 4 if a board meets more than four times a year but less than eight. If a board meets more than eight times a year which is almost double than the legal requirement, it may send a negative signal to the investors. But how bad is it compared to the case where board is not meeting at least four times? Here we need to set a score which is worse than good score of 4 (benchmark) and better than firms not meeting the legal requirements. So we set a score of 2 for such firms meeting more than eight
Nominee directors: A nominee director is a director appointed by institutional investors and is a distinct feature of Indian corporate governance system. In principle, nominee directors are considered as a good CG element so we allot a score 1 to companies with nominee director present and 0 otherwise.[e] A recent amendment by SEBI in August 2004[f] requires nominee directors to be excluded from independent directors and therefore, major policy implication for having this element is to have institutional investors' knowledge of business and incentives to monitor along with the existing business relationship with the company. However, there is no direct evidence on nominee directors and positive firm performance in India except Banaji (2004) and Nachane et al. (2005) for bank nominee directors
Leadership duality: Separating chairman and CEO of the board is an indication that management is separated from control when board leadership is concerned and therefore, should bring efficient monitoring and independence by the board.[g] We set a score of 4 when there is no duality and −1 when the two roles are played by the same person
2. Information disclosure and transparency sub-index
Remuneration committee: Setting up a remuneration committee made of independent directors is a non-mandatory recommendation by KMBC. This serves as a proxy for independence in directors' remuneration to ensure that directors are not over paid. Firms are scored 4 if firm has a remuneration committee and 0 otherwise

(continued)

Table 2 (continued)

Ownership disclosure: Ownership disclosure of 1 % or more equity holdings is required by the Clause35 of the Listing Agreement.[h] Even though it is not a mandatory requirement it could serve as a good CG element in terms of transparency and fairness in disclosing ownership and control structure within a firm. Firms with reporting of detailed ownership are allotted a score 4 and −1 otherwise. Negative score is attributed to the negative quality of CG by not disclosing the control distribution within the firm

Investors' information: If a company maintains a website which provides information on any two of the following attributes: board of directors, shareholding pattern, corporate governance report and financial results, it is scored as 4 and 0 otherwise. This element indicates firms' earnestness to supply vital information on corporate governance to existing and prospective investors

Ownership opacity: We construct a variable *opaque* similar to Sarkar and Sarkar (2008) to proxy for undisclosed ownership by controlling shareholders. This could again serve as a proxy for more appropriation from outside investors. In India controlling shareholders control the corporation through a web of cross holdings between families and group companies. A variable *opaque* is defined as the difference of unreported controlling ownership ((total share ownership by promoters + persons acting in concert) – (Total share ownership by promoters and persons acting in concert from 1 % data)). Firm is scored −1 if *opaque* is greater than 10 %, 1 if *opaque* is between 10 % and 5 %, 2 if *opaque* is between 5 % and 1 % and 4 if *opaque* is less than 1 %

International listing: Cross-listing calls for more stringent requirement about ownership, board structure and board committees. The underlying positive effect results when firms are complying with stricter disclosure rules Doidge et al. (2004). We set a score of 4 if a firm is cross-listed on any of the US stock exchanges and 0 otherwise

3. Audit sub-index

Number of auditors: There is no theoretical literature on optimum number of auditors a firm should have. An auditor's responsibility is to watch company's account and financial information. Mostly firms have internal as well as external auditors. If there is more than one auditor who will take the responsibility and who will monitor the monitor? In a wake of Arthur Anderson scandal, auditors have come under scrutiny to avoid misallocation of capital and accounting and auditing frauds. A firm is allotted a score 4 if there are 2 or less auditors and−1 otherwise

Auditor quality: Existing research on developed countries show the differential impacts of presence of Big 4 audit firms. Big 4 audit firm clients have lower equity risk premium ex ante as well as lower levels of earnings management. Indeed, Boone et al. (2010) find that Mid-tier auditor is also potentially viable. We employ presence of a Big 10 auditor by referring to the listing provided in Financial Express as of March 2005 as a proxy for audit quality and also as a corporate governance element in ensuring fair reporting of financials. Big 10 auditors have international reputation and are perceived to be more independent and hence directly related to the good quality of corporate governance.[i] We score a firm 4 if firm has a Big 10 auditor and 0 otherwise. If a firm does not report the name of auditor it is allotted a score of −1

[a]Boone et al. (2007) find that both board size and fraction of outsiders on the board increase in years since the IPO. Lehn et al. (2004) find for 81 US firms survived over the years 1935–2000 that board size is positively related to firm size and inversely related to proxies for growth opportunities. Linck et al. (2006) find that growth firms have larger and independent boards while opposite is true for cash rich firms and firms with greater information asymmetry

[b]In India traditionally boards are larger because of institutional nominees, promoters and relatives. The mandate to increase board independence by appointing independent directors who are not nominee directors has generally increased the size of Indian boards

[c]We also check for robustness of our results if we replace this category with two standard deviations from the median size which would be 14 (following Chen et al. 2007).

[d]Most of the recent theoretical research has emphasized the role of EDs to bring the firm specific knowledge to the board to enhance outside directors' advisory role with full information and

(continued)

Table 2 (continued)

knowledge on firm. NEDs do not run the company and hence are more effective in monitoring and to provide strategic advice to EDs. This argument is driven by a balance of power between inside and outside directors and at the same time to facilitate the effective communication between executive and NEDs. For example Coles et al. (2008) find that higher insider fraction on boards of diversified, larger firms and firms with higher advise needs is positively related to firm value measured by Tobin's q

[e]There have always been institutional investors on Indian boards but their role was passive in terms of monitoring. Since 2001 when most of the DFIs were privatized, role of nominee directors are under scrutiny

[f]Also recommended in Naresh Chandra Committee on CG (2002) and Narayana Murthy Committee (2001)

[g]Jensen (1993) argues that CEO becomes a Chairman as a result of internal monitoring failure and could therefore affect CEO compensations, hiring and firing of new directors (Crystal 1991)

[h]See http://www.sebi.gov.in/commreport/clause35.html for recent amendments in the Clause

[i]Research papers on U.S. data show that Big Five auditors provide better quality service than non Big Five auditors as found by Teoh and Wong (1993). For East Asia, Fan and Wong (2001) find that Big Five in East Asian firms have corporate governance roles. Other multidisciplinary research comes from Accounting practices, see for example, Francis and Wang (2008) on big 4 auditors and quality of reported earnings; Khurana and Raman (2004) on ASEAN countries and quality of audit by big 4

anti-takeover charters at company level; Black et al. (2006) –constructed CG Index for Korean companies and Chen et al. (2007) for Taiwanese companies.. Most of the recent academic research and CG indices developed by professional rating agencies like S&P, Moody's, ICRA (for India) employ a binary framework to indicate whether a specified CG practice is specified in company's charter. As we lack a stylized methodology to assign weights to elements or to sub-indices, we employ a scoring methodology to set scores with respect to each governance element between −1 and 4. Specifically, −1 indicates lowest score for (i) not meeting the mandatory legal requirement or, (ii) when such a value for an element unambiguously indicates poor CG effect and, 4 indicates the highest score. Intermediate values between 0 and 3 depend upon effectiveness of a particular element in enhancing good governance based on the hypotheses developed in the theoretical and empirical literature. In such a research design, we can address two methodological issues: (i) non-linear relationship with regard to the specified element and; (ii) relative ranking of firms across elements towards good CG.[9] Table describes individual components and scoring methodology to obtain sub-indices. Table 3 describes each of these governance elements, their means and variances for the sample firms. We combine scores for each element into sub-indices and combine sub-indices into corporate governance index (CGI). By the structure of scoring

[9] To illustrate our research design, consider the following example. Suppose a firm A has a good board structure with a score of 3. On the other hand, the firm has an opaque ownership structure which scores the company at −1 capturing the bad element in corporate governance. The overall score will be 2 for company A. Another company B has a moderate score of 2 for board structure and it has a dispersed ownership structure with no control benefits to a single shareholder which will score 2. Overall score for company B is therefore 4 actually higher than that of A.

Table 3 Benchmarking CGI

	Element1	Element2	Element3	Element4	Element5	Max total
Board index	4	4	4	4	1	17
Disclosure index	4	4	4	4	4	20
Audit index	4	4				8
CG index						49

This table shows the maximum scores within each sub-index and highest corporate governance index value

methodology, CGI internalizes the board structure. Table 2 highlights the components and assessment methodology to construct CGI. Table 3 indicates the benchmark firm with highest CGI. This benchmark firm acts as a *frontier* with highest scores for each element.[10] We then normalize each firm's CGI to 100.

5 Empirical Analyses

5.1 Univariate Analysis

Figure 1 presents the distribution of CG index for our sample of 1,330 firms. Table 4 represents descriptive statistics of CG Index and sub-indices. Pairwise correlations between overall CG index and sub-indices are represented in Table 5. There is not much correlation among sub-indices which implies that each governance index contains some specific information. Table 6 shows the descriptive statistics of the variables used in our analysis. Table 7 shows the distribution of CGI across different ownership groups. Most of Indian business groups and foreign firms have higher value of CGI.

Table 8 presents the differences on firm performance according to corporate governance and product market competition using Difference-in-Difference method. We conduct this test for full sample as well as to see these differences between firms belonging to business groups, firms with net worth more than 250 million rupees and according to divergence between control and cash flow rights. We do not find that firm characteristics affect the difference in firm value depending on the levels of product market competition and CG. The table shows that firms have significantly higher performance in more competitive industries in general. Moreover, this difference is significant in the middle deciles of firm corporate governance ratings. We can summarize the findings from above tables

[10] All sample firms takes a CGI value less than 100 because none of the firm has highest scores for all elements. Theoretically, stringent CG regulations lead to managerial lack of incentives (Burkart et al. 1997). Empirical evidence on board structure in family firms suggests meeting just a legal requirement on independent directors (e.g. Yeh et al. 2002).

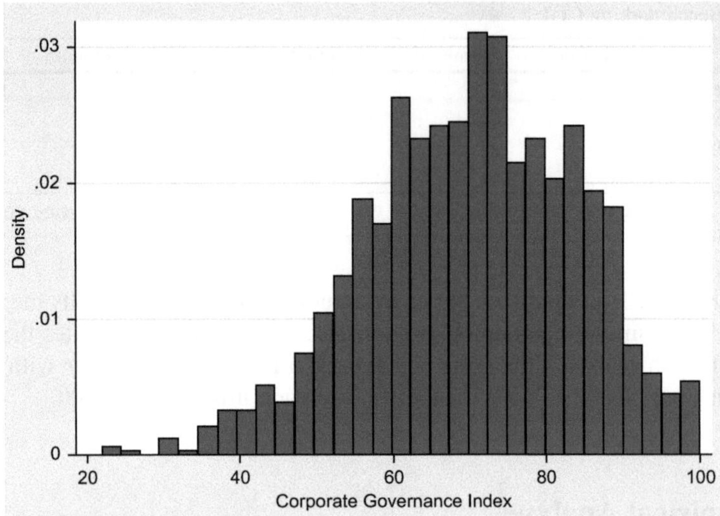

Fig. 1 Distribution of firms by corporate governance index

Table 4 Summary statistics of CG elements

	CG Element	Mean	Std. Dev	Min	Max
	Board size	8.81	2.83	3	28
	Outside directors	0.67	0.13	0.20	1
Board	Board activity	3.44	1.24	0	7
	Leadership duality	0.05	0.21	0	1
	Institutional director	0.24	0.66	0	6
	No of auditors	1.06	0.25	1	4
Audit	Big 10 auditor	0.22	0.42	0	1
	Ownership disclosure	0.97	0.17	0	1
	Remuneration committee with non-executive chairman	0.65	0.48	0	1
Disclosure	Investor information	0.65	0.48	0	1
	Ownership opacity (%)	5.04	11.59	0	85.63
	International listing	0.24	0.96	0	4

Description and summary statistics for the 11 elements included in Corporate Governance Index (*CGI*), for the 1,330 firms included in our multivariate econometric analysis. Board is board of directors sub-index, Disclosure is information disclosure and transparency sub-index and audit is audit quality sub-index

as there is certainly a possibility of interaction between product market competition and firm-level corporate governance which results in higher firm performance. Also, the interaction supports a possibility of competition and corporate governance being complements.

Table 5 Pairwise correlations: CGI and components

	CGIndex	Board sub-index	Audit sub-index	Disclosure sub-index
CG index	1.00			
Board sub-index	0.69*	1.00		
Audit sub-index	0.43*	0.12*	1.00	
Disclosure sub-index	0.75*	0.15*	0.08*	1.00

The table displays correlations between corporate governance index *CGI* and each sub-index. *indicate significance levels at 1 % levels

Table 6 Summary statistics

Variable	Obs	Mean	Median	Std. Dev	Min	Max
Qratio	1,304	0.36	0.75	0.18	0.00	1.07
Roa	1,304	0.12	.11	0.07	−0.10	0.38
CGI	1,304	64.33	54.10	12.22	11.48	93.44
Board	1,304	62.56	64.71	22.08	−5.88	100
Disclosure	1,304	58.95	50	19.61	−12.5	100
Audit	1,304	50.46	50	20.24	−6.25	100
Net worth (Million INR)	1,304	175.58	30.17	1,137.89	0.12	37,673.44
Assets (Million INR)	1,304	447.11	88.83	2,477.93	0.8	80,952.89
Age	1,304	28.69	21	20.17	2	142
Leverage	1,304	0.30	0.30	0.19	0	0.84
Expint	1,304	0.19	0.07	0.27	0	2.01
Depint	1,304	0.03	0.03	0.20	0	0.17
Advint	1,304	0.01	0.00	0.02	0	0.29
Rndint	1,304	0.004	0	0.018	0	0.44
HHI	1,304	0.82	0.93	0.08	0.01	0.98
Insider (%)	1,304	52.70	52.98	17.52	0	98.19
Foreign (%)	1,304	1.80	0	3.85	0	38.86
Group	1,304	0.413	0	0.49	0	1

This table reports statistics of variables for a sample of 1,332 firms listed on the Bombay stock exchange in the year 2005. *HHI* is lack of product market competition. *CGI* is internal corporate governance index based on board, disclosure and audit. *Board* is the score of the board of directors sub-index, *disclosure* is the score of the information disclosure and transparency sub-index, and *audit* is the score of the audit quality sub-index. *Qratio* is the firm value, which is the market value of assets (market value of equity plus book value of debt) divided by the book value of assets. *Size* is the natural log of total assets. *Levrg* is the leverage ratio (total debt/total assets)

Table 7 Distribution of CGI across ownership groups

CG index deciles	Indian group	Indian standalone	Foreign	Total
Highest	218(50.3 %)	148(34.2 %)	67(15.5 %)	433
Middle	190(42.9 %)	209(47.3 %)	43(9.7 %)	442
Lowest	139(30.4 %)	305(66.7 %)	13(2.8 %)	457
Total	547(41.1 %)	662(49.7 %)	123(9.2 %)	1,332

Table 8 Differences of firm value according to product market competition and CGI

	CGI 0–10	CGI 10–50	CGI 50–90	CGI 90–100
Qratio				
Concentrated (HHI > median)	0.65	0.80	0.94	1.25
Competitive (HHI > median)	0.80	0.90	1.06	1.24
Difference (P value)	0.15** (0.02)	0.10** (0.03)	0.11** (0.05)	0.01
ROA				
Concentrated (CINDEX < median)	0.09	0.10	0.11	0.14
Competitive (CINDEX > median)	0.08	0.12	0.13	0.14
Competitive-concentrated (P value)	0.004	0.02*** (0.002)	0.02**(0.03)	0.00

The table displays the firm values across competitiveness of the industry and CGI.
and * indicate significance levels at 5 % and 1% levels respectively

5.2 *Corporate Governance and Firm Value*

This section presents regression results after including a comprehensive set of control variables to reduce omitted variable bias and industry driven effects. Table 9 shows the regression results. Performance variables are regressed on CGI and industry dummies. CGI is highly significant across firm value after controlling for firm-specific variables such as size, age etc. In each of the regressions, observations are curtailed at 1 and 99th percentile to reduce the effects of outliers. The Table shows that CG Index variable correlates with firm performance and is both economically and statistically significant at the 1 % level. A 10 point increase in CGI predicts a 0.08 increase in Q ratio, 0.3 increase in MBVR,[11] a moderate increase of 0.004 in ROA. A worst-to-best change in CGI predicts a 0.66 change in Q ratio, compared to a sample mean of 0.94. Overall our results of positive effect of good corporate governance are consistent with the recent research employing corporate governance indices. Our results are robust to the inclusion of control variables, which suggests that the relationship between good governance and firm performance holds regardless of firm size, age etc.

Among control variables, R&D intensity, advertising intensity and leverage is positive for Q ratio. The positive sign with size variable is consistent with the argument that with increase in size companies might acquire significant to economies of scale. Positive coefficient of leverage is consistent with the signaling hypothesis that a more efficient management may signal its expertise by committing to high fixed payments (Ross 1977). The positive signs of advertising intensity and R&D are consistent with the arguments that company value tends to increase with increase in intangible assets. Positive coefficient with foreign institutional investor is consistent with the findings in the research that these investors are better monitors and hence increase the market value (Khanna and Palepu (2000); Chibber and Majumdar 1999). The negative coefficient of group dummy is consistent with the tunneling literature on Indian business groups Bertrand and Mullainathan (2002).

[11] Unreported results are available on request.

Table 9 Corporate governance and firm value

Variable	Q ratio	ROA
Intercept	0.2576	0.0095
	(0.151)	(0.668)
CGI	0.0081***	0.0004***
	(0.000)	(0.024)
Size	0.0045	0.0087***
	(0.724)	(0.000)
Age	−0.04914***	−0.0034
	(0.094)	(0.313)
Leverage	0.0004***	−0.0002***
	(0.092)	(0.000)
R&D intensity	5.264***	−0.1881
	(0.009)	(0.318)
Advertising intensity	0.0048***	0.0002**
	(0.004)	(0.060)
Depreciation intensity	0.0554	−0.0402***
	(0.653)	(0.000)
Export intensity	−0.0598	−0.0007
	(0.358)	(0.945)
Insider	0.0055***	0.0006***
	(0.000)	(0.000)
Foreign	0.0196***	0.0008
	(0.000)	(0.110)
Group	−0.0946***	−0.0164***
	(0.015)	(0.001)
Industry dummies	Yes	Yes
Sample size	1,304	1,304
Adjusted R squared	0.20	0.17
F statistics	7.48***	7.66***

Ordinary least squares regressions of Q ratio and return on assets on Corporate Governance Index (*CGI*) and control variables. Observations are curtailed for the value of dependent variable between 1 and 99 percentile to reduce the effect of outliers. *, **, and *** indicate significance levels at 10 %, 5 %, and 1 % levels. P values, based on White's heteroskedasticity-consistent standard errors, are reported in parentheses

5.3 *Product Market Competition and Corporate Governance: Compliments or Substitutes?*

We estimate Model 2 to find out the interaction between corporate governance and product market competition. Regression results are shown in Tables 10 and 11. Table 10 reports the results on direct effects of competition, corporate governance and interaction term. Positive and significant coefficients of CGI and CINDEX show that good corporate governance and competition does correlate with firm performance. This is robust to various control variables.

Table 10 Interaction of corporate governance and product market competition: effect on firm value

Variable	Q ratio	ROA
CGI	0.0082***	0.0005***
	(0.000)	(0.069)
CINDEX	0.1194	0.0099
	(0.404)	(0.590)
CGI*CINDEX	0.0002	−0.0001
	(0.936)	(0.771)
Control variables	Yes	Yes
Intercept	Yes	Yes
Industry dummies	Yes	Yes
Sample size	1,281	1,280
Adjusted R squared	0.20	0.17
F statistics	7.41***	7.39***

Ordinary least squares regressions of Q ratio and return on assets on Corporate Governance Index (*CGI*), Product Market Competition (PMC) and control variables. Observations are curtailed for the value of dependent variable between 1 and 99 percentile to reduce the effect of outliers. *, **, and *** indicate significance levels at 10 %, 5 %, and 1 % levels. P values, based on White's heteroskedasticity-consistent standard errors, are reported in parentheses

Table 11 Effect of competition on good and bad CG

	Q ratio	ROA
	Competition	Competition
	(CINDEX > median)	(CINDEX > median)
CGI (0–10)	0.1534***	0.0050
	(0.013)	(0.672)
CGI (10–50)	0.1028***	0.0135**
	(0.011)	(0.054)
CGI (50–90)	0.1281***	0.0145***
	(0.022)	(0.039)
CGI (90–100)	0.2548*	0.0329*
	(0.087)	(0.053)
Control variables	Yes	Yes
Intercept	Yes	Yes

Only coefficients of CINDEX are reported for each ordinary least squares regressions of Q ratio and return on assets on Product Market Competition (PMC). Control variables are suppressed to economize on space. Observations are curtailed for the value of dependent variable between 1 and 99 percentile to reduce the effect of outliers. *, **, and *** indicate significance levels at 10 %, 5 %, and 1 % levels. P values, based on White's heteroskedasticity-consistent standard errors, are reported in parentheses

The direct effect of competition is insignificant. However, coefficients of CG Index still appear to be positive. We also find that the interaction term appears insignificant even after controlling for firm specific variables. To better understand if corporate governance matter more in competitive industries we conduct further regressions as follows. We divided the sample into deciles based on corporate governance ratings. Then in these groups, we test the direct effects of competition. We estimate the Model 2 for all performance measures. As our objective is to see the direct effects of competition relative to the quality of corporate governance, we could replace the CINDEX with a dummy variable DCINDEX that takes value = 1 when a firm is operating in a competitive industry (i.e. CINDEX > sample median). In this way, we can compare the coefficients of DCINDEX to interpret the possible economic effects when firm is operating in a competitive industry (note that DCINDEX = 1 for all regressions). Table 11 reports the coefficients of DCINDEX across all the sub-samples. Signs and significance of control variables remain consistent with previous regressions and hence not reported. Consider the first column of the table. Coefficient of DCINDEX is 0.1534 on a sample of firms with lowest CG Index ratings. This coefficient is positive and significant which shows that competition does substitute, although to some degree, for poor corporate governance. However, this result is not consistent for other two performance measures in firm's respective product market. If we consider the coefficients of DCINDEX in the middle and higher deciles of CG Index, the effect is positive and significant across all the performance measures. This result could be interpreted as complementary effects of corporate governance and competition. As we measure the effect of competition on different levels of corporate governance at firm level, competition in firm's respective industry substantiates the positive effect.

We can also compare the values of coefficients to make a comment on economic effects of product market competition as corporate governance within firm improves from poor to good. For instance, compare the coefficients of DCINDEX in the first column −0.1028 when CG Index falls in moderately bad decile range and 0.1281 when CG Index takes values in moderately good decile range. If a firm is operating in a competitive industry, improvement in corporate governance can result in 25 % ((0.1281−0.1028)/0.1028) increase in stock valuation. We can summarize these results that effect of competition complements good corporate governance. This result is not consistent with majority of the recent empirical research on US firms that suggest that adopting good CG may be costly for firms in competitive industries. However, our results are consistent with studies that analyze European countries which are similar to Indian setting in terms of dominant shareholder. (Grosfeld and Tressel 2001; Januszewski et al. 2000).

6 Conclusion

We analyze how does product market competition and corporate governance act – as complements or as substitutes? There are two competing hypothesis relating the two mechanism. Alchian (1950), Friedman (1953) and Stigler (1958) express the view that product market competition acts as an ultimate disciplining mechanism and that managerial slack cannot survive in competitive industries. However, the modern theories of corporate governance cast doubts on role of product market competition that it alone cannot solve the problem of corporate governance due to imperfect competition and rent seeking possibilities (Shleifer and Vishny 1997). And therefore, corporate governance becomes important irrespective of competition in product markets. We contribute to the recent empirical research that has begun to address the interaction between corporate governance and product market competition to see if competition acts as a substitute for poor governance mechanism or it actually leads firms to implement better corporate governance. In this study, we investigate if corporate governance matter more in competitive industries. This question is relevant for emerging economy like India where because of predominance of business groups and family controlled businesses, corporate governance reforms focusing on internal control mechanisms might take longer to effect. Measuring product market competition is straight-forward from industrial organization literature. However, corporate governance is a multifaceted measure. To proxy for overall quality of corporate governance, we construct an index based on board structure, entrenchment, audit quality and information disclosure. These attributes of corporate governance have attained the maximum attention in corporate governance reforms in Indian corporate sector. The corporate governance index positively correlates with performance and is consistent across stock market and operating performance measures. With regard to the interaction between competition and corporate governance, our results do not support the substitution hypothesis. However, our results support the complement hypotheses that competition has a direct effect only on companies with better corporate governance index ratings. In general the empirical analysis suggests that relying on product market competition to improve corporate governance of firms may not be appropriate in the Indian setting and therefore, direct corporate governance reforms seem to be necessary and effective.

References

Aghion, P., & Dewatripont, M. (1999). Competition, financial discipline and growth. *Review of Economic Studies, 66*, 825–852.

Alchian, A. A. (1950). Uncertainty, evolution, and economic theory. *Journal of Political Economy, 50*, 211–221.

Allen, F., & Gale, D. (2000). Corporate governance and competition. In X. Vives (Ed.), *Corporate governance, theoretical and empirical perspectives*. Cambridge, MA: Cambridge University Press.

Ammann, M., Osech, D., & Schmid, M. (2010). *Product market competition, corporate governance, and firm value: Evidence from the EU-area*. Working paper.

Baily, M. N., & Gersbach, H. (1995). Efficiency in manufacturing and the need for global competition. *Brookings Papers on Economic Activity*, 307–308.

Banaji, J. (2004). Institutional investors and nominee directors. In D. Reed & S. Mukherjee (Eds.), *Corporate governance, economic reforms and development the Indian experience*. Delhi: Oxford University Press.

Berglof, E., & Von Thadden, E-L. (1999). *The changing corporate governance paradigm, implications for transition and development countries*. Manuscript. Stockholm Institute of Transition Economics.

Berle, A., & Means, G. (1932). *The modern corporation and private property*. New York: Macmillan.

Bertrand, M., Mehta, P., & Mullainathan, S. (2002). Ferreting out tunnelling, an application to Indian business groups. *Quarterly Journal of Economics, 117*, 121–148.

Black, B.S., & Khanna, V.S. (2007). *Can corporate governance reforms increase firm's market values? Evidence from India*. ECGI – Finance Working Paper. 159/2007.

Black, B. S., Jang, H., & Kim, W. C. (2006). Does corporate governance affect firms' market values? Evidence from Korea. *Journal of Law, Economics and Organization, 22*(2), 336–413.

Bloom, N., & Reenen Van, J. M. (2006). *Measuring and explaining management practices across firms and countries*. CEP Discussion Paper 716.

Boone, A. L., Field, L. C., Karpoff, M., & Raheja, C. G. (2007). The evolution and life-cycle of corporate boards: An empirical analysis. *Journal of Financial Economics, 85*, 66–101.

Boone, J., Khurana, I., & Raman, K. K. (2010). Do the Big 4 and the second-tier provide audits of similar quality. *Journal of Accounting and Public Policy, 29*, 330–352.

Bozec, R. (2005). Board of directors, market discipline and firm performance. *Journal of Business Finance & Accounting, 32*(9–10), 1921–1960.

Burkart, M., Gromb, D., & Panunzi, F. (1997). Large shareholders, monitoring, and the value of the firm. *Quarterly Journal of Economics, 112*, 693–728.

Chari, A., & Gupta, N. (2008). Incumbents and protectionism: The political economy of foreign entry liberalization. *Journal of Financial Economics, 88*(3), 633–656.

Chen, A., Kao, L., Tsao, M., & Wu, C. (2007). Building a corporate governance index from the perspectives of ownership and leadership for firms in Taiwan. *Corporate Governance: An International Review, 15*(2), 251–261.

Chibber, P. K., & Majumdar, S. K. (1999). Foreign ownership and profitability, property rights, control, and the performance of firms in Indian industry. *The Journal of Law and Economics, XLII*, 209–238.

Crystal, G. (1991). *In search of excess: The overcompensation of American executives*. New York: W.W. Norton.

Coles, J. L., Daniel, N. D., & Naveen, L. (2008). Boards, does one size fit all? *Journal of Financial Economics, 82*(2), 329–356.

Cremers, K., Martin, J., Nair, V. B., & Peyer, U. (2006). *Weak shareholder rights: A product market rationale*. Mimeo: Yale University.

Curry, B., & George, K. D. (1983). Industrial concentration: A survey. *Journal of Industrial Economics, 31*(3), 203–255.

Dalton, D., & Kesner, I. F. (1987). Composition and CEO duality in boards of directors: An international perspective. *Journal of International Business Studies, 18*, 33–42.

Doidge, C., Karolyi, A., & Stulz, R. (2004). Why are foreign firms listed in the US worth more? *Journal of Financial Economics, 71*, 205–238.

Eisenberg, T., Sundgren, S., & Wells, M. T. (1998). Larger board size and decreasing firm value in small firms. *Journal of Financial Economics, 48*, 35–54.

Fan, J.P.H., & Wong, T.J. (2001). *Do external auditors perform a corporate governance role in emerging markets? Evidence from East Asia*. In EFA 2001 Barcelona Meetings, 3rd Annual Financial Market Development Conference, Hong Kong, March, 2001. Available at SSRN: http://ssrn.com/abstract=27064.

Francis, J., & Wang, D. (2008). The joint effect of investor protection and Big 4 audits on earnings quality around the world. *Contemporary Accounting Research, 25*(1), 157–191.

Friedman, M. (1953). *The methodology of positive economics. In essays in positive economics*. Chicago: University of Chicago Press.

Giroud, X., & Mueller, H. (2010). Does corporate governance matter more in competitive industries? *Journal of Financial Economics, 95*, 312–331.

Giroud, X., & Mueller, H. (2011). Corporate governance, product market competition and equity prices. *Journal of Finance, 66*, 563–600.
Glen, J., Matthias, R., & Singh, A. (1999). *How intensive is competition in the emerging markets? An analysis of corporate rates of return from nine emerging markets*. International Monetary Fund c WP/99/32, Washington, DC.
Glen, J., Lee, K., & Singh, A. (2000). *Competition, corporate governance and financing of corporate growth in emerging markets*. Discussion papers in accounting and finance. No. AF46, Department of Applied Economics, Cambridge.
Gomes, A. (2000). Going public without governance: managerial reputation effects. *The Journal of Finance, 55*(2), 615–646.
Gompers, P. A., Ishii, J. L., & Metrick, A. (2003). Corporate governance and equity prices. *Quarterly Journal of Economics, 118*, 107–155.
Griffith, R. (2001). *Product market competition, efficiency and agency costs: An empirical analysis*. Working paper: The Institute for Fiscal Studies. WP01/12.
Grosfeld, I., & Tressel, T. (2001). *Competition and corporate governance, substitutes or compliments? Evidence from the Warsaw stock exchange*. William Davidson Institute WP N 2001–383.
Guadalupe, M., & Pérez-González, F. (2006). *The impact of product market competition on private benefits of control*. Working Paper, Columbia University.
Hart, O. (1983). The market as an incentive mechanism. *Bell Journal of Economics, 14*, 366–382.
Hermalin, B. E., & Weisback, M. S. (2003). Boards of directors as an endogenously determined institution: A survey of the economic literature. *Economic Policy Review. Federal Reserve Bank of New York, 9*(1), 7–26.
Higgs, D. (2003). The Higgs report on non-executive directors. Summary recommendations: UK.
Januszewski, S., Köke, J., & Winter, J. (2000). Product market competition, corporate governance and firm performance, an empirical analysis for Germany. *Research in Economics, 56*(3), 299–332.
Jensen, M. (1986). Agency costs of free cash flow, corporate finance and takeovers. *American Economic Review, 76*, 323–329.
Jensen, M. (1993). The modern industrial revolution, exit and the failure of internal control systems. *Journal of Finance, 48*, 831–880.
Johnson, S., La Porta, R., Lopez-Silanes F., & Shleifer A. (2000). Tunneling. *American Economic Review, 90*, 22–27.
Karuna, C. (2007). *Industry product market competition and corporate governance*. Mimeo: University of California at Irvine.
Khanna, T., & Palepu, K. (2000). Emerging market business groups, foreign investors and corporate governance. In R. Morck (Ed.), *Concentrated corporate ownership* (pp. 265–294). Chicago: University of Chicago Press.
Khanna, T., & Palepu, K. (2004). Globalization and convergence in corporate governance: Evidence from Infosys and the Indian software industry. *Journal of International Business Studies, 35*(6), 484–507.
Khurana, I. K., & Raman, K. (2004). Are Big 4 audits in ASEAN countries of higher quality than non Big 4 audits? *Asia Pacific Journal of Accounting and Economics, 11*(2), 139–165.
Klapper, L. F., & Love, I. (2002). *Corporate governance, investor protection, and performance in emerging markets*. The World Bank Development Research Group, Finance Policy Research Working Paper 2818.
Koke, J. F., & Renneboog, L. (2008). *Do corporate control and product market competition lead to stronger productivity growth? Evidence from market oriented and blockholder based governance regimes*. ECGI Finance Working Paper N14/2003.
Lehn, K., Patro, S., & Zhao, M. (2004). *Determinants of size and structure of corporate boards: 1935–2000*. Working Paper: University of Pittsburgh and Bentley College.

Linck, J. S., Jeffrey, M. N., & Tina, Y. (2006). *The effects and unintended consequences of the Sarbanes-Oxley act, and its era, on the supply and demand for directors*. Working Paper, University of Georgia.

Mohanty, P. (2002). *Institutional investors and corporate governance in India*. National Stock Exchange Research Initiative Paper 15.

Nachane, D. M., Ghosh, S., & Ray, P. (2005). *Bank nominee directors and corporate performance, micro evidence from India*. Economic and Political Weekly, MPRA Paper no 1714.

Nalebuff, B., & Stiglitz, J. (1983). Prices and incentives, towards a general theory of compensation and competition. *Bell Journal of Economics, 14*, 21–43.

Nickell, S. J. (1996). Competition and corporate performance. *Journal of Political Economy, 104*, 724–746.

Nickell, S., Nicolitsas, D., & Dryden, N. (1997). What makes firms perform well? *European Economic Review, 41*, 783–796.

Pearce, J. A., & Zahra, S. A. (1992). Board composition from a strategic contingency perspective. *Journal of Management Studies, 29*, 411–438.

Porter, M. E. (1990). *The competitive advantage of nations*. New York: The Free Press.

Randy, T., & Jenssen, J. I. (2004). Board independence and product market competition in Swedish firms. *Corporate Governance: An International Review, 12*(3), 281–289.

Ross, S. A. (1977). The determination of financial structure – The incentive-signalling approach. *The Bell Journal of Economics, 8*(1), 23–40.

Sarkar, J., & Sarkar, S. (2008). Debt and corporate governance in emerging economies. *Economics of Transition, 16*(2), 293–334.

Schmidt, K. (1997). Managerial incentives and product market competition. *Review of Economic Studies, 64*, 191–213.

SEBI Report of the Committee appointed by the SEBI on Corporate Governance Under the Chairmanship of Narayan Murthy. (2001).

SEBI Report of the Committee appointed by the SEBI on Corporate Audit and Governance Under the Chairmanship of Naresh Chandra. (2002).

Shleifer, A., & Vishny, R. W. (1997). A survey of corporate governance. *The Journal of Finance, LII*(2), 737–783.

Smith, A. (1976). *Wealth of Nations*. Chicago: University of Chicago Press.

Stigler, G. J. (1958). The economics of scale. *Journal of Law and Economics, 1*, 54–71.

Teoh, S., & Wong, T. J. (1993). Perceived auditor quality and the earnings response coefficient. *The Accounting Review, 68*, 346–366.

Veermani, C. (2001). *Analysing trade flows and industrial structure of India: The question of data harmonisation*. Unpublished working paper, Centre for Development Studies, Trivandrum, India.

White, H. (1980). A heteroscedasticity-consistent covariance matrix estimator and a direct test for heteroscedasticity. *Econometrica, 48*, 817–838.

Winter, S. (1964). Economic natural selection and the theory of the firm. *Yale Economic Essays, 4*, 225–272.

Yeh, Y.-H., & Woidtke, T. (2002). Commitment or entrenchment?: Controlling shareholders and board composition. *Journal of Banking and Finance, 29*, 1857–1885.

Yermack, D. (1996). Higher market valuation of companies with a small board of directors. *Journal of Financial Economics, 40*, 185–212.

Strong Boards, Risk Committee and Bank Performance: Evidence from India and China

Francesca Battaglia, Angela Gallo, and Anna Elvira Graziano

Abstract The recent financial crisis has raised several questions with respect to the corporate governance of financial institutions. This paper investigates whether boards of directors and risk management-related corporate governance mechanisms are associated with a better bank performance during the financial crisis of 2007/2008 for a sample of Chinese and Indian listed banks. We measure market bank performance by Tobin' Q and price-earnings ratio. In line with the previous literature on US banks, we find the general irrelevance of the standard board's variables when specific variables related to the risk committee are included in the analysis. We find that the market valuation and the expected market growth (Tobin' Q and P/E) are larger for banks with smaller risk committee. In particular, we find that the market valuation is negatively associated with the size of the risk committee and positively associated with the number of the risk committee' meetings. This seems to suggest that the market discounts as favorable the information related to "strong" risk governance.

1 Introduction

Sound financial systems serve as an important channel for achieving economic growth through the mobilization of financial savings, putting them to productive use and transforming various risks (Levine et al. 1999; King and Levine 1993; Rajan and Zingales 1996; Demirgüç-Kunt and Maksimovic 1996; Jayaratne and

F. Battaglia (✉)
University of Naples Parthenope, Naples, Italy
e-mail: francesca.battaglia@uniparthenope.it

A. Gallo
University of Salerno, Salerno, Italy

A.E. Graziano
University of Rome, "Tor Vergata", Rome, Italy

S. Boubaker and D.K. Nguyen (eds.), *Corporate Governance in Emerging Markets*, CSR, Sustainability, Ethics & Governance, DOI 10.1007/978-3-642-44955-0_4,

Strahan 1996). Strengthening financial systems has been one of the central issues facing emerging markets and developing economies. Many countries, including India and China, adopted a series of financial sector liberalization measures in the 1980s and early 1990s that included interest rate liberalization, entry deregulations, reduction of reserve requirements and removal of credit allocation. As a result of these reforms, the introduction of new rules and codes on firm's governance structure has progressively gained more and more relevance in those countries. Indeed, it is widely recognized that "good" corporate governance helps to promote corporate fairness, transparency and accountability and thus to strength financial systems.

For Asian economies, the literature has widely investigated the relationship between corporate governance and firm performance, but only few studies focus on this relationship for financial institutions. Moreover, to the best of our knowledge, no studies analyze the corporate and risk governance of banks of the emerging economies over a period of global financial crisis as the 2007–2011, which originated in the US subprime mortgage market and soon spread to other areas both in US and other European countries. In the beginning, both economists and international financial institutions claimed that this crisis would have marginal or no impact on the emerging economies of namely China and India because of the 'decoupling' effects and also because these economies have adopted market reforms, which had made these economies more efficient and competitive so that they could withstand such challenges. More recently, it has been increasingly acknowledged that the financial crisis is adversely affecting the economies of the emerging markets, and specially their banking systems. Therefore, it is significant to understand the impact of current global crisis on the Chinese and Indian banking systems. In particular, we focus on bank corporate governance because it is widely recognized that the recent financial crisis is to a large extent attributable to excessive risk-taking by banks and that shortcomings in bank corporate governance may have had a central role in the development of the crisis in the US and EU banking systems. An OECD report argues "the financial crisis can be to an important extent attributed to failures and weaknesses in corporate governance arrangements" (Kirkpatrick 2009). More recently, the National Commission on the Causes of the Financial and Economic Crisis in the US concluded "dramatic failures of corporate governance... at many systematically important financial institutions were a key cause of this crisis" (Beltratti and Stultz 2010). Some academic studies also highlight that flaws in bank governance played a key role in the performance of banks during the crisis (Diamond and Rajan 2009).

Our research aims to investigate the relationship between both standard corporate governance variables (related to the board of directors) and risk management-related variables, and bank performance for China and India over the period 2007–2011. As claimed by Aebi et al. (2012), the role of risk management is one of the main differences between financial and non-financial firms from a corporate governance point of view. The importance of a proper risk management function in the banking industry is extensively recognized and also supported by the prudential regulatory framework of the Basle Committee, but its effective role in bank corporate governance structure, defined as risk governance, still misses clear empirical evidence and interpretations for US and European banking system. To the best of our knowledge there are no studies on risk governance for non-Western countries. Based on the most recent studies on bank corporate governance, we expect banks with strong boards structure and risk control to perform better during the financial crisis.

We find the general irrelevance of the standard board's variables, when specific variables related to the risk committee are included in the analysis, in line with Aebi et al. (2012). The market valuation and the expected market growth (Tobin' Q and P/E respectively) are larger for banks with smaller risk committee. In particular, we find that the market valuation of these banks is associated with a smaller size of the risk committee and a higher number of the risk committee' meetings. This seems to suggest that the market discounts as favorable the information related to "strong" risk governance, defined as a risk committee with a low number of components and a high number of meetings.

The remainder of this chapter is organized as follows: Sect. 2 provides a brief review of relevant literature and the development of the hypotheses to test; Sects. 3 and 4 describe the institutional settings of our analysis both for Indian and Chinese banks, respectively; Sect. 5 describes data and variables, provides brief descriptive statistics of the sample and presents our empirical specifications; Sect. 6 reports the results of the analysis; and finally, Sect. 7 concludes the chapter.

2 Literature Review and Hypotheses Development

2.1 Corporate and Risk Governance in US and Europe: Evidence from the Global Financial Crisis

For US and European financial systems, a growing body of empirical literature has documented that banks with good corporate governance mechanism are generally associated with better financial performance, higher firm valuation and higher stock returns (Caprio et al. 2007; Cornett et al. 2009; de Andres and Vallelado 2008; Hanazaki and Horiuchi 2003; Laeven and Levine 2009; Macey and O'Hara 2003; Mishra and Nielsen 2000; Pacini et al. 2005; Sierra et al. 2006; Webb Cooper 2009).

A recent stream of the literature investigates the above-mentioned relationship over periods of financial turmoil. Peni and Vahamaa (2012) find a positive and significant relationship, also during the 2008 financial crisis, for large publicly traded US banks. In particular, they show that banks with stronger corporate governance (small boards and more independent directors) mechanisms have higher profitability, higher market valuations and less negative stock returns amidst the crisis. Beltratti and Stulz (2010) focus on banks in 31 countries and document that large banks with lower leverage ratios have less negative stock returns during the crisis, but also that banks with strong boards perform worse over the period from

July 2007 to December 2008 than other banks. Erkens et al. (2012) find that banks with more independent boards and larger institutional ownership gain lower stock returns over the period from January 2007 to September 2008. Pathan and Faff (2013), using a broad panel of large US bank holding companies over the period 1997–2011, find that both board size and independent directors decrease bank performance. Finally, Adams and Mehran (2012), using a sample of banking firm data that spans 34 years, find that board independence is not related to performance, as measured by a proxy for Tobin' Q. However, board size is positively related to performance.

A second body of literature that is related to our research is about risk governance and its effect on bank performance. To the best of our knowledge only two papers address this issue for US market: Aebi et al. (2012) and Ellul and Yerramilli (2013). This latter investigates whether a strong and independent risk management is significantly related to bank risk-taking and performance during the financial crisis for a sample of 74 large US bank holding companies based on a Risk Management Index (RMI). They expect that banks with strong and independent risk management functions to be less exposed to risk. Their motivation is based on the idea that an effective control and supervision of risk-taking behavior of trading desks cannot be contained through regulatory supervision or traditional external market discipline from bondholder and stockholder. Hence, they suggest that an internal risk management process is necessary to identify, measure and control risk. They find that banks with a high RMI (strong) in 2006 show a lower exposure to private-label mortgage-backed securities, are less active in trading off-balance sheet derivatives, have a lower downside risk and a higher Sharpe ratio during the crisis. Aebi et al. (2012) analyze the influence of risk specific corporate governance characteristics on the performance of banks during the financial crisis. They find that banks with better risk management structure (in particular the reporting line – the CEO reports directly to the board of directors) perform significantly better in the financial crisis 2007–2008. Notably, they find either no significant or even negative relation between a bank's performance during the crisis and standard corporate governance variables. This highlights the importance of the so-called "risk governance" to investigate the effect of the governance structure on banks performance, but also in the future reshaping of corporate governance recommendations in light of the financial crisis consequences.

2.2 *Corporate Governance in Asian Markets: Main Findings in the Literature*

The growing importance of Asian markets and businesses in the global economy has heightened interest in the corporate governance of Asian companies (Peng et al. 2010). Over the years, there have been numerous calls for reform of corporate governance models of Asian companies. While concerns about family control and state ownership of major businesses in Asia remain strong, there is substantial uncertainty about the economic consequences of the current corporate governance models prevailing in Asia, both for corporate performance at the firm level and for economic performance at the macroeconomic level (Young et al. 2008). Generalizing about corporate governance of Asian companies is perilous given variations across companies, both within individual countries as well as across countries. Nevertheless, the relevant literature highlights specific features of Asian corporate governance and links those features to the behavior and performance of Asian companies. Features of Asian corporate governance that are emphasized in the literature include: (i) concentrated ownership, (ii) extensive cross-ownership ties and pyramidal ownership structures, (iii) extensive family ownership with a high degree of overlap between controlling family ownership and management, (iv) significant state ownership with direct political influence of management appointments, and (v) the relatively limited use of professional managers in top management.

2.2.1 Corporate Governance in China: A Review of the Literature

Among the most recent studies on Chinese companies corporate governance, Cheung et al. (2008) construct a corporate governance index (CGI) for 2004 Fortune 100 largest listed Chinese companies based on a survey. Their questions are based on the Organization of Economic Cooperation and Development (OECD) principles of corporate governance, including: rights of shareholders; equitable treatment of shareholders; role of stakeholders, disclosure and transparency; and board responsibilities. They find an insignificant relationship between CGI and the market valuation of the top 100 Chinese listed companies in 2004. However, due to of the limited sample (100 companies), the study period (1 year), and the type of sampled firms, the results cannot be generalized to a wider sample over a longer period of time.

Sami et al. (2011) investigate the impact of corporate governance on firm performance and valuation in China by introducing a composite measure of corporate governance. They find that this composite measure of corporate governance is positively and significantly associated with firm performance and valuation. In order to examine how corporate governance is related to firm performance and valuation in China, they used ROA, ROE, and Tobin' Q as the dependent variables in their regression analysis. The sample is composed by the listed companies on either the Shanghai Stock Exchange or Shenzhen Stock Exchange during the period 2001–2003. The choice of using the time period 2001–2003 is due to significant changes occurred in the regulations of ownership of public companies in China.

Filatotchev et al. (2011) use a comprehensive sample of listed Hong Kong companies to evaluate how family control affects the abusive use of private information by controlling families, as well as how private information abuse risk affects company performance. They find that family leadership is negatively associated with firm performance measured by Tobin' Q. At the same time, they find that family ownership and leadership negatively moderate the impact of the expected private information abuse risk variable on performance, while board dominance positively moderates such impact. This finding suggests that family control may have an overall positive impact on corporate performance when private information abuse risks are low.

2.2.2 Corporate Governance in India: A Review of the Literature Review

Among the most recent studies on Indian companies corporate governance, Bhattacharyya and Rao (2005) analyze whether adoption of Clause 49[1] predicts lower volatility and returns for large Indian firms by comparing a 1-year period after the adoption (starting June 1, 2001) to a similar period before the adoption (starting June 1, 1998). They expect Clause 49 to improve disclosure and thus to reduce information asymmetry and thereby share price volatility. However, the authors find insignificant results for volatility.

Subramanian (2006) recognize the differences in disclosure patterns of financial information and governance attributes, as the board and management structure, the ownership structure and the investor relations for a sample of 90 Indian companies. The author reports no differences in disclosure pattern of public sector and private sector companies as far as financial transparency and information disclosure were concerned. The study also finds that private companies disclose more information under the category of board and management structure.

Jackling and Johl (2009) investigate the relationship between internal governance structures and financial performance of Indian companies. The effectiveness of boards of directors, including board composition, board size, and aspects of board leadership including duality and board busyness are addressed in the Indian context. Their study provides some support for aspects of agency theory as a greater proportion of outside directors on boards were associated with improved firm performance. However, the notion of separating leadership roles in a manner consistent with agency theory is not supported. For instance, the notion that powerful CEOs (duality role, CEO being the promoter, and CEO being the only board manager) have a detrimental effect on performance is not supported. There is some support for resource dependency theory. The findings suggest that larger board size has a positive impact on performance, by supporting the view that greater exposure to the external environment improves access to various resources and thus positively impacts on performance. The study however fails to support the

[1] In India the recommendations of the Birla Committee enacted Clause 49 of the Listing Agreements that first came into effect in 2001 with further amendments in 2004. Under Clause 49 the board of directors of a company is required to have an "optimum combination" of inside and outside directors with not less that 50 % of boards consisting of outside directors where the chairman is an insider. The requirement for outside directors on the board is reduced to 30 % where the chairman is an outsider.

resource dependency theory in terms of the association between frequency of board meetings and performance. The results show that outside directors with multiple appointments appeared to have a negative effect on performance, suggesting that "busyness" did not add value in terms of networks and enhancement of resource accessibility.

Sarkar and Sarkar (2009) extend the literature on multiple directorships, busy directors and firm performance by providing evidence from India, where the incidence of multiple directorships is high. Using a sample of 500 large firms, they find multiple directorships by independent directors to correlate positively with firm value. Independent directors with multiple positions are also found to attend more board meetings and are more likely to be present in the company's annual general meeting. Multiple directorships by inside directors are, however, negatively related to firm performance.

Raithatha and Bapat (2012) study compliance of corporate governance requirements by 30 Indian companies listed on BSE. A model is developed to calculate the corporate governance score for each company and then it is related to company attributes like size, profitability, leverage, and foreign ownership. They find no significant correlation between corporate governance and company characteristics. Factor analysis of major sub-parameters of corporate governance score, namely composition of board, audit committee, number of board meetings and remuneration committee reveals that the strength of committee and competency level of board are important factors in bank performance.

2.3 Hypotheses

Based on the prior literature, we focus on the relationship between bank performance and the following characteristics of the board's structure: the board size, the number of independent directors and the frequency of board meetings per year. Next to these, we test the relationship between bank performance and risk management-related characteristics.

The board of directors is an economic institution that, in theory, helps to solve the agency problems inherent in managing an organization (Hermalin and Weisbach 2003). We use the term "strong board" to indicate a board more representing bank shareholder interest. Following Pathan (2009), our proxies of strong boards are small board size, more independent directors and high frequency of board meetings.

As to the board size, larger boards of directors are expect to better supervise managers and bring more human capital to advise them. However, boards with too many members lead to problems of coordination, control, and flexibility in decision-making. Large boards also give excessive control to the CEO, harming efficiency. Therefore, the trade-off between advantages (monitoring and advising) and disadvantages (coordination, control and decision-making problems) has to be taken into account.

Independent directors are believed to be better monitors of managers as independent directors value maintaining reputation in directorship market but the findings in this instance are mixed (Fama and Jensen 1983). However, an excessive proportion of independent directors, which are often outside directors, could damage the advisory role of boards, since it might prevent bank executives from joining the board. Inside directors are able to provide the board with valuable information that outside directors would find difficult to gather.

The frequency of board meetings per year is a proxy of better functioning of the board. Francis et al. (2011) find that firm stock performance is positively related to the number of board meetings, consistent with Adams and Ferreira (2007), who, among others, argue that board meetings are important channels through which directors obtain firm-specific information and fulfill their monitoring role. De Andres and Vallelado (2008) argue that meetings provide board members with the chance to come together, to discuss and exchange ideas on how they wish to monitor managers and bank strategy. Hence, the more frequent the meetings, the closer the control over managers and the more relevant the advisory role of the board. We expect that a higher number of meetings might be perceived as a proxy of a more timely response of the board in stressed financial markets and thus to be associated with better bank performance.

Given the peculiar time horizon under investigation, characterized by financial uncertainty, we expect coordination and control to assume considerable relevance compared to monitoring and advising and thus that small boards are associated with better bank performance. In line with the previous literature on "strong boards" (Pathan 2009), the formal specification of our first hypothesis is the following:

Hypothesis 1 (H_1): The relationship between strong boards (i.e. small board size, more independent directors and high frequency of board meetings) and bank performance is positive during the global financial crisis.

Similarly to our hypothesis for the boards of directors, for risk-management related variables, we would expect that having a risk committee in general indicate a stronger risk management and therefore better corporate governance. As suggested by Aebi et al. (2012), most banks still seem to consider asset growth and a reduction of operational costs as the main drivers of profitability. However, the last financial crisis has clearly demonstrated that the business of banks is risk, therefore the legitimate question arises whether and to what extent the risk committee can contribute to bank performance. In particular, the literature on the topic emphasize the role of risk management-related variables in explaining bank's performance during the crisis showing that standard governance measures as used in a large body of literature on corporate governance and its valuation effect in non-financial firms may fall short in describing the relevant governance structure of banks, in particular with respect to their crisis performance.

Thus, the formal specification of our second hypothesis is as follows:

Hypothesis 2 (H_2): The relationship between strong risk-management function (a dedicated committee solely charged with monitoring and managing the risk *management efforts within the bank) and bank performance is positive during the global financial crisis.*

3 Major Aspects of Bank Corporate Governance in China: History and Institutional Framework

3.1 The Chinese Banking System

Prior to the beginning of the economic reforms in 1978, the Government largely owned the banking system and Chinese banks were generally subservient to the requirements of the central planned economy. In particular, they mainly financed the State Owned Enterprises (SOEs), that were loss-making and reliant on bank credit to continue financing their activities, but ultimately failed to repay their loans. As a result, banks' non-performing loans increased significantly: by the late 1990s the large state-owned banks' aggregate non-performing loan (NPL) ratio exceeded 30 % (Huang 2006). For these reasons, the Chinese banking system has undergone several reforms aimed to its modernization and to the spread of wider prudential lending policies, especially after 2003.

As of end-2011, the domestic Chinese banking system is composed of several categories of financial intermediaries, with different ownership structures and serving different functions, which can be broadly divided into four main categories. The first one includes the three policy banks, that are the wholly state-owned banks; the second category consists of five large commercial banks – banks previously wholly state-owned where the Chinese central government is usually the largest stockholder; the third one includes 12 joint-stock commercial banks and then there is the category of the local banks, which includes 144 city commercial banks, as well as 212 rural commercial banks, 190 rural cooperative banks and 2,265 rural credit cooperatives and one postal savings bank.

After the banking reform of 2005, China began transforming the wholly state-owned banks into joint-stock corporations, (this process is known as "equitization"), operating as commercial banks, and, as a result, only three wholly state-owned banks remain in China – the Agricultural Development Bank of China, the China Development Bank and the China Exim Bank.[2] Each of the them has a distinct mission: the Agricultural Bank of China (ABC) undertakes the rural banking business, the China Development Bank is traditionally responsible for raising funds for large infrastructure projects, while the China Exim Bank provides financial services to promote Chinese exports (particularly of high-tech and

[2] China Development Bank is reportedly to be equitized sometime in the near future, but plans for its initial public offering (IPO) have been on hold for over 2 years. There are no reported plans to equitize the Agricultural Development Bank of China or China Exim Bank.

new-tech products) and facilitates the import of technologically advanced machinery and equipment.

Referring to the large commercial banks category, the so-called equitized banks, we specify that for four of these banks the majority of the shares are non-tradable shares held by the People's Bank of China (PBOC), the Ministry of Finance (MOF), the National Council for Social Security Fund of the PRC (SSF) or other government entities.[3] Although the presence of the central government is still very strong, the large commercial banks are among the most dynamic and innovative financial institutions in China. According to the China Banking Regulatory Commission (CBRC) 2011 annual report, the five large commercial banks dominate the Chinese banking sector: they account for 47.3 % of the market shares (by total assets, as of year-end 2011).

The 12 joint-stock commercial banks have a mixture of ownership structure; they were established as commercial banks and then were subsequently transformed into joint-stock companies. In most cases, the central government remained the major stockholder (i.e. CITIC bank) after the conversion, but was allowed to divest their shares after a mandatory holding period. For at least 10 of the 12 banks, a foreign entity has purchased a significant holding of the outstanding shares.

Among the local banks the largest category is represented by the city commercial banks. These banks primarily interact with the provincial and municipal governments, but are still supervised by the PBOC and the CBRC. Like the large commercial banks, the city commercial banks have been largely transformed into private joint stock companies, with shares owned by local government agencies, investment companies and other legal entities, and individual investors.

According to the 2011 CBRC annual report, the Chinese banking system is focused on traditional financial intermediation and around 66 % of Chinese banks' income comes from these activities. Chinese banks largely fund themselves from domestic deposits (around 70 % of system liabilities); the share of banks' funding sourced from debt capital markets is fairly small. About half of banks' deposits are from non-financial corporations, with households accounting for most of the remainder. On the asset side, domestic loans represent around 50 % of banking system assets. The majority of banks' loans are to large and medium-sized non-financial corporations (including state-owned enterprises). Loans to small businesses account for around 20 % of loans, while household loans account for less than one-quarter of banks' total loans – a lower share than in many other banking systems, including those elsewhere in Asia.

[3] Such as, for example, the Central Huijin Investment Ltd., which is a wholly state-owned investment company established on 16 December 2003 under the Company Law of the People's Republic of China.

3.2 Corporate Governance of Chinese Listed Banks

Referring to the corporate governance of Chinese listed banks, we can consider the general shareholders' meeting as the power and decision-making organ of the listed companies, while the board of directors is the operational organ of the company, being responsible to the general shareholders' meeting. It takes the decisions concerning management issues under the authority of general shareholders' meeting. Moreover, the board of directors may, according to the resolution of the general shareholders' meeting, set up special committees, such as the strategy committee, the auditing committee, the nomination committee, the remuneration and appraisal committees, etc. The management is responsible to the board of directors, and it is in charge of the daily operation and management of the company. The supervisory board is the supervision organ of the company, which supervises whether directors and managers violate laws or articles of association of the company when accomplishing corporate duties, and it is entitled to inspect company's finance.

The Chinese legal framework for corporate governance comprises four levels: basic laws, administrative regulations, regulatory provisions and self-disciplinary rules. The first level consists of some fundamental laws, formulated either by the National People's Congress or its Standing Committee, including the Company Law, the Securities Law, the Criminal Law Amendment Act and the Law on the State-Owned Assets of Enterprises and the Accounting Law. The second level comprises the State Council administrative regulations, while the third level involves departmental provisions formulated by the Ministries, the People's Bank of China, the Auditing Administration and other agencies with administrative jurisdiction directly under the State Council (i.e. the Code of Corporate Governance of Listed Companies, Regulations on Information Disclosure of Listed Companies, Guidelines on Articles of Association of Listed Companies, Rules on Shareholders' Meetings of Listed Companies, etc.). Finally, the fourth level of self-disciplinary rules refers to the Rules on Listing Stocks and Trading Rules defined by the stock exchanges, among others.

We specify that the Company Law and the Securities Law provide the foundation for drawing up and developing a corporate governance framework in China. The Company Law, which was promulgated in December 1993, introduced the boards of directors and the supervisory boards and clearly provided that companies limited by shares should set up shareholders' meetings, a board of directors and a supervisory board. The previous law was revised in 2006 for the first time and stated that the main functions of the board are "to abide by the law, administrative laws and regulations, and articles of incorporation and to have the duty of loyalty and diligence to companies". The meaning of the duty of loyalty and diligence indicates that Chinese law and regulations are designed to protect the benefits of companies and shareholders. The Company Law provides that limited companies should have managers, who are hired and dismissed by the board. The corporate board may decide that a member of the board can also serve as a manager. On the one hand, the board may evaluate and supervise the operation and achievements of management by selecting managers. Companies also regularly disclose directors', supervisors' and senior managers' remuneration to shareholders. Referring to the independent directors, the Code of Corporate Governance of Listed Companies in China stipulates that they shall account for more than one-third of the board in a listed company, they shall be independent of their employer and the company's main shareholders and hold no other position but that of independent directors.

The Code of Corporate Governance of Listed Companies also stipulates that, according to the resolution of the general shareholders' meeting, a listed company's board may set up special committees on strategy, audit, nomination, remuneration and appraisal, etc. All of the special committee members are directors. Thereinafter, independent directors shall account for more than half of the committee members and act as conveners in audit committees, nomination committees and remuneration and appraisal committees.[4] In general, the special committees are the extension of the independent director system and they are good for improving the independence and effectiveness of the board's operations as well as controlling risks.

4 Major Aspects of Bank Corporate Governance in India: History and Institutional Framework

4.1 The Indian Banking System

Indian banking industry is considered as a blooming and sustainable sector in the global financial system. It has undergone major changes and reforms during economic reforms of the last decades. The reforms of Indian economy started in 1990s and materialized in a process of liberalization of the real and financial sectors, with the aim of removing barriers to the growth of businesses. Real GDP growth improved mostly during the second half of the 1990s, and more substantially during the 2000s. Real GDP growth reached 10 % in 2007 and in 2010. Though it was a part of overall economic reforms, it has changed the very functioning of Indian banks. These reforms have not only influenced the productivity and efficiency of many of the Indian Banks, but have left everlasting footprints on the working of the banking sector in India. An efficient, dynamic and effective banking sector plays a decisive role in accelerating the rate of economic growth in any economy.

The Indian reform process can be divided into two stages: a first stage of deregulation aimed at promoting competition (1992–1997) and a second stage (post 1998) aimed at strengthening financial stability. Until the end of the 1980s, the banking system in India was dominated by the presence of public banks and by a significant role of the State Bank of India. The financial regime was characterized

[4] In audit committees, at least one independent director should have an accounting background.

by an administered interest rate and a pre-emption of a large proportion of bank deposits. In the early 1990s, as part of the overall reform process in the Indian economy, banking liberalization was designed to increase competition in the banking sector and to improve the efficiency of credit allocation. The main reforms in the financial sector were implemented between 1994 and 2004. They consisted in (i) the liberalization of the interest rate, (ii) freedom for banks to choose their deposit and lending rates, (iii) facilitation of the entry of domestic and foreign private banks and (iv) diversification of the ownership of state-owned banks. Consequently, the banking system was completely transformed and private banks have now a predominant role. At the beginning of the 1990s, state-owned banks had more than 90 % share in the assets of the banking system, while in 2004 their share decreased down to 75 %. From 1998 onwards, the emphasis of the reform process focused on the stability of the banking system. For instance, prudential norms on assets classification, income recognition, provisioning on non-performing loans and risk-based capital requirements became progressively more important, particularly against the backdrop of the Asian crisis.

The whole reform process aimed to create a level playing field among different ownership; regulatory policies relating to interest rates, prudential norms and reserve requirements were applied uniformly across banking groups. However, priority sector credit requirements are still in place, with different targets for domestic and foreign bank. In 2004, 40 private domestic sector banks, 33 foreign private banks and 27 state-owned banks, in which the Government have a majority ownership, compose the Indian banking system.

In 2008, at the beginning of the crisis, the return on equity grew slightly to end at 17.34 %, while the return on assets showed an increasing trend. The net interest margin remained stable over the period at around 3 %. All but two banks recorded capital adequacy ratios of more than 10 %, above the 9 % minimum requirement in India. At aggregate level, the capital adequacy ratio reported by the Indian banking sector was 13.01 % (also thanks to government recapitalization of some public banks), while the leverage ratio has continued to decline, reaching 10.63 in 2008. The gross non-performing loans ratio fell from 11.40 % in 2001 to 2.25 % in 2008.

At 2011, India has a well-regulated and relatively stable banking sector and a well-developed capital market. It is composed by the Federal Reserve of India (RBI), the banking regulator and supervisor acting as central banks, commercial and co-operative banks, and regional rural banks. Commercial and co-operative banks cover the 88 % of whole banking system' assets, and two-third of them are publicly owned. The public sector banks (PSBs) are made of nationalized banks (19) and State of India and its associates (1 + 5), while the private sector banks are made of 21 banks. Moreover, there are 24 foreign banks operating in India. However, PSBs are still dominating the commercial banking system. Shares of the leading PSBs are listed on the stock exchanges. The RBI has given licenses to new private sector banks as part of the liberalisation process. However, at present time private and foreign banks are growing very fast and giving tough competition to the public sector banks in India.

4.2 Corporate Governance of Indian Listed Banks

The Securities and Exchange Board of India regulates the corporate governance of listed companies across all sectors through Clause 49 of the Listing Agreement. Clause 49 provides guidelines on composition of the board of directors, composition and operations of the audit committee, remuneration of the directors, board procedures, management, shareholders and reporting requirements and compliance. In addition, the Banking regulation Act of 1949, remains the foundation of the corporate governance framework for banks in India. Moreover, public sector banks are also governed by the statutes under which they are incorporated. These include the State Bank of India Act, 1955; The State Bank of India (Subsidiaries banks) Act, 1959, for the associate banks of the State Bank of India; and the Banking Companies (Acquisition and Transfer of Undertakings) Act, 1970/1980 for nationalized banks. While the framework governing ownership, board composition and operations, and fit-and-proper criteria for the public sector banks is entrenched in the legal status that govern them, the Reserve Bank of India (RBI) introduced a comprehensive policy framework for ownership and governance in private sector banks in February 2005 to ensure that boards observes sound corporate governance principles, with higher transparency and disclosure. However, there are differences between the rules that apply to public sector banks and those applying to private sector banks.

To the aim of this research, it is important to underline that the government appoints the chairman, the managing director and the executive directors and nominates non-executive directors for public sector banks. The RBI, the regulator, is also represented on the board of public sector banks, while for private sector banks RBI nominates directors only for a selection of them. Nominee directors include representative of labor unions. In general, at least one-third of board directors should be independent if the chairman is a non-executive director. If he or she is an executive chairman, or a non-executive chairman linked to the promoter (i.e., controlling shareholder), then 50 % of the directors should be independent. There is no official recommendation for a higher proportion. However, the rule outlined above is based on a mandatory recommendation from the Indian Code of Corporate Governance, published in 1999 (see Securities and Exchange Board of India, Listing Agreement, Clause 49, Indian Code of Corporate Governance of 1999, Banking Regulation Act 1949 and Companies Act 1956).

5 Sample Selection, Variables and Econometric Model

In this section, first we describe our sample and the selection strategy we adopt in order to build up it, and then we describe and analyze the variables (dependent variables, key independent variables and control variables) of the model we implement. Finally, we focus on the explanation of the estimation framework.

5.1 Sample Description

Our sample consists of all the publicly listed commercial banks, cooperative banks, bank holdings and holding companies headquartered in China and India over the period 2007–2011 having available data on corporate governance features for 2007. This results in 15 Chinese banks and 21 Indian banks. See Table 4 in the Appendix for the list of the banks in the sample.

Our empirical analysis requires information on the banks' corporate governance structures, financial information and market data, (i.e. number of outstanding shares, nominal values, market capitalizations, etc.). In detail, information on bank board structures is hand collected from the annual reports, while the financial information and the market data are obtained from Bankscope database.

Both financial and market data are published at the end of each years, while information on banks' boards and risk committees refer to the end of the year 2007. Given that the prior literature on this topic (see e.g. Black et al. 2006; Erkens et al. 2012) has suggested that corporate governance structures change slowly, we use data for year 2007 in our empirical analysis, by assuming that the strength of governance mechanism incorporated in 2007 is reflected in bank performance during the investigated period (2007–2011).

We specify that after eliminating the banks with insufficient financial and corporate governance information,[5] we obtain a sample comprising of 109 firm-year observations for the fiscal years 2007–2011.

The credit institutions included in our sample are listed in Appendix (Table 4). Despite the relatively small number of individual banks, the sample covers a substantial proportion of the total amount of banking assets in the two countries. For example, referring to the Chinese banks, we underline that our sample is composed of the 4 listed large commercial banks and of 11 listed joint-stock banks, which represent about the 63.52 % of the market share (by assets) of the Chinese banking institutions.

5.2 Variables

5.2.1 Key Independent Variables: Standard Board Variables and Risk Governance Variables

Our key independent variables are the standard governance variables relating to the definition of strong board and the risk governance variables.

[5] We drop three Chinese banks (Bank of Beijing Co Ltd, Chongqing Rural commercial Bank and Bank of Nanjing) and four Indian banks (Union Bank of India, Central Bank of India, Allahabad Bank and Syndicate Bank), not covered by governance information at the end of 2007 and for which the previous information are available only from year 2010 or 2011.

Following Erkens et al. (2012) and de Andres and Vallelado (2008), among others, the effectiveness of the board of directors in monitoring and advising managers determines its strength and we use the term "strong board" to indicate a board more representing firm shareholder interest. Thus, a strong bank board is expected to better monitor bank managers for shareholders. Our proxies of strong boards are small board size, more independent directors and high frequency of board meetings. In detail, we define board size (BS) as the number of directors on the board. Independent directors (IND) is measured by the number of the independent board directors. The frequency of the board meetings (BM) is measured as the number of the meetings held in the year 2007. This variable takes into account the internal functioning of the board (de Andres and Vallelado 2008) and how boards operate. Since meetings provide board members with the chance to come together, and to discuss and exchange ideas on how they wish to monitor managers and firm strategy, we can argue that the more frequent the meetings are and the closer the control over managers is.

Following Aebi et al. (2012), we analyze the relationship between risk governance and bank performance. In particular, for banks with a risk committee, we collect data on the number of times the risk committee of the respective banks met in 2007 (RCM) and the number of directors in the risk committee (RCS). All these variables are assigned a value of zero for banks with no risk committee.[6]

5.2.2 Dependent Variables: Bank Performance Measures

We use two alternative measures of bank performance. In particular, following de Andres and Vallelado (2008), our main performance measure is the Tobin' Q (TQ), which we calculate as the book value of assets minus the book value of common equity plus the market value of equity plus the market value of common equity divided by the book value of total assets.[7]

Then, we use another measure of bank profitability (Peni and Vähämaa 2012; Aebi et al. 2012) to test the robustness of the analysis: the price/earnings ratio (P/E). The P/E is estimated as the ratio of market price to earnings per share. In particular, we calculate the annual stock data values for each year at the closing date of each year's financial accounts.

[6] The SREI Infrastructure Finance Limited has not the risk committee referring to the year 2007.

[7] We specify that many other studies use either this measure or a similar one as the dependent variable in research on board effectiveness. See for example Adams and Mehran (2008) and Caprio et al. (2007).

5.2.3 Control Variables

Following prior studies, we include in our model a set of control variables in order to account for size, business mix, and also to take into consideration differences among countries in terms of regulation.

A first group of control variables measures differences in bank business structure. One of these control variables is bank size (SIZE), which we computed as the natural log of total bank assets (Pathan 2009; Peni and Vähämaa 2012) at the book value. The variable LOANSTA measures differences in banking business model, and it is defined as the ratio of loans to total assets at book value (de Andres and Vallelado 2008). It allows us to control for the potential differences between commercial and holding banks. The variable TIER 1 (Aebi et al. 2012) is the ratio of tier 1 capital to total risk-weighted assets and, from a regulator's point of view, is a measure of the bank capital and of its financial strength.

To investigate whether the market valuation of the firm and, therefore, the market's growth expectations, are associated with the bank performance (Aebi et al. 2012), we use the price-to-book ratio (P/B). This variable is computed as the ratio of the bank' current share price to the book value per share.

To control for potential cycle effects, common to all banks, but varying over the analyzed period, we include year fixed effects.

Finally, to account for differences among the two countries in terms of regulation, we use a "country" dummy variable that takes the value one if the analyzed bank is from China and zero if it is from India. However, the country variable does not take into account that there are similarities among the countries in legal and institutional aspects or in investors' protection rights.

See the Table 5 in the Appendix for all variables definitions.

5.2.4 Summary Statistics and Correlation Matrix

This section provides summary statistics and correlation coefficients of the variables used in the analysis. Table 1 presents the descriptive statistics for these key variables. We specify that in Table 1 variables are not winsorized.

Panel A shows the descriptive statistics for the bank performance measures. The dependent variable TQ has a mean value of 1.087 %, while P/E show a high mean value (8.414 %) during the investigated period, which comprises the financial turmoil.

Panel C reports the descriptive statistics for all governance variables. The data show that the board has a higher mean number of directors (with a minimum of 7 and a maximum of 18.00) compared to the risk committee (13.21 versus 3.96). As for the frequency of the meetings held by the board and by the risk committee, the variable BM has a mean value higher than that of RCM (11.46 versus 1.85). This information is consistent with what we expect. In fact, although the presence of the risk committee is recommended by Basel regulatory framework, this is a corporate

Table 1 Summary statistics

Variable	Obs	Mean	25th percentile	75th percentile	Std. Dev.	Min	Max
Panel A. Dependent variables							
TQ	158	1.0866	1.0331	1.0955	0.0932	1.0064	1.5249
P/E	158	8.4141	4.6770	10.9540	6.0528	1.2380	29.3830
Panel B. Governance variables							
IND	140	5.7500	4	7	2.0537	3	12
BS	140	13.2143	10	17	3.3646	7	18
BM	140	11.4643	8	14.5	3.9737	6	20
RCS	140	3.9643	2	5	2.3457	0	9
RCM	135	1.8519	1	2	1.7213	0	6
Panel C. Control variables							
SIZE	162	18.0061	16.9022	19.1574	1.5977	13.9245	21.6219
LOANSTA	160	54.1057	48.6315	61.1242	9.8142	1.9265	68.2144
TIER1	130	10.3651	8.4700	11.1800	3.1583	4.3000	26.8500
P/B	158	1.2401	0.6680	1.4850	0.8423	0.1940	4.2380

Notes: This table provides summary statistics of variables used in the paper. We calculate TQ as the book value of assets minus the book value of common equity plus the market value of equity plus the market value of common equity divided by the book value of total assets. The P/E is estimated as the ratio of market price to earnings per share. IND is the number of the independent directors on the board. BS is defined as the number of directors on the board. BM is the frequency of the board meetings, measured as the number of the meetings held by the board in the year 2007. RCS is the number of the risk committee directors. RCM is the number of the meetings held by the risk committee in the year 2007. SIZE is the natural log of total bank assets at the book value; LOANSTA is the ratio of loans to total assets at book value; TIER 1 is the ratio of tier 1 capital to total risk-weighted assets; the P/B is computed as the ratio of the bank current share price to the book value per share

body recently created, that it is still not present in all banks (as it is shown by the minimum values of the variables RCS and RCM that, for some banks, are equal to zero). Moreover, in some banks, the audit committees perform many of the functions managed by the risk committees.

As for the control variables, Panel B shows that our sample includes large credit institutions (with a mean for SIZE of 18), characterized by a high LOANSTA, our proxy to control for banks business models, and TIER1, our proxy to control for bank capital.

Table 2 presents the correlation coefficients of the independent variables used in the study. Pearson correlation coefficients are portrayed below the diagonal. Multicollinearity among regressors should not be a concern as the maximum value of correlation coefficient, between BS and SIZE, is 0.437.

5.3 Econometric Model

Since our sample is a mixture of time series and cross-sectional data, the panel data analysis is the most efficient tool to use. The panel data structure allows us to take

Table 2 Correlation matrix

	IND	BS	BM	RCS	RCM	SIZE	LOANSTA	TIER1	P/B
IND	1								
BS	0.3618*	1							
BM	−0.043	−0.147	1						
RCS	−0.218	0.106	0.245	1					
RCM	−0.030	0.340*	0.048	0.414	1				
SIZE	0.011	0.437*	−0.110	0.4211*	0.401*	1			
LOANSTA	0.116	−0.207	0.3764*	0.056	−0.250	−0.068	1		
TIER1	0.013	−0.4122*	−0.121	0.048	−0.232	−0.4058*	−0.202	1	
P/B	*0.033*	*−0.211*	*−0.151*	*−0.085*	*−0.034*	*−0.074*	*0.002*	*0.176*	*1*

Notes: This table shows the Pearson pairwise correlation matrix for the independent variables applied in the study. IND is the number of the independent directors on the board. BS is defined as the number of directors on the board. BM is the frequency of the board meetings, measured as the number of the meetings held by the board in the year 2007. RCS is the risk committee size, defined as the number of the risk committee directors. RCM is the frequency of the risk committee meetings, measured as the number of the meetings held by the risk committee in the year 2007. SIZE is the natural log of total bank assets at the book value. LOANSTA is the ratio of loans to total assets at book value. TIER 1 is the ratio of tier 1 capital to total risk-weighted assets. P/B is computed as the ratio of the bank current share price to the book value per share. Pearson (Spearman) correlations are below the diagonal

*Denotes statistical significance at the 5 %

into account the unobservable and constant heterogeneity, that is, the specific features of each bank (management style and quality, market perception, business strategy, etc.). There are several different linear models for panel data. The fundamental distinction is that between fixed-effects and random effects models. The primary estimation method is generalized least square (GLS) random effect (RE) technique. This technique is robust to first-order autoregressive disturbances (if any) within unbalanced-panels and cross-sectional correlation and/or heteroskedasticity across panels. In the presence of unobserved bank fixed-effect, panel 'Fixed-Effect' (FE) estimation is commonly suggested (Wooldridge 2002).

However, such FE estimation is not suitable for our study for two main reasons. First, time-invariant variable like IND, BS, BM, RCS and RCM cannot be estimated with FE regression, as it would be absorbed or wiped out in 'within transformation' or 'time-demeaning' process of the variables in FE.

Thus, GLS RE could be considered as an alternative to FE. However, we decided to use a pooled model or population-averaged (PA) model instead of the GLS RE model, because in the presence of a panel characterized by few individuals and by a short time horizon, the estimation of a RE could be affected by the scarcity in the randomness of the variables, while the OLS can be more easily implemented.

Pooled models assume that regressors are exogenous and simply write the error as u_{it} rather than using the decomposition $\alpha_i + \varepsilon_{it}$. Then:

$$y_{it} = \alpha + x_{it}^{'}\beta + u_{it} \tag{1}$$

Like RE estimators, consistency of the estimators requires that regressors be uncorrelated with u_{it}.

Since many of our variables have large outliers, to prevent extreme values from biasing the results of our study without losing observations, we winsorize our variables at 5 %. Winsorizing at 5 % involves assigning to outliers beyond the 5th and 95th percentiles a value equal to the value of the 5th or 95th percentile in order to limit the influence of outliers on the regression. To make sure that the results do not depend on the specific treatment of the outliers, we also rerun all calculations winsorizing our variables at 10 % and at 1 %, with no changes in the main results. For ease of exposition we do no present these findings, but all estimations and Tables are available upon request.

In all cases, observations are clustered at the bank level. In fact, because in our sample the same bank may be present in different years, it seems appropriate to allow the errors to be correlated for the same intermediary over time. Moreover, by doing so, we obtain standard errors robust to heteroscedasticity.

As we have previously noticed, in our analysis first we employ two different measures of bank performance: TQ and P/E; second, for each of these measures, we estimate the following baseline Eq. 2:

$$y_{it} = \alpha + \beta_1 IND_{i,2007} + \beta_2 BS_{i,2007} + \beta_3 BM_{i,2007} + \beta_4 RCS_{i,2007} + \beta_5 RCM_{i,2007} + \gamma CTRL_{it} + \delta YEAR\_D + \lambda COUNTRY\_D + u_{it} \quad (2)$$

where y_{it} is our dependent variable (i.e. TQ, and P/E); the β, γ, δ and λ parameters are the estimated coefficients for the key independent variables (governance variables), the control variables, the year dummies and the country dummy, respectively.

5.3.1 Endogeneity Issues

Referring to the endogeneity problem, we underline that it is a common issue in governance studies that makes interpretation of the results difficult. As pointed out by Hermalin and Weisbach (2003), the relation between board characteristics and firm performance may be spurious, because firm's governance structure and performance are endogenously determined. This issue is less likely to be problematic in our setting for two main reasons.

First, we relate corporate governance variables as at 2007 to bank performance measures in the years from 2007 to 2011. As suggested by Pathan and Faff (2013), the crisis period offers a quasi-experimental setting that provides a relatively clear test of the relation between bank boards and performance, which is robust to any endogeneity concern related to board structure variables.

Second, Wintoki et al. (2012) consider 'dynamic endogeneity' to be an important source of endogeneity that needs to be controlled for in governance and performance relation studies to obtain unbiased estimates. The term 'dynamic endogeneity' refers to the manner in which a firm's current performance affects both its future performance and its governance. However, for banks, dynamic endogeneity is less problematic because a bank's past performance, a proxy for management capability, does not affect either its board size or its composition (see also Adams and Mehran 2012).

6 Results

Table 3 presents the results of Pooled OLS estimates of Eq. 2, when considering TQ and P/E as our dependent variables, respectively. In all models we control for year fixed effects and we use a country dummy variable to control for potential unobservable difference between China and India. Coefficients and their significance are reported.

In general, the model is well fitted, with an adjusted R-square of 0.36 for TQ and 0.26 for P/E. For all the dependent variables and in all estimations we have statistically significant F-statistics.

Table 3 Pooled OLS estimates for both the dependent variables: TQ and P/E

Independent variables	*TQ* (1)	*P/E* (2)
Governance variables		
IND	−1.9404	0.1035
BS	38.5196	−0.1587
BM	−0.3781**	−0.2682**
RCS	−0.5642**	−0.2571**
RCM	0.1752**	0.4593*
Control variables		
SIZE	0.2186	0.1227
LOANSTA	−0.5487***	−0.4418**
TIER1	0.5141***	0.3155**
P/B	0.298**	0.245*
Intercept	0.9799**	0.9685***
Year dummies	Yes	Yes
Country dummy	Yes	Yes
Adjusted R2	0.3575	0.2635
F	7.29***	44.47***

Notes: This table reports Pooled OLS regression results of the effect of governance variables (i.e. standard board variables and risk governance variables) on bank performance for a sample of 15 Chinese and 21 Indian credit institutions between 2007 and 2011. In particular, we run the following equation: $y_{it} = \alpha + \beta_1 IND_{i,2007} + \beta_2 BS_{i,2007} + \beta_3 BM_{i,2007} + \beta_4 RCS_{i,2007} + \beta_5 RCM_{i,2007} + \gamma CTRL_{it} + \delta YEAR\_D + \lambda COUNTRY\_D + u_{it}$

The dependent variables are TQ and P/E. We calculate TQ as the book value of assets minus the book value of common equity plus the market value of equity plus the market value of common equity divided by the book value of total assets. The P/E is estimated as the ratio of market price to earnings per share. The governance variables are IND, BS, BM, RCS and RCM. IND is the number of the independent directors on the board. BS is defined as the number of directors on the board. BM is the number of the meetings held by the board in the year 2007. RCS is defined as the number of the risk committee directors. RCM is the number of the meetings held by the risk committee in the year 2007. Our control variables include SIZE, LOANSTA, TIER1 and P/B. SIZE is the natural log of total bank assets at the book value. LOANSTA is the ratio of loans to total assets at book value; TIER1 is the ratio of tier 1 capital to total risk-weighted assets. P/B is computed as the ratio of the bank current share price to the book value per share. *Country dummy* is a dummy variable that takes the value one if the analyzed bank is from China and zero if it is from India. All variables are winsorized at 5 %. In addition, we control for year fixed effects

*Significant at 10 %. **Significant at 5 %. ***Significant at 1 %

As for the standard board variables, we find that the variable BS is statistically insignificant for both measures of bank performance; the coefficient of IND is negative and insignificant and the coefficient of BM is negative and significant for both TQ and P/E.

Turning to analyze the risk governance variables, we find that RCM is positive and statistically significant only for TQ. RCS is significant at 1 % and negative for both P/E and TQ, our market or quasi-market based measures of bank performance.

This illustrated that, after controlling for bank and country characteristics, the performance of the banks in our sample is not strongly affected by the composition of the boards of directors and its "strength", but more by the characteristics of the risk committee. The boards of directors' variables seem only to have a limited impact on the market-based measure of performance in terms of the number of board meetings. However, the positive relationship expected by the previous evidences in the literature is not confirmed for our analysis and suggests that higher bank performance is associated with a lower board functioning. This result could be driven by specific governance rules that impose a minimum number of meetings per year, either as a recommendation or in a mandatory standard. Similarly, the insignificance of the board size's coefficients that is in contrast both with the literature on European and US banks and previous finding on Indian companies (Jackling and Johl 2009) reflect the peculiar nature of the financial institutions for these two emerging countries.

On the other hand, the general irrelevance of the standard board's variables when specific variables related to the risk committee are included in the analysis is in line with Aebi et al. (2012). We find that the market valuation and the expected market growth (TQ and P/E) are larger for banks with smaller size of risk committee. In particular, we find that the market valuation of these banks is associated with a smaller size of the risk committee and with a higher number of risk committee's meetings. This suggests that the market associates a "strong risk committee", characterized by a low number of components and a high number of meetings, with a lower performance.

All the coefficients of the bank specific variables have the expected sign and offer some significant insights. For instance, the country dummy shows that Chinese banks have on average a higher TQ, (positive and significant coefficient), but a lower P/E (negative and significant coefficient). This result is in line with the evidence of a higher uncertainty and volatility on the Indian stock market during the period under investigation. As for our two measures of bank performance, we observe a positive and significant relationship with TIER 1 and a negative and significant relationship with the variable LOANSTA. Better-capitalized and less credit-oriented banks are associated with better performance.

7 Conclusions

We analyze a sample of 36 Chinese and Indian listed banks over the period 2007–2011. Our research aims to investigate the relationship between both standard corporate governance variables (related to the board of directors) and risk management-related variables, and bank performance. We measure bank performance by Tobin'Q and price-earnings ratio. In line with the previous literature on US banks, we find the general irrelevance of the standard board's variables when specific variables related to the risk committee are included in the analysis. The market valuation and the expected market growth (Tobin' Q and P/E) are larger for banks with smaller risk committee. Moreover, the market valuation is positively associated with the frequency of the risk committee's meetings.

To summarize, the overall evidence shows that the standard governance measures, used in a large body of literature on corporate governance and its valuation effect in non-financial firms, may fall short in describing the relevant governance structure of banks. Our results highlight the importance of the so-called "risk governance" also for banks in emerging markets.

Appendix

Table 4 List of Chinese and Indian banks in our sample

No.	Bank name	Country	No.	Bank name	Country
1	Industrial and Commercial Bank of China	China	19	Bank of Baroda	India
2	China Construction Bank Corporation	China	20	Bank of India	India
3	Bank of China Limited	China	21	Canara Bank	India
4	Bank of Communications Co. Ltd	China	22	HDFC Bank Ltd	India
5	Shanghai Pudong Development Bank	China	23	AXIS Bank Limited	India
6	China Merchants Bank Co Ltd	China	24	Union Bank of India	India
7	China CITIC Bank Corporation Limited	China	25	Central Bank of India	India
8	China Minsheng Banking Corporation	China	26	Allahabad Bank	India
9	China Everbright Bank Co Ltd	China	27	Syndicate Bank	India
10	Industrial Bank Co Ltd	China	28	Corporation Bank Ltd.	India
11	Ping An Bank Co Ltd	China	29	Indian Bank	India
12	Hua Xia Bank co., Limited	China	30	Andhra Bank	India
13	Bank of Beijing Co Ltd	China	31	Kotak Mahindra Bank Limited	India
14	Chongqing Rural Commercial Bank	China	32	Bank of Maharashtra	India
15	Bank of Nanjing	China	33	Federal Bank Ltd.	India
16	State Bank of India	India	34	Jammu and Kashmir Bank Ltd	India
17	ICICI Bank Limited	India	35	ING Vysya Bank Ltd	India
18	Punjab National Bank	India	36	SREI Infrastructure Finance Limited	India

Sources: Bankscope

Notes: This table shows the names of the Chinese and Indian listed banks we analyse in the study

Table 5 Variables definition

Variable	Definition
A. Performance measures	
TQ	The book value of assets minus the book value of common equity plus the market value of equity plus the market value of common equity divided by the book value of total asset
P/E	The P/E is estimated as the ratio of market price to earnings per share; the annual stock data values for each year are calculated at the closing date of each year's financial accounts
B. Governance variables	
IND	Number of the independent directors on the boards
BS	Board size is the number of directors on the board
BM	Board meetings is the number of the meetings held by the board
RCS	Risk committee size is the number of the risk committee members
RCM	Risk committee meetings is the number of the meetings held by the risk committee
C. Other variables	
SIZE	The natural log of total bank assets at the book value
LOANSTA	The ratio of loans to total assets at book value
TIER1	The ratio of tier 1 capital to total risk-weighted assets
P/B	The ratio of the bank current share price to the book value per share; the annual stock data values for each year are calculated at the closing date of each year's financial accounts
COUNTRY_D	A dummy variable equal to one if the analyzed bank is from China and zero if it is from India

Notes: This table reports the definition of the variables used in the study

References

Adams, R. B., & Ferreira, D. (2007). A theory of friendly boards. *The Journal of Finance, 62*(1), 217–250.

Adams, R. B., & Mehran, H. (2008). *Corporate performance, board structure and their determinants in the banking industry*. Federal Reserve Bank of NY Staff Report, No 330.

Adams, R. B., & Mehran, H. (2012). Bank board structure and performance: Evidence for large bank holding companies. *Journal of Financial Intermediation, 21*(2), 243–267.

Aebi, V., Sabato, G., & Schmid, M. (2012). Risk management, corporate governance, and bank performance in the financial crisis. *Journal of Banking and Finance, 36*(12), 3213–3226.

Beltratti, A., & Stultz, R. (2010). *The credit crisis around the globe: Why did some banks perform better?* Fisher College of Business Working Paper Series, No. 2010–05.

Bhattacharyya, K. A., & Rao, S. V. (2005). *Economic impact of regulation on corporate governance: Evidence from India*, Finance 0504002, EconWPA.

Black, B. S., Jang, H., & Woochan, K. (2006). Predicting firms' corporate governance choices: Evidence from Korea. *Journal of Corporate Finance, 12*(3), 660–691.

Caprio, G., Laeven, L., & Levine, R. (2007). Governance and bank valuation. *Journal of Financial Intermediation, 16*(4), 584–617.

Cheung, Y., Jiang, P., Limpaphayom, P., & Lu, T. (2008). Does corporate governance matter in China? *China Economic Review, 19*(3), 460–479.

Cornett, M., McNutt, J. J., & Tehranian, H. (2009). Corporate governance and earnings management at large U.S. bank. *Journal of Corporate Finance, 15*(4), 412–430.

de Andres, P., & Vallelado, E. (2008). Corporate governance in banking: The role of board of directors. *Journal of Banking and Finance, 32*(12), 2570–2580.

Demirgüç-Kunt, A., & Maksimovic, V. (1996). Financial constraints, uses of funds, and deregulation. *Quarterly Journal of Economics, 111*(3), 639–670.

Diamond, D., & Rajan, R. G. (2009). The credit crisis: Conjectures about causes and remedies, American economic association. *American Economic Review, 99*(2), 606–610.

Ellul, A., & Yerramilli V. (2013). Stronger risk controls, lower risk: Evidence from U.S. bank holding companies. *Journal of Finance, 68*(5), 1757–1803.

Erkens, D., Hung, M., & Matos, P. (2012). Corporate governance in the 2007–2008 financial crisis: Evidence from financial institutions worldwide. *Journal of Corporate Finance, 18*(2), 389–411.

Fama, E. F., & Jensen, M. C. (1983). Separation of ownership and control. *Journal of Law and Economics, 26*(2), 301–325.

Filatotchev, I., Zhang, X., & Piesse, J. (2011). Multiple agency perspective, family control, and private information abuse in an emerging economy. *Asia Pacific Journal of Management, 28* (1), 69–93.

Francis, B., Hasan, I., & Wu, Q. (2011). *Do corporate boards affect firm performance? New evidence from the financial crisis*. Bank of Finland Research Discussion Papers, 11–2011.

Hanazaki, M., & Horiuchi, A. (2003). A review of Japan's bank crisis from the governance perspective. *Pacific-Basin Finance Journal, 11*(3), 305–325.

Hermalin, B. E., & Weisbach, M. S. (2003). Board of directors as an endogenously determined institution: A survey of the economic literature. *FRBNY Economic Policy Review*, *9*(1), 7–26.

Huang, B. (2006). Non-performing loan of China's banking system. *The Bulletin of Institute for Research in Business and Economics, Meiji Gakuin University, 23*, 129–152.

Jackling, B., & Johl, S. (2009). Board structure and firm performance: evidence from India's top companies. *Corporate Governance: An International Review, 17*(4), 492–509.

Jayaratne, J., & Strahan, P. E. (1996). The finance-growth nexus: Evidence from bank branch deregulation. *Quarterly Journal of Economics, 111*(3), 639–670.

King, R. G., & Levine, R. (1993). Finance and growth: Schumpeter might be right. *Quarterly Journal of Economics, 108*(3), 717–738.

Kirkpatrick, G. (2009). The corporate governance lessons from the financial crisis. *OECD Journal: Financial Market Trends, 1*, 61–87.

Laeven, L., & Levine, R. (2009). Bank governance, regulation and risk taking. *Journal of Financial Economics, 93*(2), 259–275.

Levine, R., Loayza, N., & Beck, T. (1999). *Financial intermediation and growth: Causality and causes*. World Bank Policy Research Working Paper, 2059.

Macey, J., & O'Hara, M. (2003). The corporate governance of banks. *FRBNY Economic Policy Review, 4*, 91–107.

Mishra, C., & Nielsen, J. (2000). Board independence and compensation policies in large bank holding companies. *Financial Management, 29*, 51–69.

Pacini, C., Hillison, W., Marlett, D., & Burgess, D. (2005). Corporate governance and the market impact of the financial services modernization act of 1999 on bank returns and trading volume. *Journal of Economics and Finance, 29*(1), 46–72.

Pathan, S. (2009). Strong boards, CEO power and bank risk-taking. *Journal of Banking and Finance, 33*(7), 1340–1350.

Pathan, S., & Faff, R. (2013). Does board structure in banks really affect their performance? *Journal of Banking and Finance, 37*(5), 1573–1589.

Peng, M. W., Bhagat, R. S., & Chang, S. J. (2010). Asia and global business. *Journal of International Business Studies, 41*(3), 373–376.

Peni, E., & Vähämaa, S. (2012). Did good corporate governance improve bank performance during the financial crisis? *Journal of Financial Service Research, 41*(1), 19–35.

Raithatha, M., & Bapat, V. (2012). Corporate governance compliance practices of Indian companies. *Research Journal of Finance and Accounting, 3*(8), 19–26.

Rajan, R. G., & Zingales, L. (1996). *Financial dependence and growth*, NBER Working Paper, 5758.

Sami, H., Wang, J., & Zhou, H. (2011). Corporate governance and operating performance of Chinese listed firms. *Journal of International Accounting, Auditing and Taxation, 20*(2), 106–114.

Sarkar, J., & Sarkar, S. (2009). Multiple board appointments and firm performance in emerging economies: Evidence from India. *Pacific-Basin Finance Journal, 17*(2), 271–293.

Sierra, G., Talmor, E., & Wallace, J. (2006). An examination of multiple governance forces within bank holding companies. *Journal of Financial Service Research, 29*(2), 105–123.

Subramanian, S. (2006). Management control and differences in disclosure levels: The Indian scenario. *The ICFAI Journal of Corporate Governance, 5*(1), 16–33.

Webb Cooper, E. (2009). Monitoring and governance of private banks. *Quarterly Review of Economics and Finance, 49*(2), 253–264.

Wintoki, M. B., Linck, J. S., & Netter, J. M. (2012). Endogeneity and the dynamics of corporate governance. *Journal of Financial Economics, 105*(3), 581–606.

Wooldridge, J. M. (2002). *Econometric analysis of cross section and panel data*. Cambridge, MA: MIT.

Young, M. N., Peng, M. W., Ahlstrom, D., Bruton, G. D., & Jiang, Y. (2008). Governing the corporation in emerging economies: A review of the principal-principal perspective. *Journal of Management Studies, 45*, 196–220.

Part II
Corporate Governance and Firm Behavior

Do Families Shape Corporate Board Structure in Emerging Economies?

Mohammad Badrul Muttakin, Arifur Khan, and Nava Subramaniam

Abstract This study investigates whether there are significant differences in corporate board structure between family and non-family firms using listed companies in Bangladesh where family firms are the most dominant form of public companies. The results of this study suggest that family firms in Bangladesh adopt a distinctly different board structure from non-family firms. In particular, this study finds that family firms have a lower proportion of independent directors and foreign directors than non-family firms. Further, family firms have smaller boards than non-family firms. However, family firms are likely to have more CEO duality and female directors than their non-family counterparts. The findings of this study contribute to extant research on corporate board structure. The overall findings of this study imply that families of Bangladeshi firms have a different board structure compared to non-family firms, and the structure appears to promote a close locus of control for families that facilitates family dominance to prevail.

1 Introduction

Family firms are often built by founders who are strong and passionate about their business and subsequently, such firms in turn become closely linked with the family's reputation. Consequently, there is often a strong sense of ownership and connection to the business by the family shareholders (Lee 2006; Anderson et al. 2003). This can be expected to increase the family shareholders' need to dominate the governing board, particularly in public-listed firms, leading to preferences for selecting certain types of directors to work with (Anderson and Reeb

M.B. Muttakin • N. Subramaniam
Deakin University, Burwood, Australia

A. Khan (✉)
School of Accounting, Economics and Finance, Deakin University, 221 Burwood Highway, Burwood, VIC 3125, Australia
e-mail: arifur.khan@deakin.edu.au

S. Boubaker and D.K. Nguyen (eds.), *Corporate Governance in Emerging Markets*, CSR, Sustainability, Ethics & Governance, DOI 10.1007/978-3-642-44955-0_5,

2003; Anderson et al. 2003). Thus, it is likely that family directors in family firms would prefer boards that are not only effective in terms of maximising firm performance, but also ones that would be 'yielding' to their interests. Further, it can also be argued that with a strong family commitment to business prosperity, mimicking corporate governance mechanisms designed for non-family firms may, in fact, be inefficient for family firms, as they tend to assume a greater divide between owners and management (Barney and Hansen 1994). As such, these factors have the potential to drive systematic differences in the board structure of family versus non-family firms.

Prior studies based on agency theory suggest that board effectiveness is associated with higher independent directors (Agrawal and Knoeber 1996), smaller boards (Yermack 1996), CEO non-duality (Daily and Dalton 1993), female directors (Carter et al. 2003) and foreign directors (Oxelheim and Randoy 2003). Such board characteristics are seen to provide better monitoring and lower managerial entrenchment. On the other hand, resource dependency theory states that more effective boards tend to be comprised of more independent directors (Dyer 1989), larger boards (Jackling and Johl 2009) and CEO duality (Boyed 1995), as they offer more experience and professional knowledge, which, in turn, increase the board's ability to make better business decisions.

Family firms with strong motivation to keep their business successful are, therefore, likely to invest in more effective boards. A competing argument for how family firms may structure their boards is that they are also strongly driven to dominate decision-making. From an agency Type II[1] perspective, where family owners are more inclined to expropriate the interests of minority shareholders, family firms should have fewer independent directors, a smaller board, and more CEO duality to retain control of the firm. The findings of previous studies also suggest that family firms have different board structures from non-family firms (Bartholomeusz and Tanewski 2006; Setia-Atmaja et al. 2009; Navarro and Anson 2009). However, the prior findings are deficient in three ways. First, prior studies did not assess two important board characteristics, namely, female directors and foreign directors which are increasingly seen as being critical for improving board monitoring. Second, Most of the prior studies focus on developed market and ignore emerging economies. Third, prior studies also show mixed results in terms of the proportion of independent directors and board size between family and non-family firms. Thus the purpose of this chapter is to investigate whether there are significant differences in corporate board structure between family and non-family firms in emerging economies considering Bangladesh as an example.

Bangladesh is characterised by concentrated ownership and poor investor protection and a weak legal system. Corporate ownership in Bangladesh is largely concentrated in the hands of only a few people, and the top shareholders belong

[1] Conflict between controlling and non-controlling shareholders, whereas, controlling families may seek private benefits at the expense of non-controlling shareholders (Setia-Atmaja et al. 2009).

mostly to wealthy, high profile families. Good corporate governance practices in Bangladesh are yet to be developed (Siddiqui 2010), which gives Bangladeshi family firms strong impetus to dominate the public-listed firms. Furthermore the participation of females on Bangladeshi boards is a more recent phenomenon. Female directors, who are appointed on the basis of family ties, usually increase firms' voting power or dominance. In Bangladesh, foreign directors are also becoming increasingly common because of the growth in multinational ventures.

The results of this study indicate that family firms have a lower proportion of independent directors on boards than their non-family counterparts. The size of boards in family firms is smaller than in non-family firms. Family firms are more likely to have CEO duality. The result of this study also suggests that the proportion of female directors is higher in family firms than in non-family firms. This study finds that family firms have a lower proportion of foreign directors than their non-family counterparts. The overall results indicate that family firms utilise a different combination of governance mechanisms compared to their non-family counterparts.

The rest of the chapter is structured as follows. Section 2 gives an outline of the institutional background of Bangladesh. Section 3 reviews related literature and develops hypotheses. Section 4 describes research methodology. Section 5 presents empirical results, followed by further analysis in Sect. 6. Section 7 concludes the study.

2 Institutional Background of Bangladesh

Bangladesh carries the legacy of being a British colony for about 200 years. As a consequence, although the country inherited the British legal and political systems, there were hardly any private sector enterprises owned by Bengalis. The socialist ideology adopted by the Bangladesh government after its liberation in 1971 led to the nationalisation of the limited private sector owned industries. Subsequent governments, under pressure from donor agencies such as the World Bank, adopted a privatisation policy, that, due to lack of transparency, subsequently resulted in the transfer of government controlled industries to families (World Bank 2009). Consequently, Bangladesh's capital market has evolved to comprise a high proportion of family owned public-listed companies. For example, Imam and Malik (2007) report that on an average 33 % of the shares of listed companies in Bangladesh are held by top three shareholders, who are usually from the same family.

Like many other emerging economies,[2] some of the institutional features of Bangladesh include a less developed capital market (World Bank 2009), a least weak-form efficient stock market (Islam and Khaled 2005), absence of an active market for corporate control, a passive managerial labour market, and poor incentive contracts for management (Farooque et al. 2007). The Bangladesh corporate

[2] In terms of GDP, Bangladesh is the 44th largest economy in the world (IMF 2010).

sector is characterized by high ownership concentration, reluctance of the corporate sector to raise funds through the capital markets, lack of shareholder activism, high reliance on bank financing, and poor enforcement and monitoring of regulations (Siddiqui 2010).

Though Bangladesh has a market-based system like the Anglo American firms, it lacks an active market for corporate control, strong incentive contract for management and outside directors (Farooque et al. 2007). Legal and regulatory framework and its enforcement are relatively poor in Bangladesh which critically hinders the market's potential growth. Unlike other common-law economies of wealthy nations, it represents poor-quality law enforcement (Farooque et al. 2007). In the absence of market-based monitoring and control measures, ownership based monitoring and control is expected to function as a core governance mechanism.

In summary, the above institutional background and corporate governance regulatory oversight capabilities in Bangladesh do not appear to be strong, thus increasing the risk of conflict between the dominant and the minority shareholders (also often referred to as Type II agency problem). Because of strong family dominance, poor investor protection and weak legal system, the propensity for the presence of Type II agency problem is heightened in Bangladeshi family firms with the possibility of wealth expropriation by controlling families (Farooque et al. 2007). Given that minority shareholders rely on corporate board to monitor and control family's opportunism, a better understanding of the link between board structure and family ownership and control thus becomes critical for better informing and improving internal governance mechanism in family firms.

3 Literature Review and Development of Hypotheses

3.1 Board Independence

It is argued that a higher proportion of independent directors may reduce the conflict of interest between controlling shareholders and minority shareholders, and may make management more effective through better monitoring (Andres et al. 2005). Prior studies have provided evidence which suggests that independent directors add real value to a firm (Anderson and Reeb 2004; Jackling and Johl 2009). Recently, several authors have strongly argued for the importance of an active board with independent board members in family firms (e.g., Neubauer and Lank 1998; Huse 2000). However, families usually try to minimise the presence of independent directors (Anderson and Reeb 2004) since the families often seek to entrench themselves and extract private benefits from the firm. Ward (1991) has explained possible reasons for the lack of independent directors on many family firm boards. He argues that the main reasons are that owners tend to be afraid of losing control, do not believe that the independent directors understand the firm's competitive situation, and are afraid of opening up to new, external ideas and viewpoints.

Setia-Atmaja et al. (2009) and Bartholomeusz and Tanewski (2006) document that family firms have lower levels of board independence compared to non-family firms. However, Navarro and Anson (2009) find that the proportion of independent directors does not differ between family and non-family firms. Anderson and Reeb (2004) argue that minority shareholders in family firms are best protected when there is a greater presence of independent directors on the board. Furthermore, family firms may have more independent directors on resource dependence argument. Independent directors of family firms can provide quality advice to the CEO and may also bring valuable experience and expertise to the board (Dalton et al. 1999).

Based on the above discussion, the first hypothesis of this study is as follows:

H1: The proportion of independent directors is significantly different between family and non-family firms.

3.2 Board Size

Previous empirical studies find that smaller boards enhance firm performance (Yermack 1996; Eisenberg et al. 1998). Family firms have smaller boards since individual responsibility tends to dissolve in larger groups (Ward 1991). It is argued that smaller boards in family firms facilitate communication and decision-making and are also likely to reduce the problem of free-riding. Navarro and Anson (2009) also find that family firm boards are relatively smaller than non-family firm boards. They suggest that families may be unwilling to increase the board size so as to retain control. Lane et al. (2006) suggest that smaller boards are more desirable for family firms, as larger boards inhibit full family participation and individual responsibility. Consistent with the resource dependence argument, Setia-Atmaja et al. (2009), on the other hand, contend that larger boards are affiliated with the controlling family. Larger boards may enhance performance because family members can draw on the others who may have valuable business experience, expertise, skills and social and professional networks which might add substantial business resources to the family firm.

Based on the above discussion, the second hypothesis of this study is as follows:

H2: Board size is significantly different between family and non-family firms.

3.3 CEO Duality

Having separate individuals holding the CEO and chairman positions enhances the monitoring ability of the board (Jensen 1993). Chen et al. (2005) and

Bartholomeusz and Tanewski (2006) find that CEO duality is much more likely in family firms compared to non-family firms. Within family firms, if the CEO and the chairman are the same person, or the person is a family member, the conflicts of interests may be less severe and duality may, in fact, ease family firm governance. Hence, CEO duality could be considered strength for a family firm (Navarro and Anson 2009). On the other hand, in family firms, CEO duality provides CEO entrenchment which leads to a decrease in board independence (Anderson and Reeb 2004) and increases the possibility of wealth expropriation by the families. However, a family CEO's experience, skills, expertise and powerful reputation are likely to provide valuable resources to the firm (Hillman and Dalziel 2003). Therefore, from a resource provision perspective, duality may be beneficial. The power exercised by families as large shareholders in family firms, means that duality is likely to be present to a larger extent within family firms.

Based on the above discussion, this study proposes the following hypothesis:

H3: Family firms have more CEO duality than non-family firms.

3.4 Female Directors

A more gender-diverse board is generally seen to enhance monitoring and improve board independence (Carter et al. 2003). Ruigrok et al. (2007) find evidence that there is a link between family firms and gender of the directors. They argue that females are often selected as board members based on family ties, and that they act as monitors and family delegates in family firms. Haalien and House (2005) report that there are more female directors in family firms than in non-family firms in Norway, and the number of women directors does not increase with board size. Moreover, resource dependence theorists argue that female directors facilitate the acquisition of critical resources for the organisation (Pfeffer 1972).

Though female participant at the board-level in developing countries may be recent phenomena, some companies appoint females as directors based on family ties. In most cases, the founder owners or directors appoint their wives and daughters to the boards, often with the motive of increasing family voting power or dominance (Uddin and Choudhury 2008). Therefore, it is predicted that family firms are more diverse in terms of gender than non-family firms.

Based on the above discussion the fourth hypothesis of this study is as follows:

H4: Family firms have more female directors than non-family firms.

3.5 Foreign Directors

Foreign directors are usually considered to be unaffiliated and independent of the firms. They can make the board of a family firm more effective and efficient.

However, families may seek to appoint fewer foreign directors on the board to avoid external monitors. Ruigrok et al. (2007) do not find any significant relationship between family affiliation and foreign directors. In Bangladesh, foreign directors are becoming increasingly common because of the growth in multinational ventures.

This study proposes that foreign directors can make the monitoring of the board more efficient. Their monitoring may obstruct family directors from becoming entrenched and protect the interests of general shareholders. Such directors can also improve the accountability process in the light of their foreign experience and knowledge. Therefore, family firms could be less likely to appoint foreign directors to avoid monitoring. It can also be argued that Bangladeshi family businesses may appoint them as token members just for a joint venture business. Sometimes their appointment might be made by the family firms to give signals to the market about the quality of governance.

On the basis of above discussion, this study proposes the following hypotheses:

H5: The proportion of foreign directors is significantly different between family and non-family firms.

4 Research Design

4.1 Data and Sample

The sample selection procedure is reported in Panel A of Table 1. The sample consists of all 155 non-financial companies listed with the Dhaka Stock Exchange (DSE) in Bangladesh from 2005 to 2009, producing a total sample of 775 sample year observations.[3] Missing information has meant the study had to exclude 121 firm-year observations, yielding a final sample of 654 firm-year observations. The data for the analysis comes from multiple sources of secondary data. This study collects the financial data from the annual reports of the sample companies listed on the stock exchange. Stock price data are obtained from the DataStream database. The family ownership and other corporate governance data were hand-collected from the annual reports.

[3] In 2005, there were 282 listed companies in the DSE. Out of this, 127 companies belong to the financial sector. These have been excluded since they are controlled by different regulations and are likely to have different disclosure requirements and governance structure.

Table 1 Sample description

Panel A: Sample selection	**No. of firms**	**Firm-year observations**
Number of firms	282	1,410
Less:		
Financial and utility companies	127	635
Companies without necessary information for corporate governance and family ownership data	14	121
Total	141	654

Panel B: Sample by family and non-family firms in sectors

Sector	**Family**	**Non-family**	**Total**	**Percent of family firms in industry**
Cement	17	20	37	45.95
Ceramics	13	6	19	68.42
Engineering	62	40	102	60.78
Food	68	45	113	60.18
IT	11	17	28	39.29
Jute	9	5	14	64.29
Paper and printing	10	0	10	100.00
Miscellaneous	22	30	52	42.31
Pharmaceuticals	62	30	92	67.39
Service and real estate	12	14	26	46.15
Tanneries	9	16	25	36.00
Textiles	124	12	136	91.18
Total	419	235	654	64.07

4.2 *Measuring Family Firms*

Following prior studies we identify family firms as being (1) firms in which 20% of a firm's share or voting rights (either direct or indirect) are held by the same family block holders, and (2) at least one member of controlling family holds a managerial position such as board member, CEO or chairman (Bartholomeusz and Tanewski 2006; Setia-Atmaja et al. 2009; Cascino et al. 2010). Family relationships and shareholdings pattern were collected from prospectus of the listed companies, annual reports and company websites. We use a dummy variable and set equal to 1 if the firm is considered to be family firm and 0 otherwise.

From Panel B of Table 1, it is observed that family firms are present in 64.07 % of the total sample. The family firms are prevalent in various sectors such as cement (17), ceramics (13), engineering (62), food (68), information technology (11), jute (9), paper and printing (10), miscellaneous (22), pharmaceuticals (62), service and real estate (12), tanneries (9) and textiles (124). This study controls industry affiliations for the empirical analysis.

4.3 Model Specification

To test *H1* this study uses the following OLS regression equation:

$$\begin{aligned} BIND = \alpha + \beta_1 FF + \beta_2 BSIZE + \beta_3 CEODU + \beta_4 FEMDIR + \beta_5 FORDIR \\ + \beta_6 BOWN + \beta_7 AGE + \beta_8 FSIZE + \beta_9 GROWTH + \beta_{10} LEV \\ + \beta_{11} INDDUM + \beta_{12} YEARDUM + \varepsilon \end{aligned} \tag{1}$$

The key variable family firm (FF) has already been defined in Sect. 4.2. This study defines board independence as the proportion of independent directors on the board, who do not have any material interest in the firm (*BIND*) (Anderson and Reeb 2004), whereas board size is measured based on the number of directors on the board (*BSIZE*) (Setia-Atmaja et al. 2009). It is expected that larger boards will have more independent directors. Consistent with the prior study, this study uses the CEO duality variable as a dummy variable, which is equal to 1 if the CEO and chairman are the same person, and 0 otherwise (Boyed 1995). Anderson and Reeb (2003) argue that CEO duality in a family firm increases entrenchment, resulting in lower board independence. Consistent with the prior research (Carter et al. 2003), female directors is measured as the proportion of female directors on the board (*FEMDIR*) and foreign directors is measured by the proportion of foreign directors on the board (*FORDIR*) (Oxelheim and Randoy 2003). It is argued that female and foreign directors improve monitoring and board effectiveness (Carter et al. 2003; Oxelheim and Randoy 2003). Therefore, female and foreign directors are expected to be positively related to board independence.

In the above equation this study also controls for several firm characteristics such as: Board ownership (*BOWN*) Consistent with prior studies, this study uses the board ownership (denoted as *BOWN*) variable as the percentage of directors' total shareholdings (excluding family directors' ownership) on the board (Anderson and Reeb 2003). Firm size (*FSIZE*)*:* When firm size grows over time board independence increases (Boone et al. 2007). Firm size is measured as a natural logarithm of total assets (Yermack 1996). Firm age (*AGE*)*:* Younger firms tend to have a lower proportion of independent directors than older firms because the scope and complexity are lower (Hermalin and Weisbach 1998). Age of the firm is calculated by taking the natural log of the number of years since the firm's inception (Anderson and Reeb 2003). Leverage (*LEV*)*:* Setia-Atmaja et al. (2009) argue that leverage as a governance mechanism can be used as a substitute for board independence in family firms. Leverage is measured by taking the ratio of book value of total debt and book value of total assets (Anderson and Reeb 2003). Growth (*GROWTH*)*:* Myers (1977) argues that agency costs can be relatively high for high-growth firms as managers have greater flexibility with regard to future investments. Therefore, high-growth firms may have a stronger presence of independent directors on their boards. The growth of a firm is measured as the difference between the total assets of the prior year and the current year divided by prior year total assets.

To test *H2*, this study uses the following OLS regression equation:

$$\begin{aligned} BSIZE = {} & \alpha + \beta_1 FF + \beta_2 BIND + \beta_3 CEODU + \beta_4 FEMDIR + \beta_5 FORDIR \\ & + \beta_6 LAGPERF + \beta_7 AGE + \beta_8 FSIZE + \beta_9 GROWTH + \beta_{10} LEV \\ & + \beta_{11} INDDUM + \beta_{12} YERADUM + \varepsilon \end{aligned} \tag{2}$$

The definitions of family firm and all the board structure variables and control variables are similar to those in Eq. 1. According to the agency argument, greater board independence (*BIND*) will lead to smaller board size, whereas the resource dependence argument suggests that greater board independence will lead to larger board size. CEO duality (*CEODU*) enhances CEO power, which influences the appointment of directors who are less effective monitors, or assemble larger boards which are less effective monitors (Setia-Atmaja et al. 2009). On the other hand, a powerful CEO who is also a chairman of the board might be interested in keeping the board size smaller to enhance his/her control or influence over the board. Female and foreign directors improve monitoring and board effectiveness (Carter et al. 2003; Oxelheim and Randoy 2003). Furthermore, the resource dependence argument suggests that female and foreign directors are positively related to board size.

In the above equation this study controls for several firm characteristics such as Firm size (*FSIZE*), Firm age (*FAG*), Leverage (*LEV*) and Growth (*GROWTH*). Lag Performance (*LAGPERF*) has also been controlled for as Setia-Atmaja et al. (2009) reveal that board size may be affected by prior year performance. Lag performance is measured by ROA lagged 1 year.

To test *H3*, this study uses the following logit model.

$$\begin{aligned} CEODU = {} & \alpha + \beta_1 FF + \beta_2 BIND + \beta_3 BSIZE + \beta_4 FEMDIR + \beta_5 FORDIR \\ & + \beta_6 CEOTEN + \beta_7 \; AGE + \beta_8 FSIZE + \beta_9 \; GROWTH + \beta_{10} \; LEV \\ & + \beta_{11} INDDUM + \beta_{12} YEARDUM + \varepsilon \end{aligned} \tag{3}$$

The definitions of family firms and all the board structure variables and control variables are similar to those in Eqs. 1 and 2. Board independence (denoted as *BIND*) diminishes CEO power through monitoring. Therefore, board independence is expected to be negatively related to CEO duality. Board size is measured based on the number of directors on the board (*BSIZE*). It is expected that a larger board is negatively related to CEO duality (CEODU). Since female (*FEMDIR*) and foreign directors (*FORDIR*) improve monitoring and board effectiveness (Carter et al. 2003; Oxelheim and Randoy 2003), they are expected to be negatively related to CEO duality.

In the above equation this chapter controls for several firm characteristics such as Firm size (*FSIZE*), Firm age (*FAGE*), Leverage (*LEV*) and Growth (*GROWTH*). CEO tenure is also controlled since CEO tenure (*CEUTEN*) is likely to increase CEO power, it is expected that CEO tenure is positively related to CEO duality. CEO tenure (*CEUTEN*) is measured based on the number of years served by the current CEO.

To test *H4*, this study uses the following OLS regression equation:

$$\begin{aligned} FEMDIR = \alpha &+ \beta_1 FF + \beta_2 BIND + \beta_3 BSIZE + \beta_4 CEODU + \beta_5 FORDIR \\ &+ \beta_6 FEMCEO + \beta_7\ AGE + \beta_8 FSIZE + \beta_9\ GROWTH + \beta_{10}\ LEV \\ &+ \beta_{11} INDDUM + \beta_{12} YEARDUM + \varepsilon \end{aligned} \tag{4}$$

The definitions of family firms and all the board structure variables and control variables are similar to those in previous equations. Because of the monitoring argument, board independence (*BIND*) is expected to be positively related to female directors. It is expected that a powerful CEO will appoint fewer female directors to the board. Foreign members on a board signal a higher commitment to corporate monitoring and transparency (Oxelheim and Randoy 2003).

In the above equation this chapter controls for several firm characteristics such as Firm size (*FSIZE*), Firm age (*FAGE*), Leverage (*LEV*) and Growth (*GROWTH*). This equation has also controlled for female CEO (*FEMCEO*) which is a dummy variable which equals 1 if the CEO is a female and 0 otherwise. Female directors are tougher monitors (Adams and Ferreira 2009), therefore, a positive relationship is expected between female CEOs and female directors.

To test *H5*, this study uses the following OLS regression equation:

$$\begin{aligned} FORDIR = \alpha &+ \beta_1 FF + \beta_2 BIND + \beta_3 BSIZE + \beta_4 CEODU + \beta_5 FEMDIR \\ &+ \beta_6 FOROWN + \beta_7\ AGE + \beta_8 FSIZE + \beta_9 GROWTH + \beta_{10} LEV \\ &+ \beta_{11} INDDUM + \beta_{12} YEARDUM + \varepsilon \end{aligned} \tag{5}$$

The definitions of family firms, all the board structure variables and control variables are similar to those in previous equations. Because of the monitoring argument, board independence (*BIND*) is expected to be positively related to foreign directors. Larger boards are likely to have more foreign directors. It is expected that a powerful CEO will appoint fewer foreign directors. Female directors are expected to be positively related to foreign directors, consistent with the monitoring argument.

In the above equation this chapter controls for several firm characteristics such as Firm size (*FSIZE*), Firm age (*FAGE*), Leverage (*LEV*) and Growth (*GROWTH*). This equation has also controlled for foreign ownership (*FOROWN*) as foreign ownership is expected to be positively related to foreign directors.

Table 2 Descriptive statistics

Panel A: Descriptive statistics for the full sample

Variable	Mean	Median	Std. Dev.	Max	Min	Q1	Q3
FSIZE	8.696	8.684	0.659	10.345	6.656	8.304	9.042
LEV	0.749	0.604	0.789	0.892	0.036	0.429	0.808
AGE	22.989	23.000	10.940	53.000	4.000	13.000	29.000
BOWN	0.086	0.013	0.145	0.781	0.000	0.009	0.133
BSIZE	6.742	6.500	2.073	13.000	3.000	5.000	8.000
GROWTH	0.116	0.048	0.341	5.312	−0.523	−0.022	0.145
FOWN	0.290	0.319	0.219	0.835	0.200	0.262	0.481
CEODU	0.246	0.000	0.431	1.000	0.000	0.000	1.000
BIND	0.063	0.000	0.082	0.333	0.000	0.000	0.143
FORDIR	0.055	0.000	0.157	0.250	0.000	0.000	0.000
FEMDIR	0.169	0.143	0.183	0.800	0.000	0.000	0.286

Panel B: Difference of means and medians tests

	Mean difference test			**Median difference test**		
Variable	**FF**	**NFF**	**P value**	**FF**	**NFF**	**P value**
BSIZE	6.358	7.426	0.000***	6	8	0.000***
BOWN	0.033	0.182	0.000***	0.013	0.032	0.000**
GROWTH	1.727	0.349	0.100	0.045	0.05	0.314
AGE	21.303	25.996	0.000***	22	26	0.014**
FSIZE	8.650	8.778	0.279	8.651	8.704	0.514
BIND	0.061	0.076	0.015**	0	0	–
CEODU	0.297	0.152	0.000***	0	0	–
FORDIR	0.030	0.102	0.000***	0	0	–
FEMDIR	0.240	0.050	0.000***	0.2	0	0.000***
Observations	419	235		419	235	

FF family firms, *NFF* non-family firms, *BIND* percentage of independent directors on board, *BSIZE* total number of directors on the board, *CEODU* equals to 1 if the CEO and chairman are the same person, and 0 otherwise, *FEMDIR* proportion of female directors on the board, *FORDIR* proportion of foreign directors on the board, *BOWN* percentage of directors' total shareholdings on the board, *AGE* the number of years since the firm's inception, *FSIZE* natural logarithm of total assets, *GROWTH* measured by asset growth ratio, *LEV* ratio of book value of total debt and book value of total assets

*Significant at 10 % level, **Significant at 5 % level, ***Significant at 1 % level

5 Results

5.1 Descriptive Statistics

Panel A of Table 2 presents the descriptive statistics for the full sample. The numbers of directors (BSIZE) averages around seven, 6.30 % are independent directors (BIND), 16.90 % are female directors (FEMDIR) and 5.50 % are foreign directors (FORDIR). With regard to the ownership structure, the board of directors (excluding family directors) (BOWN), and family members (FOWN), hold an average of 8.60 % and 29 % of shares, respectively. The average firm age (AGE) is nearly 23 years, and the average firm size (FSIZE) is 8.70 (natural logarithm of total assets).

Panel B of Table 2 presents difference of means and medians tests for key variables between family and non-family firms. Family firms (FF) represent 64.07 % of the sample. Family firms have a significantly lower proportion of independent directors (BIND) (6.10 % versus 7.60 %), and smaller boards (6.36 versus 7.43 directors). However, family firms have significantly higher CEO duality (CEODU) (29.7 % versus 15.20 %), and more female directors (FEMDIR) (24 % versus 5.00 %). Family firms have a lower portion of foreign directors (FORDIR) than their non-family counterparts. The univariate analysis also indicates that other variables, such as firm age (AGE) and firm size (FSIZE), are significantly lower in family firms than in non-family firms. The difference of medians test also suggests that some of the variables are significantly different between family and non-family firms.

Table 3 presents the correlation matrix for some of the key variables in the analysis. The family firm (FF) variable has a negative correlation with board size (BSIZE) and foreign directors (FORDIR). CEO duality (CEODU) and female directors (FEMDIR) are positively correlated with family ownership (FOWN). In addition, consistent with prior literature, this study also finds negative correlations between family firm (FF) and firm age (AGE), and firm size (FSIZE).

5.2 *Regression Results: Family Firms and Board Structure*

In Table 4 this study reports the individual regression results of different hypothesised board structure variables. In Model 1 of Table 4, this study examines whether the proportion of independent directors (BIND) is different between family (FF) and non-family firms (NON-FF). The result shows that the coefficient of family firms (FF) is negative and significant ($\beta = -0.021$, $p < 0.05$). This supports *H1*. This implies that family firms have a lower proportion of independent directors (BIND) than non-family firms. This is consistent with the univariate analysis (see Table 2, Panel B). The boards in family firms are usually dominated by family members, who are more likely to minimise the presence of independent directors (Anderson and Reeb 2004) since they often seek to entrench themselves and extract private benefits from the firms. Among the board structure variables, this study finds that CEO duality (CEODU) and foreign directors (FORDIR) have negative and positive impacts on independent directors, respectively. In other words, CEO duality and independent directors are substitute monitoring mechanisms, whereas foreign directors and independent directors are complementary monitory mechanisms. Board independence (BIND) is also positively related to firm age (AGE). Older firms have higher scope and face more complexity than younger firms; therefore, they appoint more independent directors (Hermalin and Weisbach 1998). Independent directors (BIND) have negative and significant relationships with leverage (LEV). In family firms, leverage allows controlling families to

Table 3 Correlation matrix

	FF	BIND	BSIZE	CEODU	FEMDIR	FORDIR	AGE	FSIZE	LEV	GROWTH
FF	1.0000									
BIND	−0.0875	1.0000								
BSIZE	−0.2473***	0.0960	1.0000							
CEODU	0.1691***	−0.1477***	−0.1583***	1.0000						
FEMDIR	0.4815***	−0.0474	−0.1669***	0.0652	1.0000					
FORDIR	−0.2150***	0.1896***	0.1520***	0.0155	−0.1429***	1.0000				
AGE	−0.1645***	0.0638	−0.0247	0.0214	−0.0284	−0.1066	1.0000			
FSIZE	−0.0933	0.0997	0.3023***	−0.0232	−0.1955***	0.2653***	−0.0182	1.0000		
LEV	−0.0649	−0.1223*	−0.0646	0.0500	−0.0816	−0.0862	0.2575***	−0.1789***	1.0000	
GROWTH	0.0512	0.0343	0.0298	0.0937	0.0181	0.1316**	−0.0715	0.1886***	−0.0520	1.0000

FF equals to 1 if the firm is considered to be family firm and 0 otherwise, *BIND* percentage of independent directors on board, *BSIZE* total number of directors on the board, *CEODU* equals to 1 if the CEO and chairman are the same person, and 0 otherwise, *FEMDIR* proportion of female directors on the board, *FORDIR* proportion of foreign directors on the board, *BOWN* percentage of directors' total shareholdings on the board, *AGE* natural log of the number of years since the firm's inception, *FSIZE* natural logarithm of total assets, *GROWTH* measured by asset growth ratio, *LEV* ratio of book value of total debt and book value of total assets

*Significant at 10 % level, **Significant at 5 % level, ***Significant at 1 % level

Table 4 Regression results: family firms and board structure

Variable	BIND (Model 1)	BSIZE (Model 2)	CEODU (Logit-model 3)	FEMDIR (Model 4)	FORDIR (Model 5)
Constant	0.192***	−0.898	−6.263***	0.459***	−0.413***
	(0.000)	(0.436)	(0.000)	(0.000)	(0.000)
FF	−0.021**	−0.638***	0.389**	0.152***	−0.092***
	(0.014)	(0.001)	(0.037)	(0.000)	(0.000)
BIND	–	0.489	−2.794*	−0.021	0.255***
		(0.647)	(0.078)	(0.792)	(0.000)
BSIZE	0.001	–	−0.185***	0.003	0.003
	(0.582)		(0.000)	(0.356)	(0.245)
CEODU	−0.017*	−0.519***	–	−0.021	0.021
	(0.089)	(0.004)		(0.192)	(0.123)
FEMDIR	0.005	0.059	0.196	–	0.023
	(0.767)	(0.905)	(0.765)		(0.524)
FORDIR	0.103***	−0.374	1.515	−0.034	–
	(0.000)	(0.486)	(0.125)	(0.376)	
BOWN	−0.051**				
	(0.032)				
AGE	0.004**	−0.014*	0.013**	0.001	−0.001**
	(0.046)	(0.077)	(0.031)	(0.906)	(0.049)
FSIZE	−0.009	0.943***	0.487	0.069***	0.062***
	(0.141)	(0.000)	(0.238)	(0.000)	(0.000)
GROWTH	0.002	−0.219	0.351	0.014	0.027*
	(0.823)	(0.332)	(0.221)	(0.346)	(0.074)
LEV	−0.016***	−0.356**	0.363	−0.002	0.027
	(0.000)	(0.023)	(0.197)	(0.844)	(0.112)
LAGPERF	–	0.443***	–	–	–
		(0.004)			
CEOTEN	–	–	0.097***	–	
			(0.000)		
FEMCEO	–	–	–	0.221***	
				(0.000)	
FOROWN	–	–	–	–	0.212***
					(0.000)
INDDUM	Included	Included	Included	Included	Included
YEARDUM	Included	Included	Included	Included	Included
Adjusted R^2/pseudo R^2	0.293	0.185	0.159	0.443	0.217
Observations	654	654	654	654	654

FF equals to 1 if the firm is considered to be family firm and 0 otherwise, *BIND* percentage of independent directors on board, *BSIZE* total number of directors on the board, *CEODU* equal to 1 if the CEO and chairman are the same person, and 0 otherwise, *FEMDIR* proportion of female directors on the board, *FORDIR* proportion of foreign directors on the board, *BOWN* percentage of directors' total shareholdings on the board, *AGE* natural log of the number of years since the firm's inception, *FSIZE* natural logarithm of total assets, *GROWTH* measured by asset growth ratio, *LEV* ratio of book value of total debt and book value of total assets, *LAGPERF* ROA lagged 1 year, *CEOTEN* number of years served by the current CEO, *FEMCEO* equals 1 if the CEO is a female and 0 otherwise, *FOROWN* proportion of ownership by foreigners

P-values are shown in parentheses

*Significant at 10 % level, **Significant at 5 % level, ***Significant at 1 % level

control more resources without diluting their voting rights, and they are unwilling to appoint independent directors (Faccio et al. 2010).

In Model 2 of Table 4 this study examines whether board size (BSIZE) is different between family (FF) and non-family (NON-FF) firms. This study finds a negative significant coefficient of family firm ($\beta = -0.638$, $p < 0.01$). It suggests that family firms have smaller boards than non-family firms. This supports *H2*. Family firms may assemble smaller boards for more effective monitoring and to retain control (Bartholomeusz and Tanewski 2006; Navarro and Anson 2009). This study also finds that CEO duality (CEODU) has a negative impact on board size (BSIZE) implying that these variables are substitute monitoring mechanisms. Firm size (FSIZE) positively influences board size. This result suggests that larger firms have a greater volume of activities that requires more advice from experts than in smaller firms (Lehn et al. 2009). Consistent with prior study, this study also reveals that prior year performance (LAGPERF) affects the board size (Setia-Atmaja et al. 2009).

In Model 3 this study tests whether family firms (FF) have more CEO duality (CEODU) than non-family (NON_FF) firms. This study documents a positive significant coefficient of family firms (FF) ($\beta = 0.389$, $P < 0.05$), implying that family firms are more likely to have CEO duality (CEODU) than their non-family counterparts. This supports *H3*. It suggests that families want to retain control over the firms with little chance for external monitoring, which is consistent with the expropriation argument. Board size (BSIZE) is negatively related to CEO duality (CEODU) which, once again, suggests that these two variables are substitute monitoring mechanisms. CEO tenure (CEOTEN) is positively related to the likelihood of CEO duality (CEODU). This study also finds a positive and significant relationship between firm age (AGE) and likelihood of CEO duality (CEODU). Older firms suffer from organisational complexity which motivates them to adopt CEO duality (Faleye 2007).

In Model 4 this study examines whether family firms (FF) have more female directors (FEMDIR) than non-family (NON_FF) firms. This study finds a positive significant coefficient of family firms (FF) ($\beta = 0.152$, $p < 0.01$), implying that family firms (FF) have more female directors (FEMDIR) than non-family firms. This also supports *H4*. In family firms female board members are often selected based on family ties, and they also act as family delegates (Ruigrok et al. 2007). Sometimes they are appointed to the board to ensure family dominance. The result of this study also supports the findings of Uddin and Choudhury (2008). This study also documents that larger firms have a higher proportion of female directors (FEMDIR). The result also suggests that firms appoint female directors (FEMDIR) when they have female CEOs (FEMCEO).

In Model 5 the study investigates whether there is a significant difference between the proportion of foreign directors (FORDIR) in family firms (FF) and non-family (NON-FF) firms. This study finds the coefficient of family firm variable (FF) ($\beta = -0.092$, $P < 0.01$) to be negative and significant. This supports *H5*. The result suggests that family firms (FF) appoint fewer foreign directors (FORDIR) than non-family counterparts because they want to avoid external monitoring. This result is also consistent with the expropriation argument. This study also finds that foreign ownership (FOROWN) is positively related to foreign directors (FORDIR). Firm size (FSIZE) and growth (GROWTH) have significant and positive impacts on foreign directors (FORDIR). Larger firms appoint more foreign directors for their expertise. Moreover, to enhance reputation in the financial market, high-growth firms may appoint more foreign directors (Oxelheim and Randoy 2003). Younger firms appoint foreign directors to create an appropriate image by signalling quality corporate governance to the market participants.

5.3 Endogeneity of Board Structure Variables

The hypothesised board structure variables used in this study are dependent on each other, that is, they are endogenous. The variables also depend on other variables such as firm size (FSIZE), firm age (AGE), and growth (GROWTH). These other variables are treated as exogenous variables. Consistent with the previous studies, this study develops a system of equations to address the issue of endogeneity (Agrawal and Knoeber 1996; Mark and Li 2001). To estimate the system of simultaneous equations empirically, this study employs the three-stage least squares (3SLS) procedure.

The endogenous variables in the system of equations are board independence (BIND), board size (BSIZE), CEO duality (CEODU),[4] female directors (FEMDIR) and foreign directors (FORDIR). There are five equations in the system of equations for the five board structure variables. In order to satisfy the order condition the equations in the system are identified, each equation must exclude at least four of the exogenous variables since each equation includes four endogenous variables as regressors (Kennedy 1998). The specification of Eqs. 1, 2, 3, 4, and 5 is partly driven by the need to satisfy this order condition. Although, as far as possible, this study relies on theory or prior research to determine the exogenous variables to be included or excluded in each of the equations, it should be recognised that the results obtained may be sensitive to what exogenous variables are included.

Table 5 reports the estimations of Eqs. 1, 2, 3, 4, and 5 using the three-stage least squares (3SLS) regression. Table 5 (second row) presents coefficients on family firm (FF) for each equation. In the CEO duality (CEODU) and female director (FEMDIR) equations, family firm (FF) variables have positive significant coefficients. It implies that family firms (FF) are more likely to have CEO duality (CEODU) than non-family (NON-FF) firms, and that these firms have a higher proportion of female directors (FEMDIR) than their non-family counterparts. Thus,

[4] The 3SLS procedure included in standard statistical software packages assumes that all the dependent variables are continuous. Therefore this study does not use the logit specification for CEO duality because OLS is generally robust to the inclusion of limited dependent variables (Greene 1997).

Table 5 Regression results: family firms and board structure (3 SLS)

Variable	BIND (Model 1)	BSIZE (Model 2)	CEODU (Logit-model 3)	FEMDIR (Model 4)	FORDIR (Model 5)
Constant	0.059	−0.975	−0.063	0.464***	−0.017
	(0.236)	(0.394)	(0.797)	(0.000)	(0.703)
FF	−0.013**	−0.607***	0.041**	0.072***	−0.062*
	(0.044)	(0.001)	(0.035)	(0.000)	(0.064)
BIND	–	0.378**	−1.441***	−0.024	0.204***
		(0.010)	(0.000)	(0.716)	(0.000)
BSIZE	0.003	–	−0.023**	0.003	0.001
	(0.125)		(0.005)	(0.317)	(0.579)
CEODU	−0.026***	−0.530***	–	−0.027	0.022**
	(0.000)	(0.002)		(0.214)	(0.033)
FEMDIR	0.007	0.032	−0.025	–	0.028
	(0.746)	(0.925)	(0.812)		(0.326)
FORDIR	0.098***	−0.541	0.370	−0.003	–
	(0.000)	(0.299)	(0.139)	(0.317)	
BOWN	−0.032				
	(0.132)				
AGE	0.001*	−0.015*	0.001	0.001	−0.002***
	(0.009)	(0.059)	(0.875)	(0.889)	(0.000)
FSIZE	−0.001	0.939***	0.038	0.049***	0.005**
	(0.241)	(0.000)	(0.180)	(0.000)	(0.042)
GROWTH	0.008	−0.221	0.070**	0.019	0.031**
	(0.363)	(0.317)	(0.040)	(0.230)	(0.013)
LEV	−0.017***	−0.329**	0.005	−0.002	0.012
	(0.000)	(0.029)	(0.818)	(0.838)	(0.172)
LAGPERF	–	0.434***	–	–	–
		(0.000)			
CEOTEN	–	–	0.013***	–	
			(0.000)		
FEMCEO	–	–	–	0.219***	
				(0.000)	
FOROWN	–	–	–	–	0.621***
					(0.000)
INDDUM	Included	Included	Included	Included	Included
YEARDUM	Included	Included	Included	Included	Included
Adjusted R^2	0.193	0.143	0.117	0.398	0.179
Observations	654	654	654	654	654

FF equals to 1 if the firm is considered to be family firm and 0 otherwise, *BIND* percentage of independent directors on board, *BSIZE* total number of directors on the board, *CEODU* equals to 1 if the CEO and chairman are the same person, and 0 otherwise, *FEMDIR* proportion of female directors on the board, *FORDIR* the proportion of foreign directors on the board, *BOWN* percentage of directors' total shareholdings on the board, *AGE* natural log of the number of years since the firm's inception, *FSIZE* natural logarithm of total assets, *GROWTH* measured by asset growth ratio, *LEV* ratio of book value of total debt and book value of total assets, *LAGPERF* ROA lagged 1 year, *CEOTEN* number of years served by the current CEO, *FEMCEO* equals 1 if the CEO is a female and 0 otherwise, *FOROWN* proportion of ownership by foreigners

P-values are shown in parentheses

*Significant at 10 % level, **Significant at 5 % level, ***Significant at 1 % level

the results provide support to *H3* and *H4*. While both the regression results (with and without addressing the issue of endogeneity) are statistically significant, the magnitude of the family firm (FF) coefficients generated by the 3SLS on CEO duality (CEODU) and female directors (FEMDIR), is smaller. In the board independence (BIND), board size (BSIZE) and foreign director (FORDIR) equations, family firm (FF) variables have negative significant coefficients. It implies that family firms have fewer independent directors, smaller boards and fewer foreign directors than non-family firms. Thus, the results provide support to *H1*, *H2* and *H5*. The magnitude of family firm coefficients generated by 3 SLS is greater than the same coefficients generated by OLS regression.

6 Further Analysis

6.1 Alternative Measure of Firm Performance

This study uses an alternative definition of family firms (FF). In particular, this study defines a family firm as one where family members hold at least 50 % of a firm's shares (voting rights) (Ang et al. 2000). Furthermore, this study requires that at least one member of the controlling family holds a managerial position (i.e., board member, CEO or chairman). This study uses a dummy variable to identify the family firms which his set equal to 1 if the firm is considered to be a family firm, and 0 otherwise. When this study uses this alternative definition, the number of family firms is reduced to 171. This study runs all the regressions that report for in Tables 4 and 5 and finds that results are consistent with the main findings.

6.2 Alternative Measure of Board Independence

This study examines whether the results are sensitive to the fact that the proportion of independent directors in family firms is, by sample construction, lower than in non-family firms. This study constructs a measure of board independence that excludes family board members in the denominator (i.e., board size) and estimates Eqs. 1, 2, 3, 4, and 5 using this measure. The results are not different from the earlier analyses.

7 Chapter Summary

This study examines whether the board structures of family and non-family firms are significantly different in an emerging economy setting, taking Bangladesh as a case. Unlike most western economies, family firms are the most dominant form of listed public companies in Bangladesh. Given that minority shareholders rely on corporate boards to monitor and control family's opportunism, the research issue addressed in regard to the relationship between board structure and family firm is particularly interesting.

The results suggest that family firms adopt distinctly different board structures from their non-family counterparts. Family firms have a lower proportion of independent directors than non-family firms. This is consistent with Anderson and Reeb (2004) who argue that families usually try to minimise the presence of independent directors since they often seek to entrench themselves and extract private benefits from the firm.

This study finds that board size is smaller in family firms than in non-family firms. This result suggests that family members want to maintain control of the firms and, therefore, prefer a smaller board. The analysis shows that family firms are more likely to have CEO duality, implying that CEO duality in family firms provides greater opportunities for managerial entrenchment and expropriation from minority shareholders.

This study also finds that family firms have more female directors than non-family firms. In Bangladeshi family firms, female board members are usually appointed based on family ties. In most of the cases the founders appoint their daughters and wives on the boards. Their appointment is also consistent with the contention of an increase in family dominance. The results of this study also suggest that family firms have fewer foreign directors than non-family firms. Family firms want to avoid external monitoring and, therefore, prefer not to have foreign members on the board.

Appendix

Variable	Measurement and operationalization	Data source
FF	Equals to 1 if the firm is considered to be family firm and 0 otherwise	Annual report
BIND	Percentage of independent directors on board	Annual report
BSIZE	Total number of directors on the board	Annual report
CEODU	Equals to 1 if the CEO and chairman are the same person, and 0 otherwise	Annual report
FEMDIR	Proportion of female directors on the board	Annual report
FORDIR	Proportion of foreign directors on the board	Annual report
BOWN	Percentage of directors' total shareholdings (excluding family directors' ownership) on the board	Annual report
AGE	Natural log of the number of years since the firm's inception	Annual report
FSIZE	Natural logarithm of total assets	Annual report
GROWTH	Difference between the total assets of the prior year and the current year divided by prior year total assets	Annual report
LEV	Ratio of book value of total debt and book value of total assets	Annual report
LAGPERF	ROA lagged 1 year	Annual report

(continued)

Variable	Measurement and operationalization	Data source
CEOTEN	Number of years served by the current CEO	Annual report
FEMCEO	Equals 1 if the CEO is a female and 0 otherwise	Annual report
FOROWN	Proportion of ownership by foreigners	Annual report

References

Adams, R. B., & Ferreira, D. (2009). Women in the boardroom and their impact on governance and performance. *Journal of Financial Economics, 94*(2), 291–309.

Agrawal, A., & Knoeber, C. R. (1996). Firm performance and mechanisms to control agency problems between managers and shareholders. *Journal of Finance and Quantitative Analysis, 31*(3), 377–397.

Anderson, R. C., & Reeb, D. M. (2003). Founding-family ownership and firm performance: Evidence from the S &P 500. *Journal of Finance, 61*(3), 1301–1328.

Anderson, R. C., & Reeb, D. M. (2004). Board composition balancing family influence in S& P 500 firms. *Administrative Science Quarterly, 49*(2), 209–237.

Anderson, R. C., Mansi, S. A., & Reeb, D. M. (2003). Founding family ownership and the agency cost of debt. *Journal of Financial Economics, 68*(2), 263–285.

Andres, P., Azofra, V., & Lopez, F. (2005). Corporate boards in OECD countries: Size, composition, functioning and effectiveness. *Corporate Governance: An International Review, 13*(2), 197–210.

Ang, J. S., Cole, R. A., & Lin, J. W. (2000). Agency costs and ownership structure. *Journal of Finance, 55*(1), 81–106.

Barney, J. B., & Hansen, M. H. (1994). Trustworthiness as a source of competitive advantage. *Strategic Management Journal, 15*(1), 175–190.

Bartholomeusz, S., & Tanewski, G. A. (2006). The relationship between family firms and corporate governance. *Journal of Small Business Management, 44*(2), 245–267.

Boone, A. L., Casares Field, L., Karpoff, J. M., & Raheja, C. G. (2007). The determinants of corporate board size and composition: An empirical analysis. *Journal of Financial Economics, 85*(1), 66–101.

Boyed, B. K. (1995). CEO duality and firm performance: A contingency model. *Strategic Management Journal, 16*(3), 301–312.

Carter, D. A., Simkins, B. J., & Simpson, W. G. (2003). Corporate governance, board diversity, and firm value. *The Financial Review, 38*(1), 33–53.

Cascino, S., Pugliese, A., Mussolino, D., & Sansone, C. (2010). The influence of family ownership on the quality of accounting information. *Family Business Review, 23*(3), 246–265.

Chen, Z., Cheung, Y., Stouraitis, A., & Wong, A. W. S. (2005). Ownership concentration, firm performance, and dividend policy in Hong Kong. *Pacific-Basin Financial Journal, 13*(4), 431–449.

Daily, C. M., & Dalton, D. R. (1993). Board of director's leadership and structure: Control and performance implications. *Entrepreneurship Theory and Practice, 17*(3), 65–81.

Dalton, D. R., Daily, C. M., Johnson, J. L., & Ellstrand, A. E. (1999). Number of directors and financial performance: A meta-analysis. *Academy of Management Journal, 42*(6), 674–686.

Dyer, W. G. (1989). Integrating professional management into a family-owned business. *Family Business Review, 2*(3), 221–235.

Eisenberg, T., Sundgren, S., & Wells, M. T. (1998). Larger board size and decreasing firm value in small firms. *Journal of Financial Economics, 48*(1), 35–54.

Faccio, M., Lang, L. H. P., & Young, L. (2010). Pyramiding vs leverage in corporate groups: International evidence. *Journal of International Business Studies, 41*, 88–104.
Faleye, O. (2007). Does one hat fit all? The case of corporate leadership structure. *Journal of Management and Governance, 13*(3), 239–259.
Farooque, O. A., Zijl, T. V., Dunstan, K., & Karim, A. K. M. W. (2007). Corporate governance in Bangladesh: Link between ownership concentration and financial performance. *Corporate Governance: An International Review, 15*(6), 1453–1468.
Greene, W. (1997). *Econometric analysis*. New York: Macmillan.
Haalien, L., & House, M. (2005). *Board of directors in Norwegian family businesses, research report 7/2005*. Oslo: Norwegian School of Management.
Hermalin, B., & Weisbach, M. (1998). Endogenously chosen boards of directors and their monitoring of the CEO. *American Economic Review, 88*(1), 96–118.
Hillman, A. J., & Dalziel, T. (2003). Boards of directors and firm performance: Integrating agency and resource dependence perspectives. *Academy of Management Review, 28*(3), 383–396.
Huse, M. (2000). Boards of directors in SMEs: A review and research agenda. *Entrepreneurship and Regional Development, 12*(4), 271–290.
Imam, M. O., & Malik, M. (2007). Firm performance and corporate governance through ownership structure: Evidence from Bangladesh stock market. *International Review of Business Research Papers, 3*(4), 88–110.
IMF (2010). *World economic outlook database*. Washington, DC: International Monetary Fund.
Islam, A., & Khaled, M. (2005). Tests of weak-form efficiency of the Dhaka stock exchange. *Journal of Business Finance & Accounting, 32*(7–8), 1613–1624.
Jackling, B., & Johl, S. (2009). Board structure and firm performance: Evidence from India's top companies. *Corporate Governance: An International Review, 17*(4), 492–509.
Jensen, M. (1993). The modern industrial revolution, exit, and the failure of internal control systems. *Journal of Finance, 48*(3), 831–880.
Kennedy, P. (1998). *A guide to econometrics* (4th ed.). Cambridge, MA: MIT Press.
Lane, S., Austrachan, J., & McMillan, K. (2006). Guideline for family business boards of directors. *Family Business Review, 19*(2), 147–167.
Lee, J. (2006). Family firm performance: Further evidence. *Family Business Review, 29*(3), 103–114.
Lehn, K., Patro, S., & Zhao, M. (2009). Determinants of the size and composition of US corporate boards: 1935–2000. *Financial Management, 38*(4), 747–780.
Mark, Y. T., & Li, Y. (2001). Determinants of corporate ownership and board structure: Evidence from Singapore. *Journal of Corporate Finance, 7*(3), 235–256.
Myers, S. (1977). Determinants of corporate borrowing. *Journal of Financial Economics, 5*(2), 147–175.
Navarro, M. S., & Anson, S. G. (2009). Do families shape corporate governance structure? *Journal of Management & Organization, 15*(3), 327–345.
Neubauer, F., & Lank, A. G. (1998). *The family business: It's governance for sustainability*. London: Macmillan.
Oxelheim, L., & Randoy, T. (2003). The impact of foreign board membership on firm value. *Journal of Banking and Finance, 27*(12), 2369–2392.
Pfeffer, J. (1972). Size and composition of corporate boards of directors: The organization and its environment. *Administrative Science Quarterly, 17*(2), 218–228.
Ruigrok, W., Peck, S., & Tacheva, S. (2007). Nationality and gender diversity on Swiss corporate boards. *Corporate Governance: An International Review, 15*(4), 546–557.
Setia-Atmaja, L., Tanewski, G. A., & Skully, M. (2009). The role of dividends, debt and board structure in the governance of family controlled firms. *Journal of Business and Accounting, 36* (7 & 8), 863–898.
Siddiqui, J. (2010). Development of corporate governance regulations: The case of an emerging economy. *Journal of Business Ethics, 91*(2), 253–274.

Uddin, S., & Choudhury, J. (2008). Rationality, traditionalism and the state of corporate governance mechanisms: Illustration from less-developed country. *Accounting, Auditing & Accountability Journal, 21*(7), 1026–1051.
Ward, J. L. (1991). *Creating effective boards for private enterprises*. San Francisco: Jossey-Bass.
World Bank. (2009). *Bangladesh: Corporate governance country assessment*. Report on the observance of standards and codes (ROSC).
Yermack, D. (1996). Higher market valuation of companies with a small board of directors. *Journal of Financial Economics, 40*(2), 185–211.

Regional Legal Protection and Earnings Management: Evidence from China

Yuyang Zhang, Konari Uchida, and Hua Bu

Abstract This chapter investigates the impact of regional legal protection on the earnings management of Chinese companies. Chinese data provide a time-variant legal protection index, which is advantageous in controlling for time-invariant, non-legal characteristics. We find that regional legal protection reduces earnings management for the period before the implementation of Split-share Structure Reform. The result is consistent with the conventional wisdom that better legal environments are associated with better earnings quality. Further analyses suggest that a significant relation exists especially between the protection of intellectual property rights and earnings management. This result proposes that legal protection mitigates earnings management that aims to prevent technology spillovers. However, there is no evidence that regional legal protection affects earnings management during the Split-share Structure Reform and after the adoption of IFRS-convergent New Accounting Standards.

1 Introduction

Previous studies suggest that a number of important differences in financial systems across countries arise from the quality of legal protection provided (La Porta et al. 1998; Mintz 2005). Researchers also have paid attention to the cross-country

Y. Zhang
Graduate School of Economics, Kyushu University, 6-19-1, Hakozaki, Higashiku, Fukuoka 812-8581, Japan

K. Uchida (✉)
Faculty of Economics, Kyushu University, 6-19-1, Hakozaki, Higashiku, Fukuoka 812-8581, Japan
e-mail: kuchida@econ.kyushu-u.ac.jp

H. Bu
School of Management, China University of Mining and Technology, University Road, Xuzhou, Jiangsu Province 221116, China

S. Boubaker and D.K. Nguyen (eds.), *Corporate Governance in Emerging Markets*, CSR, Sustainability, Ethics & Governance, DOI 10.1007/978-3-642-44955-0_6,

variation in earnings management and its relation to the country-level legal protection offered (Leuz et al. 2003; Haw et al. 2004; Shen and Chih 2005; Burgstahler et al. 2006; Lang et al. 2006). These studies find that earnings management is less pervasive in countries with strong legal protection and where insiders cannot extract substantial private benefits. However, many cross-country studies employ country-average data and inevitably discard within-country variations in earnings management (Holderness 2008; Wu et al. 2009). In addition, the relationship between country-level legal protection and earnings management potentially arises from other aspects that are correlated with legal factors (e.g., culture, religion, and peoples' thoughts).

To address these concerns, we investigate the relationship between regional legal protection and earnings management in China. China exhibits great heterogeneity in legal infrastructure across provinces due to the imbalanced economic development across regions (Qian and Weingast 1997; Jin et al. 2005). Eastern coastal regions that have benefited from the preferential policy and geographic advantages have developed considerably legal environments. However, most of the western inland areas that have suffered from weak infrastructure lag behind coastal regions in legal environment developments. Fan and Wang (2011) present a provincial legal environment index, which enables implementation of single country analyses of the relationship between legal protection and earnings management. Single country data have relatively small variations in culture and other aspects that are advantageous in avoiding non-legal factors contaminating the result. Meanwhile, Chinese provinces have improved legal environments over time (MacNeil 2002) and Fan and Wang (2011) provide a novel legal index that has time-variant properties. This data facilitates fixed effects model estimations that successfully control for time-invariant, non-legal characteristics. Among various measures of earnings management, we employ discretionary accruals that show one value for every single firm-year to take advantage of this research setting.

We investigate the relationship between legal protection and earnings management of Chinese companies from 2001 to 2009. There are two significant institutional changes – Split-share Structure Reform and introduction of International Financial Reporting Standards (IFRS) – during the sample period. On April 29, 2005, the China Securities Regulatory Commission (CSRC) initiated the Split-share Structure Reform (hereafter denoted as SSSR) that required listed companies to convert non-tradable shares (hereafter denoted as NTS), which are shown in previous studies to increase earnings management, into publicly tradable shares (hereafter denoted as TS). In 2007, the Chinese Ministry of Finance obliged listed firms to introduce IFRS-convergent New Accounting Standards (hereafter denoted as NAS). IFRS adopts accounting practices that are quite different from the Chinese traditional accounting standards and its mandatory introduction substantially changes the degree of managerial discretion on reported earnings. Accordingly, we separately address the issue for three sub-periods: before 2005 (pre-SSSR); 2005 and 2006 (during-SSSR); and 2007 and after (post-NAS).

We find that there is a negative and significant relationship between legal protection and earnings management before the SSSR after controlling for firm-fixed effects, which is consistent with the conventional idea. Fan and Wang's (2011) legal index consists of four subcomponents and further analyses suggest that a significant relation exists between the protection of intellectual property rights and earnings management before the SSSR. This result supports Fan et al.'s (2013) argument that legal protection of intellectual property rights effectively alleviates Chinese firms' earnings management, which aims to prevent technology spillovers. However, the impact of legal protection on earnings management disappears during the second and third sub-periods. Instead, the non-tradable share ratio and ownership concentration, which are substantially reduced by the SSSR, are positively related to earnings management during the second sub-period. These results suggest that legal protection does not effectively alleviate earnings management when there are considerable changes in insiders' incentives and opportunities of earnings management.

This research makes significant contributions to the literature. We present evidence that legal protection of intellectual property rights affects earnings management under specific environments after controlling for time-invariant regional and firm characteristics. We also present evidence that legal protection does not effectively alleviate earnings management during a period of substantial changes in corporate governance and accounting standards.

The remainder of the chapter is organized as follows. Section 2 presents the literature review and hypothesis development. Section 3 describes variables. Section 4 presents our sample selection and data. Regression results are reported in Sect. 5. Finally, we conclude this research in Sect. 6.

2 Hypothesis Development

Recent law and finance literature suggests that the degree of legal investor protection is associated with various aspects of corporate finance and governance, including ownership concentration (La Porta et al. 1999), dividend policy (La Porta et al. 2000), foreign listing (Doidge et al. 2004), group affiliation (Kali 1999), bankruptcy (Claessens et al. 2003) and so on. An underlying idea of these studies is that legal protection effectively mitigates the agency problem between controlling shareholders and minority shareholders (Type II agency problem), which is especially evident in firms with concentrated ownership structures. In these firms, controlling shareholders who possess control rights in excess of their equity ownership (Claessens et al. 2000; Fan and Wong 2002) extract private benefits at the expense of minority shareholders' wealth (Shleifer and Vishny 1997; Fan and Wong 2002; Firth et al. 2007; Liu and Lu 2007; Lo et al. 2010; Johnson et al. 2000; Claessens et al. 2000; La Porta et al. 2000; Dyck and Zingales 2004).

The Type II agency problem is also likely to affect firms' earnings management. If private benefits extraction is detected, outside interventions (e.g., prosecutions or penalties) are likely to discipline insiders (Zingales 1994; Shleifer and Vishny 1997). Therefore, corporate insiders have incentives to manage earnings to conceal evidence of their value-decreasing behaviors. A developed legal system imposes a high risk of future litigation and significant costs of damaged reputation on corporate insiders who extract private benefits (La Porta et al. 1998; Claessens et al. 2002; Dyck and Zingales 2004). These discussions give rise to the notion that earnings management decreases with legal protection. Indeed, Leuz et al. (2003) investigate earnings management across 31 countries worldwide and demonstrate that earnings management decreases with legal protection. By examining the properties of reported earnings of both private and public firms in the European Union, Burgstahler et al. (2006) provide evidence that earnings management is more pronounced in countries with weaker legal system and enforcement. Additionally, Lang et al. (2006) find that earnings management is more evident in cross-listing non-US firms with weak domestic investor protection. These discussions give rise to the following hypothesis.

Hypothesis 1: Chinese listed firms located in regions with less protective legal environments engage more in earnings management than firms operating in regions with a more protective legal system.

In addition to investor protection, legal protection of intellectual property rights also affects the level of earnings management. Firms with profitable technologies have an incentive to disclose opaque information to prevent technology spillovers to public and potential competitors (Fan and Wong 2002; Fan et al. 2013). This is especially true for firms located in regions with weak legal protection of intellectual property rights. Consistent with this idea, Fan et al. (2013) show evidence that income smoothing of Chinese firms is negatively related to provincial legal protection of intellectual property rights. We follow them to present a hypothesis regarding the effect of protection of intellectual property rights on earnings management.

Hypothesis 2: Chinese listed companies operating in regions with weak protection of intellectual property rights are more likely to engage in earnings management than firms in regions with strong protection of intellectual property rights.

3 Variables

3.1 Measure of Regional Legal Protection

As mentioned, Fan and Wang (2011) present the legal environment index (*LEI*) for Chinese provinces. This novel index enables the investigation of the relation between earnings management and legal protection by a single country analysis. *LEI* consists of the following components: (a) the development of market intermediaries (*LEI_1*), which is measured by the arithmetic average of the number of lawyers as the percentage of provincial population and the number of certified public accountants as the percentage of provincial population; (b) the level of protection of producers' interests (*LEI_2*), which is measured by the number of economic cases accepted by the courts divided by local GDP; (c) the level of protection of intellectual property rights (*LEI_3*), which is measured by the arithmetic mean of the number of accepted patent applications as the percentage of scientific/technical personnel and the number of approved patent applications as the percentage of scientific/technical personnel; and (d) the level of protection of consumers' interests (*LEI_4*), which is measured by the number of consumers' complaints divided by local GDP.

This index is widely adopted by previous Chinese studies to control for regional effects (Chen et al. 2006, 2009; Fan et al. 2013; Firth et al. 2009; He et al. 2012; Lo et al. 2010). Importantly, the *LEI* index is time-variant and allows us to implement fixed-effects model estimations that successfully control for time-invariant characteristics. Although the earlier studies employ Ordinary Least Squares (OLS) estimations, fixed-effects model estimations are advantageous in avoiding potential biases from unobserved, non-legal characteristics that are correlated with legal protection. As mentioned, Fan et al. (2013) show a negative relation between earnings management (income smoothing) of Chinese companies and provincial legal protection of intellectual property rights. Importantly, we develop their research by controlling for unobserved time-invariant characteristics. We follow Chen et al. (2009) to adopt the natural logarithm of the *LEI* (*LN_LEI*) in our regression analyses.

3.2 Measure of Earnings Management

To capture the magnitude of earnings management, we adopt discretionary accruals (*DA*), which are measured by the difference between total accruals (*TA*) and non-discretionary accruals (*NDA*) divided by total assets at the beginning of the year. Among various measures of earnings management, *DA* is one of the most commonly used measures in the research of earnings management (Dechow et al. 2010). Fan et al. (2013) use income smoothing to investigate the relation between legal protection and earnings management of Chinese firms. Importantly, *DA* takes one value for every single firm-year and enables implementation of firm-fixed effects model estimations. It is also noteworthy that *DA* does not use stock returns, which will be highly affected by expropriation problems.

We follow previous studies (Dechow et al. 1995; Kothari et al. 2005) to use the cross-sectional modified Jones Model to estimate *DA*. Specifically, we estimate Eq. 1 for firm-years in the same industry[1]:

[1] Industry classification is based on the Classification Guidance of Chinese Listed Companies (1998), issued by CSRC.

$$\frac{TA_{i,t}}{Assets_{i,t-1}} = \beta_0\left(\frac{1}{Assets_{i,t-1}}\right) + \beta_1\left(\frac{\Delta Sales_{i,t} - \Delta AR_{i,t}}{Assets_{i,t-1}}\right) + \beta_2\left(\frac{PPE_{i,t}}{Assets_{i,t-1}}\right) + \beta_3(ROA_{i,t-1}) + \varepsilon_{i,t} \quad (1)$$

where subscript *i* and *t* respectively indicate firm and year; *Assets* is the total assets; *ΔSales* is the change in revenues; *ΔAR* is the change in accounting receivable; *PPE* is the gross property, plant and equipment; and *ROA* is the returns on assets computed by earnings before interest and tax divided by total assets.

Following Dechow et al. (1995), we calculate *TA* as

$$TA_{i,t} = (\Delta CA_{i,t} - \Delta Cash_{i,t}) - (\Delta CL_{i,t} - \Delta STL_{i,t} - \Delta TP_{i,t}) - Depreciation_{i,t}$$

where *ΔCA* is the change in current assets, *ΔCash* is the change in cash and cash equivalents, *ΔCL* is the change in current liabilities, *ΔSTL* is the change in short-term debt included in current liabilities, *ΔTP* is the change in income tax payable, and *Depreciation* is the depreciation and amortization.

We compute *DA* as *TA* minus *NDA*, which is calculated by using the estimated coefficients for Eq. 1. Since we focus on the magnitude of *DA* rather than the direction of *DA*, the following analyses adopt the absolute value of discretionary accruals (*ADA*).

As mentioned, Chinese listed companies recently experienced two important institutional changes: the SSSR and the mandatory adoption of IFRS-convergent NAS. Previous studies suggest that these institutional changes have influence on earnings management (Jiang and Habib 2012; Liu et al. 2011; He et al. 2012; Zhang et al. 2013). Since these institutional changes potentially affect coefficients of Eq. 1, we separately estimate Eq. 1 for three sub-periods: before 2005; between 2005 and 2006 (SSSR started in 2005); and 2007 and after (NAS was introduced in 2007).

3.3 Control Variables

We employ several control variables in the following regressions of *ADA*. China has adopted a segmented ownership structure; only a minority part of shares of listed companies can be traded in the secondary market, namely tradable shares (TS). The majority of shares which have been retained mainly by the founders (usually central or local governments) are not tradable in the secondary market, which is namely, non-tradable shares (NTS). The segmented share structure was originally designed for different levels of governments to keep their control over State Owned Enterprises (SOEs), especially in key industries (e.g., agricultural, chemical and petroleum). Although NTS entitles its holders with the same voting rights as TS (one share-one vote), the existence of NTS engenders divergence between cash flow rights and control rights, since holders of NTS neither benefit from capital gains nor bear losses from stock price reductions. As a result, insiders who principally hold NTS are incentivized to extract private benefits at the expense of outside minorities' wealth (Johnson et al. 2000; Claessens et al. 2000; La Porta et al. 2000; Dyck and Zingales 2004). Those insiders are likely to engage in earnings management to conceal evidence of their value-destroying behaviors. Indeed, previous studies find that the proportion of NTS over total outstanding shares (*NTSR*) is negatively related to earnings quality (Fan and Wong 2002; Firth et al. 2007).

The largest shareholder who owns the majority of a company's shares will be released from disciplinary mechanisms (Shleifer and Vishny 1997; La Porta et al. 1999; Johnson et al. 2000; Fan and Wong 2002; Liu and Lu 2007). Consequently, a concentrated ownership structure would empower insiders to expropriate minority shareholders' wealth and to distort financial statements (Shleifer and Vishny 1997; Firth et al. 2007; Liu and Lu 2007; Lo et al. 2010). Fan and Wong (2002) and Firth et al. (2007) find that ownership concentration significantly weakens earnings quality. Therefore, we include the percentage ownership of the largest shareholder (*CONCENTRATION*).[2]

The corporate board is an important governance device that is expected to monitor insiders' behaviors. Numerous studies have investigated whether board characteristics (e.g., board size and independence) affect earnings quality (Beasley 1996; Vafeas 2000; Klein 2002; Park and Shin 2004; Ahmed et al. 2006; Firth et al. 2007; Dimitropoulos and Asteriou 2010; Xie et al. 2003; Wang et al. 2007; Liu and Lu 2007; Lo et al. 2010). We follow these previous studies and adopt the natural logarithm of the number of board members as a proxy for board size (*BOARDSIZE*). It is also a common idea that independent boards make it difficult for insiders to expropriate minority shareholders' wealth and to manage earnings (Klein 2002; Xie et al. 2003; Liu and Lu 2007; Lo et al. 2010). We employ the percentage of independent directors over total board members (*BINDEPENDENCE*) to test this idea.

Board monitoring will become more effective, as directors' personal wealth is more sensitive to firm value. High board ownership is likely to prevent insiders from conducting value-decreasing behaviors that increase their private benefits. Accordingly, earnings management is likely to decrease with board ownership. It is noteworthy that directors in Chinese listed firms typically hold no shares or only an insignificant portion of shares. The variation in directors' ownership is so limited that we employ the percentage of directors who own shares (*PDIREC_SOWN*).[3]

[2] Another feature in Chinese corporate governance is the existence of listed companies that are controlled by the governments. The governments are likely to pursue social and political objectives (e.g., employment, tax or social welfare) rather than shareholder value maximization (Liu and Lu 2007). As a result, firms controlled by the governments are likely to engender expropriation problems and to engage in earnings management. We do not explicitly address the issue, since the effect of state control is incorporated in firm-fixed effects.

[3] All board members who hold at least one share are counted in the numerator of this variable.

When board leadership and CEO power are vested in one person, the CEO is able to exert significant power and board members will find it difficult to oversee managerial behaviors (Jensen 1993; Raheja 2005). Forker (1992) and Dechow et al. (1996) find that firms that manipulate earnings are more likely to have a CEO who simultaneously serves as chairman of the board. Following them, we adopt a dummy variable that takes a value of one when the CEO also serves as chairman of the board and zero otherwise (*D_DUAL*).

China's Company Law mandatorily requires listed companies to adopt a two-tier monitoring system that consists of a board of directors and a board of supervisors. The Guidelines for Chinese Listed Companies (2006) required companies to have supervisors who were independent of directors and managers.[4] Chinese Company Law empowers a supervisory board to monitor a firm's accounting system and to request necessary changes in accounting procedures.[5] We adopt the natural logarithm of the number of supervisory board members (*SUPERSIZE*) and the percentage of supervisors who own shares over all supervisors (*PSUPER_SOWN*).[6]

It is likely that large firms engage less in earnings management due to close attention from investors and regulators (Holland and Jackson 2004). Indeed, previous studies find that disclosure quality increases with firm size (Atiase 1985; Freeman 1987). We include the natural logarithm of total assets (*SIZE*) as a proxy for firm size. Following Butler et al. (2004) and Firth et al. (2007), we include *ROA* to control for the effect of profitability on earnings management. Dhaliwal et al. (1991) suggest that firms with high leverage (high default risk) tend to exploit discretionary accounting methods to conceal poor performance (Watts and Zimmerman 1990). Therefore, we include leverage (*LEV*), which is liabilities divided by equity. Tobin's Q (*Q*), which is measured by the book value of liabilities and the market value of equity divided by the book value of total assets, is included to control for the effect of a firm's growth opportunity on earnings management. Growing firms have an incentive to manage earnings to meet earnings requirements for new security issues or to decrease costs of capital (Beaver et al. 1970; Minton and Schrand 1999). The definitions of variables are presented in Table 1.

[4] This guideline prohibits the manager, directors and financial officers of the company from being members of a supervisory board.

[5] The Code of Corporate Governance for Listed Companies allows the board of supervisors to report directly to regulatory authorities if it finds any violations of laws, regulations, accounting standards or firm charters.

[6] All supervisory members who own at least one share are counted in the numerator of this variable.

Table 1 Definition of variables

Variable	Definition
ADA	The absolute value of discretionary accruals. Discretionary accruals (*DA*) are measured by the difference between total accruals (*TA*) and non-discretionary accruals (*NDA*). A cross-sectional modified Jones Model is adopted for estimation
LN_LEI	The natural logarithm of the legal environment index. The legal environment index (*LEI*) was constructed by Fan and Wang (2011) and consists of the following components: (a) the development of market intermediaries (*LEI_1*); (b) the protection of producers' interests (*LEI_2*); (c) the protection of intellectual property rights (*LEI_3*); and (d) the protection of consumers' interests (*LEI_4*)
NTSR	The percentage of non-tradable shares over total outstanding shares
CONCENTRATION	The percentage ownership by the largest shareholder
BOARDSIZE	The natural logarithm of the number of board members
BINDEPENDENCE	The proportion of independent directors over total board members
PDIREC_SOWN	The proportion of board members who own at least one share of the firm over all board members
D_DUAL	A dummy variable that takes a value of one if the CEO also serves as the chairperson of the board
SUPERSIZE	The natural logarithm of the number of supervisory board members
PSUPER_SOWN	The proportion of supervisory board members holding at least one share of the firm over total supervisors
SIZE	The natural logarithm of total assets
ROA	Return on assets computed by earnings before interest and tax divided by total assets
LEV	Liabilities divided by equity
Q	The book value of liabilities and the market value of equity divided by the book value of total assets

4 Sample Selection and Data

Our sample consists of Chinese companies listed on the Shanghai and Shenzhen stock exchanges from 2001 to 2009. Financial and governance data are from the CSMAR (China Stock Market and Accounting Research) database and the CCER (China Center for Economic Research) database, respectively. Financial companies are excluded from our sample due to their unique regulatory environments and financial statement format (Vafeas 2000; Peasnell et al. 2005; Firth et al. 2007). We delete firms for which necessary data are not available. As a result of these procedures, our final sample consists of 10,500 firm-year observations (involving 1,316 firms). We winsorize the *ADA* at the 1st and 99th percentiles to address problems associated with outliers.

Panel A of Table 2 shows summary statistics of variables for the whole sample period. NTS accounts for a substantial part of total outstanding shares (mean *NTSR* is 49.3 %). The average largest shareholder holds 39.3 % of total outstanding shares (*CONCENTRATION*). In contrast, the mean percentage ownership by the second to fifth largest shareholders is only 15 % (the median is 12.1 %) (not reported). These

Table 2 Descriptive statistics

Variable	Mean	Median	Standard deviation	1st quartile	3rd quartile
Panel A: Descriptive statistics of variables for the whole sample period (N = 10,500)					
ADA	0.125	0.089	0.120	0.041	0.167
LN_LEI	1.877	1.841	0.537	1.488	2.243
NTSR	0.493	0.538	0.199	0.389	0.639
CONCENTRATION	0.393	0.372	0.163	0.262	0.521
Number of directors	9.641	9.000	2.297	9.000	11.000
BINDEPENDENCE	0.315	0.333	0.111	0.308	0.364
PDIREC_SOWN	0.171	0.100	0.210	0.000	0.300
D_DUAL	0.133	0.000	0.340	0.000	0.000
Number of supervisors	4.222	4.000	1.459	3.000	5.000
PSUPER_SOWN	0.198	0.000	0.276	0.000	0.333
SIZE	21.341	21.243	1.050	20.644	21.956
ROA	0.028	0.035	0.090	0.011	0.065
LEV	1.326	1.001	1.621	0.546	1.680
Q	2.262	1.784	1.519	1.321	2.612
Panel B: Pre-SSSR [2001,2004] observations (N = 4,251)					
ADA	0.112	0.083	0.105	0.038	0.148
LN_LEI	1.605	1.541	0.488	1.247	2.032
NTSR	0.602	0.620	0.114	0.539	0.689
CONCENTRATION	0.433	0.424	0.169	0.290	0.578
Panel C: During-SSSR [2005,2006] observations (N = 2,518)					
ADA	0.109	0.082	0.100	0.040	0.143
t-statistics (Z-statistics)	−1.240	−0.227			
LN_LEI	1.913	1.858	0.426	1.577	2.360
t-statistics (Z-statistics)	27.254***	25.170***			
NTSR	0.545	0.562	0.130	0.460	0.640
t-statistics (Z-statistics)	−18.278***	−17.974***			
CONCENTRATION	0.382	0.355	0.155	0.259	0.506
t-statistics (Z-statistics)	−12.593***	−11.914***			
Panel D: Post-NAS [2007,2009] observations (N = 3,731)					
ADA	0.150	0.106	0.141	0.047	0.210
t-statistics (Z-statistics)	13.615***	9.928***			
LN_LEI	2.162	2.004	0.503	1.728	2.638
t-statistics (Z-statistics)	21.000***	20.127***			
NTSR	0.333	0.350	0.210	0.185	0.493
t-statistics (Z-statistics)	−49.414***	−40.174***			
CONCENTRATION	0.354	0.334	0.151	0.231	0.470
t-statistics (Z-statistics)	−6.909***	−6.647***			

(continued)

Table 2 (continued)

Panel E: Summary statistics of ADA and LN_LEI for different province

Region	Mean of *ADA*	Mean of *LN_LEI*	Median of *ADA*	Median of *LN_LEI*	N
Anhui	0.133	1.518	0.099	1.710	337
Beijing	0.114	2.230	0.082	2.063	661
Chongqing	0.131	1.482	0.091	1.587	217
Fujian	0.121	1.810	0.085	1.858	341
Gansu	0.111	0.941	0.093	1.206	153
Guangdong	0.134	2.327	0.088	2.365	1,175
Guangxi	0.117	1.306	0.094	1.308	176
Guizhou	0.103	1.180	0.073	1.324	90
Hainan	0.143	1.358	0.100	1.335	176
Hebei	0.118	1.503	0.079	1.631	262
Heilongjiang	0.119	1.593	0.089	1.639	206
Henan	0.129	1.440	0.101	1.509	249
Hubei	0.124	1.528	0.096	1.583	484
Hunan	0.118	1.352	0.084	1.435	326
Inner Mongolia	0.111	1.426	0.079	1.488	163
Jiangsu	0.115	2.203	0.082	2.102	678
Jiangxi	0.128	1.362	0.091	1.454	188
Jilin	0.113	1.522	0.084	1.567	263
Liaoning	0.111	1.793	0.073	1.848	387
Ningxia	0.132	1.104	0.109	1.244	93
Qinghai	0.175	1.068	0.094	1.256	35
Shandong	0.130	1.774	0.095	1.815	592
Shanghai	0.121	2.598	0.086	2.553	1,120
Shaanxi	0.132	1.423	0.099	1.477	183
Shanxi	0.125	1.366	0.086	1.456	169
Sichuan	0.139	1.594	0.098	1.617	508
Sinkiang	0.123	1.498	0.098	1.517	213
Tianjin	0.130	2.136	0.082	2.141	197
Tibet	0.164	1.346	0.152	1.344	30
Yunnan	0.143	1.264	0.108	1.364	177
Zhejiang	0.126	2.437	0.090	2.482	651

Notes: *t*-statistics (Z-statistics) in Panel C are for the null hypothesis that the mean (median) is identical between the pre- and during-SSSR periods. *t*-statistics (Z-statistics) in Panel D are for the null hypothesis that the mean (median) is identical between the during-SSSR and post-NAS periods. *, ** and *** indicate significance at the 10 %, 5 % and 1 % levels, respectively. See Table 1 for the definition of variables

figures suggest that Chinese ownership structures are highly concentrated so that the largest shareholder can exert dominant control over listed companies. The average (median) board has 9.6 (9.0) members and independent directors account for about one-third of total board members (*BINDEPENDENCE*). This figure suggests that Chinese companies adopt the minimum level of independent directors required by the CSRC.[7]

Panels B to D show the statistics of key variables (including *ADA*, *LN_LEI*, *NTSR* and *CONCENTRATION*) for the three sub-periods. We find that *ADA* during the SSSR period (Panel C) tends to be lower (although the difference is statistically insignificant) compared to that for the pre-SSSR period (Panel B); whereas, there is a significant increase in *ADA* for the post-NAS period (Panel D). Although we cannot simply compare the different period *ADA*s which are separately computed, the increase in *ADA* during the post-NAS period is consistent with the finding of Zhang et al. (2013). Meanwhile, *LN_LEI* exhibits continual and significant increases over three sub-periods, which is consistent with MacNeil's (2002) argument that China has improved legal environments over time. The mean *NTSR* (*CONCENTRATION*) is about 60.2 (43.3) percent for the pre-SSSR firm-years and this becomes 54.5 (38.2) percent for the during-SSSR period. The mean and median differences in these variables are statistically and economically significant between the pre- and during-SSSR periods. Similar trends in *NTSR* and *CONCENTRATION* are found between during-SSSR and post-NAS periods. The results suggest that the SSSR considerably decreases the NTS of Chinese listed companies and thus reduces the shareholding of the largest shareholders who owned NTS before the SSSR. Panel E of Table 2 and Fig. 1 indicate mean/median values of *ADA* and *LN_LEI* by province. Results clearly suggest that regions with strong legal protection exhibit a low level of earnings management.

Table 3 exhibits the correlation matrix among variables. We find that the correlations are relatively low, except for that of *NTSR* and *CONCENTRATION*. Therefore, we include *NTSR* and *CONCENTRATION* separately as the independent variable in the following regression analysis to avoid potential multi-collinearity problems. Surprisingly, the correlation coefficient between *LN_LEI* and *ADA* is significantly positive (although the size of correlation is marginal). The firm-level earnings management is likely affected by firm-specific characteristics, which are correlated with legal environments. For example, Q is positively correlated with *ADA* as well as with *LN_LEI*. It is particularly important to control for those firm characteristics, as well as for time-invariant firm fixed effects, to accurately estimate the effect of legal environments on earnings management. Besides, untabulated results show that the correlation coefficient between *LN_LEI* and *ADA* is negative (although insignificant) for the pre- and during-SSSR periods; whereas, it is positive for the post-NAS period. The relation between legal environment and earnings management is likely to depend on the period and we should separately investigate the relation across sub-periods.

[7] The Guidance for Establishing Independent Directors System for Listed Companies, issued by the CSRC in 2001, required Chinese listed companies to gradually establish an independent directors system and to make qualified independent directors account for at least one-third of board members.

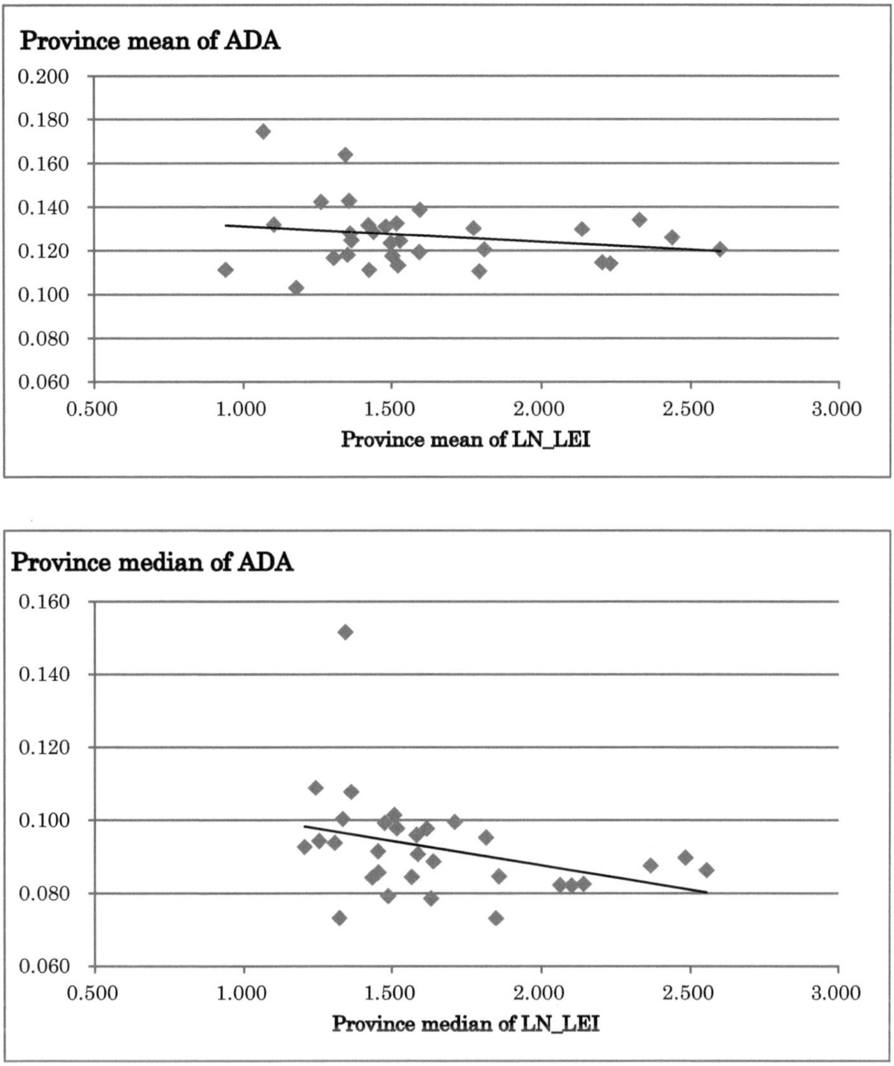

Fig. 1 *ADA* and *LN_LEI* by province. Notes: The above figure indicates the province mean of *ADA* (Y-axis) and the province mean of *LN_LEI* (X-axis). The bottom figure shows the province median of *ADA* (Y-axis) and the province median of *LN_LEI* (X-axis)

5 Regression Results

To test the notion that legal protection affects corporate earnings management, we execute regression analyses of *ADA*. The natural logarithm of the legal environment index (*LN_LEI*) is employed as a key independent variable. We estimate the following Eq. 3 by firm-fixed effects models, since unobserved, time-invariant

Table 3 Correlation matrix

	ADA	*LN_LEI*	*NTSR*	*CONCENT-RATION*	*BOARD-SIZE*	*BINDEPEN-DENCE*	*PDIREC_SOWN*	*D_DUAL*	*SUPER-SIZE*	*PSUPER_SOWN*	*SIZE*	*ROA*	*LEV*	*Q*
ADA	1.000													
LN_LEI	0.060***	1.000												
NTSR	−0.040***	−0.297***	1.000											
CONCENT-RATION	−0.026***	−0.087***	0.466***	1.000										
BOARDSIZE	−0.054***	−0.019*	0.048***	0.004	1.000									
BINDEPEN-DENCE	0.061***	0.302***	−0.269***	−0.131***	−0.085***	1.000								
PDIREC_SOWN	−0.111***	−0.057***	0.025***	0.052***	−0.005	−0.248***	1.000							
D_DUAL	0.021**	0.009	−0.013	−0.060***	−0.059***	−0.013	0.007	1.000						
SUPERSIZE	−0.052***	−0.104***	0.043***	0.071***	0.325***	−0.086***	0.016*	−0.052***	1.000					
PSUPER_SOWN	−0.081***	−0.042***	0.023**	0.024**	0.009	−0.146***	0.650***	−0.009	−0.003	1.000				
SIZE	−0.043***	0.195***	−0.119***	0.202***	0.217***	0.120***	0.114***	−0.077***	0.163***	0.101***	1.000			
ROA	−0.093***	0.077***	0.014	0.147***	0.055***	0.021**	0.064***	−0.022**	0.039***	0.033***	0.259***	1.000		
LEV	0.028***	0.029***	−0.044***	−0.051***	0.023**	0.050***	−0.061***	−0.004	0.008	−0.026***	0.150***	−0.138***	1.000	
Q	0.192***	0.064***	−0.049***	−0.068***	−0.119***	−0.091***	−0.087***	0.049***	−0.064***	−0.095***	−0.382***	−0.012	−0.159***	1.000

Notes: *, ** and *** indicate significance at the 10 %, 5 % and 1 % levels, respectively. See Table 1 for the definition of variables

firm characteristics (e.g., growth opportunities, market power, corporate culture and so on) potentially affect earnings management.[8] This is especially important in emerging markets like China, in which some companies are likely to have strong incentives of private benefits extraction and earnings management.

$$ADA_{i,t} = \beta_0 + \beta_1 LN\_LEI_{p,t} + \sum_{k=2} \beta_k Control_{k,i,t} + \varepsilon_{i,t} \quad (3)$$

where p denotes the province in which the firm i is located. $Control_k$ denotes a set of control variables.

Table 4 presents the regression results. We implement regressions separately for the three sub-periods, since we estimate *ADA* separately for these periods. The firm-fixed effects model results engender a negative and significant coefficient on *LN_LEI* (Models (1) and (2)). It suggests that firms tend to manage earnings less in regions with strong legal protection before 2005 (before the implementation of SSSR). The result is consistent with the conventional wisdom that a protective legal environment decreases earnings management. Although we find a positive correlation between *ADA* and *LN_LEI* in Table 3, the result implies that better legal environments are associated with smaller earnings management during the pre-SSSR period once we controlled for various firm characteristics. Differently from previous studies, Model (1) engenders an insignificant coefficient on *NTSR*. This is probably because *NTSR* lacks a wide variance within a single company and its effect is included in the firm-fixed effects. Indeed, *NTSR* has a positive and significant coefficient when we execute OLS estimations. *CONCENTRATION* also has an insignificant coefficient, probably for the same reason.

Models (3) and (4) suggest that during the SSSR (from 2005 to 2006), the relationship between legal protection and earnings management becomes insignificant. During this period, *NTSR* has a relatively wide variation, even within a single company, and Model (3) carries a positive and significant coefficient on *NTSR*. This result, which is consistent with the findings of Firth et al. (2007) and Zhang et al. (2013), provides support for the suggestion that the existence of NTS engenders expropriation problems and gives insiders incentives for earnings management to conceal the evidence. Similarly, *CONCENTRATION* has a positive and significant coefficient during the SSSR. A potential interpretation of the insignificant coefficient on *LN_LEI* during the SSSR period is that the NTS (ownership concentration) effect clouds out the effect of legal protection.

Models (5) and (6) (regression for the post-NAS period) also engender an insignificant coefficient on *LN_LEI*. Zhang et al. (2013) show evidence that the introduction of IFRS-convergent NAS is likely to increase managerial discretion on financial reporting. Breeden (1994) suggests that the flexibility inherent in principle-based standards (such as IFRS) is likely to entitle managers more

[8] The Hausman test results (unreported) suggest adoption of a fixed-effects model rather than a random-effects model.

Table 4 Regression results of the level of earnings management: Use *LN_LEI* as a legal protection variable

	[2001, 2004]				[2005, 2006]				[2007, 2009]			
	(1)		(2)		(3)		(4)		(5)		(6)	
	Coefficient	t-statistics	Coefficient	t-statistics	Coefficient	t-statistics	Coefficient	t-statistics	Coefficient	t-statistics	Coefficient	t-statistics
LN_LEI	−0.054**	−2.42	−0.054**	−2.41	0.002	0.05	−0.011	−0.27	0.010	0.51	0.023	1.29
NTSR	0.002	0.04			0.104***	2.83			−0.015	−0.88		
CONCENTRATION			0.004	0.09			0.097**	2.15			0.105	1.40
BOARDSIZE	0.002	0.16	0.002	0.16	−0.032	−1.28	−0.026	−1.04	0.009	0.46	0.009	0.43
BINDEPENDENCE	−0.005	−0.24	−0.005	−0.24	−0.034	−0.39	−0.038	−0.44	−0.036	−0.77	−0.034	−0.72
PDIREC_SOWN	−0.012	−0.66	−0.012	−0.66	−0.072	−1.51	−0.072	−1.52	−0.045	−0.97	−0.043	−0.92
D_DUAL	−0.002	−0.29	−0.002	−0.29	0.007	0.56	0.006	0.53	0.023*	1.88	0.023*	1.83
SUPERSIZE	−0.012	−0.77	−0.012	−0.77	−0.004	−0.15	−0.003	−0.10	−0.021	−1.00	−0.021	−1.01
PSUPER_SOWN	0.006	0.44	0.006	0.43	0.026	0.89	0.031	1.09	−0.030	−1.19	−0.031	−1.28
SIZE	0.033***	2.66	0.033***	2.71	0.053**	2.45	0.050**	2.30	0.071***	5.06	0.066***	4.73
ROA	−0.155***	−3.88	−0.155***	−3.88	−0.060	−1.20	−0.062	−1.23	0.008	0.18	0.003	0.07
LEV	−0.001	−0.37	−0.001	−0.37	−0.005*	−1.97	−0.005*	−1.96	−0.004	−1.17	−0.003	−1.09
Q	0.002	0.54	0.002	0.54	0.021***	3.02	0.020***	2.94	0.008***	3.77	0.008***	3.82
_cons	−0.486*	−1.80	−0.485*	−1.90	−1.020**	−2.21	−0.913**	−1.99	−1.389***	−4.57	−1.349***	−4.56
R^2	0.016		0.016		0.047		0.045		0.030		0.031	
N	4,251		4,251		2,518		2,518		3,731		3,731	

Notes: This table presents the regression results of *ADA*. We use firm-fixed effects models for estimation. Models (1) and (2) present the regression results for the period before 2005 (before the SSSR). Models (3) and (4) show regression results for the period between 2005 and 2006 (during the SSSR). Models (5) and (6) exhibit regression results for 2007 and after (post-NAS). *, ** and *** indicate significance at the 10 %, 5 % and 1 % levels, respectively. See Table 1 for the definition of variables.

opportunities to engage in earnings management. For instance, traditional Chinese accounting standards have allowed firms to measure trading securities at lower historical costs or market values. However, fair-value accounting in China's NAS requires firms to reflect the change in those securities' values in current earnings. He et al. (2012) suggest that this considerable change will give managers the opportunity to manipulate earnings by selling available-for-sale securities. It is likely that some companies take advantage of the increased opportunities of earnings management (this effect may be incorporated in the firm-fixed effects). The IFRS effect probably clouds out the effect of legal protection. Overall, the results suggest that the effect of legal protection on earnings management is pronounced only when there are no drastic changes in corporate governance structure and accounting standards. *NTSR* also has an insignificant coefficient after the NAS introduction, probably because many sample companies completed SSSR and the within-firm variance of NTS becomes small; thus, the NTS effect is likely incorporated in the firm-fixed effects.

With respect to other variables, firm size (*SIZE*) has a positive impact on earnings management for all the sub-periods. This result is consistent with the argument of Watts and Zimmerman (1978) that large companies are more likely to manage (decrease) earnings in order to reduce the possibility of social scrutiny and political intervention. Growing companies with higher Tobin's Q (*Q*) manage earnings more except for during the pre-SSSR period. This result is consistent with the findings of Beaver et al. (1970) and Minton and Schrand (1999). Growing firms have an incentive to manage earnings to meet requirements on earnings for issuance of new securities. These firms also attempt to reduce costs of capital by smoothing their income.

In Sect. 2, we present two alternative stories to show the prediction that legal protection alleviates earnings management. One story pays attention to minority investor protection and the other focuses on technology spillover. To investigate the mechanisms through which legal protection decreases earnings management, we replicate the analyses by replacing *LN_LEI* with *LN_LEI_1* through *LN_LEI_4*. Among the four subcomponents, *LEI_1* represents relatively general legal environments (e.g., number of lawyers and accountants). Since minority investors need well-established general legal environments to sue corporate insiders, we presume that *LEI_1* is relatively related to minority investor protection. On the other hand, *LEI_3* represents protection of intellectual property rights, and therefore, it is closely related to earnings management that aims to prevent technology spillover. To a certain degree, *LEI_2* is also related to this type of earnings management, since it represents the legal protection of company rights, although it does not focus on intellectual property rights. Finally, *LEI_4* (legal protection of consumers' rights) is not related to either of the two stories. Here, we devote our focus to the first sub-period (before 2005) for which we have found a significant relationship between legal protection and earnings management. Specifically, we estimate the following Eqs. 4, 5, 6, and 7 by firm-fixed effect models.

$$ADA_{i,t} = \beta_0 + \beta_1 LN\_LEI\_1_{p,t} + \sum_{k=2} \beta_k Control_{k,i,t} + \varepsilon_{i,t} \quad (4)$$

$$ADA_{i,t} = \beta_0 + \beta_1 LN\_LEI\_2_{p,t} + \sum_{k=2} \beta_k Control_{k,i,t} + \varepsilon_{i,t} \quad (5)$$

$$ADA_{i,t} = \beta_0 + \beta_1 LN\_LEI\_3_{p,t} + \sum_{k=2} \beta_k Control_{k,i,t} + \varepsilon_{i,t} \quad (6)$$

$$ADA_{i,t} = \beta_0 + \beta_1 LN\_LEI\_4_{p,t} + \sum_{k=2} \beta_k Control_{k,i,t} + \varepsilon_{i,t} \quad (7)$$

Results are reported in Table 5. We find that *LN_LEI_3* has a negative and significant coefficient. Consistent with Fan et al.'s (2013) finding, this result suggests that the protection of intellectual property rights is the most influential legal factor for corporate earnings management. Firms are likely to manage earnings (opacity) if they feel that their technology is likely spilled over. This is the case for firms located in regions with poor legal protection of intellectual property rights. Noticeably, we show this evidence after controlling for unobserved time-invariant regional and company characteristics. *LN_LEI_1* has an insignificant coefficient, which does not support the story that firms manage earnings to conceal evidence of expropriation of minority shareholders. However, we cannot reject this story, since *LEI_1* is not a direct measure of minority investor protection.

In unreported analyses, we replicate the analyses by using the non-logged value of *LEI*. This analysis engenders a negative and significant coefficient on *LEI_2* and the coefficient of *LEI_3* becomes insignificant. We argue that this result is also consistent with the technology spillover story, since *LEI_2* is likely to include protection of company rights on intellectual property. We also replicate the analyses of Table 5 for the second and third sub-periods. Again, the analyses carry an insignificant coefficient on all the indices. As mentioned, important institutional changes are likely to have considerable impacts on earnings management during these sub-periods, and therefore, earnings management that aims to prevent technology spillover becomes less evident. Finally, we replicate the analyses by using OLS and province-fixed effects models. These estimations engender an insignificant coefficient on all the legal environment indices. As mentioned, different companies have different incentives of earnings management. We interpret the result that unobserved, time-invariant characteristics (e.g., corporate culture) representing the firm's unique incentive of earnings management are highly associated with the level of earnings management. The effect of legal protection on earnings management becomes evident only after controlling for these firm-fixed effects.

Table 5 Regression results of the level of earnings management: Use *LN_LEI_1* to *LN_LEI_4* as legal protection variables

	(1)		(2)		(3)		(4)		(5)		(6)		(7)		(8)	
	Coefficient	*t-stat*	Coefficient	*t-stat*	Coefficient	*t-stat*	Coefficient	*t-stat*	Coefficient	*t-stat*	Coefficient	*t-stat*	Coefficient	*t-stat*	Coefficient	*t-stat*
LN_LEI_1	−0.014	−0.90	−0.014	−0.92												
LN_LEI_2					−0.007	−0.86	−0.007	−0.85								
LN_LEI_3									−0.015*	−1.78	−0.014*	−1.77				
LN_LEI_4													−0.019	−1.48	−0.019	−1.47
NTSR	0.013	0.21			0.012	0.20			0.009	0.15			0.010	0.17		
CONCENTRATION			0.014	0.32			0.011	0.25			0.007	0.16			0.008	0.20
BOARDSIZE	0.002	0.21	0.003	0.23	0.002	0.18	0.002	0.19	0.003	0.22	0.003	0.23	0.002	0.13	0.002	0.14
BINDEPENDENCE	−0.026	−1.37	−0.026	−1.36	−0.026	−1.34	−0.026	−1.34	−0.009	−0.47	−0.009	−0.47	−0.019	−0.98	−0.019	−0.98
PDIREC_SOWN	−0.007	−0.40	−0.008	−0.41	−0.008	−0.43	−0.008	−0.43	−0.010	−0.52	−0.010	−0.53	−0.010	−0.57	−0.010	−0.57
D_DUAL	−0.002	−0.22	−0.002	−0.22	−0.002	−0.22	−0.002	−0.21	−0.002	−0.23	−0.002	−0.23	−0.002	−0.22	−0.002	−0.21
SUPERSIZE	−0.012	−0.78	−0.012	−0.78	−0.012	−0.80	−0.012	−0.81	−0.012	−0.79	−0.012	−0.79	−0.012	−0.81	−0.012	−0.81
PSUPER_SOWN	0.007	0.51	0.006	0.49	0.006	0.49	0.006	0.48	0.006	0.45	0.006	0.44	0.007	0.55	0.007	0.54
SIZE	0.031**	2.52	0.031**	2.56	0.032**	2.59	0.032***	2.63	0.033***	2.65	0.033***	2.69	0.033***	2.61	0.032***	2.65
ROA	−0.150***	−3.80	−0.150***	−3.81	−0.150***	−3.80	−0.150***	−3.80	−0.151***	−3.82	−0.151***	−3.83	−0.153***	−3.84	−0.153***	−3.84
LEV	−0.001	−0.39	−0.001	−0.39	−0.001	−0.40	−0.001	−0.41	−0.001	−0.40	−0.001	−0.40	−0.001	−0.37	−0.001	−0.37
Q	0.004	1.09	0.003	1.08	0.003	1.07	0.003	1.06	0.002	0.73	0.002	0.73	0.003	0.86	0.003	0.85
_cons	−0.529*	−1.92	−0.520**	−2.00	−0.550**	−2.01	−0.541**	−2.09	−0.556**	−2.04	−0.549**	−2.13	−0.527*	−1.95	−0.519**	−2.03
R^2	0.014		0.014		0.014		0.014		0.015		0.015		0.015		0.015	
N	4,251		4,251		4,251		4,251		4,251		4,251		4,251		4,251	

Notes: This table presents the regression results of *ADA* for the period before 2005. In this table, we employ one of the four subcomponents of *LEI* instead of *LEI*. We use firm-fixed effects models for estimation. *, ** and *** indicate significance at the 10 %, 5 % and 1 % levels, respectively. See Table 1 for the definition of variables

6 Conclusions

We investigate the effect of regional legal protection on earnings management by using data from a single country (China). Single country data have relatively small variations in culture and other aspects, and therefore, are advantageous in avoiding non-legal factors contaminating the relationship between legal protection and earnings management. China offers us an appropriate research setting to address the issue, since China exhibits great heterogeneity in legal infrastructure across provinces (Qian and Weingast 1997; Jin et al. 2005) and improves its legal environments over time (MacNeil 2002). Fan and Wang (2011) present China's provincial legal environment index, which enables implementation of single country analyses of the relationship between legal protection and earnings management. Importantly, Fan and Wang's index is time-variant and enables the use of firm-fixed effects models that can control for unobserved, time-invariant region- and firm-characteristics.

Although we do not find evidence that strong regional legal protection decreases earnings management for the whole sample period, there is a negative and significant relationship between regional legal protection and earnings management before the SSSR. The result is consistent with the conventional wisdom that a protective legal environment decreases corporate earnings management. Further analyses suggest that the effect of legal protection on earnings management before the SSSR is attributable to the protection of intellectual property rights. Consistent with Fan et al.'s (2013) finding, this result suggests that legal protection of intellectual property rights mitigates earnings management that aims to prevent technology spillovers. The presented analyses make contribution to the literature by showing this evidence with controlling for unobserved, time-invariant region- and firm-characteristics.

The relationship between legal protection and earnings management becomes insignificant during the SSSR. During this period, earnings management is significantly related to the non-tradable share ratio and ownership concentration. This result suggests that changing insiders' incentives clouds out the effect of the legal environment. Similarly, legal protection does not have a significant impact on earnings management after the introduction of IFRS-convergent NAS. These results imply that legal protection does not have a visible effect on earnings management when corporate governance and accounting standards are in the transition process.

Acknowledgements We would like to thank the financial support provided by the JSPS KAKENHI Grant Number 23330107.

References

Ahmed, K., Hossain, M., & Adams, M. (2006). The effects of board composition and board size on the informativeness of annual accounting earnings. *Corporate Governance: An International Review, 14*, 418–431.

Atiase, R. (1985). Predisclosure information, firm capitalization, and security price behavior around earnings announcements. *Journal of Accounting Research, 23*, 21–36.

Beasley, M. (1996). An empirical analysis between the board of director composition and financial statement fraud. *The Accounting Review, 71*, 443–466.

Beaver, W., Kettler, P., & Scholes, M. (1970). The association between market determined and accounting determined risk measures. *The Accounting Review, 45*, 654–682.

Breeden, R. (1994). Foreign companies and U.S. markets in a time of economic transformation. *Fordham International Law Journal, 17*, S77–S96.

Burgstahler, D. C., Hail, L., & Leuz, C. (2006). The importance of reporting incentives: Earnings management in European private and public firms. *The Accounting Review, 81*, 983–1016.

Butler, M., Leone, A. J., & Willenborg, M. (2004). An empirical analysis of auditor reporting and its association with abnormal accruals. *Journal of Accounting and Economics, 37*, 139–165.

Chen, G. M., Firth, M., Gao, D. N., & Rui, O. M. (2006). Ownership structure, corporate governance, and fraud: Evidence from China. *Journal of Corporate Finance, 12*, 424–448.

Chen, G. M., Firth, M., & Xu, L. P. (2009). Does the type of ownership control matter? Evidence from China's listed companies. *Journal of Banking and Finance, 33*, 171–181.

Claessens, S., Djankov, S., & Lang, L. H. P. (2000). The separation of ownership and control in East Asian corporations. *Journal of Financial Economics, 58*, 81–112.

Claessens, S., Djankov, S., Fan, J., & Lang, L. (2002). Disentangling the incentive and entrenchment effects of large shareholdings. *Journal of Finance, 57*, 2741–2772.

Claessens, S., Djankov, S., & Klapper, L. (2003). Resolution of corporate distress in East Asia. *Journal of Empirical Finance, 10*, 199–216.

Dechow, P. M., Sloan, R. G., & Sweeney, A. P. (1995). Detecting earnings management. *The Accounting Review, 70*, 193–225.

Dechow, P. M., Sloan, R. G., & Sweeney, A. P. (1996). Causes and consequences of earnings manipulation: An analysis of firms subject to enforcement actions by the SEC. *Contemporary Accounting Research, 13*, 1–36.

Dechow, P. M., Ge, W. L., & Schrand, C. (2010). Understanding earnings quality: A review of the proxies, their determinants and their consequences. *Journal of Accounting and Economics, 50*, 344–401.

Dhaliwal, D., Lee, K., & Fargher, N. (1991). The association between unexpected earnings and abnormal security returns in the presence of financial leverage. *Contemporary Accounting Research, 8*, 20–41.

Dimitropoulos, P. E., & Asteriou, D. (2010). The effect of board composition on the informativeness and quality of annual earnings: Empirical evidence from Greece. *Research in International Business and Finance, 24*, 190–205.

Doidge, C., Karolyi, A., & Stulz, R. (2004). Why are foreign firms listed in the US worth more? *Journal of Financial Economics, 71*, 205–238.

Dyck, A., & Zingales, L. (2004). Private benefits of control: An international comparison. *Journal of Finance, 59*, 537–599.

Fan, G., & Wang, X. L. (2011). *NERI index of marketization of China's provinces*. Beijing: Economic Science Press (In Chinese).

Fan, J. P. H., & Wong, T. J. (2002). Corporate ownership structure and the informativeness of accounting earnings in East Asia. *Journal of Accounting and Economics, 33*, 401–425.

Fan, J. P. H., Gillan, S. L., & Yu, X. (2013). Property rights, R&D spillovers, and corporate accounting transparency in China. *Emerging Markets Review, 15*, 34–56.

Firth, M., Fung, P. M. Y., & Rui, O. M. (2007). Ownership, two-tier board structure, and the informativeness of earnings: Evidence from China. *Journal of Accounting and Public Policy, 26*, 463–496.

Firth, M., Lin, C., Liu, P., & Wong, S. M. L. (2009). Inside the black box: Bank credit allocation in China's private sector. *Journal of Banking and Finance, 33*, 1144–1155.

Forker, J. J. (1992). Corporate governance and disclosure quality. *Accounting and Business Research, 22*, 111–124.

Freeman, R. (1987). The association between accounting earnings and security returns for large and small firms. *Journal of Accounting and Economics, 9*, 195–228.

Haw, I., Hu, B., Hwang, L., & Wu, W. (2004). Ultimate ownership, income management, and legal and extra-legal institutions. *Journal of Accounting Research, 42*, 423–462.

He, X. J., Wong, T. J., & Young, D. Q. (2012). Challenges for implementation of fair value accounting in emerging markets: Evidence from China. *Contemporary Accounting Research, 29*, 538–562.

Holderness, C. G. (2008). *Do differences in legal protections explain differences in ownership concentration?* Working Paper, Boston College.

Holland, K., & Jackson, R. H. G. (2004). Earnings management and deferred tax. *Accounting and Business Research, 34*, 101–123.

Jensen, M. C. (1993). The modern industrial revolution, exit, and the failure of internal control systems. *Journal of Finance, 48*, 830–881.

Jiang, H. Y., & Habib, A. (2012). Split-share reform and earnings management: Evidence from China. *Advances in Accounting, incorporating Advances in International Accounting, 28*, 120–127.

Jin, H., Qian, Y., & Weingast, B. (2005). Regional decentralization and fiscal incentives: Federalism, Chinese style. *Journal of Public Economics, 89*, 1719–1742.

Johnson, S., La Porta, R., Lopez-De-Salinas, F., & Shleifer, A. (2000). Tunneling. *American Economic Review, 90*, 22–27.

Kali, R. (1999). Endogenous business networks. *Journal of Law, Economics, and Organization, 15*, 615–636.

Klein, A. (2002). Audit committee, board of director characteristics, and earnings management. *Journal of Accounting and Economics, 33*, 375–400.

Kothari, S. P., Leone, A. J., & Wasley, C. E. (2005). Performance matched discretionary accrual measures. *Journal of Accounting and Economics, 39*, 163–197.

La Porta, R., Lopez-de-Silanes, F., Shleifer, A., & Vishny, R. W. (1998). Law and finance. *Journal of Political Economy, 106*, 1113–1155.

La Porta, R., Lopez-de-Silanes, F., & Shleifer, A. (1999). Corporate ownership around the world. *Journal of Finance, 54*, 471–518.

La Porta, R., Lopez-de-Silanes, F., Shleifer, A., & Vishny, R. W. (2000). Agency problems and dividend policies around the world. *Journal of Finance, 55*, 1–33.

Lang, M., Raedy, J. S., & Wilson, W. (2006). Earnings management and cross listing: Are reconciled earnings comparable to US earnings? *Journal of Accounting and Economics, 42*, 255–283.

Leuz, C., Nanda, D., & Wysocki, P. D. (2003). Earnings management and investor protection: An international comparison. *Journal of Financial Economics, 69*, 505–527.

Liu, Q., & Lu, Z. (2007). Corporate governance and earnings management in the Chinese listed companies: A tunneling perspective. *Journal of Corporate Finance, 13*, 881–906.

Liu, C. H., Yao, L. J., Hu, N., & Liu, L. (2011). The impact of IFRS on accounting quality in a regulated market: An empirical study of China. *Journal of Accounting, Auditing and Finance, 26*, 659–676.

Lo, A. W. Y., Wong, R. M. K., & Firth, M. (2010). Can corporate governance deter management from manipulating earnings? Evidence from related-party sales transactions in China. *Journal of Corporate Finance, 16*, 225–235.

MacNeil, I. (2002). Adaptation and convergence in corporate governance: The case of Chinese listed companies. *Journal of Corporate Law Studies, 2*, 289–344.
Minton, B., & Schrand, C. (1999). The impact of cash flow volatility on discretionary investment and the costs of debt and equity financing. *Journal of Financial Economics, 54*, 423–460.
Mintz, S. M. (2005). Corporate governance in an international context: Legal systems, financing patterns, and cultural variables. *Corporate Governance: An International Review, 13*, 582–597.
Park, Y. W., & Shin, H. H. (2004). Board composition and earnings management in Canada. *Journal of Corporate Finance, 10*, 431–457.
Peasnell, K., Pope, P., & Young, S. (2005). Board monitoring and earnings management: Do outside directors influence abnormal accruals. *Journal of Business Finance and Accounting, 32*, 1311–1346.
Qian, Y., & Weingast, B. (1997). Federalism as a commitment to preserving market incentives. *Journal of Economic Perspectives, 11*, 83–92.
Raheja, C. (2005). Determinants of board size and composition: A theory of corporate boards. *Journal of Financial and Quantitative Analysis, 40*, 283–306.
Shen, C. H., & Chih, H. L. (2005). Investor protection, prospect theory, and earnings management: An international comparison of the banking industry. *Journal of Banking and Finance, 29*, 2675–2697.
Shleifer, A., & Vishny, R. W. (1997). A survey of corporate governance. *Journal of Finance, 52*, 737–775.
Vafeas, N. (2000). Board structure and the informativeness of earnings. *Journal of Accounting and Public Policy, 19*, 139–160.
Wang, H. C., Liu, T. L., & Lu, C. (2007). Corporate governance and earnings quality: Evidence from China. *China Soft Science, 11*, 122–128 (In Chinese).
Watts, R. L., & Zimmerman, J. L. (1978). Towards a positive theory of the determination of accounting standards. *The Accounting Review, 53*, 112–134.
Watts, R. L., & Zimmerman, J. L. (1990). Positive accounting theory: A ten year perspective. *The Accounting Review, 56*, 131–156.
Wu, S. N., Xu, N. H., & Yuan, Q. B. (2009). State control, legal investor protection, and ownership concentration: Evidence from China. *Corporate Governance: An International Review, 17*, 176–192.
Xie, B., Davidson, W. N., & DaDalt, P. J. (2003). Earnings management and corporate governance: The role of the board and the audit committee. *Journal of Corporate Finance, 9*, 295–316.
Zhang, Y., Uchida, K., & Bu, H. (2013). How do accounting standards and insiders' incentives affect earnings management? Evidence from China. *Emerging Markets Review, 16*, 78–99.
Zingales, L. (1994). The value of the voting right: A study of the Milan stock exchange experience. *Review of Financial Studies, 7*, 125–148.

Corporate Form, Institutional Complementarity, and Organizational Behavior: Open versus Closed Joint-Stock Companies in Russia

Ichiro Iwasaki

Abstract The vast majority of Russian corporations are still compelled to become closed joint-stock companies that lack a modern fundraising mechanism in order to attract capital from a wide range of private investors. This is due to factors such as significant insider ownership, a strong orientation among managers toward closed organizations, slumping needs for corporate finance, and underdeveloped local financial institutions. The impact of ownership structure on the choice of corporate form exists, even if we assume that the two elements are determined endogenously. Under these circumstances, however, a significant number of closed companies attempt to develop more open internal organizational structures that are virtually the same as those of open companies. Nonetheless, an institutional coupling of a closed corporate form and an open internal organizational structure is far from effective in resolving the serious in-house problems facing Russian firms, such as the prevention of infighting among executives and shareholders and the implementation of discipline among top management.

1 Introduction

One of the most distinguishing features of the Russian corporate sector is the preponderance of closed joint-stock companies (JSCs) over open JSCs. According to unpublished official statistics, as of January 1, 2005, there were only 58,400 open JSCs registered in Russia, compared with as many as 389,200 closed JSCs. Regarding large-scale companies that require raising funds from outside sources, the number of open JSCs exceeds that of closed JSCs, with the latter number still being fairly significant. In fact, a survey conducted in 2003 by the Federal State Statistics Service found that, of the 32,266 JSCs surveyed, excluding micro- and

I. Iwasaki (✉)
Institute of Economic Research, Hitotsubashi University, Tokyo, Japan
e-mail: iiwasaki@ier.hit-u.ac.jp

S. Boubaker and D.K. Nguyen (eds.), *Corporate Governance in Emerging Markets*, CSR, Sustainability, Ethics & Governance, DOI 10.1007/978-3-642-44955-0_7,

small enterprises, 19,407 were open companies, and the remaining 12,859 were closed ones (Federal State Statistical Service 2004). In other words, 4 of every 10 medium-sized and large Russian corporations were operating under a governance mechanism that put rigorous restrictions on the liquidity of their own shares.

In Russia, both open and closed JSCs are statutory legal forms of incorporation, as defined in the Federal Law on Joint-Stock Companies (hereinafter, the Law on JSCs). As we will later detail, these two corporate forms refer to the legal names of the two types of JSCs that are decisively different from each other in terms of share transferability to a third party. All JSCs established in Russia must choose either of the two company types as their statutory organizational form. There are clear distinctions between closed and open JSCs in terms of not only the restrictions on the number of shareholders but also the modes of securities issuance, the required levels of minimum capital, and disclosure obligations. From this viewpoint, Russia has an extremely unique legal framework in comparison with the developed economies. Moreover, as reported above, even though almost all of the Russian leading companies are former state-owned firms, about 40 % of them are still operated as closed JSCs after more than 10 years of mass privatization. This highlights the sharp contrast with the situation of closed corporations in the United Kingdom and the United States, most of which are family-run or privately held companies.

Inspired by the economic theory on internal organization that has been developed from suggestions made by Coase (1937), a large number of empirical studies have been conducted with regard to the determinants of organizational choice and the relationship between organizational form and behavior, including corporate performance. Surprisingly, however, except for a valuable case study by Karpoff and Rice (1989), there is little empirical work investigating organizational choices by JSCs and their possible impacts on corporate governance and firm performance. Thus, the corporate forms of Russian JSCs are an important research subject to be explored from the viewpoint of the study of law and economics as well as organizational economics.

Furthermore, this topic is of great significance in understanding the Russian economic system. It is quite possible that the high degree of orientation toward closed organization in the Russian business sector is deeply rooted in its poor corporate governance practices and investment behavior, which remains inactive regardless of significant economic recovery in recent years. In other words, it is highly likely that there are severe agency problems within these Russian closed companies that prevent the enhancement of their corporate value. In order to redress this situation, it is critical to empirically examine what factors drive many Russian firms to choose to become closed companies and how much harm is done to corporate management and maximization of shareholder wealth by this choice. Therefore, particular attention should also be given to research on the legal forms of incorporation of JSCs in the context of Russian economic studies.

In this chapter, we deal with this significant but yet-to-be explored issue on the basis of a large-scale enterprise survey. The survey was conducted in 2005 within the framework of a Japan-Russia joint research project. It covers 822 manufacturing and communications firms located throughout the Russian Federation. All samples were JSCs, and the average number of workers per company was 1,884 (standard deviation: 5,570; median: 465). Regarding the regional and sectoral composition of the surveyed firms, they formed a representative sample of large and medium-sized Russian firms. As for their corporate form, open and closed JSCs account for 67.3 % (553 firms) and 32.7 % (269 firms) of the 822 surveyed firms, respectively, and this composition corresponds closely to the results of the 2003 survey by the Russian statistical office mentioned above.[1]

Relying upon the results of the joint survey, we first examine a variety of factors as to why Russian firms elect to become closed JSCs. In the latter part of this chapter, we examine the relationship between the corporate forms and the internal organizational structures in addition to the impact of these institutional couplings on organizational behavior, including firm performance. Through these research steps, we intend to provide new perspectives on the relationship between corporate forms and organizational behavior.

The remainder of the chapter is organized as follows: Section 2 looks into the legal framework regulating the corporate forms of Russian JSCs as well as its significance in the context of corporate management. Section 3 examines the determinants of corporate form choice between open and closed JSCs. Section 4 focuses on the institutional complementarity of corporate forms and internal organizational structures. Section 5 empirically assesses the impact of the institutional equilibrium of a corporate organization on corporate governance and firm performance. Section 6 concludes.

2 Corporate Forms of Joint-Stock Companies in Russia: Institutional Framework and Its Significance for Company Management

As reported in the Introduction, an investor who intends to establish a joint-stock company in Russia must choose to make it either an open JSC or a closed JSC as required by the provisions of Russian corporate law,[2] which provides for statutory

[1] The closed JSCs covered by the joint survey include four workers' joint-stock companies (people's enterprises). Because the workers' JSCs are run under a system that is substantially different from that of standard closed JSCs (Iwasaki 2007a), we have excluded all workers' JSCs from the observations when they are inappropriate to include in empirical analysis. See Dolgopyatova et al. (2009, Appendix) for more detailed information on the joint survey. Other research outcomes based on the same dataset used in this chapter include: Abe and Iwasaki (2010) and Iwasaki (2008, 2011, 2013a, b).

[2] These provisions refer to the Civil Code, Part I, Chap. 4, Articles 96 to 104, and to the Law on JSCs. This section was written taking into account the laws and regulations that were effective in Russia during the period in which the enterprise survey was conducted and which was used as the base material for this empirical study.

distinctions between these two types of corporate forms in the following six areas: (a) share transferability, (b) method for issuing securities, (c) required minimum capitalization, (d) number of shareholders, (e) government funding, and (f) disclosure obligations (Table 1).

First, a shareholder of an open JSC may freely transfer his/her shares to any third party other than another shareholder of the company or the company itself; on the other hand, a shareholder of a closed JSC must sell his/her shares first to another shareholder of the company or the company itself due to the right of preferential purchase. Specifically, a shareholder of a closed JSC who intends to transfer his/her shares to a third party must, at his/her own expense, notify all other shareholders of the company and its executives in writing concerning the selling price of the shares by the selling shareholder as well as other terms and conditions included in an agreement between the seller and the purchasing third party. This is done in order to confirm whether any of the other shareholders of the company or the company itself wishes to execute its right of preferential purchase. This obligation enables a closed JSC and its shareholders to detect in advance every action by any shareholder seeking to transfer his/her shares to a third party and to allow the other shareholders to effectively prevent a stock drain to outside parties by bearing the necessary expenses to purchase these shares.

Second, unlike open JSCs, whose shares issued at the time of formation may be allocated to the company founders and to the general public (i.e., establishment with outside offering), closed JSCs are only required to issue shares to their founders and to other investors specified in advance. Even after incorporation, closed JSCs are not allowed to offer new shares to the general public, although they may issue corporate bonds other than convertible bonds on the securities market as a means of raising funds from outside sources.

Third, the minimum capitalization (share capital) for open JSCs needs to be at least 1,000 times the statutory minimum wage at the time of their registration, while closed JSCs are required to secure only 100 times the statutory minimum wage. For example, the effective statutory minimum wage for the period from January to August 2005 was 720 rubles (about USD25) monthly.[3] Therefore, there is a difference of 648,000 rubles (about USD23,000) between these two legal forms of JSCs established during this period with respect to their minimum share capital as required by the Law on JSCs, not a trivial difference for small and venture businesses seeking incorporation.

Fourth, closed JSCs may not have more than 50 shareholders. If the number of shareholders exceeds this limit, they must reduce it to 50 or fewer, turn the firm into an open JSC, or dissolve within a period of one year. However, this regulation does not apply to closed companies established by the end of 1995, before the enforcement of the current Law on JSCs. A large number of closed JSCs still have 50 or more shareholders, because many of these companies are either former state-owned enterprises or ex-municipal companies that were privatized in the process of the

[3] Refer to Article 1 of the amended Federal Law on Minimum Wages of December 29, 2004.

Table 1 Differences in the legal framework between open and closed joint-stock companies in Russia

	Open JSC	Closed JSC
Share transferability	No restrictions are imposed on share transfers. No preferred purchase rights may be arranged for any shareholders, including the company, with regard to the transfer of shares to third parties (Art. 7(2)).	The company shareholders have the right to purchase the shares of other shareholders in preference to third parties. The company may only exercise such a preferred purchase right when no shareholder elects to do so (Art. 7(3)).
Share subscription	Open JSCs are incorporated by having all of their shares subscribed by their promoters or by having some of their shares subscribed by their promoters and the remaining shares subscribed by other investors (Art. 7(2)). After incorporation, they can make a public share placement without any restriction (Art. 39(1); Art. 39(2)).	Closed JSCs are incorporated only by having all of their shares subscribed by their promoters. All of their shares issued after incorporation must be offered only to their promoters or persons specified in advance (Art. 7(3); Art. 39(2)).
Issuance of company bonds	Open JSCs may issue any kind of bonds (including convertible bonds) to the public in accordance with the procedures set by law (Art. 39(2)).	Closed JSCs are prohibited from issuing convertible bonds to the public (Art. 39(2)).
Statutory minimum capitalization requirement	1,000 times the minimum statutory wage on the date of registration (Art. 26)	100 times the minimum statutory wage on the date of registration (Art. 26)
Number of shareholders	No upper limit is placed on the number of shareholders (Art. 7(2)).	The upper limit on the number of shareholders is 50 (Art. 7(3)). However, this limit does not apply to closed JSCs established by the end of 1995 (Art. 94(4)).
State involvement in investment	In principle, the state may not become the promoter of a joint-stock company (Art. 10(1)). However, state agencies may become the promoters of open JSCs in certain cases as provided for by law (Art. 7(4)).	Only former state-owned enterprises and other former municipal enterprises may become promoters of closed JSCs (Art. 7(4)).
Disclosure requirements	Open JSCs are required to disclose certain information as requested by the Law on JSCs and other statutes and by government agencies (Art. 92(1)).	Closed JSCs that issue bonds or securities at the same price and in the same manner as instructed by the Federal Financial Markets Service (FFMS) are required to disclose certain information in accordance with the rules adopted by the FFMS (Art. 92(2)).

Note: This table shows the differences between legal frameworks of open and closed joint-stock companies according to the Civil Code and the Federal Law on Joint-Stock Companies of the Russian Federation, which were effective in 2005.

mass-privatization policy in the early 1990s or affiliates of private firms and brand-new companies opened in those days.

Fifth, no state authority, including a local government, can be the founder of a JSC in principle. In addition, even when a JSC is established by a government or state organization using a company separation package in which the newly established joint company inherits the assets of the government or state organization, that newly established company must be an open JSC. However, this regulation does not apply to cases in which a corporation is established by a government or state agency as a result of its separation from a privatized firm. This is one of the reasons there are still many closed JSCs whose shares are held by the state.

Lastly, open JSCs are obliged to disclose information such as annual business reports, financial statements, asset securities reports, and other materials required by statute or requested by the Federal Financial Markets Service (FFMS) and other government authorities. On the other hand, closed JSCs are not subject to such disclosure requirements except in cases in which they issue bonds and other securities using the schemes and prices specified by financial authorities.

The results of the Japan-Russia joint enterprise survey, in which company executives were asked to explain how they perceived the significance of the aforesaid legal framework in the context of their corporate management as well as to indicate the most important reason for them to keep their company in the current corporate form, revealed that many of the respondents recognized that the choice between an open and a closed JSC had a considerable impact on their management strategies. Of 793 firms that provided valid responses to the survey, 602 (75.9 %) replied that their corporate form choice would or might affect their business development; this is far more than the 191 (24.1 %) who answered that there was no connection between these two factors. The difference between the group of open JSCs and the group of closed JSCs covered in the survey regarding the proportion of firms that confirmed a connection between their organizational choice and their business development is statistically significant at the 10 % level ($\chi^2 = 3.209, p = 0.073$), but in actuality, it was quite small (77.8 % vs. 72.0 %). Of the 602 firms that said their performance was influenced by their corporate form, 518 (86.0 %) perceived such an influence to be positive for their business growth, many more than the 84 firms (14.0 %) that regarded it as negative. The difference between the group of open JSCs and the group of closed JSCs regarding the number of firms that positively perceived such an influence on their performance was very small (85.7 % vs. 86.7 %) and not statistically significant ($\chi^2 = 0.098, p = 0.754$). Regardless of the difference in the corporate form of their companies, a great number of corporate executives see a close relationship between their organizational choice and business activities.

Table 2 summarizes the answers given by company managers to the question about the comparative advantages of each of the two corporate form options. Of the enterprises reporting that open JSCs were institutionally superior to closed JSCs, many of them answered that open JSCs were better than closed JSCs at building a reliable relationship with investors and partners (235 out of 753 firms) or at raising funds from outside financial sources (160 out of 753 firms). This number is greater

Table 2 Comparative advantages of open and closed companies over an alternative corporate form of joint-stock company

	All companies		Open JSCs		Closed JSCs	
	No. of affirmative respondents	Share (%)	No. of affirmative respondents	Share (%)	No. of affirmative respondents	Share (%)
(a) Advantages of open JSCs over closed JSCs[a]						
Company transparency can be emphasized to business partners and investors.	235	31.2	202	38.3	33	14.6
Corporate governance can be improved.	85	11.3	60	11.4	25	11.1
Better access to financial markets and increased ability to attract potential investors	160	21.2	97	18.4	63	27.9
Shareholders may sell stocks freely.	96	12.7	67	12.7	29	12.8
Others	2	0.3	2	0.4	0	0.0
There is no comparative advantage.	175	23.2	99	18.8	76	33.6
Total	753	100.0	527	100.0	226	100.0
(b) Advantages of closed JSCs over open JSCs[b]						
Managers can effectively control companies.	60	8.4	30	6.5	30	12.0
Very strict regulations imposed by the state on open joint-stock companies can be avoided.	131	18.3	92	19.8	39	15.6
The transfer of stock to outsiders can be prevented, and companies are protected from hostile takeover.	350	49.0	218	47.0	132	52.8
Even a small-scale enterprise could be set up as joint-stock company.	43	6.0	29	6.3	14	5.6
Others	0	0.0	0	0.0	0	0.0
There is no comparative advantage.	130	18.2	95	20.5	35	14.0
Total	714	100.0	464	100.0	250	100.0

Note: This table shows the results of the answers from company managers participating in the joint enterprise survey to a question about the comparative advantages of open and closed JSCs over an alternative corporate form. Closed JSCs include four workers' joint-stock companies (people's enterprises).

[a]Test for the equality of the composition of the responding firms by corporate form that gave a positive answer to each item: $\chi^2 = 51.079$ ($p = 0.000$).

[b]Test for the equality of the composition of the responding firms by corporate form that gave a positive answer to each item: $\chi^2 = 12.480$ ($p = 0.014$).

than the number of firms reporting that an organizational advantage of open JSCs is the flexibility of share transfers, which reflects their current focus (96 out of 753 firms). A substantial and statistically significant difference is evident between the open and closed JSCs in the breakdown of their answers to this question. Compared with the respondents of open JSCs, those of closed JSCs pay more attention to the fact that open JSCs enjoy good fundraising capabilities. At the same time, however, many managers of closed JSCs do not see any advantage in the corporate form of open JSCs. As for closed JSCs, most executives, regardless of whether they are working for closed or open JSCs, agree that closed companies can more effectively prevent their firms from transferring stocks to outsiders (350 out of 714 firms) and avoid the threat of hostile takeovers (131 out of 714 firms). There is statistically significant, but no remarkable difference between the two company groups in the breakdown of their answers to the above question.

Table 3 contains the results of the answers of our respondents to the question of what was the most important reason for their companies' maintaining their current corporate form. Compared with 11.8 % (93 out of 791 firms), who identified it as being related to legal restrictions concerning the number of shareholders and the minimum required capital, 75.5 % replied that it was because of the mass-privatization policy in the early 1990s or because of a management decision made on their own or by their shareholders. The fact that 54.4 % of the open JSCs reported that they had become open JSCs due to the mass-privatization policy is quite understandable, given that the federal government had strongly encouraged soon-to-be-privatized enterprises to become open JSCs by facilitating a swap between privatization vouchers distributed to the general public free of charge and the shares of state-owned and municipal enterprises. On the other hand, in consideration of the fact that managers are still the dominant shareholders in many Russian firms and in light of the strong orientation of these company insiders toward organizational closedness, it is reasonable for them to favor a closed JSC as the legal form of incorporation for their company due to the uncertain social environment typical of a period of transition.

3 Determinants of Corporate Form Choice

In Russia, the growing trend toward a market economy and its integration into the global economy is forcing domestic firms to tackle the issue of optimal adaptation to ever-changing business environments. Hence, it is common for Russian firms to make a major change in their company profile, including their form of incorporation. For instance, companies change from limited to joint-stock stature and *vice versa* much more frequently than they do in Western countries. Needless to say, transformations from open JSCs to closed JSCs and *vice versa* take place all the time, although the latter can only take place by amending the company charter through a special resolution at a general shareholders' meeting and then officially registering such an amendment.

Table 3 Most important reason for being in the current corporate form

	All companies		Open JSCs		Closed JSCs[a]	
	No. of affirmative respondents	Share (%)	No. of affirmative respondents	Share (%)	No. of affirmative respondents	Share (%)
Legal restrictions on the number of shareholders, minimum required capitalization (minimum share capital)	93	11.8	58	10.8	35	13.7
Mass-privatization policy for state-owned enterprises	349	44.1	291	54.4	58	22.7
Judgment by the managers and shareholders	248	31.4	133	24.9	115	44.9
Lack of consensus among managers and shareholders	7	0.9	3	0.6	4	1.6
Time and cost of changing the corporate form	21	2.7	10	1.9	11	4.3
Others	73	9.2	40	7.5	33	12.9
Total	791	100.0	535	100.0	256	100.0

Note: This table shows the results of the answers from company managers participating in the joint enterprise survey to the question of what was the most important reason for their companies having the current corporate form. Closed JSCs include four workers' joint-stock companies (people's enterprises).

[a]Test for the equality of the composition of the responding firms by corporate form that gave a positive answer to each item: $\chi^2 = 74.240$ ($p = 0.000$)

The law on JSCs stipulates that the amendment of a company charter must be made through a special resolution passed by a majority of at least three-fourths of the votes cast by the shareholders with voting shares in attendance. Nevertheless, this provision is not a serious obstacle to such amendments. This is due to the fact that, in many Russian companies, a small number of shareholders own a significant amount of the total shares, which means that, for the top management and major shareholders of Russian JSCs, the issue of whether their firms should be open or closed JSCs is just an "operational" variable, even after their establishment.

The discussion in the previous section highlights the differences between open and closed JSCs as a corporate form option available in Russia and the significance of these two corporate forms from the viewpoint of corporate management as well as the impact of the mass-privatization policy on the decision-making process of stock-issuing companies with respect to whether they should be open or closed JSCs. Based on these fact findings, the next three subsections theoretically consider and empirically analyze the determinants of corporate form choice by Russian firms.

3.1 Hypothesis Development

Basing on the arguments and survey results reported in Sect. 2, we expect that the differences between the institutional settings of open and closed JSCs would affect the incentives and decision-making processes of management executives and shareholders with respect to their choice of corporate form through the following three mechanisms.

The first mechanism is the asset effect of restrictions on share transfers. Any restrictions imposed on a closed company's share transfers will undermine the liquidity and value of such shares as financial commodities. Furthermore, as explained in Sect. 2, a shareholder of a closed JSC intending to transfer his/her shares to a third party must bear all the costs needed to confirm whether any of the other shareholders in the closed JSC or the company itself wishes to execute their right of preferential purchase. Therefore, those who invest money mainly to gain a capital return on their investment (i.e., portfolio investors) will buy the shares of open JSCs rather than those of closed JSCs, *ceteris paribus*. By the same logic, company managers would prefer the corporate form of an open company from the standpoint of issuing securities to raise funds from outside sources, since a closed company must pay for all the marginal capital costs equal to the transaction costs for the transfer of its own shares to a third party and the cost of a low liquidity premium on its own shares. Closed JSCs are further placed at a disadvantage over open JSCs due to the ban on issuing any convertible bonds. Furthermore, as indicated in Table 2, choosing to adopt the open company as its legal form of incorporation will increase the transparency of a firm's management, making it easier for the firm to receive loans from banks and other financial institutions. Considering these conditions, we hypothesize that:

H_1: *The higher a firm's fundraising demand, the more likely it is to be operated as an open JSC.*

The second mechanism is the governance effect of share transfer restrictions. Tight restrictions imposed on a closed JSC as to the transfer of its shares significantly decrease the possibility of a change in its internal control or ownership that might otherwise come about due to an "exit" from the company of its shares sold, a tender offer, a proxy fight, or a bankruptcy. Such restrictions pose a serious impediment to achieving effective management discipline and to reshuffling of a management team with poor performance. Therefore, from the standpoint of which corporate form has a relatively better corporate governance mechanism, shareholders are more inclined to invest in open JSCs. On the other hand, as illustrated in the previous section, the understanding by company executives that the biggest advantage of a closed company lies in the protection against outside environments suggests that they have a strong inclination toward managerial entrenchment that enables them to eliminate supervision and intervention from outside as much as possible and to avoid external discipline. Accordingly, we predict that corporate managers who wish to retain their managerial discretion to behave in an opportunistic way or who wish to avoid the risk of hostile takeover will choose to establish and maintain their firms as closed-stock companies.

The third mechanism is the information effect of state disclosure regulations. The disclosure obligation imposed only on open JSCs by the state produces the effect of alleviating the information asymmetry between company managers and investors in favor of the latter. This, in turn, causes more shareholders to invest in open JSCs, which have a better governance system than closed JSCs, and more managers to operate their firms as closed companies. The discussions on both the second and the third mechanisms as to the organizational choice of a corporate form can be summarized in the following hypothesis:

H_2: *The influence of non-managerial shareholders increases the possibility of firms becoming open JSCs, while the influence of managers increases the possibility of firms becoming closed JSCs.*

In addition to the three mechanisms above, it is necessary to focus on the widespread existence of business groups (i.e., financial-industrial groups or holding companies) as a factor having a significant impact on the organizational choices between open and closed JSCs in Russia. In fact, the joint survey revealed that 35.7 % of the manufacturing companies (268 of 751 firms) and 77.5 % of the communications companies (55 of 71 firms) are controlled by certain business groups through stock ownership. A company's participation in a business group is effective in protecting it from outside threats, especially intervention into company management by state administrations and public bureaucrats, which is a serious problem for Russian firms. This is due to the countervailing political power of the business group the company belongs to and the corrective cohesion among member firms (Iwasaki and Suzuki 2007). As a result, the organizational advantages of a closed JSC as an "institutional defense barrier" may become less important for managers of group companies. Furthermore, it is undesirable for management of a holding company or a core company of a business group to impose severe restrictions on the transfer of shares by its controlling companies, not only from the standpoint of a large shareholder of the group firms, but also from that of the group's goal of ensuring effective asset management within the group. Therefore, we assume that:

H_3: *A firm's affiliation with a business group increases the possibility of the firm being operated as an open JSC.*

However, with the hierarchy within such business groups expanding, enterprises in the lower echelons are more likely to be established by their hierarchically upper companies as wholly owned subsidiaries or dummy firms for account-rigging or tax-evasion purposes, and these enterprises are usually closed companies bound by less strict disclosure obligations. Consequently, we also predict that:

H_4: *The organizational scale of a business group is positively correlated with the proportion of closed JSCs in the member firms of that group.*

Lastly, as explained above, taking into account the background of Russia's privatization policy and its legal restrictions on state investment, the past policies on company start-ups may have a historical, path-dependent impact on organizational choices between open and closed JSCs. Hence, we hypothesize that:

H_5: *Privatized enterprises and companies separated from state-owned or municipal companies or former state-owned, now privatized, companies are more likely to choose to operate as open JSCs in comparison with private companies newly established after the fall of the communist regime.*

3.2 Empirical Methodology

Next, to empirically examine the testable hypotheses presented in Sect. 3.1, we estimate discrete choice models that take a value of 1 for closed JSCs as the dependent variable (*CLOCOM*) using a probit maximum likelihood estimator. On the right-hand side of the regression models, we introduce (a) ownership variables representing the influence of shareholders and managers over organizational strategies, (b) variables concerning the constraints affecting capital demand and supply of the company, (c) variables regarding the linkage between a company with a business group and the organizational scale of that group, (d) variables concerning the impact of past policies on company start-ups, and (e) other control variables. The detailed variable definitions are as follows.

The variables of outside ownership utilized in our estimation are the 6-point-scale ownership share of non-managerial shareholders, excluding domestic individuals (*OWNOUT*),[4] and the ownership share of the state (*OWNSTA*) and private shareholders (*OWNPRI*), each of which is further classified into the federal government (*OWNFED*), regional and local governments (*OWNREG*), commercial banks (*OWNBAN*), investment funds and other financial institutions (*OWNFIN*), non-financial corporate shareholders (*OWNCOR*), and foreign investors (*OWNFOR*). As for company managers, we use a large management shareholder dummy (*MANSHA*) that assigns a value of 1 if a company has a specific manager or a specific managerial group as its large shareholder.

As a proxy for a company's capital demand, a securities-issuing planning variable (*SECPLA*) is used. If the company has a plan to issue securities in Russia in the near future, this variable takes a value of 1, whereas if the company has a plan to issue shares and bonds in foreign financial markets, where more stringent rules than those in Russia are enforced with respect to organizational management and disclosure, it is assigned a value of 2. If neither of these two conditions applies, it is assigned a value of 0. A relationship-banking dummy (*RELBAN*) is used for companies with a long-term credit relationship with a certain commercial bank. On the other hand, as a proxy for representing the constraints affecting the capital procurement of a company, the number of financial institutions per 1,000

[4] The ownership share of domestic individual shareholders is completely excluded from *OWNOUT*. This is to eliminate the ownership effects from the management executives' family members, relatives, or friends as well as those of the employees, all of whom are formally categorized as outside shareholders.

non-financial corporations in a federal district where the company is located (*NUMFIN*) is introduced because, except in a few big cities, local commercial banks and investment firms play a critical role in the field of investment financing and financial consulting services for the local corporate sector, and the development of these local financial institutions is an overriding factor affecting the fundraising abilities of local companies.

In order to examine how affiliation with a business group affects the choice of corporate form, we introduce a group firm dummy variable (*GROFIR*) with a value of 1 if the company is a member of a holding company or another business group through stock ownership. We also use a core group firm dummy (*GROCOR*) and an affiliate firm dummy (*GROAFF*) to test a possible asymmetric impact of the company's group membership on the two. The organizational size of the business group is represented by the natural logarithm of the total number of its member firms (*GROSIZ*).

The impact of past policies on company start-ups is assessed using two dummy variables from the standpoint of the importance of the mass-privatization policy and the statutory regulations on investments by state agencies. Namely, *PRICOM* is a dummy variable for former state-owned (ex-municipal), now privatized, companies; *SPIOFF* captures firms spun off from state-owned (municipal) enterprises or privatized companies by a value of 1.[5] The control variables include the natural logarithm of the total number of employees representing the company size (*COMSIZ*) and industry dummy variables to control the fixed effects in each industry that are unobservable for econometricians.

In accordance with our theoretical predictions in Sect. 3.1, we expect that the ownership by non-managerial shareholders represented in *OWNOUT* and other variables is negatively correlated with the choice of a closed JSC. The sign of *MANSHA* cannot be specified at this stage, as it varies depending on which element is more powerful: the marginal assessment value of shares owned by a manager or group of managers or the additional benefits the manager obtains by operating a closed company. All three variables concerning capital demand and supply (*SECPLA*, *RELBAN*, and *NUMFIN*) are expected to be negative. The three dummy variables representing a company's participation in a business group (*GROFIR*, *GROCOR*, and *GROAFF*) would be negatively correlated with the choice of a closed JSC, whereas *GROSIZ* would have a positive sign. *PRICOM* and *SPIOFF* would be negative. *COMSIZ* is also expected to be estimated with a negative sign because the larger the size of a company is, the more shareholders and capital the company has, and the requirements for choosing the corporate form of an open JSC are thus gradually fulfilled.

Table 4 compares open and closed JSCs using the above independent variables. As this table shows, open JSCs, regardless of their type, have a higher average outside ownership than closed JSCs, and the difference between the two forms of

---

[5] Newly established private firms after the collapse of the Soviet Union are treated as the default category in our estimation.

Table 4 Comparison between open and closed joint-stock companies regarding the ownership structure, capital demand and supply constraints, relationship with business groups, past policies on company start-ups, and company size

	Open JSCs			Closed JSCs		
	N	Mean/ proportion	Median	N	Mean/ proportion[a]	Median[b]
Outsider ownership share (*OWNOUT*)	448	2.21	2.00	223	1.18***	0.00###
State ownership share (*OWNSTA*)	473	0.66	0.00	236	0.12***	0.00###
Federal government agencies (*OWNFED*)	480	0.49	0.00	238	0.09***	0.00###
Regional and local government agencies (*OWNREG*)	478	0.23	0.00	237	0.05***	0.00###
Private ownership share (*OWNPRI*)	449	1.72	0.00	223	1.06***	0.00###
Commercial banks (*OWNBAN*)	470	0.19	0.00	231	0.07**	0.00###
Investment funds and other financial institutions (*OWNFIN*)	465	0.31	0.00	233	0.09***	0.00###
Non-financial corporations (*OWNCOR*)	463	1.06	0.00	237	0.69***	0.00###
Foreign investors (*OWNFOR*)	469	0.37	0.00	234	0.31	0.00##
Proportion of firms with a large managerial shareholder (shareholder group) (*MANSHA*)	527	0.43	0.00	255	0.58†††	1.00###
Proportion of firms planning to issue securities in the near future (*SECPLA*)	449	0.12	0.00	256	0.08	0.00
Proportion of firms with a long-term credit relationship with a certain commercial bank (*RELBAN*)	529	0.85	1.00	256	0.76†††	1.00###
Proportion of member companies of a business group (*GROFIR*)	553	0.41	0.00	269	0.36	0.00
Proportion of core corporations of a business group (*GROCOR*)	553	0.05	0.00	269	0.06	0.00
Proportion of affiliated companies of a business group (*GROAFF*)	553	0.35	0.00	269	0.31	0.00
Total number of member companies of a business group to which a company belongs (*GROSIZ*)	536	7.67	0.00	261	9.98	0.00
Proportion of former state-owned or ex-municipal privatized firms (*PRICOM*)	553	0.78	1.00	269	0.51†††	1.00###
Proportion of firms that separated from a state or privatized company (*SPIOFF*)	553	0.09	0.00	269	0.11	0.00
Average number of employees (*COMSIZ*)	553	2414.77	600.00	269	794.19***	300.00###

Note: This table shows results from the univariate comparison of open and closed JSCs based on the results of the joint enterprise survey. Workers' joint-stock companies (people's enterprises) are excluded from observations. "Ownership share" means an ownership share rated on the following 6-point scale: 0: 0 %; 1: 10.0 % or less; 2: 10.1–25.0 %; 3: 25.1–50.0 %; 4: 50.1–75.0 %; 5: 75.1–100.0 %. *OWNOUT* and *OWNPRI* exclude ownership by domestic individual shareholders. *MANSHA*, *SECPLA*, *RELBAN*, *GROFIR*, *GROCOR*, *GROAFF*, *PRICOM*, and *SPIOFF* are dichotomous variables, which take a value of 1 to corresponding firms. The Appendix provides detailed variable definitions.

[a] ***The difference of the means in comparison with open JSCs is significant at the 1 % level according to the *t*-test (the Welch test was performed instead of the *t*-test when the null-hypothesis that the two samples have the same population variance was rejected by *F*-test for homoskedasticity); **at the 5 % level; †††the difference of the proportions in comparison with open JSCs is significant at the 1 % level according to the χ^2 test.

[b] ###The difference in comparison with open JSCs is significant at the 1 % level according to the Wilcoxon rank-sum test; ##at the 5 % level.

incorporation in this regard is statistically significant at the 5 % or less significance level for all types of non-managerial shareholders. In contrast, the percentage of companies with large management shareholding in all closed JSCs is 15 % higher than in open JSCs, and the difference between them is statistically significant at the 1 % level. Furthermore, the differences between open and closed JSCs regarding the proportion of companies having a long-term credit relationship with a specific commercial bank, the proportion of privatized firms, and the average number of employees are also statistically significant and consistent with our predictions.

The basic sample for our estimation consists of 557 observations, excluding all companies that have already issued securities in the past (Sample type I). In order to validate the robustness of the estimation results, a supplementary estimation is performed using the following three subsamples: Sample type II, which is made up of the firms included in Sample type I, excluding all communications firms; Sample type III, which excludes firms whose number of employees exceeds the mean of the number of employees of the closed JSCs ± 1 standard deviation from the basic sample set; and Sample type IV, which consists of firms with a stable ownership structure that did not experience changes in major shareholders from 2001 to 2004. An estimation using the former two subsamples focuses on the estimation bias arising from the characteristics of newly emerged telecommunications businesses and those of mega corporations. On the other hand, the estimation using Sample type IV deals with the possible endogeneity between corporate forms and ownership structures. As an alternative way to deal with the endogeneity of two factors, we also conduct a two-stage probit estimation[6] by introducing the following four variables to be utilized as additional instruments together with all exogenous variables on the right-hand side in the first stage of regression: a dummy variable of shareholding by an incumbent CEO (or president) (*CEOSHA*); a dummy variable for firms with a dominant shareholder (*DOMSHA*); the age level of the CEO or company president (*CEOAGE*); and a 3-point-scale assessment of the intensity of competition with domestic firms in a product market (*COMDOM*).[7]

To compute standard errors, we use White's heteroskedasticity-consistent estimator.

3.3 Estimation Results

Table 5 shows the estimation results. In this table, the regression coefficients represent marginal effects.

---

[6] The two-stage procedure would be to estimate the reduced forms for ownership variables by probit or ordered probit maximum likelihood and estimate the corporate form choice model by probit after substituting the predicted values for ownership variables.

[7] The correlation coefficients for *CLOCOM* and each of the newly introduced four variables range between −0.032 and 0.019 and are statistically insignificant.

Except for the ownership variables of financial institutions and foreign ownership, all of the independent variables for Models [1] through [4] estimated using the basic sample have the predicted signs with high statistical significance. The presence of non-managerial shareholders diminishes the probability that a firm they own will become a closed JSC. In this respect, it is noteworthy that the marginal effect of state ownership is much stronger than that of private owners. The impact of capital demand and the development of local financial institutions also reduce the probability of the choice of closed JSC as a corporate form. Companies linked with a business group through stock ownership tend to choose open JSC as their corporate form. However, the larger a business group becomes, the higher the number of closed companies that are included among its member firms. Privatized firms are more likely to be open companies, as are JSCs spun off from state-owned or municipal enterprises or from privatized companies. In addition, as the company size grows, the likelihood of the company operating as a closed JSC significantly decreases.

In contrast, the estimation result that a large management shareholder dummy (*MANSHA*) is significant and positive implies that Russian managers place far more importance on maintaining effective control of their company than on obtaining capital gains by owning stock in their companies. This result also suggests that they have a strong desire to prevent outside intervention into their company management and discipline by shareholders, even at the cost of a somewhat reduced value and lowered transferability of their own shares.[8] In other words, the inclination toward managerial entrenchment is significant among Russian managers. We conjecture that one of the most attractive reasons for Russian managers to operate their firms as closed JSCs is the variety of fringe benefits they obtain by doing so. Even at the time of the joint survey, which was 14 years after the systemic transformation to a market economy, it was highly likely that many corporate executives still held such perceptions, given the underdeveloped capital and managerial markets in Russia.

It is logical that *SECPLA* for Models [5] and [6] is slightly less significant than that for the other models, since the sample set does not include any communications companies, which represent the emerging industry in Russia, or the largest corporations that have substantial financial needs and are highly motivated to raise equity capital. It is not surprising that *GROFIR* and *GROSIZ* for Model [7] are estimated to be insignificant, considering that 46.4 % of the surveyed firms (110 of 237) that experienced a substantial change in their ownership structure from 2001 to 2004 were almost part of a business group. What is more important from the viewpoint of the statistical robustness of the estimation results is that the explanatory power and statistical significance of the ownership variables in Model [7] are almost at the same level as those of the estimates for Model [1]. In addition, the result of a

[8] This is closely associated with the fact that the sample firms used for the empirical analysis in this section, as well as the overwhelming majority of Russian companies, are unlisted and have stock prices that are not particularly sensitive to management performance, which leads to an extremely low incentive effect of stock ownership by managers.

two-stage probit estimation of Model [8] also strongly suggests that there is a statistically significant relationship between the corporate form and the ownership structure even if we assume that both of them are determined endogenously.

In summary, our empirical evidence supports that the five organizational-choice mechanisms stated in Sect. 3.1 are effectively functioning in reality. Consequently, we conclude that there are four primary economic problems that cause many JSCs to choose the corporate form of a closed company in Russia. They are (a) a concentrated insider ownership structure, (b) persistent orientation toward organizational closedness among management executives, (c) sluggish capital demand in the corporate sector, and (d) an underdeveloped regional financial sector. In contrast, corporatization through state asset privatization and the formation of business groups positively affect the choice of an open company. These findings strongly suggest that the peculiarities of the transition economy and the massive presence of closed JSCs are inseparably linked in Russia.

4 Institutional Complementarity Between the Corporate Form and the Internal Organizational Structure

Choosing which corporate form to adopt is an important step for a Russian JSC in order to determine its organizational openness and the relationship between its managers and shareholders. However, this objective is ultimately fulfilled when the company has finalized its internal organizational structure by drawing up a corporate charter and establishing the corporate bodies required by law, and so forth. This section further examines this issue by focusing on the institutional complementarity between the corporate form and the internal organizational structure.

4.1 A New Approach to Institutional Complementarity: Function-Enhancing Complementarity versus Function-Neutralizing Complementarity

A general perception by economists of the concept of institutional complementarity is represented in the following statement by Aoki (2000):

> If the institutional structure of a particular economy reflects equilibrium strategies in its underlying evolutionary game, complementarity is likely to exist between the elements of that structure. That is, *the operations of one institution will be reinforced by the existence of other institutions*. This is referred to as "institutional complementarity" [emphasis added]. (ibid., pp. 57–58)

The concept of institutional complementarity not only refers to the institutional compatibility in a particular economic system but also implies a positive assessment of the synergistic effects of different institutions functionally enhancing one

Table 5 Probit regression analysis of the corporate form choice

Dependent variable	*CLOCOM*							
Sample constraints[a]	Type I				Type II	Type III	Type IV	Type I
Model	[1]	[2]	[3]	[4]	[5]	[6]	[7]	[8]
OWNOUT	−0.055***			−0.056***	−0.058***	−0.058***	−0.050***	−0.169**
	(0.01)			(0.01)	(0.01)	(0.01)	(0.01)	(0.07)
OWNSTA		−0.120***						
		(0.03)						
OWNFED			−0.106***					
			(0.03)					
OWNREG			−0.143***					
			(0.04)					
OWNPRI		−0.041***						
		(0.01)						
OWNBAN			−0.023					
			(0.05)					
OWNFIN			−0.071					
			(0.04)					
OWNCOR			−0.057***					
			(0.01)					
OWNFOR			0.019					
			(0.03)					
MANSHA	0.100**	0.093**	0.099**	0.102**	0.104**	0.105**	0.110**	0.210*
	(0.05)	(0.05)	(0.05)	(0.05)	(0.04)	(0.05)	(0.05)	(0.11)
SECPLA	−0.131*	−0.124*	−0.129*	−0.133**	−0.113	−0.116	−0.175*	−0.124**
	(0.07)	(0.07)	(0.07)	(0.07)	(0.08)	(0.08)	(0.10)	(0.06)
RELBAN	−0.148**	−0.153**	−0.146**	−0.149**	−0.138**	−0.158**	−0.134*	−0.143**
	(0.06)	(0.06)	(0.06)	(0.06)	(0.06)	(0.06)	(0.07)	(0.07)
NUMFIN	−0.188***	−0.191***	−0.194***	−0.192***	−0.164**	−0.185***	−0.142*	−0.146**

	(0.06)	(0.07)	(0.07)	(0.06)	(0.07)	(0.07)	(0.08)	(0.07)
GROFIR	−0.217**	−0.216**	−0.209**		−0.179*	−0.253***	−0.169	−0.225**
	(0.10)	(0.09)	(0.09)		(0.10)	(0.09)	(0.14)	(0.09)
GROCOR				−0.232***				
				(0.08)				
GROAFF				−0.196**				
				(0.10)				
GROSIZ	0.098**	0.088*	0.085*	0.094**	0.084*	0.115**	0.067	0.122**
	(0.05)	(0.05)	(0.04)	(0.05)	(0.05)	(0.05)	(0.07)	(0.05)
PRICOM	−0.390***	−0.383***	−0.403***	−0.394***	−0.376***	−0.388***	−0.423***	−0.392***
	(0.06)	(0.06)	(0.06)	(0.06)	(0.06)	(0.06)	(0.07)	(0.06)
SPIOFF	−0.173***	−0.162**	−0.166***	−0.178***	−0.160***	−0.168**	−0.200***	−0.180***
	(0.06)	(0.06)	(0.06)	(0.06)	(0.06)	(0.07)	(0.07)	(0.06)
COMSIZ	−0.062**	−0.058**	−0.060**	−0.064**	−0.049*	−0.070**	−0.068**	−0.037
	(0.03)	(0.03)	(0.03)	(0.03)	(0.03)	(0.03)	(0.03)	(0.03)
Industry dummies	Yes	Yes	Yes	Yes	Yes	Yes	Yes	Yes
N	557	555	555	557	525	534	389	527
Pseudo R^2	0.19	0.20	0.21	0.19	0.16	0.19	0.17	0.17
Log likelihood	−295.70	−290.69	−286.06	−295.44	−283.83	−284.18	−211.91	−282.43

Note: This table reports results from the regressions of the choice between open and closed JSCs on the variables reflecting the ownership structure, capital demand and supply constraints, relationship with business groups, past policies on company start-ups, and company size. Workers' joint-stock companies (people's enterprises) are excluded from observations. We estimate models that take *CLOCOM*, a qualitative variable with a value of 1 assigned to closed JSCs, as the dependent variable using a probit estimator. Model [8] endogenizes corporate form and ownership structure. *OWNOUT* and *MANSHA* are instrumented by all exogenous variables on the right-hand side and a dummy variable of shareholding by an incumbent CEO (or president) (*CEOSHA*); a dummy variable that takes a value of 1 if there is a shareholder or a shareholder group who substantially controls corporate management (*DOMSHA*); the age level of the CEO or company president (*CEOAGE*); and a 3-point-scale assessment of the intensity of competition with domestic firms in a product market (*COMDOM*). The Appendix provides detailed variable definitions. The coefficients represent marginal effects. White's heteroskedasticity-consistent standard errors are shown in parentheses.

[a]Type I: basic sample (available observations without firms that already issued securities in the past); Type II: excluding communications firms from the basic sample; Type III: excluding those with the total number of employees exceeding the mean of number of employees of closed JSCs (794.19 person) ±1 standard deviation (3,149.14) from the basic sample; Type IV: excluding those that experienced a change in major shareholders from 2001 to 2004 from the basic sample.

***Significant at the 1 % level; **at the 5 % level; *at the 10 % level.

another. Nevertheless, we emphasize that such complementarity may exist in a way that causes one institution to functionally undermine the other. This means that even if the functional level of an institution is excessive for a particular economic entity and it would be impossible to fine-tune that institution, another institution would work to inhibit the function of others in order to optimize the entire system. More specifically, if an institutional complementarity that causes institution Ψ^+ to reinforce the function of institution Ω^+ or causes both of these institutions to functionally enhance each other can be called a "function-enhancing complementarity" and an institutional arrangement that is established based on such institutional complementarity and represented in a matrix form as (Ω^+, Ψ^+) may be referred to as a "function-enhancing complementarity equilibrium," then an institutional complementarity that causes institution Ψ^- to work to offset or mitigate the function of institution Ω^+ or causes these two institutions to functionally neutralize each other may be called a "function-neutralizing complementarity," and an institutional arrangement based on this (Ω^+, Ψ^-) may be referred to as a "function-neutralizing complementarity equilibrium."

A function-neutralizing complementarity equilibrium tends to be achieved when institution Ω^+ is exogenous to a given economic entity or when it is still under development in its evolutional process. If institution Ω^+ transforms into Ω^{++} with the desired functional level by becoming endogenous to a given economic entity or gaining perfection over time, it is presumed that there is also a change in institution Ψ^-, leading to the emergence of a new, non-function-neutralizing complementarity equilibrium expressed as (Ω^{++}, Ψ^{++}). In this sense, an institutional arrangement with function-neutralizing complementarity characteristics generates only a short-term equilibrium. As seen in the relationship between law and business, however, the wider the social hierarchy is between a particular economic entity (enterprise) and an institutional builder (legislative body) for institution Ω^+, the more difficult it is for the former to achieve long-term equilibrium. Therefore, a function-neutralizing complementarity equilibrium may exist for a substantial period of time in our incomplete real world, even though it is theoretically transient. With this in mind, the impact of a function-neutralizing complementarity equilibrium on the economic performance under assessment cannot be disregarded.

As is probably quite evident, this chapter provides a good opportunity for an empirical study of the two examples of institutional complementarity, making it possible to observe both the function-enhancing and function-neutralizing aspects of institutional complementarity by looking at various combinations of corporate forms and internal organizational structures. The dichotomous options of statutory corporate form enforced by the Russian corporate law, i.e., the choice between an open and a closed company, are probably not satisfactory to the JSCs, whose ownership structures and business environments are diverse because the ideal degree of organizational openness differs from company to company. In addition, it is unlikely that an enterprise can solve conflicts of interest between shareholders and company managers solely by determining its legal form of incorporation.

For instance, some investors in closed JSCs may persistently complain that the restrictions on share transferability imposed by the Law on JSCs unreasonably increase a company's organizational closedness, which can potentially hamper effective monitoring of top management. On the other hand, some open JSC managers, fearing governmental intervention into their companies and hostile takeovers by strategic investors, may continue to feel cautious about the statutory rights of shareholders to freely transfer shares, as well as about the disclosure requirements, due to the possible risk of the company being excessively exposed to the outside environment. Of course, there also may be shareholders and managers who regard the institutional effect of the corporate form they have chosen as insufficient. These people try to affect the functional strength of their companies' corporate forms and achieve more adequate organizational openness for their own benefit by amending their corporate charters to include their original provisions on share transfers and by exercising their influence over the decision-making process to determine the composition and rules of management and supervisory bodies.

In the case described above, open (closed) JSCs are regarded to have attained a function-enhancing complementarity arrangement by coordinating the organizational openness (closedness) of their internal structures. Conversely, enterprises that chose an open (closed) JSC as their corporate form and adjusted their internal structures to have closed (open) characteristics are considered to have selected a function-neutralizing complementarity equilibrium as their institutional arrangement. By applying the above criteria to our firm-level dataset, in the next subsection, we look at the actual behavior of Russian corporations in this respect.

4.2 *Institutional Arrangement of the Corporate Form and Internal Structure in Russian Firms*

First of all, we need to measure the organizational openness of the internal structure as a whole of each surveyed firm. To this end, we adapt Hayashi's quantification method III for 24 qualitative variables (categorical data) collected from 553 firms, representing the characteristics of a statutory corporate structure in terms of the content of a corporate charter regarding shareholders' ownership and their voting rights, general shareholders' meetings, the board of directors, the collective executive board,[9] the audit committee (auditors), and an external auditor. This measure

[9] A collective executive board headed by the company president (the general director), which is an internal executive organization voluntarily set up by a company, "takes leadership in daily corporate management except for exclusive competence of the general shareholder meeting and the board of directors" (Article 69(2) of the Law on JSCs). In addition, Article 66(2) of that law prohibits members of a collective executive board from making up more than one quarter of the board of directors. In view of these provisions, it is assumed that the presence of a collective executive board functions to clarify management responsibilities and to enhance the independence of the board of directors from management. For more details on this management body, see Iwasaki (2007a, 2013a).

aims to obtain sample scores of the second eigenvalues that best represent the organizational openness of a company's internal structure.

The variables used in the analysis are listed in Table 6. These variables contain information about the existence of corporate charter provisions that limit the number of shares owned per shareholder or restrict shareholder voting rights as well as about the composition of its membership, frequency of meetings, and authority of management and supervisory bodies. In this table, the response rate of these variables for each corporate form is also shown. The χ^2 test of differences of proportions revealed that the difference between open and closed JSCs is statistically significant for 16 of the 24 categories. As expected, these results clearly suggest that closed JSCs generally have a more closed internal structure than open JSCs.

The sample scores calculated on the basis of the categorical quantity of the second eigenvalue listed at the far right of Table 6 are hereinafter referred to as openness scores (*OPESCO*), which are used as indices to quantify the openness of the internal organizational structure. *OPESCO* ranges from −2.910 to 2.020, and its mean (median) is −0.093 (−0.052). The mean (median) *OPESCO* for open JSCs is 0.045 (0.023), that for closed JSCs is −0.472 (−0.510), and the difference in the means between these two company groups is significant at the 1 % level ($t = 5.180$, $p = 0.000$; Wilcoxon $Z = 4.896, p = 0.000$). Obviously, there is a substantial and statistically significant difference between open and closed companies in terms of the openness of their internal structures.

The determinants of the openness of an internal structure of a company may overlap with the factors affecting its choice of corporate form discussed in Sect. 3.2. In particular, both the bargaining power of shareholders and top executives over management and the company's membership in a business group are expected to have a significant impact on the openness of an internal structure, since the mode of the internal organizational structure is directly related to how the company divides its managerial control. As we reported in Sect. 2, because the formation of an open organizational architecture enables company managers to demonstrate a more transparent management style to business partners and potential investors, a firm's demand in fundraising may be positively related to the openness of its internal structure.

To verify the above presumptions, we conduct an OLS estimation to regress *OPESCO* on the variables representing ownership share by shareholders and managers, capital demand and supply constraints, and affiliation with a business group, controlling the difference in past policies on company start-ups, company size, and industry fixed effects.[10] Table 7 shows the results. It indicates that (a) ownership by shareholders and managers adversely affects the formation of a company's internal structure; (b) affiliation with a business group increases the openness of the internal structure of its member firms against the background that

[10] The basic sample for the OLS estimation consists of 417 observations. Sample constraints are the same for the corporate form choice models described in Sect. 3.2.

Table 6 Comparison between open and closed joint-stock companies regarding their internal organizational structure

Upper categories	Lower categories	Response rate: Open JSCs	Response rate: Closed JSCs[a]	Categorical quantity of the second eigenvalue[b]
Corporate charter restricting ownership and voting rights	Ownership limits are set by the corporate charter.	0.12	0.19**	−2.234
	Voting rights limits are set by the corporate charter.	0.16	0.19	−1.847
General shareholders meeting	General shareholders meeting has a high degree of influence over management decisions.[a]	0.79	0.87***	−0.345
Board of directors	Managerial directors constitute the majority (51 % or more) of the board of directors.	0.34	0.55***	−1.995
	Employee directors constitute the majority of the board of directors.	0.01	0.05***	−3.641
	Outsider directors, including those representing the state, constitute the majority of the board of directors.	0.58	0.33***	1.581
	Private outside directors constitute the majority of the board of directors.	0.51	0.33***	1.705
	The chairman of the board of directors is an outsider.	0.33	0.26**	0.342
	The board of directors includes a director(s) who represents non-employee minor shareholders.	0.19	0.12**	0.919
	The board of directors includes an independent director(s).	0.21	0.14**	1.307
	A board of directors' meeting is convened at least once a month.	0.46	0.34***	−0.336
	The board of directors has a high degree of influence on management decisions.[a]	0.93	0.93	−0.048
	The chairman of the board of directors has a high degree of influence on management decisions.[a]	0.84	0.83	0.076
Collective executive board	A collective executive board is in place.	0.39	0.24***	0.257
	A meeting of the collective executive board is convened at least once a month.[b]	0.83	0.72*	0.329
	The collective executive board has a high degree of influence on management decisions.[a]	0.33	0.23***	0.530

(continued)

Table 6 (continued)

Upper categories	Lower categories	Response rate: Open JSCs	Response rate: Closed JSCs[a]	Categorical quantity of the second eigenvalue[b]
Audit committee (auditors)	Auditors representing employees and their union constitute the majority of the audit committee.	0.46	0.51	−1.553
	Outside auditors constitute the majority of the audit committee.	0.51	0.46	1.383
	The audit committee members include a professional expert(s).	0.27	0.26	1.172
	A meeting of the audit committee is convened at least once per quarter.	0.44	0.37	−0.749
	The audit committee has a high degree of influence on management decisions.[a]	0.49	0.46	−0.373
External auditors	The external auditor is a foreign incorporated audit firm.	0.10	0.05*	1.762
	A meeting between management and the external auditor is held at least once per quarter.	0.72	0.63**	−0.225
	The external auditor has a high degree of influence on management decisions.[a]	0.49	0.42*	0.182

Note: This table shows results from the univariate comparison of open and closed JSCs in terms of internal organizational structure using the results of the joint enterprise survey. Workers' joint-stock companies (people's enterprises) are excluded from observations. The data used for comparison are qualitative variables (categorical data) collected from 553 surveyed firms. The right column presents the categorical quantity of the second eigenvalue computed by Hayashi's quantification method III to measure the openness of the internal organizational structure in each sample firm. The second eigenvalue, its contribution rate, and correlation coefficient are 0.221, 15.3 %, and 0.470, respectively.

[a]Indicates firms that replied "there is a certain degree of influence" or "there is a high degree of influence".

[b]Covering only firms with a collective executive board.

***The difference in proportions when compared with open JSCs is significant at the 1 % level according to the χ^2 test; **at the 5 % level; *at the 10 % level.

the holding company and core group companies try to secure effective monitoring and corporate governance in affiliated companies; and (c) the significant and positive estimate of *RELBAN* corresponds to our assumption that constraints on capital supply and demand tend to discourage the organizational openness of a company. These results strongly indicate that many common factors have the same direction of impact both on the choice of corporate form and on the formation of the internal structure. In other words, they appear as driving forces to promote the coevolution and function-enhancing institutional arrangements of a company's legal form of incorporation and its internal organizational structure.

Table 7 OLS regression analysis of the openness of the internal organizational structure

Dependent variable	*OPESCO*			
Sample constraints[a]	Type I	Type II	Type III	Type IV
Model	[1]	[2]	[3]	[4]
Const.	0.233	0.112	0.526	0.621
	(0.38)	(0.39)	(0.44)	(0.58)
OWNOUT	0.072***	0.071***	0.071***	0.071**
	(0.03)	(0.03)	(0.02)	(0.03)
MANSHA	−0.748***	−0.750***	−0.749***	−0.641***
	(0.10)	(0.10)	(0.10)	(0.12)
SECPLA	−0.044	0.062	−0.122	−0.063
	(0.11)	(0.13)	(0.13)	(0.15)
RELBAN	0.244*	0.265*	0.266*	0.316**
	(0.13)	(0.14)	(0.14)	(0.16)
NUMFIN	−0.053	−0.074	−0.036	−0.128
	(0.15)	(0.16)	(0.15)	(0.17)
GROFIR	0.353***	0.347***	0.346***	0.505***
	(0.11)	(0.11)	(0.11)	(0.13)
PRICOM	−0.018	−0.009	−0.036	−0.218
	(0.13)	(0.13)	(0.14)	(0.16)
SPIOFF	0.001	0.004	−0.023	−0.179
	(0.19)	(0.19)	(0.20)	(0.23)
COMSIZ	−0.002	−0.022	−0.049	−0.030
	(0.05)	(0.05)	(0.06)	(0.06)
Industry dummies	Yes	Yes	Yes	Yes
N	417	396	401	284
Adjusted R^2	0.24	0.21	0.23	0.25
Breusch-Pagan test (χ^2)	29.27**	27.61**	27.67*	21.83

Note: This table reports results from the regressions of the openness of the internal organizational structure on the variables reflecting the ownership structure, capital demand and supply constraints, relationship with business groups, past policies on company start-ups, and company size. We estimate models that take *OPESCO* (the openness score of the internal organizational structure) as the dependent variable by OLS. The Appendix provides detailed variable definitions. Standard errors are shown in parentheses. White's heteroskedasticity-consistent standard errors are given when the null-hypothesis of homoskedasticity is rejected at the 5 % level by the Breusch-Pagan test.

[a]Type I: basic sample (available observations without firms that already issued securities in the past); Type II: excluding communications firms from the basic sample; Type III: excluding those with the total number of employees exceeding the mean of number of employees of closed JSCs (794.19 person) ±1 standard deviation (3,149.14) from the basic sample; Type IV: excluding those that experienced a change in the major shareholders from 2001 to 2004 from the basic sample.

***Significant at the 1% level; **at the 5% level; *at the 10% level.

Meanwhile, the following interesting fact is found by looking at *OPESCO* from a different angle. As referred to in Sect. 2, the respondents were asked whether they believed that the corporate form of their company was beneficial to the growth of their business. When comparing the *OPESCO* values for companies that answered "beneficial" with those for companies that answered "detrimental," the sample group of open JSCs had a mean/median ratio of 0.033/0.150 (265 firms) to −0.090/0.010 (43 firms), whereas that for the sample group of closed JSCs was −0.606/−0.609 (97 firms) to 0.095/0.115 (14 firms), suggesting that JSCs whose managers have a negative view of their own corporate form are inclined to develop an internal structure with function-neutralizing characteristics. In particular, the difference between closed JSCs with a positive view and closed JSCs with a negative view is statistically quite significant ($t = 2.217$, $p = 0.029$; Wilcoxon $Z = 2.070$, $p = 0.039$).[11] In other words, closed companies that are not satisfied with their closed disposition in terms of the corporate form are much more likely to achieve function-neutralizing complementarity institutional arrangements than are open companies. This result suggests the possibility that dissatisfaction with the corporate form of a closed JSC comes from its closed organizational nature, represented by severe restrictions on share transferability imposed by the Russian corporate law.

As is clear from the above examination, the distribution of *OPESCO* for open and closed JSCs is diverse, and there is a general tendency for open companies to try to make their internal structures more open to the outside and for closed companies to act in the reverse. Hence, looking at the overall picture of the current state of Russian JSCs, their dynamic and systematic efforts to attain a function-enhancing complementarity equilibrium for their internal structures are noticeable. However, as illustrated in Fig. 1, many open JSCs have internal structures with openness levels that are the same or lower than the average internal structures in closed JSCs. At the same time, a significant number of closed JSCs have open internal structures. In fact, when categorizing the surveyed firms into companies with open internal structures and companies with closed internal structures on the basis of whether their *OPESCO* values are larger than the median of all samples, 43.3 % of the responding open JSCs (176 of 406) have closed internal structures, whereas 32.0 % of the responding closed JSCs (47 of 147) have open structures. To summarize, according to the discussions in Sect. 4.1, 4 of 10 of the surveyed firms have already achieved or are in the process of achieving a function-neutralizing complementarity equilibrium as the institutional arrangement for the internal governance system.

5 Institutional Equilibrium and Organizational Behavior

As noted in the previous section, an asymmetrical institutional arrangement between a corporate form and its internal structure is a noticeable phenomenon that divides medium- and large-scale JSCs, which are a core component of the

---

[11] The result of the same test for open companies is: $t = -0.752$, $p = 0.452$; Wilcoxon $Z = -0.556$, $p = 0.578$.

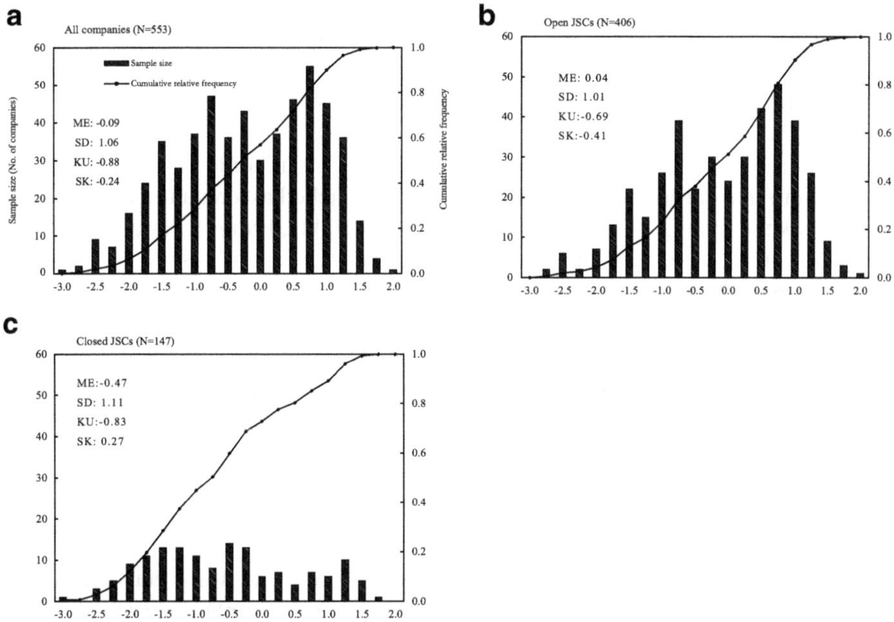

Fig. 1 Distribution of the openness score of the internal organizational structure. Note: This figure shows the distribution of the openness score of the internal organizational structure (*OPESCO*) in 553 firms participated in the joint enterprise survey. *OPESCO* is computed by Hayashi's quantification method III using 24 qualitative variables (categorical data), which represent the characteristics of a statutory corporate structure. Table 6 reports its results. ME, S.D., KU, and SK denote mean, standard deviation, kurtosis, and skewness, respectively

Russian business sector, into two types. Therefore, as long as the qualitative differences in an institutional equilibrium affect corporate governance and firm performance in these companies to a certain degree, that fact may be of great significance not only to their businesses but also to the Russian economy as a whole. In this section, we empirically examine this issue.

5.1 Hypothesis Development

The theoretical study of institutional diversity and imperfect institutions has made remarkable progress in recent years (Young 1998; Aoki 2001; Eggertsson 2005; Ostrom 2005). Although such research lacks precision in assessing how an institutional equilibrium affects the behavioral pattern of an economic entity, it provides highly suggestive clues to elucidating this mechanism. The organizational economics also gives helpful hints on this topic. Based on recent developments of institutional and organizational studies in economics, we propose three testable hypotheses with regard to the possible impact of institutional arrangements of corporate forms and internal organizational structures of Russian JSCs on corporate governance and firm performance.

First, the institutional arrangement of corporate form and internal organizational structure in a stock company may be closely linked with the probability of the occurrence of infighting between management and shareholders. An institutional equilibrium in a corporate organization, which is reached as a result of a bargaining game between managers and owners over control rights, brings a certain degree of stability to the company management but does not prevent all conflicts of interest between the two parties stemming from changes in the outer environment and opportunistic behavior of the management executives. The probability of such a disagreement on company management between the managers and the shareholders developing into serious infighting largely depends on the degree of freedom shareholders have to voice their opinions to the management and exit ownership. Accordingly, we hypothesize that:

H_1: *The more institutionally open a company is, the more effective it will be at reducing the risk of internal conflict between shareholders and management.*

Second, in terms of the marginal effect to restrain infighting between shareholders and company managers, function-neutralizing complementarity between the corporate form and the internal structure is inferior to function-enhancing complementarity as institutional coordination. The reasons for the relatively low degree of the marginal functional strength of a function-neutralizing complementarity equilibrium are that no synergetic effects between functionally compatible institutions can be expected and that systemic distortion (coordination loss) may occur by coupling function-incompatible institutions. Hence, we expect that:

H_2: *Function-neutralizing complementarity between corporate forms and internal structures is inferior to function-enhancing complementarity in the sense that the additional openness of the internal organizational structure in closed JSCs may be less effective at deterring internal conflicts between corporate managers and shareholders than is the structure in open companies, ceteris paribus.*

Finally, the institutional equilibrium of corporate form and internal structure in a JSC has only an indirect impact on its productivity, investment, and restructuring activities. There are two rationales for this discussion. First, although it is true that the institutional coordination of corporate form and internal structure plays a significant role in disciplining corporate officers and ensuring organizational stabilization, it is equally true that firm performance in Russia is also largely affected by the business environment, the human capital quality of its top management, labor-management relationships, financial constraints, and interrelationships with business partners and the state. Particularly, in transitional Russia, corporate management is seriously crippled by hardening budget constraints due to the uncertain political and economic situation and the underdeveloped capital market and banking system. Therefore, it is quite possible that these factors have a more definitive impact on the performance of the corporate management of Russian firms in comparison with the potential impact of the institutional equilibrium of corporate form and internal structure.

The second rationale, although not as realistic as the first one, is that many Russian firms determine their organizational arrangements for the purpose of optimizing their performance. As reported in Sect. 2, most of the managers of the surveyed firms replied that the current corporate form, whether an open or a closed JSC, was more beneficial to the development of their companies than the alternative form. This may suggest that many of the surveyed firms chose the corporate form most appropriate for the pursuit of firm performance. If the same logic is applicable to the formation of internal corporate structures and to the institutional arrangements of a company as a whole, there are no statistically significant correlations among firm performance and its corporate form, its internal structure, and the institutional equilibrium of the two. Based on the two rationales discussed above, we predict that:

H_3: *It appears difficult to find a statistically significant relationship between the institutional equilibrium of corporate form and internal structure of a Russian stock company and the firm's performance.*

5.2 Impact of Institutional Equilibrium on Corporate Governance

To verify hypotheses H_1 and H_2 presented in Sect. 5.1, we perform a probit estimation of discrete choice models using the following two dependent variables. One is an internal-conflict dummy variable (*INTCON*), which is assigned a value of 1 if a company has experienced harsh infighting between managers and shareholders at least once from 2001 to 2004. "Infighting between managers and shareholders," as reported here, refers to a situation in which the conflict was brought to the court's attention as a criminal or civil case or became a scandal attracting local and national media coverage. The other dependent variable is a CEO-displacement dummy (*CEOTUR*), in which a value of 1 is assigned to companies that saw CEO turnover at the request of shareholders at least once during the same period. According to the survey results, 206 (26.8 %) of the 768 firms had more than one internal conflict, and 170 (20.7 %) of the 821 firms changed their top management as a result of pressure from shareholders. Karpoff and Rice (1989) regard managerial turnover as a proxy variable to measure the magnitude of a control contest or shareholder disagreement. Our *CEOTUR* variable may have the same function. However, managerial turnovers in Russia are generally regarded as an arbitration process applied to reduce conflict between managers and shareholders and reach settlements outside of court. In fact, of the 158 surveyed firms that answered they had a CEO displacement from 2001 to 2004, only 53 companies (33.5 %) reported that they also experienced an internal conflict in the same period. In other words, companies that can attain a CEO displacement relatively easily are able to settle conflicts effectively between managers and shareholders as to the reported CEO displacement. Consequently, these companies may prevent themselves from getting involved in a grave scandal attracting the attention of the court and mass media. Therefore, we predict that a corporate organization open to non-managerial shareholders deters internal conflicts between shareholders and management and increases the likelihood of shareholder-initiated CEO turnovers, *ceteris paribus*.

To examine the impact of corporate form and internal structure of a JSC and its institutional arrangement on the probability of such organizational behavior, we perform probit regression to estimate the individual effects of the corporate form and internal structure as well as the synergistic effects generated by the institutional coordination of these two elements. The individual effects of the corporate form and internal structure are estimated using an equation that takes an open JSC dummy (*OPECOM*) and *OPESCO* as independent variables together with variables controlling ownership structure (*OWNOUT*, *MANSHA*); affiliation with a business group (*GROFIR*); gross sales change from 2001 to 2004 (*SALGRO*), which represents the firm performance; company size (*COMSIZ*); and industry fixed effects.

The synergistic effect of the institutional coordination of a corporate form and an internal structure is estimated on the basis of two subsamples of open and closed JSCs using the above equations without the *OPECOM* variable. In consideration of the possible reverse-causality, in which an internal conflict or CEO turnover that occurred in the past may directly or indirectly affect the current state of the governance system, the empirical analysis in this subsection is limited to the firms that did not experience changes in major shareholders from 2001 to 2004, that is, companies whose ownership structure remained almost stable during that period. This sample constraint is considered to be quite effective in ruling out the possibility of the aforementioned reverse-causality, since it is a well-known fact that almost all large-scale internal structural changes in Russian firms are triggered by a shift in dominant shareholders resulting from a hostile takeover or merger.

Table 8 shows the results of univariate analysis. Both the χ^2-test and the Wilcoxon rank-sum test confirm that there is a statistically significant difference between open and closed JSCs in terms of the probability of shareholder-initiated CEO turnover at the 5 % level. On the other hand, the difference between two company groups divided on the basis of the median value of *OPESCO* is significant both at the 10 % level in terms of the probability of an internal conflict between shareholders and management executives as well as at the 1 % level with regard to the probability of CEO turnover.

The results of multivariate regression analysis are reported in Table 9.[12] As the table shows, the corporate form alone does not have any significant impact on the probability of an internal conflict or a CEO turnover. Moreover, the internal structure alone does not effectively deter internal conflicts. On the contrary, an

[12] Again, all of the correlation coefficients among the independent variables used in these models were below a threshold of 0.70.

Table 8 Comparison between open and closed joint-stock companies and between the two groups of companies divided by the openness of the internal organizational structure in terms of the probability of an internal conflict between shareholders and management and shareholder-initiated CEO turnover

	Corporate form						Openness of the internal organizational structure					
	Open JSCs			Closed JSCs			*OPESCO* > −.052			*OPESCO* < −.052		
	N	Occurrence rate	Median	N	Occurrence rate[a]	Median[b]	N	Occurrence rate	Median	N	Occurrence rate[a]	Median[b]
Internal conflict in 2001–2004 (*INTCON*)	355	0.21	0.00	182	0.23	0.00	165	0.19	0.00	194	0.25†	0.00$^{\#}$
Shareholder-initiated CEO turnover in 2001–2004 (*CEOTUR*)	374	0.20	0.00	188	0.12††	0.00$^{\#\#}$	172	0.25	0.00	195	0.12†††	0.00$^{\#\#\#}$

Note: This table shows results from the univariate comparison between open and closed JSCs and between the two groups of companies divided by the median of the openness of the internal organizational structure (*OPESCO*) in terms of the probability of an internal conflict between shareholders and management and shareholder-initiated CEO turnover in the period of 2001–2004 using the results of the joint enterprise survey. *OPESCO* is computed by Hayashi's quantification method III using 24 qualitative variables (categorical data), which represent the characteristics of a statutory corporate structure. Table 6 reports its results. The Appendix provides detailed variable definitions of *INTCON* and *CEOTUR*.

[a] †††The difference in the proportions in comparison with its counter category is significant at the 1 % level according to the χ^2 test; ††at the 5% level; †at the 10 % level.

[b] $^{\#\#\#}$The difference in comparison with its counter category is significant at the 1 % level according to the Wilcoxon rank-sum test; $^{\#\#}$at the 5 % level; $^{\#}$at the 10 % level.

Table 9 Probit regression analysis of the impacts of the institutional coordination of corporate form and internal organizational structure in a joint-stock company on the probability of internal conflicts between shareholders and management and shareholder-initiated CEO turnover

Dependent variables	*INTCON*			*CEOTUR*		
Sample constraints	All companies	Open JSCs	Closed JSCs	All companies	Open JSCs	Closed JSCs
Model	[1]	[2]	[3]	[4]	[5]	[6]
OPECOM	−0.023			0.010		
	(0.06)			(0.05)		
OPESCO	−0.024	−0.056*	0.050	0.046**	0.054**	0.028
	(0.03)	(0.03)	(0.06)	(0.02)	(0.03)	(0.02)
OWNOUT	0.045***	0.040***	0.076**	0.017*	0.019	0.011
	(0.01)	(0.01)	(0.03)	(0.01)	(0.01)	(0.01)
MANSHA	0.045	0.051	0.005	−0.173***	−0.149***	−0.169
	(0.05)	(0.06)	(0.12)	(0.05)	(0.05)	(0.11)
GROFIR	−0.047	−0.069	−0.132	0.066	0.150**	−0.034
	(0.06)	(0.07)	(0.12)	(0.05)	(0.06)	(0.03)
SALGRO	−0.021	−0.010	−0.090**	0.011	−0.003	0.014
	(0.02)	(0.02)	(0.04)	(0.02)	(0.02)	(0.01)
COMSIZ	0.006	0.024	−0.073	−0.015	−0.025	0.008
	(0.02)	(0.03)	(0.05)	(0.02)	(0.02)	(0.01)
Industry dummies	Yes	Yes	Yes	Yes	Yes	Yes
N	317	238	74	321	237	73
Pseudo R^2	0.07	0.08	0.14	0.17	0.17	0.43
Log likelihood	−157.42	−115.93	−35.13	−121.27	−96.15	−15.53

Note: This table reports results from the regressions of the internal conflicts between shareholders and top management and the shareholder-initiated CEO turnover on the variables reflecting corporate form, openness of the internal organizational structure, ownership structure, relationship with business groups, past firm performance, and company size. We estimate models that take *INTCON*, a qualitative variable that takes a value of 1 for firms that have experienced harsh infighting between managers and shareholders at least once from 2001 to 2004, or *CEOTUR*, a qualitative variable in which a value of 1 is assigned to companies that saw CEO turnover at the request of shareholders at least once during the same period, as the dependent variable using a probit estimator. The Appendix provides detailed variable definitions. White's heteroskedasticity-consistent standard errors are shown in parentheses.

***Significant at the 1 % level; **at the 5 % level; *at the 10 % level.

increase in the openness of an open company's internal structure positively affects the prevention of corporate infighting and expansion of shareholders' influence over the managerial selection process, and its magnitude and statistical significance are larger than those for an internal structure's individual effects. In contrast, a closed company's attempts to design a more open internal structure yield no statistically significant result. These results strongly suggest that the function-enhancing complementarity between corporate form and internal structure in a JSC can produce considerable synergistic effects and, conversely, that the function-neutralizing institutional complementarity may be accompanied by a serious coordination loss to corporate management.

On the other hand, empirical evidence on the corporate governance of Russian firms suggests that *OWNOUT* has a positive sign with statistical significance in many cases and that *MANSHA* is negative and significant in Models [4] and [5], taking *CEOTUR* as the dependent variable.[13] Furthermore, the estimation result that *SALGRO* is not significant for the probability of an internal conflict and CEO turnover except for Model [3] is consistent with those of preceding studies that repeatedly maintain that the managerial turnover in Russian firms was not sensitive to their performance (Iwasaki 2007c; Abe and Iwasaki 2010). It is possible that, in Russia, corporate infighting and CEO turnover need to be seen in the context of power struggles between managers and outside investors rather than in the context of shareholders' complaints blaming managers for poor performance or company scandals.

5.3 Impact of Institutional Equilibrium on Firm Performance

Hypothesis H_3, regarding the relationship between institutional equilibrium and firm performance, is also supported by the survey data. Table 10 shows the results of univariate comparative analysis of two sample groups classified by corporate form and by the degree of openness of their internal structure on the basis of 13 criteria. Six of them, including labor productivity and changes in gross sales, are related to business performance for the past several years. The remaining seven, including the intensiveness of investment activities and changes in research and development (R&D) expenditure, reflect restructuring activities.

In each of these two types of comparison, no significant difference is observed in more than half of the criteria. In addition, the statistical differences found in the remaining criteria do not necessarily demonstrate an advantage of an open JSC over a closed JSC, nor do they suggest any advantage of an open internal structure over a closed one, and *vice versa*. Moreover, none of the regression analyses conducted with these performance indices as the dependent variables (not reported) produced systematically significant estimates of *OPECOM*, *OPESCO*, and the interaction term of these two variables.[14] To sum up, these empirical results indicate that an institutional equilibrium between corporate form and internal organizational structure in a Russian JSC is less likely to have a direct impact on firm performance.

---

[13] We re-estimated all models in Table 9, excluding ownership variables from the independent variables, and confirmed that this treatment did not have any influence on estimates of *OPECOM* and *OPESCO*.

[14] In almost all of these regression results, the independent variables representing the affiliation with a business group, company size, and financial constraints are estimated with high statistical significance. This also supports hypothesis H_3.

Table 10 Comparison between open and closed joint-stock companies and between the two groups of companies divided by the openness of the internal organizational structure in terms of firm performance

	Corporate form						Openness of the internal organizational structure					
	Open JSCs			Closed JSCs			*OPESCO* > −.052			*OPESCO* < −.052		
	N	Mean/ proportion	Median	N	Mean/ proportion[a]	Median[b]	N	Mean/ proportion	Median	N	Mean/ proportion[a]	Median[b]
Gross sales per employee in 2004 (1,000 rubles)[c]	328	3502.94	387.31	166	2917.03	341.67	156	6645.31	400.00	180	1452.89	333.33###
Changes in gross sales in 2000–2004[e]	371	1.65	2.00	187	1.51	2.00	168	1.83	2.00	195	1.38***	1.00###
Changes in the total number of employees in 2001–2005[f]	373	−0.13	0.00	189	0.27***	0.00###	170	−0.19	0.00	195	0.06*	0.00##
Changes in average wages in 2000–2004[e]	369	1.98	2.00	189	1.89	2.00	169	2.14	2.00	195	1.85***	2.00###
Financial/economic situation (at the time of the survey)[f]	373	0.36	0.00	187	0.33	0.00	170	0.41	0.00	195	0.22	0.00
Frequency of dividend payments in 2001–2003[g]	365	1.05	0.00	187	0.75**	0.00##	167	0.95	0.00	195	0.99	0.00
Intensiveness of investment in 2001–2004[h]	364	1.16	1.00	184	0.98***	1.00##	167	1.23	1.00	194	1.05**	1.00##
Changes in R&D expenditure in 2001–2004[i]	370	1.42	2.00	186	1.36	2.00	169	1.48	2.00	194	1.46	2.00
Changes in marketing and advertising expenditure in 2001–2004[i]	370	2.28	3.00	188	2.16	2.00#	170	2.21	3.00	195	2.47**	3.00#
Introduction of new production facilities in 2001–2004[j]	366	0.66	1.00	183	0.68	1.00	167	0.63	1.00	192	0.69	1.00
Employment of new technology in 2001–2004[j]	364	0.54	1.00	184	0.51	1.00	167	0.54	1.00	192	0.53	1.00
Development of new products or services in 2001–2004[j]	368	0.60	1.00	184	0.54	1.00	170	0.58	1.00	193	0.58	1.00
ISO certification obtained for own products in 2001–2004[j]	360	0.48	0.00	182	0.31†††	0.00###	166	0.49	0.00	189	0.41	0.00

Note: This table shows the results of univariate comparison between open and closed JSCs and between the two groups of companies divided by the median of the openness of the internal organizational structure (*OPESCO*) in terms of business performance and restructuring activities using the results of the joint enterprise survey. *OPESCO* is computed by Hayashi's quantification method III using 24 qualitative variables (categorical data), which represent the characteristics of a statutory corporate structure. Table 6 reports its results.

[a] ***The difference in the means in comparison with its counter category is significant at the 1 % level according to the *t*-test (the Welch test was performed instead of the *t*-test when the null-hypothesis that the two samples have the same population variance was rejected by *F*-test for homoskedasticity); **at the 5 % level; †††the difference of the proportions in comparison with its counter category is significant at the 1 % level according to the χ^2 test.

[b] ###The difference in comparison with its counter category is significant at the 1 % level according to the Wilcoxon rank-sum test; ##at the 5 % level; #at the 10 % level.

[c] Excluding discordant value.

[d] The changes are rated on the following 5-point scale: −1: decreased; 0: no change; 1: increased by less than 1.5 times; 2: increased by 1.5 or more but less than 2.0 times; 3: increased by 2.0 or more times.

[e] The changes are rated on the following 5-point scale: −2: decreased by 20 % or more; −1: decreased by less than 20 %; 0: no change; 1: increased by less than 20 %; 2: increased by 20 % or more.

[f] This item is rated on the following 5-point scale: −2: bad; −1: poor; 0: average; 1: good; 2: fairly good.

[g] Excluding all firms established after 2001.

[h] This item is rated on the following 3-point scale: 0: no investment made; 1: small-scale investment made; 2: large-scale investment made.

[i] This item is rated on the following 4-point scale: 0: no spending; 1: expenditure decreased; 2: expenditure remained unchanged; 3: expenditure increased.

[j] This item takes a value of 1 to corresponding firms.

6 Conclusion

In Russia, an overwhelming number of JSCs choose to become closed companies despite the fact that this corporate form strays far from the primary nature of joint-stock companies that work as an economic mechanism to raise capital from a wide range of private investors and to increase shareholder wealth as effectively as possible. This trend is also true for medium- and large-scale enterprises in the manufacturing and communications sectors. In this study, we theoretically and empirically examined this interesting economic phenomenon using the results of a nationwide enterprise survey conducted in 2005.

In the first part of this chapter, we explored the mechanism behind the organizational choice between two alternative corporate forms and identified the following four factors that encourage many Russian firms to be closed: (a) a widespread insider-dominating corporate ownership structure emerging as a result of the mass-privatization policy, (b) a strong orientation among managers toward closed corporate organization due to underdeveloped capital and managerial markets, (c) slumping needs for corporate finance, and (d) insufficient financial support from local financial institutions. The relationship between ownership structure and corporate form does exist, even if the endogeneity of the two factors is assumed. The fact that the above four factors still have a significant impact on the behavioral patterns of Russian companies 14 years after the collapse of the Soviet Union reminds us of the difficult and time-consuming transition process from a centrally planned to a market-oriented economic system. In addition to the four determinants outlined above, we also found that the historical path dependency of the enterprise privatization in the early 1990s and the intense formation of business groups have a significant impact on the choice of corporate form by Russian firms.

In the second half of this chapter, we examined the institutional coordination between corporate forms and internal organizational structures in Russian stock companies and their effect on corporate governance and firm performance. The provisions of the Law on JSCs force Russian firms to choose between an open and a closed JSC as their legal form of incorporation, resulting in the emergence of the two contrasting types of institutional equilibrium. The reason some Russian enterprises try to add a reverse-functional aspect to their internal structures needs to be understood in the context of their economically rational organizational behavior to adjust the excessive functional strengths of their corporate form, which are exogenous to them. Such an organizational reaction of Russian firms to corporate law probably plays an important role in enabling them to perform stable business operations. According to the empirical evidence reported in the previous section, however, compared with a function-enhancing complementarity equilibrium coupling functionally compatible institutions, the function-neutralizing complementarity equilibrium is quite ineffective for preventing serious internal conflicts between shareholders and company managers and for allowing shareholders to dismiss managers, both of which are critical challenges facing corporate governance in Russia today.

Now Russia is required to build a legal framework that can eliminate the need for enterprises to maintain the inefficient institutional equilibrium of firm organization. Yet it will be difficult to achieve this objective in a way that forces all JSCs to become open companies, as has been proposed by the lower house of the Federal Assembly (*The State Duma*) and is currently being discussed within the federal government (Osipenko 2005). The most essential policy solution is to facilitate an environment that motivates Russian firms to voluntarily unlock their organizations. Without this condition, the convergence policy of the corporate forms into open JSCs may drive more companies toward a function-neutralizing complementarity equilibrium. After all, the sound development of the Russian business sector can be achieved only by promoting the transition to a market economy in parallel with an effort to move forward with appropriate and comprehensive structural reforms. There is no shortcut to this process.

Acknowledgments This chapter presents research outcome from a Japan-Russia joint research project titled "Corporate Governance and Integration Processes in the Russian Economy" launched by the Institute of Economic Research, Hitotsubashi University, and the Institute for Industrial and Market Studies, National Research University – Higher School of Economics. It is a substantially revised and extended version of Iwasaki (2007b, 2009). This research was financially supported by a grant-in-aid for scientific research from the Ministry of Education and Sciences in Japan (No. 23243032), the Joint Usage and Research Center of the Institute of Economic Research, Hitotsubashi University, and the Japan Securities Scholarship Foundation (JSSF). I also thank Naohito Abe, Sabri Boubaker (book coeditor), Tatiana G. Dolgopyatova, Martin Gilman, Satoshi Mizobata, Duc K. Nguyen (book coeditor), and Andrei Yakovlev for their valuable comments and suggestions, and Dawn Brandon and Jim Treadway for their careful editorial assistance. Needless to say, all remaining errors are mine.

Appendix

Definition, descriptive statistics, and data source of variables used for empirical analysis

Variable name	Definition	Descriptive statistics Mean	S.D.	Min.	Max.
CLOCOM	Closed JSC dummy[a]	0.33	0.47	0	1
OPECOM	Open JSC dummy[a]	0.67	0.47	0	1
OWNOUT	Outsider ownership share[b, c]	1.87	2.14	0	5
OWNSTA	State ownership share[b]	0.37	1.02	0	5
OWNFED	Ownership share by federal government agencies[b]	0.23	0.82	0	5
OWNREG	Ownership share by regional and local government agencies[b]	0.17	0.70	0	5
OWNPRI	Private ownership share[b, c]	1.26	1.90	0	5
OWNBAN	Ownership share by commercial banks[b]	0.11	0.50	0	5
OWNFIN	Ownership share by investment funds and other financial institutions[b]	0.16	0.68	0	5

(continued)

Variable name	Definition	Descriptive statistics			
		Mean	S.D.	Min.	Max.
OWNCOR	Ownership share by non-financial corporate shareholders[b]	0.88	1.65	0	5
OWNFOR	Ownership share by foreign investors[b]	0.22	0.88	0	5
MANSHA	Large managerial shareholder dummy[a]	0.51	0.50	0	1
SECPLA	Securities issuance planning dummy[a]	0.06	0.29	0	2
RELBAN	Relationship-banking dummy[a]	0.82	0.39	0	1
NUMFIN	Number of financial institutions per 1,000 firms in the location	1.19	0.31	0.54	2.18
GROFIR	Business group participation dummy[a]	0.33	0.47	0	1
GROCOR	Core business group member dummy[a]	0.05	0.22	0	1
GROAFF	Business group affiliation dummy[a]	0.28	0.45	0	1
GROSIZ	Natural logarithm of the total number of member firms of a business group	0.68	1.13	0	6.40
PRICOM	Dummy for former state-owned or ex-municipal, now privatized, companies[a]	0.69	0.46	0	1
SPIOFF	Dummy for firms separated from state-owned or privatized companies[a]	0.10	0.30	0	1
COMSIZ	Natural logarithm of the total number of employees	6.16	0.93	4.66	9.42
CEOSHA	Dummy of shareholding by incumbent CEO (or company president)[a]	0.63	0.48	0	1
DOMSHA	Dummy of a shareholder or shareholder group dominating corporate management[a]	0.87	0.33	0	1
CEOAGE	Age level of incumbent CEO (or company president)[d]	2.43	0.91	0	5
COMDOM	Intensity of competition with domestic firms in product market[e]	1.50	0.69	0	2
OPESCO	Indicator of the openness of the internal organizational structure[f]	−0.09	1.06	−2.91	2.02
INTCON	Internal conflict dummy[a]	0.27	0.44	0	1
CEOTUR	Shareholder-initiated CEO turnover dummy[a]	0.21	0.41	0	1
SALGRO	Changes in gross sales[g]	1.62	1.27	−2	2

Source: *NUMFIN* was calculated by the author based on Federal State Statistical Service (2005) and the Central Bank of the Russian Federation (2005). Other variables are based on the results of the joint enterprise survey.

Note: [a]Dichotomous variable, which takes a value of 1 to corresponding firms.

[b]"Ownership share" means an ownership share rated on the following 6-point scale: 0: 0 %; 1: 10.0 % or less; 2: 10.1–25.0 %; 3: 25.1–50.0 %; 4: 50.1–75.0 %; 5: 75.1–100.0 %.

[c]Excluding ownership by domestic individual shareholders.

[d]Age level is rated on the following 6-point scale: 0: 30 years old or younger; 1: 31–40 years old; 2: 41–50 years old; 3: 51–60 years old; 4: 61–70 years old; 5: 71 years old or older.

[e]The intensity of competition is rated on the following 3-point scale: 0: no competition; 1: not very competitive; 2: very competitive.

[f]Sample score computed by Hayashi's quantification method III using 24 qualitative variables (categorical data), which represent the characteristics of a statutory corporate structure. Table 6 reports its results.

[g]The changes are rated on the following 5-point scale: −2: decreased by 20 % or more; −1: decreased by less than 20 %; 0: no change; 1: increased by less than 20 %; 2: increased by 20 % or more.

References

Abe, N., & Iwasaki, I. (2010). Organisational culture and corporate governance in Russia: A study of managerial turnover. *Post-Communist Economies, 22*(4), 449–470.

Aoki, M. (2000). *Information, corporate governance, and institutional diversity: Competitiveness in Japan, the USA, and the transitional economies*. New York: Oxford University Press.

Aoki, M. (2001). *Toward a comparative institutional analysis*. Cambridge/London: MIT Press.

Central Bank of the Russian Federation. (2005). *Biulleteni bankovskoi statistiki: regional'noe prilozhenie* (Bulletin of banking statistics: Regional features), *1*(17). (in Russian).

Coase, R. H. (1937). The nature of the firm. *Economica, 4*(4), 386–405.

Dolgopyatova, T., Iwasaki, I., & Yakovlev, A. (Eds.). (2009). *Organization and development of Russian business: A firm-level analysis*. Basingstoke: Palgrave Macmillan.

Eggertsson, T. (2005). *Imperfect institutions: Possibilities and limits of reform*. Ann Arbor: University of Michigan Press.

Federal State Statistical Service. (2004). *Struktura i osnovhye pokazateli deyatel'nosti predpriyatii (bes subientov malogo predprinimatelistva) za 2003 god po dannym strukturnogo obsledovaniya* [Structure and basic indicators of enterprise activities (excluding small firms) in 2003 based on the structural survey]. Moscow: Federal State Statistical Service (in Russian).

Federal State Statistical Service. (2005). *Rossiiskii statisticheskii ezhegodnik 2004* [Russian statistical yearbook 2004]. Moscow: Federal State Statistical Service (in Russian).

Iwasaki, I. (2007a). Corporate law and governance system in Russia. In B. Dallago & I. Iwasaki (Eds.), *Corporate restructuring and governance in transition economies* (pp. 213–249). Basingstoke: Palgrave Macmillan.

Iwasaki, I. (2007b). Legal forms of joint stock companies and corporate behavior in Russia. *Problems of Economic Transition, 50*(5), 73–86.

Iwasaki, I. (2007c). Enterprise reform and corporate governance in Russia: A quantitative survey. *Journal of Economic Surveys, 21*(5), 849–902.

Iwasaki, I. (2008). The determinants of board composition in a transforming economy: Evidence from Russia. *Journal of Corporate Finance, 14*(5), 532–549.

Iwasaki, I. (2009). Legal form of incorporation. In T. Dolgopyatova, I. Iwasaki, & A. Yakovlev (Eds.), *Organization and development of Russian business: A firm-level analysis* (pp. 62–88). Basingstoke: Palgrave Macmillan.

Iwasaki, I. (2011). *Economic transition, firm organisation and internal control: determinants of audit structure in Russian firms*. EBRD Working Paper No. 126. London: European Bank for Reconstruction and Development.

Iwasaki, I. (2013a). Firm-level determinants of board system choice: Evidence from Russia. *Comparative Economic Studies, 55*(4), 636–671.

Iwasaki, I. (2013b). Global financial crisis, corporate governance, and firm survival: The case of Russia. *Journal of Comparative Economics*. http://dx.doi.org/10.1016/j.jce.2013.03.015. (Advance online publication, 28 Mar 2013)

Iwasaki, I., & Suzuki, T. (2007). Transition strategy, corporate exploitation, and state capture: An empirical analysis of the former Soviet states. *Communist and Post-communist Studies, 40*(4), 393–422.

Karpoff, J. M., & Rice, E. M. (1989). Organizational form, share transferability, and firm performance: Evidence from the ANCSA corporations. *Journal of Financial Economics, 24*(1), 69–105.

Osipenko, O. (2005). Kosenke obnarodovannoi kontseptsii reformirovaniya federalinykh institutov korporativnogo upravleniya (An assessment of the published concept on the reform of the federal institutions of corporate governance). *Rossiiskii Ekonomicheskii Zhurnal*, (1), 34–44. (in Russian)

Ostrom, E. (2005). *Understanding institutional diversity*. Princeton/Oxford: Princeton University Press.

Young, H. P. (1998). *Individual strategy and social structure: An evolutionary theory of institutions*. Princeton/Oxford: Princeton University Press.

Big 4 Conservatism Around the World

Richard Chung, Michael Firth, Jeong-Bon Kim, and Lei Pang

Abstract Conservatism is a long-established underlying principle of accounting but its implementation has come under the spotlight in recent years following the spate of well-publicized corporate collapses in the U.S. and elsewhere. Previous studies have shown that the Big 4 audit firms are more conservative than the non-Big 4 *in the U.S*. The current study examines whether the U.S. findings extend to other countries. In doing so, we make use of a relatively new measure of conservatism, namely, the C-score developed by Khan and Watts. We find that the conclusion drawn from U.S. studies, namely that the Big 4 are more conservative, extends to the international setting but only under certain conditions. Specifically, the Big 4 are more conservative in those countries where litigation and reputation risks, broadly defined, are high. This increase in conservatism represents a rational response by the Big 4 auditors to their greater exposure, vis-a-vis the non-Big 4 auditors, to litigation and reputation loss in those countries.

R. Chung (✉)
Department of Accounting, Finance and Economics, Griffith University, Gold Coast, QLD 4222, Australia
e-mail: r.chung@griffith.edu.au

M. Firth
Department of Finance and Insurance, Lingnan University, Tuen Mun, Hong Kong
e-mail: mafirth@Ln.edu.hk

J.-B. Kim
Department of Accountancy, City University of Hong Kong, Kowloon, Hong Kong
e-mail: jeongkim@cityu.edu.hk

L. Pang
Department of Finance and Decision Sciences, Hong Kong Baptist University, Kowloon, Hong Kong
e-mail: lpang@hkbu.edu.hk

S. Boubaker and D.K. Nguyen (eds.), *Corporate Governance in Emerging Markets*, CSR, Sustainability, Ethics & Governance, DOI 10.1007/978-3-642-44955-0_8,

1 Introduction

Conservatism is an old-established concept that underlies financial accounting practices and standards in many countries. Broadly defined, conservatism implies that, given a number of ways to calculate profit, a firm will choose to report the lowest profit. Thus, the reported earnings will be at the lower bound and reflect pessimistic rather than optimistic outcomes. For example, accounting principles usually dictate that no credit should be taken for revenue until it has been realized, but losses should be immediately recorded for all known liabilities. This leads to a bias 'that will tend to understate profit and undervalue assets' (Lewis and Pendrill 1996, p. 29). Explicit examples of conservatism include higher provisions for bad debts and higher impairment charges for declines in the value of assets. Conservatism acts as a bulwark against the natural tendency of many managers to report optimistic earnings or to report earnings that help achieve managers' opportunistic objectives.

Recent research studies have investigated conservatism in a variety of settings. Watts (2003a, b) and Givoly et al. (2007) provide a concise review of the U.S. literature: non-U.S. studies include Giner and Rees (2001), Raonic et al. (2004), and Huijgen and Lubberink (2005). The basic research design in most of these studies follows Basu (1997). He defined conservatism in financial statements 'as the more timely recognition in earnings of bad news regarding future cash flows than good news' (Basu 1997, p. 33). Basu proposed the use of positive stock returns as a proxy for good news and negative stock returns as a proxy for bad news. Using U.S. data, he finds a larger contemporaneous association between bad news and earnings, than for good news and earnings. Thus, bad news is incorporated in a firm's earnings much more rapidly than is good news; good news filters through to reported earnings over a number of future years. Two major contributions of Basu's work are, one, to develop a model for assessing conservatism, and, two, to demonstrate empirically that conservatism is a common trait in the U.S.

Subsequent studies have examined conservatism across a number of countries. Ball et al. (2000) find that conservatism is greater in common-law countries (e.g., Anglo-American influence) than in code-law countries. Furthermore, they conclude that regulation, taxation, and litigation explain variations in conservatism among countries with a common law heritage. For example, they report that, within common law countries, British firms have less conservative accounting and they attribute this to lower litigation costs and a lower reliance on public debt. However, Pope and Walker (1999) dispute their conclusions and argue that once differences in reporting practices are acknowledged, U.K. firms recognize bad news faster than U.S. firms do. In a later study, Ball et al. (2003) conclude that accounting standards are not the prime driver of conservatism. They examine the accounting conservatism of four East Asian countries (Hong Kong, Malaysia, Singapore, and Thailand) and find that despite adopting Anglo-American style accounting standards, firms' earnings are less conservative than in many code-law countries. Ball et al. (2003) argue that preparers' incentives for conservative accounting are particularly important, and in the case of Hong Kong, Malaysia, Singapore, and Thailand, the incentives are weak. Thus, the adoption of Anglo-American standards and a common law heritage (for Hong Kong, Malaysia, and Singapore) do not provide a sufficient condition for conservatism. Law enforcement, along with political, legal, and economic institutions, affect financial reporting incentives and thus the level of conservatism applied to financial statements in different countries (Ball et al. 2008; Bushman and Piotroski 2006; Watts 2006).

The earnings reported in a firm's financial statements are a function of judgments and decisions made by both company managers and the external auditor. Chung et al. (2003) argue that in the U.S., large auditors have incentives to impose more conservative accounting on their audit clients. These incentives relate to avoiding costly litigation. Their empirical tests confirm the prediction that Big 6 clients[1] adopt more conservative accounting, and the results are robust across a variety of conditions.

In this paper, we extend the work of Chung et al. (2003) in two different ways. First, we examine the role of auditors in influencing conservatism in client financial statements across a large number of countries. Cross-country studies are important because of the increasingly global nature of financial markets and the multi-national scope of institutional investors and financial service providers, including auditors. We are interested in discovering whether the differences in attitudes towards conservatism between large and small auditors found in the U.S. is replicated in other countries that have different legal and institutional regimes. For example, does the more conservative stance of Big 4 auditors observed in the U.S. extend to other national jurisdictions? Is there a conservatism culture within an audit firm that transcends national borders? Alternatively, does the legal, political economy, and financial market environment within a country shape views on conservatism such that audit firms' cultures are subdued? Our research will shed light on these questions. Our study contributes to the expanding literature that examines the extent to which legal and institutional factors help explain cross-country differences in accounting, corporate performance, and financial structure (Ball et al. 2000; Bushman et al. 2004; La Porta et al. 1997, 1998, 2000; Leuz et al. 2003).

Second, we make use of a new approach to measure conservatism developed by Khan and Watts (2008, 2009). Instead of using the coefficient on negative stock returns as a measure of conservatism (i.e., the Basu approach), we use the C-score measure advocated by Khan and Watts.[2] The Basu approach has come in for

[1] The auditors of listed firms are very concentrated. At various times, the largest eight, six, five, and four auditors have dominated audit markets worldwide. Because of mergers and the demise of one auditor, Arthur Andersen, the Big Eight are now the big Four (Big 4). The Big 4 are Deloitte Touche Tohmatsu (DTT), Ernst and Young (EY), KPMG, and PriceWaterhouseCoopers (PWC). When we review prior studies, we use Big 8, Big 6, Big 5, and Big 4, as appropriate. In our analyses, we use the term Big 4 even though at the beginning of our sample period it was the Big 8. The Big 4 is an internationally well-known term for the four largest audit firms.

[2] The Basu measure of conservatism has previously been used by Chung et al. (2004) in a study of Big 4 firms using data from around the world. They reported that the Big 4 audit firms had a

criticism in recent years (Beaver and Ryan 2005; Dietrich et al. 2007; Givoly et al. 2007; Khan and Watts 2009) and there are increasing doubts about its ability to adequately measure conservatism. Several studies have concluded that the Basu measure of conservatism is unrelated to, or even negatively related to, other measures of conservatism. This issue limits the usefulness of the Basu model in empirical studies. C-score has been used in several recent studies as a measure of conservatism (Dhaliwal et al. 2010; Frankel and Roychowdhury 2009; Kim and Zhang 2011; Louis et al. 2011; Srivastava and Tse 2010; Wittenberg-Moerman 2008).

Using a sample of 108,088 firm-year observations from 36 countries for the period 1991–2007, we investigate whether Big 4 clients use more conservative accounting than non-Big 4 clients. Our results show that whether Big 4 clients adopt more conservative accounting than the clients of the non-Big 4 is conditional on the legal and institutional environment of the country where the client is domiciled. We find that the clients of Big 4 auditors use more conservative accounting than the clients of non-Big 4 auditors *if* they are located in jurisdictions with stronger investor protection. However, when the legal and institutional structures are weak, Big 4 clients are indistinguishable from non-Big 4 clients in terms of adopting conservative accounting. We argue that the observed differences in conservatism across clients are due partly to differential pressure from their Big 4 versus non-Big 4 auditors. Our findings are consistent with Big 4 auditors having flexible views on conservatism, and these views are shaped by the legal and institutional environment they operate in. If there are costs to the auditor for not reporting conservatively these are differentially greater for the Big 4. The higher conservatism of Big 4 auditors represents a rational response to the increased threat of litigation, sanctions, and loss of reputation they face in more litigious and investor-friendly jurisdictions. The premise that Big 4 auditors adopt a single global brand image of being more conservative than non-Big 4 auditors across all countries is not supported by the results.

Our paper contributes to the literature in several ways. First, anecdotal evidence, as well as the promotional materials from the auditors themselves, suggests that Big 4 auditors work hard to create a global brand image of high quality conservative audits but our results imply this image does withstand rigorous international scrutiny. Big 4 auditors are opportunistic in the sense that the level of conservatism they apply to their clients' financial statements depends on the jurisdiction of their clients' businesses. Thus, the Big 4 auditors use conservatism to signal audit quality and distinguish themselves from their non-Big 4 brethren only in those countries where the litigation risk and reputation costs to them are high. This study complements the work of Bushman and Piotroski (2006), who carefully articulate why

uniform level of quality across countries, a finding which is opposite to that reported here. This indicates that the correct measurement of conservatism is extremely important. In a later study, Francis and Wang (2008) also use the Basu approach. Francis et al. (2004) use earnings management to examine audit quality differences between Big 4 and other auditors using international data.

there are different levels of conservatism across countries. Our extension examines the role of the Big 4 and non-Big 4 auditors in explaining differences in conservatism across clients and across countries. Second, we demonstrate the use of a conservatism measure, C-score, rather than the traditional Basu approach. C-score has useful properties that make it more suitable as a measure of conservatism than the Basu measure. In particular, the use of C-score allows us to conduct a cross-sectional analysis of the effect of Big 4 conservatism on firm-level accounting conservatism using cross-country data.

The paper proceeds as follows. In the next section, we discuss the concept of conservatism and explain the differences attached to conservatism across countries. Importantly, we articulate the role of auditors in influencing their clients' accounting conservatism and debate whether, and under what conditions, there are differences between Big 4 auditors and non-Big 4 auditors. We then describe the research design and the data used to test our hypotheses. We then discuss the results, and follow it with a summary and conclusion.

2 Factors That Influence Conservatism

Several forces have led to conservatism in financial reporting (Watts 2003a, b; Bushman and Piotroski 2006; LaFond and Watts 2008). The main objective of many of them is to increase the confidence of outside investors and creditors in using financial statements. Confidence in the veracity of financial statements is vital for investors and creditors when deciding whether to invest or extend credit and whether to write contracts based on accounting numbers. Because of information asymmetry between managers and outsiders, investors and creditors may restrict the equity, debt, and credit financing they provide to the company and/or they make the cost of financing more expensive. To mitigate the costs imposed by information asymmetry, managers voluntarily adopt conservative accounting practices, and, recognizing this, investors and creditors become more willing to help finance the company. This view of conservative accounting is widely held. For example, Ball et al. (2000, p. 2) state that conservative accounting 'facilitates monitoring of managers, and of debt and other contracts, and is an important feature of corporate governance.'

The voluntary acts of companies to adopt conservative accounting led regulators and professional accounting bodies to enshrine conservatism into rules, standards, and recommended codes of practice. The aim of the regulations is to help protect the interests of investors and creditors, and thereby improve the functioning of commerce and finance. The profession emphasizes conservatism as it wishes to maintain and improve its reputation for financial probity. Financial scandals and the ensuing litigation have often been the impetus for the adoption of more conservative accounting (Mitchell et al. 1991). In the U.S., Statement of Financial Accounting Concepts No. 2 (SFAC 2) requires the use of conservatism, and this underlies the other standards of the FASB. Conservatism also receives backing from the standards and promulgations of regulatory agencies and professional bodies in other national jurisdictions.

Another force behind conservative accounting is the threat of litigation that alleges fraudulent financial statements and especially the overstatement of earnings. In the U.S., litigation involving financial statement fraud has been commonplace for many years, and this feature of American corporate life is becoming increasingly prevalent in other countries as well (Likierman 1989; London Economics 2006; Samsonova et al. 2010). The money involved in litigation cases has increased dramatically, and it has the potential to bankrupt the recipients of the lawsuits. To reduce the chances of litigation in the first place, and to provide a defense when litigation does arise, managers voluntarily select conservative accounting methods.

While accounting standards prescribe required practices, these are not all-encompassing and do not cover all aspects of business transactions. Furthermore, accounting standards often permit a choice of methods and estimates. Thus, managers have some latitude in choosing what accounting methods to adopt and some of them select more conservative methods than others choose. Managers may have incentives to increase current reported earnings and this will lead them to use less conservative accounting (Kim and Zhang 2011). Current earnings can be boosted by recognizing future gains early and delaying the recognition of expenses to future periods. Reasons why managers might want to boost current earnings include attempts to increase executive compensation and bonuses that are tied to reported earnings, to avoid violating debt covenants, and to increase the perceived attractiveness of the firm when raising new equity or debt finance.

Managers' choices of accounting methods are constrained by the external auditors. In effect, auditors are the enforcers of accounting standards. In many cases, a company will discuss accounting methods or changes in methods with their auditor before implementation. The external auditor also influences accounting choice at the time of the audit and can insist on changes in method if a clean audit report is to be given. In the U.S., there is documented evidence that large auditors prefer conservative accounting methods (e.g., Chung et al. 2003; Kim et al. 2003), and this may also apply in other national jurisdictions as well. Litigation is a major factor that drives auditors to prefer conservative accounting in the U.S. Simunic and Stein (1996) and Shu (2000) show that litigation risk is a major factor in the supply decisions of audit firms. The litigation factor differentially affects large and small auditors, and it is the large auditors that have the most wealth at risk.[3] Class action lawsuits are more likely to involve large auditors because of their 'deep pockets'. Therefore, large auditors will insist on clients using conservative accounting methods so as to reduce the chances of litigation and so as to provide a defense if litigation does occur. Early evidence from the U.S. showed no instances where auditors were sued for understatement of earnings, while there were many instances of litigations over alleged over-statement of

[3] Litigation costs include fines, penalties, and court and lawyers' fees. However, auditors also bear costs relating to sanctions from regulators and professional bodies and from loss of reputation.

earnings (St. Pierre and Anderson 1984). Large auditors are more likely to be able to insist that their listed clients adopt conservative accounting. Because they have many listed clients, large auditors can afford to lose some of them if there is a disagreement on accounting matters. In contrast, small audit firms may be very loath to lose a listed client as this is seen as a very prestigious client to them; in this circumstance, small audit firms may be willing to approve the less conservative accounting choices of listed clients. Chung et al. (2003) provide evidence that Big 8/6 auditors (a proxy for large auditors) are associated with more conservative accounting in the U.S. An alternative explanation for an association between conservative accounting and large auditors is that some companies use conservative accounting and hire a large auditor to signal this policy. In this study, we employ a two stage 'treatment effects' model to control for this simultaneity problem.

A recent strand of research has emerged that examines reasons for differences in corporate governance and performance across countries. Here, studies have found that the legal and institutional environment within a country has an important impact on managerial behavior, ownership structure, and corporate and investment practices (e.g., La Porta et al. 1997, 2000). Strong investor protection laws and the ability to enforce laws and obtain legal remedies have been shown to be vital ingredients of good corporate governance. Strong protection for investors' rights is associated with greater transparency and higher quality disclosures of firm-specific information. In countries with strong minority investor protection, accounting standards are more developed, earnings are more value relevant (Ali and Hwang 2000; Ball et al. 2000; Hung 2001), the extent of earnings management is lower (Leuz et al. 2003), and more firm-specific information is incorporated into stock prices (Kim and Shi 2011; Morck et al. 2000). Bushman and Piotroski (2006) consider in detail the influences that shape conservatism and how these differ across countries. In particular, they examine the influence of the legal regime, securities laws, political economy, and tax policy on conservatism. We extend their study by examining the influence of audit firm type: Big 4 and non-Big 4.

As described earlier, the Big 4 auditors are associated with more conservative accounting in the U.S. and we attribute this to the legal environment where auditors are routinely subject to lawsuits. It follows, therefore, that company managers and auditors may be less conservative in accounting matters in those countries that are characterized as having weak investor protection. The penalties for allowing clients to pursue more aggressive accounting are largely absent in weak legal environments and so auditors may give management more discretion and latitude in reporting income. This can apply to all auditors and so large auditors may become indistinguishable from smaller auditors as regards their stance on conservatism. Based on this view of the world, the operational standards of the Big 4 vary depending on the legal jurisdiction in which they operate. By allowing more aggressive accounting in low investor protection environments, the auditors endear themselves to managements who then have more latitude in preparing the financial statements.

An alternative hypothesis is that a large auditor develops a culture of strong conservatism that pervades its world-wide operations. This is consistent with a large auditor building a global brand image based on conservatism. Education, training, and inter-country exchange of staff all help to inculcate a uniform approach to conservatism within a multi-national audit firm. Under this alternative hypothesis, we expect that a large auditor will be more conservative than a small auditor in all types of legal and financial market environments. Of course, a Big 4 auditor may pursue a brand name enhancing strategy of conservatism and, at the same time, increase the conservatism premium even more in those countries where litigation risk is high.

3 Research Design

3.1 A Measure of Conservatism

Although the concept of conservatism is well understood, it has proved very difficult to derive a quantitative measure of it that can be used in empirical studies. Basu (1997) constructed a measure of conservatism based on the asymmetric timeliness of earnings, where earnings more rapidly incorporate bad news than good news. While prior research studies have extensively used Basu's news-dependent conservatism measure to address various accounting issues (e.g., Bushman and Piotroski 2006; Roychowdhury and Watts 2007), several researchers have recently noted some problems inherent in the Basu conservatism measure, particularly when research questions are related to firm-level variation in accounting conservatism (e.g., Givoly et al. 2007; Khan and Watts 2008; Penman and Zhang 2002).

Recently, Khan and Watts (2008, 2009) proposed an alternative approach to measure conservatism. While their approach is similar in spirit to Basu, it avoids the problems associated with that model. In particular, their model allows us to measure the extent of firm-level conservatism, which is called C-score, using cross-sectional data. A firm's size, market to book ratio, and leverage are theoretically and empirically linked to conservatism (Khan and Watts 2009; Roychowdhury and Watts 2007; Watts 2003a, b) and these variables are used to estimate a firm's C-score. C-scores vary across firms and over time. Although the model uses just three characteristics of a firm, Khan and Watts (2009), using a variety of validation tests, demonstrate that the resulting C-scores provide robust estimates of conservatism.

The first step in the procedure to calculate C-scores is to run a regression of earnings against stock returns and negative stock returns, and their interactions with firm size, market to book ratio, leverage, and a country-level law enforcement index. Thus:

$$\begin{aligned} X_{cit} = {} & \beta_1 + \beta_2 D_{cit} \\ & + R_{cit}(\mu_1 + \mu_2 SIZE_{cit} + \mu_3 MB_{cit} + \mu_4 LEV_{cit}) \\ & + D_{cit} R_{cit}(\lambda_1 + \lambda_2 SIZE_{cit} + \lambda_3 MB_{cit} + \lambda_4 LEV_{cit}) + \varepsilon_{cit} \end{aligned} \tag{1}$$

where, for country *c*, company *i*, and year *t*, all variables are as defined below.

X	=	Earnings before extraordinary items deflated by lagged market capitalization;
D	=	A dummy variable coded one (1) if the stock return (R) is negative, and coded zero (0) otherwise;
R	=	Stock return, inclusive of dividends, over the fiscal year;
SIZE	=	Log of equity market capitalization (share price times shares outstanding in millions of U.S. dollars);
MB	=	Market to book ratio;
LEV	=	Total liabilities divided by total assets.

In the second, step, we use the coefficients from regression model (1) to measure firm-specific conservatism, denoted by *C-score*. Specifically:

$$\text{C-score}_{cit} \equiv \hat{\lambda}_1 + \hat{\lambda}_2 SIZE_{cit} + \hat{\lambda}_3 MB_{cit} + \hat{\lambda}_4 LEV_{cit} \tag{2}$$

Since C-score is not normally distributed, we convert it to a decile ranking (*Cdec*).

3.2 *Self-selection Issue*

To test whether Big 4 auditors are more conservative than non-Big 4 auditors across different legal environments we use cross-sectional regressions of C-score decile rankings on auditor-type (and control variables). However, we recognize that managers not only make accounting choices but also select the auditor. To the extent that companies with conservative accounting practices are more likely to appoint Big 4 auditors, the results of single-equation regressions may suffer from a self-selection bias. To address this concern, we estimate a two-stage treatment effects model (Greene 1997; Hogan 1997; Kim et al. 2003; Maddala 1983).

In the first stage, we estimate a multivariate probit model, where the dependent variable, *Pr(B4)* is the probability that managers select a Big 4 auditor. The model is based on Choi and Wong (2007). This model has been used in several studies of auditor choice (e.g., Choi et al. 2008; Gul et al. 2010). The model is:

$$\begin{aligned} Pr(B4)_{cit} = {} & \delta_0 + \delta_1 LNTA_{cit} + \delta_2 CAPINT_{cit} + \delta_3 INVREC_{cit} + \delta_4 LEV_{cit} \\ & + \delta_5 LOSS_{cit} + \delta_6 CROSS_{cit} + \delta_7 ENF_{cit} + \delta_8 FDI_{ct} + \delta_9 STK_{ct} + \delta_{10} GDP_{ct} + \varepsilon_{cit} \end{aligned} \tag{3}$$

where, for country *c*, firm *i* in year *t*, the variables are as defined below:

Pr(B4)	=	Ex ante probability that a company appoints one of the Big 4 auditors, which is ex post coded one (1) for a Big 8/6/5/4 client, and zero (0) otherwise: To aid exposition, we use the term "Big 4" for the Big 8, Big 6, Big 5, and Big 4.
LNTA	=	Log of total assets (in millions of U.S. dollars);
CAPINT	=	Fixed assets divided by total assets;
INVREC	=	Inventory and receivables divided by total assets;
LEV	=	Total liabilities divided by total assets;
LOSS	=	A dummy variable coded one (1) if the firm reports a loss in the prior year, and zero (0) otherwise;
CROSS	=	A dummy variable coded one (1) if a firm has a listing on more than one market, and zero (0) otherwise;
ENF	=	A law enforcement variable for the country where the company is located. It is equal to 0.5* (rule of law index) + antidirectors rights. The variable is taken from Choi and Wong (2007), who use data from La Porta et al. (1997). We update the antidirectors rights index by using the anti-self-dealing index from Djankov et al. (2008);
FDI	=	Net foreign direct investment (scaled by total GDP) for the country in each sample year;
STK	=	The total market capitalization scaled by total GDP for the country in each year;
GDP	=	Gross domestic product per capita (in thousands of U.S. dollars) for the country in each year;
ε	=	Unspecified random factors.

Our choice of independent variables draws on Choi and Wong (2007). *LNTA* and *CAPINT* represent the scope and complexity of an audit and a large client with complex operations may believe that a Big 4 auditor has greater resources and superior skills necessary for the audit. The valuation of short-term assets, *INVREC*, involves some management judgment and this might have an impact on the selection of the auditor. *LEV* and *LOSS* are associated with a client's financial health and this may have an impact on auditor choice. Companies that are listed on more than one national exchange (*CROSS* = 1) may choose a Big 4 auditor as they will have more experience and a greater presence in many countries. Lang et al. (2003) find that non-U.S. firms that cross-list in the U.S. have higher quality accounting reports. In more advanced legal enforcement regimes (*ENF* = 1), clients may seek to hire a Big 4 auditor to give them assurance that financial statements are credible and will not be a source for lawsuits. *FDI*, *STK*, and *GDP* are added as control variables.

In the second stage, we estimate the following regression that links our measure of accounting conservatism to our test variables, control variables, and the inverse Mills ratio, denoted by *LAMBDA*, which is computed from the first stage probit regression.

$$\begin{aligned}\mathrm{Cdec}_{\mathrm{cit}} = \alpha_1 + \alpha_2 \mathrm{Big4}_{\mathrm{cit}} + \alpha_3 \mathrm{SIZE}_{\mathrm{cit}-1} + \alpha_4 \mathrm{MB}_{\mathrm{cit}\text{-}1} + \alpha_5 \mathrm{LEV}_{\mathrm{cit}-1} \\ + \alpha_6 \mathrm{CROSS}_{\mathrm{cit}} + \alpha_7 \mathrm{LAMBDA}_{\mathrm{cit}} + \varepsilon_{\mathrm{cit}}\end{aligned} \tag{4}$$

where, for country *c*, company *i*, and year *t* (or *t-1*), *Cdec* represents our measure of conservatism, estimated from the pooled regression in Eq. 2. *SIZE*, *M*/*B*, *LEV*, and *CROSS* are as defined earlier; and other variables are defined below:

Big4	=	A dummy variable coded one (1) if the auditor is a member of the Big 8/6/5/4, and coded zero (0) otherwise;
LAMBDA	=	The inverse Mills ratio generated from the self selection model in Eq. 3 using the pooled OLS procedure.

We include three important determinants of conservatism, *SIZE, M/B,* and *LEV*, in a *lagged* form (in year t − 1) as control variables to minimize possible mechanical correlations between our measures of conservatism in year t and these three determinants in year t. As indicated in Eq. 2, C-score is measured as a function of firm size, market-to-book ratio, and leverage in the current year t. As such, *SIZE, M/B*, and *LEV* in current year t could be mechanically correlated with our measures of C-score. We therefore use lagged terms. A cross-listing on a foreign stock market might affect conservatism and so we control for this using the dummy variable *CROSS*.

3.3 Legal and Institutional Factors That Influence Conservatism

The main experimental variable of interest is *Big4*, which captures the difference in conservatism between Big 4 and non-Big 4 client companies. If the coefficient on *B4* is significantly positive, this indicates that Big 4 client companies are more conservative than non-Big 4 client companies. To see if the Big 4 conservatism effect is conditional on the legal and institutional environment of the country where the client is domiciled, we partition countries by whether they are characterized as having strong investor protection rights and strong institutional structures or whether they are characterized as having weak investor protection rights and weak institutional oversight. We use a variety of indices to measure the legal and institutional factors of a country because there is no single universally accepted indicator of country-level legal and institutional quality. All these indices have been used in prior research. We do not combine the indices into a single score as there is no obvious way to weight the individual factors. Instead, we examine whether the results are robust to the choice of legal or institutional environment index.

We group country-specific legal and institutional factors into five types: auditor litigation risk, legal institutions, securities law, political economy, and financial market factors. The specific indices and their sources are listed in Appendix 1. Auditor litigation risk is explicitly proxied by the Wingate (1997) litigation index, ease of being sued, and the severity of sanctions, denoted by *Litigate, Sue,* and *Sanction*, respectively. The Wingate litigation index captures the litigiousness of doing business as an auditor in a country and is based on assessments made by an international insurance underwriter who specialized in providing indemnity insurance for auditors (Wingate 1997). A high score is given for countries where the insurance cost is high. Previous studies have used the Wingate litigation index as a proxy for country-level litigation risk (e.g., Choi and Wong 2007; Choi et al. 2008).

The other two auditor litigation risk variables reflect the ease of suing or sanctioning the auditor with a high score given to countries where it is very easy to sue and where sanctions are easily imposed.

A country's legal system is often described as being either common law or code law. Common law emphasizes the use of case law and judicial precedent in interpreting laws whereas code law emphasizes adherence to the legal statutes. Ball et al. (2000) and Bushman and Piotroski (2006) argue that common law countries may be more inclined toward conservative accounting. Thus, we distinguish between common law and code law countries. Other legal/judicial regime indices relate to the efficiency of the judiciary, the quality of legal enforcement, liability standards, public enforcement of laws, disclosure requirements, and laws related to enhancing shareholders' rights in dealing with directors (Anti-self dealing). In all cases, a high score indicates a more efficient legal system where plaintiffs can more easily take legal actions, including suing the auditor. Greater disclosure will facilitate plaintiffs' actions against the auditor. The political economy factor is measured by how easy it is for the government to expropriate assets (risk of expropriation), state owned enterprises' share of the national economy, and how high the tax burden is. Bushman and Piotroski (2006) include these variables in their study of conservatism.

Some countries have higher stock price synchronicity than other countries (Morck et al. 2000), which implies that stock prices in these countries co-move more with common (market and/or industry-wide) factors than with firm-specific factors. In contrast, in countries with low synchronicity, firm-specific information is very important in determining stock prices. Here, a firm's financial statements assume more importance for investors. Auditors should therefore have a bigger role to play in countries with low synchronicity. By extension, auditors may face greater scrutiny in these countries.

When the proportion of shares held by minority shareholders is high (i.e., the score for "ownership concentration" is low), investors place greater reliance on a firm's financial statements and the external audit. Litigation pressure on the auditor will therefore be higher when firms have a widely-held share capital. Furthermore, Big 4 auditors may be more conservative in dealing with clients in countries with diffuse ownership patterns. Countries with a lot of insider trading might have a lesser need for high quality financial statement information as shareholders base their investment decisions on the actions of the insiders. In contrast, countries with better regulated insider trading have a greater need for high quality financial statements and the Big 4 have incentives to be more conservative. The extent to which stock markets make it easy for new firms to make IPOs may also have an impact on conservatism. IPO companies have biases towards optimistic financial reporting as they want to maximize their values for listing purposes. In heavily regulated markets (i.e., where there are more barriers to making an IPO or SEO) there will be more penalties against auditors if the new IPOs and SEOs fail to live up to expectations. We therefore expect the Big4 auditors will be more conservative in such countries.

The scores for the legal and institutional factors for each of our 36 countries are shown in Appendix 2. A few countries have no scores for auditor litigation risk (Litigate), stock price comovement or synchronicity (VWR^2), insider trading (Insider), and access to equity. This is because the countries were not covered by the indexes we use. We categorize each country that has a score into those with an above median score (High) and those with a below median score (Low). Appendix 3 shows the High and Low scores for each country along each legal and institutional dimension. In the case of risk of expropriation, state-operated business, tax burden, insider trading, and access to capital, we reverse the scoring so that a low score in Appendix 2 receives a High score in Appendix 3. This coding means that countries with a high risk of expropriation, high state involvement in business, high taxes, high insider trading, and high access to capital are coded High in Appendix 3. Bushman and Piotroski (2006) use this same approach. In the case of severity of auditor sanction (Sanction), there are many ties. We therefore classify scores of 0 and 0.5 as Low and a score of 1 as High (0, 0.5, and 1 are the only scores for sanction). As an example of the coding of High and Low, India has a score of 0.66 for liability standards (Liab Std) in Appendix 2 and this is above the median for the 36 countries. India is therefore classified as having a high score for Liab Std (see Appendix 3).

3.4 Data

The sample consists of 108,504 firm-year observations and 14,864 firms from 36 countries around the world for the period 1992–2007. In some of our tests the sample size is less than 108,504 observations because we do not have scores for some legal and institutional factors for some countries. We obtain global financial data from the *Worldscope* database. Information on institutional or legal environment are obtained from Wingate (1997), La Porta et al. (1997, 1998), La Porta et al. (2006); Djankov et al. (2008), Jin and Myers (2006), Hartland-Peel (1996), and Schwab et al. (1999). GDP per capita, market capitalization scaled by GDP (STK), and net foreign investment scaled by GDP (FDI) are extracted from the *International Financial Statistics* published by the World Bank. To be included in the sample, a firm must have the necessary information on their stock return, auditors, assets and lagged financial data. We exclude financial firms (SIC code 6000–6999). We require that the total assets and book value of equity for each firm be greater than zero. We delete firms with missing data on market capitalization (*SIZE*), total assets (*LNTA*), fixed assets (*CAPINT*), market-to-book ratio (*MB*), leverage (*LEV*), inventory and receivables (*INVREC*), earnings (*X*) and stock returns (*R*). We require at least 100 firm-year observations within a country. All continuous variables used in the regression analyses are deleted if their values are below the 1 % and above the 99 % cutoffs to mitigate potential effects of outliers on our results. Appendix 4 defines the variables.

Table 1 Summary statistics

Country	*X*	*R*	*SIZE*	*MB*	*LEV*	*LNTA*	*CAPINT*	*INVREC*	*LOSS*	*CROSS*	*BIG4*	*C-score*	*Cdec*	N. observations
Argentina	0.160	0.111	4.955	1.130	0.271	5.786	0.559	0.289	0.274	0.202	0.769	0.023	0.401	416
Australia	0.001	0.264	4.052	2.629	0.168	3.977	0.445	0.247	0.459	0.142	0.659	0.154	0.674	5,835
Austria	0.137	0.093	4.937	1.785	0.264	5.747	0.379	0.400	0.194	0.185	0.601	0.050	0.463	702
Belgium	0.127	0.103	5.472	2.086	0.242	5.968	0.325	0.417	0.189	0.066	0.666	0.042	0.452	850
Brazil	0.001	0.382	4.989	1.302	0.285	6.173	0.631	0.345	0.313	0.269	0.688	0.023	0.398	1,856
Canada	0.055	0.206	5.219	2.412	0.219	5.298	0.557	0.253	0.403	0.000	0.828	0.073	0.508	6,345
Chile	0.129	0.138	5.677	1.758	0.232	5.954	0.596	0.265	0.102	0.168	0.949	0.024	0.395	922
Colombia	0.244	0.177	5.183	0.886	0.129	6.142	0.567	0.195	0.171	0.000	0.842	0.050	0.467	158
Denmark	0.141	0.141	4.655	1.925	0.266	5.138	0.385	0.447	0.187	0.026	0.772	0.068	0.518	1,303
Egypt	0.238	0.357	5.862	2.676	0.232	5.971	0.574	0.289	0.089	0.000	0.580	0.048	0.462	112
Finland	0.145	0.176	5.141	2.011	0.261	5.543	0.353	0.388	0.163	0.057	0.862	0.049	0.472	1,122
France	0.111	0.117	5.022	2.111	0.226	5.643	0.223	0.496	0.239	0.060	0.414	0.070	0.522	5,344
Germany	0.093	0.081	5.143	2.390	0.196	5.692	0.308	0.437	0.254	0.064	0.637	0.084	0.551	5,132
Greece	0.108	0.198	4.705	2.406	0.253	5.095	0.389	0.527	0.244	0.016	0.288	0.087	0.553	1,351
Hong Kong	0.070	0.231	4.378	1.729	0.187	4.948	0.325	0.339	0.298	0.153	0.703	0.100	0.591	3,764
India	0.288	0.258	4.302	2.339	0.299	4.930	0.471	0.456	0.141	0.021	0.125	0.089	0.558	3,541
Indonesia	0.216	0.230	3.607	1.457	0.367	4.598	0.471	0.372	0.279	0.013	0.519	0.068	0.527	1,677
Ireland	0.087	0.184	5.030	2.640	0.225	5.172	0.396	0.305	0.339	0.247	0.844	0.089	0.544	454
Israel	0.079	0.144	5.474	2.116	0.243	5.824	0.298	0.309	0.344	0.163	0.915	0.043	0.449	553
Italy	0.132	0.090	5.808	1.828	0.256	6.534	0.312	0.429	0.258	0.090	0.904	0.012	0.366	1,697
Japan	0.073	0.028	5.559	1.556	0.253	6.331	0.317	0.379	0.206	0.038	0.709	0.015	0.373	27,669
South Korea	0.308	0.262	4.613	1.063	0.300	5.870	0.406	0.362	0.261	0.010	0.614	0.028	0.414	4,579
Malaysia	0.075	0.066	4.010	1.354	0.241	4.698	0.450	0.368	0.279	0.018	0.683	0.087	0.575	4,773
Mexico	0.205	0.126	6.154	1.528	0.257	6.856	0.611	0.276	0.240	0.475	0.832	−0.016	0.286	768
New Zealand	0.130	0.147	5.198	2.111	0.257	5.331	0.538	0.308	0.123	0.084	0.929	0.051	0.469	521
Norway	0.118	0.192	5.191	2.243	0.305	5.587	0.428	0.311	0.293	0.104	0.843	0.040	0.433	1,063
Peru	0.239	0.359	4.389	2.370	0.211	4.897	0.506	0.334	0.157	0.145	0.797	0.115	0.574	344
Portugal	0.132	0.111	4.921	1.684	0.318	5.821	0.439	0.374	0.227	0.055	0.529	0.029	0.414	493

Singapore	0.084	0.170	4.273	1.572	0.205	4.774	0.387	0.374	0.237	0.048	0.799	0.094	0.592	2,864
South Africa	0.217	0.203	5.105	2.133	0.145	5.448	0.371	0.472	0.148	0.232	0.789	0.093	0.584	1,760
Spain	0.141	0.172	6.040	2.175	0.231	6.496	0.446	0.407	0.109	0.051	0.837	0.021	0.398	1,224
Sri Lanka	0.316	0.134	3.413	1.240	0.255	4.343	0.551	0.332	0.129	0.000	0.903	0.107	0.643	124
Sweden	0.095	0.161	5.389	2.430	0.198	5.550	0.283	0.420	0.242	0.080	0.892	0.073	0.523	1,724
Thailand	0.170	0.139	3.632	1.281	0.317	4.469	0.475	0.335	0.236	0.043	0.624	0.077	0.547	2,510
Turkey	0.227	0.281	4.790	2.296	0.197	5.024	0.505	0.576	0.246	0.018	0.566	0.097	0.595	1,123
United Kingdom	0.064	0.091	4.683	2.619	0.178	4.859	0.354	0.402	0.301	0.088	0.684	0.120	0.629	13,831
Mean	0.143	0.176	4.916	1.924	0.241	5.458	0.434	0.368	0.233	0.095	0.711	0.063	0.498	

This table reports summary statistics for test and control variables across countries. To be included in the sample, a firm must have stock returns, auditors, assets and other financial data in the *Worldscope* database for the period 1992–2007 and have lagged financial data as well. Financial firms are omitted (SIC 6000–6999). All variables are defined in Appendix 4. Reported numbers, except in the last column and the last row represent mean statistics across firms in each country. The last row reports the grand mean across all countries

Table 2 Pearson correlation matrix. All variables are defined in Appendix 4. p-values are reported below the correlation coefficient

	X	R	SIZE	MB	LEV	INTA	NFA	INVREC	CROSS	BIG4	C-score	Cdec
X	1.000											
R	0.226	1.000										
	0.00											
SIZE	0.071	0.127	1.000									
	0.00	0.00										
MB	−0.088	0.225	0.230	1.000								
	0.00	0.00	0.00									
LEV	0.066	−0.077	0.007	−0.057	1.000							
	0.00	0.00	0.02	0.00								
LNTA	0.149	−0.015	0.874	−0.059	0.238	1.000						
	0.00	0.00	0.00	0.00	0.00							
CAPINT	0.071	0.075	0.072	−0.049	0.188	0.091	1.000					
	0.00	0.00	0.00	0.00	0.00	0.00						
INVREC	0.143	0.028	−0.104	0.027	−0.035	−0.064	−0.298	1.000				
	0.00	0.00	0.00	0.00	0.00	0.00	0.00					
CROSS	−0.019	0.004	0.280	0.041	0.028	0.261	0.056	−0.098	1.000			
	0.00	0.00	0.00	0.00	0.00	0.00	0.00	0.00				
BIG4	0.012	0.010	0.321	0.027	−0.025	0.294	0.044	−0.085	0.111	1.000		
	0.00	0.00	0.00	0.00	0.00	0.00	0.00	0.00	0.00			
C-score	−0.140	0.090	−0.579	0.501	−0.533	−0.786	−0.175	0.110	−0.190	−0.203	1.000	
	0.00	0.00	0.00	0.00	0.00	0.00	0.00	0.00	0.00	0.00		
Cdec	−0.126	0.070	−0.638	0.282	−0.575	−0.826	−0.181	0.140	−0.199	−0.211	0.923	1.000
	0.00	0.00	0.00	0.00	0.00	0.00	0.00	0.00	0.00	0.00	0.00	

Table 1 reports the country-level mean values of the financial variables. The overall mean stock return is 0.176 and the overall mean earnings to market value ratio is 0.143. The average leverage is 24 % and about 9.5 % of observations have cross-listings. The Big 4 penetration across the 36 countries is 71 %, and ranges from 94 % in Chile to 12 % in India. Table 2 shows the correlation matrix.

4 Results

4.1 C-scores

Table 3 shows the estimated results of the conservatism model. The results for our multi-country sample are similar to the U.S. results of Khan and Watts (2008). Our measure of C-score is computed using Eq. 1. Since C-scores are not normally distributed, we use the decile rankings of C-score to calculate *Cdec*. We compute *Cdec* across all firms for all years. The mean *Cdec* for each country is shown in Table 1.

4.2 Auditor Choice Model

Table 4 reports the results of the auditor selection model in Eq. 3. Firms that are bigger, profitable, and cross-listed are more likely to select Big 4 auditors. Those firms that have lower inventory and receivables and lower leverage are more likely to hire Big 4 auditors. Firms located in countries with stronger legal enforcement and stronger investor protection rights (*ENF*), and with well-developed equity markets (*STK*), are more likely to appoint Big 4 auditors. The probit models generate firm specific inverse Mills ratios (*LAMBDA*) that we use in Eq. 4 to control for self-selection bias.

4.3 Big 4 Test Results

To test for a Big 4 effect we include the *Big4* variable in Eq. 4. We partition the sample into observations in high litigation and reputation cost countries and those in low litigation and reputation cost countries. An alternative approach would be to use the raw legal and institutional variable scores but we reject this research design for a variety of reasons. These reasons include: (1) the raw variables are non-normal; (2) the different scales make comparisons across variables more difficult; and (3) raw variables are noisier than using the dichotomy of above-and below-median indicator variables and result in greater measurement error.

Table 3 Regression results of the conservatism model for all firms in 36 countries

	Pooled regression		
	Coefficient	t-stat.	p-value
Intercept	0.110	87.00	0.00
D	−0.009	−4.03	0.00
R	0.043	10.08	0.00
R*SIZE	0.002	2.93	0.00
R*MB	−0.014	−40.65	0.00
R*LEV	0.282	42.24	0.00
D*R	0.311	30.23	0.00
D*R*SIZE	−0.048	−24.61	0.00
D*R*MB	0.036	22.60	0.00
D*R*LEV	−0.329	−20.63	0.00
Adj. R square	0.102		
N.observations	108,504		

This table reports the regression results of the conservatism model for all firms in 36 countries for the period of 1992–2007. The dependent variable, X, is earnings before interest and taxes scaled by beginning of year market capitalization. All other variables are defined in Appendix 4. Two tailed t-statistics and p-values are reported. The coefficients and the test statistics are based on the following regression model:

$$X_{cit} = \beta_1 + \beta_2 D_{cit} + R_{cit}(\mu_1 + \mu_2 SIZE_{cit} + \mu_3 MB_{cit} + \mu_4 LEV_{cit}) + D_{cit}R_{cit}(\lambda_1 + \lambda_2 SIZE_{cit} + \lambda_3 MB_{cit} + \lambda_4 LEV_{cit}) + \varepsilon_{cit}$$

Table 4 Regression results on probit regression for all firms in 36 countries

		Pooled probit regression		
	Expected sign	Coefficient	χ^2	p-value
Intercept		2.326	517.38	0.00
LNTA	+	0.272	8925.91	0.00
CAPINT	+	−0.010	0.42	0.52
INVREC	+/−	−0.346	325.25	0.00
LEV	+/−	−0.709	853.66	0.00
LOSS	+/−	−0.088	81.90	0.00
CROSS	+	0.217	112.18	0.00
ENF	+	0.099	1296.53	0.00
FDI	+	−0.162	2.40	0.12
STK	+	0.001	206.55	0.00
GDP	−	−0.139	1284.81	0.00
Pseudo r square		0.1261		
N.observations		108,504		

This table reports the logistic regression results of the auditor selection model for all firms in 36 countries for the period of 1992–2007. The dependent variable, Big4, is equal to 1 if a company appoints one of the Big 4 auditors, and 0 otherwise. All other variables are defined in Appendix 4. χ^2 and p-values are reported. The coefficients and the test statistics are based on the following probit regression model:

$$Pr(Big4)_{cit} = \delta_0 + \delta_1 LNTA_{cit} + \delta_2 CAPINT_{cit} + \delta_3 INVREC_{cit} + \delta_4 LEV_{cit} + \delta_5 LOSS_{cit} + \delta_6 CROSS_{cit} + \delta_7 ENF_{cit} + \delta_8 FDI_{cit} + \delta_9 STK_{cit} + \delta_{10} GDP_{cit} + \varepsilon_{cit}$$

Table 5 Influence of auditor litigation risk on Big 4 conservatism

Legal institutions	Whole sample	Wingate (1997) litigation index Low	Wingate (1997) litigation index High	Easiness of auditor being sued Low	Easiness of auditor being sued High	Severity of auditor sanction Low	Severity of auditor sanction High
Intercept	1.047	1.101	1.042	1.014	1.055	0.982	1.051
	(34.92)	(25.38)	(29.56)	(22.22)	(30.78)	(29.45)	(23.31)
Big4	0.007	0.005	0.010	0.000	0.012	0.008	0.010
	(2.60)	(1.00)	(2.66)	(0.08)	(3.17)	(1.95)	(2.11)
lagSIZE	−0.103	−0.117	−0.102	−0.104	−0.103	−0.096	−0.102
	(−19.05)	(−19.38)	(−17.14)	(−19.96)	(−15.54)	(−16.83)	(−15.12)
lagMB	0.039	0.059	0.037	0.054	0.036	0.038	0.041
	(6.35)	(12.07)	(5.55)	(14.06)	(5.49)	(5.27)	(6.11)
lagLEV	−0.791	−0.827	−0.777	−0.828	−0.776	−0.786	−0.828
	(−57.10)	(−26.58)	(−60.91)	(−41.00)	(−55.73)	(−50.84)	(−34.31)
CROSS	0.015	0.002	0.023	0.007	0.023	0.020	0.008
	(1.32)	(0.19)	(1.90)	(0.84)	(1.87)	(1.70)	(0.98)
LAMBDA	0.100	0.061	0.106	0.122	0.096	0.145	0.121
	(4.12)	(1.90)	(3.77)	(3.50)	(3.40)	(5.06)	(2.85)
Country clustering	Yes	Yes	Yes	Yes	Yes	Yes	Yes
Year dummies	Yes	Yes	Yes	Yes	Yes	Yes	Yes
Adj. r-squared	0.802	0.793	0.810	0.822	0.800	0.810	0.778
N.observations	108,504	20,283	80,388	28,394	80,110	82,340	26,164
Difference in coefficients for Big4 high minus low (t-value)		4.96		9.25		1.02	

This table reports the regression analysis on auditor litigation risk on Big 4 conservatism. The high versus low groups are defined according to the median level of auditor litigation risk variables across countries in our sample. The sample consists of 108,504 firm-year observations drawn from 36 countries for the period of 1992–2007. The dependent variable, Cdec, is the decile ranking of C-score, estimated from Eq. 2 in a pooled regression. All other variables are defined in Appendix 4. *t-statistics* are calculated using adjusted standard errors corrected for country-level clustering (Petersen 2009). The first line shows the coefficient and the second line shows the t-statistic (in parenthesis). The coefficients and the test statistics are based on the following regression model:

$$Cdec_{cit} = \alpha_1 + \alpha_2 Big4_{cit} + \alpha_3 SIZE_{cit-1} + \alpha_4 MB_{cit-1} + \alpha_5 LEV_{cit-1} + \alpha_6 CROSS_{cit-1} + \alpha_7 LAMBDA_{cit} + Year\ dummies + \varepsilon_{cit}$$

Bushman and Piotroski (2006) also use the dichotomy of High and Low partitions rather than using the raw country scores. For Law origins, firms in code law countries are classified as Code and firms in common law countries are classified as Common. Tables 5, 6, 7, 8, and 9 show the regression results. Reported t-values are on an adjusted basis using robust standard errors corrected for clustering at the firm level (Gow et al. 2010; Petersen 2009). As we control for self-selection bias, positive coefficients on *Big4* will imply that it is the Big 4 auditors that exert pressure on companies to report conservatively rather than companies who report conservatively (on their own volition) choosing Big 4 auditors.

Table 6 Influence of legal institutions on Big 4 conservatism

	Law origins		Efficiency of the judiciary		Law enforcement	
Legal institutions	Code	Common	Low	High	Low	High
Intercept	1.022	1.028	1.096	1.030	1.059	1.060
	(30.86)	(37.01)	(20.62)	(33.02)	(21.02)	(33.92)
Big4	0.003	0.011	0.003	0.009	−0.001	0.011
	(1.64)	(3.77)	(1.06)	(2.55)	(−0.20)	(3.17)
lagSIZE	−0.106	−0.094	−0.112	−0.101	−0.109	−0.105
	(−21.22)	(−21.76)	(−14.63)	(−16.67)	(−15.01)	(−17.98)
lagMB	0.054	0.030	0.050	0.037	0.050	0.038
	(8.96)	(7.87)	(5.20)	(5.56)	(5.59)	(5.77)
lagLEV	−0.809	−0.779	−0.792	−0.787	−0.817	−0.777
	(−58.52)	(−33.19)	(−29.81)	(−50.76)	(−30.45)	(−60.27)
CROSS	0.024	0.002	0.004	0.022	0.007	0.018
	(2.05)	(0.26)	(0.32)	(1.90)	(0.70)	(1.34)
LAMBDA	0.122	0.110	0.055	0.118	0.081	0.089
	(4.28)	(5.46)	(1.40)	(5.07)	(2.27)	(3.30)
Country clustering	Yes	Yes	Yes	Yes	Yes	Yes
Year dummies	Yes	Yes	Yes	Yes	Yes	Yes
Adj. r square	0.831	0.757	0.792	0.807	0.789	0.807
N.observations	61,629	46,875	23,978	84,526	22,830	85,674
Difference in coefficients for Big4, Common minus code (t-value); high minus low (t-value)	13.13		3.02		6.85	

This table reports the regression analysis on legal institutions on Big 4 conservatism. The high versus low groups are defined according to the median level of legal institutions variables across countries in our sample. The sample consists of 108,504 firm-year observations drawn from 36 countries for the period of 1992–2007. The dependent variable, Cdec, is the decile ranking of C-score, estimated from Eq. 2 in a pooled regression. All other variables are defined in Appendix 4. *t-statistics* are calculated using adjusted standard errors corrected for country-level clustering (Petersen 2009). The first line shows the coefficient and the second line shows the t-statistic (in parenthesis). The coefficients and the test statistics are based on the following regression model:

$$Cdec_{cit} = \alpha_1 + \alpha_2 Big4_{cit} + \alpha_3 SIZE_{cit-1} + \alpha_4 MB_{cit-1} + \alpha_5 LEV_{cit-1} + \alpha_6 CROSS_{cit-1} + \alpha_7 LAMBDA_{cit} + Year\ dummies + \varepsilon_{cit}$$

In the first column of Table 5, we report the results of regression Eq. 4 using the Whole Sample: we find that the *Big4* variable is statistically significant with an expected positive sign, suggesting that the Big 4 are more conservative than the non-Big 4. We find that the coefficients on *lagSIZE* and *lagLEV* are significantly negative, suggesting that large firms and highly levered firms have lower conservatism. These results are in line with the following view: large firms tend to be monitored more closely and there is a lot of information about them. Therefore, they have less need for conservative accounting reports. Similarly, highly levered firms are closely monitored and also have a lower need for conservative accounting. Cross-listed firms (*CROSS*) have positive coefficients but they are not significant.

Table 7 Influence on security law on Big 4 conservatism

Security law	Liability standard		Public enforcement		Disclosure requirements		Anti-self dealing	
	Low	High	Low	High	Low	High	Low	High
Intercept	1.062	1.049	1.114	1.026	0.976	1.085	1.068	1.072
	(23.90)	(32.10)	(47.28)	(32.65)	(21.35)	(32.04)	(24.11)	(34.69)
Big4	−0.004	0.010	0.003	0.012	0.000	0.006	0.000	0.010
	(−0.80)	(2.39)	(1.69)	(3.79)	(0.04)	(1.68)	(0.04)	(3.47)
lagSIZE	−0.110	−0.098	−0.118	−0.097	−0.093	−0.107	−0.108	−0.106
	(−18.49)	(−14.43)	(−36.87)	(−21.41)	(−9.55)	(−20.01)	(−20.30)	(−18.17)
lagMB	0.056	0.031	0.062	0.032	0.035	0.043	0.048	0.038
	(12.12)	(3.61)	(14.01)	(8.32)	(2.82)	(7.83)	(8.17)	(5.66)
lagLEV	−0.796	−0.812	−0.821	−0.776	−0.808	−0.802	−0.813	−0.782
	(−41.64)	(−34.96)	(−70.35)	(−40.35)	(−36.00)	(−48.54)	(−31.26)	(−47.17)
CROSS	−0.001	−0.003	0.025	−0.003	−0.019	0.005	−0.001	0.021
	(−0.16)	(−0.35)	(2.24)	(−0.37)	(−1.38)	(0.54)	(−0.13)	(1.83)
LAMBDA	0.086	0.113	0.042	0.106	0.184	0.059	0.074	0.074
	(2.07)	(3.19)	(2.20)	(4.18)	(3.70)	(1.79)	(2.41)	(2.80)
Country clustering	Yes	Yes	Yes	Yes	Yes	Yes	Yes	Yes
Year dummies	Yes	Yes	Yes	Yes	Yes	Yes	Yes	Yes
Adj. r square	0.824	0.765	0.845	0.767	0.783	0.791	0.811	0.801
N.observations	25,476	83,028	52155	56349	22,340	86,164	25,898	82,606
Difference in coefficients for Big4 high minus low (t-value)	11.63		8.36		9.48		6.69	

This table reports the regression analysis on security law and Big 4 conservatism. The high versus low groups are defined according to the median level of security laws variables across countries in our sample. The sample consists of 108,504 firm-year observations drawn from 36 countries for the period of 1992–2007. The dependent variable, Cdec, is the decile ranking of C-score, estimated from Eq. 2 in a pooled regression. All other variables are defined in Appendix 4. *t-statistics* are calculated using adjusted standard errors corrected for country-level clustering (Petersen 2009). The first line shows the coefficient and the second line shows the t-statistic (in parenthesis). The coefficients and the test statistics are based on the following regression model:

$$Cdec_{cit} = \alpha_1 + \alpha_2 Big4_{cit} + \alpha_3 SIZE_{cit-1} + \alpha_4 MB_{cit-1} + \alpha_5 LEV_{cit-1} + \alpha_6 CROSS_{cit-1} + \alpha_7 LAMBDA_{cit} + Year\ dummies + \varepsilon_{cit}$$

Table 8 Influence of political economy and tax regime on security law on Big 4 conservatism

	Risk of expropriation		Stated-owned enterprises		Tax burden	
Political economy	Low	High	Low	High	Low	High
Intercept	1.025	1.083	1.055	1.066	1.064	0.975
	(25.83)	(34.95)	(26.26)	(31.25)	(27.17)	(59.57)
Big4	0.012	0.000	0.011	0.006	0.008	0.011
	(2.69)	(0.07)	(2.78)	(2.50)	(2.02)	(2.90)
lagSIZE	−0.101	−0.108	−0.104	−0.110	−0.106	−0.094
	(−15.42)	(−20.08)	(−16.98)	(−25.10)	(−15.60)	(−31.95)
lagMB	0.037	0.046	0.035	0.056	0.039	0.041
	(5.18)	(5.81)	(5.85)	(19.33)	(5.00)	(6.89)
lagLEV	−0.779	−0.811	−0.775	−0.827	−0.785	−0.804
	(−58.60)	(−30.98)	(−52.92)	(−39.77)	(−58.93)	(−26.03)
CROSS	0.025	−0.002	0.018	0.010	0.020	0.002
	(2.22)	(−0.27)	(1.34)	(1.15)	(1.46)	(0.20)
LAMBDA	0.118	0.075	0.089	0.090	0.089	0.149
	(3.75)	(2.74)	(2.51)	(3.38)	(2.87)	(8.25)
Country clustering	Yes	Yes	Yes	Yes	Yes	Yes
Year dummies	Yes	Yes	Yes	Yes	Yes	Yes
Adj. r square	0.816	0.768	0.804	0.815	0.798	0.812
N.observations	78,173	30,331	75,637	32,867	79,301	29,203
Difference in coefficients for Big4 high minus low (t-value)	−6.69		−4.77		2.24	

This table reports the regression analysis on political economy and tax regime and Big 4 conservatism. The high versus low groups are defined according to the median level of political economy and tax regime variables across countries in our sample. The sample consists of 108,504 firm-year observations drawn from 36 countries for the period of 1992–2007. The dependent variable, Cdec, is the decile ranking of C-score, estimated from Eq. 2 in a pooled regression. All other variables are defined in Appendix 4. *t-statistics* are calculated using adjusted standard errors corrected for country-level clustering (Petersen 2009). The first line shows the coefficient and the second line shows the t-statistic (in parenthesis). The coefficients and the test statistics are based on the following regression model:

$$Cdec_{cit} = \alpha_1 + \alpha_2 Big4_{cit} + \alpha_3 SIZE_{cit-1} + \alpha_4 MB_{cit-1} + \alpha_5 LEV_{cit-1} + \alpha_6 CROSS_{cit-1} + \alpha_7 LAMBDA_{cit} + Year\ dummies + \varepsilon_{cit}$$

Higher growth firms (*lagMB*) have more conservative accounting. *LAMBDA* is significant indicating that it is important to control for self-selection.

The Whole Sample results show that the Big 4 auditors are more conservative. But does this effect apply to both High and Low legal and institutional environments? If the answer is Yes, then this suggests the Big 4 have a uniform approach towards conservatism that transcends national boundaries and legal and institutional differences. If the answer is No, then this implies a Big 4's views on conservatism are flexible and depend on the legal and institutional environment.

For the partition based on auditor litigation risk (which we proxy with the Wingate litigation index), we see that *Big4* is positive and significant in the High partition regression but not in the Low partition regression. Furthermore, the

Table 9 Influence of financial market factors on Big 4 conservatism

	Stock price comovement		Concentrated ownership		Insider trading		Access to equity	
Contracting and litigation	Low	High	Low	High	Low	High	High	Low
Intercept	0.980	1.115	1.032	1.066	1.062	0.971	1.016	1.072
	(49.42)	(46.39)	(26.08)	(47.69)	(32.05)	(18.06)	(39.86)	(22.88)
Big4	0.019	0.003	0.009	0.003	0.010	0.000	0.013	0.002
	(8.23)	(1.77)	(2.15)	(0.85)	(2.69)	(−0.10)	(4.39)	(1.58)
lagSIZE	−0.091	−0.117	−0.101	−0.105	−0.105	−0.097	−0.095	−0.113
	(−28.80)	(−28.75)	(−15.10)	(−24.16)	(−17.74)	(−12.11)	(−24.39)	(−16.73)
lagMB	0.029	0.058	0.039	0.041	0.038	0.047	0.033	0.058
	(9.01)	(7.96)	(5.21)	(5.62)	(5.61)	(5.73)	(7.55)	(6.10)
lagLEV	−0.767	−0.820	−0.795	−0.785	−0.788	−0.808	−0.789	−0.793
	(−41.84)	(−56.26)	(−47.11)	(−30.36)	(−51.05)	(−23.93)	(−33.67)	(−51.46)
CROSS	0.006	0.026	0.016	−0.012	0.022	0.005	0.003	0.021
	(1.01)	(2.36)	(1.51)	(−1.28)	(1.92)	(0.51)	(0.57)	(1.50)
LAMBDA	0.146	0.053	0.108	0.095	0.088	0.162	0.124	0.080
	(8.78)	(2.48)	(3.33)	(4.08)	(3.15)	(3.18)	(7.32)	(2.13)
Country clustering	Yes	Yes	Yes	Yes	Yes	Yes	Yes	Yes
Year dummies	Yes	Yes	Yes	Yes	Yes	Yes	Yes	Yes
Adj. r square	0.782	0.831	0.813	0.765	0.807	0.790	0.772	0.833
N.observations	42,896	59,915	84,759	23,745	87,858	20,534	57,357	51,023
Difference in coefficients for Big4 high minus low (t-value)	−15.04		−5.02		−7.44		−11.54	

This table reports the regression analysis on contracting and litigation and Big 4 conservatism. The high versus low groups are defined according to the median level of contracting and litigation variables across countries in our sample. The sample consists of 108,504 firm-year observations drawn from 36 countries for the period of 1992–2007. The dependent variable, Cdec, is the decile ranking of C-score, estimated from Eq. 2 in a pooled regression. All other variables are defined in Appendix 4. *t-statistics* are calculated using adjusted standard errors corrected for country-level clustering (Petersen 2009). The first line shows the coefficient and the second line shows the t-statistic (in parenthesis). The coefficients and the test statistics are based on the following regression model:

$$Cdec_{cit} = \alpha_1 + \alpha_2 Big4_{cit} + \alpha_3 SIZE_{cit-1} + \alpha_4 MB_{cit-1} + \alpha_5 LEV_{cit-1} + CROSS_{cit-1} + \alpha_7 LAMBDA_{cit} + Year\ dummies + \varepsilon_{cit}$$

coefficient on *Big4* in the High partition ($\alpha_2 = 0.010$) is larger than the coefficient on *Big4* in the Low partition ($\alpha_2 = 0.005$) and the difference is statistically significant (t = 4.96). We obtain similar results when the sample is partitioned using the easiness of auditor being sued. The *Big4* coefficient is positively significant only in countries where it is easy to sue the auditor (the High subsample). The *Big4* coefficient is positive and significant for firms located in countries where the severity of auditor sanctions is high. In contrast, *Big4* is not significant at the 0.05 level in the Low severity subgroup. However, the difference in the *Big4* coefficients across the High and Low partitions is not significant (t = 1.02). This lack of significant difference may be the result of the difficulty in identifying the high and low categories for severity (see the earlier discussion). The results reported in Table 5, taken together, suggest that the Big 4 auditors are more conservative for clients based in countries where litigation risk is high. Although the coefficients on *Big4* are also positive in the Low subsamples, they are not statistically significant. The other independent variables have similar coefficients and significance levels across the High, Low and Whole sample regressions.

The pattern of results shown in Table 5 is repeated for the legal institutions and securities laws factors. As shown in Tables 6 and 7, the Big 4 are more conservative in common law countries (law origins) and countries with high judicial efficiency, effective law enforcement, high liability standards, high public enforcement of laws, high disclosure requirements, and high (i.e., tough) anti-self dealing regulations. In all cases, the coefficients on the *Big4* variable for the High legal standard countries are statistically higher than the coefficients on the *Big4* variable in the Low legal standard countries. The results in Tables 5, 6, and 7 are unequivocal: the Big 4 are more conservative than their non-Big 4 brethren in countries where auditors are more likely to face litigation or sanctions. When litigation and sanctions are low, the Big 4 are indistinguishable from the non-Big 4.

Next, we turn our attention to factors that we group under the umbrella of political economy. Although these factors do not bear directly on auditor litigation, we argue that they can have an influence over the way auditors view conservatism and can create differences between Big 4 and non-Big 4 auditors. A high score for risk of expropriation indicates that the government is more likely to expropriate or nationalize private firms. When the risk of expropriation is low, firms have more freedom and face more market competition. This may result in firms using aggressive accounting. We argue that the Big 4 are more vigilant about conservatism than the non-Big 4 auditors in this situation. Hence we expect that the Big 4 will be more conservative in countries with a low risk of expropriation. The results shown in Table 8 give support to our argument. Specifically, *Big4* is positive and significant for the Low risk of expropriation subsample but is not significant in the High subsample. Furthermore, the *Big4* coefficient is statistically higher in the Low subsample (t = −6.69).

The proportion of state-owned enterprises within an economy is one indicator of economic freedom. Aggressive accounting is more likely when freedom is high and state influence is low. In this situation, we argue that Big 4 auditors will be more conservative than non-Big 4 auditors. This argument is similar to the one for expropriation of assets. Consistent with our argument above, we find that the Big 4 auditors are even more conservative than the non-Big 4 auditors in countries characterized as having low government control (i.e., few state-owned enterprises). In particular, the difference in *Big4* coefficients (0.011 in the Low subsample and 0.006 in the High subsample) is statistically significant (Table 8).

When tax rates are very high, firms may want to report conservatively as lower earnings may translate to lower taxable profits. The Big 4 have more skill in identifying conservative accounting practices and their clients will have high C-scores. Table 8 confirms our expectation that the Big 4 auditors are more conservative than the non-Big 4 auditors in countries where the tax burden is high.

Table 9 shows the results from partitioning countries into High and Low groups based on financial market factors. Some countries are characterized as having high stock price synchronicity where the stock price co-moves with the market index. Here, a firm's stock price is largely determined by the movement of the stock market index and firm-specific information is less important. This implies investors rely less on a firm's financial statements and thus there may be less risk for the auditor. In contrast, when the stock price co-movement is low (i.e., low synchronicity, low VWR^2), firm-specific information is more important. When investors use firm-specific information, the auditors will face more risk and so we expect Big 4 auditors to be more conservative than the non-Big4 auditors in this setting. The results in Table 9 confirm our hypothesis. The Big4 are more conservative when stock price co-movement is low.

We code firms with highly concentrated ownership as High and firms with widely held shares as Low. Stockholders in widely held firms are more likely to rely on financial statements as agency costs are larger when managers and blockholders own fewer shares. We argue that the Big 4 will be more likely to be conservative in those countries with more widely held listed firms. The results reported in Table 9 bear out our argument. The difference in the *Big4* coefficients between the Low and High subsamples is significant ($t = -5.02$). Thus, the Big 4 are more conservative than non-Big 4 auditors in countries where share ownership is widely held.

When there is a lot of insider trading, financial statements become less important. Instead, investors attempt to mimic the insiders' trading. As financial statements become less important so does auditing. In contrast, financial statements play a more important role in countries with relatively less insider trading. We therefore argue that Big 4 auditors will be more conservative in countries where insider trading is low. The results in Table 9 show that the *Big4* coefficient in the Low subsample is statistically greater than the *Big4* coefficient in the High subsample. Thus, the results confirm our prediction.

In some countries there are few restrictions on raising capital on the stock market and so access to capital is easier. Other countries place more regulations on accessing capital markets and the auditor's role becomes more important. We argue that Big 4 auditors are more likely to demand conservative accounting in countries characterized as having heavily regulated IPO and SEO markets. Our results are consistent with this expectation (Table 10). In particular, the coefficient

Table 10 WLS regression results

Auditor litigation	Whole sample		Wingate (1997) litigation		Easiness of auditor being sued		Severity of auditor sanction	
			Low	High	Low	High	Low	High
Big4	0.003		0.007	0.008	−0.002	0.009	0.003	0.007
	(1.03)		(1.35)	(1.64)	(−0.40)	(2.19)	(0.75)	(1.63)
Difference in coefficients for Big4 high minus low (t-value)			4.11		12.10		2.61	
Legal institutions			Law origins		Efficiency of the judiciary		Law enforcement	
			Code	Common	Low	High	Low	High
Big4			0.001	0.007	−0.004	0.012	−0.008	0.013
			(0.14)	(1.41)	(−0.85)	(3.35)	(−1.14)	(4.10)
Difference in coefficients for Big4 high minus low (t-value)			9.72		7.90		10.34	
Security law	Liability standard		Public enforcement		Disclosure requirements		Anti-self dealing	
	Low	High	Low	High	Low	High	Low	High
Big4	−0.004	0.010	0.004	0.002	0.000	0.006	−0.003	0.007
	(−0.80)	(2.39)	(0.78)	(0.54)	(0.04)	(1.68)	(−0.44)	(1.48)
Difference in coefficients for Big4 high minus low (t-value)	11.63		1.08		9.48		5.27	
Political economy			Risk of expropriation		State-owned enterprises		Tax burden	
			Low	High	Low	High	Low	High
Big4			0.012	−0.006	0.004	0.004	−0.001	0.011
			(3.15)	(−1.12)	(0.64)	(0.92)	(−0.15)	(2.75)
Difference in coefficients for Big4 high minus low (t-value)			−9.74		−1.15		4.81	
Financial market factors	Stock return comovement		Concentrated ownership		Insider trading		Access to equity	
	Low	High	Low	High	Low	High	Low	High
Big4	0.016	−0.002	0.011	−0.005	0.012	−0.009	0.014	−0.005
	(3.85)	(−0.58)	(2.72)	(−0.91)	(3.69)	(−1.59)	(4.85)	(−1.11)
Difference in coefficients for Big4 high minus low (t-value)	−11.73		−10.77		−13.21		−12.53	

This table reports the weighted-least-square (WLS) regression results. The weight applied for each firm is the inverse of the number of firms for that country. The high versus low groups are defined according to the median level of country-level variables across countries in our sample. The sample consists of 108,504 firm-year observations drawn from 36 countries for the period of 1992–2007. The dependent variable, Cdec, is the decile ranking of C-score, estimated from Eq. 2 in a pooled regression. All other variables are defined in Appendix 4. Intercepts, coefficients on control variables and year dummies are not reported for parsimony. *t-statistics* are calculated using adjusted standard errors corrected for country-level clustering (Petersen 2009). The first line shows the coefficient and the second line shows the t-statistic (in parenthesis)

on *Big4* in the Low subsample regression is statistically higher than the coefficient on *Big4* in the High subsample regression (t = −11.54).

4.4 Sensitivity Checks

As shown in Table 1, Japan and the U.K. have a large number of observations (observations = 27,669 and 13,831), relative to other countries. To alleviate a concern over potential problems that may arise from this unequal distribution of sample firms across the 36 countries, we apply weighted least squares (WLS) procedures by assigning smaller weights to countries with the largest number of sample firms. The weighting applied to each firm within a country is the inverse of the number of firms for that country. In the interests of parsimony, we just show the coefficients and statistical significances for our variable of interest, *Big4*, from the WLS regressions (Table 10). The results are consistent with these using the unweighted OLS regressions shown in Tables 5, 6, 7, 8, and 9.

We also repeat the OLS analyses in Tables 5, 6, 7, 8, and 9 but exclude observations from Japan and the U.K. The coefficients and statistical significances of *Big4* are shown in Table 11. The results and conclusions are broadly the same as those shown in Tables 5, 6, 7, 8, and 9. Overall, the results in Tables 10 and 11 suggest that the results reported in Tables 5, 6, 7, 8, and 9 are robust to the unequal distribution of sample firms across different countries.

We also run firm fixed effect models to control for unobserved firm-specific factors. The coefficients for the *Big4* variable are shown in Table 12. The results are similar to those shown in Tables 5, 6, 7, 8, 9, 10, and 11. In sum, the results are robust to alternative samples and regression specifications.

5 Conclusion

Conservatism is a concept that underscores accounting practice and formal professional standards. It is widely accepted that companies use conservative accounting although the degree of conservatism varies according to legal and institutional circumstances (Bushman and Piotroski 2006). As the auditor heavily influences a company's accounting choices, we argue that the auditor is a major driver of conservatism. One reason for an auditor's conservatism is their concern about lawsuits and loss of reputation that may result if the client adopts less conservative accounting and reports inflated earnings. However, we contend that auditors do not have homogeneous views on conservatism. In particular, large audit firms have a lot more to lose from litigation and loss of reputation and so they will be more conservative than small audit firms. One open question, however, is whether large audit firms will maintain a conservatism premium, vis-à-vis smaller audit firms, in those jurisdictions that are less litigious and where investor protection and

Table 11 Robustness checks: Excluding Japan and United Kingdom

Auditor litigation	Whole sample		Wingate (1997) litigation		Easiness of auditor being sued		Severity of auditor sanction	
			Low	High	Low	High	Low	High
Big4	0.006		0.005	0.010	0.000	0.012	0.006	0.010
	(2.28)		(1.04)	(2.30)	(0.11)	(4.35)	(1.66)	(2.14)
Difference in coefficients for Big4 high minus low (t-value)			5.44		9.30		0.21	
Legal institutions			Law origins		Efficiency of the judiciary		Law enforcement	
			Code	Common	Low	High	Low	High
Big4			0.003	0.010	0.003	0.012	−0.001	0.012
			(0.86)	(3.03)	(1.08)	(3.62)	(−0.19)	(4.06)
Difference in coefficients for Big4 high minus low (t-value)			7.78		4.92		7.22	
Security law	Liability standard		Public enforcement		Disclosure requirements		Anti-self dealing	
	Low	High	Low	High	Low	High	Low	High
Big4	0.002	0.010	0.004	0.009	0.002	0.010	0.000	0.011
	(0.46)	(2.23)	(1.04)	(2.73)	(0.46)	(2.23)	(0.04)	(3.33)
Difference in coefficients for Big4 high minus low (t-value)	9.14		3.39		5.93		7.32	
Political economy			Risk of expropriation		State-owned enterprises		Tax burden	
			Low	High	Low		Low	High
Big4			0.014	0.000	0.009	Big4	0.014	0.000
			(3.01)	(0.12)	(1.75)		(3.01)	(0.12)
Difference in coefficients for Big4 high minus low (t-value)			−6.79		−6.32		2.95	
Financial market factors	Stock return comovement		Concentrated ownership		Insider trading		Access to equity	
	Low	High	Low	High	Low	High	Low	High
Big4	0.020	0.001	0.009	0.003	0.010	0.000	0.014	0.001
	(5.95)	(0.51)	(1.87)	(0.85)	(2.52)	(−0.10)	(4.38)	(0.31)
Difference in coefficients for Big4 high minus low (t-value)	−8.98		−5.38		−7.69		−7.45	

This table reports the regression results excluding firms from Japan and United Kingdom. The high versus low groups are defined according to the median level of country-level variables across countries in our sample. The sample consists of 67,704 firm-year observations drawn from 34 countries for the period of 1992–2007. The dependent variable, Cdec, is the decile ranking of C-score, estimated from Eq. 2 in a pooled regression. All other variables are defined in Appendix 4. Intercepts, coefficients on control variables and year dummies are not reported for parsimony. *t-statistics* are calculated using adjusted standard errors corrected for country-level clustering (Petersen 2009). The first line shows the coefficient and the second line shows the t-statistic (in parenthesis)

Table 12 Firm fixed effect regression

Auditor litigation	Whole sample		Wingate (1997) litigation		Easiness of auditor being sued		Severity of auditor sanction	
			Low	High	Low	High	Low	High
Big4	0.008		0.009	0.008	−0.002	0.012	0.007	0.013
	(5.08)		(3.13)	(4.49)	(−0.68)	(6.30)	(4.09)	(4.31)
Difference in coefficients for Big4 high minus low (t-value)			2.04		10.31		2.00	
Legal institutions			Law origins		Efficiency of the judiciary		Law enforcement	
			Code	Common	Low	High	Low	High
Big4			0.002	0.014	0.003	0.011	−0.001	0.011
			(1.16)	(5.61)	(1.07)	(6.16)	(−0.28)	(6.18)
Difference in coefficients for Big4 high minus low (t-value)			13.19		3.19		6.95	
Security law	Liability standard		Public enforcement		Disclosure requirements		Anti-self dealing	
	Low	High	Low	High	Low	High	Low	High
Big4	−0.004	0.012	0.003	0.012	0.005	0.008	0.000	0.010
	(−1.61)	(6.50)	(1.99)	(5.46)	(1.46)	(4.87)	(0.08)	(5.72)
Difference in coefficients for Big4 high minus low (t-value)	10.58		8.06		3.19		6.77	
Political economy			Risk of expropriation		State-owned enterprises		Tax burden	
			Low	High	Low	High	Low	High
Big4			0.010	0.004	0.005	0.010	0.008	0.008
			(5.27)	(1.36)	(2.14)	(5.33)	(4.50)	(2.88)
Difference in coefficients for Big4 high minus low (t-value)			−4.65		4.79		−2.19	
Financial market factors	Stock return comovement		Concentrated ownership		Insider trading		Access to equity	
	Low	High	Low	High	Low	High	Low	High
Big4	0.018	0.004	0.011	0.002	0.010	−0.001	0.017	0.001
	(6.78)	(2.22)	(6.21)	(0.46)	(6.16)	(−0.18)	(7.67)	(0.58)
Difference in coefficients for Big4 high minus low (t-value)	−13.54		−4.50		−5.80		−13.46	

This table reports the firm fixed effect regression analysis. The high versus low groups are defined according to the median level of country-level variables across countries in our sample. The sample consists of 108,504 firm-year observations drawn from 36 countries for the period of 1992–2007. The dependent variable, Cdec, is the decile ranking of C-score, estimated from Eq. 2 in a pooled regression. All other variables are defined in Appendix 4. Intercepts, coefficients on control variables and year dummies are not reported for parsimony. *t-statistics* are calculated using adjusted standard errors corrected for firm-level clustering (Petersen 2009). The first line shows the coefficient and the second line shows the t-statistic (in parenthesis)

regulatory oversight is weaker. On the one hand, large auditors could establish a strong global image for conservatism that is impervious to the legal and institutional environments of where they operate. On the other hand, large audit firms may be more flexible in their application of conservative accounting practices and take into account the probabilities and costs of litigation in the client's country of domicile. This is the central question in our study.

We use the model developed by Khan and Watts (2008, 2009) to capture conservatism. The conservatism score (C-score) avoids the problems associated with the Basu model, which has been widely used in the past. To the best of our knowledge, this is one of the first applications of the C-score and first one to use international data. We use the Big 4 as a proxy for large audit firms. Self-selection bias may affect the results, and so we use a two-stage 'treatment effects' research design to alleviate this concern.

Using a large sample of client firms from 36 countries, we find that Big 4 clients use more conservative accounting when clients are located in countries that are litigious and where investor protection rights are strong. This represents a rational response to the increased threat of litigation and loss of reputation that come from such environments. We also find that the political economy and financial market factors of a country can have an impact on the conservatism premium of a Big 4 audit. Our study adds to the literature by demonstrating that the Big 4 have flexible views on conservatism, which depend on the threat of litigation within a specific country.

Acknowledgement We thank Jong-Hag Choi, Jere Francis, Annie Qiu, Dan Simunic, and participants at the PhD/DBA Research Seminars at The Hong Kong Polytechnic University and City University for constructive comments on earlier versions of the paper. The usual disclaimer applies.

Appendix 1

Definitions of litigation and other country institutions variables and data sources

Description	Variable	Definition of variable and data source
Wingate (1997) litigation index	*Litigate*	Natural log of the Wingate (1997) litigation index. This index is derived from an assessment of litigiousness for doing business as an auditor in each country and was developed by an international insurance underwriter for one of the Big 4 auditors. This index ranges from 1 to 15 with the U.S. taking the highest value of 15 among our sample countries (Source: Wingate (1997))
Easiness of auditor being sued	*Sue*	Index of the procedural difficulty in recovering losses from the auditors in a civil liability case for losses due to misleading statements in the audited financial information accompanying the prospectus. Equals one when

(continued)

Description	Variable	Definition of variable and data source
		investors are only required to prove that the audited financial information accompanying the prospectus contains a misleading statement. Equals two-thirds when investors must also prove that they relied on the prospectus and/or that their loss was caused by the misleading accounting information. Equals one-third when investors must also prove that auditor acted with negligence. Equals zero if restitution from the auditor is either unavailable or the liability standard is intent or gross negligence (Source: The World Bank)
Severity of auditor sanction	*Sanction*	An index of criminal sanctions applicable to auditor (or its officers) when the financial statements accompanying the prospectus omit material information. Equals zero if the auditor cannot be held criminally liable when the financial statements accompanying the prospectus are misleading. Equals one-half if the auditor can be held criminally liable when aware that the financial statements accompanying the prospectus are misleading. Equals one if the auditor can also be held criminally liable when negligently unaware that the financial statements accompanying the prospectus are misleading (Source: The World Bank)
Law origins	*Law*	Equals one if a country has a common law legal origin and zero otherwise (Source: La Porta et al. (1998))
Anti-director rights	*Antidir*	This index of Anti-director summarizes the protection of minority shareholders in the corporate decision-making process. The index is formed by summing: (1) vote by mail; (2) shares not deposited; (3) cumulative voting; (4) oppressed minority; (5) pre-emptive rights; and (6) capital to call a meeting. The range for the index is from zero to six (Source: Djankov et al. (2008))
LawRule	*LawRule*	Assessment of the law and other conditions in the country produced by the country risk rating agency International Country Risk (ICR). Average of the months of April and October of the monthly index between 1982 and 1995. Scale from 0 to 10, with lower scores for less tradition for law and other (Source: La Porta et al. (1998))
Law enforcement	*Enf*	Calculated as 0.5*(rule of law index) + anti-director rights
Efficiency of the judiciary	*EffJud*	Assessment of the efficiency and integrity of the legal environment as it affects business, particularly foreign firms, produced by the country risk rating agency International Country Risk (ICR). It 'may be taken to represent investors' assessment of conditions in the country in question.' Average between 1980 and 1983. Scale from 0 to 10, with lower scores representing lower efficiency levels (Source: La Porta et al. (1998))
Liability standard	*LiabStd*	The index of liability standards equals the arithmetic mean of: (1) Liability standard for the issuer and its directors; (2) Liability standard for the distributor; and (3) Liability standard for the accountant. The index ranges from 0 to 1, with higher values indicating less procedural difficulty

(continued)

Description	Variable	Definition of variable and data source
		in recovering losses from agents (Source: La Porta et al. (2006))
Public enforcement	*PubEnf*	The index of public enforcement equals the arithmetic mean of: (1) Supervisor characteristics index; (2) Rule-making power index; (3) Investigative powers index; (4) Orders index; and (5) Criminal index. The variable is ranked between 0 (weak public enforcement) to 1 (strong public enforcement) (Source: La Porta et al. (2006))
Disclosure requirements	*DisclReq*	An index of disclosure requirements relating to: (1) prospectus; (2) compensation of directors and key officers; (3) ownership structure; (4) inside ownership; (5) contracts outside the ordinary course of business; and (6) transactions between the issuer and its directors, officers, and/or large shareholders. The index ranges from 0 to 1; with higher values indicating more extensive disclosure requirements (Source: La Porta et al. (2006))
Anti-self-dealing index	*Anti-self-dealing index*	Average of ex ante and ex post private control of self-dealing. Index of ex ante control of self-dealing transactions is based on the average of approval by disinterested shareholders and ex ante disclosure. Index of ex post control over self-dealing transactions is based on the average of disclosure in periodic filings and ease of proving wrongdoing. First principal component of: (1) approval by disinterested shareholders; (2) disclosures by Buyer; (3) disclosures by the insider self-dealer; (4) independent review; (5) each of the elements in the index of disclosure in periodic filings; (6) standing to sue; (7) rescission; (8) ease of holding the insider self-dealer liable; (9) ease of holding the approving body liable; and (10) access to evidence. The index ranges from zero (weak private enforcement) to one (strong private enforcement) (Source: Djankov et al. (2008))
Risk of expropriation	*RiskExp*	International Country Risk (ICR)'s assessment of 'outright confiscation' or 'forced nationalization.' Average of the months of April and October of the monthly index between 1982 and 1995. Scale from 0 to 10, with lower scores for higher risks (Source: La Porta et al. (1999))
State-operated business	*SOE*	Governance enterprises and investment as a percentage of GDP. Data on the number, composition and share of output supplied by State-operated enterprises and government investment as a share of total investment were used to construct the 0 (high percentage)-to-10 (low percentage) ratings. All country-year observations are based on 2001 ratings (Source: Economic Freedom of the World: 2002 Annual Report)
Tax burden	*Burden*	Data on the top marginal tax rate and the income thresholds at which they take effect used to construct a rating of taxation. Countries with higher marginal tax rates that take effect at lower income thresholds receive lower ratings. Rankings based on a scale from 0 (low) to 10 (high). All country-year observations are based on the

(continued)

Description	Variable	Definition of variable and data source
		2001 ratings (Source: Economic Freedom of the World: 2002 Annual Report)
Stock return comovement	*VWR*^{2}	Value-weighted R^2, a measure of stock price synchronicity. Following Morck et al. (2000), R^2 is estimate from an expanded market model regression. Jin and Myers (2006) measure a country's stock market synchronicity by its average R^2 for each year. Lower R^2 reflects larger firm-level information content in stock price and indicates higher stock return variation (Source: Jin and Myers (2006))
Concentrated ownership	*Concer*	Average percentage of common shares owned by the top three shareholders in the ten largest non-financial, privately-owned domestic firms in a given country. A firm is considered privately-owned if the State is not a known shareholder in it (Source: La Porta et al. (1999), Hartland-Peel (1996) for Kenya, Bloomberg and various annual reports for Ecuador, Jordan, and Uruguay)
Insider trading	*Insider*	Prevalence of insider trading. The score ranges from 1 to 7. 1 = pervasive; 7 = extremely rare (Source: Schwab et al. (1999))
Access to equity	*Access*	Index of the extent to which business executives in a country agree with the statement "Stock markets are open to new firms and medium-sized firms." Scale from 1 (strongly agree) though 7 (strongly disagree) (Source: Schwab et al. (1999), La Porta et al. (2006))

Appendix 2

Details on auditor litigation risk, legal institutions, security law, political economy, and financial market factor

Country	*Litigate*	*Sue*	*Sanction*	*Law*	*LawRule*	*AntiDir*	*Enf*	*EffJud*	*LiabStd*	*PubEnf*	*DisclReq*	*Anti-self dealing*	*RiskExp*	*SOE*	*Burden*	*VWR*[2]	*Concentrated ownership*	*Insider*	*Access*
Argentina	–	0.33	0	0	5.35	2	6	4.68	0.22	0.58	0.5	0.34	5.91	10	8	0.27	0.53	3.5	3.23
Australia	10	0.66	0.5	1	10	4	10	9.00	0.66	0.9	0.75	0.76	9.27	10	3	0.22	0.28	5.7	6
Austria	3.6	0	0.5	0	10	2.5	9.5	7.50	0.11	0.17	0.25	0.21	9.69	10	2	0.24	0.58	5.5	4.89
Belgium	4.8	0.66	1	0	10	3	9.5	8.00	0.44	0.15	0.42	0.54	9.63	10	1	0.24	0.54	5.1	5.7
Brazil	–	0.33	0	0	6.32	5	5.75	8.16	0.33	0.58	0.25	0.27	7.62	10	5	–	0.57	4	4.05
Canada	8.1	1	1	1	10	4	9.25	9.00	1	0.8	0.92	0.64	9.67	10	5	0.21	0.40	5.2	6.39
Chile	2.4	0.33	0.5	0	7.02	4	7.25	7.51	0.44	0.6	0.58	0.63	7.5	6	5	0.22	0.45	4.3	4.8
Colombia	–	0.33	0.5	0	2.08	3	7.25	4.04	0.33	0.58	0.42	0.57	6.95	0	5.5	0.21	0.63	4	2.78
Denmark	4.8	1	0	0	10	4	10	9.00	0.55	0.37	0.58	0.46	9.67	10	5	0.2	0.45	5.5	5.87
Egypt	–	0.33	0.5	0	4.17	3	6.5	5.09	0.22	0.3	0.5	0.2	6.3	4	7	–	0.62	-	5.2
Finland	3.6	0.66	0.5	0	10	3.5	10	8.50	0.66	0.32	0.5	0.46	9.67	8	2	0.22	0.37	5.5	6.37
France	6.2	0.33	0.5	0	8.98	3.5	8	7.99	0.22	0.77	0.75	0.38	9.65	4	1	0.23	0.34	5.1	5.75
Germany	6.2	0	0.5	0	9.23	3.5	9	8.12	0	0.22	0.42	0.28	9.9	6	4	0.24	0.48	4.9	5.93
Greece	3.6	0.33	0.5	0	6.18	2	7	5.09	0.5	0.32	0.33	0.22	7.12	8	4	–	0.67	3.2	5.28
Hong Kong	10	0.66	1	1	8.22	5	10	9.11	0.66	0.87	0.92	0.96	8.29	10	10	0.27	0.54	4.4	5.5
India	2.4	0.66	1	1	4.17	5	8	7.09	0.66	0.67	0.92	0.58	7.75	6	8	0.32	0.40	3.5	5.3
Indonesia	3.6	0.66	0.5	0	3.98	4	2.5	5.99	0.66	0.62	0.5	0.65	7.16	4	6	0.14	0.58	2.8	4.53
Ireland	6.2	0.66	1	1	7.8	5	8.75	8.90	0.44	0.37	0.67	0.79	9.67	10	4.5	0.2	0.39	5.4	5.29
Israel	–	0.66	0.5	1	4.82	4	10	6.41	0.66	0.63	0.67	0.73	8.25	2	2.5	–	0.51	4.9	5.35
Italy	6.2	0.33	0.5	0	8.33	2	6.75	6.17	0.22	0.48	0.67	0.42	9.35	6	3	–	0.58	4.2	4.41
Japan	4.8	0.66	0	0	8.98	4.5	8.66	8.99	0.66	0	0.75	0.5	9.67	7	5	0.28	0.18	5.1	4.92
South Korea	3.6	0.33	0.5	0	5.35	4.5	6	7.18	0.66	0.25	0.75	0.47	8.31	7	5.5	0.28	0.23	4.4	5.02
Malaysia	3.6	0.66	1	1	6.78	5	9	8.39	0.66	0.77	0.92	0.95	7.95	0	8	0.29	0.54	4.4	5.11
Mexico	4.8	0.33	0.5	0	5.35	3	6	5.68	0.11	0.35	0.58	0.17	7.29	10	5	0.24	0.64	3.8	3.9
New Zealand	10	0.66	0	1	10	4	10	9.00	0.44	0.33	0.67	0.95	9.69	10	5	0.22	0.48	5.6	5.82
Norway	6.2	0.66	1	0	10	3.5	10	8.50	0.39	0.32	0.58	0.42	9.88	8	3.5	0.22	0.36	4.1	5.57

Peru	–	0.66	0.5	0	2.5	3.5	6.75	4.75	0.66	0.78	0.33	0.45	5.54	7	6.5	0.23	0.56	3.5	3.84
Portugal	3.6	0.66	0	0	8.68	2.5	5.5	6.84	0.66	0.58	0.42	0.44	8.9	6	4	0.2	0.52	4.9	4.5
Singapore	4.8	0.66	1	1	8.57	5	5	9.29	0.66	0.87	1	1	9.3	8	9	0.27	0.49	5.5	5.5
South Africa	–	0.66	0.5	1	4.42	5	6	7.21	0.66	0.25	0.83	0.81	6.88	4	4	0.23	0.52	4.3	5.94
Spain	4.8	0.66	0.5	0	7.8	5	6.25	8.90	0.66	0.33	0.5	0.37	9.52	4	5	0.27	0.51	4.1	5.09
Sri Lanka	–	0.66	0.5	1	1.9	4	7	4.95	0.39	0.43	0.75	0.39	6.05	4	7	–	0.60	4.2	–
Sweden	4.8	0.33	0.5	0	10	3.5	10	8.50	0.28	0.5	0.58	0.33	9.4	6	0.5	0.22	0.28	5	6.15
Thailand	–	0	1	1	6.25	4	3.25	7.13	0.22	0.72	0.92	0.81	7.42	4	7	0.24	0.47	3.3	4.24
Turkey	2.4	0.33	0.5	0	5.18	3	4	5.59	0.22	0.63	0.5	0.43	7	6	4.5	0.34	0.59	3.8	5.03
United Kingdom	10	0.66	0.5	1	8.57	5	10	9.29	0.66	0.68	0.83	0.95	9.71	10	5	0.21	0.19	6.2	6.26

Classification of auditor litigation risk, legal institutions, security law, political economy, and financial market factor variables: high versus low realization

	Auditor litigation risk			Legal institutions			Security law			
Country	Wingate litigation index	Easiness of auditor being sued	Severity of auditor sanction	Law origins	Efficiency of the judiciary	Law enforcement	Liability standard	Public enforcement	Disclosure requirements	Anti-self dealing
Argentina	–	Low	Low	Low	Low	Low	Low	High	Low	Low
Australia	High	High	Low	High	High	High	High	High	High	High
Austria	Low	Low	Low	Low	High	Low	Low	Low	Low	Low
Belgium	High	High	High	Low	High	High	Low	Low	Low	High
Brazil	–	Low	Low	Low	Low	High	Low	High	Low	Low
Canada	High	High	High	High	High	High	High	High	High	High
Chile	Low	Low	Low	Low	Low	Low	Low	High	Low	High
Colombia	–	Low	Low	Low	Low	Low	Low	High	Low	High
Denmark	High	High	Low	Low	High	High	High	Low	Low	Low
Egypt	–	Low	Low	Low	Low	Low	Low	Low	Low	Low
Finland	Low	High	Low	Low	High	High	High	Low	Low	Low
France	High	Low	Low	Low	High	High	Low	High	High	Low
Germany	High	Low	Low	Low	High	High	Low	Low	Low	Low
Greece	Low	Low	Low	Low	Low	Low	High	Low	Low	Low
Hong Kong	High	High	High	High	High	High	High	High	High	High
India	Low	High	High	High	High	Low	High	High	High	High
Indonesia	Low	High	Low	Low	Low	Low	High	High	Low	High
Ireland	High	High	High	High	High	High	Low	Low	High	High
Israel	–	High	Low	High	High	Low	High	High	High	High
Italy	High	Low	Low	Low	Low	Low	Low	Low	High	Low
Japan	High	High	Low	Low	High	High	High	Low	High	High
Korea	Low	Low	Low	Low	Low	Low	High	Low	High	High
Malaysia	Low	High	High	High	High	High	High	High	High	High
Mexico	High	Low	Low	Low	Low	Low	Low	Low	Low	Low
New Zealand	High	High	Low	High	High	High	Low	Low	High	High

Norway	High	High	High	Low	High	High	Low	Low	Low	Low
Peru	–	High	Low	Low	Low	Low	High	High	Low	Low
Portugal	Low	High	Low	Low	Low	Low	High	High	Low	Low
Singapore	High	High	High	High	Low	High	High	High	High	High
South Africa	–	High	Low	High	Low	Low	High	Low	High	High
Spain	High	High	Low	Low	Low	High	High	Low	Low	Low
Sri Lanka	–	High	Low	High	Low	Low	Low	Low	High	Low
Sweden	High	Low	Low	Low	High	High	Low	Low	Low	Low
Thailand	–	Low	High	High	Low	Low	Low	High	High	High
Turkey	Low	Low	Low	Low	Low	Low	Low	High	Low	Low
United Kingdom	High	High	Low	High	High	High	High	High	High	High

Appendix 3

	Political economy			Financial market factors			
Country	Risk of expropriation	State–operated business	Tax burden	Stock return comovement	Concentrated ownership	Insider trading	Access to equity
Argentina	High	Low	Low	High	High	High	High
Australia	Low	Low	High	Low	Low	Low	Low
Austria	Low	Low	High	High	High	Low	High
Belgium	Low	Low	High	High	High	Low	Low
Brazil	High	Low	Low	–	High	High	High
Canada	Low	Low	Low	Low	Low	Low	Low
Chile	High	High	Low	Low	Low	High	High
Colombia	High	High	Low	Low	High	High	High
Denmark	Low	Low	Low	Low	Low	Low	Low
Egypt	High	High	Low	–	High	–	High
Finland	Low	Low	High	Low	Low	Low	Low
France	Low	High	High	Low	Low	Low	Low
Germany	Low	High	High	High	Low	Low	Low
Greece	High	Low	High	–	High	High	Low
Hong Kong	High	Low	Low	High	High	Low	Low
India	High	High	Low	High	Low	High	Low
Indonesia	High	High	Low	Low	High	High	High
Ireland	Low	Low	High	Low	Low	Low	Low
Israel	High	High	High	–	High	Low	Low
Italy	Low	High	High	–	High	High	High
Japan	Low	Low	Low	High	Low	Low	High
Korea	High	Low	Low	High	Low	Low	High
Malaysia	High	High	Low	High	High	Low	High
Mexico	High	Low	Low	High	High	High	High
New Zealand	Low	Low	Low	Low	Low	Low	Low
Norway	Low	Low	High	Low	Low	High	Low
Peru	High	Low	Low	Low	High	High	High
Portugal	Low	High	High	Low	High	Low	High
Singapore	Low	Low	Low	High	Low	Low	Low
South Africa	High	High	High	Low	High	High	Low
Spain	Low	High	Low	High	High	High	High
Sri Lanka	High	High	Low	–	High	High	–
Sweden	Low	High	High	Low	Low	Low	Low
Thailand	High	High	Low	High	Low	High	High
Turkey	High	High	High	High	High	High	High
United Kingdom	Low	Low	Low	Low	Low	Low	Low

Appendix 4

Definitions of Firm Specific Variables

X	is earnings before interest and taxes deflated by lagged market capitalization.
R	is stock return, inclusive of dividends, over the fiscal year.
SIZE	is the natural log of market capitalization at the end of the fiscal year (in USD, $million).
MB	is the ratio of market value of equity to the book value of equity, measured at the end of the fiscal year.
LEV	is the total liability divided by total assets, measured at the end of the fiscal year.
LNTA	is the natural log of total assets at the end of the fiscal year (in USD, $million).
CAPINT	is the fixed assets divided by total assets at the end of the fiscal year.
INVREC	is the sum of inventory and receivables divided by total assets, measured at the end of the fiscal year.
LOSS	is equal to 1 if net income before extraordinary is negative in the prior year and 0 otherwise.
CROSS	is equal to 1 if a company trades ADRs (American Depository Receipts) and 0 otherwise.
BIG4	is equal to 1 if a company appoints one of the Big 4 auditors and 0 otherwise.
C-score	is estimated from Eq. 2 in a pooled regression.
Cdec	is decile ranking of C-score, estimated from Eq. 2 in a pooled regression.
Industry indicators	are based on the two-digit SIC code.
FDI	is the net foreign investment scaled by total GDP for the country in each year.
STK	is the total market capitalization to scaled by total GDP for the country in each year.
GDP	is the natural log of Gross Domestic Investment (in thousands of US dollars) for the country in each year.

References

Ali, A., & Hwang, L. S. (2000). Country-specific factors related to financial reporting and the relevance of accounting data. *Journal of Accounting Research, 38*, 1–21.

Ball, R., Kothari, S., & Robin, A. (2000). The effect of international institutional factors on properties of accounting earnings. *Journal of Accounting and Economics, 29*, 1–51.

Ball, R., Robin, A., & Wu, J. (2003). Incentives versus standards: Properties of accounting income in four East Asian countries. *Journal of Accounting and Economics, 36*, 235–270.

Ball, R., Robin, A., & Sadka, G. (2008). Is financial reporting shaped by equity markets or by debt markets? An international study of timeliness and conservatism. *Review of Accounting Studies, 13*, 168–205.

Basu, S. (1997). The conservatism principle and the asymmetric timeliness of earnings. *Journal of Accounting and Economics, 24*, 3–37.

Beaver, W., & Ryan, S. (2005). Conditional and unconditional conservatism: Concepts and modeling. *Review of Accounting Studies, 10*, 269–309.

Bushman, R., & Piotroski, J. (2006). Financial reporting incentives for conservative accounting: The influence of legal and political institutions. *Journal of Accounting and Economics, 42*, 107–148.

Bushman, R., Piotroski, J., & Smith, A. (2004). What determines corporate transparency? *Journal of Accounting Research, 42*, 207–252.

Choi, J. H., & Wong, T. J. (2007). Auditors' governance functions and legal environments: An international comparison. *Contemporary Accounting Research, 24*, 13–46.

Choi, J.-H., Kim, J.-B., Liu, X., & Simunic, D. A. (2008). Audit pricing, legal liability regimes, and Big 4 premiums: Theory and cross-country evidence. *Contemporary Accounting Research, 25*, 55–100.

Chung, R., Firth, M., & Kim, J.-B. (2003). Auditor conservatism and reported earnings. *Accounting and Business Research, 33*, 19–32.

Chung, R., Firth, M., & Kim, J. -B. (2004). *Big 4 conservatism around the world*. Working Paper, The Hong Kong Polytechnic University.

Dhaliwal, D. S., Huang, S. X., Khurana, I., & Pereira, R. (2010) *Product market competition and accounting conservatism*. SSRN eLibrary.

Dietrich, J., Muller, K., & Riedl, E. (2007). Asymmetric timeliness tests of accounting conservatism. *Review of Accounting Studies, 12*, 95–124.

Djankov, S., La Porta, R., Lopez-de-Silanes, F., & Shleifer, A. (2008). The law and economics of self-dealing. *Journal of Financial Economics, 88*, 430–465.

Francis, J. R., & Wang, D. (2008). The joint effect of investor protection and Big 4 audits on earnings quality around the world. *Contemporary Accounting Research, 25*, 157–191.

Francis, J. R., Wang, D., & Nikitkov, A. (2004). *The effect of legal environment on Big Five conservatism around the world*. Working Paper, University of Missouri.

Frankel, R. M., & Roychowdhury, S. (2009). *Are all special items equally special? The Predictive Role of Conservatism*. SSRN eLibrary.

Giner, B., & Rees, W. (2001). On the asymmetric recognition of good and bad news in France, Germany and the United Kingdom. *Journal of Business Finance and Accounting, 28*, 1285–1331.

Givoly, D., Hayn, C., & Natarajan, A. (2007). Measuring reporting conservatism. *The Accounting Review, 82*, 65–106.

Gow, I., Ormazabal, G., & Taylor, D. (2010). Correcting for cross-sectional time-series dependence in accounting research. *The Accounting Review, 85*, 483–512.

Greene, W. (1997). *Econometric analysis* (3rd ed.). Upper Saddle River: Prentice Hall.

Gul, F. A., Kim, J.-B., & Qiu, A. (2010). Ownership concentration, foreign shareholding, audit quality, and stock price synchronicity: Evidence from China. *Journal of Financial Economics, 95*, 425–442.

Hartland-Peel, C. (1996). *African equities: A guide to markets and companies*. London: Euromoney Publications.

Hogan, C. E. (1997). Costs and benefits of audit quality in the IPO market: A self-selection analysis. *The Accounting Review, 72*, 67–86.

Huijgen, C., & Lubberink, M. (2005). Earnings conservatism, litigation, and contracting: The case of cross-listed firms. *Journal of Business Finance and Accounting, 32*, 1275–1310.

Hung, M. (2001). Accounting standards and value relevance of financial statements: An international analysis. *Journal of Accounting and Economics, 30*, 401–420.

Jin, L., & Myers, S. (2006). R^2 around the world: New theory and new tests. *Journal of Financial Economics, 79*, 257–292.

Khan, M., & Watts, R. (2008). *Estimation and validation of a firm-year measure of conservatism.* Working Paper, The Sloan School of Management, Massachusetts Institute of Technology, Cambridge, MA.

Khan, M., & Watts, R. (2009). Estimation and empirical properties of a firm-year measure of accounting conservatism. *Journal of Accounting and Economics, 48*, 132–150.

Kim, J. -B., & Shi, H. (2011). *International financial reporting standards, analyst following, institutional infrastructure, and stock price synchronicity around the world.* Working Paper, City University of Hong Kong and Fudan University.

Kim, J. -B., & Zhang, L. (2011). *Does accounting conservatism reduce stock price crash risk? Firm-level evidence.* Working Paper, City University of Hong Kong.

Kim, J.-B., Chung, R., & Firth, M. (2003). Auditor conservatism, asymmetric monitoring, and earnings management. *Contemporary Accounting Research, 20*, 323–359.

La Porta, R., Lopez-de-Silanes, F., Shleifer, A., & Vishny, R. (1997). Legal determinants of external finance. *Journal of Finance, 52*, 1131–1150.

La Porta, R., Lopez-de-Silanes, F., Shleifer, A., & Vishny, R. (1998). Law and finance. *Journal of Political Economy, 106*, 1113–1155.

La Porta, R., Lopez-de-Silanes, F., & Shleifer, A. (1999). Corporate ownership around the World. *Journal of Finance, 54*, 471–518.

La Porta, R., Lopez-de-Silanes, F., Shleifer, A., & Vishny, R. (2000). Investor protection and corporate governance. *Journal of Financial Economics, 58*, 3–27.

La Porta, R., Lopez-de-Silanes, F., & Shleifer, A. (2006). What works in securities laws? *Journal of Finance, 61*, 1–32.

Lafond, R., & Watts, R. L. (2008). The information role of conservatism. *The Accounting Review, 83*, 447–478.

Lang, M., Raedy, J. S., & Yetman, M. H. (2003). How representative are firms that are cross-listed in the United States? An analysis of accounting quality. *Journal of Accounting Research, 41*, 363–386.

Leuz, C., Nanda, D., & Wyscocki, P. D. (2003). Earnings management and investor protection: An international comparison. *Journal of Financial Economics, 69*, 505–527.

Lewis, R., & Pendrill, D. (1996). *Advanced financial accounting* (5th ed.). London: Pitman Publishing.

Likierman, A. (1989). *Professional liability: Report of the study teams.* London: Department of Trade and Industry, HMSO.

London Economics. (2006). *Study on the economic impact of auditors' liability regimes.* Final Report to EC-DG Internal Markets and Services.

Louis, H., Lys, T. Z., & Sun, A. X. (2011). *Conservatism and analyst earnings forecast bias.* SSRN eLibrary.

Maddala, G. (1983). *Limited-dependent and qualitative variables in econometrics.* New York: Cambridge University Press.

Mitchell, A., Puxty, A., Sikka, P., & Willmott, H. (1991). *Accounting for change: Proposals for reform of audit and accounting.* London: Fabian Society.

Morck, R., Yeung, B., & Yu, W. (2000). The information content of stock prices: Why do emerging markets have synchronous stock price movements? *Journal of Financial Economics, 58*, 215–260.

Penman, S., & Zhang, X. J. (2002). Accounting conservatism, the quality of earnings, and stock returns. *The Accounting Review, 77*, 237–264.

Petersen, M. A. (2009). Estimating standard errors in finance panel data sets: Comparing approaches. *Review of Financial Studies, 22*, 435–480.

Pope, P., & Walker, M. (1999). International differences in the timeliness, conservatism, and classification of earnings. *Journal of Accounting Research, 37*(Supplement), 53–87.

Raonic, I., McLeay, S., & Asimakopoulos, I. (2004). The timeliness of earnings, market to book and conservatism in financial reporting. *Journal of Business Finance and Accounting, 31*, 151–165.

Roychowdhury, S., & Watts, R. L. (2007). Asymmetric timeliness of earnings, market-to-book and conservatism in financial reporting. *Journal of Accounting and Economics, 44*, 2–31.

Samsonova, A., Humphrey, C., & Kokkali, S. (2010). *Re-thinking auditor liability: The case of the European Union's regulatory reform.* Conference Paper, APRIA, Sydney.

Schwab, K., Porter, M., Sachs, J., Warner, A., & Levinson, M. (1999). *The global competitiveness report.* New York: Oxford University Press.

Shu, S. Z. (2000). Auditor resignations: Clientele effects and legal liability. *Journal of Accounting and Economics, 29*, 173–205.

Simunic, D. A., & Stein, M. T. (1996). The impact of litigation risk on audit pricing: A review of the economics and the evidence. *Auditing: A Journal of Practice and Theory, 15*(Supplement), 119–134.

Srivastava, A., & Tse, S. Y. (2010). *The contribution of delayed gain recognition to trends in conservatism: A re-examination using a new approach to measuring accounting conservatism.* SSRN eLibrary.

St. Pierre, K., & Anderson, J. (1984). An analysis of the factors associated with lawsuits against public accountants. *The Accounting Review, 59*, 242–263.

Watts, R. (2003a). Conservatism in accounting, Part I: Explanation and research implications. *Accounting Horizons, 17*, 207–221.

Watts, R. (2003b). Conservatism in accounting, Part II: Evidence and research opportunities. *Accounting Horizons, 17*, 287–301.

Watts, R. (2006). What has the invisible hand achieved? *Accounting and Business Research, 36* (Special Issue), 51–61.

Wingate, M. L. (1997). An examination of cultural influence on audit environments. *Research in Accounting Regulation, 11*(Supplement), 129–148.

Wittenberg-Moerman, R. (2008). The role of information asymmetry and financial reporting in quality in debt trading: Evidence from the secondary loan market. *Journal of Accounting and Economics, 46*, 240–260.

Corporate Governance in Emerging Markets: What We Can Learn from a Privatisation Context

Jaime Guerrero-Villegas, Gloria Cuevas-Rodríguez, and Ramón Valle-Cabrera

Abstract This chapter analyses the changes observed in the corporate governance of companies after privatisation. Specifically, the study focuses on the analysis of how boards change their two main functions – control and provision of resources – when the company is transferred from public to private hands. This serves as a reference to emerging countries that use privatisation as a mechanism for economic development. Regarding the control function, the study shows the key role played by directors appointed before the Chief Executive Officer (CEO) in monitoring managers. This study also establishes the influence of external factors – such as regulation and competition in the sector – on the control function. Regarding the provision of resource role, the results highlight the importance of changing the configuration of the boards after privatisation – in terms of the profile of the directors – in order to acquire the necessary resources in the private stage of the firm. In this respect, the study indicates that directors who are business experts play a greater role after privatisation, and highlights the important presence of support specialists with specific skills at each stage of the company. The study also emphasises the limitations of some variables traditionally associated with the control function – leadership structure (non-duality) and outside directors – and with the provision of resources role – board size.

1 Introduction

Emerging markets have captured the attention of academics and practitioners in the last two decades (Luo 2003). Emerging markets are countries that are restructuring their economies along market-oriented lines and offer a wealth of opportunities in trade, technology transfers, and foreign direct investment (Aghara et al. 2011).

J. Guerrero-Villegas (✉) • G. Cuevas-Rodríguez • R. Valle-Cabrera
Management Department, Pablo de Olavide University, Carretera de Utrera, Km.1, Seville 41013, Spain
e-mail: jguevil@upo.es; gcuerod@upo.es; rvalcab@upo.es

S. Boubaker and D.K. Nguyen (eds.), *Corporate Governance in Emerging Markets*, CSR, Sustainability, Ethics & Governance, DOI 10.1007/978-3-642-44955-0_9,

These markets present challenges for firms from developed countries, leading to high returns and portfolio risk diversification (Movassaghi et al. 2004).

Recently, the study conducted by Claessens and Yurtoglu (2013), focusing on emerging markets, pointed out the key role played by corporate governance in companies. According to their study, better corporate governance benefits firms through greater access to financing, lower cost of capital, enhanced performance, and more favourable treatment of all stakeholders. The authors identified issues requiring further study, specifically the corporate governance issues of State-Owned Enterprises (SOEs) and how privatisation and corporate governance interact. In this regard, one of the main mechanisms pushing economic development in emerging markets has been the privatisation of SOEs, since this provides much of the capital needed to develop the domestic economy. Investors will put in their funds and technical expertise to improve the quality of the management and output of the privatised organisation (Aghara et al. 2011). Therefore, the importance of analysing privatisation from the perspective of corporate governance in emerging markets is highlighted. Despite this fact, most studies have mainly focused on analysing the effects of privatisation on business performance (Megginson and Sutter 2006).

Research into the central governing mechanism – the board of directors – in a privatisation context has focused primarily on describing changes in the structure and composition of the board after the organisation passes into private hands (Bozec et al. 2004). This line of research has neglected to analyse the key role played by directors. Additionally, studies examining the functions of directors have largely only dealt with the control function, offering a partial view of the functioning of boards. Indeed, there is literature highlighting other board activities that remains almost entirely unexplored (Daily et al. 2003), for example, activities of providing resources (Hillman and Dalziel 2003). The partial view of board functions has hindered a full understanding about how directors perform their functions. Hence, an approach that takes into account all of the board's functions is complex to analyse, but nonetheless of great interest when it comes to understanding how boards operate.

The aim of this chapter is to analyse the changes that take place within a company's corporate governance following privatisation. Specifically, the study focuses on analysing how boards change their two main functions – control and provision of resources – when the company passes from public to private hands. The interest and importance of this study lies in the key role played by boards in the success of the privatisation process and its effect on increasing business performance (Omran 2009).

To conduct the study, multiple case studies were used. The cases examined are not an arbitrary selection but rather aim to include companies from different industries and belonging to strategic Spanish sectors (Endesa, Iberia and Repsol). It uses information from interviews, questionnaires and secondary sources in order to triangulate the information (Yin 1989). Aspects are considered that are both internal and external to the organisation. Internal issues include leadership structure, the size and composition of the board, and the profiles of the board's members.

External factors encompass regulation and competition in the sectors where the companies operate. Focusing on the Spanish context could enrich the debate surrounding corporate governance research that has been dominated by the pattern of investor-management relationships typical of Anglo-Saxon countries. Although there is a growing tendency towards capital markets in Spain these days, historically they have been considered somewhat underdeveloped. This fact, together with the weak market for corporate control, low investor protection and the characteristics of the legal and financial systems could explain the emergence of different types of blockholders as an alternative control mechanism in the Spanish context. By introducing the debate around these issues, this article further clarifies the consequences of privatisation on this corporate governance model.

The results highlight changes in control role and provision of resources role once firms are privatised. Regarding the control function, the study shows that the privatisation of SOEs leads to an increase in the board's control function over top management. The study shows the central role played by directors appointed before the CEO in monitoring managers, and the influence of external factors – such as regulation and competition in the sector – on the control function. Regarding the provision of resources role, the results highlight the importance of changing the configuration of boards after privatisation – in terms of the profile of the directors – in order to acquire the necessary resources in the private stage of the firm. Specifically, companies increase the number of *business experts* as a consequence of privatisation while *support specialists* are equally important in SOEs and privatised companies. However, the resources provided by the support specialists are different in the public and private phases. Whereas communication channels with the government and other public agencies are more important in SOEs, financial and insurance counsel and advice, and access to financial and other resources become more important in privatised firms. This study also emphasises the limitations of variables traditionally associated with the control role and provision of resources role, such as leadership structure (duality/non-duality), size, and composition (in terms of insiders and outsiders) of the board of directors.

In following sections we review the literature, then we present the method and discuss the empirical results. Finally, the study's main conclusions are set out, providing a reference to emerging countries that use privatisation as a mechanism for economic development.

2 Board Roles

The literature often focuses specifically on studying the board of directors, both in academic and professional contexts, because of the board's decisive influence on company outcomes (Pearce and Zahra 1992). Hillman and Dalziel (2003) maintain that boards of directors perform two key functions: (1) monitoring (control), which is related to control over managers and monitoring the firm's performance to safeguard shareholder interests (Fama and Jensen 1983); and (2) provision of resources, which consists of facilitating key resources that may favour the survival and success of a company (Johnson et al. 1996). The next section analyses the control role and provision of resources role in a privatisation context.

2.1 Control Role and Privatisation

Regarding the control function, and according to agency theory, the board of directors and managers have a different role. While managers are concerned with making decisions in the company, the directors are responsible for overseeing these decisions (Fama and Jensen 1983).

The agency conflict, and the underlying problem with the overseeing of management, occurs in both the private sector and SOEs. However, in SOEs, due to their unique agency relationship and their being unable to assert property rights, the problem of monitoring the "agents" deepens (Melle 1999). The main reasons are:

1. The political nature of SOEs, where appointments are not focused on effective management capacity, but rather on allegiance to the political group in government (González-Páramo 1995).
2. The disparity of objectives (Laffont 1995). Generally, the public purpose is translated into a series of objectives in the spheres of political and social welfare. These are different depending on governments and according to their programmes. Consequently, these objectives are often vague, multiple, volatile, and sometimes contradictory (Hernández de Cos 2004).
3. Greater dispersion in the ownership of SOEs. According to agency theory, when the ownership of a company is spread, the incentive for owners to control managers is low. By contrast, when ownership is concentrated, the owners are more interested in control, especially when their wealth is not diversified (Hoskisson and Turk 1990). Private companies also suffer from poor control over agents, especially companies with very large and dispersed ownership structures (Jensen and Meckling 1976). However, in the case of SOEs, the distribution of ownership is always higher because the ultimate shareholders are citizens (Alchian and Demsetz 1972), thereby causing a double agency problem (Cuevas et al. 2007).

Regarding the ownership structure, the active role of the controlling shareholders in corporate governance has been analysed in numerous studies (e.g., Hernández and López de Castro 2000). In this respect, some authors have pointed out that the success of privatisation is linked to the existence of stable shareholders with significant blocks of shares (Boycko et al. 1996; Melle 1999). The success of the privatisation process is also linked to the business knowledge of stable shareholders, as they can improve control over managers (Cuervo 2003).

Overall, privatisation changes the identity of the owners, creating an alignment of ownership rights, greater ownership concentration (Cragg and Dyck 2000) and improved functioning of the control systems (Boycko et al. 1996). Consequently, the new owners will be highly motivated to increase the value of the company (Lioukas et al. 1993) and, thus, they will be more interested in controlling the activities performed by managers.

2.2 Provision of Resources Role and Privatisation

Resource dependence theory posits that organisations constantly require external resources, and the environment, therefore, has an impact on these organisations (Pfeffer and Salancik 1978). The literature shows the key role played by the board of directors as resource providers based on the links that the directors embody between the firm and its environment (Johnson et al. 1996; Zahra and Pearce 1989).

Following Pfeffer and Salancik (1978), and Hillman and Dalziel (2003), the resources provided by directors could be categorised as follows: (1) *counsel and advice* (Jones et al. 2008); (2) *legitimising and bolstering a firm's public image* (Certo et al. 2001; Pfeffer and Salancik 1978); (3) *facilitation of access to resources* (Mizruchi and Stearns 1994); and (4) *building external relationships* (Peterson and Philpot 2009).

These four groups of resources provided by directors help firms cope with uncertainty arising from the environment. Nevertheless, private firms are more sensitive to environmental uncertainty than SOEs (Megginson et al. 1994). Therefore, private firms are expected to develop strategies to cope with uncertainty. In contrast, SOEs count on government support – which guarantees firm survival – although SOEs also require specific resources to respond to political objectives and the general interests of citizens. Additionally, SOEs present certain peculiarities. Firstly, SOEs are rarely diversified (Cragg and Dyck 2000). This means that they usually focus their activity on a unique product or service. Second, SOEs are geographically limited to a national territory (Ocaña and Salas 1983). Furthermore, SOEs are usually oligopolistic or monopolistic (Ocaña and Salas 1983). These peculiarities could affect the need for specific resources in SOEs. For example, it could be expected that SOEs have less need for directors experienced in competitive markets and strategic decision-making.

Privatised firms depend on their own resources to cope with environmental uncertainty and achieve goals that are clearly oriented towards efficiency and productivity (Shleifer and Vishny 1994). Following privatisation, the company and its interests depend on the market flow. This change creates a new scenario in which the company's primary objective is survival (Zahra et al. 2000). According to Zahra and Hansen (2000), privatisation increases the pressure to work hard, conserve resources and develop skills that fulfil market demands.

Bearing this idea in mind, the resources required by privatised companies and SOEs can be understood to be different. This argument points out the necessity of analysing the specific characteristics that a board of directors should possess to provide the resources appropriate to a firm's status (private or public).

3 The Idiosyncrasy of Privatisation in Spanish Corporate Governance

In accordance with the above literature, privatised firms can be expected to exhibit improved control mechanisms over managers' activities, and their board of directors should provide the appropriate resources for the new environmental requirements. Although these issues are to be expected on the basis of agency theory and resource dependence theory, the idiosyncrasy of Spanish corporate governance should be acknowledged. A number of literature reviews, concluding that evidence regarding what drives board effectiveness is mixed, recommend that future studies adopt a more contextually sensitive approach because a difference in national context can, for example, limit the applicability of standard agency theory assumptions of investor risk preferences, managerial behaviours and ultimately the functions of the boards (Yoshikawa and Phan 2005). Hence, Pedersen and Thomsen (1997) argue different national patterns of ownership structures regarding several country-specific variables such as the size and liquidity of the stock market, the concentration of the banking sector, the existence of dual class shares, and the openness of the economy to international capital.

Aguilera (2005, p. 198) suggests that the case of Spain, along with that of Italy, and to some extent France, follows the so-called Latin model characterised by strong state intervention, weak labour participation at a company level, and concentrated firm ownership. These Spanish features are to some extent the legacy of 40 years of dictatorship under Franco when the State (with extensive industry ownership) and a privileged banking system were the main providers of capital to firms, and little competition existed in either capital or product markets. Overall, according to Aguilera (2005), the current Spanish corporate governance scene is composed of newly privatised firms owned by core investors (some of them foreign), a weak market for corporate control, and sporadic use of Anglo-Saxon practices, although certain reforms have been undertaken to increase the transparency and accountability of firms, as well as the efficiency of boards of directors.

4 Research Methodology

4.1 Case Studies

Given the context and complexity of the phenomenon studied, an examination of multiple case studies is the most suitable method to understand the dynamic changes of firms (Yin 1994). A qualitative analysis facilitates the elaboration of an in-depth study.

In line with Yin's (1994) suggestions, the cases examined are not an arbitrary selection, but rather aim to include different combinations related to two control variables: (1) the industrial sector (in other words, the companies studied should represent a variety of industries); and (2) the companies should belong to strategic Spanish sectors. In addition, the following restriction is applied: the companies selected for study were fully privatised after 1996. The reason for this restriction is related to the fact that the privatisation process in Spain is divided into two different periods (Caixa 1999). The first period includes privatisations that occurred from 1985 to 1996, when the Spanish government was aiming to reform the public sector rather than implement a privatisation policy per se. A second period of privatisation in Spain started after 1996 with the Modernisation Programme of the Public Sector. This programme encouraged the privatisation of efficient SOEs. Meanwhile, others were preparing to make them profitable. This second period witnessed a complete process of privatisation. Following the above-mentioned requirements, three privatised Spanish companies were analysed: Endesa, Iberia and Repsol (see Table 1).

4.2 Data Collection

Contact was made the companies' CEOs by telephone and e-mail. This initial communication invited the CEOs to participate in the study and requested information, such as the composition of the board and top management team, and reports, for the 5 years before and after privatisation.

The sample population was composed of 114 directors (Endesa: 37; Iberia: 35; Repsol: 42) and 114 top managers (Endesa: 54; Iberia: 34; Repsol: 26). After numerous communications with the three companies, 30 interviews were conducted between May 19, 2009, and February 22, 2010, corresponding to 18 directors and 12 top managers (Table 2), giving a response ratio of 15.8 % and 10.5 %, respectively. Among those interviewed were four CEOs and two managing directors.

Interviews and a questionnaire survey were used simultaneously. A questionnaire was constructed with structured questions. This was divided into two columns to enable the interviewees to assess their answers in the pre- and post-privatisation periods. The information for each of the firm's phases was obtained from the directors and top managers, that is, from two different perspectives corresponding to the principal and agents.

To analyse board structure and board composition, the 5 years prior to and after privatisation were considered (10 years). Secondary information sources were used, such as annual reports, company websites, the National Securities Market Commission, databases, Who's Who and various business publications.

4.3 Measures

Leadership structure (duality). Following previous research (Lin 2005), this study assumes that CEO duality exists when a firm's CEO also serves as chairman of the board of directors.

Table 1 Main characteristics of firms analysed

	Endesa	Iberia	Repsol
Sector	Electrical	Airline	Hydrocarbon
Year of complete privatisation	1998	2001	1997
Times of privatisation, percentage sold, and privatisation method	1988:(20.4 %) Public Offering (PO) 1994:(8.7 %)PO 1997:(25 %)PO 1998:(33 %)PO 1998:(8.19 %) Capital Reduction (CR)	1999:(10 %)Direct Sale (DS) 1999:(30 %)DS 2001:(48.51 %)PO	1989:(4.2 %)DS 1989:(26.4 %)PO 1989:(2.9 %)DS 1992:(2.1 %)DS 1992:(10 %)Bond Issue (BI) 1993:(13.3 %)PO 1993:(0.6 %)BI 1994:(0.1 %)BI 1995:(19.4 %)PO 1996:(11 %)PO 1997:(10 %)PO
Major shareholders	Caixa (5 %); Caja Madrid (5 %); BSCH (3 %); BBVA (3 %)	NEWCO (10 %); Caja Madrid (10 %); BBVA (7.3 %); Logista Aeroportuaria, S.A (6.7 %); Corte Inglés (3 %); Ahorro Corporación S.A (3 %)	Caixa (5 %); BBVA (7 %); PEMEX (5 %)
Company size (year complete privatisation)			
Sales (in millions of euros)	6,836.5	4,581	19,287.2
Employees	19,479	27,523	21,440
Profits (in millions of euros)	1,097.2	29.4	757.9

Source: Authors' own data

Outsider representation. This variable was measured as the percentage of outside directors sitting on the board (Young et al. 2000).

Board members appointed before the CEO's appointment. This variable was measured as the percentage of board members who were appointed before the CEO had taken office (Young et al. 2000).

Board size. The number of directors on the board was taken into account (Linck et al. 2008).

Director profile. Following previous research (Hillman et al. 2000), directors were classified into one of three profiles (business experts, support specialists and community influentials). The type of director included in each category is shown in Table 3. A total of 114 director profiles were analysed.

Ownership structure. To measure ownership structure, the Index of Concentration of Ownership (ICON) was used, specifically considering the percentage of shares held by blockholders, i.e., stakeholders holding more than 5 % of the capital (Tosi and Gómez-Mejía 1989).

Table 2 Interviews

	Endesa	Iberia	Repsol	Total
Directors	7	6	5	18
Managers	7	3	2	12
Total	**14**	**9**	**7**	**30**

Table 3 Type of director

Director category	Types of directors in category
Business experts	Directors and executives in big companies with profit-making aims
Support specialists	Lawyers, bankers, insurance representatives and public relations experts
Community influentials	Political leaders, university faculty and leaders in social organisations

Source: Adapted from Hillman et al. (2000)

Sector regulation. In order to measure this variable, a list was developed of the most important aspects related to regulation (Helland and Sykuta 2004), prices, production, purchasing, investments, location, and diversification policy (see Appendix).

Sector competition. In order to measure this variable, the scale developed by Sarin and Mahajan (2001) was used, made up of four items (see Appendix). Its purpose is to measure the degree of rivalry in the sector.

Control role. Seven statements from the research by Carpenter and Westphal (2001), and Wan and Ong (2005) were used to capture the control role. Control questions asked about the extent to which board oversees the decisions made by top managers, evaluates the performance of top managers, and the degree to which board engages in succession planning for the CEO and top managers. Examples of items are "Board monitors top management decision-making" and "Board formally evaluates the performance of company executives". The items selected from the scales of the authors mentioned above are shown in Appendix.

Provision of resources role. Questions about the provision of resources role were worded according to the resource classifications in the literature (Hillman and Dalziel 2003; Pfeffer and Salancik 1978), and referred particularly to the specific activities undertaken by the board. Specifically, four types of resources were identified: (1) counsel and advice (on business management, legal, financial, insurance and public relations issues), (2) legitimising and bolstering the firm's public image, (3) facilitating access to resources (financial and others), and (4) building external relationships (communications channels with the government and other public agencies, and communications channels with firms) (see Appendix).

4.4 Data Analysis and Quality of Findings

Wilcoxon non-parametric tests (Siegel and Castellan 1988) were used to test for statistically-significant differences in control activities and the resources provided by directors before and after privatisation. The open questions enabled the respondents to provide information that they considered relevant in terms of the specific control activities and resources provided by the directors.

The analysis was performed using the Atlas/ti software package for qualitative analysis. Atlas/ti is a powerful tool for coding and interpreting textual data (Muhr 2006). The central themes of this research – the control and provision of resources – served as the initial coding categories (referred to as families in Atlas/ti). Sub-categories (referred to as codes in Atlas/ti), which were formulated according to the research framework proposed, were subsumed under these families. Additionally, following the recommendations of Yin (1994), some of the significant interviews responses are reproduced.

As in previous research (Plakoyiannaki et al. 2008), and to ensure the quality of the case study findings, the researchers followed numerous practices recommended in the literature to increase the validity and reliability of the case study evidence, such as the theory to structure the list of interview topics (Eisenhardt 1989), and data and between-method triangulation to capture phenomena investigated from different perspectives (Yin 1989). Data triangulation is based on the collection and comparison of data from multiple respondents (e.g., directors and top managers) in the organisation (Denzin 1989). In a similar vein, between-method triangulation relied on the use of multiple methods, such as interviews, questionnaires and secondary sources, to examine the role of the directors in control activities and providing resources (Denzin 1989).

5 Findings

Below are the main results of the change in board roles as a result of privatisation. They are divided into two sections: firstly control role and secondly the provision of resources role.

5.1 Privatisation and Change in the Control Function of the Board

Regarding the public stage of the firm, one of the aspects highlighted is the difficulty for directors to perform their control role. This difficulty is largely due to the ambiguity of objectives. In this regard, the interviews show the influence of public authorities in setting goals and making decisions. The more important the decisions, the greater the influence exerted by the government. This influence reached its peak when there was a change of government. One of the managers interviewed said that "*... when there was a change of government, the company was like the new toy that came to power ...*". This lack of clarity and stability in the objectives of the company made it difficult or even impossible to control and monitor their achievement. A director of Repsol said "... *it is very difficult to control the performance of top managers without having previously established a clear business objective* ...". He added, "... *the government was focused on the degree of achievement of policy objectives rather than business objectives* ...".

The results clearly show the passive attitude of boards in the evaluation and control of top managers in the firm's public stage.

One important aspect that is highlighted after privatisation is the emergence of blockholders in the ownership of the companies analysed.

Table 4 shows the results of the ICON in the pre- and post-privatisation phases for each of the companies. Before privatisation, it was above 41 % in all three companies, due to the high stakes held by the State. After privatisation, although it declines, the ICON continues to display high values: 10.01 %, 39.36 %, and 21.60 % of Endesa, Iberia and Repsol respectively, due to the presence of blockholders. In this regard, despite the emergence of major shareholders in the three companies, there are some aspects which are noteworthy. Firstly, in Iberia the percentage of capital held by blockholders is significantly higher than in the other two companies, reaching almost 40 %. Moreover, the profile of these blockholders in Iberia is more heterogeneous than in the other case studies. Specifically, the ownership of this airline included financial institutions (Caja Madrid and BBVA), airlines (British Airways and American Airlines), and a distribution company (Logista). However, in both Endesa and Repsol, the blockholders' profile is more homogeneous, largely financial institutions: in Endesa, Caja Madrid and La Caixa, and in Repsol, Caixa and BBVA – plus PEMEX.

The new ownership structures of the firms show that privatisation replaced the public sector ownership position with a dual ownership structure. On the one hand, most of the equity of privatised firms was in the hands of institutional or industrial investors, comprising the hardcore. These hardcore groups are generally well-known entities. They purchased the shares but had to agree that they would not transfer the stock. This was a state-mandate stipulation intended to guarantee a certain stability in the composition of the firm's capital. On the other hand, the involvement of minority shareholders was encouraged in the newly privatised firms. This is consistent with the government objective of promoting popular capitalism. In fact, security market law reforms were approved in 1998 to stimulate activity in the Spanish stock market (historically small and geographically segmented) and help to develop a small investor culture (Aguilera 2005, p. 206).

Although the concentration of capital declined in firms following privatisation, the average percentage in the hands of important shareholders remained high. The main shareholders were financial institutions and different types of shareholders – industrial shareholders, financial institutions and non-financial institutions. In this regard, the profile of the shareholders could determine the way in which companies were managed. For example, in the case of Iberia, the experience and knowledge of the air industry brought by British Airways and American Airlines helped to introduce changes in the way the company was managed right before the whole firm was privatised. In fact, the role of these shareholders was critical to consolidate

Table 4 Stakes held by blockholders (ICON)

	Endesa (%)		Iberia (%)		Repsol (%)	
	Before	After	Before	After	Before	After
ICON	63.49	10.01	93.04	39.36	41.68	21.60

Source: Authors' own data

the market position of Iberia in the air industry, which had been highly deregulated and competitive right before the firm's privatisation.

Another of the changes arising from privatisation was related to business objectives. Once privatised, the companies' objectives clearly focused on business growth, international expansion, improving market share, and reducing costs. For example, in Endesa, in 1999 (1 year after privatisation), 53 % of the company's electrical market was outside Spanish territory (Annual Report, 1999). In Iberia, these measures led the company to obtain a net profit of 159.8 million euros in 2002, triple that of the previous year. This meant a 12 % return on equity (Annual Report, 2002). Finally, Repsol's results show the efforts made to reduce the operating costs of exploration and production by almost 10 %.

Analysis of the information provided by the questionnaires showed an increase in the boards' control over managers' activities. For example, after privatisation, greater attention was paid to the formal evaluation of management performance, supervision of managers' strategic decision-making and the succession planning of directors. However, although all three companies showed a significant increase in the board's control activity, it was more intense in Iberia (Wilcoxon p-value = .042) compared to Endesa (Wilcoxon p-value = .083) and Repsol (Wilcoxon p-value = .080).

After analysing the increase in board control as a result of privatisation, it seems appropriate to analyse the behaviour of factors that can influence the board's control role. These can be divided into internal and external factors. Among the internal factors are: (1) leadership structure (duality/non-duality) (Lin 2005), (2) board composition (Lehn et al. 2009), and (3) the time directors are appointed (Young et al. 2000). Among the external factors, literature identifies the key role played by sector regulation (Cuervo 1997; Vickers and Yarrow 1991) and sector competition (Cuervo 1998).

5.1.1 Internal Factors

Regarding leadership structure, analysis of the cases reveals two distinct behaviours. In Iberia and Repsol, on the one hand, the positions of chairman and CEO are held by the same person, both in the pre- and in the post-privatisation period. In Endesa, on the other hand, a situation of non-duality was observed when the company passed into private hands (Table 5).

The second factor analysis is related to the composition of the board. In this respect, there was a decrease, following privatisation, in the percentage of outside directors in Endesa and Iberia. However, this decrease was greater in Iberia (from

Table 5 Duality, board composition and directors appointed before CEO (before and after privatisation)

	Duality		Board composition (% outsiders)		Directors appointed before CEO (%)	
	Before	After	Before	After	Before	After
Endesa	Yes	No	88	86	6	0
Iberia	Yes	Yes	92	85	22	58
Repsol	Yes	Yes	78	93	7	18

Source: Authors' own data

92 % to 85 %) than in Endesa (from 88 % to 86 %). In contrast, after privatisation, Repsol saw a significant increase in the presence of non-executive directors from 78 % to 93 % (Table 5).

This latter variable is related to the time directors are appointed. The data reflect an increase in the presence of directors appointed before the CEO in two of the companies after privatisation. However, this increase occurs with greater intensity in the company that, in turn, has a greater intensity of board control: Iberia. Thus, whereas in Iberia this metric value shoots up from 22 % to 58 % after privatisation, in Repsol, moderate changes were found, from 7 % to 18 % (Table 5).

To sum up, with regard to internal factors, two considerations can be highlighted. Firstly, the data do not suggest a clear relationship between leadership structure and the presence of outside directors, and the board's control role. Secondly, there seems to be some influence from the presence of directors appointed before the CEO and greater board control after privatisation.

5.1.2 External Factors

Related to regulation, the behaviour of the electrical and hydrocarbon sectors – which Endesa and Repsol respectively own – has been similar. Both sectors underwent major deregulation once the companies were privatised.

For the electrical sector, the adoption of Act 54/1997, which entered into force in 1998, established the legislative framework for the liberalised Spanish electrical system. In that year, power was no longer considered a state-owned service. The results of the Wilcoxon test (p-value = .043) show evidence of the decline in the level of regulation in the sector, indicating significant differences when comparing the period before and after privatisation.

Meanwhile, Act 34/1998 in the hydrocarbon sector also meant a drastic change in the level of regulation in certain areas, such as opening up the market for liquid fuels, the elimination of the price-cap system, and the liberalisation of the natural gas sector. The Wilcoxon test results support the decline in the level of global regulation after Repsol was privatised (p-value = .039).

The airline industry, however, follows a different pattern. The market was already highly liberalised before the privatisation of Iberia. Specifically, liberalisation measures were implemented during the years 1987–1997 (Button 2001), with biggest change being in 1993. The Wilcoxon test supports these arguments showing the absence of significant differences in both periods (p-value = .285). Although the year 1993 marked a turning point in the airline industry deregulation process, after the privatisation of Iberia (in 2001), some deregulatory measures also occurred, although they were more minor.

Analysis of the results shows that, after privatisation, in the three sectors there was a decrease in the level of regulation (not significant in the airline industry) and a higher level of board control. Given these data, it could be stated that firms tend to raise the level of board control when the deregulation of the sector decreases, since both variables (board control and regulation) follow an opposite pattern. This relationship clearly arises for two of the three cases, Endesa and Repsol. By way of an example, average values in the level of regulation went from 3.36 to 2.22, and from 4.04 to 1.69, comparing the pre-and post-privatisation situation in the electrical and hydrocarbon sectors, respectively. However, the case of Iberia impedes any clear conclusions regarding the level of regulation, because although it decreases after privatisation, there were no significant changes (from an average value of 3.05–2.33).

Finally, regarding the role of competition in the board control function, data analysis showed, as in the case of regulation, two distinct patterns: on the one hand, the electrical and the hydrocarbons sectors and, on the other hand, the airline industry. In the case of the electrical sector, drastic changes were seen in the level of competition after the privatisation of Endesa. The company's market share in Spain fell from 54 % in 1995 to 42.6 % in 2003 (Annual Report, 1995, 2003). Meanwhile, regarding the hydrocarbon market, and according to the Ministry of Industry (1995), 86 % of the fuel market in Spain was owned by three companies – Repsol, 54 %, Cepsa, 25 %, and British Petroleum (BP), 7 %. Three years after the privatisation of Repsol (in 2000), the market share of the three major oil companies fell by 11 %, placing it at 75 % (Repsol 43 %, Cepsa 22 %, and BP 10 %). Increased competition in both sectors is reflected by the results of the Wilcoxon test, showing a p-value = .042 for Endesa and Repsol.

However, in the case of Iberia, the level of competition in the airline industry did not experience significant changes once the company was privatised. The liberalisation measures were implemented before the privatisation of Iberia, over a 10-year period (1987–1997). The lack of significant differences in the degree of competition in the airline sector in both periods was corroborated by the results of the Wilcoxon test (p-value = .285).

All the information taken together, the three sectors – electricity, airline and hydrocarbons – showed an increase in the level of competition (although not significant for the airline sector). Thus, both the level of competition in sectors and the control exercised by boards intensified after privatisation. This is clearly reflected in the data collected from the questionnaires. For example, in the electricity sector, competition rose from an average value of 1.78–4.03 after privatisation. In the case of the hydrocarbon sector, these values were 1.82 and 4.55 in the public and private stages of the company, respectively. However, as with regulation, once again the case of Iberia does not help to clarify this relationship, because it is placed in an environment in which competition does not undergo any major variations (the average value goes from 3.69 to 4.83).

5.2 *Privatisation and Change in the Provision of Resources Function of the Board*

According to resource dependence theory, two factors determine the capacity of boards of directors as resource providers: size and composition (Johnson et al. 1996).

Data for the size and composition of the boards of directors are summarised in Table 6. Regarding size, the results show a tendency to maintain the same number of members in the board once the company is privatised. Therefore, there is no clear relationship between the number of directors and the public and private phases of the firms.

Regarding board composition, as mentioned previously, the results do not show a clear relationship between the presence of outsiders and the public and private phases of the firms.

Additionally, the data show that changes occurred in the director profiles pre- and post-privatisation (Table 6). The following section provides an in-depth analysis of the changes in director profiles and the resources provided by each director type before and after privatisation.

5.2.1 Business Experts

The aggregated data showed a clear tendency towards an increase in the number of business experts after privatisation (from 32 % to 55 %).

Analysis of the questionnaire responses and the interviews reveals the utility of the counsel and advice provided by business experts after privatisation (Table 7, item 1). These results were supported with a Wilcoxon non-parametric test (Siegel and Castellan 1988), which showed statistically significant differences (p-value = .004) between scores for advice and counsel provided by board members about business management and internal firm operations before and after privatisation.

In line with these arguments, one of the chairmen interviewed said that, "... *the counsel and advice provided by directors who are experts in business became more important after privatisation. Their training and background provide a better definition of business management and so they improve the position of the firm in the market*".

The evidence obtained through the documentation analysed shows a greater need for the counsel and advice of this type of director in business management in all three case studies. For example, the Endesa results show a clear increase in

Table 6 Composition of the board of directors before and after privatisation

	Endesa		Iberia		Repsol		*Mean*	
	Before	After	Before	After	Before	After	Before	After
Size of the board	13.3	14.6	12.8	11.8	14.6	14.2	**13.6**	**13.5**
Inside directors (%)	12	14	8	15	22	7	**14**	**12**
Outside directors (%)	88	86	92	85	78	93	**86**	**88**
Business experts (%)	21	48	28	58	46	60	**32**	**55**
Support specialists (%)	22	23	10	8	13	5	**15**	**12**
Community influentials (%)	57	29	62	34	42	34	**54**	**32**

Source: Authors' own data

Table 7 Resources provided by the board of directors before and after privatisation

			Before	After	Wilcox. Test
Item 1	(1)	Counsel and advice on business management (decision-making, competitive environments and so on)	2.92 (1.093)	4.59 (.507)	p = .004
Item 2	(2)	Counsel and advice on legal issues	3.73 (.724)	4.06 (.827)	p = .317
Item 3	(2)	Counsel and advice on specific issues (financial, insurance, etc.)	2.69 (.788)	4.29 (.772)	p = .005
Item 4	(2)	Counsel and advice on public relations issues	3.31 (.679)	3.82 (.809)	p = .102
Item 5	(1) (2) (3)	Contribute to prestige and reputation of the firm	2.92 (.845)	4.53 (.624)	p = .003
Item 6	(1) (2) (3)	Contribute to legitimising the firm	3.23 (.652)	4.18 (.809)	p = .013
Item 7	(1) (2) (3)	Contribute to improving the image of the firm	2.88 (.653)	4.29 (.772)	p = .002
Item 8	(2)	Facilitate access to financial resources	1.88 (.588)	3.53 (1.125)	p = .002
Item 9	(2)	Facilitate access to other resources (other than financial ones)	2.38 (.637)	4.00 (1.225)	p = .003
Item 10	(2)	Provide communications channels with the government and other public agencies	4.81 (.567)	2.71 (.772)	p = .002
Item 11	(1)	Provide communications channels with other firms	2.81 (.801)	4.29 (1.047)	p = .004
Item 12	(3)	Provide communications channels with non-business organisations (associations, foundations)	3.50 (.510)	3.94 (.966)	p = .785
Item 13	(3)	Provide communications channels with other social groups	3.46 (.859)	4.06 (.748)	p = .129

Notes: (1) Business experts; (2) Support specialists; (3) Community influentials.

business experts after privatisation (from 21 % to 48 %). An increase in business experts could be a logical consequence of the new business orientation taken by the firm once its ownership goes into private hands.

Iberia shows a similar evolution in business experts, comparing Iberia and Endesa. The presence of business experts doubles once the company becomes private (from 28 % to 58 %). In 2000, Iberia initiated a new management plan, which was in force until 2003. This plan mainly focused on consolidating the company in the market and improving financial and operating profitability ratios to achieve better shareholder value. Iberia increased its European and worldwide air routes.

As for Repsol, the number of business experts also increased after privatisation from a minimum value of 33 % before privatisation to a minimum value of 54 % after privatisation. As it did for Endesa and Iberia, the privatisation of Repsol meant a change in the company's business management. After privatisation, the company adopted an unprecedented strategy of international expansion. Repsol's strategic priority was to initiate the firm's expansion in Latin America as a worldwide energy company. Therefore, the entry of private shareholders promoted the internationalisation of the company – specifically in Latin-America–, greater diversification in its activities, and an increase of petroleum production and oil exploration. In 1999, when the company acquired Yacimientos Petrolíferos Fiscales, Repsol became the largest private energy company in Spain and Latin America.

In short, in the three companies analysed, a business reorientation occurred after privatisation and greater attention was paid to customers and markets, and to recruiting directors with a knowledge of business management and decision-making.

In addition to counsel and advice in business management, another resource provided by business experts consists of facilitating communication channels with other companies (Hillman et al. 2000). The data collected show that after privatisation, the board of directors in these case studies allowed for more effective communication channels of this kind. The results were also supported by a Wilcoxon test (see Table 7, item 11), which indicates significant differences (p-value = .004). In this respect, one director stated that this type of communication channel improves market analysis, not only in the sector in which the firm is operating, but also in other sectors. Sometimes the communication channels were made into strategic alliances, facilitating the firm's international expansion. Examples of such developments include the business partnership in 2003 between Iberia and British Airways, which led to the companies' later merger, the agreements between BP and Repsol regarding the acquisition of assets in Trinidad and Tobago in 2000, and the agreements reached between Endesa and Morgan Stanley Dean Witter, the global financial services company, in 2000.

Finally, another resource provided by business experts consists of helping to improve the firm's image and reputation. Analysis of the questionnaire responses (see Table 7, items 5, 6 and 7) and the interviews showed the importance of this resource after privatisation.

In brief, according to the information gathered in the interviews and questionnaires, the resources provided by this type of director becomes increasingly relevant after privatisation because it is then that firms make important decisions regarding investment, diversification and alliances with the objective of expanding their business nationally and internationally.

5.2.2 Support Specialists

The aggregated results regarding support specialists show that the presence of this type of director decreases from an average of 15–12 % before and after privatisation, respectively. The individual data only show relevant differences at Repsol, whereas the ratio remains almost constant at Endesa and Iberia.

Advice provided by support specialists on matters such as finance and insurance significantly increases after privatisation. A Wilcoxon test supports these differences, showing a p-value of .005 (Table 7, item 3). In this connection, certain top managers and directors highlight the importance of these resources after privatisation and note that firms tend to invest more after privatisation. This leads to an increased presence of specialists to improve profitability.

Additionally, the results show a significant increase in the role played by support specialists when they facilitate access to resources, (e.g., financial resources) after privatisation. Wilcoxon tests show significant differences in access to financial (p-value = .002) (Table 7, item 8) and other resources (p-value = .003) (Table 7, item 9). These differences reveal that when a firm is state-owned, resources – mainly financial resources- are provided by the government directly or indirectly. However, when a firm is privatised, it must generate its own resources.

Data also show an increase in counsel and advice provided on legal issues after privatisation, though the differences found before and after privatisation were not significant (Table 7, item 2). This fact is corroborated by a Wilcoxon non-parametric test, which supports the null hypothesis of similarity between average scores before and after privatisation (p-value = .317). This outcome reveals that specialists in legal issues are important both in public and private companies.

However, public-relations advice and counsel do not undergo significant changes in the corresponding public and private phases. The Wilcoxon test showed a p-value of .102 (Table 7, item 4).

Additionally, privatisation seems to imply a decrease in the number of communication channels with the government and other public agencies (Table 7, item 10). These results are corroborated by a Wilcoxon non-parametric test that did not support the null hypothesis of similarity between average scores before and after privatisation (p-value = .002). In the words of one director, "... *When the company was state-owned, the board was composed of a large number of directors linked to the government ..., so it allowed the government to ensure its influence and control over the decisions made by the board of directors*".

Finally, similar to business experts, support specialists contribute to legitimising the firm and improving its image and reputation. These results corroborate the increase of this type of resource (see Table 7, item 5, 6 and 7).

Thus, the resources provided by the support specialists are different in the public and private phases. Whereas communication channels with the government and other public agencies are more important in SOEs, financial and insurance counsel and advice, and access to financial and other resources become more important in privatised firms.

5.2.3 Community Influentials

Finally, analysis of the cases presented here reveals changes in this director profile. This fact may be due to the changes within this director profile.

The percentages in relation to the last category mentioned are clearly higher during the period in which the company depends on the state. In this connection and following an in-depth longitudinal analysis, there are two important aspects to consider. The first aspect is the large number of politicians included on the boards before privatisation. The second aspect is the increasing number of directors linked to the academic world and representatives of social organisations after privatisation. At Endesa, the number of community influential directors decreased after privatisation from 57 % when the firm was state-owned to 29 %. The same tendency appears in the other cases studied: privatisation meant a decrease in community influentials on the boards of Iberia (reducing them by half) and Repsol (from 42 % to 34 %). Nonetheless, once a firm is privatised, the number of politicians decreases significantly. This leads to a general reduction of board members who are community influentials.

The communication channels with non-business organisations (institutions, foundations, and others) provided by this type of director do not seem to undergo significant changes pre- and post-privatisation (Table 7, item 12). This result is supported by a Wilcoxon test (p-value = .785) and ties in with the interview responses, in which one managing director stated, "... *This kind of communication channel offered by directors is very important not only for SOEs but also for private firms. For SOEs, because of political reasons and general public interest, whereas for privatised companies, communication channels are more aimed at improving the public image of the firm* ...". Additionally, the communication channels with other social groups (Table 7, item 13) offered by this type of director do not undergo any relevant changes after privatisation (Wilcoxon test, p-value = .129). Moreover, of particular note are the high scores of the resources obtained pre- and post-privatisation.

Finally, the results of the interviews and questionnaires show that privatisation involves using the reputation and prestige of the directors to legitimise the firm. These results are corroborated by a Wilcoxon test that does not support the null hypothesis of similarity between average scores before and after privatisation. Table 7 (items 5, 6 and 7) shows the results of the Wilcoxon non-parametric test for each of the three items related to this resource (prestige and reputation; legitimacy; image of the firm).

Generally, the findings related to the legitimacy, reputation and image of the firm reveal that regardless of the director profile, privatisation requires that the directors contribute to legitimising the firm and improving its image. In the words of one company chairman, "... *Regardless of the profile of directors, when the firm*

Table 8 Summary of main findings

Observed changes after privatisation
Presence of blockholders
Company objectives: Business growth, international expansion, improve market share
Relationship between **directors appointed before CEO** and board control
Certain effects from **regulation and competition** of the sector on board control
Greater need for resources provided by "Business Experts": Advice and counsel on business management; Communications channels with other firms
Differences in the need for resources provided by "Support Specialists" before and after privatisation:
Before → Communications channels with the government and other public agencies
After → Advice and counsel on financial and insurance issues; Access to resources (financial and others)
Lower presence of "Community Influentials"
Higher need for contributions from directors **to improving the image of the firm**

Source: Authors' own data

includes a new top manager or a director, it is because there is certainty about their professional reputation and positive public image ..., this is vital for its influence on the image and reputation of the firm ...".

Table 8 summarises the main findings of this study.

6 Conclusions

Case studies conducted in the Spanish context allow for certain conclusions to be reached regarding changes in the control and provision of resources roles once companies are privatised. The findings can act as a reflection and reference for emerging countries that use the privatisation of SOEs as a mechanism for economic development.

The study shows that the privatisation of SOEs causes an increase in the board's control over top managers as a result of the new ownership. In-depth analysis of the cases identifies certain factors that help to explain changes in the control activities of boards. Of particular note are the ownership structure and internal factors, such as board composition. In addition, external factors are considered, such as regulation and competition in the sector in which the companies operate.

Regarding the ownership structure, the key role played by blockholders in the increase in control is shown. In addition to ownership concentration, it is worth noting the importance of considering the profile and heterogeneity of these blockholders. The analysis of case studies highlights the positive influence of blockholder profile heterogeneity on the board's control activity. In this respect, whereas Endesa and Repsol blockholders are mainly financial institutions – except PEMEX in Repsol–, Iberia's situation is different. In the capital of the airline there are also institutional – financial and non-financial – and industrial blockholders

(British Airways and American Airlines) directly related to the activity of Iberia. One possible explanation for these results may be due to the knowledge that industrial blockholders have of the sector. The cases analysed seem to adhere to the characteristics of corporate governance in the Continental European and more specifically the so-called Latin model regarding the presence of major shareholders (i.e., financial institutions, family groups and other companies), which usually act as a core that holds a sufficiently high proportion of a company's shares to exercise a high degree of control over the company (Fernández and Arrondo 2005). From 1996 to 2003, the Spanish government actively promoted the maintenance of stable investors – mainly banks – as part of the privatisation efforts (Tribo et al. 2007).

Regarding internal factors, the composition of the board is highlighted. In this respect, the results show the key role played by the CEO's lack of involvement in the appointment of directors and its influence on monitoring managerial behaviour. It is noted how directors appointed before the mandate of the current CEO are best placed to monitor and evaluate the top management team.

The study also emphasised two aspects relevant to board composition. Firstly, the results do not appear support the traditional variables considered by agency theory, which were associated with the greater capacity of boards to develop the control role. No relationship is found between the existence of a shared leadership structure (non-duality) and the increased presence of outside directors, and greater board control. Secondly, the results show a tendency of firms after privatisation to have a greater presence of directors appointed before the CEO (i.e., independent directors) when there is duality. That is, it appears that companies try to compensate for the concentration of power that causes duality with a greater number of independent directors in order to ensure control over the top management team.

Finally, with regard to external factors, the level of regulation and competition in the sector is seen to exert some influence on the degree of control exercised by boards of directors. A joint assessment of these factors points to the following conclusion. The change of ownership seems to trigger increased levels of control in all companies. However, it appears that the characteristics of the sector can mitigate or enhance the board's overseeing of management. For example, looking at the case of Iberia, there has been little change in regulation and market competition. This has been accompanied by a major increase in the level of control exercised by the board. On the contrary, in the case of Endesa and Repsol, large variations in the levels of regulation and market competition are accompanied by smaller increases in control. This highlights the need to take these two variables into consideration in order to better understand the changing control role of boards in privatisation processes.

The data analysis performed in this study reflects on how firms modify the structure and composition of their boards of directors to obtain the resources they need.

In short, the findings show the limitations of traditional variables, such as the size and composition (in terms of insiders and outsiders) of the board of directors. These variables have been traditionally used in resource dependence theory to identify the ability of the board to provide the organisation with resources.

Furthermore in-depth study is needed to examine the specific role played by each director as a resource provider that analyses not only the variety of director profiles but also the specific resources provided in different contexts.

The data show that companies increase the number of business experts as a consequence of privatisation. One possible explanation for this increase lies in the differences that characterise SOEs and privatised companies as perceived from a business management standpoint. In general, directors at SOEs do not have complete freedom of action in relation to strategic activities (Cragg and Dyck 1999) as they are constrained by bureaucratic control. Additionally, they have less freedom to influence recruitment, choice of suppliers, the price of products or services, financing or company expansion (Cragg and Dyck 2000). Moreover, action taken within SOEs is politically and geographically restricted. In contrast, a privatised company can expand the scope of its activity and geographical markets. Such companies evolve from an orientation towards production and agents' interests to being oriented towards the market and customers (Cuervo 1997). Communication channels between firms, provided by business experts, are more relevant after privatisation. These changes explain the large increase in this director profile once a company goes into private hands.

Support specialists are equally important in SOEs and privatised companies, although the aggregate results do not support the theoretical assumption about the maintenance of this type of director. A detailed analysis of individual cases reveals that the specialisation of the directors and the resources they provide change. In this regard, whereas financial and insurance advice and counsel, and access to resources – financial and other – are more important in privatised firms, communication channels with the government and other public agencies are more important in SOEs.

Results also show a clear decrease in the third director profile – community influentials – after privatisation. The reason may be that political representatives play a crucial role in this group. When companies are state-owned, political leaders are clearly relevant. However, after privatisation they are no longer necessary. Therefore, the tendency may be to reduce the size of this particular group. Nonetheless, there is an increase in the number of board members who are leaders of social organisations and university representatives. Additionally, the communication channels provided by community influentials with non-business organisations (institutions, foundations) and other social groups are equally important in the public and private phases of a firm. Moreover, the contribution made by this director profile to a firm's legitimacy and public image increases in relevance once the firm is privatised.

6.1 Practical Implications for Emerging Markets

Although the results of this research should be interpreted with caution because of the sample selection bias (low response rate ratio) and the idiosyncrasy of Spain and its industries, the functioning of the board of directors in the context of privatisation could provide a reference to emerging countries that are also involved in privatisation processes.

Firstly, it highlights the importance of considering, after privatisation, the profile and heterogeneity of new shareholders and their influence on the performance of the board's control role. In this regard, a link is found here between greater blockholder heterogeneity and increased control activities of the board. At the same time, a relationship is also revealed between the presence of blockholders related to the activity of the privatised firm and greater board control. Secondly, the importance of having independent directors in order to properly monitor the behaviour of the top management team should be noted. Along these lines, it seems that it is more important to have directors appointed before the CEO than it is to have shared leadership (non-duality) or an increased presence of outside directors. Thirdly, it is also important to consider the influence of market functioning (levels of regulation and competition), as this can have an effect on board functions. And finally, this study points to the importance of changing the configuration of the boards after privatisation in terms of the profile of directors, in order to acquire the necessary resources in the private stage of the firm. In this respect, after privatisation, companies should incorporate into their boards a higher number of business experts with knowledge and skills in business management and the ability to establish links with other businesses. The important presence of support specialists with specific capabilities in both periods of the company is also to be stressed. This could be because certain resources provided by these directors are more relevant than others depending on the stage of the firm (pre- and post-privatisation). For example, whereas government ties are more important in the public stage, access to resources and knowledge in financial matters become relevant after privatisation.

Appendix (Survey Items)

Control Role

To what extent does the board . . .?
(the response scale ranged from "minimally" 1, until "very much so" 5)

1.	Delegate strategic decision-making to top managers
2.	Monitor top managers in decision-making
3.	Formally evaluate the performance of top managers
4.	Constructively criticise the strategic decisions made by managers
5.	Request information from the top managers about the company
6.	Engage in succession planning for the CEO
7.	Engage in succession planning for top managers besides the CEO

Provision of Resources Role

To what extent does the board . . .?
(the response scale ranged from "minimally" 1, until "very much so" 5)

1.	Provide counsel and advice on business management (decision-making, competitive environments, and so on)
2.	Provide counsel and advice on legal issues
3.	Provide counsel and advice on specific issues (financial, insurance, etc.)
4.	Provide counsel and advice on public relations issues
5.	Contribute to the prestige and reputation of the firm
6.	Contribute to legitimising the firm
7.	Contribute to improving the image of the firm
8.	Facilitate access to financial resources
9.	Facilitate access to other resources (other than financial ones)
10.	Provide communications channels with the government and other public agencies
11.	Provide communications channels with other firms
12.	Provide communications channels with non-business organisations (associations, foundations)
13.	Provide communications channels with other social groups

Sector Competition

To what extent do you agree with these statements . . .?
(the response scale ranged from "strongly disagree" 1, until "strongly agree" 5)

1.	Competitive pressures have led to firms in this industry spending a great deal of money on marketing
2.	Firms in this industry aggressively fight to hold onto their share of the market
3.	Competition in this industry is intense
4.	Firms in this industry follow a philosophy of peaceful coexistence

Sector Regulation

Indicate the level of sector regulation on each of the issues below:
(the response scale ranged from "minimally" 1, until "very much so" 5)

1.	Prices
2.	Production
3.	Purchasing

(continued)

4.	Investments
5.	Location
6.	Diversification

References

Aghara, V., Anyanwu, A., Nwaizugbo, I., Okpala, C., & Oparah, P. (2011). World Journal of Enterprenuership. *Management and Sustainable Development, 7*(1), 81–95.

Aguilera, R. (2005). Corporate governance and employment relations: Spain in the context of Western Europe. In H. P. Gospel & A. Pendleton (Eds.), *Corporate governance and labour management: An international comparison* (pp. 197–225). Oxford: Oxford University Press.

Alchian, A., & Demsetz, H. (1972). Production, information cost and economic organization. *American Economic Review, 62*, 777–795.

Boycko, M., Shleifer, A., & Vishny, R. (1996). A theory of privatization. *Economic Journal, 106*, 309–319.

Bozec, R., Zéghal, D., & Boujenoui, A. (2004). The effect of the reform of Canadian state-owned enterprises on major corporate governance mechanisms. *Australian Journal of Public Administration, 63*(2), 79–94.

Button, K. (2001). Deregulation and liberalization of European air transport markets. *Innovation: The European Journal of the Social Sciences, 14*(3), 255–275.

Caixa. (1999). *Una década de privatizaciones en España*. Estudios especiales. Informe mensual

Carpenter, M. A., & Westphal, J. D. (2001). The strategic context of external ties: Examining the impact of director appointments on board involvement in strategic decision making. *Academy of Management Journal, 44*(4), 639–660.

Certo, S. T., Daily, C. M., & Dalton, D. R. (2001). Signaling firm value through board structure: An investigation of initial public offerings. *Entrepreneurship Theory & Practice, 26*, 33–50.

Claessens, S., & Yurtoglu, B. (2013). Corporate governance in emerging markets: A survey. *Emerging Markets Review, 15*, 1–33.

Cragg, M. I., & Dyck, I. J. (1999). Management control and privatization in the United Kingdom. *Rand Journal of Economics, 30*, 475–497.

Cragg, M. I., & Dyck, I. J. (2000). Executive pay and U.K. privatization: The demise of one country, two systems. *Journal of Business Research, 47*, 3–18.

Cuervo, A. (1997). *La privatización de la empresa pública*. Madrid, Ed. Encuentro.

Cuervo, A. (1998). La privatización de las empresas públicas. Cambios de propiedad, libertad de entrada y eficiencia. *Información Comercial Española, 772*, 45–57.

Cuervo, A. (2003). La empresa pública entre 1978 y 2003. De la justificación a la privatización. *Economía Industrial, 349*(350), 233–248.

Cuevas, G., Alvarez-Dardet, C., & Valle, R. (2007). Incentives management during privatization: An agency perspective. *Journal of Management Studies, 44*(4), 536–560.

Daily, C., Dalton, D., & Cannella, A. (2003). Corporate governance: Decades of dialogue and data. *Academy of Management Review, 28*, 371–382.

Denzin, N. K. (1989). *Interpretive interactionism*. Newbury Park: Sage.

Eisenhardt, K. M. (1989). Building theories from case study research. *Academy of Management Review, 14*, 532–551.

Fama, E., & Jensen, M. C. (1983). Separation of ownership and control. *Journal of Law and Economics, 26*, 301–325.

Fernández, C., & Arrondo, R. (2005). Alternative internal controls as substitutes of the board of directors. *Corporate Governance: An International Review, 13*(6), 856–866.

González-Páramo, J. M. (1995). Privatización y eficiencia: ¿es irrelevante la titularidad? *Economistas, 63*, 32–43.
Helland, E., & Sykuta, M. (2004). Regulation and the evolution of corporate boards: Monitoring, advising, or window dressing? *Journal of Law and Economics, 47*(1), 167–193.
Hernández De Cos, P. (2004). Empresa pública, privatización y eficiencia. *Estudios Económicos: Banco de España, 75*, 1–112.
Hernández, N., & López De Castro, L. (2000). *Privatizaciones, liberalización y bienestar*. Cuadernos de Regulación y Políticas Públicas, Granada (Spain), Ed. Comares, SL.
Hillman, A. J., & Dalziel, T. (2003). Boards of directors and firm performance: Integrating agency and resource-dependence perspectives. *Academy of Management Review, 28*, 383–396.
Hillman, A. J., Cannella, A., & Paetzold, R. (2000). The resource dependence role of corporate directors: Strategic adaptation of board composition in response to environmental change. *Journal of Management Studies, 37*, 235–256.
Hoskisson, R. E., & Turk, T. A. (1990). Corporate restructuring: Governance and control limits of the internal capital market. *Academy of Management Review, 15*(3), 459–477.
Jensen, M. C., & Meckling, W. H. (1976). Theory of the firm: Managerial behaviour, agency costs and ownership structure. *Journal of Financial Economics, 3*, 305–360.
Johnson, J., Daily, C. M., & Ellstrand, A. E. (1996). Board of directors: A review and research agenda. *Journal of Management, 22*(3), 409–438.
Jones, C. D., Makri, M., & Gomez-Mejia, L. R. (2008). Affiliate directors and perceived risk bearing in publicly traded, family-controlled firms: The case of diversification. *Entrepreneurship: Theory and Practice, 32*(6), 1007–1026.
Laffont, J. J. (1995). Econometrics and economic theory in the 20th century: The Ragnar Frisch Centennial Symposium. In S. Ström (Ed.), *Frisch, hotelling and the marginal cost pricing controversy* (pp. 319–342). Cambridge, UK: Cambridge University Press.
Lehn, K., Patro, S., & Zhao, M. (2009). Determinants of the size and structure of corporate boards: 1935–2000. *Journal of the Financial Management, 38*, 747–780.
Lin, Y. (2005). Corporate governance, leadership structure and CEO composition: Evidence from Taiwan. *Corporate Governance: An International Review, 13*, 824–835.
Linck, J. S., Netter, J. M., & Yang, T. (2008). Determinants of board structure. *Journal of Financial Economics, 87*, 308–328.
Lioukas, S., Bourantas, D., & Papadakis, V. (1993). Managerial autonomy of state-owned enterprises: Determining factors. *Organization Science, 4*(4), 645–666.
Luo, Y. (2003). Market-seeking MNEs in an emerging market: How parent-subsidiary links shape overseas success. *Journal of International Business Studies, 34*(3), 290–309.
Megginson, W. L., & Sutter, N. (2006). Privatisation in developing countries. *Corporate Governance, 14*, 234–265.
Megginson, W. L., Nash, R., & Van Randenborgh, M. (1994). The financial and operating performance of newly-privatized firms: An international empirical analysis. *Journal of Finance, 49*(2), 403–452.
Melle Hernández, M. (1999). Algunos resultados efectivos de las privatizaciones en España: una primera aproximación. *Economía Industrial, 330*, 141–158.
Mizruchi, M. S., & Stearns, L. B. (1994). A longitudinal study of borrowing by large American corporations. *Administrative Science Quarterly, 39*, 118–140.
Movassaghi, H., Bramhandkar, A., & Shikov, M. (2004). Emerging vs. developed markets closed-end funds: A comparative performance analysis. *Managerial Finance, 30*(3), 51–62.
Muhr, T. (2006). *Atlas/ti version 5.2*. Berlin: Scientific Software Development: GMBH. http://www.atlasti.com
Ocaña, C., & Salas, V. (1983). La teoría de la agencia. Aplicación a las empresas públicas españolas. *Cuadernos Económicos de I.C.E., 22/23*, 157–182.
Omran, M. (2009). Post-privatization corporate governance and firm performance: The role of private ownership concentration, identity and board composition. *Journal of Comparative Economics, 37*, 658–673.

Pearce, J. A., & Zahra, S. A. (1992). Board compensation from a strategic contingency perspective. *Journal of Management Studies, 29*, 411–438.

Pedersen, T., & Thomsen, S. (1997). European patterns of corporate ownership: A twelve-country study. *Journal of International Business Studies, 28*(4), 759–778.

Peterson, C. A., & Philpot, J. (2009). Roles of academic directors on US Fortune 500 boards. *Corporate Governance, 9*(2), 202–215.

Pfeffer, J., & Salancik, G. R. (1978). *The external control of organizations: A resource dependence perspective*. New York: Harper & Row.

Plakoyiannaki, E., Tzokas, N., Dimitratos, P., & Saren, M. (2008). How critical is employee orientation for customer relationship management? Insights from a case study. *Journal of Management Studies, 45*(2), 268–293.

Sarin, S., & Mahajan, V. (2001). The effect of reward structures on the performance of cross-functional product development teams. *Journal of Marketing, 65*, 35–53.

Shleifer, A., & Vishny, R. W. (1994). Politicians and firms. *Quarterly Journal of Economics, 109*, 995–1025.

Siegel, S., & Castellan, J. (1988). *Nonparametric statistics for the behavioural sciences*. New York: McGraw-Hill.

Tosi, H. L., & Gómez-Mejía, L. R. (1989). The decoupling of CEO pay and performance: An agency theory perspective. *Administrative Science Quarterly, 34*, 169–189.

Tribo, J. A., Berrone, P., & Surroca, J. (2007). Do the type and number of block-holders influence R&D investments? New evidence from Spain. *Corporate Governance: An International Review, 15*(5), 828–842.

Vickers, J., & Yarrow, G. (1991). Economic perspectives on privatization. *Journal of Economic Perspectives, 5*, 111–132.

Wan, D., & Ong, C. H. (2005). Board structure, process and performance: Evidence from public-listed companies in Singapore. *Corporate Governance: An International Review, 13*(2), 277–290.

Yin, R. K. (1989). *Case study research – Design and methods*. Newbury Park: Sage.

Yin, R. K. (1994). *Case study research: Design and methods* (2nd ed.). Beverly Hills: Sage.

Yoshikawa, T., & Phan, P. H. (2005). The effects of ownership and capital structure on board composition and strategic diversification in Japanese corporations. *Corporate Governance, 13* (2), 303–312.

Young, G., Stedham, Y., & Beekun, R. (2000). Boards of directors and the adoption of a CEO performance evaluation process: Agency- and institutional-theory perspectives. *Journal of Management Studies, 37*(2), 277–295.

Zahra, S., & Hansen, C. (2000). Privatization, entrepreneurship and global competitiveness in the 21st century. *Competitiveness Review, 10*(1), 83–103.

Zahra, S., & Pearce, J. (1989). Boards of directors and corporate financial performance: A review and integrative model. *Journal of Management, 15*, 291–334.

Zahra, S., Ireland, R., Gutierrez, I., & Hitt, M. (2000). Privatization and entrepreneurial transformation: Emerging issues and a future research agenda. *Academy of Management Journal, 25*, 509–524.

Part III
Corporate Governance Practices in Emerging Markets

Corporate Governance in Ukraine: Major Standards and Emerging Trends

Alexander Kostyuk, Markus Stiglbauer, Patrick Velte, Yuliya Lapina, and Dmitriy Riabichenko

Abstract The level of corporate sector development depends not only on historical processes and factors, but also on the legal framework, which is actual at the certain time. Corporate governance in Ukrainian companies is developing constantly, e.g. under the influence of intense change legislation, so first we systematize the results of previous studies, second we carry out cross-sector analysis of the corporate governance performance in the financial and non-financial companies, and third we try to determine whether Ukrainian emerging corporate governance trends are moving to the worldwide accepted standards or not.

1 Introduction

Ukraine is an emerging country with a high number of more than 26,000 joint stock companies (JSCs). Obviously, the adoption of the Joint Stock Companies Act in 2009 caused massive reorganizational processes of open and closed JSCs in public and private, which led to a decrease of their total number by 7 % they notwithstanding produce about 75 % of GDP and, besides, more than 60 % of industrial potential of the country is concentrated in their activities. Surprisingly, only 24 JSCs have their own corporate governance codes.

The National Bank of Ukraine, banking market regulator, within supervisory functions' fulfillment defines that JSC is the only possible form of incorporation.

A. Kostyuk • Y. Lapina • D. Riabichenko
International Center for Banking and Corporate Governance, Ukrainian Academy of Banking of the National Bank of Ukraine, Sumy, Ukraine

M. Stiglbauer (✉)
School of Business and Economics, University of Erlangen-Nürnberg, Erlangen, Germany
e-mail: Markus.Stiglbauer@wiso.uni-erlangen.de

P. Velte
School of Business, Economics and Social Sciences, University of Hamburg, Hamburg, Germany

S. Boubaker and D.K. Nguyen (eds.), *Corporate Governance in Emerging Markets*, CSR, Sustainability, Ethics & Governance, DOI 10.1007/978-3-642-44955-0_10,

Since a national corporate governance code does not exist so far, the absence of specific standards in this sphere for micro- and macro-level causes differentiated developments of corporate governance in banks. Foreign companies are actively expanding into the Ukrainian market over the last 10 years. The share of foreign capital exceeds 50 % in many sectors of the national economy, including banking. Therefore, the issue of the implementation of corporate governance principles to ensure the competitiveness of domestic companies is still urgent.

The initial stage of market relations formation in Ukraine was characterized by the extensive privatization processes that had a significant influence on the corporate governance implementation in the country. But rapid development of globalization processes and, as a result, the necessity of maintaining the sufficient competitiveness level triggered the change of corporate governance system from its initial designs to more complicated ones. Thus, on the modern stage of Ukrainian economy development one of the most important transformations of the corporate governance is the implementation of its principles in companies' daily activities.

Ukrainian legislation which regulates some issues of companies' activity is changing permanently. This stimulates the development of corporate governance practice, so the objective necessity to study the level of development of corporate governance in Ukraine in accordance with current legislation exists. The results of previous research characterize only separate corporate governance problems. Moreover, some of them are out of date because of significant changes in Ukrainian legislation recently. That's why we initiated our own study in this field to give reader actual information.

The study of corporate governance practice in Ukrainian companies and banks allows to summarize that there are no significant differences in the level of development of corporate standards, but due to the specificity of banking activities, in particular in terms of risk management, the banking sector is facing more stringent regulation, including corporate governance issues. The study also revealed that despite the existence of many problems in this sphere, corporate governance practice in Ukraine is moving to world standards very fast.

Our chapter is structured as follows: first, we describe the evolutionary development of Ukrainian legislation; second, we give a brief overview of the modern Law concerning corporate governance; third, we examine the evolution of ownership structure and corporate control; fourth, we touch upon board of directors' issues; fifth. we analyze the level of financial accountability and disclosure; sixth, we describe the difference between bankruptcy process in financial and non-financial sectors and seventh, we describe the mechanism of minority shareholders' rights protection in Ukraine. We finish up with a conclusion.

2 Literature Review

Nowadays the system of corporate governance is functioning in such way that minority shareholders don't take evident participation in corporate governance. Accordingly, their interests are ignored in the activity process and during received income distribution. The basic contradiction is based on the conflict of interests between managers and shareholders of the corporation, especially minority shareholders. The main reason for this is the imperfect corporate governance legislation, where many aspects of corporate governance are not covered by the legal framework. This applies to major corporate rights: corporation governance, dividend policy, liquidation procedures; information access (Wojciechowska and Wojciechowska 2009; Pigyl 2011).

The legal regulation of Ukrainian companies has significant drawbacks, such as issues about the protection of minority shareholders and investors' rights. Corporate conflicts in JSCs cause distrust among the strategic investors in major financial instruments (Bayura 2009). In 2011, the State Commission on Securities and Stock Market received 4,339 written appeals regarding the rights and legitimate interests of participants in the securities market, which is 14 % higher compared to 2010. Seventy-five percent of the total number of requests is complaints of minority shareholders, concerned about violation of their rights.

Iorhachova (2011) examines the types of corporate conflicts, particularly between majority and minority shareholders finding that "weak corporate governance in Ukraine enables for owners of primary shares to strengthen its position by capital erosion, transfer pricing". Brynza (2011) overviews the main peculiarities of Ukrainian law and comes to the conclusion that the rule "everything which less than 50 % + 1 share, is zero" still exists. Ownership concentration can ensure better company performance than a dispersed ownership structure, and this gap is particularly large in countries with weak protection of minority rights and low transparency of a company environment, e.g. Ukraine (Andreyeva and Dean 2000): "in a system like the Ukrainian one, outsiders, even with controlling shares, often cannot dismiss ineffective management". The effect of ownership structure on the performance of privatized Ukrainian enterprises is non-linear: increasing in a range below majority shareholding but decreasing above a threshold close to majority ownership (Zaplatinsky 2002). For manager and employee shareholding, this non-monotonicity by the stakeholding interests of those owner groups is explained. The non-linearity of foreign ownership effects, which tends to be the most robust one, are due to an institutional environment still adverse to foreign majority ownership (Akimova and Schwodiauer 2003).

Selected issues of Executive and Supervisory Board interaction are disclosed in recent investigation: Bilyk et al. (2009) analyze the impact of the size of supervisory boards on CEO turnover; Shum (2010) examine both the effects of different forms of incentive compensations to supervisory board and the impact of SB composition on CEOs turnover.

Ukrainian stock market is characterized by a lack of liquidity. The negative impact of this factor also makes a general decline in world stock markets, strengthening of listing requirements (in particular, the requirements for capital, disclosure and transparency), which led some enterprises to delisting (Belyalov 2008). Mergers and acquisition as a way out in crisis for many companies are not widespread in Ukraine.

3 Main Findings

3.1 Legislative Framework of Corporate Governance in Ukraine: An Evolutionary Approach

For a long time the Law of Ukraine "On Economic Companies" (1991) was the main regulatory act for JSCs. According to this document general shareholders' meeting, supervisory board, the executive body (management) and the audit committee are the main bodies of corporate governance. General shareholders' meeting is recognized as the supreme body of JSCs having practically unlimited competence, for the company charter may refer other issues to the competence of general shareholders' meeting except for those stipulated in Article 41. Amendments introduced to "On Economic Companies" in 1997 determine the circle of aspects comprising exclusive competence of general shareholders' meetings and these issues cannot be delegated for consideration and resolution to other bodies of JSCs.

Supervisory boards can be elected in JSCs, but its installation is mandatory for companies where the number of shareholders exceeds 50 persons, shall represent the interests of the shareholders in the period between the holding the general shareholders' meetings. The main function of the board of directors is to secure control over the activities of executive body (OECD 2001). In accordance with the company's charter, the supervisory board may be delegated with some functions referred to as the competence of general shareholders' meetings. Company charter may also stipulate exclusive competence for the supervisory board. Alongside with this, the range of these issues is not stipulated on the level of legislation. Issues referred to exclusive competence of the supervisory board by company charter may not be delegated for consideration to the executive body.

As it was stipulated in Article 47 of "On Economic Companies", the executive body of a joint stock company implements the guidance of its current activities. An executive body can have another name, which shall be stipulated in the company charter. The executive body shall solve all the issues of company's activities, except for those that belong to the competence of general shareholders' meeting and the board of directors. General shareholders' meetings can adopt decisions on transfer of the part of the rights that belong to them to the competence of the executive body, except for those issues, which comprise the exclusive competence of general shareholders' meetings. All shareholders, irrespective of the quantity and type of shares they hold, are entitled with the right to participate in the general shareholders' meetings. Voting at general shareholders' meeting is realized in accordance with the "one share – one vote"-principle. Members of executive body holding no company shares may participate in the general shareholders' meetings with the right of deliberative vote. The supervisory board shall be elected by the shareholders at the general shareholders' meeting. Representatives of trade unions or of some other body authorized by the working collective and having concluded collective agreement on the behalf of the working collective may participate in the work of the supervisory board with the right of deliberative vote.

The audit committee of a JSC implements control over the financial and economic activities of management and shall be elected by the shareholders of the company. The members of the audit committee are entitled with the right to participate in the meetings of the executive body with the right of deliberative vote. Ukrainian law excludes the possibility of combining participation in the activities of JSC governance bodies for certain persons. The members of the supervisory board cannot be members of executive body or of the audit committee (Article 46); neither executive body members, nor the members of the supervisory board as well as any other company officers cannot be members of the audit committee (Article 49).

Functions, competence and organizational principles of activities for the bodies of corporate governance of the JSC are just outlined in the general form in "On Economic Companies". As a rule, these aspects find their detailed reflection in internal by-laws of the companies: in the by-law on the general shareholders' meeting, on the supervisory board, on the executive body and on the audit committee. As these documents are adopted within the company and by the company and possess local characteristics, realization of corporate governance functions is stipulated with considerable deviations and differences.

In 2004, the Civil Code introduced a novel rule dealing with conflict of interest transactions between the company and a shareholder. It provides that a shareholder does not have the right to vote at the general shareholders' meeting on decisions regarding a transaction or dispute between the company and such shareholders. Corporate governance provisions are also part of the new Code, but the provisions are too general and mostly contain references to special legislation in particular areas of law (Asaul et al. 2006). These documents lay the legal foundation for organizing and operating entrepreneurial subjects as entities regulated by private law. They also define the specific characteristics of stock companies. The Civil Code gives shareholders the exclusive right to vote to elect and remove the members of the supervisory board, executive body and audit committee.

The need to implement a special law which could regulate all the aspects of JSCs' activity was caused primarily by the fact that "On Economic Companies" in 1991 didn't provide the protection of both large and small shareholders, could not effectively regulate matters arising in the corporate governance process and generated a number of corporate conflicts. In addition, its rules were outdated and contained conflict with the Civil and Commercial Code, which were adopted later. The necessity thus to adopt the Law "On Joint Stock Companies" was caused by the requirements of the Civil Code, which contains provisions governing JSCs, but does not describe in detail the procedure for their application and has a link to a special law (Ivasiv 2008).

"On Join Stock Companies" (2009) contains some innovations regarding the establishment and legal status of JSCs: an accurate definition of "joint stock company"; a new typological distinction between private and public JSCs, certain restrictions on the legal status of companies' participants are imposed, and owners of JSCs are allowed to form the authorized capital by property., The general concept of the law is to strengthen the protection of shareholders by placing additional duties of the supervisory board, the executive body, officials, the registration procedures, the general shareholders' meeting or the acquisition and disposition of shares are clearly defined.

3.2 Modern Legislation Concerning Corporate Governance in Ukraine: Brief Overview

The level of corporate governance is a key factor that determines the investment climate in the state, affects the efficiency of companies, and determines the degree of protection of investors' rights and the interests of other stakeholders. The state's role in regulating this issue is to create a proper legal framework. As of today there are a few legislative acts in this sphere in Ukraine:

- Joint Stock Companies Act, 2008 – Chapters VII–X define the feature of corporate governance in Ukraine. Section "General Meeting of JSC" defines the competence, procedure of general shareholders' meetings, voting procedure, etc. The next part "The Supervisory Board of JSC" contains a detailed list of issues, which the supervisory board takes responsibility for. The section "Company's Executive Body" includes the basic principles of the executive body activities. This Act also contains a separate section on defining the rules for identifying the officers of the company and their responsibilities;
- Civil Code, 2003 – Section 5 "Join Stock Company" of Chapter 8 contains the rules, which regulate the activity of commercial companies including the aspects of corporate governance. Article 159 defines the exclusive competence of the general shareholders' meeting, period of the meetings and voting procedure. Regarding the executive body, the Civil Code Article 161 states that the executive body of the company that takes care of operating management in the executive body or other authority specified by the statute;
- Commercial Code, 2003 – Chapter 9 "Business Partnerships" regulates property relations (Articles 85–87), the rights and obligations of participants (Article 88) and certain management, accounting and reporting issues (Articles 89–90);
- Securities and the Stock Market Act, 2006 – regulates the issues of registration and issuance of shares of JSC;

- Principles of Corporate Governance, 2003 – includes the key principles for corporate relations in Ukraine and specific recommendations for quality and transparent management of a JSC in accordance with international standards (rights of shareholders, supervisory board and executive body, disclosure and transparency, control over financial and economic activity of company and stakeholders).

The role of banks as market players under modern economic conditions is determined by their ability to attract temporarily available cash and effectively use accumulated resources to meet the financial needs of both corporate and individuals. Due to the specific of banking activities, government bodies (including the National Bank of Ukraine) conduct regulation and supervision in this market. The main legislative acts in the field of corporate governance in banks are as follows:

- Banks and Banking Activity Act, 2000 – specifies the questions of corporate governance in more details such as defining the functions of general shareholders' meeting, supervisory board, executive body and audit committee;
- Guidelines for Improving Corporate Governance in Banks of Ukraine, 2007 – covering such matters of corporate governance in banks: the role of shareholders in protecting depositors and other stakeholders; professional behavior and honesty of bank employees, the division of responsibilities, competencies and responsibilities between shareholders, the supervisory board and the executive body, strategy development in banks and overseeing its implementation; disclosure and transparency;
- Guidelines on the Organization and Functioning of Risk Management in Banks of Ukraine, 2004 – functions and duties of bodies in the field of risk governance are clarified.

3.3 Evolution of Ownership Structure and Corporate Control

The ownership structure of Ukrainian companies was formed during the privatization process that took place after Ukraine became independent, with all their features and flaws. The emergence and development of corporate control is accompanied by the evolution of the enterprises' legal form. Because of the mass privatization of large industrial facilities and associations in Ukraine capital formed the corporate sector, which represented business entities. These processes intensified development of corporate governance in the country. This was due to the need for efficient business activity with increasing capital and settlement of relations between individuals of corporate relations with balancing their interests.

In 1991 with the adoption of the "On Economic Companies", Ukraine formed a collective legal form of companies founded mainly on combining assets of participants. The law provided for the emergence of various types of business entities, but the most prevalent were JSCs, which mainly constitute the Ukrainian corporate sector. The Ukrainian companies are usually created in the form of a limited liability company (LLC) and JSCs. The founders can be both individual persons and corporate bodies. Under current law, LLC were established with the participation of one or more members. When the LLC is created with one member, it should be aware that an individual person or corporate body may be the sole founder of only one of this LLC type.

According to the State Statistics Committee of Ukraine, in 1992, nearly 90.5 thousand enterprises in Ukraine changed their ownership form, which indicated that privatization process was quite extensive. First of all, it affected industry; artificially of October 2004 there were only 14 % of state-owned companies in this sphere. Over the period of 1992–2001 more than 600 thousand Ukrainian enterprises changed their ownership structure, state ownership decreased from over 90 % to almost 25 %. It is a strong performance in quantitative terms, but in qualitatively – such privatization has not reached its goal of improvement the economic situation in the country. This is the result of constant struggle between the parliament and the government on the privatization strategy and tactics (which led to the instability of the legal framework of privatization), lack of adequate infrastructure for the operations of private companies (which was influenced by non-developed stock market, and therefore, lack of proper support for businesses with new forms of property); rigid state tax policy and high interest rates (which created significant barriers to the reformed enterprises' expansion).

Today the public sector isn't longer a dominant one in all spheres of economic activity. The share of private sector in electricity production is on average 40–60 %, and up to 99 % in the chemical industry and light industry. Denationalization of enterprises property, organizations and institutions in the last decade, carried out mainly through the purchase of privatization objects: in 2002: minus 80.1 % of total denationalized companies, in 2003; minus 88 %, in 2004: minus 49.35 %; and by selling at auction. It should be noted that the redemption is the main method of privatization in most economic activities. The auction is being used for the privatization of assets under construction. The least amount of companies that have changed their ownership structure over the entire period of reform in the economic activities accounted for transport and communication: minus 3 %.

The most important institutional feature of post-privatization period in Ukraine is lack of property relations transparency – it is virtually impossible to define real and nominal owners. The vast majority of domestic stock companies shares moved to insider ownership – management, former directors, personnel, etc. that were formed extremely concentrated corporate ownership. The lack of property relations and agreements transparency leads to transaction costs increase. Over the past 3 or 4 years, a lot of Ukrainian companies have improved the ownership structure disclosure, increasing its transparency. But the limited disclosure of the actual beneficiary/owner continues to dominate the companies on the full range of Ukrainian companies.

It should be noted that one of the main factors that have the biggest impact on the state of corporate relations in Ukraine today is the role of the government in its relations with corporations. Many companies in Ukraine are controlled either by a narrow range of private shareholders/individuals or the state. In addition, the majority shareholders often hold managerial/executive positions, which may limit the ability of minority shareholders to verify or challenge the decision management. The main problem in this area is the lack of a unified government policy on the corporate governance development.

3.4 Board of Directors' Issues

Using corporate standards set out in 1999 by the Organization for Economic Co-operation and Development and supplemented by the British Standards Institute in 2012, which are recognized in all developed and developing countries, allows shareholders of large organizations to control the activities of management properly. In Ukraine, these documents are a methodological basis for internal corporate governance codes.

Directors of domestic firms are still significantly behind of their foreign colleagues in development and implementation of corporate standards. According to research conducted by the Ukrainian investment company "Concorde Capital" in 2007 corporate governance has been assessed as fully consistent to international principles only in 7 domestic companies out of the 118 largest ones. This is reasoned by many factors: high level of concentration in the ownership of companies (majority shareholders own 40–99 % of shares), limited availability of information about their activities (banks provide only 42 % of the required data), an impact of real owners on the supervisory boards and the executive body, as well as imperfect and superficial legislation in this area.

Compliance with corporate standards associated with the disclosure of a large amount of information can be used in the competition. At the same time in contrast to other countries, it is quite difficult to find a qualitative analysis of corporate governance practices in Ukraine, because such information is very easy to hide, staying within the law, even in spite of the fact, that corporate transparency in a country is controlled by one of the biggest investment companies – "Concorde Capital". The principle of transparency is common for global market players, because precisely the level of disclosure of information about an organization and its financial condition. Strategic risk and ownership structure influences the decisions of portfolio investors to invest their money in it.

It's worth noting that there is a decision of the State Commission for Securities and the Stock Market "On Approval of the Principles of Corporate Governance" in the country since 2003, and since 2007 series of guidelines of the National Bank on the improvement of corporate governance in banks of Ukraine exist, and also each individual organization may have its own code of corporate governance. All these documents are just recommendations and are not binding on the company to take specific actions for improving corporate standards. If we compare them with international standards in the functioning of the executive body, it is worth noting that the Ukrainian company describes its work in a more general way, often leaving the questions of election conditions, term of activity, order of termination of its members powers open, as well as regulating the meetings frequency, giving the opportunity to the members of the board to schedule them. We may conclude that in practice members of the executive body in Ukrainian firms are rarely guided in their activities by these documents. That's why they are more formalized and have a nominative character.

In 2005, when Ukrainian business environment was characterized by continuing growth of the securities market of domestic institutions, and investment capital arrived into the country, the International Finance Corporation (2005) decided to help a few Ukrainian banks in improving corporate governance standards, and funded a 2-year project ("Ukraine Banking Corporate Governance Project", worth $1.5 million. The project was not eventually successful, because less than a year after forming in selected banks temporary administrations two of them were liquidated (public JSC "Dnestr Bank", public JSC "Ukrprombank"), one bank was nationalized (public JSC "Ukrgasbank"), one of them has gradually lost market share (public JSC "TAS-Commerzbank"), and there were no qualitative changes in the performance of the latter one (public JSC "Megabank"). However, national scientists have concluded that banks in Ukraine are generally well informed about the principles and benefits of corporate standards, but they lack of motivation or resources to improve their practices over the minimum standards established by legislation. Banks don't seem to face enough pressure from shareholders, and therefore don't see the need to disclose information about the company. As well as the appointment applicants to key positions by largest shareholders became a common practice in the country, they are not able to determine adequately the functional role of their controls (in particular the supervisory board).

In Ukraine, the evolution of the supervisory board consisted of three stages, during which the concept of the supervisory board was developing as the most important governing body (Fig. 1).

Thus, the evolution of the structure and composition of the supervisory board in Ukraine was proportional to the requirements that appeared with the development of the domestic financial market, but has not yet reached its conclusion in several of issues, for example, the issue of formation of special committees of that body. While shareholders of foreign companies persistently initiate the establishment of special committees, they are not as popular in Ukrainian enterprises (on average only 4–25 % of companies have one or another committee in a supervisory board).

The law "On Banks and Banking Activity" (2000) regulates creation of three compulsory committees – credit committee, tariff committee and committee on asset and liability management. If we consider the structure of three largest banks in Ukraine (public JSC "Privatbank", public JSC "Oschadbank", public JSC "Raiffeisen Bank Aval"), they have created four committees, adding to others the budget committee. At the same time they don't have such a strategically important structural part as the risk committee. The problem is that in Ukraine there are no uniform requirements for the participants of committees, their powers and accountability, as well as there is no binding legislative act, which would regulate the principles of their independence. Thus, the members of the supervisory board

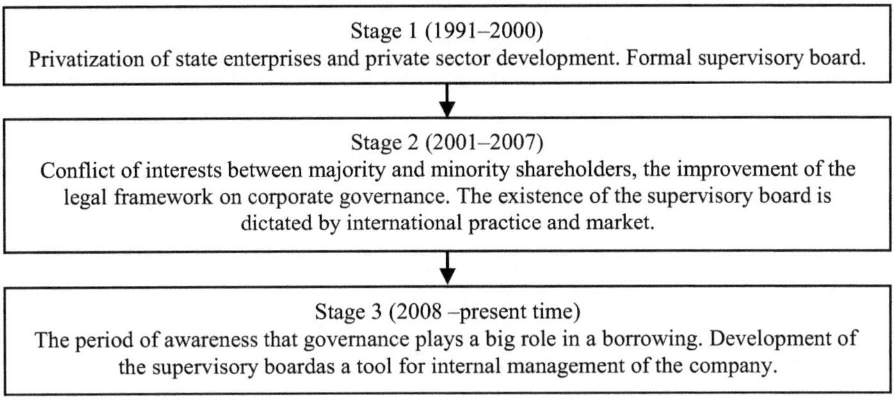

Fig. 1 Evolution the supervisory board in Ukraine

should assume functions of strategy development, operating, monitoring, as well as remuneration of their own. If we compare this aspect with an international practice, in almost all foreign companies remuneration committees are composed of independent directors.

One more obstacle for development of investment business in Ukraine is unavailable information about compensations of the supervisory board members and executive directors. The problem arises in the preparatory stage: it's impossible to hire an experienced manager, not knowing the amount of his previous pay. Although the statutory documents of the companies often guarantee disclosure of such information, but in practice it remains inaccessible.

3.5 *Financial Accountability*

On May 2, 2011 the Supreme Council amended the law "On Accounting and Financial Reporting in Ukraine" (1999), which raised the issue of the transition of the Ukrainian companies to international financial reporting standards. Already in 2012, public JSCs, banking institutions, insurance companies, and companies that are engaged in activities approved by the Cabinet of Ministers of Ukraine, are required to prepare and publish financial statements and consolidated financial statements according to international standards. Companies those are not included in the above list, given the opportunity to make their own decision on the use of IFRS for reporting. In addition, any company can keep records, guided solely by international standards, but in this case it is necessary to inform about such decision to the public agency.

The main difference with IFRS and national standards in the field of accounting is the principle of the prevalence of substance over form. This principle is one of the most fundamental in the management of accounting under IFRS. In spite of the fact that national standards also declare this principle, the majority of Ukrainian companies did not comply, and display operations solely on the basis of the legal form, ignoring the economic substance. If the company in the conduct of accounting complies with national standards and has no operations that can be interpreted in two ways, there will be no difficulties in the transition to IFRS in accounting. If we analyze and compare the requirements for preparation of the financial statements and consolidated financial statements IFRS and national accounting standards, there does exist a lot of difference. IFRS requires additional disclosures, notes and analysis of financial indicators that are not covered by national standards. National standards provide a clear form of reports that are part of the financial information. IFRS gives choice to the form in which to prepare reports, adjusting only the basic methodological approaches (Baryshnikova 2012).

In Ukrainian audit committee plays an important role in preparing the financial statements. The main function of the audit committee is to exercise control over financial and economic activity of the supervisory board. Ukrainian regulatory framework establishes provisions under which a member of the audit committee should include only shareholders of JSCs. Members of the audit committee may not be members of the executive body, the supervisory board and other officials. Procedure of the audit committee and its quantitative composition approved by the general meeting of shareholders in accordance with the charter of the company. Typically, an average-size Ukrainian JSC creates an audit committee out of three people, although quantitative structure may be different.

Typically, the audit committee reports on the results of its inspections of the general meeting of the company. In addition, the audit committee without a general meeting of shareholders does not have the right to approve the balance (Kostyuk et al. 2010).

Branches of the main world's leaders in auditing the "Big Four" (Ernst & Young, Deloitte & Touche, PricewaterhouseCoopers and KPMG) are presented in Ukraine. In Ukraine the activity of auditing firms and received earnings vary considerably by region, confirming statistics newsletters Audit Chamber of Ukraine. The situation that occurs in the market for audit services in Ukraine, says that one of the major problems is the pricing audit. It is necessary to develop a specific mechanism that would regulate the determination of audit firms for their services, setting its lower limit. As of 2012 there were registered a total of 1,680 audit entrepreneurs in Ukraine who were entered in the Register of Audit Chamber of Ukraine (Business Decisions 2011). The market share controlled by foreign audit corporations, especially by the "Big Four", has been steadily increased, creating very significant competition to domestic auditors (Table 1).

3.6 Bankruptcy System

Ukrainian bankruptcy system has a lot of weaknesses: the rate of repayment to creditors is only 9 % in Ukraine, while it's about 28 % in Eastern Europe and Central Asia. Moreover, 42 % of the total value of enterprise is spent on procedures

Table 1 Top-10 of the main auditing companies in Ukraine, 2010

Place	Company name	Net income, mln USD	Net profit, mln USD	Profitability, %	Staff
1	Deloitte & Touche	21.04	2.09	10.0	302
2	Ernst & Young	21.78	1.33	6.1	203
3	PricewaterhouseCoopers	13.64	0.06	0.4	53
4	KPMG	10.38	0.08	0.7	188
5	BDO	5.98	0.68	15.7	180
6	Baker Tilly Ukraine	5.70	0.25	4.3	200
7	EBS	2.53	0.31	12.2	90
8	Nexia DK Auditors & Consultants	1.96	0.30	15.0	88
9	"UPK Audit"	2.01	0.04	1.6	52
10	MGI Consulting	1.23	0.03	2.4	48

related to bankruptcy (13 % in Eastern Europe and Central Asia). The process of restoring the solvency in Ukraine takes about 3 years and in most cases (90 %) leads to liquidation. This procedure is more complicated in the banking sector and, despite legal restrictions, can take a long time. For example, JSC "Gradobank" is in liquidation for more than 10 years (National Bank of Ukraine 2013).

Ukrainian legislation on bankruptcy should be divided into three groups: (1) laws which regulate general aspects for enterprises: Civil Code, 2003; Commercial Code, 2003; Law "On Restoring the Debtor's Solvency or Bankruptcy", 1992; (2) laws which regulate bankruptcy of banks: Law "On Banks and Banking Activity", 2000; Law "On the Deposit Guarantee System", 2012; (3) laws which regulate separate aspect: relationships with employees: Law "On Employment", 2012; Labor Code, 1971; tax issues (Tax Code, 2010; Instruction "On the Registration of Taxpayers", 2011) and others.

It should be mentioned, that liquidation is not the only way to sort the problem of debtors' solvency out. Article 5 (Law "On Restoring the Debtor's Solvency or Bankruptcy" (Verkhovna Rada of Ukraine 1992)) determines the list of possible measures: disposition of debtors' property; settlement agreement; rehabilitation (restoring solvency) of the debtor; liquidation. At the same time there are different subjects who have an opportunity to initiate the bankruptcy procedure (Fig. 2).

Banks have some peculiarities in their activity compared to enterprises, so the order of payments to creditors (Table 2) differs significantly. To protect the rights of individual depositors (natural persons) to the banks the Deposit Guarantee Fund was established. In 1998, the President of Ukraine signed the Decree "On Measures to Protect the Rights of Physical Persons as Depositors of Commercial Banks in Ukraine" which approved the establishment of the Deposit Guarantee Fund and procedures regulating the use of the Fund's resources. The Decree also established that the depositors could be reimbursed for the deposits to the commercial banks from the date of the deposits inaccessibility at the amount of UAH 500.

On September 20, 2001, the Verkhovna Rada (Parliament of Ukraine) approved the Law "On Deposit Guarantee Fund", which took effect on October 24, 2001.

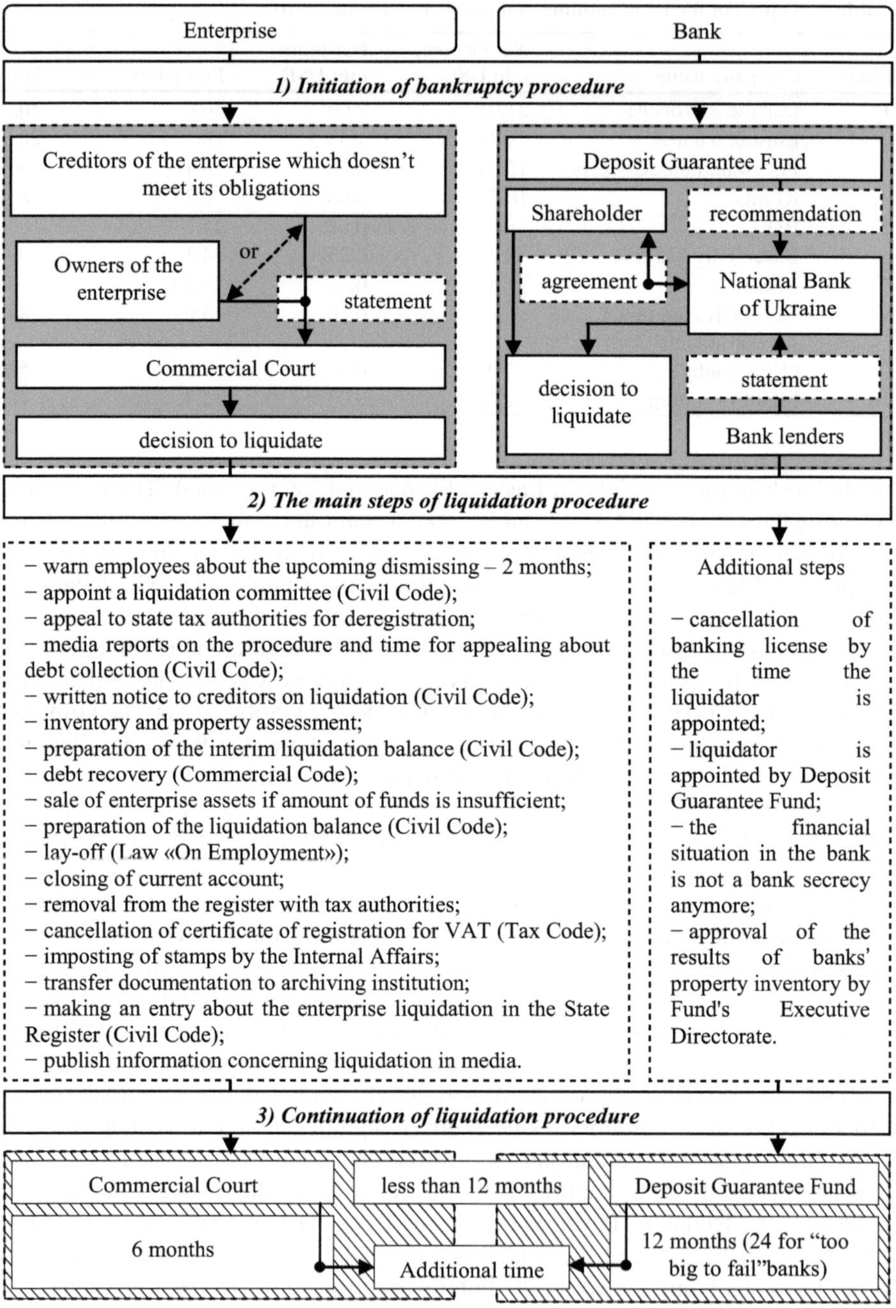

Fig. 2 The procedure of bankruptcy in Ukraine

Table 2 The order of payments to creditors

Enterprise	Bank
(1.1) Secured claims;	(1) Liabilities arising from injury to life and health of citizens;
(1.2) Claims for arrears of wages;	(2) Monetary claims for wages;
(1.3) Creditors' claims under insurance contracts;	(3) The requirements of the Fund;
(1.4) Legal costs and costs of liquidation committee;	(4) The requirements of investors-individuals in the amount that exceed the amount paid by the Fund;
(2) Claims arising from the liabilities of the bankrupt to employees, except the requirements satisfied in the first place;	(5) The requirements of the National Bank of Ukraine;
(3) Claims for taxes and duties (mandatory payments);	(6) Claims of individuals, whose fees or charges are locked (except individuals-entrepreneurs);
(4) Unsecured claims;	(7) Other requirements except subordinated debt;
(5) Requirements for the return of contributions from members of the personnel in the authorized capital;	(8) Subordinated debt.
(6) Other requirements.	

According to the law the Fund guaranteed reimbursement of the deposits including the interest accrued for every depositor to the Fund member (temporary member) banks at the amount of UAH 1,200. The coverage amount could be increased by the decision of the administrative board of the Fund depending on the market trends (Deposit Guarantee Fund 2013).

On February 2012, the Parliament of Ukraine approved the Law "On Households Deposit Guarantee System" that came into force on September, 2012. The law extended the mandate of the Deposit Guarantee Fund in the field of bank resolution, including provisional administration and liquidation of insolvent banks. The law provided for provisional administration of banks for a term of up to 3 months, during which a decision on the least cost resolution method should be taken. It cancelled the concept of the "temporary Fund member". According to the present law all duly licensed banks in Ukraine are members of the Fund. The only bank which is not a member of the Fund is public JSC "Derzhavniy Oschadniy Bank Ukrainy" (the National Savings Bank of Ukraine). A depositor is entitled to receive a guaranteed amount (within 25,000 USD) after deciding to revoke banking licenses and liquidate the bank, but the real practice shows that chronological difference between the date of insolvency and the date of taking decision to liquidate exists. A bank is insolvent in the following cases: (1) if the bank was recognized as ailing and did not correct existing violations within 180 days; (2) if the amount of the bank's regulatory capital falls below 30 % of the minimum set by legislation; (3) if the bank doesn't meet its obligations to depositors and other creditors within 10 days. The bank will be placed under the control of the Deposit Guarantee Fund when the decision on insolvency is taken. From that point temporary administration operates. This entails a moratorium on the payment of claims of depositors and the abolition of the interest accrual during this period. According to Article 34 of the law “On the Deposit Guarantee System” the maximum term for temporary administration to be introduced is 3 months (6 months for “too big to fail bank”). Only after this procedure, the bank may be declared bankrupt. It takes a lot of time and all the depositors are unable to have their money returned if the temporary administration regime is declared.

3.7 Minority Shareholders’ Rights Protection

In the Global Competitiveness Report 2009–2010 Ukraine takes 132nd place in the ranking of countries that protect the rights of minority shareholders, having a worse index than most countries with a market economy. Seventy-five percent of the total number of applications to the National Securities and Stock Market Commission (2012) are minority shareholders’ complaints about the violation of their rights during decision making process in JSCs. They include: violation of the right to equal treatment of all shareholders, to participate in the JSC, to get the information about the activities of the company and to receive part of profits as dividends. The fact is that Ukraine had a lot of problems in this sphere what could be proofed by the Corporate Governance Annual Report (Concorde Capital 2011). The analysis showed that most companies have an average level of protection (45 %). Poor protection is in 44 % of all companies. Only 11 % of the companies have a good base to protect minority shareholders’ rights.

The l “On Joint Stock Companies” is the main legislative act, which regulates the instrument of minority shareholders’ rights protection in Ukrainian companies. With the introduction of this law a list of information available to shareholders has increased substantially compared to previous legislation. The order of the company’s supervisory board formation is one of the most noteworthy elements of the minority shareholders’ protection mechanism. Indeed, the supervisory board is an agent that guarantees the realization of shareholders’ rights protection, among which the important place is given to minorities. Article 53 of “On Joint Stock Companies” established that members of the supervisory board of a public company are only through cumulative voting. In turn, members of the private company supervisory board are the principle of representation in the supervisory board of shareholders’ representatives or by cumulative voting. Cumulative voting is the election of the people of the society in which the total number of shareholder votes multiplied by the number of body members of the company, elected as a shareholder may give all counted votes for one candidate or distribute them among several candidates. What matters here is that the mechanism of electing the supervisory board by cumulative voting is intended to help ensure that even a minority shareholder who owns a small number of shares, can significantly affect the composition of the supervisory board. But under the conditions stipulated by the law “On Joint Stock Companies” to amendments there to February 3, 2011, it was impossible to implement such a mechanism of cumulative voting. As in Article 42 old wording stated that the elected body of the corporation shall be the candidate who received the most votes among those who scored over 50 % of the votes. Clearly, provide 50 % of the vote minority shareholder could not, because of a small number of voting shares. Thus, this rule does not only level the benefits of cumulative voting by incomplete enable a minority shareholder of his right to participate in the governance of the company, but also paralyzed the process of formation of the supervisory board.

Moreover, the law "On Securities and the Stock Market" is important as well, especially Article 44 about the insider information. It regulates the non-disclosure of information about the issuer for its transfer to the minority shareholder. But there could be another option. Information on a minority shareholder transferred issuer who then tries to redeem his shares. And it is also illegal use of insider information. If we consider the protection of minorities in general, we see that there are a number of problems. The use of derivative lawsuits is the effective legal rights protection mechanism and legitimate interests of minority shareholders. This mechanism is widespread in practice in most countries with a developed market economy. In Ukraine, one of the key problems of the regulatory protection of shareholders and members of societies is the failure to recognize by the Ukrainian Courts Institute of indirect (derivative) action. But since the current legislation of Ukraine recognizes the European Convention on Human Rights and the European Court of Human Rights as a source of law, the case law, including the rights of shareholders and the invalidation of related party transactions should be applied more widely in Ukraine. Seek protection in the European institutions can also be an effective mechanism for the protection of shareholders' rights.

To prevent fraud and make maximum protection of the rights and legitimate interests of minority shareholders of large companies, can provide a requirement to publish complete information of the general meeting on companies' websites no later than 30 days before the meeting. Thus, minority shareholders have few sources of relevant information about the meeting, which will surely be a positive thing for the protection of his rights. On the other hand, minority shareholders have some power. For example, to prevent majoritarian decisions necessary for the development of the enterprise. When the majority shareholders have at least 75 % of the shares, but cannot increase the authorized capital or to change the charter without the consent of the minority shareholders.

4 Conclusion

In conclusion, the level of corporate governance practices in Ukraine, although is not perfect, but is under active development. It should be noted that the current domestic economic realities do not allow explicitly adopt and replicate the experience of developed countries in terms of corporate governance. This is reasoned by the national features of business and banking activity in Ukraine. Since Ukraine became independent the track of the development and reforms in the sphere of corporate governance practices are clearly defined, and in addition during this time many laws and regulations, adapted to modern business environment, appeared, which have formed a legal framework that promotes corporate relations development.

The importance of having the adequate corporate governance system is connected with such key element in decision-making processes of potential investors as their interests' protection. Business is the game with its own rules, and these rules are international. Ukrainian and foreign companies have to deal with similar problems; tools developed abroad can successfully be used in Ukrainian corporate governance with national characteristics and changes in standards of business conduct, albeit with some delay, come into Ukrainian businesses.

References

Akimova, I., & Schwodiauer, G. (2003). *Ownership structure, corporate governance and enterprise performance: Empirical results for Ukraine*. Institute for Economic Research and Policy Consulting. [Online] Available from: http://pdc.ceu.hu/archive/00001671/01/wp_21_eng.pdf. Downloaded 9 Jan 2013.

Andreyeva, T., & Dean, J. (2000). *Privatization, ownership structure and company performance: The case of Ukraine*. Institute of Macroeconomic Analysis and Development. [Online] Available from: http://www.umar.gov.si/fileadmin/user_upload/konference/07/14_andreyeva.pdf. Downloaded 9 Jan 2013.

Asaul, A., Pavlov, V., Beskier, F., & Myshko, O. (2006). *Formation of the corporate ownership in Ukraine*. [Online, in Russian] Available from: http://www.aup.ru/books/m2/3_2_1.htm. Downloaded 9 Jan 2013.

Baryshnikova, E. (2012). *International financial reporting standards as a reflection of globalization and the realities of Ukraine*. Business Education Alliance. [Online, in Russian] Available from: http://www.bea.com.ua/ru/articles/127-stifrs. Downloaded 9 Jan 2013.

Bayura, D. (2009). *Corporate governance system in Ukraine: Situation and prospects*. Kyiv: Kyiv University.

Belyalov, T. (2008). Issues, trends and characteristics of the development of modern business environment. *Journal of Culture of Black Sea Region, 126*, 9–14.

Bilyk, O., Grechaniuk B., & Muravyev, B. (2009). *Firm performance and managerial turnover: The case of Ukraine*. Institute for the Study of Labor. [Online] Available from: http://mpra.ub.uni-muenchen.de/13685/1/MPRA_paper_13685.pdf. Downloaded 9 Jan 2013.

Brynza, M. (2011). *Protection of minority shareholders' rights in joint-stock companies in Ukraine*. Kyiv School of Economics. [Online] Available from: http://www.academia.edu/1437712/Protection_of_minority_shareholders_rights_in_joint-stock_companies_in_Ukraine. Downloaded 9 Jan 2013.

Business Decisions. (2011). *Rating of audit firms*. [Online, in Russian] Available from: http://www.dk.ua/download/108a1df635e7ab64131f0ed0ddcd300155d/. Downloaded 9 Jan 2013.

Concorde Capital. (2011). *Corporate governance in Ukraine*. [Online] Available from: http://rs.concorde.ua/files/Image/Corporate_GovernanceOctober_2011_Special_Report_ENGLISH.pdf. Downloaded 9 Jan 2013.

Deposit Guarantee Fund. (2013). *About the Deposit Guarantee Fund*. [Online] Available from: http://www.fg.gov.ua/about/info/. Downloaded: 10 Jan 2014.

International Finance Corporation. (2005). *Ukraine banking corporate governance project*. [Online] Available from: http://ifcext.ifc.org/ifcext/pressroom/ifcpressroom.nsf/1f70cd9a07d692d68525 6ee1001cdd37/853f80475afbe81885257012005200ec?OpenDocument. Downloaded 10 Jan 2014.

Iorhachova, M. (2011). Corporate conflicts in Ukraine: Types and role. *Journal Economics and Management Issues, 698*, 170–180.

Ivasiv, I. (2008). Corporate governance issues in Ukrainian banks. *Journal of European Economics, 2*, 232–241.

Kostyuk, A., Takeda, F., & Hosono, K. (2010). *Anti-crisis paradigms of corporate governance in Banks: A new institutional outlook*. Sumy: Virtus Interpress.

Ministry of Finance of Ukraine. (2011). *Instruction "On the Registration of Taxpayers" № 1394*. [Online, in Ukrainian] Available from: http://zakon2.rada.gov.ua/laws/show/z1369-11. Downloaded 9 Jan 2013.

National Bank of Ukraine. (2013). *Key performance indicators of banks*. [Online] Available from: http://www.bank.gov.ua/control/en/publish/article?art_id=37942&cat_id=37937. Downloaded 9 Jan 2013.

National Securities and Stock Market Commission. (2012). *Investors' rights protection*. [Online] Available from: http://www.nssmc.gov.ua/fund/investorsrights. Downloaded 9 Jan 2013.

OECD. (2001). *Corporate governance in Ukraine*. [Online] Available from: http://www.oecd.org/daf/corporateaffairs/corporategovernanceprinciples/1930958.pdf. Downloaded 9 Jan 2013.

Pigyl, N. (2011). Corporate governance in Ukraine: Problems and ways of its solution. *Problems and Prospects of Development of the Banking System of Ukraine, 2*, 58–60.

President of Ukraine. (1998). *Decree "On Measures to Protect the Rights of Physical Persons as Depositors of Commercial Banks in Ukraine" № 996-98*. [Online, in Ukrainian] Available from: http://zakon2.rada.gov.ua/laws/show/996/98. Downloaded 9 Jan 2013.

Shum, V. (2010). *Does incentive compensation to supervisory boards affect CEO turnover*. Kyiv School of Economics. [Online] Available from: http://kse.org.ua/uploads/Shum20103105.pdf. Downloaded 9 Jan 2013.

The National Bank of Ukraine. (2004). *Guidelines on the organization and functioning of risk management in banks of Ukraine № 361*. [Online, in Ukrainian] Available from: http://zakon.nau.ua/doc/?uid=1045.5598.0. Downloaded 9 Jan 2013.

The National Bank of Ukraine. (2007). *Guidelines for improving corporate governance in banks of Ukraine № 98*. [Online, in Ukrainian] Available from: http://www.bank.gov.ua/doccatalog/document?id=45211. Downloaded 9 Jan 2013.

The State Commission on Securities and Stock Market. (2003). *Decision "On Approval of the Principles of Corporate Governance" № 571*. [Online, in Ukrainian] Available from: http://zakon.nau.ua/doc/?code=vr571312-03,%20vr052312-08. Downloaded 9 Jan 2013.

Verkhovna Rada of Ukraine. (1991). *Law of Ukraine "On Economic Companies" № 1576-XII*. [Online, in Ukrainian] Available from: http://zakon1.rada.gov.ua/laws/show/1576-12. Downloaded 9 Jan 2013.

Verkhovna Rada of Ukraine. (1992). *Law of Ukraine "On Restoring the Debtor's Solvency or Bankruptcy" № 2343-XII*. [Online, in Ukrainian] Available from: http://zakon2.rada.gov.ua/laws/show/2343-12. Downloaded 9 Jan 2013.

Verkhovna Rada of Ukraine. (1999). *Law of Ukraine "On Accounting and Financial Reporting in Ukraine" № 996-XIV*. [Online, in Ukrainian] Available from: http://zakon1.rada.gov.ua/laws/show/996-14. Downloaded 9 Jan 2013.

Verkhovna Rada of Ukraine. (2000). *Banks and Banking Act № 2121-III*. [Online, in Ukrainian]. Available from: http://zakon2.rada.gov.ua/laws/show/2121-14. Downloaded 9 Jan 2013.

Verkhovna Rada of Ukraine. (2001). *Law of Ukraine "On Deposit Guarantee Fund" № 2740-III*. [Online, in Ukrainian] Available from: http://zakon2.rada.gov.ua/laws/show/2740-14. Downloaded 9 Jan 2013.

Verkhovna Rada of Ukraine. (2003). *Civil Code № 435-IV*. [Online, in Ukrainian] Available from: http://zakon2.rada.gov.ua/laws/show/435-15. Downloaded 9 Jan 2013.

Verkhovna Rada of Ukraine. (2003). *Commercial Code № 436-IV*. [Online, in Ukrainian] Available from: http://zakon1.rada.gov.ua/laws/show/436-15. Downloaded 9 Jan 2013.
Verkhovna Rada of Ukraine. (2006). *Securities and the Stock Market Act № 3480-IV*. [Online, in Ukrainian] Available from: http://zakon2.rada.gov.ua/laws/show/3480-15. Downloaded 9 Jan 2013.
Verkhovna Rada of Ukraine. (2008). *Joint Stock Companies Act № 514-IV*. [Online, in Ukrainian] Available from: http://zakon2.rada.gov.ua/laws/show/514-17. Downloaded 9 Jan 2013.
Verkhovna Rada of Ukraine. (2012). *Law of Ukraine "On Employment" № 5067-VI*. [Online, in Ukrainian] Available from: http://zakon1.rada.gov.ua/laws/show/5067-17. Downloaded 9 Jan 2013.
Verkhovna Rada of Ukraine. (2012). *Law of Ukraine "On Households Deposit Guarantee System" № 4452-VI*. [Online, in Ukrainian] Available from: http://zakon2.rada.gov.ua/laws/show/4452-17. Downloaded 9 Jan 2013.
Verkhovna Rada of USSR. (1971). *Labor Code № 322-VIII*. [Online, in Ukrainian] Available from: http://zakon2.rada.gov.ua/laws/show/322-08. Downloaded 9 Jan 2013.
Wojciechowska, Y., & Wojciechowska, V. (2009). Corporate governance problems in Ukraine and ways of its solution. *Journal of Economics and Management Issues, 64*, 244–247.
World Economic Forum. (2009). *The global competitiveness report 2009–2010*. [Online] Available from: http://www3.weforum.org/docs/WEF_GlobalCompetitivenessReport_2009-10.pdf. Downloaded 9 Jan 2014.
Zaplatinsky, V. (2002). *Features of privatization in Ukraine*. [Online, in Russian] Available from: http://vasilievaa.narod.ru/ptpu/12_4_02.htm. Downloaded 9 Jan 2013.

Corporate Governance Development in a Rapidly Changing Economy: Trends and Challenges in Estonia

Ruth Alas and Tiit Elenurm

Abstract Implications of the Estonian privatization and the two-tier board model on corporate governance development are discussed. Despite implementing OECD corporate governance guidelines the stock market has still limited role in Estonian economy. The chapter reflects empirical research conducted at the Estonian Business School in the field of corporate governance at different stages of Estonian integration to the European Union and in the change management context. Technology-based new ventures create situations, where entrepreneurs are choosing new owners able to offer smart capital. These examples cannot be fully explained by applying the traditional principal-agent logic. Cases presented by participants of training workshops highlight conflicts between owners with different future vision and difficulties of entrepreneurs to differentiate the role of corporate governance from the daily management of business operations.

1 Introduction

Corporate governance in a small open economy is influenced by many global and regional factors, including economic growth and crisis, integration to the European Union, foreign investments and development trends of the knowledge-based economy. Holistic approach to corporate governance in Central and Easter Europe has to take into consideration macro-level variable implications of the privatization process on the emerging corporate governance practices, clear property rights, institutions and mechanisms that support transparent and growth-enhancing business environment (Hardi and Buti 2012). Estonian society has after the collapse of the Soviet command economy and regaining independence in 1992 accomplished rapid transition to the market economy and integration to the European Union. At present,

R. Alas (✉) • T. Elenurm
Estonian Business School, Tallinn, Estonia
e-mail: Ruth.Alas@ebs.ee

S. Boubaker and D.K. Nguyen (eds.), *Corporate Governance in Emerging Markets*, CSR, Sustainability, Ethics & Governance, DOI 10.1007/978-3-642-44955-0_11,

a challenge is to change the structure of the economy towards more knowledge-based products and services and to diminish the role of subcontracting that does not create high added value for owners and sustainable income increase for local workforce.

Present chapter integrates results of several studies that have conducted in Estonia by authors of the present paper and their colleagues during the process of corporate governance development. These studies reflect the institutional framework and regulations influencing the corporate governance but also practical challenges and change trends. The central research problem is how corporate governance regulations and principles can enhance co-operation between owners and managers in small and large business organization facing change management challenges and crises, taking into consideration the role of local and foreign ownership and development of knowledge-based enterprises.

The framework for developing corporate governance in a small open economy is at first analyzed. Section 2 will start from presenting implications of the relatively rapid privatization in Estonia and the two-tier model of corporate governance bodies that has been taken over from the German corporate governance system. Survey results that reflect composition and work practice of supervisory boards and boards are presented. This section also discusses the role of the Commercial Code and implications of the OECD Corporate Governance Recommendations. Section 3 focuses on relations between corporate governance and change management. Change trends in co-operation between owners and managers are analyzed by using data from an expert survey. Special attention is paid to growing small enterprises as the Estonian stock market still has small number of listed companies and exercises quite limited influence on corporate governance practices. Cases of knowledge-based innovative companies are discussed in order to highlight some corporate governance challenges in such enterprises that have born global potential. Finally, the role of corporate governance bodies is linked to crisis management issues in companies.

2 Developing Corporate Governance in a Small Open Economy

2.1 *Privatization and Corporate Governance*

Already in the early stages of privatization in the transition economies of Central and Eastern Europe, Saul Estrin (1994) pointed out the dangers of insider privatization that would not facilitate rapid restructuring of enterprises. Orientation on finding core owners has been stressed among the success factors in Estonian privatization (Terk 2000). Estrin (2002) stressed that only governments in Hungary and Estonia were willing or able to sell an appreciable share of formerly state-owned assets to foreigners. In 1992 Estonian authorities decided to implement the

German 'Treuhand' model for accelerating the process of large-scale privatization and a special body, the Estonian Privatization Enterprise was established. By the beginning of 1995, the period of privatization in Estonia was predominantly over and the first legislative framework related to the operation of corporations in the Western sense had started to develop.

Terk and Elenurm (1996) in case studies of employee-owned enterprises revealed that such enterprises were able to increase operational efficiency. Employee-owners however lacked corporate governance experience and strategic vision in order to decide on long-term investments. A few years after privatization of some transport enterprises to insiders, some employees had retired and insisted on paying out dividends although the need to invest to new vehicles had become even more topical than at the time of privatization.

Jones et al. (2003) have studied the process of ownership change in Estonia after privatization and concluded that ownership change from employees to owners-outsiders has speeded up restructuring of companies. Manager-owned firms have however, according to their research results, displayed better business performance than enterprises owned by domestic owners-outsiders or employee-owned enterprises. Eamets et al. (2008) have studied the development of employee financial participation in Estonian enterprises and concluded that there is no historical tradition of employee share ownership in Estonia and during years after privatization owner-managers and outside owners have become dominant. The discussion on implementing EU regulations that would support financial participation of employees and employee representations in corporate governance bodies of *Societas Europaea,* could however make employee ownership more topical especially in knowledge-based companies.

The ownership structures of Estonian enterprises are relatively concentrated as the result of applying the Treuhand privatization model despite using the privatization process for jump-starting the Tallinn stock exchange. Minority shares of some large privatized companies were sold for the privatization vouchers but these vouchers were tradable and interested investors could start concentrating ownership already at this stage. This privatization practice made the Estonian case different from the so-called Anglo-American system, where ownership is more diffused, and also from the so-called German practice, where the role of banks in corporate governance of industrial companies is very high, as the participation of Estonian institutional investors (banks and other financial institutions, including pension funds) in domestic share trading has also been low. Some features of the Estonian ownership landscape are more similar to the Italian model, as many enterprises are family-owned, but the concentration of domestic outsiders and foreign investors is also high (Hannula 2006, p. 81).

2.2 Two-Tier Model of Corporate Governance Bodies

There are considerable differences between the Anglo-American, German and Japanese corporate governance systems that reflect corporate governance development traditions but also broader institutional context. Many developing and emerging economies are only in the process of developing the most basic market institutions. Kuznetsov and Kuznetsova (2012) claim that large and medium-size companies have failed to gain legitimacy among the vast strata of Russian society. From the corporate social responsibility point of view the Anglo-American theory of corporate governance, which concentrates mostly on the problems of stock ownership, is not exactly adequate in a situation where the ownership structure is in rapid transition and where ownership concentration is in progress.

Development of different types of corporate governance models could be observed in various countries, for example, in Poland the German type and in Russia the Anglo-American type. Slovenian enterprises adopted the German model of corporate governance (Rozman 2006). So did also Czech enterprises with some modifications (Maly 2006). Martynova and Renneboog (2011) point out that the countries of German legal approach and the countries that joined the European Unions in 2004 in principle give more decision rights directly to shareholders. At the same time countries of English legal heritage and the EU 2007 accession countries give more control to trustees and representatives of shareholders in the board of directors but still provide the highest quality of governance standards. Bedo et al. (2011) analysed governance and employment relations in Eastern and Central Europe and stated a key distinction between Ango-American style liberal market economies and coordinated economies in continental Europe. They interpret development of the Baltic countries as moving particularly closely to neo-liberalism.

The stakeholder perspective of corporate governance is strongly represented in the corporate governance practices of the continental Europe but in-depth interviews in 26 Estonian organisations demonstrated that during the rapid economic growth period before the global economic crisis, stakeholder interests and corporate relations with society and environment had not yet been considered important issues in business organisations (Kooskora 2008).

In the German model, governance is assigned to two boards: supervisory board and the management board. Foo and Witkowska (2011) discuss the view that German-Japanese model of more concentrated ownership with active role of such intermediaries as banks and employee-owners may be more appropriate for transition countries than Anglo-American model of dispersed owners. Concentrated corporate ownership can be seen as a tool for active shareholding monitoring and developing closer ties between more active and dominating owners and managers in order to respond to the agency problem. Such trend can however lead to contradictions between controlling versus minority shareholders.

2.3 The Commercial Code

In Estonia the main source of corporate governance rules is the Commercial Code, which entered into force in 1995 and has been amended on numerous occasions since its adoption. The Commercial Code provides for the general corporate governance rules to public limited companies (Aktsiaselts), private limited companies (Osaühing) and for other types of legal entities that can be used for setting up a business. It is commonly understood in Estonia that developing transparent corporate governance with wide opportunities for the investors to control the use of the funds creates a perfect ground for attracting new investments to the country and ensuring continuous economic growth.

The Commercial Code and Estonian corporate governance regulations in general are mainly based on the German version of the Continental corporate governance model. Governance is performed through three main bodies of the company. Corporate governance bodies include general meeting of the shareholders, the supervisory board and the management board. Establishing a supervisory board is compulsory in all public limited companies. The Commercial Code clearly specifies the roles of different corporate governance bodies, assuming that owners of the public limited company are interested to use such legal form to be listed at the stock exchange and are ready to differentiate clearly the role of the supervisory board as the corporate governance body that supervises and strategically directs the management board but is not involved in routine business decisions or in representing the company in daily business transactions.

By establishing a two-tier system, the aim was to bring clarity to the legal landscape in Estonia. Compared to the one-tier system, the roles of managers and owners are more clearly separated in the two-tier system and that played a decisive role in selecting between these two systems. The supervisory board determines the course of action for the company, elects the members of management board and supervises the activity thereof. In order to fulfil its tasks, the supervisory board has the right to examine all the documents of the company and to audit the accuracy of accounting, the existence of assets and the conformity of the activities of the company with the law, the articles of association and resolutions of the general meeting. The consent of the supervisory board is required for conclusion of transactions which are beyond the scope of everyday economic activities. The management board in Estonia at the same time represents the company in business transactions. Every member of the board has the authority to represent the company, whereas in case the articles of association have set forth joint representation, such an arrangement has effect on third persons dealing with the company only if such joint representation is registered in the Commercial Register.

In Estonia members of the management board cannot simultaneously be members of the supervisory board. Entrepreneurs and controlling shareholders in public limited companies have to decide if they prefer to be in the management board as CEO or other management team member in order to accomplish business transactions as representatives of the company that do not need authorization or they want to be in the supervisory board that elects management board members, sets goals for their activities and accepts or rejects large investment proposals made by the management board.

2.4 Supervisory Boards and Management Boards in Practice

In 2007 researchers of the Estonian Business School and the Estonian Institute of Future Studies conducted survey that included 373 companies randomly selected by the Estonian Statistics Bureau (Alas and Tafel 2008). In one third of all domestic companies in the sample, the company belonged 100 % to the CEO or top management team and to their closest family members. The majority of management boards had one or two members (38.5 % and 22.2 % respectively), 14.5 % had three members and 10.3 %, four members. Management boards meet 1 or 2 times per month, on average 1.5 times per month. In 11 % of cases the supervisory board formed a special committee for dealing with issues such as compensation or remuneration for members of the top management team, strategy, finances, issues connected with purchasing raw materials, investments, evaluating assets and changing top managers. As much as 44 % of supervisory boards had three members that possess voting power on the supervisory board. Only 11 % of them were elected by the employees. In foreign firms, most of the supervisory board members are foreign residents. Thirty-seven percent of supervisory board members have the job of CEO or a similar top executive role in some other company. Sixty-five percent of supervisory board members had no business ties to the firm. It can be concluded that at least part of them can be seen as independent supervisory board members. Although supervisory board meetings on average take place 4 times per year, formal board decisions are also made outside regular face to face board meetings using phone meetings, e-mails and faxes instead. In 35 % of companies, the work of board members was compensated, but only 15 % had explicit rules for compensating their work. Contributions by the supervisory board was assessed to be the most significant in controlling business results and business decisions, followed by the function of replacing top management if needed. The survey results highlighted that conflicts in the supervisory board arise most often in discussions about what is best for the firm (Tafel-Viia and Alas 2009).

2.5 Implementing OECD Corporate Governance Principles

Trying to develop a system of good corporate governance in new EU member states is made difficult by problems such as complex corporate ownership structures, vague and confusing relationships between the state and financial sectors, weak legal and judicial systems, absent or underdeveloped institutions and scarce human resource capabilities (Tafel et al. 2006).

OECD has contributed to developing corporate governance in Estonia already in 1990s (Gerndorf et al. 1999) although Estonia was invited to join OECD only in 2007. The major stock market index in Estonia was originally TALSE (derived from the Tallinn Stock Exchange name), now renamed as OMX Tallinn. The OMX has been from 2008 integrated with NASDAQ.

Only 13 companies were listed in the main list of the Tallinn Stock Exchange as of March 2013. Secondary list comprises companies that do not meet quantitative admission requirements (free float, capitalization). In the secondary list 3 companies were listed. Tallinn Stock Exchange is one of the OMX Nordic Exchanges, which also operates Helsinki Stock Exchange and Stockholm Stock Exchange.

The role of the Tallinn Stock Exchange in the market for corporate financing changed during the economic crises at the end of 1990s, where large Scandinavian banks took over the majority ownership stake in the leading Estonian banks, former Hansapank and Eesti Ühispank have been now fully integrated as 100 % owned subsidiaries to Swedish Swedbank and Svenska Enskilde Banken corporate structures. After gaining the full corporate control Estonian subsidiaries of these international banks were withdrawn for the Tallinn Stock Exchange in 2008. On September 20, 2008, the shares of Saku Õlletehase AS (Saku Brewery) were delisted from the Tallinn Stock Exchange after the Carslberg Group had acquired shares of other shareholders. TeliaSonera Group delisted Eesti Telekom in 2010 after acquiring the stake of Estonian state and minority shareholders in this company that offers wide range of telecommunication services.

Bistrova and Lace (2012) have studied the influence of high quality corporate governance on firms financial performance in Central and Eastern European listed companies. Twenty-one assessment criteria based on best practices recommended by stock exchanges in the region were grouped into four major categories: supervisory board, management team, investor relations and information transparency. Estonian, Latvian, Lithuanian and Slovakian companies obtained in their research high scores mainly thanks to high stability of their management teams and logical organisational structures compared to Czech and Slovenian companies. However, in the whole region, when comparing 25 % of the best and 25 % of the worst companies from corporate governance perspective, researchers discovered that companies with the best corporate governance ratings, delivered below average profitability. The only financial ratio, which was better in the best corporate governance companies, was the equity ratio. These companies followed conservative capital management policy having higher than 45 % of equity ratio in their total assets. Companies that by the corporate governance criteria were among 25 % worst performers, had in average 35 % equity ratio. Bistrova and Lace (2012) see as one explanation that utility companies that cannot offer huge growth try to attract potential investors by demonstrating excellent corporate governance. But they do not exclude the possibility of the earnings manipulation in their sample.

Due to the liberal economic policy and high involvement of investors from more advanced Nordic countries in large and medium-sized Estonian companies, the current legislation with its low level of regulation frequently gives advantages to majority shareholders. In order to avoid machinations and manipulations, corporate governance practices need to be improved, especially where it concerns the protection of small shareholders (Steger et al. 2006). In companies partly controlled by foreign investors that could mean developing the regulations that deal with transfer pricing between large foreign corporate owners and their Estonian subsidiaries. In smaller enterprises that are controlled by the local capital it assumes clarification of the role of larger block owners that are simultaneously top managers.

2.6 The Corporate Governance Recommendations

In Estonia, the Corporate Governance Recommendations approved by the Financial Supervision Authority (2005) and introduced at the Tallinn Stock Exchange in 2006 follow the principle "comply or explain". Recommendations deal with arranging general meetings of shareholders in order to exercise shareholder rights, management board and supervisory board's composition, duties and charge, cooperation between management and supervisory boards, publication of information, and financial reporting and audit. Equal treatment of all shareholders, avoiding conflicts of interests and transparency are stressed in recommendations. In these recommendations public limited companies listed on the stock exchange are also asked to disclose their CEO compensation schemes. CEO compensation in non-listed enterprises is, however, a field that so far has been reflected mainly in general salary surveys that do not disclose links between components of the executive compensation package and specific corporate governance practices. Public discussions about compensation packages of board members have in recent years focused on companies, where the state is the main shareholder. In 2012 chairman of the Estonian Air management board Tero Taskila was dismissed after failing to implement his ambitious expansion strategy. The supervisory board and also the Ministry of Economy and Communications were criticized for accepting the contract that allowed to pay to Taskila 33,000 € guaranteed monthly salary that was higher than salaries paid to Estonian president and prime minister.

A survey among representative of companies listed at Tallinn Stock Exchange and a sample of investors Raadik (2008) revealed that issuers were 2 years after introducing the corporate governance recommendations to the stock exchange quite well informed about their essence. Many investors, even regular ones, were at the same time not aware about content of recommendations and potential benefits of related company reports for making sound investment decisions. In recent years information about recommendations has become more widespread but following or not following principles of this document has still not become a topical issue when discussing the quality of corporate governance.

The OECD report on corporate governance in Estonia (2011) reached a positive overall view on Estonia's corporate governance framework. The report mentions among weaknesses a small listed market that tends to be dominated by core, controlling shareholders. Investors are not active, and stock market mechanisms play a limited role in providing incentives for good corporate governance. OECD experts suggest that Estonia's voluntary corporate governance recommendations should be reviewed to consider making some provisions mandatory, while clarifying more the nature of reporting requirements and their enforcement. Provisions to protect "whistle-blowers" informing about irregularities in corporate governance and provisions about developing codes of ethics could be added. Authors of the report also insist on more specific reporting requirements related to company objectives, to the independence, qualifications and remuneration of board members.

3 Corporate Governance and Change Management

3.1 Cooperation Between Managers and Owners

Good corporate governance should not be seen as a static system but as a change management framework. Changes in corporate strategies and adaptation to crises situations create moments of truth, where conflicts between owners and managers or between owners themselves can lead to new development visions but sometimes to delays in restructuring companies or in initiating new profitable business projects.

The classical organization development (OD) approaches do not pay much attention to possible conflicts of interest between owners and their representative corporate governance bodies versus company managers. Although aligning the strategic priorities of the wider circle of stakeholders inside and outside organizational boundaries has become more integrated into organizational development programs during recent decades, conflicts between the strategic views of owners and managers are not the key focus of OD initiatives. The same applies to the learning organization concept that identifies systemic archetypes (Senge 1990) inhibiting sustainable strategic solutions, but does not specify the roles of managers and owners in dealing with the underlying mechanisms enabling the organizational learning process. In the emerging market economy context, however, it would be especially important to understand the functions and dysfunctions of owners in the organizational learning process, as the first learning challenge for many inexperienced owners is to clarify their identity in this new role.

Interaction between owners and managers has to be understood in order to predict the results of organizational change processes. A survey by Cvelbar (2007) in Slovenia on the effectiveness of management turnover as a corporate governance mechanism presents evidence that the supervisory board in not an efficient corporate governance mechanism for changing underperforming managers. Furthermore, representatives of owners in the supervisory board do not protect the interests of the shareholders better than representatives of employees and managers. This conclusion can be related to specific features of the Slovenian heritage of employee ownership, which is also reflected in its present corporate governance practices.

Beside the owners' control function, no lesser importance can be attached to their "soft" mechanism – their role in defining the vision, mission, values, etc. of the organization – in other words, the motives behind establishing the organization. Although the visionary role of the top management and his/her management team is essential, it can be argued that the business vision starts from the owners (Alas et al. 2010a).

3.2 Change Trends in Corporate Governance Practices

The Estonian Business School and the Estonian Institute for Future Studies have studied co-operation between executives and owners by interviewing experts that represent the main business sectors in Estonia and have long, more than 10 years of experience in both roles. The interviewees had the most extensive experience as owners and managers in the following business sectors: banking, real estate, wholesale and retail, logistics, energy, hotels, publishing, telecommunications, information technology, food processing and clothing. Results of this study indicate the main corporate governance change trends between the 1990s of the last century and the first decades of this century, and on the other hand, differences between companies based on foreign and domestic capital. Local Estonian owners in 1990s were looking for developer-type managers that sometimes took over the strategic role of owners. When owners moved later towards preferring maintainer-type of top managers for more mature markets, this indicated a change towards less radical organizational changes. Recent economic crisis has forced some block owners to be more actively involved in company down-sizing decisions.

The interviews provided evidence that in the context of a transition economy, the managers do not often trust the strategic visions offered by owners that were successful as entrepreneurs during the earlier stages of economic transition. Managers are skeptical about the abilities of many owners as strategists, especially if the business environment has changed and the original business success model might not be sustainable. They tend to share the view that becoming an owner in a transition economy was more often the result of being in the right place at the right time rather than an indication of more entrepreneurial competence than they themselves possess. The central problems causing stress among the managers were, first, the issue of the managers being left out of possible strategic decision-making by the owners, and, secondly, the owners' excessive interference in operations, which would obstruct the manager's opportunities to operate according to an established strategic plan. According to the managers, the owners are remote and less informed, but often do not acknowledge it and start interfering. It was claimed to be especially frequent if the owners have been earlier operating as managers in the same sector. Approximately half of the interviewed managers considered more long-term, clearer and complex strategies necessary. The owners were described as immediately addressing numbers in the strategy discussions instead of conceptual debates and quickly descending to the level of next year's business plan.

The owners in their interpretations set apart the businesses, with which they were actively connected, either as authors of the business idea or sometimes because of personal interest, and where they view the manager's role primarily as the executive and implementer. They displayed a different attitude towards the enterprises, which have achieved stability and whose owner/founder has turned his attention to other business projects. In these cases the CEO was expected to show initiative, which would help to retain or restore the growth trend. Managers were in this situation seeking for a greater strategic decision-making role in enterprises with multiple owners, whose expectations regarding its development need not coincide and some of whom had, in the CEO's opinion, accidentally become owners.

There are different mechanisms used by domestic and foreign owners to influence organizational change. Owners in foreign-owned companies may accomplish their corporate governance functions through the supervisory board, but if the subsidiary in a transition economy is part of a larger transnational corporation, they may prefer to use the chain of command linking functional units of the corporate headquarters to management board of their overseas subsidiary. In this case the role of the supervisory board tends to be rather formal. In practice the interference of foreign owners in a more regulated and reporting-based compared to unforeseen actions by local owners. The results of the interviews enable us to conclude that local owners in Estonia can be often described as interfering owners that try to be involved in the daily management of the management board but are not enough focused on long-term strategic objectives supported by incentive schemes for top managers that should be developed by representatives of owners in the supervisory board. Foreign owners, especially strategic foreign owners, impose many more instructions on top managers and much greater formalized restrictions on the top manager's freedom of action than Estonian owners. In fact, involvement of larger transnational corporations on the Estonian business landscape has resulted in more detailed procedures and reporting rules.

In recent years the need for more innovative, high value-added business models has emerged as a result of economic convergence with the European Union. It can be anticipated that development towards a knowledge-based economy may in future again lead to higher demand for developer-type managers, especially as partners for risk capitalists that invest into high tech ventures.

3.3 Corporate Governance Challenges in Small Growing Enterprises

Redefining the role of owner-entrepreneur in the business growth process of a small enterprise is an essential issue in the corporate governance discourse. In addition to different aims of managers and owners, asymmetric information can also lead to conflicts between these two roles. These reasons are reflected in the research that sees separation of ownership and control as a reason decreasing business performance (Andres 2008).

Ramdani and Witteloostuijn (2012) have used data from the World Bank Enterprise Surveys that also included Estonia among 51 countries in other to establish the likelihood of firm bribery depending on the shareholder-manager relationship. They have found that the principal-owner gender and the equity share of the largest shareholder have significant impact on likelihood of trying to bribe public officials in order to get some advantages for owner's business. A conclusion based on samples from all countries is that male principal-owners are more likely to be engaged in bribery than female principal owners. The effect of separation of ownership and control was not established but enterprises where the largest shareholder has large equity share have lower bribery likelihood.

Information about firm bribery cases in Estonia has been mainly linked to state procurements, where large construction companies have been involved, and transactions for exchanging plots in Natura 2000 environment protection areas to land in city areas that are interesting for real estate developers.

In Estonia formal procedures of setting up a company are not too complicated. A limited liability company (Osaühing), the typical legal form for a start-up company, can be registered by filling in online application at the Company Registration Portal http://www.rik.ee/en/company-registration-portal without physically visiting public notary or the Commercial Register's office. Identity of the applicant-company founder is proved with the help of ID-card or by using an online banking link.

Our group work during training workshops for entrepreneurs have however revealed several cases, where founders of a new venture did not anticipate growth-related challenges for corporate governance when they were in hurry to register their limited liability company. They used the standard statutes template and made only minimalistic agreement between founders that did not specify how to solve situations, where one of founding partners wants to exit the company or there is no consensus how to invest for company growth. When using the standard statutes template, such founders did not discuss which articles should be customized in order to set the qualified majority requirement for some strategic decision. Insufficient regulations in the company statutes and missing agreements between founders usually lead to conflicts if company is in crisis but also at some stage of rapid business growth. Rapid growth usually assumes additional investments. Often additional owners are needed in order to expand to foreign markets. When making growth-related decisions, situations where consensus-seeking does not succeed have to be regulated beforehand.

Cases of participants discussed during training events have also indicated that involving relatives and friends to key positions in growing companies have often lead to conflicts if these persons appear to have limited management skills for a larger company. Family-owned businesses have in Estonia better track record in gardening and retailing compared to knowledge-intensive business fields.

In Estonia the number of portfolio investors and serial entrepreneurs is still limited and for this reason owners that have hired a managing director for their growth enterprise tend to have difficulties in differentiating their governance role as the principal form the management of daily operations that they should delegate to the managing director as their agent. Many experienced entrepreneurs started their first business during the collapse of the Soviet command economy are now close to the retirement age. They do not want to be involved any more in daily business. Their first business success experience 20–25 years ago is however based on such interpretations of the principle "trust but control", where control was accomplished through direct observation of employee activities and the owner was constantly generating ideas for using new "windows of opportunity" as an early mover. Such experience drives owners to interfere to daily operations instead of defining long-term priorities and resources for company value growth.

3.4 Corporate Governance Development as Learning by Doing

New private ventures were created by local entrepreneurs for the first time experiencing the role of private owners. That has resulted in learning by doing processes, where corporate governance and strategic management practices are shaped by the changing institutional framework and business environment but also by conflicting priorities and role models of managers and owners at different stages of the transition to the market economy and internationalization of the Estonian corporate structures. Since the year 2000 retained earnings in Estonia have been exempt from profit taxation. The aim has been to stimulate investments through availability of internally accumulated funds. Frankel (2012) has presented this taxation rule as one example of new approaches that small countries can teach to the world. Such taxation has supported organic growth on new ventures that have growth potential, need to re-invest their profit and have consensus of majority owners to follow long-term growth strategy. Management does not have motivation to manipulate profits downwards in their financial accounting statements in order to decrease profit taxation of company as only dividend payments are taxed.

Hobdari et al. (2010) have used a representative sample of Estonian enterprises for analysing liquidity constraints of business organisations. They have concluded that firms owned by insiders, especially by non-managerial employees, are more prone to be liquidity constrained in their investment rates than other ownership structures.

A typical situation that has inhibited strategic efforts in many locally owned growing ventures is that founder-owners of the limited liability company keep jobs in the management hierarchy that do not correspond to their competencies in a growing company. The question when it is the right time for an entrepreneurial owner to pass his managerial tasks to a professional manager is also topical in advanced market economies. In a new market economy one could however more often find cases, when in the role of owner-founders of a new company or partners in the privatization process were friends or persons that happened to be at the right place in the right time. Management jobs were distributed as a compensation for commitment of founders and following the need to fill in the gaps in the management team at the first stage of company development. New strategic challenges of growing companies and more fierce business competition have revealed mismatch between being one of important owners and at the same time a bad performer compared to other members of the management team. During recent years a solution in many companies has been that all key owners, including excellent and bad management performers, give up their membership in the management board and move to the supervisory board. That will distance them more clearly from the operations management and set the supervisory board to the role of the team that has to assess the performance and strategic ideas of non-owner managers without the tough job of assessing the managerial performance of other owner-founders of the company. However, supervisory boards are at present a voluntary governance body for limited liability companies and many entrepreneurs in growing medium-sized companies prefer to avoid the two-tier corporate governance bureaucracy if possible.

Business opportunity exploitation includes business concept development, business planning and business creation (Ardichvili et al. 2003). Growth opportunities mean also business risks. The mainstream theory of corporate governance views one of the main problems of agency relationship in frequent risk aversion of the executive managers and too short-term interests, at least as compared to the owners. In advanced market economies the owners have dispersed their risks between the various objects of investment but the manager has invested his entire human capital in the enterprise where he works, meaning that his risks are not dispersed. He has significantly more to lose than the owners-shareholders. Several reasons allow presuming that such managerial risk mechanism need not dominate in Estonia. A special survey carried out by the Estonian Business School established that in case of approximately 40 % of the surveyed enterprises, the manager desired a higher level of risk than that accepted by the owner when assessing new business opportunities. In other words, the above problem of agent relationship was not observed. The risk aversion of top managers could be observed more in case of enterprises owned by domestic rather than by foreign capital, in case of very young and very old managers and less in case of middle-aged managers (Elenurm et al. 2008).

3.5 Corporate Governance in Innovative Knowledge-Based Ventures

Mainela and Puhakka (2011) suggest that international new venture emergence assumes an entrepreneurial process that involves four major elements that link networks to international business opportunities: venture drafting, resourcing, learning & creation and finally legitimizing the emerging venture. The "blue ocean" concept (Kim and Mauborgne 2005) explains business opportunities of value innovations that focus on new markets and on new ways of satisfying client needs not yet discovered by competitors stacked in fierce competition in existing "red oceans". The innovative entrepreneur faces the choice of developing in his/her entrepreneurial venture core competences sufficient for implementing a value innovation or relying on complementary core competences of business partners and customers as co-creators of changes. A challenge for knowledge-based new ventures is to integrate technological, international marketing and governance competencies of entrepreneurs and risk capital provides.

Research on relationships between export activities, local managers' independence and decision-making in five new member states of the European Union that used the data set of 434 foreign-invested firms in Poland, Hungary, Slovenia, Slovakia and Estonia demonstrated the positive impact of foreign investor's ownership and control over strategic decisions on the export intensity (Filatotchev et al. 2008). Allen and Aldred (2011) criticized Nölke and Vliegenthart's (2009) view that Central and East European market economies are mainly in the role of assembly platforms based on innovations that are made at transnational corporation's headquarters and then transferred to CEE subsidiaries. They present a more optimistic vision of the role of these subsidiaries in using the tacit knowledge for innovation and stress the benefits of spillover from the foreign-owned subsidiary to host-country firms that try to move to higher value-added activities in international networks. Allen and Aldred (2011) also raise the question about the role of banks in financing investment and export activities under different corporate governance models. They argue that in the German and other co-ordinated market economies banks provide "patient capital" for long-term strategic initiatives of client companies, have more detailed understanding of the investment and strategic decisions of companies and are represented in company supervisory boards. At the same time banks are reluctant to support strategies that aim to offer new products to new markets and prefer to support incremental up-grading of products. In liberal market economies such as USA and UK, company managers feel more the pressure of owners to attain short-term business targets of institutional investors.

Technology-based companies from a small open economy already at early growth stage have a challenge to obtain credibility among international clients. Regio is a company in Tartu, second largest city in Estonia located at the southern part of the country. Their aim is to become a premium provider of location-based solutions in the Eastern Hemisphere for telecom, transport and infrastructure sectors. Regio has four fields of activity: mapping, geospatial data, geographical information systems and mobile positioning. Regio was founded in 1990. As a matter of fact their first business action started even earlier, in 1989, when Regio as an university spin-off (having unique combination of roots from Tallinn Pedagogical University and Tartu University) was the first to publish the map of Estonian roads that was not deliberately distorted. Due to security considerations of Soviet authorities it had not been possible to publish non-distorted maps before the Soviet empire started to collapse. The evolution of the company since 1990 has gone through different corporate governance stages: at the beginning an university spin-off, then an employee-owned company, followed by the venture capital-fuelled company stage, after that being part of an international stock exchange listed technology corporation, and finally, management buy-out. In the years 1994–1998 Regio team was involved in developing Estonian geoinformatics standards and development concepts. It was a period of stable sales growth, many innovative ideas and "club spirit". This led the founders of the company to the logical conclusion that all "club members" (i.e. employees) should become also shareholders. However, as shares were given free of charge to employees and the share distribution was the sole discretion of founders without clear criteria, Regio did not become a typical partnership. In order to get resources to speed up sales and profit growth and to transform Regio from the "club" to a "normal company", the Baltic Small Equity Fund was involved in 1998 as an investor. The risk capital owners remained fairly passive, but the fund was of great help when it came to negotiating in the second round of financing. Risk capital could open doors to new contacts and networks. Regio management understood that it is not possible to finance mobile technology sales all over Europe only by using the Estonian capital. The problem was not only about limited capital, it was also about image. They started to think how to use the image of Finland as an innovative country to enter the global technology market from a unknown country at the edge of Europe. It was decided to sell Regio to a Finnish company Done Corporation that had been listed at the Helsinki stock exchange. The crises however hit both information and mobile technology sectors at the global scale in the year 2000 and the Finnish parent company soon faced bankruptcy. Regio management offered to the trustees of the bankrupt's estate management buy-out solution and in 2002 Regio again became an independent company owned by Estonian capital. Although Done Corporation was not sustainable, being part of this venture gave to Regio credibility to offer its services to Ericsson and other large international customers. This client capital appeared to be valuable for business growth and international recognition of Regio services after 2002. Regio case demonstrates that the role of ownership structures in accessing global markets. Technology-driven companies need smart capital but also ownership structures that enable co-operation with large international customers and integration to some international value chain for developing and applying advanced technologies. Traditional principal-agent thinking does not reflect fully such situations. In high-tech companies entrepreneurs-developers in the role of managers are actively looking for new owners that would add value to their venture.

During the first decade of the twenty-first century development of technology-based start-up firms has raised some new corporate governance issues. Estonians were active in developing Skype internet phone application. Although Scandinavians had the key role in commercializing Skype and selling it to eBay, Estonian developers also received substantial capital gains from this transaction. Ambient Sound Investments (ASI) was established in 2003 as an equal partnership by four founding engineers at Skype Technologies to hold a minority stake in Skype. At the end of 2005 ASI sold its stake to eBay and now operates as a private investment vehicle. Today they are a team of about ten people managing 100 million Euros of the partners' assets and growing an independent investment vehicle spanning multiple generations. They consider themselves more as a "family trust' than a typical venture capital firm" Although ASI partners themselves have strong track record of building cutting-edge P2P networks, they declare that they are not constrained by a particular industry focus and are ultimately free to invest in the best people and ideas from different business fields. However, so far they have demonstrated investment skills mainly in such fields, where understanding internet and telecommunication technologies has enabled them to represent smart capital in these particular fields. In September 2012 ASI, together with co-investors the Estonian Development Fund and Caplia Invest announced that they had successfully realized the exit of one of their first risk capital investments, Modesat Communications, assets of which were acquired by Xilinx, a World leader in the programmable logic devices sector. The deal entailed the sale of substantially all of Modesat's assets (http://www.asi.ee/company).

The case of Ambient Sound Investments demonstrates how technology-driven developers can move to the role of risk capitalists. But it also draws attention to the need to prepare entrepreneurs in start-up ventures for presenting the potential of their team to potential risk capitalists and for co-operation with more than one smart capital provider in order to access global markets and to find the right position in the global value chain.

3.6 Corporate Governance and Crisis Management

Crisis challenges the public's sense of safety, values and appropriateness (Sapriel 2003). The failure to manage crisis effectively leads to even more risk-laden eventualities for the organization and its stakeholders (Ulmer et al. 2007). Earlier research on the Swedish financial crisis of the early 1990s and later has demonstrated that severe results of crisis for companies were caused by overconfidence, control illusion, and herd mentality but also by shortcomings in management and corporate governance (Fromlet 2012).

In 2008, 67 interviews were conducted in Estonian companies in order to study crisis management in Estonia. The companies were from various industries, with different sizes and ages – 20.6 % of the companies had 1–10 employees, 16.2 % had 11–25 employees, 16.2 % had 26–100 employees, 20.6 % had 101–500 employees, 25.0 % had more than 500 employees. According to industry, 25.0 % were from production, 25 % from trade, 11.8 % from consultation, 8.8 % from banking, 1.5 % from telecommunications, 2.9 % from entertainment, 7.4 % from the public sector, 2.9 % from repair and transport and 4.4 % from services companies. In 35.3 % of companies the top manager of the company answered the questions. The content analysis was done using interviews in order to find types of crisis that companies have faced. Almost half (41.8 %) of the crises in companies in 2008 were connected to human resources, reputation and economics were both crises for 23.9 % of companies (Alas et al. 2010b). Even in 2008 lack of qualified labor was seen among main situations, where crisis management is needed in a company and deteriorating global financial situation and market demand was not seen as the

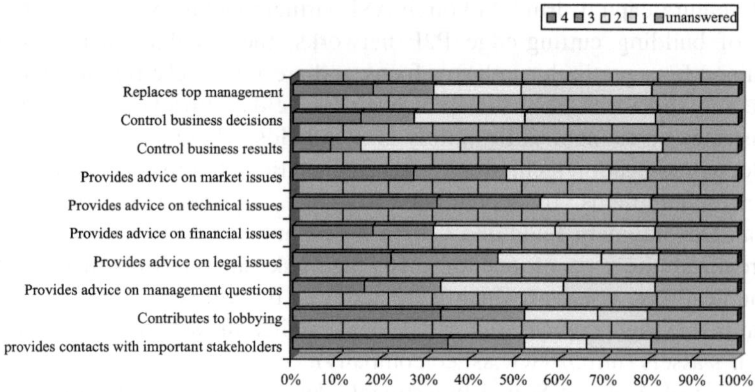

Fig. 1 Contributions by the supervisory board to different issues (1 = significant contribution . . .4 = does not deal with this)

main determinant of crisis management. Only a few companies had adopted a profound proactive crisis management strategy at that time. Figure 1 indicates the contribution made by the supervisory board. Most attention was paid to the firm's business results, next came business decisions and then replacing the top management.

After 7.5 % GDP growth in 2007, Estonian GDP declined 4.2 % in 2008 and 14.1 % on 2009. In 2010 there was moderate growth 3.3 % and in 2011 Estonian GDP growth was the highest in the European Union, 8.3 % (Eurostat 2013). Owners in an economy so dependent on international markets should be able to forecast risks created by decline of foreign markets and make sound decision for strengthening the capital base of the company in order to be prepared for sharp sales decline.

Main banks in Estonia belong to Nordic banking corporations and remained well-capitalized during the financial crisis. Estonian government did not need to bail out banks. Estonian policy makers and public opinion have during the global financial crisis and euro crisis become more aware of the contribution good corporate governance makes to financial market stability, investment and economic growth. As companies play a pivotal role in our economies and we rely increasingly on financial institutions to manage personal savings and secure retirement incomes, good corporate governance is important to broad growing segments of the population.

4 Conclusions

Estonian privatization process in general supported involvement of foreign investors in shaping the corporate governance landscape and facilitated restructuring of companies. There is no strong historical tradition of employee share ownership in

Estonia and as the result during years after privatization the dominance of owner-managers and outside foreign and domestic owners has mainly directed changes in the corporate governance practices. When discussing protection of small shareholders, challenge is the dominance of large block owners that simultaneously are top managers.

The German two-tier corporate governance model has been implemented already in 1990s through the Commercial Code but its application in many small and medium-sized companies has been rather formal as owners have preferred more the role of "hands-on" decision makers and considered two-tier system too slow and complicated for executing their functions in ownership and management. Managers at the same time do not trust the strategic visions of owners that were successful as entrepreneurs during the earlier stages of economic transition. It will take time before a larger number of active owners will emerge that are prepared to implement their ownership functions through corporate governance tools, without desire to be involved in daily management operations. Training and coaching both owners and managers for co-operation can help to align the corporate governance legal framework and practices of boards and supervisory boards. Aligning perceptions concerning reasonable business risks and strategic teamwork both for growth and crisis governance are essential fields of such development activities that also enable action research on corporate governance problems and development priorities. Anticipating future crisis situations are among important skills for professional owners and investors.

A future research field is holistic study of the influence that the global financial crisis has had on corporate governance in Estonia as in a country, where the banking sector did not need any bailout and many companies were able to cut their costs in order to react to the rapid decline in the export demand.

Technology-based new ventures that have to gain credibility at global markets face situations, where the ownership structure influences their credibility for large international customers. Smart capital creates new opportunities but also new challenges for entrepreneurs in Estonia and in other rapidly changing economies. This is an avenue for future research in order to develop new corporate governance approaches for knowledge-based economies.

References

Alas, R., & Tafel, K. (2008). Corporate governance in Estonia. *Corporate Ownership and Control, 5*(1), 296–302.

Alas, R., Elenurm, T., & Tafel-Viia, K. (2010a). Who is driving the change? Corporate governance and organizational change in Estonia. *Journal of Baltic Studies, 41*(1), 23–43.

Alas, R., Gao, J., & Vanhala, S. (2010b). The crisis management in Chinese and Estonian organizations. *Chinese Management Studies, 4*(1), 18–36.

Allen, M., & Aldred, M. (2011). Varieties of capitalism, governance, and high-tech export performance. *Employee Relations, 33*(4), 334–355.

Andres, C. (2008). Large shareholders and firm performance: An empirical examination of founding-family ownership. *Journal of Corporate Finance, 14*, 431–445.
Ardichvili, A., Cardozo, R., & Ray, S. (2003). A theory of entrepreneurial opportunity identification and development. *Journal of Business Venturing, 18*(1), 105–123.
Bedo, Z., Demirbag, M., & Wood, G. (2011). Introducing governance and employment relations in Eastern and Central Europe. *Employee Relations, 33*(4), 309–315.
Bistrova, J., & Lace, N. (2012). Quality of corporate governance system and quality of reported earnings: Evidence from CEE companies. *Economics and Management, 17*(1), 55–61.
Cvelbar, L. K. (2007). The relationship between supervisory board structure and CEO turnover: The empirical evidence of Slovenia'. *Nase Gospodarstvo, 5*(6), 53–62.
Eamets, R., Mygind, N., & Spitsa, N. (2008). The development of employee financial participation in Estonia. *Baltic Journal of Management, 3*(2), 218–231.
Elenurm, T., Terk, E., & Andresoo, J. (2008). Cooperation patterns between capital owners and managers in the strategic management process. Case Estonia. *Corporate Governance: The International Journal of Business in Society, 8*(5), 637–648.
Estrin, S. (1994). Privatization in the transitional economies of Central and Eastern Europe – Issues and progress. *Business Strategy Review, 5*(4), 81–96.
Estrin, S. (2002). Competition and corporate governance in transition. *Journal of Economic Perspectives, 16*(1), 101–124.
Eurostat. (2013). *Real GDP growth rate*. http://epp.eurostat.ec.europa.eu/tgm/table.do?tab=table&init=1&plugin=1&language=en&pcode=tec00115. Accessed 20 Mar 2013.
Filatotcev, I., Stephan, J., & Jindra, B. (2008). Ownership structure, strategic controls and export intensity of foreign-invested firms in transition economies. *Journal of International Business Studies, 39*, 1133–1148.
Financial Supervision Authority. (2005). *Corporate governance recommendations*. http://www.nasdaqomxbaltic.com/files/tallinn/bors/press/HYT_eng.pdf. Accessed 20 Feb 2013.
Foo, J., & Witkowska, D. (2011). The role of corporate governance in transition countries. *International Journal of Latest Trends in Finance, Economic Sciences, 1*(2), 43–53.
Frankel, J. (2012). What small countries can teach to the World. *Business Economics, 47*, 97–103.
Fromlet, H. (2012). Predictability of financial crises: Lessons from Sweden to other countries. *Business Economics, 47*, 262–272.
Gerndorf, K., Elenurm, T., & Terk, E. (1999). *Corporate governance in Estonia, OECD (homepage)*. www.oecd.org/dataoecd/60/36/1931752.pdf, Accessed 6 June 2013.
Hannula, H. (2006). Identifying patterns in ownership changes and their implications for enterprise: Restructuring in the Estonian manufacturing sector. *EBS Review, 1*(21), 76–93.
Hardi, P., & Buti, K. (2012). Corporate governance variables: Lessons from a holistic approach to Central-Eastern European practice. *Corporate Governance, 12*(1), 101–117.
Hodbari, B., Jones, D. C., & Mygind, N. (2010). Corporate governance and liquidity constraints: A dynamic analysis. *Comparative Economic Studies, 52*, 82–103.
Jones, D. C., Kalmi, P., & Mygind, N. (2003). *Choice of ownership structure and firm performance: Evidence from Estonia* (Vol. 7). Helsinki: Bank of Finland, Institute for Economics in Transition.
Kim, W. C., & Mauborgne, R. (2005). *Blue ocean strategy: How to create uncontested market space and make competition irrelevant*. Cambridge, MA: Harvard Business School Press.
Kooskora, M. (2008). Corporate governance from the stakeholder perspective, in the context of Estonian business organizations. *Baltic Journal of Management, 3*(2), 193–217.
Kuznetsov, A., & Kuznetsova, O. (2012). Business legitimacy and the margins of corporate social responsibility in the Russian context. *International Studies of Management and Organization, 42*(3), 35–48.
Mainela, T., & Puhakka, V. (2011). Role for networks in emergence of international new ventures. *International Journal of Entrepreneurial Venturing, 3*(1), 5–25.
Maly, M. (2006). Board structure and competencies after mass privatization – The case of the Czech Republic. *EBS Review, 1*(21), 117–125.

Martynova, M., & Renneboog, L. D. R. (2011). Evidence on the international evolution and convergence of corporate governance regulations. *Journal of Corporate Finance, 17*(5), 1531–1557.

Nölke, A., & Vliegenthart, A. (2009). Enlarging the varieties of capitalism: The emergence of dependent market economies in East Central Europe. *World Politics, 61*(4), 670–702.

OECD. (2011). *Corporate governance in Estonia 2011*. Corporate Governance, OECD Publishing. doi.org/10.1787/9789264119079-en

Raadik, A. (2008). *Investors' and issuers' awareness of the corporate governance recommendations*. Master's Thesis, Estonian Business School.

Ramdani, D., & Witteloostuijn, A. (2012). The shareholder-manager relationship and its impact on the likelihood of firm bribery. *Journal of Business Ethics, 108*(4), 495–507.

Rozman, R. (2006). Some organizational corporate governance issues in Slovenian enterprises. *EBS Review, 1*(21), 104–116.

Sapriel, C. (2003). Effective crisis management: Tools and best practices for the new millennium. *Journal of communication management, 7*(4), 348–355.

Senge, P. (1990). *The fifth discipline, the art and practice of the learning organization*. London: Random House.

Steger, T., Tafel, K., & Alas, R. (2006). *Good corporate governance in transition countries – A comparison of experts' perceptions in East Germany, Estonia and Hungary*. Berlin: IFSAM VIIIth World Congress. http://www.ctw-congress.de/ifsam/download/track_8/pap00719.pdf. Accessed 6 June 2013.

Tafel, K., Terk, E., & Purju, A. (2006). Corporate governance in post-socialist countries – Theoretical dilemmas, peculiarities, research opportunities. *EBS Review, 1*(21), 7–26.

Tafel-Viia, K., & Alas, R. (2009). Differences and conflicts between owners and top managers in the context of social responsibility. *Engineering Economics, 4*(64), 86–94.

Terk, E. (2000). *Privatisation in Estonia: Ideas, process, results*. Tallinn: ETI Publishing.

Terk, E., & Elenurm, T. (1996). Employee ownership in Estonia. Conclusions from case studies. In N. Mygind & P. N. Pedersen (Eds.), *Privatization and financial participation in the Baltic countries. Case studies* (pp. 1–15). Copenhagen: Copenhagen Business School.

Ulmer, R. R., Sellnow, T. L., & Seeger, M. W. (2007). *Effective crisis communication: Moving from crisis to opportunity*. Thousand Oaks: Sage.

Audit Committees in Polish Supervisory Boards: Common Practice and New Challenges

Izabela Koładkiewicz

Abstract The objective behind this chapter is an assessment of the functioning of audit committees in the supervisory boards of companies listed on the Warsaw Stock Exchange in Poland. It is made up of three parts. The first encompasses the history of the origins of the audit committee in Polish supervisory boards and presents its basic characteristics – i.e. size, composition, and scope of activities. The second part presents the opinions and views of 34 interviewed board members with respect to their experiences in connection with the functioning of audit committees. The third part of the chapter is a presentation of the results of an analysis of recommendations relating to the functioning of audit committees as found in the post–crisis versions of corporate governance best practice in Western Europe.

The conducted analysis indicates that under Polish conditions the audit committee continues to be a young institution. Among key benefits tied with its activities is its role as an institution bringing order and improving the efficiency of the supervisory board, which is especially important in the case of large boards.

In spite of the observed benefits provided by the presence of an audit committee, the rate of the process of its spreading among Polish boards is slow.

As to the challenges that must be faced by audit committees in Poland, among them is the need to pass into a higher level of maturity expressed in the character and complexity of performed tasks.

I. Koładkiewicz (✉)
Center for Management Studies, Kozminski University, 57/59 Jagiellonska St., 03-301 Warsaw, Poland
e-mail: izabela@kozminski.edu.pl

S. Boubaker and D.K. Nguyen (eds.), *Corporate Governance in Emerging Markets*, CSR, Sustainability, Ethics & Governance, DOI 10.1007/978-3-642-44955-0_12,

1 Introduction

Most present day assessments on the usefulness of an audit committee in the life of the supervisory board (improvement in the quality of its work) and of the company itself (improvement in financial reporting and increased trust on the part of investors) are dominated by positive opinions. Confirmation may mainly be found in the experience of the audit committees of Anglo–Saxon countries such as the United States. However, American observations clearly demonstrate that the key impulse in transforming an audit committee into an effective body was the introduction of "hard law" regulating its operations. The Sarbanes–Oxley Act (SOX) passed by the United States Congress in 2002 incorporated the soft recommendations developed in 1999 by the Blue Ribbon Committee (BRC), an organization made up of representatives of the NYSE and NASD, which were intended to increase the effectiveness of audit committees (Myers and Ziegenfuss 2006, pp. 48–49). It should also be stressed that the United States is not alone in such moves. Recent times have seen major world capital markets taking action to incorporate "soft" best practice defining the framework and operations of audit committees into legal regulations with increasing frequency. An analysis of the character of regulations defining the tasks and principles of the functioning of audit committees in the boards of companies listed on the stock exchanges of 40 of the world's largest capital markets indicates that its presence in those boards has become obligatory in 31 countries. This was achieved through code/legislative solutions or stock market regulations governing the given market. In the case of the European Union, the passage in 2006 of Directive 2006/43/EC on the Statutory Audit of Annual Accounts and Consolidated Accounts was of particular significance in this process. Most member states of the European Union have applied this Directive (Fichtner 2010, p. 233).[1]

The audit committee, like the board of directors/supervisory board, is a rather difficult object to examine. It is often compared to a "black box." What goes in and what the final outcome of its work should be is known. However, relatively little is known about the processes going on within it (Spira 1998, p. 30). To a great extent this is the result of the fact that access is problematic. The main barrier is the sensitivity of information. Among the main reasons for reluctance on the part of board members in sharing knowledge relating to their work is the fear that such information might have a negative impact on their relations with investors or with other board members. A significant role is also played by fear of increased risk of legal action by shareholders as a result of the divulging the inner workings of board operations. Apprehension against being sued by the other board members also

[1] At the time when J. R. Fichtner was conducting his research, the presence of an audit committee was obligatory in the supervisory boards of companies in Spain (introduced in 2002), Austria (2006), Portugal (2006), Finland (2008), France (2008), the Netherlands (2008), Romania (2008), Great Britain (2008), Belgium (2009), the Czech Republic (2009), Denmark (2009), Germany (2009), Greece (2009), and Poland (2009) (Fichtner 2010, p. 234).

limits any tendency to share information with researchers about what goes on during board meetings (Payne et al. 2009, p. 705).

In spite of these limitations and difficulties, each successive year sees an increase in the number of studies devoted to audit committees and with them growth in knowledge about them. To a great extent, the results received indicate its usefulness to boards. These observations have been confirmed by the results of studies carried out by Bédard and Gendron (2010) who conducted an analysis of 113 articles on the effectiveness of audit committees published over the years 1994–2008 in 18 scientific journals. Their analysis showed that the results of research mostly indicated the usefulness of such committees as compared with results showing an absence of influence or a negative impact on processes within the sphere of committee responsibility (Bédard and Gendron 2010, p. 199).

Research results also indicate that the audit committee has recently undergone significant changes. These modifications should be assessed positively. It is thanks to them that the process of transformation of some committees from mere ornaments of the board into institutions conducting active monitoring of critical spheres of company activity has been observed. A key change shown by the results of the research is without any doubt an increase in specialized expertise in the realms of finance and accounting as held by members of the audit committee. In its turn, this expertise serves as a basis for the primary activity of the audit committee, which is the directing of questions to collaborating actors – the managerial staff, external auditors, internal auditors, and the internal control staff. This questioning as well as the committees' ability to verify received results is mainly intended to guarantee the reliability and quality of company financial results (Cohen et al. 2010, p. 752, p. 754). However, not all audit committees are going down the above road. A certain group has no intention of changing and continues to remain an adornment serving as an adjunct to the board without bringing with it any added value.

In light of the fact that topical literature is dominated by the results of analyses of the experiences of audit committees that are primarily found in economically developed countries, an interesting challenge is a look at experience in the area of the development and activities of such institutions in developing countries. Thus, it is the audit committees that are active in Polish supervisory boards that are at the focus of this chapter.

The aim of this chapter is to assess the functioning of audit committees in supervisory boards listed on the Warsaw Stock Exchange (WSE). This investigation encompasses two components:

- An assessment of the current practice of audit committees in the supervisory boards of companies listed on the WSE, including the identification of factors determining their effectiveness as well as an indication of challenges facing them, and
- An assessment of the scope to which Polish audit committees are keeping pace with European reforms contained in post–crisis versions of corporate governance best practice as well as whether the practice of Polish committees is similar to challenges faced in economically developed countries, where the

baggage of experience in the realm of corporate governance is decidedly greater than in Poland.

Data from primary as well as secondary sources have been used in preparing this chapter. Empirical materials for analysis were received through interviews that were conducted with 34 respondents, members of the supervisory boards of 27 companies listed on the WSE. The interviews were conducted between April and June of 2011. The average duration of each interview was 1 h.

The basic secondary information source consisted of reports on studies conducted by professional companies as well as the results of the work of Polish researchers.

This chapter is made up of three parts. The first encompasses the history of the origins of the audit committee in Polish supervisory boards and presents its basic characteristics – i.e. size, composition, and scope of activities.

The second part presents the opinions and views of 34 interviewed board members with respect to their experiences in connection with the functioning of audit committees. The weight of these experiences is linked to the fact that the companies on whose boards the respondents sit are major listed companies in terms of capitalization (the top 40). This translates into the level of complexity of the functioning of those companies as well as just how complicated the challenges faced by their boards, including its committees, actually are.

At the center of attention of interviewed board members are matters relating to the functioning of audit committees in those boards:

- An assessment of the usefulness of the audit committee, including benefits stemming from its establishing in the board, and
- Factors prerequisite to effective action on the part of the audit committee.

The third part of the chapter is a presentation of the results of an analysis of recommendations relating to the functioning of audit committees as found in the post–crisis versions of corporate governance best practice in Western Europe. They form the starting point for comparisons of Polish experience in audit committees and the expectations articulated with respect to audit committees on mature capital markets.

The chapter ends with a summary of current audit committee experience subject to Polish conditions and an indication of successive challenges facing them.

2 The Audit Committee in Poland

2.1 Audit Committees in Poland: Legal Regulations

The watershed year in the process of implementing the audit committee in Polish supervisory boards was 2009. The determining factor was the passage of the Act of May 7 2009 on Certified Public Accountants and Their Professional Associations,

Entities Empowered to Audit Financial Reports, and Public Oversight (Act on Auditors). In line with its provisions, entities of public interest, such as listed companies, must have an audit committee established as a part of their supervisory board; it is to be composed of members of that board (Article 86.1.). The basic determinant of its creation is the size of the board, where the threshold is set at five members. In cases in which the board is made up of five members, the tasks of the audit committee may be entrusted to the board itself (Article 86.3.). Prior to the introduction of the above Act, only writers of corporate governance best practice saw the need for the establishing of audit committees in Polish boards. That need was first articulated in the recommendations of 2005 (the second version of Polish best practice). The authors advocated the establishing of at least two committees in the board – i.e. an audit committee and a remuneration committee – whose tasks should be detailed in the bylaws of the supervisory board (CGF 2004, p. 7). They also recommended that "at least two independent members and at least one member holding qualifications and experience in accounting and finance" (Principle #28) be on the audit committee (CGF 2004, p. 8).

As time passed, recommendations suggesting the creation of committees in the board were "relaxed" with respect to the number of committees and the number of independent members forming them. January 2008 marked the approval of a third version of corporate governance best practice under the title of "Best Practice for Companies Listed on the WSE." This time, the authors only recommended that in establishing audit committees in boards, their composition "should include at least one member independent of the company and other entities with significant links to the company and hold competencies in the area of accounting and finance. In companies where the supervisory board is made up of the minimal number of members required by law (5), the tasks of the committee may be performed by the supervisory board" (Principle #III.7.) (WSE 2007, p. 10). At the same time, as a source of information on guidelines relating to the tasks and functioning of audit committees, the above version of best practice made reference to a document entitled "Commission Recommendation of 15 February 2005 on the role of non–executive or supervisory directors of listed companies and on the committees of the (supervisory) board" in its Attachment No. I (Principle #III.8.) (WSE 2007, p. 10).

Currently, matters related to the manner of appointing members to the committee as well as the scope of audit committee tasks is regulated by Chap. 8 of the Act. In line with its provisions, the basic tasks of the audit committee include (Article 86.7.):

- Monitoring of the financial reporting process;
- Monitoring of the effectiveness of the internal control system, internal auditing, and risk management;
- Monitoring of financial audits;
- Monitoring the independence of the external auditor and entities empowered to audit financial reports.

The legislator was also precise in indicating the scope of jurisdiction of the audit committee, recommending that the supervisory board have a body empowered to audit financial reports as well as for conducting financial audits of the entity, where decisions should be taken by the board as a whole, however (Article 86.8.).

Lawmakers also specified the size of the audit committee, recommending that it be composed of at least three members, including at least one meeting the condition of independence and holding qualification in the field of accounting or financial auditing (Article 86.4.). As to the independent board member, the legislator provided the following criteria defining independence (Article 86.5. and Article 56, Clause 3, Subclauses 1, 3, and 5):

- Holds no shares, stock, or other ownership titles in the entity where that member performs financial audit functions or in any other related entity,
- Has not been a party to bookkeeping or drafting financial reports for the entity where the member performed any financial audit over the past 3 years, and
- Has no spouse, relative, or direct kin to the second degree who is a member of any supervisory, management, or administrative body of the entity.

At the same time, it is worth adding that the above criteria defining the independence of an audit committee member are the same as in the case of auditor/certified public accountant.

In analyzing the functioning of audit committees in Polish supervisory boards, it should also be remembered that the Commercial Company Code, which contains the basic legal regulations defining company operations, lacks any provisions regulating the activities of audit committees. The placement of the audit committee in the board is derived from the Act on Auditors as well as company charters or board bylaws (Domański and Jagielska 2011, p. 20).

In summarizing the characteristics of the legal regulations governing the creation and the scope of activities of audit committees subject to Polish conditions, it should be stated that regulations give it the role of a permanent working group of the board, which in no way restricts the board's freedom in decision–making, where the committee has no powers to act in the name of the company or represent the board with respect to other bodies and entities (Domański and Jagielska 2011, p. 20). The tasks performed by the audit committee are analytic, preparatory, and opinion–generating in nature, where the final decision is taken by the board (Domański and Jagielska 2011, p. 20; Czerniawski and Rapacka 2007, p. 141). Stability and continuity of composition are seen as important factors fostering the work of the committee. This guarantees a steady level of knowledge about the company (Czerniawski and Rapacka 2007, p. 147). It should be stressed that the presence of the committee in the board in no way changes the scope of responsibility of board members, regardless of whether the given member is a member of the audit committee or not.

2.2 *Audit Committee Practice in Poland: Basic Characteristics*

The year 2012 marked 3 years as of the introduction in 2009 of the Act on Auditors. To a great extent, this fact determined the volume and character of experiences stemming from the activities of audit committees in Polish supervisory boards. There can be no doubt that the introduction of this Act forced an increase in the activeness of the boards of listed companies in establishing audit committees.[2] An analysis looking at the presence of audit committees in all boards of WSE listed companies conducted at the end of 2012 showed their presence in only 41 % of the boards. More detailed analysis, taking into account company size as expressed by listing on a stock market index, showed that audit committees were present in all the boards of the largest companies in terms of capitalization listed on the WIG20 (95 %), with the exception of a single WIG20 company board that failed to establish a committee. Research results also demonstrate that as company size diminishes, interest on the part of boards in creating audit committees decidedly drops. Thus, 72 % of WIG40 company boards established audit committees, the figure for WIG80 company boards was only 52 %, while a mere 37 % of companies not listed on any of these indexes decided to take such a step (Szułdrzyński et al. 2013, p. 23).

At this point it is worth adding that the conducted research analyzing the presence of audit committees in listed company boards after the elapse of a year (2010) and 2 years (2011) as of the introduction of the Act shows that levels of committee presence are just slightly lower. Committee presence was observed in almost 40 % of the boards of these companies (Szułdrzyński and Spiechowicz 2012, p. 7 and p. 38). A comparison of the data – 41 % of boards in 2012 and just under 40 % in 2010 and 2011 with audit committees – indicates low dynamics of change. One explanation for this phenomenon might be the fact that the boards of companies listed on the WSE are not particularly populous. Studies conducted by Bohdanowicz (2011, p. 79) show that the average number of members of a supervisory board of a non–financial company listed on the WSE over the years

[2] Research results show that successive versions of corporate governance best practice recommendations for establishing audit committees in boards in 2005 and 2008 did not engender any increased interest on the part of listed company boards. Studies of declarations regarding the application of best practice as submitted in 2005 by 250 companies listed on the WSE showed that Principle #28, which speaks of the establishing of an audit committee and a remuneration committee in the supervisory board, was among the least applied. A total of 165 from among 250 then listed companies declared that they do not apply the principle (Campbell et al. 2006, p. 367). In its turn, an analysis of the application of principles conducted in December 2008, 1 year after the introduction of the modified version of best practice, showed that Principle #III.7. is among the most frequently non–applied principles of "Best Practice for Companies Listed on the WSE" by listed companies. Among the main reasons for failure to apply was primarily difficulties in meeting all conditions –i.e. the presence of an independent member holding expertise in the area of finance and accounting (Gontarek 2008).

2005–2008 was 5.79. This means that five–member boards dominate in such companies. They took the functions and tasks of the audit committee on themselves when the Act on Auditors came into effect.

As to the size of the committees created, the practice of listed company boards in Poland demonstrates that they most often consist of three members, which is in agreement with the minimum recommendations found in the Act of Auditors (Szułdrzyński and Spiechowicz 2012, p. 8). Usually, committee members are people who professionally fill posts on the management boards of other companies or provide independent advisory services (28 %). Members of the scientific community and individual investors are also appointed to audit committees at times (17 %, each). A cause for concern might be the fact that only one out of four members is professionally involved in finance (Szułdrzyński and Spiechowicz 2010, p. 10). There is probably no need to convince anyone of the importance of experience in finance and accounting brought in by members of the audit committee and that it is in fact a key to its effectiveness. Among primary key competencies that should be held by members of audit committees are:

- Proficiency in reading and interpreting financial results;
- Familiarity with financial engineering basics;
- Expertise relating to financial markets;
- Skill in drawing proper conclusions (Dobija et al. 2011, p. 70).

In 2010 the frequency of meetings of the audit committees in boards of listed companies was five. The year 2011 saw a minimal increase to 5.5 meetings (Szułdrzyński and Spiechowicz 2012, p. 18).

To a great extent, it is the scope of activity that determines the maturity of an audit committee. That audit committees in the boards of companies listed on the WSE continue to be young institutions is seen in their concentration on traditional areas – i.e. analysis of financial reports and the reports of auditors/certified public accountants. Monitoring the effectiveness of internal control systems, risk management, internal audits, and financial management in its broad sense continue to be challenges for most (Szułdrzyńki and Spiechowicz 2012, p. 22).

Among areas that continue to require a change in the alignment of powers between the audit committee and the company management is the matter of the commissioning of an external auditor, monitoring that auditor's work, and defining the level of the auditor's remuneration. It is still the management that deals the cards "in this game." However, worth adding is the fact that certain changes are beginning to make their appearance in this area. Among them is the growing tendency to hold regular meetings of the audit committee with the external auditor (Dobija et al. 2011, p. 72).

It may be assumed that the rate at which domestic audit committees mature is, to a great extent, determined by their composition. This primarily concerns the presence of people with expertise and experience that is adequate to meet needs. The results of research conducted in 2011 pointed to positive changes that took place in the make up of Polish audit committees starting with 2010. These certainly include an increase in participation by auditors/certified public accountants and professional board members (Szułdrzyński and Spiechowicz 2012, p. 9). Thus, it may be assumed that the improvement in the professionalism of audit committees in Poland is going in a desirable direction.

There is a cause for concern in the context of performance of audit committee tasks, however. The Act on Auditors does not guarantee, by way of legislative obligation, the presence on the board of members qualified in the fields of accounting and financial audits in cases when that board decides not to establish an audit committee and, instead, assigns its tasks to the board as a whole. That requirement only appears with respect to the audit committee (Szułdrzyński and Spiechowicz 2010, p. 5). This makes it possible for a situation to exist whereby a board performing the duties of an audit committee has no member with expertise and experience in the above areas (Szułdrzyński et al. 2013, p. 24). This is a significant problem, as 59 % of the boards of companies listed on the WSE in 2012 had not established any audit committee. This means that the entire five–member board of these companies fills the function of an audit committee. At this point it should be added that failure to establish an audit committee in the supervisory board is beginning to be seen by capital market participants, including by the supervisory boards themselves, as a significant risk factor (Deloitte et al. 2012, p. 12).

The list of problems that Polish audit committees must tackle as seen by members of listed company boards includes a lack of time on the part of committee members to perform their tasks (62 % of indications in 2010 and over 70 % in 2011) and a dearth of specialists with the relevant competencies and experience in the area of accounting, internal audits, and risk management (40 % of those interviewed in 2010) (Szułdrzyński and Spiechowicz 2010, pp. 26–27; Szułdrzyński and Spiechowicz 2012, p. 5 and p. 33). The reason identified behind the difficulties in attracting suitable specialists to fill positions as audit committee members is unsuitable remuneration for compensating a dual–function board member. At this point it should be added that most chairmen and members of audit committees in Poland are not compensated for their work on the audit committee (Szułdrzyński and Spiechowicz 2012, p. 5 and p. 33).

As to the requirements of the Act on Auditors relating to the independence of an audit committee member, only approximately 20 % of respondents in 2010 and 2011 saw this as a factor restricting the development of audit committees in Poland (Szułdrzyński and Spiechowicz 2010, p. 26; Szułdrzyński and Spiechowicz 2012, p. 33). In analyzing the question of the independence of a board member it is necessary to bear in mind that independence formally meeting legislative criteria may be insufficient for the member of the board and committee to be truly independent. Decidedly more desirable is independence understood as a "state of the mind," including being guided by one's own views or even intuition. It is primarily the interests of the company that should be at the center of attention of the independent member. Action undertaken by such a member should chiefly be targeted at the good of the company (Dobija et al. 2011, p. 70).

3 Audit Committee Practice Assessment

3.1 Audit Committee Usefulness and Its Key Role

Interesting observations on the operations of audit committees in the supervisory boards of the largest companies listed on the WSE in terms of capitalization (top 40) have been provided thanks to interviews conducted in 2011 with 34 of their members. In practice, all of the examined board members had contact with the committee, either through collaboration, as board members where such a committee existed in the board, or directly as committee members. An analysis of their opinions indicates that in spite of the fact that the audit committee is still a relatively young institution under Polish conditions, their experience with respect to it is decidedly positive. A prevailing opinion among interviewed board members is the conviction that the audit committee is useful for improving the quality of work of the board. This was particularly stressed in the case of major listed companies. The tying of committee presence with company size is explained by the view of respondents of its role as something of a "safety valve" for the board. This safety aspect stems from the structuring of board work, which finds expression in the assigning of defined tasks to members of the audit committee. These assigned tasks also foster a more in–depth and detailed "getting into" the given subject matter by its members. This also leads to growth in the level of transparency in terms of member responsibilities. Interviewed board members see a significant benefit derived from the creation of a several–member audit committee in the board in the form of facilitated mutual communication and a safeguard against undue talk during meetings.

The experience of the respondents shows that, in practice, being active on the audit committee most often means that its members "get their teeth" into such spheres of company operations as financial reporting, internal audits, internal control, risk management, and collaboration with external auditors. In their activities, members of this committee go beyond simple collaboration with the management. Sources of their information also include lower level staff members who work on the above areas directly. This expanded scope of collaboration also finds expression in greater information flow that translates into increased knowledge on the part of audit committee members on what is happening inside the company. This provides a basis for the audit committee to develop solutions that are adequate with respect to company needs. Subsequently, such solutions are presented to the entire board, which should take a look at them in its entirety. Benefits flowing from the subdivision of work in the board as introduced by the committee that are seen by some of the interviewed board members is the achieving of a better level of information for the board as well as better prepared materials for its meetings. One of the persons interviewed summed up the usefulness of the audit committee as follows: "[...] in general, those boards in which committees function actively do better than those where they do not." However, it should be remembered that each board is different. Their needs are different. It is dependent on the board just how the practice of their operations unfolds. This also applies to the audit committee.

The respondents simultaneously stressed that the audit committee can only serve as a body providing support for the board. Its activities should take on the form of recommendations for solutions developed by its members, where decisions should be taken by the board. It is also the board that remains responsible for those decisions.

3.2 Quality Determinants in Audit Committee Operations

The audit committee, like other committees in the board, creates the potential for delving deeper into company matters. Certain conditions must be met in order for the audit committee to benefit from this potential, however. The experience of interviewed board members shows that a key to this potential is the presence on the committee of people with professional competencies that are up to the tasks as well as sufficient time resources. The character of competencies determines the spheres of activity that should be encompassed in the operations of the audit committee (i.e. financial reporting, internal audits, internal control, risk management, and collaboration with external auditors). In practice, this means a need for the composition of the committee to include people with the relevant expertise and experience in the realms of finance and accounting. One respondent underscored the need for selecting audit committee members while keeping in mind their propensity to "work with numbers."

Making sure the committee has people who like and understand numbers, which means people who have skills and experience in the area of finance and accounting, is an important factor defining the quality of committee work. However, this is not the only factor. In the view of many interviewed board members, the basis for success on the part of the committee in performing its tasks is guaranteeing access to a broad spectrum of information to its members, including financial information, information on key risks facing the company, and information on the existing system of risk management and internal control. An important component of the stream of information flowing to the audit committee also includes information on internal audit activity. Such information is vital with respect to spheres monitored by the committee that are a part of its operations.

A successive important factor determining the quality of the work of the audit committee is the availability of time on the part of its members. The question of work outlay required of members pops up often in the views of respondents. Their statements indicate that being a member of an audit committee is tied with a significantly greater workload. This in and of itself signifies a need on the part of its members for more time to devote to it, which stems from not only a need for a greater number of meetings as compared with the number of meetings of the entire board, but primarily of the necessity to review larger volumes of materials relating to diverse spheres of audit committee activities. Moreover, audit committee meetings are not brief. Analysis of the opinions of respondents makes it possible to put forward the conclusion that appropriate reserves of time on the part of members must be treated as one of the major factors prerequisite for efficient operation.

Statements made by interviewed board members indicate that the list of determinants behind effective action on the part of audit committees is not complete when it restricts itself to only the above–mentioned factors. According to them, a factor that without any doubt should find its way onto such a list is the will of committee members to become involved in their work. In its absence, the usefulness of resources such as experience and expertise as brought in by them remains small.

According to the interviewed board members, an important factor fostering the involvement of committee members in committee work is shareholder awareness that they put in greater amounts of work as compared to "single–function" board members. In their view, a basic indication of the understanding of this fact should be the offering of higher compensation for serving two functions. Unfortunately, under Polish conditions, additional remuneration for membership in a board committee is not very common. Interviewed board members decidedly postulate the necessity of implementing changes in this sphere. It might be worth adding that, in their view, the absence of financial compensation for additional work outlay as incurred by audit committee members may be one of the reasons behind the development of audit committees in Polish boards being inadequate in terms of needs.

In identifying other factors limiting the development of audit committees under Polish conditions, the respondents indicated insufficient numbers of board members with the relevant expertise and experience in the realm of finance and accounting.

In concluding this presentation of the opinions and views of the 34 interviewed board members on the functioning of audit committees, worth showing are the limitations and weaknesses that they noted stemming from a committee presence in the board. The possibility of a conflict of interest among members representing various groups of shareholders was also deemed as a primary and significant threat to the results of the work of an audit committee. Moreover, nobody needs convincing that the appearance of a constellation of conflicting interests in this body can significantly upset the effectiveness of its operations. In its turn, this cannot remain without an impact on the quality of work of the board as a whole. Moreover, the list of potential weaknesses of an audit committee as forwarded by respondents included the committee's acceptance of an orientation targeting day–to–day action and the passivity of its members. Ultimately, this can lead to the undertaking by the committee of mock activity. Thus, the board will not feel expected benefits from its presence.

An interesting aspect as seen by the interviewed board members is the "danger" that may be ushered in through the presence of an audit committee in the form of the potential threat of "languor" within the supervisory board. A symptom of this may be the "automatic" acceptance of committee recommendations without any desire on the part of the remaining board members to get involved in the details of the solutions proposed by that committee. The absence of discussions on audit committee recommendations by the board as a whole can significantly lower the effectiveness of committee operations (Fig. 1).

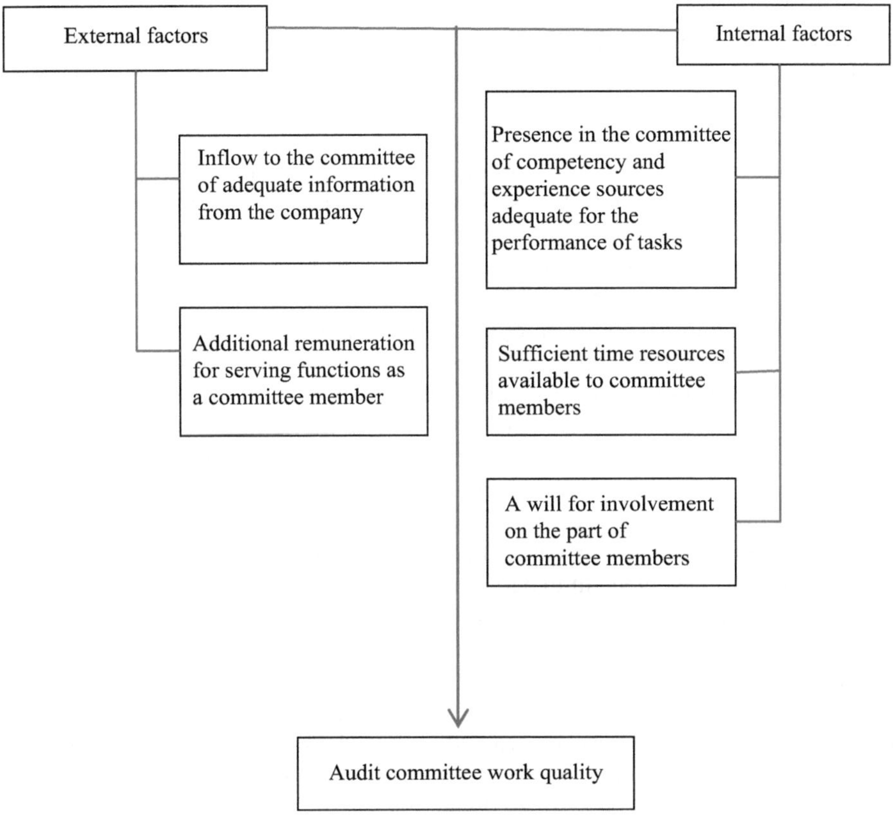

Fig. 1 Factors determining the quality of audit committee activity (Source: Own research)

4 Corporate Governance Best Practice Recommendations in Western European and Polish Practice

An analysis of post–crisis sets of best practice in Western Europe indicates that, in practice, they all include recommendations pointing to a need to create audit committees in boards of directors/supervisory boards.[3] At the same time, some of

[3] The selection criterion for choosing best practice for analysis was its year of appearance on the capital market. Documents that were developed in 2008 and over the successive three post–crisis years were subject to analysis. A successive selection criterion was place of origin. The starting point in choosing countries from Western Europe was their having been encompassed by research by Heidrick and Struggles in 2009. A preliminary analysis of available documents in line with the year of appearance criterion narrowed the sample down to 12 best practice sets. The analyzed pool of documents included recommendations from such countries as Austria, Belgium, Denmark, Finland, France, the Netherlands, Germany, Portugal, Sweden, Switzerland, Italy, and Great Britain.

them allowed for the possibility of their function being served by the whole board. Depending on perceived needs on the given capital market, the authors of the analyzed documents formulated recommendations that ranged from the relatively general to significant levels of detail. The establishing of an audit committee (as well as other committees) in the board is tied with the hope that the committee's presence will have a positive impact on the effectiveness as well as the quality of the work of the board (e.g. AWGfCG 2009, p. 26; KfgS 2011, p. 15; SMA 2010, p. 13; GConGCGC 2010, p. 10; CCG 2011, p. 21). This stems from the fact that the audit committee – a permanent working group in the board – will be specialized in overseeing such sensitive spheres of company activities as finance and accounting, external audits, internal audits, internal control, and risk management. Among key factors determining the meeting of hopes accompanying the committee, there is no doubt that composition is one. It should guarantee independence of action as well as efficient movement among company activities within its jurisdiction. It is agreed that a basic determinant for the latter is not only specialized expertise in the area of finance and accounting, external audits, and internal audits, but also embracing internal control systems and audit management systems. Also strongly accented is the need for members of this committee to have practical experience, which can also be linked to management experience.

As to the size of an audit committee, the most frequently met proposal is that it be made up of at least three members (e.g. BCGC 2009, p. 19; KfgS 2011, p. 15; SMA 2010, p. 14; SCGB 2010, p. 20; CCG 2011, p. 20; FRC 2010, p. 19). Among these there should be at least one independent board member or independent members should make up its majority (this second suggestion is among the most often recommended solutions) (e.g. AWGfCG 2009, p. 26; BCGC 2009, p. 30; KfgS 2011, p. 15; SCGB 2010, p. 20; Economiesuisse 2008, p. 16). As to a member holding specialized expertise and experience, the dominant position was for the composition of the audit committee to have at least one member meeting this competency criterion. It should be stressed that in the case of a board of directors, committee members should be selected out of the group of non–executive board members (e.g. BCGC 2009, p. 30; Economiesuisse 2008, p. 16).

An important aspect of the operations of an audit committee, as seen by the designers of the corporate governance recommendations, is its positioning in the role of an "advisor" formulating proposals and recommendations within its field of tasks on the basis of conducted in–depth analyses. Thus, the committee should propose and consult specific solutions, but the final decision remains with the board. The committee's presence cannot upset the collegiate activities of the board and it also cannot take over the board's responsibility for decisions (albeit, certain best practice authors allow for certain decision–making powers on the part of a committee, Austria and Sweden, for example) (e.g. AWGfCG 2009, p. 26; SCGB 2010, p. 10).

The authors of the analyzed sets of recommendations see the board as responsible for the development and writing down of guidelines for committee operations, including its role and objective, the defining of tasks, and principles of operations as well as the specifying of forms of reporting to the board as a factor facilitating the functioning of the audit committee. These guidelines can take on various forms (such as audit committee charters, board resolutions, committee bylaws, and terms of reference) (e.g. BCGC 2009, p. 19; KfgS 2011, p. 15; SMA 2010, p. 15). However, of particular significance is availability to other members of the capital market. Stockholders and other actors should be equally informed of the composition of the audit committee as well as the results of its activities, including meetings held. A basic tool for communication with the market on the activities and effectiveness of the work of the audit committee is the company annual report, its webpages, and declarations of the application of corporate governance best practice, also referred to as the report on corporate governance (e.g. KfgS 2011, p. 15; AFG 2011, p. 18; CMVM 2010, p. 9; FRC 2010, p. 20; CCG 2011, p. 20).

In summarizing the above presented observations relating to the expectations of mature markets with respect to audit committees as expressed by the authors of corporate governance best practice, it should be stated that the basic factor determining the quality of its activities is considered to be committee composition. Its members should guarantee independence of action as well as hold specialized expertise and practical experience adequate to meet the needs of committee tasks. In juxtapositioning the above expectations with the practice of audit committee operations in Poland, it may be stated that current Polish legal regulations strive in the same direction as Western European recommendations. In line with the Act on Auditors, independence of action by the committee is guaranteed by the presence of at least one independent member holding qualifications in the area of accounting or financial audits. The weight postulated by the designers of best practice for independent committee members has also been noted under Polish conditions. However, greater stress is placed on the independence of views and assessments rather than on the mere meeting of defined criteria for the independence of a member as contained in the Act or found in best practice principles.

The authors of Polish regulations as well as the authors of corporate governance best practice documents were also in agreement that three members is the minimum size of a committee. Their alignment of views is also visible in assigning the audit committee the role of an advisory group recommending solutions, where decision–making is left with the board itself.

Observation of the practice of Polish audit committee operations indicates that the greatest challenge 3 years after the introduction of the Act on Auditors continues to be the guaranteeing of an audit committee composition that is appropriate in terms of competencies. A significant restriction in this respect is the limited resources of board members holding competencies and experience in the area of finance and accounting. Yet another barrier under Polish conditions is that not providing remuneration for serving as a member of the committee remains commonplace.

5 At What Point of Development Are Polish Audit Committees?

In summarizing the above–presented collection of Polish experiences in the area of audit committee activities in the Polish supervisory boards of listed companies, it is necessary to stress that subject to Polish conditions the audit committee continues to be a young institution. Perceiving it in this way is, to a great extent, determined by the concentration of audit committees on traditional areas such as analysis of financial and auditor's reports. Overseeing the effectiveness of systems for internal control and risk management, internal audits, and broadly understood financial management continue to challenge most Polish audit committees. In spite of the fact that in today's Poland the audit committee is still in its developmental phase, board members who have had contact with such committees, both directly and indirectly, see its usefulness in most cases. However, it must be stressed that there are certain dangers stemming from its presence. Among these the taking on of a role of a ceremonial body and the unthinking acceptance of committee proposals by the remaining members of the board were identified.

Some key benefits tied with the activities of audit committees are its role as an institution bringing order and improving the efficiency of the supervisory board, which is especially important in the case of large boards. The ability of an audit committee to delve into the details of activities that form a central sphere of the company, including the preparing of financial reports, external and internal audits, internal control systems, and risk management systems, increases the sense of safety of the board. This is determined by the ability of committee members to take a more in–depth look at the above spheres, the greater effectiveness of its operations, including easier communication, and usually a greater number of meetings as compared with the board as a whole. However, it should not be forgotten that in addition to the above structural factors, the main determinants of the effectiveness of committee work is for its members to hold competencies and experience in accounting and finance. Another key is the amount of time that they can devote to work on the committee as well as their real desire to get involved in the performance of its tasks. Faced with a lack of desire to act, competencies and time are not enough. Decidedly less weight is applied to the meeting of the criterion of independence of the committee member in line with the definition contained in the Act. Much more importance is placed on a member's independence of views and assessments.

In spite of the observed benefits provided by the presence of an audit committee, the rate of the process of its spreading among Polish boards is slow. Among basic factors retarding it is the limited participation in boards of people holding competencies in the area of finance and accounting. A second important factor limiting the potential for committee development in Polish boards is remuneration, which is presently inadequate with respect to work outlay by its members. Moreover, it should not be forgotten that the multiplicity and complexity of audit committee tasks makes it necessary for its members to have sufficient time resources. Their absence may be an important reason for refusing an invitation to sit on it.

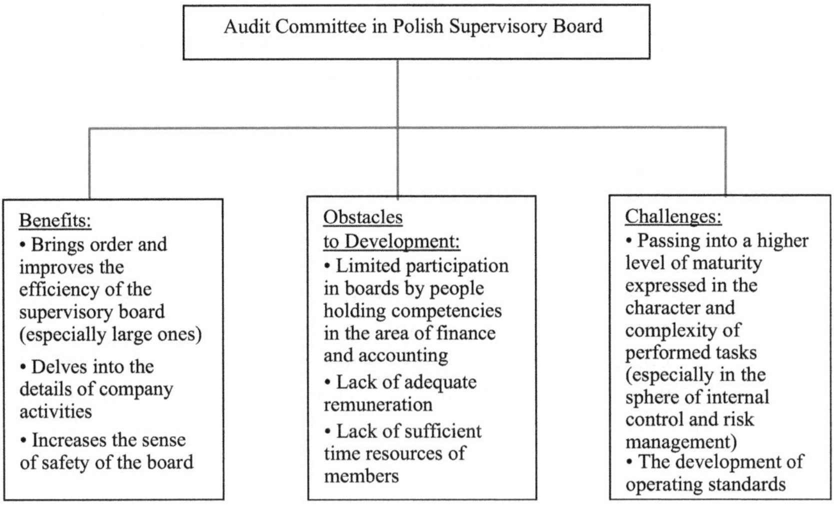

Fig. 2 Audit committee in Poland – benefits, obstacles for development, and future challenges (Source: Own research)

As to the challenges that must be faced by audit committees in Poland, among them is the need to pass into a higher level of maturity expressed in the character and complexity of performed tasks. Among areas that are particularly desirable and where there should be an increase in Polish audit committee activity is the sphere of internal control and risk management. Another important challenge facing Polish audit committees is the need for the development of operating standards that are adequate with respect to needs. (Fig. 2)

6 Conclusion

In summarizing, it is necessary to stress that in the case of Polish supervisory boards made up of more than five members that operate in large and complex companies, the audit committee is seen as an important board working group. Experience to date in the functioning of the audit committee indicates that its usefulness in such boards is appreciated. Its presence makes it possible to introduce a subdivision of labor in the boards as well as make clear assignments of tasks and responsibilities to individual board members. However, an important challenge remaining is the awareness that it is the supervisory board that makes the decisions, while the audit committee only makes recommendations.

It should also be remembered that in the population of companies listed on the WSE in Warsaw there are companies that have not established audit committees. They assign audit committee tasks to the supervisory board as a whole when that board consists of five members (pursuant to the Act on Auditors). It may be assumed that these are smaller companies in which the supervisory function does not have to be expanded in the form of supervisory board committees. A cause for concern is the fact that the Act on Auditors fails to regulate the matter of the guaranteeing of qualifications in the area of accounting and financial auditing when such a solution is used. Thus, an important challenge facing shareholders is undoubtedly the guaranteeing of an appropriate level of competencies and independence on such board making possible the autonomous execution of tasks assigned to audit committees.

There can be no doubt that the audit committee under Polish conditions continues to be an interesting object of study. However, research undertaken should already move beyond better–understood matters, such as descriptions of its characteristics – i.e. committee size, composition, and tasks. Spheres that remain practically unexplored include the dynamics of committee behavior, its relationship with the board and other stakeholders, including the external and internal auditor.

References

Act of May 7, 2009 on Certified Public Accountants and Their Professional Associations, Entities Empowered to Audit Financial Reports, and Public Oversight [in Polish].

AFG – Association Française de la Gestion Financière. (2011). *Recommendations on corporate governance – Revised 2011*. France.

AWGfCG – Austrian Working Group for Corporate Governance. (2009). *Austrian Code of corporate governance*. Austria.

BCGC – Belgian Corporate Governance Committee. (2009). *The 2009 Belgian Code on corporate governance*. Belgium.

Bédard, J., & Gendron, Y. (2010). Strengthening the financial reporting system: Can audit committees deliver? *International Journal of Accounting, 14*(2), 174–210.

Bohdanowicz, L. (2011). Obecność kobiet w organach statutowych polskich spółek publicznych: Perspektywa teorii instytucjonalnej oraz teorii zasobowej", [The presence of women in the charter bodies of Polish public companies: Institutional and resource theory perspectives]. *Master of Business and Administration*, special issue, No. 2(112), 68–87 [in Polish].

Campbell, K., Jerzemowska, M., & Najman, K. (2006). Wstępna analiza przestrzegania zasad nadzoru korporacyjnego przez spółki notowane na GPW w Warszawie w 2005 r. [Preliminary analysis of observations of corporate governance by companies listed on the WSE in 2005]. In S. Rudolf (Ed.), *Tendencje zmian w nadzorze korporacyjnym* [Tendencies for change in corporate governance], Łódź: University of Łódź Press, 357–372 [in Polish].

CCG – Comitato per la Corporate Governance. (2011). *Codice di Autodisciplina* [Corporate Governance Code], Dec 2011. Borsa Italiana, Italy.

CGF – Polish Corporate Governance Forum. (2004). *Best practices in public companies in 2005*. Warsaw.

CMVM – Comissão do Mercado de Valores Mobiliários. (2010). *CMVM Corporate Governance Code 2010 (recommendations)*. Portugal.

Cohen, J., Krishnamoorthy, G., & Wright, A. (2010). Corporate governance in the Post–Sarbanes–Oxley era: Auditors' experiences. *Contemporary Accounting Research, 27*(3), 751–786.

Commission Recommendation of 15 February 2005 on the Role of Non–Executive or Supervisory Directors of Listed Companies and on the Committees of the (Supervisory) Board (2005/162/EC).

Czerniawski, R., & Rapacka, A. (2007). *Pomiędzy prawem a finansami. Poradnik członka rady nadzorczej spółki akcyjnej* [Between the law and finance: A manual for members of joint stock company supervisory boards]. Warsaw: Wolters Kluwer Polska, [in Polish].

Deloitte, Komisja Nadzoru Finansowego [Financial Supervision Authority], Polski Instytut Dyrektorów [Polish Institute of Directors]. (2012). Raport: Współczesna rada nadzorcza 2013 [The contemporary supervisory board report]. Praktyka ładu korporacyjnego w Polsce [The practice of corporate governance]. Deloitte Polska, [in Polish].

Dobija, D., Koładkiewicz, I., Cieślak, I., & Klimczak K. (2011). *Komitety rad nadzorczych* [Supervisory board committees]. Warsaw: Wolters Kluwer Business, [in Polish].

Domański, G., & Jagielska, M. (2011). *Rada nadzorcza w spółce akcyjnej. Powoływanie, kompetencje, funkcjonowanie – aspekty prawne* [The supervisory board in a joint stock company: Establishing, competencies, and functioning – legal aspects]. Warsaw: Wolters Kluwer Polska, [in Polish].

Economiesuisse. (2008). *Swiss code of best practice for Corporate Governance*. Switzerland.

Fichtner, J. R. (2010). The recent international growth of mandatory audit committee requirements. *International Journal of Disclosure and Governance, 7*(3), 227–243.

FRC – Financial Reporting Council. (2010). *The UK Corporate Governance Code*. United Kingdom.

GConGCGC – Government Commission on the German Corporate Governance Code. (2010). *German Corporate Governance Code as amended on May 26, 2010*. Germany.

Gontarek, A. (2008). Best practice: Report on the application of principles [in Polish], presented at the First Year in the Functioning of Best Practices in Companies Listed on the WSE Conference. WSE, Warsaw.

KfgS – Komité for god Selskabsledelse. (2011). *Recommendations on Corporate Governance*. Denmark.

Myers, P. M., & Ziegenfuss, D. E. (2006). Audit committee pre–Enron efforts to increase the effectiveness of corporate governance. *Corporate Governance, 6*(1), 49–63.

Payne, G. T., Bensons, G. S., & Finegold, D. L. (2009). Corporate boards attributes, team effectiveness and financial performance. *Journal of Management Studies, 46*(4), 704–731.

SCGB – Swedish Corporate Governance Board. (2010). *The Swedish Code of Corporate Governance*. Sweden.

SMA – Securities Market Association. (2010). *Finnish Corporate Governance Code 2010*. Finland.

Spira, L. F. (1998). An evolutionary perspective on audit committee effectiveness. *Corporate Governance: An International Review, 6*(1), 29–38.

Szułdrzyński, K., & Spiechowicz, P. (2010). Komitety audytu w Polsce w 2010 roku. Badanie spółek publicznych notowanych na GPW [Audit committees in Poland in 2010: Research into public companies listed on the WSE]. Warsaw: PwC, SEG, PID, and KomitetAudytu.pl, [in Polish].

Szułdrzyński, K., & Spiechowicz, P. (2012). Komitety audytu w Polsce w roku 2011. Badanie spółek publicznych notowanych na GPW [Audit committees in Poland in 2011: Research into public companies listed on the WSE]. Warsaw: PwC, SEG, PID, and KomitetAudytu.pl, [in Polish].

Szułdrzyński, K., Koładkiewicz, I., & Magda, T. (2013). Rady nadzorcze 2013. Skuteczność rad nadzorczych w spółkach publicznych notowanych na GPW badanie 2011–2012 [Supervisory boards 2013: Supervisory board effectiveness in public companies listed on the WSE as examined in 2011–2012]. Warsaw: PwC and AMROP, [in Polish].

WSE – WSE. (2007). *Code of best practice for WSE listed companies*. Warsaw.

Multinationals as Vectors of Corporate Governance Improvement in Emerging Economies in Eastern Europe: A Case Study

Nadia Albu, Ioana Lupu, and Raluca Sandu

Abstract Emerging economies are characterized by a reduced level of transparency and accountability of their business environment. Previous research on corporate governance practices in these economies has highlighted the difficulties of implementing corporate governance codes, the reduced level of compliance with these codes and the reluctance of local businesses to change the manner in which they are managed. In this context, multinational corporations (MNCs) are often perceived as "knowledge transfer" agents contributing to the improvement of local practices. However, the transfer is not unilateral, but it should be rather seen as a process of mutual transformation and adaptation. The aim of this chapter is to investigate the role of multinationals in improving corporate governance practices in emerging economies. We conduct a case study on the privatization of Petrom, the largest company listed on the Romania's Bucharest Stock Exchange (BSE). The case suggests that the alignment of Petrom's practices with the new owner's (Austrian company OMV) vision and strategy, besides contributing to superior performance and accountability of the company itself, led to a significant improvement of the local corporate governance. This is a story of successful privatization which sheds light on the mechanisms of globalization and on how economic progress is obtained.

N. Albu (✉)
The Bucharest University of Economic Studies, Bucharest, Romania
e-mail: nadia.albu@cig.ase.ro

I. Lupu
Rouen Business School, Rouen, France

R. Sandu
SKEMA Business School, Univ Lille 2 Nord de France, Lille, France

S. Boubaker and D.K. Nguyen (eds.), *Corporate Governance in Emerging Markets*, CSR, Sustainability, Ethics & Governance, DOI 10.1007/978-3-642-44955-0_13,

1 Introduction

Despite an increasing body of literature, corporate governance remains understudied in emerging economies. The interest of this case study is justified by the richness of the East-European field. First, this is induced by the variations between countries and even between firms within the same country in adopting good practices (Przbyłowski et al. 2011), and second, by the multiplicity of factors influencing the output of reforms, such as local traditions and regulations (Przybyłowski et al. 2011), informal rules (Boytsun et al. 2011), and general economic change (Megginson and Netter 2001). While initially post-communist economies had similar institutional structure (the command economy), reforms and institutional transformations produced a variety of outcomes (Mickiewicz 2009).

Companies in these economies needed improvements of their governance systems in order to successfully adapt to a market economy. Privatization was one of the means of triggering or supporting these changes. Previous findings suggest a large variation of outcomes of the privatization process, especially in emerging economies (Gołębiowska-Tataj and Klonowski 2009; Omran 2009; Denisova et al. 2012). Issues related to the legitimacy of the privatization process (Denisova et al. 2012), the local rules and regulations (Young 2010) and to firms' characteristics (Black et al. 2012) are put forward in order to explain the variety of privatization's outcomes. However, the manner in which Western practices are transferred (Ezzamel and Xiao 2011), the evolution of corporate governance practices within the local context and the role of privatization in this process (Megginson and Netter 2001) are still insufficiently explored.

The aim of this chapter is to investigate the role of multinationals in improving corporate governance practices in emerging economies,[1] in the context of the privatization of a company based in an ex-communist country. We conduct a case study on Petrom, the biggest oil company in Central and Eastern Europe and the largest company listed on the BSE. Petrom's privatization took place in 2004, when the Romanian Government sold the controlling interest in the company to the Austrian group OMV. While it was at times viewed as a controversial privatization, with political implications and conflicting public opinions, Petrom is now considered to be a successful company, a model of best practices, and embracing such values as ethics, respect, corporate citizenship and a viable management strategy. The case study method was preferred as it allows an in-depth analysis of improvements and transformations undergone by Petrom after its privatization. Additionally, this case is an opportunity to discuss how global corporate governance models and practices are transferred and implemented in an entity, and how this transfer contributes to enhancing cross-national cooperation and co-ordination.

[1] The focus of this paper is on the positive role of MNCs in the evolution of practices in local context, though we recognize that they have also been criticized for their negative impact (cf. Gołębiowska-Tataj and Klonowski 2009; Stiglitz 2008).

Our case study suggests that the alignment of Petrom's practices with OMV's practices and strategy, besides contributing to a superior performance and accountability of the company itself, led to significant improvement of the local corporate governance. As such, this case may constitute a model for other local companies while shedding light on the mechanisms of globalization and economic progress. The transfer of knowledge and practices is not unilateral, but it should be seen rather as a process of mutual transformation and adaptation, as MNCs have to take into account the local context, the local cultural and societal codes. Thus, transitional European countries and MNCs are somehow shaping each other, and in this process they are also shaping and challenging the concept of corporate governance. These results contribute to an emerging literature concerned with how global models and standardization projects interact with the local institutions and practices (Megginson and Netter 2001; Mennicken 2008; Gołębiowska-Tataj and Klonowski 2009; Ezzamel and Xiao 2011).

As privatizations and knowledge transfers from multinationals are still on going in many countries, this study is both relevant and timely, and our results might be of interest to investors, policy makers and other researchers in this area.

The remainder of this chapter is organized as follows: after a literature review on the privatization effects in emerging economies and the role of multinationals, the research methodology is presented. A detailed analysis of the case follows, and the results and conclusion close the chapter.

2 Literature Review

2.1 Privatizations and Corporate Governance in Emerging Economies

Corporate governance is viewed as a set of institutional and market-based mechanisms used to reduce agency costs (Omran 2009), or to improve information flows and increase accountability (Dyck 2001). Corporate governance mechanisms became important in emerging economies, especially in ex-communist ones, where the market-based orientation emerged as a necessity in the business environment. However, difficulties appeared when changes had to be implemented in companies that were used to function in a centralized system.

Most local managers in such countries were found to have communist ideological legacies, little competence and determination to make changes in line with the market-based economy model (Young 2010). Corporate governance systems were absent or very weak immediately after the fall of communism, and sometimes even considered undesirable (Earle and Sapatoru 1994). Djankov and Murrell (2002) find that new entrepreneurial management was implemented in order to generate improvements in the business environment. Privatizations represented another means. Besides the need to promote economic efficiency, privatizations raised revenue for the state and introduced competition (Megginson and Netter 2001).

A variety of privatization strategies was employed in emerging economies, ranging from mass privatization, the creation of private ownership funds, direct sales to domestic and foreign investors, and public offerings (Earle and Sapatoru 1994). However, changes were slow, at least in some countries, and transition took more than a decade. Besides privatization programs, there were legislation changes and alignment with international standards was visible, at least after 2000. In this regulatory framework, corporate governance became an important topic as privatizations stimulated reflection on how entities should be owned and controlled, showing the need for sound rules and practices in order to protect and encourage foreign investment (Becht et al. 2005).

However, the outcomes of these changes varied in emerging economies (Omran 2009; Denisova et al. 2012). On the one hand, corporate governance systems are the result of "the effects of legal systems, business practices, institutions, and past histories of countries" (Costello and Costello 2004, p. 8) and therefore the change process is neither linear nor predictable. On the other hand, imported practices or rules may not lead to the intended outcome because corporate governance models are institution and firm-specific (Boytsun et al. 2011; Black et al. 2012).

Prior research investigated the impact of several factors on the outcome of the privatization process, as well as the effects of governance mechanisms. Some studies suggest that ownership identity, in particular foreign and strategic investors, have a positive impact on firms' performance (Claessens et al. 1997; Dyck 2001; Djankov and Murrell 2002; Omran 2009). Moreover, the existence of foreign owners is a strong indicator of restructuring (Dyck 2001; Djankov and Murrell 2002). Djankov and Murrell (2002) consider that a successful privatization should result in increased efficiency, profitability, and stronger financial health. A positive impact of corporate governance good practices on performance is also assumed (Black et al. 2012; Gołębiowska-Tataj and Klonowski 2009; Djankov and Murrell 2002). The outcomes of the privatization process, may range from no impact on performance to significant improvements (Omran 2009). Also, there are variations in the manner in which organizations respond to change pressures and restructuring plans (Djankov and Murrell 2002). Gołębiowska-Tataj and Klonowski (2009) illustrates how the participation of Western partners in an entity from Poland did not result in improvements in practices and performance, but in ignoring corporate governance principles.

In conclusion, existing literature provides a limited understanding of the changes generated by privatization and their interrelation with changes in the local business environment. Corporate governance, and its link with organizational controls, actions and conflicts, especially in the case of MNCs is a rich area for research. Emerging economies offer a unique opportunity to study the local–global dialectic and how change occurs.

2.2 Multinational Corporations and Practice Transfer

One of the consequences of the privatization process in emerging economies was the entrance of MNCs on local markets. The opportunities triggered by the globalization process and the fall of communism in emerging economies led to increasing attractiveness of these countries to MNCs. The impact of MNCs on local regulations and practices in emerging economies, on global and local economic development has recently become a hot topic in business research (Rugraff and Hansen 2011).

Transitional, East European countries such as Romania have been undergoing major post-communist restructuring projects, which meet the European restructuring industrial project, with cross-border foreign direct investment representing an important mechanism of the Single Market project. In this context, MNCs benefit from their international position, and gain "ability to arbitrage cross-national differences in tax, employment, credit, and other regulations as means by which to earn monopoly rents" (Rahman 2009, p. 86). This situation calls for a new reflection on corporate governance.

In many cases, governments in emerging economies are "too inexperienced and inept to regulate behavior" (Earle and Sapatoru 1994, p. 63), and therefore international models and requirements are an important vehicle for change. In this context, MNCs may bring to emerging economies new technology, knowledge, and skills (Rugraff and Hansen 2011), and therefore contribute to their economic development. However, in some cases, resistance to change and conflicts with informal rules may occur (Boytsun et al. 2011), or the legitimacy of the privatization process may hamper the positive economic effects (Denisova et al. 2012). Also, negative effects of MNCs entrance in emerging markets might also occur, especially when they bring low-level activities, use anti-competitive practices, provide poor quality products and services because of the quest for profits, divert profits, default on tax and wages payments, and do not reinvest the profits in the same country (Dyck 2001; Becht et al. 2005; Rugraff and Hansen 2011).

Communication between headquarter and subsidiaries and the manner in which coordination and cooperation occur within the group impact their competitiveness, the corporate governance model and their performance. Moreover, the corporate governance mechanisms of subsidiaries are influenced by the corporate governance systems of the home and host countries (Costello and Costello 2004) but also by informal rules (Boytsun et al. 2011). In exchange, the corporate governance of the subsidiary influences not only the cooperation with the headquarters, but also the wealth created and the share of this wealth going to the stakeholders (Costello and Costello 2004). Corporate governance mechanisms are influenced by the network of actors, because the role and actions of each governance actor (shareholders, board of director, government, or employees) are shaped by institutions, interests and generate conflicts and coalitions (Aguilera and Yip 2004). These actors play a very important role in the knowledge transfer and learning process. Moilanen (2007) discusses the accounting knowledge transfer from Western headquarters to a subsidiary in a former communist country and explores the interaction between past and present forces, the learning barriers and facilitators, and the balance between transferring practices and allowing for local adaptability and flexibility.

Some questions related to the role of MNCs in emerging economies are still under research: how do MNCs contribute to the development of the local environment, how does foreign ownership participation make corporate governance practices better (Rugraff and Hansen 2011), and how is it that the transfer of knowledge and practices is more successful in some cases than in others? Our study is presenting a case of success, as acknowledged by local actors, despite the pressure created around Petrom's controversial privatization contract. In addition to that, this case allowed us to identify different corporate governance paradigms that coexist in the MNCs, as a consequence of the encounter with different contexts and actors.

3 Context and Research Methodology

In order to provide an in-depth analysis of improvements and transformations following a privatization in an emerging economy, and also to explore the actions and attitudes of various actors, our case study is set in Romania.

Romania is a relevant setting because of the various paces of change characterizing different periods after the fall of communism in 1989, and because of the variety in the outcomes of the privatization process. Cojocar (2013) provides examples of successful privatizations, which generated successful restructuring and economic performances, but also bankruptcies, delayed and unsuccessful restructuring, and negative economic and social effects. Under these circumstances, a case study approach is useful to understand how change was realized.

After the fall of communism, which set in motion a long process of transition marred by slow reforms and wrong political choices, especially beginning with the years 2000 a sound macroeconomic management and restructuring process started in Romania (Young 2010). An alignment to international standards was attempted, including in the field of corporate governance. A project to improve the corporate governance with the support of international organizations was launched and resulted in a Corporate Governance Code in 2001, revised and improved later, in 2008 (Olimid et al. 2009). However, implementing Western-based standards is not necessarily sufficient in order to improve practices, and there is evidence that "one size does not fit all firms in all countries" (Black et al. 2012, p. 935).

Despite recent progress, several studies suggest that disclosures and transparency still need improvement in Romania (Cuc and Kanya 2009; Young 2010; Răileanu et al. 2011). In analyzing the transparency index for 58 Romanian listed entities, Cuc and Kanya (2009) find out that Petrom has the highest level of transparency and identify significant differences between Romanian entities. Other studies also present Petrom as having sound corporate governance and financial reporting practices (Albu et al. 2011). However, Petrom had a controversial privatization which raised legitimacy issues (Lupu and Sandu 2010). These conflicting previous findings make Petrom an interesting case to study the implementation of corporate governance practices and their impact on the company's performance and transparency.

Petrom is the biggest oil company in Central and Eastern Europe and the largest company listed on the BSE. Petrom's privatization took place in 2004, when the Romanian Government sold the controlling interest to the Austrian group OMV. While privatization was, as noted, controversial, Petrom is currently considered a successful company, a model of good practices, and embracing such values as ethics, respect, partnership and a viable management vision. Starting in 2008, the company annually issues a Corporate Social Responsibility (CSR) report. Following privatization, Petrom was restructured in terms of processes, IT systems, rules and people's training. It became one of the most profitable Romanian companies and obtained massive profits even during the actual economic crisis. Its net profit grew in 2011 by 72 %, and while the 2012 increase was of only 5 %, the profit obtained (over 900 million EUR) is a record for Romania. Petrom's Romanian CEO, Mariana Gheorghe, was deeply involved in the restructuring process and is perceived as having contributed to Petrom's performance. She was the first Romanian to be included in Fortune 50 International Most Powerful Women in 2012 (an annual ranking of businesswomen worldwide). She is also Chairwoman of the BSE's Corporate Governance Board (responsible for issuing the Corporate Governance Code).

As a major limit of prior studies is the limited period of time for observations and their focus immediately before and after the privatization (Omran 2009), we employ a longitudinal case study covering a longer period of time (4 years). Thus we take a process view of the privatization, which allows us to understand its long-term implications. Archival data are collected from the annual reports and other information made available by the company, but also from press materials and prior research on Petrom. A content analysis of the annual reports of Petrom was performed in order to analyze the disclosures in corporate governance areas such as compliance with standards, social and environmental issues. Also, eight semi-structured interviews with IR officers from other major companies in Romania, as well as with relevant representatives of the financial community (financial analysts, brokers) were conducted.

We used the content analysis of four post-privatization annual reports of Petrom SA in order to identify the impact of privatization on the volume and quality of corporate disclosures. Also, we identified the type of corporate governance paradigm which characterizes these disclosures, by differentiating between the shareholders' market based model, and the stakeholders' relationship based model. The unit of analysis was the clause. These were grouped in 16 relevant topics. The clauses could be related to more than one topic and thus counted more than once. About 2,500 units of analysis were identified, following a cross-numbering protocol, and then allocated to the corresponding topic.

Content analysis relies on the postulate that repetition of units of analysis (words, expressions, sentences, paragraphs) reveals the interests and the concerns of the authors (Krippendorff 1980). The text is split and organized according to the choice of research objectives, and following an accurate coding method.

Our objective was to identify the main topics that emerged in Petrom's corporate communication, after the privatization of the company. We used a manual treatment for the classification of disclosures in the annual report, and a semi-manual treatment for the numbering (the filters, the subtotals and the grand total are automatically generated). The cross-numbering increases the reliability of our searching and classification. The titles, tables, images, and graphics, or the localization of the information were not taken into account.

4 Results and Discussion

The 16 topics were partly derived from the literature review, partly derived from the particular context (according to the first part of this chapter) and partly inspired by the structure of the annual reports. Particular attention was given to defining the topics, so as to increase the reliability of the content analysis. The process implied developing additional classification rules, when specific questions were raised, with a constant care for coherence in classification. A final general consensus between the three coders was achieved, thus ensuring the reliability of the results (see Table 1 below).

Our analysis of corporate disclosures showed that even if pragmatic disclosures directly aimed at the shareholders were prominent, during the fours years of our analysis there is an important shift towards disclosure targeted at different categories of stakeholders, especially employees, customers, local communities, and society in general. MNCs have to face different audiences which, especially in the context of privatization, are not always favorable to the company, which often leads to increased legitimizing needs. The corporate governance market-based view, with a focus on shareholders, is not enough in these contexts. Stakeholders' relationship models might prove more adapted, as we will see in the following discussion. The following sections present the four main themes under which were grouped the 16 research topics identified through the content analysis of the annual reports: compliance with standards, pragmatic issues, social issues, and strategy and self-assessment.

4.1 Compliance with Standards

The main strategy adopted by Petrom to gain legitimacy is showing that it abides by the laws, regulations, national and international or group standards. The main actions we identified are: *compliance with group standards and compliance with national/international standards*. Manipulation of the environment could also be identified, for example if we compare the declarations concerning environmental

Table 1 Results of the quantitative content analysis of the annual reports of Petrom

	Year			
Topic	2004	2005	2006	2007
Compliance with standards	**10**	**60**	**34**	**23**
Group standards		24	14	11
National/international standards	10	36	20	12
Pragmatic issues	**127**	**331**	**443**	**537**
Corporate governance		15	21	55
Development of the business	21	33	67	85
Economic, financial & technical issues	39	71	134	177
Investments	18	29	44	31
Prices	11	11	16	9
Quality improvement		6	18	7
Restructuring, reorganization & modernization	38	166	143	173
Social issues	**44**	**124**	**204**	**116**
Employee relations	7	20	54	17
Environmental issues	18	35	31	22
Health & safety	17	27	53	38
Community involvement	2	42	66	39
Strategy and self-assessment	**54**	**80**	**128**	**179**
Corporate strategy	12	33	53	89
Defensive tactics	6	29	27	26
Self-confidence	36	18	48	64
Total	**235**	**595**	**809**	**855**

issues with the facts. For nine times in 2006 the maximum fine was imposed to Petrom for violation of the laws regarding the protection of the environment (Curentul 2006) and in May 2007 one of the two refineries of Petrom was temporarily shut down by the Romanian Authority of Environment Protection because of its lack of conformity with environmental standards (Ziarul Financiar 2007).

Compliance with predefined, accepted standards, whether these are OMV's standards or national and international regulations, represents a major topic in the year following privatization, and it tends to plateau afterwards. Compliance with group standards can be directly related to privatization and its benefits, as pressures coming from different categories of stakeholders increased the need to legitimize the new status.

> During 2005, it was agreed that Petrom would be fully aligned with OMV Group targets and strategy for 2010. (Annual Report 2005)
>
> ...implementing security standards at OMV level is of great importance. (Annual Report 2006)
>
> 2007 saw the establishment of an effective gas marketing business. The small gas distribution network was spun off into a wholly-owned company, Petrom Distributie Gaze srl, achieving compliance with the EU unbundling regulations. (Annual Report 2007)

Previous research has acknowledged that corporations are increasingly taking on, beside their role as economic actors, roles of political actors (Palazzo and

Scherer 2006; Scherer et al. 2006). However, corporations' acts of self-regulation (political activism, as Scherer et al. 2006 calls it) are regarded with mistrust by the public. As Scherer et al. (2006) puts it: "The self-imposed standards are often not the result of a broader and inclusive discourse with civil society. They are often implemented without any form of neutral third-party control. It is sometimes 'business as usual' that takes place behind the veil of well formulated ethical rules" (Rondinelli 2002).

4.2 Social Issues and Community Involvement

Care for the environment and prevention of environmental accidents are an important component of the corporate social responsibility, and as such, a powerful instrument of legitimacy towards the stakeholders:

> …the company tried to meet its own environment objectives, by implementing several measures in line with the EU requirements. These measures related to the production technologies as well as product distribution. (Annual Report 2004)
>
> The economic growth of the company implies also a great responsibility for the employees' health and safety and for the environment. (Annual Report 2005)
>
> Being a responsible industrial company, Petrom is committed to supporting efficient and well-managed utilization of energy sources and products, taking into account the needs of today's consumers and the interest of future generations with respect to environmental protection. (Annual Report 2006)
>
> The transformation and modernization of Petrom not only encompasses the company business, but also its role in the Romanian society. Consequently, management's effort was also focused on transforming Petrom into a truly socially responsible company, involved in various areas of social development. (Annual Report 2007)

The declarations of the management concerning the measures taken to increase *the health and the security* of company's employees represent a means to show that Petrom acts as a responsible employer concerned with the well-being of its human resources. These aspects are especially of interest for companies such as Petrom operating in hazardous industries, such as the energy industry.

> A series of actions were taken in order to improve personnel working conditions in order to maintain production without incidents. These covered all elements of the work place system: operator//equipment//work task//work environment. (Annual Report 2004)
>
> Petrom attaches utmost importance to providing high-quality medical care to its employees. Thus, we aim at promoting the health of our staff, maintaining their capabilities and improving their general well being. (Annual Report 2006)
>
> The priority for 2007 was the implementation of the Petrom health concept, aimed at offering employees state-of-the-art medical services (occupational health, preventive and curative, and health management). (Annual Report 2007)

Petrom's *community involvement* concerns the responsibility of the corporation towards the society at large. In Carroll's (1979) theorization of CSR, this topic is to be found as the philanthropic responsibility of the company to contribute to various kinds of social, educational, recreational, or cultural purposes. Social responsibility is a major part of the legitimacy strategy of Petrom, as the amount of disclosure increases substantively over the four years post privatization, and is completed by a dedicated section in the company's web site, and the creation of a department of CSR. This corresponds to the policy and structure of the OMV group.

> We are a responsible company, perfectly aware of the importance required by health, safety and environment; Petrom is a company which has always been involved and will continue to be part of the community life, through actions developed for persons in need, said Mr Gheorghe Constantinescu, CEO of Petrom (Corporate News 2005).
>
> We want to become not only a role model for the business community but also a responsible "citizen" of the community we are living in. (Annual Report 2006)
>
> In order to enforce our social responsibility message, we created in 2007 a platform named "Respect for the future" under which we develop all our CSR programs. (Annual Report 2007)

The role of the company as defined by the company's management is a role of education of the community, of a setter of high standards and of a responsible citizen.

> As one of the largest companies in Romania we are aware of the impact of our activities on the Romanian society and we assume this important role by bringing our contribution to increasing the people's confidence in the EU integration process, by applying high business standards, health and safety measures, both internally and externally, and by developing related projects. (Annual Report 2006)

The topic *employees' relations* included assertions about the training and career of the employees. Petrom addresses employees directly, as a special stakeholder category, recognizing their contribution to the company's prosperity:

> One fundamental indicator of any company's performance is the quality of its work force and the working conditions it provides its own employees. Petrom is a responsible employer committed to treating every employee with respect and dignity, providing a safe, hospitable and quality working environment, and to developing its management team through evaluation and definition of staff development measures, talent management programs, comprehensive training programs at European standards for all existing and future managers, as well as leadership and management programs. *We recognize that a motivated, well-trained and diversified workforce represents a strong competitive advantage and a must have in the achievement of our target.* (Annual Report 2006)

4.3 Pragmatic Issues: The Shareholders' View

Besides disclosing information with a socially responsible color, Petrom also uses the disclosure of more pragmatic information such as: the development of the business, economic, financial and technical information, quality improvement, corporate governance, investments, and the evolution of prices.

In the topic *development of the business* we included the assertions regarding the expansion of the business, on the internal market as on the external market. This represents a way to obtain legitimacy based on the role of large corporations in the economic development of the region, and it can be related to the general welfare.

> The privatization itself, through a significant capital increase and new forms of management, created the grounds of the most important growth of the company. (Annual Report 2004)
>
> The sustainable and profitable growth of our company is of benefit to our shareholders, clients, employees and the Romanian economy in general and is therefore at the focus of all our activities. (Annual Report 2005)

An improved corporate communication with all the stakeholders and the creation of a *corporate governance* code is an important means of building legitimacy. The statements were mainly related to corporate governance issues and the target audiences being the shareholders and the analysts and in only a few cases the trade unions.

> Starting with 2005 the Investor Relations function was established, enlarging the scope of work of the existing office dealing with the large individual investor base.(Annual Report 2006)
>
> Petrom strongly believes that high corporate governance standards are essential tools to achieving business integrity and performance. This report sets out the policies and practices that Petrom applied during the year. (Annual Report 2007)

In 2007, the structure of the annual reports changed, a report of the Supervisory Board was introduced and the weight of the disclosure on corporate governance issues increased. Moreover, the company voluntary adopted in 2007 a corporate governance code, because no local code was available at that time.

> Given that OMV Aktiengesellschaft has committed itself to fully observing the Austrian Code of corporate governance and because such a Code is not yet available in Romania, Petrom voluntarily adopted a corporate governance policy that outlines the governance principles and structures, focusing on the long term interests of shareholders and ensures the integrity of the governance process. (Annual Report 2007)

Assertions about *prices* comprised management's declarations, justifying the increase in or the decrease of the price and the assessment of its effects on the company's results. In the post-privatization context, the liberalization of prices appeared as a highly sensitive issue. Important pressure was placed by the political power on the management of the company to consider Romania's economic and social situation in establishing the prices. The company tried to justify the increase in the prices on two bases – aligning prices to international quotations and increasing the profitability. Additionally, the management of the company proposed to contribute to the setting of a governmental fund to help those in need to cope with price increases.

> In 2006, the international Platts quotations have registered big fluctuations. Acting according to its 2005 pricing policy, Petrom has adjusted its prices for terminal deliveries and retail pump sales to the price fluctuations at international level. The highest quotations in 2006 were registered in July, due to geo-political reasons (Iran and Middle East) and speculations on international commodity markets (there were fluctuations of USD 200 per ton in gasoline and USD 100 per ton in diesel). (Annual Report 2006)

Statements on *quality improvement* show an increased preoccupation with customer satisfaction, and are often related to innovation and modernization, as part of the new strategy. This sheds a favorable light on the privatization process.

> As part of its newly defined strategy, the company aims to provide its customers with the best products and services available on the market. (Annual Report 2005)
>
> The quality of the remaining chemical products was improved to international standards allowing access to more international customers. (Annual Report 2006)
>
> The Exploration and Production Services division, following the acquisition of oil service business of Petromservice for EUR 328.5 mn, which will allow us to enhance the quality and efficiency of the operations and to support the reduction of production costs and the increase of production. (Annual Report 2007)

The quality improvement is a consequence of the modernization process. In 2006, we can notice an increased focus on assertions focusing on quality improvement and justifying prices increases.

A large part of the company's assertions underline past accomplishments and future changes concerning the processes of *restructuring, reorganization and modernization* within the company. Restructuring, reorganization and modernization are key processes triggered by privatization and mark a fundamental change for the company:

> 2006 was a remarkable year for Petrom. The projects we implemented focused mostly on modernization, efficiency and profitability increase and on international expansion. ... The Service Center Petrom Solutions and the introduction of the most important enterprise resource planning system, SAP, are just two of the projects that will lead to efficiency increase and cost reduction. The year 2006 was a landmark with regards to company reorganization, which is on track. (Annual Report 2006)
>
> In 2007, the management will further continue to focus on efficiency improvement throughout the company by further implementing the modernization program that Petrom has embarked on during 2005. (Annual Report 2006)
>
> 2007 was a year of significant restructuring and modernization achievements and the laying of solid foundations for future growth and sustainable development. (Annual Report 2007)

It should be noted however, that the management only presents the favorable aspects of the process. For instance, since December 31st 2004 when Petrom had around 50,000 employees, the number of employees decreased to almost 33,000 employees due to the restructuring, and in consequence we would have expected more disclosure on this topic. This situation is at the core of the debate on new corporate governance models and the MNCs. As we could see, OMV is following the Austrian corporate governance code, based on a German stakeholder relationships model. Petrom, as part of OMV, has to follow both OMV's corporate governance rules, and local regulations. However, at least from the disclosure point of view, it seems that employees are not as well represented as expected, and this can be the effect of a local dilution, based on a different cultural and societal setting. With an increasing number of cross-border mergers and acquisitions inside the European Union, we are facing now new challenges for the labor law and protection of employees,[2] with an impact on corporate governance rules.

[2] With freedom of movement, the MNCs might be tempted to choose the less restrictive settings, from an employee protection point of view (e.g. the case of Viking, and Laval in EU).

An important means to build legitimacy, preponderantly used in the annual reports is to make use of numbers in order to show the evolution of the company's financial and economic indicators. This type of strategy focuses on the usefulness of the activities for the immediate audiences, such as shareholders and customers. The information that did not match under any of the previous themes was included under the *economic, financial & technical issues.*

> Petrom's refineries will further increase efficiency and production to meet the rising market demand for petroleum products and the refineries will be in a position to fully process Petrom's domestic oil production. (Annual Report 2004)

Investments appear as an important theme in the declarations of the management of the company, as a means to legitimate the new ownership of the company.

As part of the privatization contract, investments constantly appear in the annual report. In 2004, assertions regarding future investments are dominant, whereas in the following years achieved investments and plans of investments occupy a larger part in company's disclosures:

> The new fuels are the result of the revamping and modernization processes carried out in Petrobrazi and Arpechim supported by investments of approximately EUR 1 bn until 2010, declared Mr. Jeffrey Rinker, Member of the Managing Committee, in charge of Refining and Petrochemicals. (Corporate News 2006)

Investments are acknowledged regularly in the annual reports, being at the core of Petroms's development strategy, and an important topic communicated to shareholders.

> The growth of our business is fuelled by important investments aiming at improved efficiency and increased production. (Annual Report 2007)

4.4 Strategy and Self-Assessment

The presentation of the *company's strategy* is an important theme in the annual reports, occupying more and more space as the years go by.

> Our strategy aims towards turning Petrom into a more profitable company through modernization and implementation of information technology. (Annual Report 2004)
>
> We committed ourselves to becoming the leading oil and gas company in South Eastern Europe, to investing in abating the effects of the natural decline and in stabilizing production in Romania. (Annual Report 2006)

In 2007, the information on corporate strategy occupied a more important weight as the company set its objectives for the year 2010.

> We committed ourselves to becoming the leading oil and gas company in South-Eastern Europe leveraging on our role as the OMV Group operational hub for marketing in South-Eastern Europe and for exploration and production in Romania and the Caspian region. (Annual Report 2007)

This topic allows us to detect a "life cycle" of the company's strategy which began in 2004 through defining some of the long-term objectives and which is re-launched in 2007.

After privatization, the company underwent a transfer of managerial knowledge from the Austrian mother company. In this transfer, as we could see, the corporate governance and investor relations held a structuring role, as they helped to improve constantly the corporate communication of the newly privatized company.

4.5 Assessments Made by Other Actors

As we could see in the previous analysis, the new management of Petrom assumed the role of educating the population in the spirit of market economy. This, in addition to extensive communication on the knowledge transfer and on the positive effects of the privatization for the different stakeholders, shows that the management took seriously the positive role of MNCs in the transition process.

Petrom's performance as a good communicator was acknowledged through different awards obtained (for example – The Silver PR award for CSR communication in 2011, or the Golden PR award for non-commercial communication in 2007). In addition to that, representatives from the company were invited to different conferences on corporate reporting and investor relations, in order to talk about their practices, considered as best practices on the market (for example, the Amsterdam conference organized in 2008 by USAID).

In addition to these formal ways of recognition, we had the opportunity to interview several investor relations representatives from companies listed on the BSE, and other actors of the financial market (brokers, financial analysts), in order to confront their views with the image communicated by the management.

> In general, multinationals that bought something (in Romania) didn't find any interest in staying. And they didn't have the elegance to be transparent. There are some exceptions. Petrom for instance is transparent. (*local broker, working with MNCs*)
>
> We have always taken example from Petrom, which is a company listed on the Romanian market, but with Austrian influences. From this point of view it is very easy if you have a parent company that helps you with procedures, or at least with some lessons already learned, with experience in business, they can at least tell you what and how to learn. (*Investor Relations representative of a company listed on the BSE*)

Other local actors (from the market authority, and PR firms specialized in financial communication) confirmed the positive role that Petrom has played on the local market, from the point of view of good corporate communication practices and corporate governance. Compliance is related to the existing code, based on a shareholders' model, and from this point of view the best practices promoted by Petrom on the local market are well acknowledged.

However, we could see in the content analysis that pressure coming from different stakeholders imposed enhanced communication towards non-shareholder audiences. Based on these findings, we will introduce in the next section a new debate, on the role of the MNC in arbitraging between different corporate governance models.

4.6 Corporate Governance Reports

We have chosen to study the 4 years following Petrom's privatization, focusing mainly on the annual reports. This analysis allowed us to observe increased disclosure aiming different stakeholders. Corporate governance issues represented an important chapter in corporate communication and a way for the company to promote a favorable image, especially for shareholders.

Moreover, the company issues a corporate governance report, under the Bucharest Stock Exchange regulations (the 2008 code). As mentioned in this report, Petrom wants to align with best international practices. On the company website, it is also stipulated that in addition to local regulations, the company is held to follow the internal standards of OMV (as we could also see in the previous analysis). From a corporate governance point of view, these are two different models, a local one of Anglo-Saxon inspiration, and the parent company one, of German inspiration. Therefore, if the BSE's code acknowledges in a general manner the recognition of employees' interests, the Austrian code is explicitly providing a direct role to employees' representatives in the various governance instances of the corporation.

Rahman (2009) makes a thorough analysis of the differences between the German and the Anglo-Saxon model, and considers that "as the corporate landscape in the EU is transformed by the Single Market project, the prevalence of firms with multinational scope favors the adoption of explicit roles in corporate governance by non-shareholding stakeholders" (Rahman 2009, p. 92).

Based on our case study, we could observe that Petrom's corporate communication gradually shifted towards non-shareholding stakeholders. This was on the one hand the effect of privatization, with pressure coming from various categories of stakeholders, and on the other hand it was the consequence of a new governance system coming from the mother company. From this point of view, we argue that emerging countries and transitional economies in particular represent a setting where the corporate governance models are challenged. However, we should note that disclosure is not in itself a guarantee for good corporate governance, as there is always a difference between corporate discourses and substantive action.

5 Conclusion

Our research is motivated by the complexity of the change processes in the field of corporate governance in emerging economies. Studies in this area are useful to assess the development of the corporate sector and the degree of adaptation to the business principles of the market economy (Abe and Iwasaki 2010). In this chapter we contributed to the debate on the role of MNCs in improving corporate governance in emerging markets. While it is considered that transfer of practices from the MNCs to the local firms is achievable, with positive impact on performance (Gołębiowska-Tataj and Klonowski 2009), the existing literature provides a variety of experiences in emerging economies (Omran 2009).

Exploring the case of Petrom, the largest Romanian listed entity on the BSE, we find that the role of MNCs as a vector of improvement for corporate governance in emerging economies can be explored at two different levels. First, at the local level, because MNCs set best practices, and become a benchmark for corporate reporting and corporate governance practices. Second, at the global level, as MNCs are confronted with new contexts, with complex stakeholder structures and various sources of pressure, they can represent a vector for future mutations in corporate governance models.

Therefore, these settings make possible the encounter between different models of corporate governance. This opens new debates on the convergence of corporate governance codes in the European Union, and on the role of MNCs as a vehicle for these models, and a source of hybridization. Future research should look into the transformation that is brought by the encounter between different social and cultural norms, and emerging countries represent an ideal setting for such research.

References

Abe, N., & Iwasaki, I. (2010). Organisational culture and corporate governance in Russia: A study of managerial turnover. *Post-Communist Economies, 22*(4), 449–470.

Aguilera, R. V., & Yip, G. S. (2004). Corporate governance and globalization: Toward an actor-centered institutional analysis. In A. Arin, P. Ghemawat, & J. E. Ricard (Eds.), *Creating value through international strategy* (pp. 55–77). New York: Palgrave Macmillan.

Albu, N., Albu, C. N., Bunea, S., Calu, D. A., & Gîrbină, M. M. (2011). A story about IAS/IFRS implementation in Romania – An institutional and structuration theory perspective. *Journal of Accounting in Emerging Economies, 1*(1), 76–100.

Annual Report. (2004). *Petrom's annual report*. http://www.petrom.com/portal/01/petromcom/petromcom/Petrom/Raport_Anual. Accessed 12 June 2010.

Annual Report. (2005). *Petrom's annual report*. http://www.petrom.com/portal/01/petromcom/petromcom/Petrom/Raport_Anual. Accessed 12 June 2010.

Annual Report. (2006). *Petrom's annual report*. http://www.petrom.com/portal/01/petromcom/petromcom/Petrom/Raport_Anual. Accessed 12 June 2010.

Annual Report. (2007). *Petrom's annual report*. http://www.petrom.com/portal/01/petromcom/petromcom/Petrom/Raport_Anual. Accessed 7 May 2011.

Becht, M., Bolton, P., & Röell, A. (2005). *Corporate governance and control*. ECGI Working paper series in, Finance, 2, www.ecgi.org/wp. Accessed 15 Sept 2013.

Black, B. S., de Carvalho, A. G., & Gorga, E. (2012). What matters and for which firms for corporate governance in emerging markets? Evidence from Brazil (and other BRIK countries). *Journal of Corporate Finance, 18*(4), 934–952.

Boytsun, A., Deloof, M., & Matthyssens, P. (2011). Social norms, social cohesion, and corporate governance. *Corporate Governance: An International Review, 19*(1), 41–60.

Carroll, A. B. (1979). A three-dimensional conceptual model of corporate performance, academy of Management. *The Academy of Management Review, 4*(4), 497–505.

Claessens, S., Djankov, S., & Pohl, G. (1997). *Ownership and corporate governance. Evidence from the Czech Republic*. Policy Research Working Paper 1737. World Bank.

Cojocar, A. (2013) Industria trece printr-un val de închideri care afectează creşterea economică. Care sunt cauzele dezindustrializării de după'89 şi unde s-a greşit? Am privatizat prea mult sau prea puţin? De ce nu am atras destui noi investitori? (in Romanian) [The industry undergoes a wave of shut-downs which affect the economic growth. What are the causes of de-industrialization after'89 and what went wrong? Have we privatized too much or not enough? Why did we not attract more investors?], *Ziarul Financiar*, 7 Mar 2013.

Corporate News. (2005). *Petrom corporate news*, 26 May 2005. http://www.petrom.com/portal/01/petromcom/petromcom/Petrom/Relatia_cu_investitorii/Noutati_investitori/Noutati_investitori_2005. Accessed 11 Dec 2008.

Corporate News. (2006). Petrom launches a new line of fuels [10 Apr 2006], http://www.petrom.com/portal/01/petromcom/petromcom/Petrom/Biroul_de_presa/Arhiva_presa/Arhiva_2006. Accessed on 2 Feb 2008.

Costello, A. O., & Costello, T. G. (2004). *Corporate governance in multinational corporations*. Midwest Academy of Management annual conference, Minneapolis.

Cuc, S., & Kanya, H. (2009). Corporate governance – A transparency index for the Romanian listed companies. *Annals of Faculty of Economics, 2*(1), 60–66.

Curentul. (2006). *Garda Naţională de Mediu "arde" Petromul* [in Romanian]. http://www.curentul.ro/curentul.php?numar=20061020&cat=7&subcat=100&subart=45534. Accessed 15 June 2011.

Denisova, I., Eller, M., Frye, T., & Zhuravskaya, E. (2012). Everyone hates privatization, but why? Survey evidence from 28 post-communist countries. *Journal of Comparative Economics, 40* (1), 44–61.

Djankov, S., & Murrell, P. (2002). Enterprise restructuring in transition: A quantitative survey. *Journal of Economic Literature, 40*(3), 739–792.

Dyck, A. (2001). Privatization and corporate governance: Principles, evidence, and future challenges. *The World Bank Research Observer, 16*(1), 59–84.

Earle, J. S., & Sapatoru, D. (1994). Incentive contracts, corporate governance, and privatization funds in Romania. *Atlantic Economic Journal, 22*(2), 61–79.

Ezzamel, M., & Xiao, J. (2011). Accounting in transitional and emerging market economies. *European Accounting Review, 20*(4), 625–637.

Gołębiowska-Tataj, D., & Klonowski, D. (2009). When East meets West: corporate governance challenges in emerging markets of Central and Eastern Europe – The case of Polish Aggregate Processors. *Post-Communist Economies, 21*(3), 361–371.

Krippendorff, K. (1980). *Content analysis: An introduction to its methodology*. London: Sage.

Lupu (Ioan), I., & Sandu, R. (2010). *Legitimacy strategies in the annual reports – What turn to social responsibility in post-privatization context*. 33rd European Accounting Association (EAA) Annual Congress, Istanbul [working paper].

Megginson, W. L., & Netter, J. M. (2001). From state to market: A survey of empirical studies on privatization. *Journal of Economic Literature, 39*(2), 321–389.

Mennicken, A. (2008). Connecting worlds: The translation of international auditing standards into post-Soviet audit practice. *Accounting, Organizations and Society, 33*(4–5), 384–414.

Mickiewicz, T. M. (2009). Hierarchy of governance institutions and the pecking order of privatization: Central-Eastern Europe and Central Asia reconsidered. *Post-Communist Economies, 21*(4), 399–423.

Moilanen, S. (2007). Knowledge translation in management accounting and control: A case study of a multinational firm in transitional economies. *European Accounting Review, 16*(4), 757–789.

Olimid, L., Ionaşcu, M., Popescu, L., & Daniel, V. (2009). *Corporate governance in Romania. A fragile start*. The Proceedings of the 5th European Conference on Management Leadership and Governance, Athens, 5–6 Nov 2009.

Omran, M. (2009). Post-privatization corporate governance and firm performance: The role of private ownership concentration, identity and board composition. *Journal of Comparative Economics, 37*(4), 658–673.

Palazzo, G., & Scherer, A. G. (2006). Corporate legitimacy as deliberation: A communicative framework. *Journal of Business Ethics, 66*(1), 71–88.

Przybyłowski, M., Aluchna, M., & Zamojska, A. (2011). Role of independent supervisory board members in Central and Eastern European countries. *International Journal of Disclosure and Governance, 8*(1), 77–98.

Rahman, M. (2009). Corporate governance in the European Union: Firm nationality and the 'German' model. *Multinational Business Review, 17*(4), 77–98.

Răileanu, A. S., Dobroţeanu, C. L., & Dobroţeanu, L. (2011). Probleme de actualitate cu privire la măsurarea nivelului de guvernanţă corporativă în România (in Romanian) [Current issues in measuring the level of corporate governance in Romania]. *Audit Financiar, 2011*(1), 11–15.

Rondinelli, D. A. (2002, Winter). Transnational corporations: International citizens or new sovereigns? *Business and Society Review, 107*(4), 391–413.

Rugraff, E., & Hansen, M. W. (2011). Multinational corporations and local firms in emerging economies: An introduction. In E. Rugraff & M. W. Hansen (Eds.), *Multinational corporations and local firms in emerging economies* (pp. 13–47). Amsterdam: Amsterdam University Press.

Scherer, A. G., Palazzo, G., & Baumann, D. (2006). Global rules and private actors: Toward a new role of the transnational corporation in global governance. *Business Ethics Quarterly, 16*(4), 505–532.

Stiglitz, J. E. (2008). Foreword. In G. Roland (Ed.), *Privatization: Successes and failures*. New York: Columbia University Press.

Young, P. T. (2010). Captured by business? Romanian market governance and the new economic elite. *Business and Politics, 12*(1), 1–38.

Ziarul Financiar. (2007). *Petrom: The closing down of the refinery won't have a major impact on the results*, 30 May 2007.

Corporate Governance in the Philippines and Switzerland—A Comparison of the Institutional Environment and Practices

Marie dela Rama, Christophe Volonté, and Simon Zaby

Abstract This chapter reviews the corporate governance environment of the Philippines and Switzerland by comparing and contrasting the experiences and practices of businesses in these two countries. The comparison between an economically developed country and a developing one provides an insight into the challenges both countries face in implementing corporate governance reforms. The theoretical scope is explored by emphasizing the institutional framework of both countries. Underlying economic measures are also provided placing the context of corporate ownership and board experience.

1 Introduction

Our chapter aims to compare corporate governance practices between a developing (or emerging) market (the Philippines) and a developed market (Switzerland) by highlighting the objectives and challenges of such control mechanisms within distinct institutional contexts.

This chapter also demonstrates how pervasive corporate governance reforms and practices—often demanded by international investors as a result of global capitalism—have been over the past decade and how this has impacted two, economically different countries. Corporate governance is shaped by each country's history and inherent socio-cultural norms.

One main goal of corporate governance is to ensure that the owners of the corporation—the shareholders—receive an adequate risk-adjusted return to their investment. The mechanisms of corporate governance reduce the possibilities of

M. dela Rama
Management Discipline Group, UTS Business School, University of Technology Sydney, Sydney, NSW, Australia

C. Volonté (✉) • S. Zaby
Department of Financial Management, University of Basel, Basel, Switzerland
e-mail: christophe.volonte@unibas.ch

S. Boubaker and D.K. Nguyen (eds.), *Corporate Governance in Emerging Markets*, CSR, Sustainability, Ethics & Governance, DOI 10.1007/978-3-642-44955-0_14,

managers to expropriate money from the shareholders by setting rules, monitoring and incentives. The legal system sets boundaries and protects shareholders from illegal behavior. Corporate legal rules typically prevent managers from basic expropriation of shareholders such as stealing and/or tunneling. Corporate governance mechanisms are mostly voluntarily installed devices protecting shareholders. The legal environment—written legislation and law enforcement—differs across countries. These differences affect the way optimal corporate governance structures should be implemented. The requirements of the system of corporate governance practices also depend on the legal and corporate environment. For instance, in countries where shareholders' money may be used for corruption, other governance mechanisms may be important. The situation is the same if companies are actively controlled by families; that makes other corporate governance strategies necessary.

First of all, we relate the development of both countries to corporate governance and the institutional environment. Then, we briefly describe the historical development of both economies with regard to the economic and legal environment, and the corporate landscape, but also culture and politics. Based on that, we then point out differences in corporate governance practices that might arise because of these country-specific characteristics.

In this context, we show how—because of a differing institutional environment—the ownership structure and the board of directors may vary and how this is related to the structures of firms. Since corporate governance practices in Switzerland follow predominantly best practice, we stress practices in the Philippines in our comparison. Finally, the chapter will compare and contrast the similarities and differences in both systems.

2 Theoretical Scope

2.1 Corporate Governance and the Development of Countries

In general, countries can be divided into two categories according to their economic development: advanced (or developed) countries and emerging (or developing) countries (see IMF 2012).

In **developed countries**, the basic law generally protects the interests of stakeholders. Basic legal rules protect contractual rights and law is effectively enforced. Legal investor protection is higher than in less developed countries and corporate governance is seen as additional (voluntarily) devices ensuring that corporate managers do not waste shareholder' resources. Covenants are protected by debtor rights; criminal law is enforced to reduce corruption, environmental pollution etc. Labor law governs the relationship between employers and employees. Given these basic rules, one main purpose of corporate governance is providing practices and rules that optimize agency relationship, protecting of shareholder interests and creating a sense of trust that the managers and directors act in the best interest of the corporation. This becomes obvious due to the fact that, in developed countries, corporations typically are widely held and the fraction of institutional ownership such as pension funds is substantial.

In **developing countries**, legal reforms are aimed at sustaining economic development and trade, e.g., by protecting property rights. Investor protection is less developed and, as a result, corporate ownership is usually concentrated in the hands of a few (e.g. such as a high net-worth individuals and/or families) (see Claessens et al. 2000). In these countries, illegal economic activities such as corruption and bribery often are prevalent and should be addressed by corporate governance and corporate social responsibility (CSR) which take other stakeholders such as the wider community into account as well.

Corporate governance protects shareholders from firm value-reducing activities of management. Corporate failures, as a consequence of weak corporate governance, create mistrust and can lead to bad resource allocations. As a result, corporate governance supports economic development by ensuring that investments from investors are not expropriated and economic confidence is assured. This is especially important for institutional-building and development of emerging economies, which in turn benefits society as a whole.

2.2 *A Country's Institutional Framework*

In general, institutions are the outcome of human organizing and interaction. They are normally indigenous structures that are the result of social, economic, historical, judicial, political and religious relationships. Institutions are made up of both "informal constraints" and "formal rules" and are a reflection of socio-economic motives:

> Institutions provide the incentive structure of an economy; as that structure evolves, it shapes the direction of economic change towards growth, stagnation, or decline. (North 1991, p. 1)

The importance of the institutions of law and regulation in studies of societies was also expounded by Edelman and Stryker (2005). Laws and enforcement thereof, provide institutional legitimacy to the state, but also certainty to society. Laws, regulations, government policies and official edicts oil the wheels of commerce by providing boundaries in the field. The absence of these tools is an obstacle to a well-functioning society as social norms are poor substitutes for legitimate social actions. Supporting the importance of the law in economic development also comes from La Porta et al.'s (1998) study on Law and Finance which tracked the historical evolution of legal development across different jurisdictions.

Altogether, the institutional framework within a country **defines the scope and terms of its corporate governance rulings** because it sets strict rules of investor protection and indirectly influences the configuration of corporate governance at firm level (see Easterbrook and Fischel 1989). In a series of papers, La Porta et al. (1997, 1998, 2000, 2002) show that lower investor protection is related to weaker financial markets, higher ownership concentration and lower corporate valuation and affects corporate governance. Transparency International (2009) underlines the importance of corporate governance to counter corruption and fraud. Wu (2005) detects a positive relationship between good corporate governance and a reduced level of corruption.

Countries with insufficient legal enforcement are observed to have difficulty in attracting external capital (Shleifer and Vishny 1997). Furthermore, the importance of an appropriate legal environment was acutely described by Adam Smith:

> Commerce and manufacturers can seldom flourish long in any state which does not enjoy a regular administration of justice, in which the people do not feel themselves secure in the possession of their property, in which the faith of contracts is not supported by law, and in which the authority of the state is not supposed to be regularly employed in enforcing the payment of debts from all those who are able to pay. Commerce and manufactures, in short, can seldom flourish in any state in which there is not a certain degree of confidence in the justice of government.—Smith (1776)

To put it in a nutshell: The institutional environment of a country is **fundamental to its future success and growth**. As Lazonick aptly put it: "History shows, that the driving force of successful capitalist development is not the perfection of the market mechanism but the building of organizational capacities" (Lazonick 1991, p. 8). A distinct view of the role institutions play in economic development was taken by Lin and Nugent (1995). They looked at the reality and struggles of institutions in developing countries. More often than not, developing countries are politically unstable and institutions have to work around this instability.

Institutions influence the **pace and level of economic development**, while economic development can trigger institutional changes (Lin and Nugent 1995, p. 2303). Institutions in economic development are divided into two types: market and non-market. Market institutions deal directly with contracts, commodity and factor markets. Usually, they are government institutions such as courts, securities commissions (or market regulators), stock exchanges, and economic ministries. Non-market institutions are the firms and communities. Both market and non-market institutions complement each other due to their interconnectedness and interdependency with each other (Lin and Nugent 1995, p. 2312).

Where there is **underdevelopment**, the most important institutions are "the family, the tribe and the kin group" (Lin and Nugent 1995, p. 2313). When rich countries undergo economic crises or economically regress, these familiar institutions are rediscovered because they are fundamental. In developing countries, strong family or kin ties are a safeguard for mutual survival, and insurance against hunger or starvation (Lin and Nugent 1995, p. 2317).

3 Comparison of the Philippines and Switzerland

The Philippines is an island archipelago located in South East Asia with a population of 104 million. It is considered a lower middle income country with a nominal gross national income per capita of USD 2,319 in 2012 (CIA 2013).

In recorded history it was a colony for several centuries under Spain and then nearly half a century by the USA. In the period since the end of World War II, it has suffered various political instabilities with a period of dictatorship under Ferdinand Marcos (Celoza 1997). The country continues to be erratic politically and economically, not yet achieving the stability that has marked the growth of its neighbors in the region. It is currently a democracy-in-progress with the most recent presidential elections held in May 2010. Instability in the country has meant a large outflux of its citizens and the economy is reliant on remittances which makes a significant proportion of its GDP (Bayangos and Jansen 2011). **Switzerland** is situated in the midst of Europe with a population of roughly more than eight million. The country comprises three major language areas (German, French and Italian) and a small Rhateo-Romanic fraction. The country, while not member of the European Union, is highly internationalized with around 25 % of the population being non-Swiss citizens. The Swiss economy is relatively successful in international comparison and has a reputation of a so called "safe haven". In 2012, the nominal gross national income per capita was ranked 4th in the world (USD 78,754) (CIA 2013). Switzerland's position is also due to a stable and strong institutional environment: it is one of the most developed economies and has one of the strongest democracies in the world, where the people can have the last word concerning single laws, after government, parliament and other stakeholders. As Switzerland is a country with only few natural resources, there is a strong emphasis and focus on its intellectual resources such as the high tech industry which aims to develop new innovative products in the fields of e.g. biotech, medical engineering, new materials, greentech etc.

3.1 Institutional Environment

3.1.1 Philippines

Institutional reforms in developing countries with absolute rulers are difficult to verify due to the power struggle that can exist between a president and the bureaucracy (Lin and Nugent 1995, p. 2338). Typically, the former usually prevails over the latter and a heavily politicized bureaucracy is the result. Politicization of the bureaucracy in developing countries is a common, albeit problematic, phenomenon (Ilchman and Uphoff 1998, pp. 30–48). Where a working bureaucracy exists, the institutions will have to work around the whims of the incumbent and vice versa. Such a scenario can end up in a catch-22 situation where institutional reforms cannot be initiated at all due to the fear and uncertainty changes might bring to the pre-existing power-political structure (Lin and Nugent 1995, p. 2340).

The Philippines is plagued by weak institutions in the aftermath of Marcos' lengthy dictatorship. Democracy has returned to the country but the institutions are not of robust standard with political representation made of oligarchical families. This means government institutions and regulators are frequently politicized.

The system of government is modeled after the USA, its former colonial ruler, with a strong executive; however, the legislative and bureaucratic arms are not independent from the executive in practice.

The impact of a politicized bureaucracy results in the "primarily loss of confidence in the fairness of government institutions" (Peters and Pierre 2004, p. 8). In the context of the Philippines, there is a history of politicization in the civil service compounded under the tenure of Marcos. It has been rare for instances of impartiality to occur within the bureaucracy since the end of the dictatorship. In a study of the performance appraisal of the civil service in Singapore, Thailand and the Philippines, Vallance (1999) found the Philippine bureaucracy as highly politicized, fundamentally traumatized, and debilitated by a culture of patronage:

> Under Marcos, the distinction between politics and administration became increasingly blurred as the president appointed undersecretaries from the ranks of elected legislators. Patronage in the civil service became entrenched during the Marcos regime and notions of civil service neutrality were irreparably damaged. Despite President Aquino's vow to 'de-Marcosify' the Philippine civil service (Cariño 1989, p. 214), the trend of politicization has continued. Under President Ramos it is estimated that slightly more than half of all senior civil servants in the Philippines are political appointees (Vallance 1999, p. 82).

In a comprehensive 2003 report prepared by the World Bank and the ADB for the Government of the Philippines on improving the efficiency of government organizations, politicisation was singled out as a significant obstacle in the effective functioning of government. The report articulated the main problems of a politicised bureaucracy in the Philippines: its function "too much as an adjunct of the political executive", hierarchical culture, emphasis political influence and patronage, appointments based on patronage rather than merit, and poor salary compensation making some sections prone to graft and corruption (World Bank and ADB 2003, pp. 106–107). To be effective, institutional development requires political will, a relatively de-politicised bureaucracy, and a culture that is willing to be responsive and adapt to the changing needs of the country. Politicization of the Philippine bureaucracy hinders the country's performance and frustrates meaningful economic development (dela Rama 2012). This is a fundamental institutional challenge for the country.

3.1.2 Switzerland

The Swiss confederation was founded on 1 August 1291.[1] In 1499, the country virtually was separated from the Holy Roman Empire. Since then, in spite of various wars and disputes—also among different parts within the country—Switzerland stayed independent, even during World War II.

[1] A synopsis of Switzerland's history and development can be found in e.g. Maissen (2012). For the institutional System see Schweizerische Eidgenossenschaft (2012).

The institutional system of the country is characterized by a highly developed and deeply rooted democracy, as the Swiss people can decide on single laws at all levels of the confederation. There is a federal level, a cantonal level (comparable to single federal-states) and also a communal authority level. In addition, Switzerland does not have a capital city as known in virtually all countries of the world; the city of Bern is called the "federal city". The historical independence is elementary for the institutional system of the country.

The Swiss federal government comprises members of all the strongest political parties of the country, and therefore is not only constituted by one political wing. Switzerland does not have a person as a head of state as well as no prime minister; these tasks are jointly fulfilled by the federal government as a whole. On the federal level there are two houses of parliament, both fully elected by the people: First, the national assembly, and second, the Council of States which represents the Swiss cantons. The 26 cantons are have their own governments and parliaments.

The above mentioned history of independence also is a crucial fact for the institutional system of Switzerland in an international perspective. Only in 2002, the Swiss people decided to join the UN. At the same time, it was the first country ever in history, where there was a popular vote about an UN membership. Also, the country is not member of the European Union and the people also refused to join the EU's European Economic Area.

Moreover, the country has an historical, international, humanitarian tradition. A well-known example is the International Red Cross, which was founded in Switzerland in 1863.

Switzerland's institutional environment is strong, democratic and a competitive advantage for the country.

3.1.3 Comparative View

Since we are discussing corporate governance in two very distinct countries, it is important to compare differences in the countries' characteristics. For that reason we use figures from the CIA (2013) Factbook about general economic and legal factors. In addition, we used broad indices (and sub-indices) made available by the Heritage Foundation (2013) and Transparency International (2012) to evaluate economic freedom and corruption, transparency, and governance, respectively, in the two countries.

Table 1 shows significant differences between the two countries in economic terms. The Philippines is the 12th largest country in terms of population and has over 100 million inhabitants. Switzerland with its roughly eight million people is only ranked 95th from 239 countries. However, gross domestic product (GDP) is higher in Switzerland than in the Philippines which translate into an almost 34 times lower GDP per capita.

It is interesting to note the comparison of the size of the respective stock markets. The stocks listed on the Philippine Stock Exchange are worth 202 Billion US Dollars in 2010 while the figure of the SIX Swiss Exchange is 1,229 Billion US

Table 1 CIA Factbook

	Philippines	Switzerland
Government type	Republic	Confederation
Legal system	Civil law/French[1]	Civil law/German
Main religion(s)	Catholicism	Catholicism/Protestantism
Population[2]	103,775,002	7,925,517
GDP[3]	240,700	622,900
Stock Market value[4]	202,300	1,229,000
GDP per capita	2,319	78,594
Stock Market value/GDP	0.84	1.97

Source: Stulz and Williamson (2003), [1]CIA (2013) describes the legal system in the Philippines as being a mixed legal system of civil, common, Islamic, and customary law. [2]July 2012 est. [3] in Million Dollars, official exchange rate, 2012 est. [4] in Million Dollars, 31 December 2010

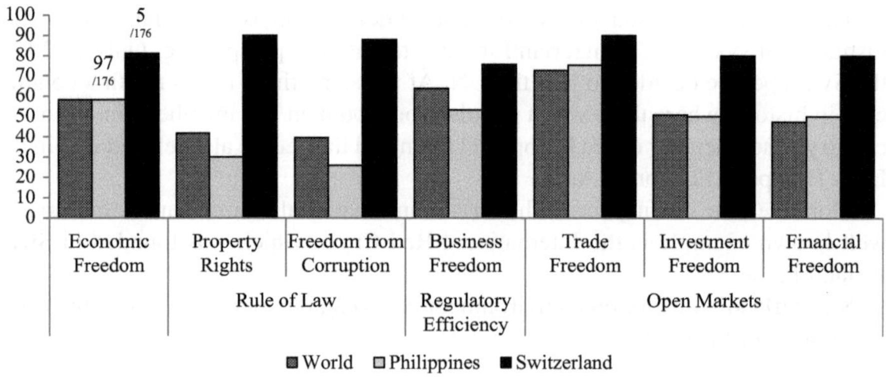

Fig. 1 Index of economic freedom (Source: Heritage Foundation 2013)

Dollars. The ratio of market value of publicly traded shares to GDP is 0.84 in the Philippines and 1.97 in Switzerland. However, the stock market is relatively important in Switzerland due to some multinational companies such as Nestlé, Novartis, Roche and UBS. In comparison, the ratios are 1.09 in the United States, 0.42 in Germany, and 0.57 in China.[2] Hence, the importance of the stock exchange also in the Philippines is relatively high suggesting that the legal environment and corporate governance are important factors.

To compare the Philippines and Switzerland, we also looked at the so-called "Index of Economic Freedom", developed by the Heritage Foundation (Fig. 1).

It becomes obvious that Switzerland has a degree of economic freedom above the world's average. Switzerland has one of the strongest systems for enforcing property rights, whereas the Philippines is below other countries in this context. This also holds account in terms of business freedom and investment freedom.

[2] Ratios: United States: 17,140,000 (market value of publicly traded shares in 2010)/15,650,000 (GDP in 2012). Germany: 1,430,000/3,367,000. China: 4,763,000/8,250,000.

Table 2 Corruption, transparency, and governance

		Philippines	Switzerland	World
Corruption Perceptions Index (2012)	Rank	105/176	6/176	
	Score	34/100	86/100	43/100
Control of Corruption (2010)	Percentile rank	22 %	96 %	
	Score	(−0.8)	(2.1)	(1.3)
Bribe Payers Index (2011)	Rank	n.a.	1/28	
	Score (max 10)	n.a.	8.8	7.9
Financial Secrecy Index (2011)	Rank	33/71	1/71	
	Score	(254)	(1879)	(350)
Press Freedom Index (2011–2012)	Rank	140/179	8/179	
	Score	(65)	(−6)	(39)
Rule of Law (2010)	Percentile rank	35 %	96 %	
	Score	(−0.5)	(1.8)	(0)
Judicial Independence (2011–2012)	Rank	102/142	5/142	
	Score (max 7)	(2.9)	(6.4)	(4)

Source: Transparency International (2012)

However, the trade freedom and financial freedom of the Philippines shows clear signs of an upswing in that country's development.

Furthermore, we also looked three factors of corruption, transparency and governance to compare the institutional system of the two countries (Table 2).

The Corruption Perceptions Index ranks Switzerland on the 6th and the Philippines on the 105th position from 176 countries surveyed (see Transparency International 2012). Accordingly, the control of corruption differs significantly between the two countries (Philippines 22 %; Switzerland 96 %). The differences and relative positions of the Philippines and Switzerland are unaltered with respect to financial secrecy, press freedom, rule of law and judicial independence.

According to Hofstede (1980), culture is a set of shared values that separate one group of people from another. While it is difficult to assess a country's culture and hence its values, we use characterizations provided by Hofstede (2013) to approximate culture in both countries and make general comparisons (Fig. 2).

Power-distance measures bias towards hierarchical structures. Filipinos and Swiss French are inclined to accept hierarchical structures where people accept their position within a society. In contrast, Swiss Germans are more egalitarian and prefer decentralization. Both language groups in Switzerland are equally individualistic and value self-responsibility. In the Philippines, belonging to a group (e.g., family), loyalty, and responsibility for each other is important. In terms of the role of competition in a society, there are low differences between the countries. In both countries, people value success more than the quality of life. Filipinos do not value the avoidance of uncertainty in contrast to the Swiss who are rules-orientated with strong regard for precision or punctuality. In the Philippines practice comes before principles and there is a higher tolerance of crossing the norm. Both countries' people value traditions and are affected by social peer-pressure to succeed in life.

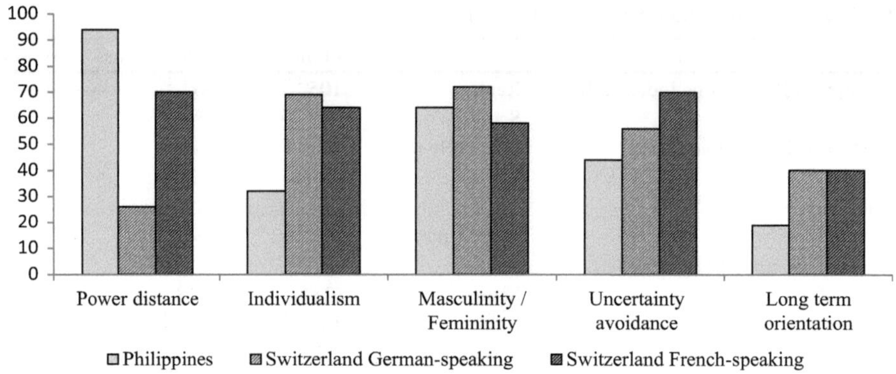

Fig. 2 National cultural dimensions (Source: Hofstede 2013)

Because there are significant differences on the economic, legal, and societal level, it is very interesting to note the corporate governance responses to these differences.

3.2 *Corporate Governance Practices*

3.2.1 In General

Corporate governance practices aim to reduce agency costs which accrue from the conflict of interests between shareholders and managers. A variety of mechanisms protects shareholders from managerial misbehavior, ensures that shareholders' interests are respected and thereby mitigates the so-called principal-agent problem. Good corporate governance reduces the likelihood of bad management decisions. On the one hand, lower risk leads to lower costs of capital. On the other hand, investment solely into positive net present value projects leads to higher free cash flows. Both effects have a positive impact on firm performance. In addition, a CSR strategy takes also other stakeholders into account. For instance, risk management, which is also a board task, has to consider corporate actions that may negatively affect society; these in turn lead to reputational costs. Recommendations for corporate governance practices or reforms have to account for a country's institutional environment and firm-specific characteristics.

Even though corporate governance is important, its form and implementation are largely left to the discretion of the firms and can be formulated differently across countries. This flexibility and the fact that one unique corporate governance system does not exist is probably one of the reasons why the topic has grew in interest in the recent years. The corporate scandals in the United States and Europe at the beginning of the twenty-first century have led to debates about corporate governance in society. People, especially in developed countries, are typically invested into stocks or pension funds and are thereby materially dependent on corporations that generate high returns.

Countries providing weak legal investor protection and firms with poor corporate governance tend to have difficulty obtaining financial resources (Shleifer and Vishny 1997). Empirical studies have documented a positive relationship between strong corporate governance and firm value (see e.g., La Porta et al. 2002; Gompers et al. 2003).

The effectiveness of corporate governance devices such as the board of directors, large shareholders, the market for corporate control, the capital structure, executive compensation, and, not least, competition at various firm levels is affected by a country's institutional framework.

Additionally, CSR accounts for wrong managerial behaviour that may financially or non-financially affect a variety of stakeholders. CSR becomes especially important if the state is not able to maintain a basic legal system that protects stakeholder interests and ensures that corporations are held liable for their potential misbehavior. The legal environment in emerging countries is typically less developed than in advanced countries and therefore responsibility for all stakeholders becomes especially important for corporations doing business in such environments.

Philippines

To understand corporate governance practices in the Philippines, the context in which these practices occur must take into account the pre-existing business-economic condition: the Philippines is a developing country with underdeveloped institutions, a small private sector controlled by a few families, a large public sector with a sometime predatory state.

The first corporate governance code was introduced in the Philippines in 2002, in the wake of the region-wide reform backed by the IMF, World Bank and Asian Development Bank after the East Asian Crisis of 1997. Parts of the code look at board governance, shareholder rights and disclosure. The 2002 code is overseen by the Securities and Exchange Commission (SEC). Corporations are expected to follow the code but due to resource issues, the code suffers from mandatory regulatory enforcement. Blue-chip companies tend to subscribe to the intentions of the code in order to assure foreign investor confidence. The board governance element codifies the introduction and existence of independent directors. However, this has been difficult to implement due to the largely family-controlled insider boards of the major corporations of the country. Nevertheless, unlike companies in developed countries, excessive managerial remuneration is not an issue.

Corporations in the country, by and large, have engaged in stakeholder relationships given the wide gulf between the haves and have-nots in the country. There is an inherent obligation on the former to contribute to the community and address issues of poverty. Programs of CSR are well established in the country such as providing infrastructure (e.g. work-sanctioned days off to build homes for the poor), and scholarships for students who are socio-economically disadvantaged.

The analogy of the Philippine corporation as an extended family takes a far more significant and socially embedded function in society. As religion is an important part of the society, large companies have their own chapels and places of worship. In shopping malls, masses are conducted daily. Work stops for the conduct of daily masses and prayers in-house at 9 a.m., 12 p.m. and 3 p.m. Social clubs exist in companies such as dance, photography, or art clubs. The relationship between an employer and employee in the Philippines is far more socially embedded than in other countries—the employment contract extends to a social contract with a strong emphasis on loyalty and reciprocity.

Switzerland

Until recently, Swiss corporation law is relatively flexible concerning corporate governance-related rules and leaves much freedom to firms. The law prescribes directors to act in the best interest of the corporation. The *Swiss Code of Best Practice for Corporate Governance (SCBP)* consists of unbinding recommendations. These recommendations focus on shareholder interests as is customary in Anglo-Saxon countries. However, in contrast to the typical dispersion of ownership prevalent at U.S. companies, many Swiss firms are controlled by large shareholders, notably families and private individuals. Hence, a corporate governance strategy is also affected by the values advocated by these dominant shareholders (see Gantenbein and Volonté 2012).

Since Switzerland is host to many large multinational firms, international corporate governance standards have been adopted without being imposed by Swiss law. For instance, most firms have installed an audit, compensation, and nomination committee. In addition, their international orientation gives them special responsibilities when dealing in different parts of the world, especially in emerging markets. Swiss law does not stipulate a CSR strategy, however, particularly those firms operating in emerging markets have introduced codes of conduct (e.g., Syngenta), maintain educational or health care programs for people in emerging markets (e.g., Nestlé and Novartis).

3.2.2 Corporate Ownership

Corporate governance mitigates problems arising from the separation of ownership and control. If the owner is also the manager (e.g. sole-proprietorship) there are no conflicts of interest because the principal and the agent are the one and the same, and thus requires no specific corporate governance mechanisms. In contrast, modern corporations with capital-intensive production processes as prevalent in modern economies are frequently financed by capital markets. As a consequence, many economic actors provide finance, and ownership is typically separated from control which potentially leads to agency costs. Hence, agency costs do also depend on how ownership is linked to control. If ownership and control largely overlap, as is often the case with family-controlled firms, agency costs should be lower.

The voting right is the most important legal right to shareholders as legal owners of the corporation (Shleifer and Vishny 1997). Therefore, the ownership structure is the most frequently discussed corporate governance device (see Aguilera and Jackson 2010). Agency costs accrue from a principal-agent conflict when ownership and control are separated.

In many countries, corporations are held by controlling families or individual shareholders. On the one hand, their control allows them to monitor more effectively the management and agency costs potentially decrease (see Shleifer and Vishny 1986). On the other hand, they may also influence corporate policies for their own private benefits of control creating a principal-principal agency problem. Such private benefits are difficult to measure and include influence over the firm's resources, prestige or perquisites (Fama and Jensen 1983; Dyck and Zingales 2004). In this situation, the protection of minority shareholders' interests becomes especially crucial.

Shleifer and Vishny (1997) argue that the conflict between controlling and minority shareholders is stronger than the classical conflict between managers and shareholders in many countries. This is especially the case if controlling positions are based on a deviation of voting rights from cash flow rights such as dual class equity structures (see Masulis et al. 2009; Gompers et al. 2010). In Asia, but also in Continental Europe such structures are common and typically negatively related with firm value (see La Porta et al. 1999; Claessens et al. 2000; Faccio and Lang 2002; Volonté and Zaby 2012). In contrast, Li et al. (2011) indicate that large foreign shareholders have a positive effect on firms in emerging markets and Kim et al. (2010) show that higher levels of corporate governance attract foreign investors.

In addition, in emerging markets, firms often belong to business groups which are typically owned by families connecting multiple member firms through direct, pyramidal, and/or cross-holding structures which enhance control (see Masulis et al. 2011). This corporate structure has its own problems. Korean chaebol-affiliated firms, for instance, have lower shareholder values than other firms (see Ferris et al. 2003). The lower valuation is associated with typical problems of diversified firms, the "diversification discount" caused, e.g., by subsidizing weak branches of the group.

Philippines

In developing countries, ownership is highly concentrated. Ownership concentration is a manifestation of economic control (see Berle and Means 1933 and Sales 1979 for classifications of control). In the ground-breaking study by Claessens et al. (2000) of 2,980 East Asian listed corporations, the authors found more than two thirds of firms are controlled by a single shareholder. In the Philippines, the top 15 families control 55 % of corporate assets, and 46 % of the GDP.

According to the 2002 World Development Report, there is a link between high concentrated corporate ownership and the efficacy of legal protection in countries. That is, "concentrated ownership tends to substitute for weak legal protections" (2001, p. 58). This view complements and supports resource dependence theory and the resource based view of the firm in developing countries: where there is an unstable political environment, the conglomerate form is the preferred method of organising. Investors in weak institutional environments also place a premium on firms who are part of conglomerates due to the perception that "concentrated ownership delivers great benefits when those owners in control have appropriate incentives and when owners outside the firm have more leverage" (World Bank 2001, p. 58).

The other side to this is that the treatment of minority shareholders is a pressing corporate governance issue in countries with concentrated ownership. Even where the prevalence of business groups is a private response to weak government institutions, the concentration of wealth in a few people, families or groups is a "formidable barrier to policy reform" and could negatively affect "the evolution of the legal and other institutional frameworks for corporate governance and the manner in which economic activity is conducted" (Claessens et al. 2000, p. 110). Concentration of ownership in the private sector of the Philippines and most of East Asia is manifested in the widespread corporate form of family-owned business groups or conglomerates (Granovetter 2001, pp. 69–70). Family-owned business groups dominate the private sector landscape of the country with the Ayala Group and SM Group as prime exemplars. However, this corporate form is not unusual as business group structure dominate across the East Asian region with Japanese keiretsus and Korean chaebols (as the previous section mentioned) being prime examples of this type of private sector organizing.

Another perspective on their dominance can be situated from the resource based view of the firm (Penrose 2009), which posits the firm as a collection of productive resources (Penrose (1959, 2010), pp. 21–23, 58–77). The relevance of the resource-based view of the firm for business groups in developing countries was highlighted in Guillen's (2000) seminal work on business groups. The resource based view of business groups provides reasons for their affiliated firms to be widespread and dominate across a diversity of industries (2000, pp. 368–369) and their advantages over foreign competitors (2000, p. 376) due in large part to "asymmetric trade and investment conditions" (2000, p. 368).

However, unlike the institutional view of business groups the resource-based view gives business groups a superior advantage to others due to their conglomerate structure and allowing a sharing and cross-over of resources between companies within a business group. This view of the business group as highly protectionist may overlook some of the historical reasons for their establishment, growth and persistence. The other side to the resource-based view of a business group in a developing country is where the internal resources of a firm interact with the external environment. Indeed, the resource-based view of the firm is closely related and complements the resource dependence theory perspective.

For Philippine business groups, the internal resource-based view of the firm poses the following question: how are resources administered (or protected) within a predatory state environment?

Under the dictatorship of Marcos, there were moves by the President to expropriate businesses owned by conglomerates and transfer them to his cronies. Where majority ownership in a firm was below 50 %, the firm was more prone to being taken over by the President's cronies. Therefore, a strategy adopted by some of the family-owned business groups was to attract a foreign investor to take a minority interest in a business to offset the political risk of expropriation. The raison d'être being if Marcos expropriated the business, a foreign government would intervene and put pressure on Marcos not to expropriate the business. There was an assumption that a foreign government would interfere to defend the ownership stake of the foreign investor.

This resource-based view of the firm also justifies the continued dominance of family business groups in developing economies. If a fickle government came into power with the view of expropriating company assets, the interests of business groups are diversified enough to survive such a political move. This is one reason why the ownership strategy of business groups in developing countries such as the Philippines, is to ensure majority control is consistent and an explanation for their reluctance to relinquish majority ownership. A long-term view of the firm with majority control was far more important than a valuation discount in the short-term. In the Philippines, minority ownership made a firm vulnerable to state-backed expropriation as what happened with the brewery San Miguel Corporation during Marcos' dictatorship.

The business group structure is a deliberate response to the external pressures of an organisation. The idea of organisational survival "to acquire and maintain resources" (Pfeffer and Salancik 1978, p. 2) has manifested itself with the conglomerate structure or group affiliation in order to withstand the political turmoil of the country and provide a bulwark against a predatory state.

Switzerland

In modern industrialized economies such as Switzerland, large complex corporations user their competitive advantage in producing innovative goods and providing high quality services. These types of firms are typically financed by equity investors. In Switzerland, 60 % of all exchange-listed companies are controlled by shareholders owning over 20 % of voting rights. While these firms are smaller in size on average, there are also large firms that are controlled by shareholders. For instance, Roche and Richemont are majority-controlled by families. However, both firms are exhibiting a dual-class equity structure which discriminates minority shareholders in their voting rights (see Volonté and Zaby 2012).

In March 2013, the Swiss people approved an initiative aimed to strengthen shareholder rights. Most importantly, managerial salaries now have to be approved by the general meeting. This mandatory "say-on-pay" is meant to reduce the leeway of so called "fat cats". As a result, flexibility of the Swiss corporation law is significantly reduced by these new corporate rules. In addition, Swiss pension funds are now required to vote on all agenda items in the best interests of their assureds and to disclose their voting behaviour. Switzerland has a mandatory pension plan system consisting of a federal social security fund (since 1948) and mostly privately organized employee benefit schemes (since 1985). In consequence, similar to the United States, a relatively high fraction of personal wealth is invested in the equity market and people depend on its development. It will thus be interesting to observe how pension fund managers who have been used to be rather passive interpret their new roles as active shareholders.

3.2.3 Boards

Board of directors are an essential factor in corporate governance. Corporate directors are delegates of, and elected by, shareholders to represent them and lead the company. They have the duty to act in the best interest of the corporation which, in general, is equal to looking after shareholder interests. This implies that its primary responsibility, upon which its legitimacy rests, is to reduce agency costs. The directors' responsibility is monitoring and advising the management board which is charged with the daily operational business and therefore board composition and structure is an important issue in corporate governance.

Major topics in this respect include CEO duality, the independence of board members from managers (especially the CEO), and the busyness of directors etc. The board is regularly blamed if corporations fail for not having protected shareholder interests, colluding with management, and for being too passive in general.

Philippines

Consensus-building is a fundamental feature of Philippine boards—a dysfunctional board rarely works and a conflicted board has a flow-on effect to the rest of the organisation. The role and nature of the relationship between the CEO and Chairman is pivotal in the board. If the CEO and Chair roles are unified, this is commonly referred to as CEO duality and power is heavily concentrated:

> The power of the chairman added to the power of the chief executive presents a formidable combination. (Cadbury 2002, p. 110)

CEO duality may lead to what Finkelstein and D'Aveni (1994) point out its double-edged sword: "forcing boards to choose between the contradictory objectives of unity of command and [CEO] entrenchment avoidance" (1994, p. 1080). When the roles are separated, the Chairman must decide whether they are an executive or non-executive chair.

For Philippine corporations, the roles are normally combined. Or if they are separated, then the two individuals come from the same ownership interests or from the same business family typically with a founder generation-son/daughter combination. This duality is a reflection of the business being an extension of the family with the family's "identity or reputation" intricately linked to the business (Gersick et al. 1997, p. 37). This also reinforces the need for control by the family owners and a signal to the stock market the family's enduring interest.

With regards to board membership, most companies have the requisite board committees. The SEC Code also requires two independent directors. Their introduction to a family-insider and controlled board has been a revolutionary element in Philippine corporate governance. Unlike Anglo-American countries where the majority of company boards have independent directors reflecting the highly-dispersed ownership, Asian company boards have strong reluctance to have independent directors on their board. This is not only the case in the Philippines but also in other countries of the region such as Japan, Hong Kong and South Korea where a majority of the company board membership are made of executive, and not independent, directors.

Switzerland

Swiss corporation law imposes corporate directors the duty to act in the best interest of the company. SCBP states that shareholders' interests should be met, however, it consists only of recommendations, also in what is the best configuration of the board. Nevertheless, Swiss boards orientate themselves by these recommendations and best practices at the international level. For instance, the roles of the CEO and the chairman are separated in 87 % of all firms (see Volonté 2013).

The flexibility of the Swiss law manifests in the use of board system used by the companies. Swiss boards can either be one-tiered or two-tiered. One-tier boards such as in Anglo-Saxon countries or France can consist of executive (e.g., CEO) as well as non-executive directors, while two-tier boards strictly separate the management board from the board of directors such as in Germany. Volonté (2013) shows that culture is likely to affect the decision which board system to choose: boards in Swiss-French areas and in Roman Catholic cantons are more likely to be one-tiered and thus more hierarchical; Swiss-German boards and boards in Protestant cantons are more likely to be two-tiered where powers are strictly separated. Both structures correspond to values attributed to those four cultural groups and to the two language regions' closest neighbours (France and Germany).

Since many Swiss companies are big multinational players, international standards of corporate governance do also affect the board membership of directors. Most boards are composed by independent and internationally experienced directors. About a quarter of all directors are foreigners and almost half of all board members have been working abroad. In addition, other business experiences of

Table 3 Comparative corporate governance practices between The Philippines and Switzerland

Corporate governance elements	The Philippines	Switzerland
Institutional environment	Developing country, weak regulatory enforcement, post-dictatorship environment	Developed country, strong regulatory enforcement, old stable democracy
Main legal reform	SEC Corporate Governance Code 2002	New corporation law currently is on the way to legislative process
Corporate ownership	Majority blockholders, usually family owners, concentrated shareholder base, weak minority investor protection	Controlling shareholders notably families and private individuals, extensive shareholder rights
Boards	One-tier board, majority of the board members are executives, two independent directors, chairman and CEO are from the same ownership interests	One-tier and two-tier boards, mostly independent directors, chairman and CEO are predominantly separated

directors are high too: 50 % of all directors have served or serve as CEO, 59 % have financial experience, and 56 % depict industrial experience (see Gantenbein and Volonté 2013).

Some companies do also explicitly address CSR. In such a setting boards are likely to introduce ethical standards, codes of conduct an install specific board such as committees that govern compliance with CSR (see Gantenbein and Volonté 2012).

A summary of comparing the practices between the two countries is provided in the Table 3 below:

4 Discussion and Conclusion

The role of the government in developing countries is a pivotal one. The absence of government cannot be filled by the private sector alone as the latter does not have the legitimacy and isn't sufficiently capable—ideologically and operationally otherwise—to completely discharge its stakeholder responsibilities to fulfil wider community expectations. Functional government, rather than a functional private sector, is overwhelmingly far more important for a developing country than a dysfunctional government.

The government sets rules via its legal system that encourages economic activity. For instance, the enforcement of property rights is crucial for doing business and a source of competitive advantage.

This chapter has shown how important the institutional environment is for the strength of a country's corporate governance system and private sector development. In emerging countries such as the Philippines where politicised government institutions still dominate, regulatory enforcement of existing laws and codes become problematic. The private sector is asked to take on some of the public roles that government is unable to fulfil. This filters down to the way the companies and boards react to unstable political situations and how corporate governance reform is shaped and continues to be shaped by the existing private sector environment.

In developing countries, such basic rules are factual and the legal system is increasingly improved to guarantee minority shareholders protection and other corporate governance-related rules. Improving corporate governance has been argued to enhance capital allocation and is thereby beneficial for the whole society.

In Switzerland, the law provides basic rules to protect shareholders (e.g., duty of care of directors) and stakeholders (e.g., labour law), however, corporate governance-related rules are until now relatively unspecific. Many corporations influenced by the unbinding SCBP and their international orientation standards have adapted international standards of corporate governance. Many firms are controlled by families or individuals. However, most boards are composed by internationally experienced and independent directors, and CEO and chairman positions are predominantly separated.

This chapter showed that corporate governance in the Philippines and Switzerland has been shaped by their respective histories, institutions and ownership structure. The practice of corporate governance continues to be an important element in attracting and assuring investor confidence. The experiences of companies in these two countries show the diversity of experience but also the global nature of corporate governance reforms.

References

Aguilera, R. V., & Jackson, G. (2010). Comparative and international corporate governance. *The Academy of Management Annals, 4*(1), 485–556.

Bayangos, V., & Jansen, K. (2011). Remittances and competitiveness: The case of the Philippines. *World Development, 39*(10), 1834–1846.

Berle, A. A., & Means, G. C. (1933). *The modern corporation and private property*. New York: Commerce Clearing House.

Cadbury, A. (2002). *Corporate governance and chairmanship: A personal view*. Oxford: Oxford University Press.

Cariño, L. (1989). Bureaucracy for a democracy: The struggle of the Philippine political leadership and the civil service in the Post-Marcos period. *Philippine Journal of Public Administration, 33*(3), 207–252.

Celoza, A. F. (1997). *Ferdinand Marcos and the Philippines: The political economy of authoritarianism*. Westport: Greenwood Publishing Group.

CIA. (2013). *Library, The World Factbook*. www.cia.gov

Claessens, S., Djankov, S., & Lang, L. H. P. (2000). The separation of ownership and control in East Asian corporations. *Journal of Financial Economics, 58*(1/2), 81–112.

Dela Rama, M. (2012). Corporate governance and corruption: Ethical dilemmas of Asian business groups. *Journal of Business Ethics, 109*(4), 501–519.

Dyck, A., & Zingales, L. (2004). Private benefits of control: An international comparison. *The Journal of Finance, 59*(2), 537–600.

Easterbrook, F. H., & Fischel, D. R. (1989). The corporate contract. *Columbia Law Review, 89*(7), 1416–1448.

Edelman, L. B., & Stryker, R. (2005). A sociological approach to law and the economy. In N. J. Smelser & R. Swedberg (Eds.), *The handbook of economic sociology* (2nd ed., pp. 527–551). Princeton: Princeton University Press.

Faccio, M., & Lang, L. H. P. (2002). The ultimate ownership of Western European corporations. *Journal of Financial Economics, 65*(3), 365–395.

Fama, E. F., & Jensen, M. C. (1983). Separation of ownership and control. *The Journal of Law and Economics, 26*(2), 301–325.

Ferris, S. P., Kim, K. A., & Kitsabunnarat, P. (2003). The costs (and benefits?) of diversified business groups: The case of Korean chaebols. *Journal of Banking & Finance, 27*(2), 251–273.

Finkelstein, S., & D'Aveni, R. A. (1994). CEO duality as a double-edge sword: How boards of directors balance entrenchment avoidance and unity of command. *Academy of Management Journal, 37*(5), 1079–1108.

Gantenbein, P., & Volonté, C. (2012). Corporate social responsibility and the board's role in Switzerland. In S. Boubaker & D. K. Nguyen (Eds.), *Board directors and corporate social responsibility* (pp. 202–214). Basingstoke: Palgrave Macmillan.

Gantenbein, P., & Volonté, C. (2013). *Directors' business experience, firm strategy, and firm performance* (Working paper), University of Basel.

Gersick, K. E., Davis, J. A., McCollom Hampton, M., & Lansberg, I. (1997). *Generation to generation: Life cycles of the family business*. Cambridge, MA: Harvard Business School Press.

Gompers, P. A., Ishii, J., & Metrick, A. (2003). Corporate governance and equity prices. *The Quarterly Journal of Economics, 118*(1), 107–156.

Gompers, P. A., Ishii, J., & Metrick, A. (2010). Extreme governance: An analysis of dual-class firms in the United States. *Review of Financial Studies, 23*(3), 1051–1088.

Granovetter, M. (2001). Coase revisited: Business groups in the modern economy. In G. Dosi, D. J. Teece, & J. Chytry (Eds.), *Technology, organisation and competitiveness: Perspectives on industrial and corporate change* (pp. 67–103). Oxford: Oxford University Press.

Guillen, M. F. (2000). Business groups in emerging economies: A resource-based view. *Academy of Management Journal, 43*(3), 362–380.

Heritage Foundation. (2013). *Index of economic freedom*. www.heritage.org

Hofstede, G. (1980). *Culture's consequences: International differences in work-related values*. Beverly Hills: Sage.

Hofstede, G. (2013). *National cultural dimensions*. www.geert-hofstede.com

Ilchman, W. F., & Uphoff, N. T. (1998). *The political economy of change*. Piscataway: Transaction Publishers.

IMF. (2012). *World Economic Outlook: Growth resuming, dangers remain*. www.imf.org

Kim, I. J., Eppler-Kim, J., Kim, W. S., & Byun, S. J. (2010). Foreign investors and corporate governance in Korea. *Pacific-Basin Finance Journal, 18*(4), 390–402.

La Porta, R., Lopez de Silanes, F., Shleifer, A., & Vishny, R. W. (1997). Legal determinants of external finance. *The Journal of Finance, 52*(3), 1131–1150.

La Porta, R., Lopez de Silanes, F., Shleifer, A., & Vishny, R. W. (1998). Law and finance. *Journal of Political Economy, 106*(61), 1113–1155.

La Porta, R., Lopez de Silanes, F., & Shleifer, A. (1999). Corporate ownership around the world. *The Journal of Finance, 54*(2), 471–517.

La Porta, R., Lopez-de-Silanes, F., Shleifer, A., & Vishny, R. W. (2000). Investor protection and corporate governance. *Journal of Financial Economics, 58*(1), 3–27.

La Porta, R., Lopez de Silanes, F., Shleifer, A., & Vishny, R. W. (2002). Investor protection and corporate valuation. *The Journal of Finance, 57*(3), 1147–1170.

Lazonick, W. (1991). *Business organisation and the myth of the market economy*. Cambridge: Cambridge University Press.

Li, D., Nguyen, Q. N., Pham, P. K., & Wei, S. X. (2011). Large foreign ownership and firm-level stock return volatility in emerging markets. *Journal of Financial and Quantitative Analysis, 46*(4), 1127–1155.

Lin, J. Y., & Nugent, J. B. (1995). Institutions and economic development. In J. Behrman & T. N. Srinivasan (Eds.), *Handbook of development economics* (Vol. 3A, pp. 2303–2370). Amsterdam: Elsevier Sciences.

Maissen, T. (2012). *Geschichte der Schweiz* (4th ed.). Baden: Hier + Jetzt, Verlag für Kultur und Geschichte.

Masulis, R. W., Wang, C., & Xie, F. (2009). Agency problems at dual-class companies. *The Journal of Finance, 64*(4), 1697–1727.

Masulis, R. W., Pham, P. K., & Zein, J. (2011). Family business groups around the world: Financing advantages, control motivations, and organizational choices. *Review of Financial Studies, 24*(11), 3556–3600.

North, D. (1991). Institutions. *Journal of Economic Perspectives, 5*(1), 97–112.

Penrose, E. (2009). *The theory of the growth of the firm* (4th ed.). Oxford: Oxford University Press.

Penrose, E. (1959, 2010). *The theory of the growth of the firm* (4th ed.). Oxford: Oxford University Press.

Peters, B. G., & Pierre, J. (Eds.). (2004). *Politicization of the civil service in comparative perspective: The quest for control.* London: Routledge.

Pfeffer, J., & Salancik, G. R. (1978). *The external control of organisations: A resource dependence perspective.* New York: Harper & Row.

Sales, A. (1979). *La bourgeoisie industrielle au Québec.* Québec: Les Presses de L'Université de Montréal.

Schweizerische Eidgenossenschaft. (2012). *Der Bund kurz erklaert* (34th ed.). Bern: Schweizerische Eidgenossenschaft.

SEC. (2002). *Securities and Exchange Commission of the Philippines' Corporate Governance Code of 2002.* www.sec.gov.ph. Accessed 2 May 2013.

Shleifer, A., & Vishny, R. W. (1986). Large shareholders and corporate control. *Journal of Political Economy, 94*(3), 461–488.

Shleifer, A., & Vishny, R. W. (1997). A survey of corporate governance. *The Journal of Finance, 52*(2), 737–783.

Smith, A. (1776). *Wealth of nations.* London: Strahan and Cadell.

Stulz, R. M., & Williamson, R. (2003). Culture, openness, and finance. *Journal of Financial Economics, 70*(3), 313–349.

Transparency International. (2009). *Transparency in reporting on anti-corruption: A report on corporate practices, Berlin, Germany: Transparency International.* http://archive.transparency.org/content/download/44358/710959. Accessed on 28 Jan 2014.

Transparency International. (2012). *Corruption Perceptions Index 2012.* www.transparency.org

Vallance, S. (1999). Performance appraisal in Singapore, Thailand and the Philippines: A cultural perspective. *Australian Journal of Public Administration, 58*(3), 78–95.

Volonté, C. (2013). *Is culture a determinant of corporate governance?* (Unpublished working paper), University of Basel.

Volonté, C., & Zaby, S. (2012). *The minority investors' voice option and its impact on firm performance* (Unpublished working paper), University of Basel.

World Bank. (2001). *World Development Report 2002: Building institutions for markets.* Washington, DC: World Bank.

World Bank, Asian Development Bank (ADB). (2003). *Philippines: Improving government performance = discipline, efficiency and equity in managing public resources* (Report No. 24256). www-wds.worldbank.org. Accessed 29 Apr 2009.

Wu, X. (2005). Corporate governance and corruption: A cross-country analysis. *International Journal of Policy, Administration and Institutions, 18*(2), 151–170.

Corporate Governance Practices in Nigeria

Chris Ogbechie and Dimitrios N. Koufopoulos

Abstract Recent global happenings regarding high-profile corporate failures have put back on the agenda and intensified debate on corporate governance and board practices. Business regulatory agencies in many countries – Nigeria specifically – have responded by enacting governance codes as a means of better oversight and to align with international best practice. In Nigeria, there are three main codes that cover mostly public and private business organizations.

The authors in their research found that Nigerian companies have been compliant with these codes on structural factors. As regards the process factors, more needs to be done specifically in board evaluation and the quality of directors.

It is recommended that there should be a harmonization of all the codes so that the same set of rules and regulations can be used to evaluate companies irrespective of industry. In addition, the culture promoting whistle blowing in firms should be encouraged.

1 Introduction

The global concern for good corporate governance has also been extended to Nigeria as a result of various global corporate governance challenges that have arisen in a number of publicly quoted companies over the past 10 years. This has made corporate governance one of the most debated business issues in Nigeria and has prompted a number of regulatory institutions to enact directives to firms to set up corporate governance structures.

C. Ogbechie (✉)
Strategy department, Lagos Business School, Pan-Atlantic University, Lagos, Nigeria

Strategy department, Strathmore Business School, Strathmore University, Nairobi, Kenya
e-mail: cogbechie@yahoo.com

D.N. Koufopoulos
Strategy department, Brunel Business School, Uxbridge, UK

S. Boubaker and D.K. Nguyen (eds.), *Corporate Governance in Emerging Markets*, CSR, Sustainability, Ethics & Governance, DOI 10.1007/978-3-642-44955-0_15,

Noticeably, each round of corporate scandals over the years sets off a fresh round of debate and corporate governance enhancements. The Asian financial crisis in the late 1990s led to the focus on insider trading. The Enron and WorldCom scandals in 2002 led to the focus on the roles of audit committees and external auditors and board independence. The global financial crisis that erupted after the collapse of Lehman Brothers in 2008 led to the focus on executive remuneration.

Several corporate governance scandals had also taken place in Nigeria mainly in the private sector, in such companies as Unilever Nigeria and African Petroleum in the late 1990s, Cadbury Nigeria in 2006 and in the Nigerian banking industry in 2008/2009. These scandals led to the introduction of some good governance initiatives. In 2001 the Securities and Exchange Commission (SEC) of Nigeria set up a committee that came up with a code of Best Practices for Public Companies in Nigeria ("the Code") which became operational in 2003, and was updated in 2012. In 2005 the Institute of Directors of Nigeria set up a Center for Corporate Governance to champion the cause of good corporate governance amongst its members. Furthermore in March 2006, the Central Bank of Nigeria (CBN) issued corporate governance guidelines for banks operating in Nigeria. In January 2013, the Federal Ministry of Trade and Investment set up a committee, under the financial Reporting Council (FRC), to produce a unified Nigerian code of corporate governance that will harmonise all the various codes and be in line with global best practices (Omoh 2013).

At the heart of these corporate governance reforms and enhancements is a common interest in ensuring good corporate governance and effectiveness of boards of directors in Nigeria. Several authors have commented on the importance of effective corporate governance in both the public and private sectors of Nigeria (Dabor and Adeyemi 2009; Ahmed 2007; Olusa 2007; Wilson 2006; Roe 2003), however, several events in the country in the last decade indicate that there are entrenched challenges to good corporate governance in Nigeria.

Corporate governance aims at building and strengthening corporate transparency, accountability, credibility, integrity and trust. Its major goal is to enhance the directors' fiduciary duties, uprightness and utmost commitment in directing the corporation's affairs. Moreover, good governance practices maintain the integrity of business transactions and in so doing strengthen the rule of law and democratic governance. A powerful antidote to corruption, corporate governance clarifies private rights and public interests, preventing abuses of both. The recent happenings in the Nigeria banking sector and the scandals regarding some directors' involvement in financial crimes and money laundering have necessitated the need for better regulatory oversight and once more put corporate governance and board effectiveness on the front burner of business issues in Nigeria.

This chapter aims to examine the state of corporate governance in Nigeria and the factors hindering good corporate governance practices. Corporate governance is particularly important in Nigeria because of the prevalence of relationship-based institutions in both the economic and political sphere, since the various regulatory institutions tend to be weak. This scenario has given rise to countless abuse of corporate privileges by corporate insiders and their allies, which has resulted in the expropriation problem. These weak regulatory institutions in Nigeria have further strengthened the need for strong corporate governance and effective boards to ameliorate these weaknesses (Wilson 2006). The effectiveness of boards in Nigeria will therefore have a significant impact on the state of corporate governance in companies and may help in transforming governance in the public sector. Hence, the need to understand the issues that make these boards effective is important.

This chapter thus becomes germane and will be of great usefulness to corporate governance professionals, researchers, academic and policy makers as it critically examines and unravels corporate governance issues and challenges in Nigeria especially in areas of board characteristics; board committee; and board processes and roles. Readers will also find this chapter interesting as issues looked at are substantiated with empirical evidences as it relates to Nigeria companies. It is relatable to also state that relevant data used for the purpose of analysis was elicited via the administration of questionnaires mailed to all directors and chairpersons of publicly quoted companies in Nigeria.

The chapter starts with the overview of Nigeria in terms of social and economic issues, and then looks at the history and development of corporate governance in Nigeria. Next it explores the state of corporate governance in Nigeria and discusses key issues on board development in Nigeria. Finally, the chapter also features recommendation to the corporate governance challenges in Nigeria and how it could be improved; and the reference pages which enlist the various materials used for the chapter.

2 Overview of Nigeria

Nigeria is a country in West Africa with land area of 924,000 square metres and an estimated population of 163 million in 2012 (OECD 2008; Oduh et al. 2012). The country, which was a colonial territory of the British, is an assemblage of people of different tribes, cultures, languages and religions, necessitated by the colonial interests of the then British government to ease the governance of the country. The predominant ethnic groups and languages in Nigeria are the Hausas in the North, Yorubas in the West and Igbos in the East. The country's government and politics have been conditioned and be-devilled by the problems of uniting several diversities: ethnic, linguistic (there are between 250 and 400 distinct languages), geopolitical, religious (there is a deepening cleavage between Christians and Muslims), and class (Joshua 2013; Haliru 2012; Onapajo 2012; Salawu 2010; Saheed 2012; Akindele and Adegbite 1992). Nevertheless, English serves as the official language and medium of communication in schools and in business (Olofin 2012).

In economic terms, Nigeria has the second largest economy in Sub-Sahara Africa and one of Africa's leading powerhouses given its sheer size and resource base. Only recently, the country was documented to be the 36th largest economy in the world in terms of gross domestic product (GDP) (Olokor 2013). However, the

Nigerian economy is largely dependent on its oil sector, which accounts for about 95 % of the country's foreign exchange earnings as at 2012. The country is a large supplier of oil to the US, although the growing exploitation of unconventional oil and gas supplies in North America will mean that Nigeria will need to look for alternative markets over the longer term. Despite its abundant natural resources, Nigeria has a per capita income of around US$1,460 per annum and life expectancy of 48.4 years (UNDP Human Development Report 2010).

Over the last few years the Nigerian government had operated with significant deficit budget every year and this deficit had been around the 3–5 % of GDP level. Deficits of this level are considered sustainable, provided that the efficiency of expenditure is steadily increased and translate into higher longer-term economic growth. The deficit had been financed largely by domestic borrowing but in 2010 the government indicated its intention to borrow a greater share debt from external sources. This was to allay fears locally that government borrowing was crowding out the private sector. A debut US$500m Eurobond was launched successfully in January 2011 and based on that success there has been suggestions that the government might return to international capital markets in the future.

Going forward, the government is targeting more prudent fiscal policy, and the generally favourable oil price environment will make this possible via strong revenue. However, expenditure control will prove more difficult. Economic expansion will be buoyed by robust performance in the non-oil sector and real GDP growth is expected to average above 7 % in the near future. Tighter monetary and fiscal policy should help control inflation but stronger growth and higher commodity prices could see it increase.

However, the public sector is very weak and, on top of this, corruption threatens to ruin the country. As such, compared with the Western standard, there is a near collapse of governance in Nigeria. Corruption has increased the cost of doing business in the country. According to Transparency International, 2012 Report Nigeria ranked 139 out of 174 countries in its corruption index.

In sum, businesses wishing to operate in Nigeria face many constraints, including poor infrastructure, particularly road networks and electricity supply; inadequate physical security; corruption; weak enforcement of contracts, and the high cost of finance (Iarossi et al. 2009). These factors have deterred foreign entrepreneurs from investing in Nigeria and induced many Nigerians to take their capital and skills abroad (National Planning Commission 2004: xv). The World Bank Report "Doing Business 2012", rates Nigeria 131 out of 185 countries (125 in 2010) in terms of ease of doing business. The World Bank, in an investment assessment report, showed that 80 % of businesses in Nigeria offer bribes to government officials (Boswell 2013). It also adds that the country remains the most attractive investment destination in Africa despite the high rate of corruption.

3 History and Development of Corporate Governance in Nigeria

Most of Nigeria's prestigious firms originated within the context of colonial imperialism and further evolved within the milieu of modernisation and contact with the Western world. Before the contact with the Western world the mode of production and trade in the territories now known as Nigeria was largely agrarian and communal. The first generation of Nigerian firms evolved towards the end of the slave trade.

The United Africa Company (UAC), founded by George Goldie in 1879, was one of the earliest modern firms that operated in the area that later became Nigeria (Amaeshi et al. 2006). Guobadia (2000) make clear that the first law governing firms operating in Nigeria was the Companies Ordinance of 1912. The law was a local ratification of the Companies (Consolidation) Act 1908 of England; even the subsisting company law of Nigeria (now known as the Companies and Allied Matters Act 1990, CAMA) is largely modelled on the UK Company Act 1948 (Amao and Amaeshi 2008). By the end of the colonial era in 1960, expatriates dominated the investment opportunities and sources of capital accumulation in Nigeria. This inhibited the accumulation and reinvestment of capital by Nigerian investors who were not economically strong to compete with the foreign investors and multinational corporations. This inability to compete made the Nigerian investors to become intermediaries between the foreign entrepreneurs and the Nigerian state, or, was made to turn to the state as a source of capital. This resulted in an increased intervention of the state in investment and entrepreneurship, which in turn arrogated to the state and the members of the political class a huge advantage of monopoly over economic investments and highly profitable government contracts. Politics has also become one of the primary sources of capital accumulation by Nigerians, as most major players have always come out richer. This fuelled corruption in the country.

The post-independence (after 1960) Nigerian economy was public sector-driven with government at both Federal and State levels investing in most sectors. In the 1970s the government embarked on a massive indigenization program which aimed at achieving some level of economic independence by getting more Nigerians involved in the private sector at the expense of foreign investors in all sectors of the economy. The 1980 and 1990s was the era of privatization, with government divesting from businesses and moving the economy to become private sector-driven. This did not result in dispersion of ownership but rather created companies with core and dominant investors. These dominant investors determined the composition of the boards of the companies they own, influence the way they are run and even the people/institutions they do business with.

In Nigeria, most businesses are not publicly listed companies. Onyema (2012), states that there are 199 companies that are listed in the Nigerian Stock Exchange (NSE). While the rest, numbering in hundreds of thousands operate outside the ambit of legislations governing the capital market. These companies are mainly small and family owned. In contrast to the Anglo-Saxon world, where corporate ownership is typically dispersed among many shareholders, a high percentage of listed companies in emerging markets such as Nigeria have dominant shareholders (Barton and Wong 2006). This ownership structure has significant effect on corporate governance practice as the dominant shareholders tend to have control over top management and directors appointments and decisions.

Today, the basic law that guides the operations of companies in Nigeria is the Companies and Allied Matters Act (CAMA) of 1990. It clearly specifies the duties and responsibilities of directors and recognises the board of directors as the most important body that can ensure good corporate governance practices in a firm. The CAMA 1990 requires every private company registered in Nigeria to have at least two directors on its Board. The directors have a statutory duty to act at all times in what they believe to be the best interests of the company as a whole so as to preserve its assets, further its business and promote the purposes for which the company is formed. They must prepare financial statements, which reflect a "true and fair" view of the company's affairs during the financial year and must be presented to shareholders for their approval at the annual general meeting (AGM). Lastly, directors are obliged to also prepare a Directors' Report providing an overview of the company's development, its principal activities during the year and any significant changes in those activities. These provisions are aimed at ensuring the effectiveness of boards and their accountability to shareholders and other stakeholders.

3.1 The Code of Best Practices for Public Companies in Nigeria

The Nigerian code of Corporate Governance is primarily aimed at ensuring that managers and investors of companies carry out their duties within a framework of accountability and transparency. This should ensure that the interests of all stakeholders are recognized and protected as much as possible.

The code of Best Practices for Public Companies in Nigeria ("the code") is voluntary even though it is recommended that all Nigerian publicly quoted companies comply with the code . In addition, publicly listed companies are required to state reasons for non-compliance should they at any time fail to comply with it. Unlisted companies are also being encouraged by the Securities and Exchange Commission to adopt the code provisions as measure to improve corporate governance best practices.

The code outlines the main duties and responsibilities of the board to include balancing the interests of the stakeholders, ensuring that the company performs to high business and ethical standards and providing sound advice to management. In particular the board is expected to oversee the management and conduct of the business, in terms of risk management and effective internal control systems;

appointment, training, remuneration and replacement of board members and senior management. The board is also to ensure that the company compliances with the laws of Nigeria and maintain high ethical standards. The high incidence of corruption in the country implies that boards have not performed well in this area.

The code recommends that the board of directors shall be composed of executive and non-executive directors under the leadership of a chairperson, such as not to exceed 15(fifteen) persons or be less than 5(five) persons in total. The code recommends that the roles of the chairman and the CEO should be separate and where the chairman is also the Chief Executive, it is important to have a "strong independent element" on the board. It also recommends that the number of non-executive directors should be more than the number of executive directors and the appointment of at least one independent director to ensure further independence of the board. However, many governance experts are of the opinion that one independent director is too minimal for this purpose. Companies who seek to practice good corporate governance tend to appoint at least two independent directors.

An independent director (non-executive) is defined by the code as one who is not a substantial shareholder of the company, has not more than 0.1 % of the company's paid up capital either directly or indirectly. He should not be a representative of an influential shareholder, has not been employed by the company or the group of which it currently forms part, and has not served in any executive capacity in the company or group for the preceding 3 financial years. In addition, he should not be a member of the immediate family of an individual who is, or has been in any of the past 3 financial years, employed by the company or the group in executive capacity. Finally, such a person should not have business relationship either directly or indirectly with the firm and should be free of any relationship with the company or management that may impair the director's ability to make independent judgments. Unfortunately many companies in Nigeria have difficulties in finding independent directors that meet these criteria and also possesses the qualities and expertise of competent directors they want.

The code recommends that members of the board should be individuals with upright personal characteristics, relevant core competences and entrepreneurial spirit. They should have a record of tangible achievement and should of knowledgeable in board matters. Members should possess a sense of accountability and integrity and be committed to the task of good corporate governance. The code also recommends that non-executive directors should be provided with positive environment for the effective discharge of their duties and that adequate and comprehensive information on all Board matters should be provided in a timely manner. Board papers should be made available to them at least 1 week ahead of Board or committee meetings.

Another interesting recommendation of the code is that directors should not be members of boards of companies in the same industry to avoid conflict of interest, breach of confidentiality and misappropriation of corporate opportunity. It also recommends that not more than two members of the same family should sit on the board of a public company at the same time, in order to safeguard the independence of the Board.

On board committees, the code recommends the establishment of the following board committees: the Audit Committee; Governance/Remuneration Committee; Risk Management Committee and such other committees as the Board may deem appropriate, depending on the size, needs or industry requirements of the company. The chairman of the Board should not be a member of any committee.

The code recommends that the Board should establish a system to undertake a formal and rigorous annual evaluation of its own performance, that of its committees, the Chairman and individual directors. The evaluation system should include the criteria and key performance indicators and targets for the Board, its committees, the Chairman and each individual committee member.

Finally, the code recommends continuous director development at the company's expense, to assist directors to fully and effectively discharge their duties to the company. The code does not recommend tenure limits for directors but regular refreshing of the board.

The Table 1 below shows the Nigeria's code of corporate governance recommended by SEC, CBN and National Insurance Commission (NAICOM) in comparison to the OECD principles of corporate governance.

3.2 The Central Bank of Nigeria (CBN) Code

At the end of the consolidation exercise in the Nigerian banking industry, the Central Bank of Nigeria (CBN), in March 2006, released the Code of Corporate Governance for Banks operating in Nigeria, to complement and enhance the effectiveness of the SEC code, which was implemented at the end of 2006. The four major governance issues that attracted the attention of the regulators are directors' dealings (related party transactions), conflict of interest, quality of internal control systems and creative accounting. The main objective was to restore public confidence in the banking industry through the enthronement of good corporate governance.

The CBN code is mandatory to all banks operating in Nigeria which are expected to comply while CBN inspectors are supposed to enforce the compliance. The code recommends a board size of 5–20 directors, the separation of the positions of the CEO and chairperson, majority non-executive directors, and the appointment of two independent directors. The code also recommends tenure limit of 10 years for CEO and 12 years for directors, a recommendation that is not in the SEC code.

The CBN code also recommends annual performance evaluation of the board and individual directors and the evaluation report presented to the shareholders at the annual general meeting and a copy sent to the CBN. The establishment of the following committees are recommended by the code, Audit, Credit, Risk Management, and Governance. The code also recommends that whistle blowing procedures should be put in place by banks.

Table 1 Nigeria's code of corporate governance vis-à-vis OECD corporate governance principles

Code of corporate governance	Nigeria	OECD
Shareholders' right	1. Right to the appointment and removal of directors	1. Right to secure ownership registration
	2. Right to equal treatment irrespective of the amount of shares held	2. Right to convey and transfer shares
	3. Shareholder's representation on a board is proportionate to the size of shareholdings	3. Right to obtain relevant and timely information
		4. Right to vote in general meetings
		5. Right to elect or remove members of the board
		6. Right to share the profit of the corporation
		7. Right to participate in fundamental decision making such as amendment of statutes or articles of association
Disclosure and transparency	The code recommend the following disclosure in the annual accounting reports:	1. Disclosure of material information such as: finance and operating results, company's objective, major share ownership and voting right, remuneration policy of board member, related party transaction, foreseeable risk factors, issues regarding employees and other stakeholders
	1. Company's capital structure	2. Information disclosure should be in accordance with high quality standards of accounting and financial and non-financial disclosure
	2. Corporate governance reports	3. Disclosure of the annual audit conducted by independence auditors
	3. Accounting and risk management issues	4. Disclosure of the channels for the dissemination of information to users
	4. Summary of the company's performance for the periods under review and future prospects	5. Disclosure of the analysis that is relevant and aid investors in decision making
	5. Statement of the degree of compliance to the corporate governance code	
	6. Disclosure of the significant contract with controlling shareholder(s) in case of public companies	
	7. Related third party transactions	

(continued)

Table 1 (continued)

Code of corporate governance	Nigeria	OECD
Responsibility of board	1. The board should define the strategic goal of the company and ensure the deployment of human and financial resources towards the attainment of the set goals	1. The board should act in good faith, with due diligence and care in the best interests of the company and the shareholders
	2. The principal responsibility of the board is to ensure that the company is properly managed and enhance shareholders' value and other stakeholders	2. Board should treat all shareholders fairly
	3. The board should ensure compliance with the Article of Association and the Memorandum of Association and other ethical standards	3. The board should apply high ethical standard taking into account the interests of the stakeholders
	4. The board is responsible for the affairs and performance of the company	4. Board should exercise independence judgment on corporate issues
		5. Board should have access to accurate, relevant and timely information
Shareholders equality	The code recommends all shareholders be treated equally irrespective of the number of shares held	1. The code recommends equitable treatment to all shareholders including minority and foreign shareholders
		2. All shareholders should have the opportunity to obtain effective redress for violation of their rights

Source: Authors' compilation from SEC, CBN, NAICOM and OECD code of corporate governance

The Central Bank of Nigeria code is also being reviewed as a result of corporate governance failures that led to the near collapse of 10 of the 24 banks operating in Nigeria in 2009.

3.3 The Code of Good Corporate Governance for the Insurance Industry in Nigeria

The regulatory agency of the Nigerian Insurance Industry, the National Insurance Commission, in 2009 issued its own code of good corporate governance for the industry that is mandatory to all players. The main objective of the code is to promote transparent and efficient market that is anchored on effective and accountable boards.

The code recommends a board size of minimum of 7 directors and a maximum of 15 directors, the separation of the positions of chairperson and CEO and that no two members of the same extended family shall occupy the position of the chairperson and CEO at the same time. It also recommends that the number of non-executive directors should not be less than 40 % of the members and that at least one of them will be an independent director. The desired qualities of the directors are the same as those of the SEC and CBN codes.

The code expects the Regulator to organize mandatory regular training for directors on insurance principles and practices, directors' responsibilities and liabilities, and update on insurance market.

The code recommends the establishment of the following board committees; Audit and Compliance (to be headed by an independent director), Enterprise Risk Management, Establishment and Governance (with independent director being a member), Investment, and Finance and General Purposes (Table 2).

4 The State of Corporate Governance in Nigeria

Nigeria is one country where public accountability is seriously hampered by the political elite and the country's corporate governance mechanism is driven more by political considerations. The extent to which the laws are enforced is largely dependent on the disposition of the political party in power (Adekoya 2011).

The significant levels of corruption, corporate misdemeanours and insider abuses of corporate privileges in Nigeria are indications of weak corporate governance environment. The mechanisms for ensuring good corporate governance exist in Nigeria but the major challenge lies in the weakened, inefficient and inadequate regulatory agencies responsible for ensuring enforcement and monitoring compliance (Amaeshi et al 2006; Okike 2007). In Nigeria, the Corporate Affairs Commission (CAC) is the prime government agency that is saddled with the responsibility of regulating, controlling and supervising all companies' related matters, but this agency is deliberately weakened by government negligence and is perfunctory in performing its duties (Okike 2007). Legal compliance can only be ensured by a virile and well-funded agency. The struggle to survive at all costs is making most businesses in Nigeria to close their eyes to governance, ethical, social and environmental issues.

The dismissal of the boards of directors of eight Nigerian banks in 2009 for bad corporate governance, insider abuse and mismanagement of shareholders and depositors funds, just 3 years after the introduction of the CBN's mandatory code, manifests the difficulties of enforcement in Nigeria. Although these banks, which are listed companies, were reporting incredible economic performances and receiving accolades and awards locally and internationally, the CBN could not assure the integrity of the figures that the banks were reporting to the public.

To empirically determine the state of corporate governance in Nigeria, this study employed a structured questionnaire to survey the sample of quoted companies at the Nigeria Stock Exchange. The research instrument, covering about 106 response items, was mailed to all the directors and chairpersons of all the companies. Closed-ended questions with ordered answered choices were mainly used in the

Table 2 Summary of corporate governance codes in operation in Nigeria

Board attributes	CBN Code 2006	PENCOM Code 2008	NAICOM Code 2009	SEC Code 2011
Board size	Prescribes no minimum but maximum number of 20 directors	No limit	Minimum of 7 directors and maximum of 15	Minimum of 5 directors
Level of compliance	Mandatory	Mandatory	Mandatory	Voluntary
CEO/Chairman duality	Separate	Separate	Separate	Separate
Independence	Non executive directors should dominate board membership and at least two (2) non-executive board members should be independent directors	The number of non-executive members of the board shall at all times, in the minimum, equate the number of executive members, if applicable. And , the board shall have at least one independent director	No non-executives should comprise 60 % of board membership and with at least one independent director	Majority of board members should be non-executive directors and at least one director should be an independent
Multiple directorship	Silent	Silent	Silent	No limit on the number of directorships a director of a company may hold
Board committees	Prescribes as a minimum, the presence – Risk Management, Audit, and the Credit Committees	Stipulates that there should be Audit, the Investment Strategy , the Risk Management, and the Nominating Committees	Advocates the establishment of five (5) committees i.e. Finance and General Purposes, Investment, Risk Management, Audit and Compliance and Establishment and Governance	Advocates at the minimum the establishment of audit, governance/remuneration and risk management
Meetings of the board	The board should meet regularly at a minimum of four (4) regular meetings in a financial year	The board shall meet at least once every quarter of the financial year i.e. four times annually	The board shall meet not less than four (4) times in a year. Each member is expected to attend not less than 75 % of the meetings annually	The board shall meet once every quarter i.e. four (4) times in a year. And, members are required to attend two thirds of all board meetings

Source: Authors' research on SEC, CBN, NAICOM and PENCOM codes of corporate governance

questionnaire. Seven-point (7) scales (Likert and Semantic) were consistently used with the same order throughout the questionnaire. The questions and statements were kept as short as possible in order to increase respondents' comprehension (Leitz 2008; Holbrook et al. 2006). The questions employed the active rather than the passive voice (Dornyei 2003) and the researcher avoided using leading questions, generalisations, ambiguous expressions (Leitz 2008; Martin 2006). Prior to mailing out the questionnaires, a validation test was carried out on a sample of chief executive officers attending the Chief Executive Program (CEP) of the Lagos Business School in 2010. We discuss the results from the analysis of the data on board size, independence and diversity in the section below.

4.1 *Board Characteristics*

This section presents three important issues that capture the profile of Corporate Boards: The board size, the issue of independence and the degree of diversity.

4.1.1 Board Size

Highlights of the results show that the average size of boards of publicly quoted companies in Nigeria in 2010 was about 10.6 directors. This figure was higher than the average in Europe and the US, which is 8. The relatively large board size in Nigeria is accounted for by banks that have an average board size of about 12/13. Another reason why Nigerian boards tend to be larger is the demand by many significant shareholders to have seats on the board.

4.1.2 Board Independence

Board independence is considered at two levels: at one level is the chairperson – CEO separation and at the other level is the dominance of outside directors on the board.

Most of the boards, about 97 %, had separated the positions of chairperson and CEO, which is in line with global best practice. This might indicate some degree of board independence, but in practice, many chairpersons and CEOs are nominees of the dominant or major shareholders. Such chairpersons or CEOs work in the interest of these shareholders and as such cannot be regarded as independent. A common practice found in many public companies in Nigeria is the appointment of former CEOs as chairpersons of boards (Ogbechie and Koufopoulos 2007). Such appointments might not enhance board independence.

The second level of board independence is the dominance of outside directors on the board. Outside directors are usually independent of the firm's management and so can be more objective and provide independent supervision of the firm's management (Fama and Jensen 1983). Boards of publicly quoted companies in Nigeria have more non-executive directors than executive directors, by a ratio of 64:36, which again is in line with global best practice. However, the degree of independence of the non-executive directors is doubtful as their appointment tends to be influenced by either the chairperson or the CEO or the dominant shareholder.

4.1.3 Board Diversity

Diversity is a factor that is considered in the evaluation of board performance and effectiveness. Board diversity implies that the directors have different skills, knowledge and experience, and they are also from different age groups and social status. Some researchers suggest that board diversity leads to a greater board knowledge base, creativity and innovation because of the diverse experience of members of the board (Watson et al. 1993). Nigerian boards are diverse in nature with the key professions represented being accountants, engineers, lawyers and economists with sound management experience in various industries. Directors are expected to have a working knowledge of financial matters, have a fair understanding of the industry their firm operates in and a good understanding of the business of their firm. Unfortunately, the percentage of female on Nigerian boards is on the low side. Furthermore, a recent investigation, by the authors on the presence of female directors on Nigerian boards yielded gender diversity level of 14 %, which is slight higher than what obtains other emerging market peers like Indonesia and South Africa which report figures of 11.2 % and 12.8% respectively (Azmi and Barret 2013; Lehobo 2011). However, compared with figures reported of industrialised countries, the figure is poor. Data released by GMI Ratings (2013) reveal that women constitute 36.1 %, 27.0 %, 26.8 % and 17.0 % of Norwegian, Swedish, Finnish and Dutch boardrooms respectively. Pande and Ford (2011) also informs that 15.2 % of board directors in the U.S. and 12.2 % in the UK (Fortune 500 and the FTSE 100) as of the female gender.

Board diversity in Nigerian state owned firms is not actually an independent factor in the sense that it is determined by a constitutional provision known as the Federal Character principle. This requires that national appointments in the public sector reflect the principle of equal representation of all the distinct political geographies of the Nigerian state. This principle is also known as the quota system. Following this, it is interesting to note that boards in Nigeria are constitutionally mandated to reflect the same degree of diversity arising from the diversity of geo-political nationalities characterizing the state. This policy is informed by the agitation for equitable distribution of national resources amongst the various ethnic groups. Federal character or the quota system in Nigeria is similar to the affirmative action policy of the United States of America and the equal opportunity principle practiced by many countries.

The letter and spirit of the Federal Character principle imply the composition of the government of the federation or any of its agencies and the conduct of its affairs in such a manner as to reflect the Federating units of Nigeria, the need to promote national unity, and also to command national loyalty, thereby ensuring that there be no dominance of persons from a few units in the government or in any of its agencies. Although this principle does not yet apply to States and Local Governments, the principle has however filtered into the private sector even though the constitution does not demand it. Diversity has therefore been engraved into the psyche of Nigerians. Any firm in Nigeria is very conscious of multi-stakeholder issues and therefore, the diversity problem in the country. Some firms operating in the country have consciously spread their board and top management appointments to reflect the diversity of the country.

The importance of true and effective implementation of federal character in public appointments to reflect the variables of a multi-cultural, multilingual, multi-religious Nigeria society cannot be over emphasized in the interests of sustainable peace and national development. It is important, particularly, in a plural society such as Nigeria, that all citizens feel a sense of equal voice, equal representation and equal participation. The sectional polarization has, in recent times, manifested itself in what is now known as "ethnic militias" that have led to several social unrests in the country. It is argued that these groups emerged to protect their collective ethnic or regional interests.

The adverse effect of Federal Character is the promotion of mediocrity or neglect of merit in appointments. This is because professionals and experienced individuals could be over-looked due to the fact that they are more in one part of the country than the other. In addition, ethnicity and religion are two issues that have also played dominant roles in the way of life and governance in Nigeria and Africa in general. The corporate governance implications of Federal Character in board appointments include having directors that are not competent and knowledgeable, and parochial loyalty to shareholders that are responsible for their appointment.

However, research results present that most Nigerian boards favour ensuring diversity on the basis of educational and occupational background than by any other means.

4.2 Board Committees

The effectiveness of boards will, to some extent, depend on the type and quality of board committees. The key board committees that were in existence include Audit, Risk Management, Remuneration, Credit (for banks), Governance, Nomination, and Succession. These are also the kind of committees that exist in developed markets. In most companies, the chairperson is usually not a member of any of the committees.

The audit committee (statutory) is the mandatory CAMA ordered committee that is made of up equal representation of shareholders and non-executive directors. This audit committee is not regarded as a board committee but shareholders' committee. The committee has the key objective of ensuring the integrity and efficiency of the audit process. It has oversight responsibility for the firm's financial statements, ensuring that they are prepared in accordance with the legal and accounting requirements and agreed ethical policies. However, it is not unusual to find another audit committee, particularly in banks, regarded as board audit committee and with the additional responsibility of enterprise risk management.

The risk management committee has the responsibility of assisting the Board in fulfilling its oversight responsibility in relation to the management of all (enterprise) risks within the firm. It also evaluates the effectiveness of the internal control system and ensures compliance with legal and regulatory requirements.

Many firms tend to have a committee to handle governance and personnel issues. This committee handles all corporate governance matters and also human capital issues at senior management level. It is responsible for director recruitment and development, director/executive compensation, and board/directors' evaluation.

4.3 Board Processes and Roles

Many Nigerian boards see their roles as overseeing activities of management, offering relevant advice to them, assisting them in business development using their social capital, and being involved in strategy development. These roles can only be performed effectively with the right board processes. There are several board processes that enable the board to perform its roles effectively, which enhance good board performance, and hence effective corporate governance within the Nigerian business environment. These include the process of recruiting the right directors, the quality and timeliness of board papers, conduct of board meetings, leadership style of the chairperson, degree of teamwork, board decision-making, conflict resolution, and board evaluation.

Board evaluation is still not wide spread but the Nigerian Securities and Exchange Commission (SEC) has made annual board evaluation mandatory for quoted companies. The most common approaches employed by companies include the use of external consultants and the use of governance committee to handle board and directors' evaluation.

Director remuneration is another thorny governance issue in Nigeria. Non-executive directors' remuneration is in two components – an annual director's fee, usually paid quarterly and sitting allowance paid after every meeting. The various codes are silent on the limit of remuneration and shareholders are expected to approve directors' remuneration at the annual general meeting. Share options and bonuses are not usually part of non-executive compensation package in Nigeria.

Many boards in Nigeria expect their directors to sign a code of conduct that guides their behaviour and actions as directors and are expected to abide by the code. In study conducted by Ogbechie (2012) show that most companies (87.4 %) hold board meetings quarterly (every 3 months); high deal of team spirit and take their board roles seriously.

5 Key Issues on Board Development in Nigeria

Shareholder vigilance in Nigeria is rather lax and external pressure on corporate management is also weak. Boards are therefore required to be major drivers of good corporate governance in Nigeria. The general roles played by boards, including those in Nigeria, can be classified into three broad categories. First, directors are expected to monitor senior executives, select and dismiss them, evaluate their performances and design their compensation packages. Second, directors should be part of defining, selecting and implementing corporate strategy. Third, directors should perform ceremonial functions that enhance the company's legitimacy (Pearce and Zahra 1992; Stiles and Taylor 2001).

How to enhance board effectiveness has become a focus of attention and debate amongst corporate governance experts and researchers. In the last few years there has been more pressure on boards to show how they add value to their companies. In Nigeria, the debate has gained momentum following a recent scandal involving Cadbury Nigeria which seems to have exposed the limited knowledge of boards in Nigeria and has brought to question the effectiveness of the board and individual directors. There was a deliberate overstatement of the company's financial position over a number of years (2003–2006) to the tune of N15 billion ($100 million) and the board did not pick it up over those years. Cadbury Nigeria had projected an ambitious growth target in a highly competitive market and it appeared that the board did not ask the right questions in connection with this growth target. Management of the company could not realistically achieve this target and so embarked on falsifying accounting figures through abuse of its systems and controls. This led to the firing of the Managing Director and Finance Director by the board. This corporate governance breach made the Securities and Exchange Commission (SEC) to penalize and reprimand the external Auditors and Registrars of Cadbury Nigeria.

After a forensic audit had been done by an independent auditor, SEC sent a query to the board of Cadbury Nigeria expressing concern on issues arising from the report in the areas of declining profitability, worsening leverage ratio, deteriorating cash flow, inadequate disclosure, non-compliance with Corporate Governance Code, and obtaining loans for the payment of dividends to shareholders contrary to SEC regulations. It was also discovered that an undocumented and undisclosed offshore account was maintained and operated by the company from which the managing director and executive directors were paid offshore remunerations without the approval of the Committee responsible for fixing remunerations of Executive Directors and not recorded in the company's financial report and account. All the directors were sacked and new ones appointed.

In Nigeria, like most developing countries, good corporate and public governance are critical to economic development and growth. It is therefore important to understand the role of boards in ensuring good governance practices. Recent and current developments in Nigeria's financial services industry have added more pep to the discussion on board effectiveness and good corporate governance. A number of financial failures, frauds and questionable business practices had adversely affected investors' confidence and customers' trust in the industry.

The corporate governance failures in the terminally distressed banks included insider abuses by executive and non-executive directors, related party loans that were not repaid, chief executive officers that built bank branches with loans from the banks and leasing these buildings to the bank, CEOs taking personal loans from other banks and using depositors' funds in their banks as collateral. Other financial engineering acts included recognising interest due from non-performing loans as income and using depositors' funds to pay the interest charges on some non-performing loans to give the impression that they are performing. Directors of the distressed banks were dismissed and had to face all kinds of legal charges ranging from insider abuses to economic crimes.

In Nigeria, the institutions that help guard against corporate malfeasance – Securities Exchange Commission, Nigeria Stock Exchange, the Judiciary, Institutional Investors, Professional Associations, and a probing Media – are still relatively weak or lack critical mass (Ettah 2008). Boards may therefore be the most reliable line of defence for good corporate governance. It is therefore important to understand how boards function and how best to make them effective and add value to the firm.

Many companies in Nigeria, particularly quoted companies, are responding to pressure from regulators for higher standards of corporate governance. Boards now appoint truly independent directors; have board committees such as audit, risk management, nomination (governance) and remuneration. They also invest in director training and development and embark on annual board/director evaluation.

Our study also shows that many board characteristics, apart from job diversity and professional human capital, do not have significant impact on board effectiveness. However, we found that board processes have significant impact on board effectiveness. The insignificance of board characteristics can be seen to be contrary to board reforms throughout the world in the last decade. The study shows the critical importance of board job diversity, professional human capital, board cohesiveness, board decision-making and board operation in ensuring board effectiveness. In effect, board processes including more preparation for board meetings, better decision-making, less personal conflicts and more usage of all the available skills on the board are more important than board structure. Overall, the results support the idea that board design involves both structural and process variables as propounded by Forbes and Milliken (1999), Finkelstein and Mooney (2003), Pye and Pettigrew (2005), Roberts et al (2005), and boards that want to be more effective must devote more attention to their processes and not just focus on the structure.

6 Recommendation

As the Nigerian economy grows towards becoming the leading economy in Africa in the next 20 years, it will attract more foreign investors and more Nigerian transnational companies will emerge. Good corporate governance will be critical in achieving this economic growth. The growth of institutional investors, such as pension funds, will also favour improvements in corporate governance. However, there is the urgent need to organise the various associations of shareholders to play more useful role in ensuring good corporate governance. There is a need for a regulatory body, just as SEC, to regulate their performance.

The various codes are adequate to ensure good corporate governance behaviour however; SEC and other regulatory bodies have to be more active in their enforcement roles. Regulatory agencies have to be strengthened in terms of human capital, competencies and other resources needed for effective operation.

Furthermore, there is a need for harmonization of all the codes into a single document so that the same set of rules and regulations can be used to evaluate companies irrespective of industry. Compliance with the code of corporate governance should be a pre-condition for listing in the stock exchange and quoted companies who do not adhere strictly to the code should be de-listed.

Quite importantly, a culture of whistle blowing should be encouraged as it would enhance good corporate governance practices. However, such promotion should start within companies to push for more decent behaviours. The SEC and Corporate Affairs Commission (CAC) should set up complaints hotlines and email addresses where whistle blowers can lodge their complaints. In addition, the culture of whistle blowing will also require the protection of crime investigating units and law enforcement agencies against political pressures and influences from the political office holders.

Finally, it is well established that good corporate governance practices is predicated by good public governance in the society. Thus, a political system or process that ensures public accountability is necessary for ensuring good corporate governance. The campaign for accountability and fight against corruption at national level should be supported by both public and private sector firms as well as the state.

7 Conclusion

The SEC code and the three industry specific currently in use in Nigeria have helped to facilitate good corporate governance practices in Nigeria to a large extent. However, this study has unveiled some major loopholes in corporate governance practices in Nigeria which require attention. For instance, despite the increase of company compliance to the various codes, findings have shown that, the Nigerian boards are yet to experience independence. It will be pertinent here for researchers to investigate the behaviour of directors particularly in emerging markets as regards corporate governance. Secondly, some directors are usually nominated by the dominant shareholders and as a consequence these board members likely to compromise their integrity to satisfy these powerful shareholders groups. Additionally research might be relevant in examining the role(s) of affiliated non-executive directors, their compensation, and degree of independence on board effectiveness and firm performance in emerging markets. In terms of board diversity, Nigeria boards appear to be well endowed with directors with diverse professional backgrounds. However, unfortunately women directors seem to be a rare breed as most board positions are occupied by men. Most Nigerian boardrooms are extensions of the old boys' network clubs. The federal character principle which is gradually is finding root in the private sector in Nigeria could breed mediocrity in the boards thus adversely affect corporate practices in Nigeria. Thus, it might useful to undertake empirical studies to analyse the impact such diversity in the board has on firm market performance.

References

Adekoya, A. (2011). Corporate governance reforms in Nigeria: Challenges and suggested solutions. *Journal of Business Systems, Governance and Ethics, 6*(1), 38–50.

Ahmed, M. (2007, March 30). *Corporate governance: A new fad or an important development prerequisite?* Paper presented at *British Council's Management Express Forum*, Calabar, Nigeria. Calabar: British Council.

Akindele, F., & Adegbite, W. (1992). *The sociology and politics of English in Nigeria: An introduction*. Ile-Ife: OAU Press.

Amaeshi, K., Adi, B. C., Ogbechie, C., & Amao, O. O. (2006). Corporate social responsibility in Nigeria: Indigenous practices or Western influences? *Journal of Corporate Citizenship, 24*(39), 83–99.

Amao, O., & Amaeshi, K. (2008). Galvanising shareholder activism: A prerequisite for effective corporate governance. *Journal of Business Ethics, 82*(1), 119–130.

Azmi, I. A. G., & Barrett, M. A. (2013). Women on boards and company financial performance: A study of Malaysian SMEs. In *Proceedings of 3rd global accounting, finance and economics conference*, Melbourne, Australia.

Central Bank of Nigeria. (2006). *Code of corporate governance for banks in Nigeria post-consolidation*. Abuja: CBN Publications.

Barton, D., & Wong, S. C. Y. (2006). Improving board performance in emerging markets. *The McKinsey Quarterly, 1*, 35–43.

Boswell, N. Z. (2013). Ethics in a global economy: 'Code red' bribery and corruption in the world. *Drake Management Review, 2*(2), 1–7.

Dabor, E. L., & Adeyemi, S. B. (2009). Corporate governance and credibility of financial statements in Nigeria. *Journal of Business Systems, Governance and Ethics, 4*(1), 13–24.

Doing Business. (2012). *Doing business 2012: Doing business in a more transparent world*. Washington, DC: The International Bank for Reconstruction and Development/The World Bank Publishers. http://www.doingbusiness.org/reports/global-reports/doing-business-2012

Dornyei, Z. (2003). *Questionnaires in second language research: Construction, administration and processing*. New Jersey: Lawrence Erlbaum Associates.

Ettah, L. (2008). *Governance, size, and diversity: Multiple roles of boards*. Annual conference of the Institute of Chartered Secretaries and Administrators of Nigeria (ICSAN). Lagos: ICSAN publication. [Online] Available at: http://www.unacnplc.com/news/publications /ICSAN.doc. Accessed 6 Mar 2013.

Fama, E. F., & Jensen, M. C. (1983). Separation of ownership and control. *Journal of Law and Economics, 26*(2), 301–325.

Finkelstein, S., & Mooney, A. C. (2003). Not the usual suspects: How to use the board process to make boards better. *Academy of Management Executive, 17*(2), 101–113.

Forbes, D. P., & Milliken, F. J. (1999). Cognition and corporate governance: Understanding boards of directors as strategic decision-making groups. *Academy of Management Review, 24*(3), 489–505.

Gladman, K., & Lamb, M. (2013). *GMI ratings' 2013 women on Boards survey*. [Report] GMI ratings. Retrieved from: http://www.fortefoundation.org/site/DocServer/GMIRatings_WOB_042013.pdf?docID=19201. Accessed 10 July 2013.

Guobadia, A. (2000). Protecting minority and public interests in Nigeria company law: The Corporate Affairs Commission as a corporation's ombudsman. In F. McMillan (Ed.), *International Company Law Annual* (pp. 1–81). Oxford/Portland: Hart Publishing.

Haliru, T. (2012). Ethnicity and political violence in Nigeria: Challenges of democratic governance. *Journal of Research in Peace, Gender and Development, 2*(4), 89–94.

Holbrook, A., Cho, Y. I., & Johnson, T. (2006). The impact of question and respondent characteristics on comprehension and mapping difficulties. *Public Opinion, 70*(4), 565–595.

Iarossi, G., Mousley, P., & Radwan, I. (2009). *Private sector development: An assessment of the investment climate in Nigeria*. Washington, DC: The International Bank for Reconstruction and Development/The World Bank.

Joshua, S. (2013). Democracy and violent conflicts in Nigeria: Implications for national development. *An International Multidisciplinary Journal, 7*(3), 324–339.

Lehobo, L. (2011). *The relationship between gender diversity and corporate profitability: The top 100 companies on the JSE Ltd.* (Master's Thesis), University of Johannesburg. Accessed at https://ujdigispace.uj.ac.za/bitstream/handle/10210/8120/Lehobo.pdf?sequence=1

Leitz, P. (2008). *Questionnaire design in attitude and opinion research: Current state of an art*. Technical report number: For 655, Jacobs University Bremen.

Martin, E., (2006). *Survey questionnaire construction*. Research report series (Survey Methodology #2006–13), Washington, DC: U.S. Census Bureau.

National Insurance Commission Code. (2009). *Code of corporate governance for insurance companies in Nigeria*. Abuja: NAICOM Publications.

National Planning Commission. (2004). *National Economic Empowerment and Development Strategy (NEEDS)*. Abuja: Communications Development Incorporated. Available at: www.ng.undp.org/documents/NEEDS/NEEDS.pdf. Accessed 6 Apr 2013.

Oduh, M. O., & Oduh, M. O. (2012). Homogenous Economic policy and heterogeneous consumer economy: Empirical analysis of the vulnerability of the regions to macroeconomic policy in Nigeria. *European Journal of Business and Management, 4*(14), 129–138.

Ogbechie, C. (2012). *Key determinants of effective boards of directors: Evidence from Nigeria*. Ph.D. thesis, Brunel Business School, Brunel University.

Ogbechie, C., & Koufopoulous, D. N. (2007). Corporate governance practices in publicly quoted companies in Nigeria. *International Journal of Business Governance and Ethics, 3*(4), 350–381.

Okike, E. N. M. (2007). Corporate governance in Nigeria: The status quo. *Corporate Governance, 15*(2), 173–193.

Olofin, A. O. (2012). Effects of English language on national development. *Greener Journal of Social Sciences, 2*(4), 134–139.

Olokor, F. (2013, July 26). Nigeria's global GDP ranking now 36th – Jonathan. *Punch* [online]. Available at: http://www.punchng.com/business/business-economy/nigerias-global-gdp-ranking-now-36th-jonathan/. Accessed 26 July 2013.

Olusa, M. (2007). Corporate governance vs. Cadbury Nigeria. *Guardian* [online]. Available at: http://www.guardiannewsngr.com/editorial_opinion/article 03/160107. Accessed 10 Feb 2013.

Omoh, G. (2013). FG inaugurates committee on code of corporate governance. *Punch* [online]. Retrieved at: http://www.vanguardngr.com/2013/01/fg-inaugurates-committee-on-code-of-corporate-governance/. Accessed 11 Mar 2013.

Onapajo, H. (2012). Politics for God: Religion, politics and conflict in democratic Nigeria. *The Journal of Pan African Studies, 4*(9), 42–66.

Onyema, O. (2012). *The stock exchange as a financing option for long-term business expansion.* Paper presented at Academy for Entrepreneurial Studies (AES) Excellence Club meeting, Lagos. Accessed at:http://www.nse.com.ng/MarketNews/CEOs%20Presentation/The%20Stock%20Exchange%20as%20a%20Financing%20Option%20For%20Long-Term%20Business%20Expansion.pdf

Organization for Economic Co-operation and Development [OECD]. (2008). *African economic outlook: Nigeria* [online]. Available at: www.oecd.org/dev/emea/40573969.pdf. Accessed 6 Apr 2013.

Pande, R., & Ford, D. (2011). *Gender quotas and female leadership: A review.* Background paper for the world development report on gender. Retrieved at: http://www.hks.harvard.edu/fs/rpande/papers/Gender%20Quotas%20-%20April%202011.pdf. Accessed 16 July 2013.

Pearce, J., & Zahra, S. (1992). Board composition from a strategic contingency perspective. *Journal of Management Studies, 29*(4), 411–438.

Pye, A., & Pettigrew, A. (2005). Studying board context, process and dynamics: Some challenges for the future. *British Journal of Management, 16*, S27–S38.

Roberts, J. T., Mc Nulty, P., & Stiles, P. (2005). Beyond agency conceptions of the work of the non-executive directors: Creating accountability in the boardroom. *British Journal of Management, 16*(1), S5–S6.

Roe, M. J. (2003). *Political determinations of corporate governance: Political context, corporate impact.* Oxford: Oxford University Press.

Saheed, Z. S. (2012). Impact of social crises on economic development: Theoretical evidence from Nigeria. *American International Journal of Contemporary Research, 2*(6), 176–184.

Salawu, B. (2010). Ethno-religious conflict in Nigeria: Causal analysis and proposals for new management strategies. *European Journal of Social Sciences, 13*(3), 345–353.

SEC Code. (2011). *Security and Exchange Commission revised code of corporate governance for public listed companies in the Nigerian Stock Exchange.* Retrieved at: http://www.sec.gov.ng/code-of-corporate-governance-.html. Accessed 11 Mar 2013.

Stiles, P. (2001). The Impact of the board on strategy: An empirical examination. *Journal of Management Studies, 38*(5), 627–650.

Stiles, P., & Taylor, B. (2001). *Boards at work: How directors view their roles and responsibilities: How directors view their roles and responsibilities.* Oxford: Oxford University Press.

United Nations Development Programme [UNDP]. (2010). *The real wealth of nations: Pathways to human development* (UNDP Report). Retrieved at: http://hdr.undp.org/en/media/HDR_2010_EN_Complete_reprint.pdf. Accessed 17 Sept 2012.

Watson, E., Kumar, K., & Michaelsen, L. (1993). Cultural diversity's impact on interaction process and performance: Comparing homogeneous and diverse task groups. *Academy of Management Journal, 36*, 590–603.

Wilson, I. (2006). Regulatory and institutional challenges of corporate governance in Nigeria post – Banking consolidation. [Online] *Nigerian Economic Summit Group (NESG) Economic Indicators, 12*(2), 1–10. Available at: http://www.templars-law.com/media/regulatory%20and%20intitutional%20challenges.pdf. Accessed 7 Feb 2013.

Corporate Governance in Bangladesh: A Comparison with Other Emerging Market Countries

Chowdhury Saima Ferdous, Chris Mallin, and Kean Ow-Yong

Abstract Corporate governance has developed a higher profile in recent years in many emerging markets. Bangladesh as an emerging country provides an interesting case study. Whilst its economy has achieved an impressive growth rate, weak governance has caused an increasing number of companies to fail. Governance codes have been developed in many other emerging countries including Bangladesh and a comparative analysis may ascertain if their provisions are internationally compatible. This chapter discusses the theoretical framework and outlines the various governance codes and guidelines in Bangladesh and contrasts them with the OECD Principles of Corporate Governance as well as those codes in India and Pakistan. Using case studies and examples, we illustrate the key corporate governance characteristics typically found in companies in these countries. We highlight the common governance features and discuss their differences. Our chapter outlines a number of the practical and policy implications for corporate governance in the emerging markets of Bangladesh, Pakistan and India.

1 Introduction

Emerging countries do not need to be reminded about the failure of large multinational companies like Enron or Parmalat to highlight the necessity of ensuring good corporate governance. In recent years many of them have reported some significant

C.S. Ferdous
Department of International Business, The University of Dhaka, Dhaka, Bangladesh

C. Mallin (✉)
Norwich Business School, University of East Anglia, Norwich, UK
e-mail: C.Mallin@uea.ac.uk

K. Ow-Yong
Birmingham Business School, University of Birmingham, Birmingham, UK

S. Boubaker and D.K. Nguyen (eds.), *Corporate Governance in Emerging Markets*, CSR, Sustainability, Ethics & Governance, DOI 10.1007/978-3-642-44955-0_16,

home-grown company scandals and failures. Bangladesh suffered two massive capital market crashes (1996 and 2011) where deficiencies in governance standards were alleged to be a contributing factor (Imam and Malik 2007). Hence, it is not surprising to find that there has been an increasing interest among emerging countries, through issuing governance codes and guidelines, to emphasize the importance of good corporate governance practice. Studies have empirically shown that companies' disclosure of compliance with best practice recommendations not only has a positive impact on the stock market (e.g. Fernández-Rodríguez et al. 2004; Igor et al. 2006) and improves performance (Bauwhede 2009; Mallin and Ow-Yong 2012), but also helps the country to remain up-to-date with recent changes (Akkermans et al. 2007).

The evidence of companies not complying with their respective governance codes prompted countries to try and narrow the gap between the standards and reality through reforming and revising their codes (e.g. MacNeil and Li 2006; Parsa et al. 2007). Moreover, a recent study (Claessens and Yurtoglu 2013) on the corporate governance practices in emerging markets stated that the development of codes of corporate governance is vital particularly for the emerging countries, because it helps to improve the governance standard, which in turn benefits companies by allowing greater access to financing, strengthens the capital market, ensures lower cost of capital, better financial performance and more favorable treatment of all stakeholders – and these benefits are vital for sustainable economic growth in the emerging market countries.

However, developing a code is not an easy task. In response to the need for an international benchmark of good governance the 'OECD Principles of Corporate Governance' were issued in (1999) and subsequently amended in 2004. Today, the OECD Principles (2004) are widely accepted as a global benchmark which is considered as adaptable to varying social, legal and economic contexts in individual countries (Krambia-Kapardis and Psaros 2006). Donor agencies and institutional investors are thus prioritizing this kind of benchmark to be reflected in code provisions and that is one of the reasons behind the similarities in the content of governance codes around the world (Aguilera and Cuervo-Cazurra 2009). Nevertheless, domestic pressures are causing divergence in governance codes. Emerging countries are expected to revise the provisions of a benchmark governance code to reflect local circumstances.

Researchers (e.g. Rwegasira 2000; Wanyama et al. 2009) argue that in the absence of a strong legal system and adequate infrastructure, the differences in political and cultural background found in emerging countries make it difficult to design a governance code where its provisions are internationally compatible and at the same time, reflect the local needs. Nevertheless, countries like India, have developed their own governance codes and revised them subsequently. For instance, India has established the whistle blowing concept and has expanded its provisions relating to the appointment and authority of an independent director; whilst Pakistan, realizing the challenges, has in its revised Code, made it mandatory for directors to attend training including training on corporate governance.

Although Bangladesh started its journey with a more voluntary approach for Code compliance, in its revised form, the policy-makers have placed more emphasis on Code compliance, i.e. the expectation is that the listed companies will comply with the provisions as a listing requirement. In instances where they cannot comply, they can explain their non-compliance. However, designing an appropriate code for emerging markets has become even more difficult because, there is a controversy in the appropriateness of governance codes in emerging market countries. An increasing number of studies (Adu-Amoah et al. 2008; Bhagat and Black 2002) strongly argue that the codes reflecting the Anglo-American model of governance are not suitable for emerging markets. Instead it is the stakeholder model which would be the better alternative. One effective way to respond is to go beyond the one size fits all approach, and concentrate on the local needs when designing more appropriate corporate governance practices (Letza et al. 2004). Hence, research should be carried out on the ways in which countries are adapting the governance code provisions which will guide other countries with a similar corporate infrastructure.

This chapter addresses this need by taking the case of Bangladesh and contrasting it with its neighboring countries, India and Pakistan (the 'emerging market countries' generally referred to in this chapter) which share many common political and other socio-economic characteristics. Thus a comparison with these two countries will help Bangladesh policy makers to understand how, whilst bearing similar kinds of socio-economic and cultural issues, these neighbours are facing up to the challenges of good governance.

This chapter also explores the theories underpinning the development of codes (Sect. 2); draws a comparative analysis of the code contents (Sect. 3); and analyzes the corporate structure (Sect. 4) – which will help the policy makers to understand how different countries are dealing with similar kinds of issues via codes of corporate governance (Sect. 5). The chapter ends by drawing concluding thoughts in the light of the overall findings.

2 Regulation, Corporate Governance Codes and Guidelines

The corporate governance structures in Bangladesh, India and Pakistan have evolved through a long historical and political change. Bangladesh emerged from its war of independence in 1971 with extreme poverty, overpopulation, and a ravaged corporate and socio-economic infrastructure. A visible corporate governance structure started taking shape after its independence and in the last two decades in particular (Mir and Rahaman 2005). In order to overcome the economic disaster, the Government (since 1972) made some industrial reformation policies and also reviewed business and corporate level strategies to promote public and private sector of Bangladesh.[1] The effort of government initiatives (along with the support of different national and international associations) were successful in changing the pessimistic opinion on the possibilities for Bangladesh, and made it one of the fastest growing economies. Historically, public enterprises were the mainstay of the Bangladesh economy (Sarker 2011) following the nationalization of major industrial units. However, due to corruption, political intervention, bureaucracy, lack of management efficiency and over-staffing these public sector units turned into loss-making concerns (Farooque et al. 2007). As a result of these failures and the world-wide trend towards privatization, the successive governments in Bangladesh pursued the principles of a market economy, particularly since the 1990s.

In recent years, more emphasis has been placed on export oriented industrial development led by the private sector. Rapid industrialization was seen as a key strategy for achieving faster economic development (Belal and Owen 2007); strengthening the stock exchange and then establishing a Securities and Exchange Commission (SEC) for developing and controlling private sector capital. The low labor cost and Bangladesh's government undertakings to pursue market economic policies in the country have attracted huge foreign investment since 1980.[2] Corporate governance issues thus have become prominent in Bangladesh in recent times as its domestic economy integrates with the global economy, and firms are under pressure to maintain international competitiveness.

The *Bangladesh Enterprise Institute* (BEI) a donor-funded private think-tank was formed in 2000 and is actively involved in shaping the corporate governance regulations in Bangladesh.[3] BEI took a remarkable step in corporate governance by developing the voluntary Code of Corporate Governance for Bangladesh (2004),[4] which is the only voluntary code for Bangladesh. Later in 2006, the Securities and Exchange Commission of Bangladesh introduced a very brief corporate governance guideline (hereafter the "SEC Guidelines") for its members, which was revised in 2012. Table 1 (panel A) provides a brief summary of the available codes of corporate governance in Bangladesh.

---

[1] The major policies were related to: (i) privatization of poorly governed public enterprises (ii) encouraging public enterprises and foreign investors, while progressively discouraging the growth of the public sector (iii) improving the import regime, and introducing investment and export incentives, (iv) improving the efficiency of public sector industrial enterprises through financial restructuring and (v) improvements in pricing policies (Palit 2006).

[2] The World Investment Report 2011, published by The United Nations Conference on Trade and Development shows that although "FDI to South Asia declined due to recession, inflows to Bangladesh increased by nearly 30 % to $913 million" http://www.unctad.org

[3] BEI was established as a non-profit research centre. Its Board of Governors includes business personalities, political members and bureaucrats. BEI provides training to directors of companies, conducts dialogue with policy-makers and different stakeholder groups.

[4] The international donors that assisted in organizing the Taskforce on Corporate Governance and supported the development of the Code for Bangladesh: namely, the Department for International Development (DFID), the Commonwealth Secretariat and the Global Corporate Governance Forum (GCGF).

Table 1 Codes of corporate governance in Bangladesh, India and Pakistan

Panel A: codes of corporate governance in Bangladesh		
Code	**Issued by**	**Year issued**
Code of Corporate Governance for Bangladesh	Bangladesh Enterprise Institute	2004
Corporate Governance Guidelines	Securities and Exchange Commission of Bangladesh	2006
Corporate Governance Guidelines (revised)	Securities and Exchange Commission of Bangladesh	2012
Panel B: codes of corporate governance in India		
Code	**Issued by**	**Year issued**
Desirable Corporate Governance: A Code	Confederation of Indian Industry (CII)	1998
Kumar Mangalam Birla Committee on Corporate Governance	Securities and Exchange Board of India	2000
Naresh Chandra Committee on Corporate Audit and Governance	Government of India, Ministry of Finance and Corporate Affairs	2002
Narayan Murthy Committee on Corporate Governance	Securities and Exchange Board of India	2003
Corporate Governance Voluntary Disclosure	Ministry of Finance and Corporate Affairs/CII	2009
Panel C: codes of corporate governance in Pakistan		
Code	**Issued by**	**Year issued**
Stock Exchange Code of Corporate Governance	Securities and Exchange Commission of Pakistan	2002
Code of Corporate Governance (revised)	Securities and Exchange Commission of Pakistan	2002
Code of Corporate Governance (revised)	Securities and Exchange Commission of Pakistan	2012

Source: European Corporate Governance Institute (www.ecgi.org); Dhaka stock exchange (www.dsebd.org); Narayanaswamy et al. (2012)

The history of the corporate governance development in India is similar to Bangladesh. India also adopted a socialistic approach to industrial production which continued until 1991 when the government embarked on some major policies and successive governments followed the path of economic liberalization (Narayanaswamy et al. 2012). The government, regulators and private sectors have taken initiatives to reform corporate governance and financial reporting in India. "Desirable Corporate Governance: A Code" was the first Indian governance code issued in 1998 by the Confederation of Indian Industry (CII). This outlined a number of recommendations with the aim to protect investor interest, especially small investors, promotion of transparency and ensuring international compatibility in reporting. However, the four later Indian governance codes were issued either by the government or the regulators. Table 1 provides a brief summary of these Indian governance codes.

Panel B of Table 1 suggests that unlike Bangladesh, the Indian Government and its agencies have to a large extent, taken the initiative in developing the country's governance codes. In Pakistan, the first Code of Corporate Governance issued in 2002 and its subsequent two revisions were made by the country's stock market regulator as indicated in Panel C of Table 1. In terms of corporate governance code development, the analysis suggests that in emerging market countries, they are mainly developed by the regulators and governments. The role of the private sector varies across countries, but the institutional investors and other stakeholders' associations are almost silent in developing or revising governance codes.

3 Comparative Analysis of Corporate Governance

This section analyses the corporate governance codes in Bangladesh, India and Pakistan by comparing a number of their key features using a matrix[5] table. We focus on three main areas namely: the extent to which the governance codes meet international recommendations (i.e. OECD Principles of Corporate Governance 2004); how they vary with each other; and finally, we discuss how the provisions in these governance codes deal with board issues, shareholders' participation and disclosure.

3.1 Features of the Corporate Governance Codes

Table 2 compares the fundamental features of the Codes. These Codes are generally issued by the stock market regulators or government bodies with the exception of the Bangladeshi governance code which was issued by BEI, a private think-tank.

Previous studies (e.g. Conyon and Mallin 1997; Zattoni and Cuomo 2008) have stated that compliance with governance codes is voluntary and has no specific legal basis. Table 2 suggests that except for Pakistan, both Bangladesh and India promote voluntary compliance using the comply-or-explain mechanism and thus are in line with the OECD recommended principles. However, emerging countries need to increase the efficiency of the internal corporate governance (i.e. via the board of directors) and support from external market forces to ensure the credibility of the voluntary compliance mechanism in their corporate environment. That is perhaps why the SEC of Bangladesh, placed more emphasis on making the provisions mandatory. Whilst the SEC Guidelines 2006 followed a comply-or-explain mechanism, it was later revised in 2012 to 'comply' only.

[5] In the case of India and Pakistan, their most recent codes were used for comparison. i.e. from India the "Corporate Governance Voluntary Disclosure" (2009), and from Pakistan the "Code of Corporate Governance" (2012).

Table 2 The corporate governance codes

		Bangladesh		Developing countries	
	OECD principles	Code – Bangladesh	SEC guidelines	Code – India	Code – Pakistan
Issuer and year issued	OECD; 2004	BEI (a private think-tank); 2004	SEC; 2012	The Government of India; 2009	SEC; 2012
Enforcement mechanism	Voluntary	Voluntary	Comply	Voluntary	Mandatory
Scope of the code	Policymakers, regulators and market participants in OECD and Non-OECD countries	Private companies, financial institutions, SOEs and NGOs	Listed companies	Public and private companies	Listed companies
Coverage of the code	Board CG framework Shareholders Stakeholders Disclosure and transparency	Board Shareholders Disclosure Sector-specific provisions	Board Audit committee Auditors Subsidiary Company CEO and CFO Duties	Board Audit committee Auditors Whistle blowing	Board Disclosure Compliance
Aims of the code	Improve the confidence of domestic investors Reduce the cost of capital Functioning of financial markets Stable sources of financing	Improve CG practices and performance Reduce cost of capital Attract quality personnel Greater investment Attract quality investors Efficient allocation of resources	Enhance corporate governance for investors and capital market	Enhance the value of company and stakeholders Provide a global benchmark for good CG	Improves CG practices Makes capital market transparent Protects rights of minority shareholders Sustainable economic growth

Source: European Corporate Governance Institute (www.ecgi.org); Dhaka stock exchange (www.dsebd.org); Bangladesh Enterprise Institute (www.bei-bd.org)

Notes: *CG* stands for Corporate Governance, *SEC* Securities and Exchange Commission

The comparison of the scope of the governance codes, i.e. the type of companies considered by the codes, indicates that similar to the OECD Principles, all of the codes cover public limited companies.

Zattoni and Cuomo (2008) also report that most of the codes contents apply to companies listed in national stock exchanges. Perhaps that is the reason why Conyon and Mallin's (1997) study found that publicly traded companies tend to respond to the main code recommendations Nevertheless, as Table 2 indicates, the Codes of Bangladesh and India have also included private companies, whilst the Code of Bangladesh has extended its scope a bit further to cover state-owned enterprises (SOEs) and non-governmental organizations (NGOs).

Table 2 also contains a comparison of the main provisions covered by each code. It suggests that governance codes are almost similar in terms of their main provisions. For instance, all the codes reflect OECD Principles in emphasizing issues relating to board matters, financial and non-financial disclosures and audit. However, among the three governance codes, the Indian governance code is focused more on board issues and made no reference to shareholder rights and disclosures. The Indian governance code is in fact unique among the sample codes because it has provisions on whistle-blowing. The Bangladeshi governance code extended its coverage by including sector-specific provisions. The SEC Guidelines for Bangladesh also extended their coverage by emphasizing more on Independent Directors (as in the Indian governance code), identifying provisions for subsidiary companies and the duties of the CEO and CFO.

Overall, the coverage of the sample governance codes suggests that the agency theory prevails and that the core code recommendations are board centric with an emphasis on the check and balance to control agency costs. The three key provisions in the sample governance codes are discussed in the following sections.

Globalization offers developing and less developed countries an opportunity to increase private investment, modernize technologies, raise employment and accelerate economic growth. The ability of developing countries to harness these benefits will depend on how quickly and effectively they can resolve the socio-economic issues, strengthen their capital markets, and establish ethical and overall governance standards. Perhaps that is the reason why the codes are broadly similar to the OECD Principles in articulating their functions.

3.2 The Code Provisions Relating to Board Issues

Table 3 contains a comparison of the governance code provisions relating to the board. As an international benchmark for good governance, the OECD Principles recommend that the role of chief executive and chairman should be split in order to strengthen objectivity in judgment, achieve an appropriate balance of power, and increase accountability – and all three sample governance codes conform to this approach. It is interesting to note that the original Pakistani governance code

Table 3 Board related issues

		Bangladesh		Developing countries	
Board issues	OECD principles	Code – Bangladesh	SEC – guidelines	Code – India	Code – Pakistan
CEO/Chairman split	Strongly recommended	Yes	Yes	Yes	Yes
ID on board	Strongly recommended	Yes	Yes	Yes	Yes
Multiple directorships	Restrictions on multiple directorship and emphasized on attending board meetings	Not more than 6 boards; -at least 50 % attendance in board meetings	Need to disclose the number of directorships	Not more than 7 boards	Not more than 7 boards
Board code of conduct	Strongly recommended	Yes	Yes	No provision	No provision
Evaluation of board performance	For board, CEO and chairman	Yes (for board and chairman; collectively and individually)	No specific provision or general statement	Yes (for board, committees, and individual directors)	Yes (for board)
Training for board members	Both in-house and outside	Yes	No specific provision or general statement	Yes	Yes
Board committees	Audit Remuneration Nomination Ethics	Audit Remuneration Nomination	Audit	Audit Remuneration Nomination	Audit Human resource and remuneration

Source: European Corporate Governance Institute (www.ecgi.org); Dhaka stock exchange (www.dsebd.org); Bangladesh Enterprise Institute (www.bei-bd.org)

introduced in 2002 did not make it mandatory for the listed companies to split the roles of Chair/CEO, but the updated version (2012) did.

The Indian governance code is relatively stricter on this provision. In order to promote the balance of power, it recommends that even the physical location of the offices of the CEO and Chairman should be separated. Nevertheless, all of them recommend that the Chairman should be elected from amongst the non-executive directors.

The OECD Principles also recommend that a sufficient number of board members will need to be independent to exercise objective judgment; boards must declare who they consider to be independent and why they are independent; and independent members must be included in different committees created by the board. As shown in Table 3, all of the sample governance codes have, to varying degrees, conformed with these recommendations. The Bangladeshi governance code identifies the appropriate range of the board size[6] and recommends including different competence levels. To ensure effective board decisions and better transparency like the other codes it also emphasizes inclusion of non-executive directors (NEDs) on the board. However, the Bangladeshi governance code gives more emphasis to NEDs over independent directors (ID) claiming that the companies are not yet ready to appoint independent directors.

Due to the dominance of family businesses, the independent status of an ID would be questioned in many of the emerging markets (Aggarwal 2010). However, the necessity to include IDs on a board is further reflected by the SEC Guidelines of the country. Whilst the initial Guideline issued by the SEC in Bangladesh strongly recommended the presence of IDs, in its updated version it strengthened this provision by adding a provision to ensure the independence of the ID. For instance, it clarified the definition of ID and to ensure that an ID is able to give sufficient time to his/her responsibilities it limits the number of boards an ID could serve on to three. Moreover, as Indian and Pakistani companies operate in a similar environment, their respective governance codes addressed these issues too by adding some additional provisions. The Indian governance code requires the board to put in place policies for specifying attributes of independent directors, their expertise, foresight, management quality and ability to understand financial statements. It also suggests that the independent directors should provide a detailed 'Certificate of Independence' at the time of their appointment and thereafter annually. The Pakistani governance code too expanded its criteria for assessing the independence of the ID.

Table 3 also indicates that all of the sample governance codes adhere to the OECD Principles that recommend a limit to multiple board directorships in order to ensure board members have sufficient time and ability to commit themselves effectively to their responsibilities. With the exception of the Bangladeshi SEC

[6] Although the Code of Corporate Governance for Bangladesh does not specify any number but referring internationally to successful companies it states 7–15 is an ideal size to ensure that the size of the board is large enough to include directors with diverse expertise and experience, but not too large to preclude involvement by all directors.

Guidelines, the rest of the sample governance codes set a maximum number of board directorships to be held by a director. The Bangladeshi SEC Guidelines merely require that the listed companies declare the number of directorships held by each director. The OECD Principles 2004 also recommend the disclosure of the number of board meetings attended by each board member. None of the sample governance codes made this recommendation apart from the Bangladeshi governance code which further recommends that directors who have not attended at least 50 % of the board meetings (without a leave of absence) during the reported year should not be eligible for re-election to the board.

The OECD Principles recommend that appropriate codes of conduct or behavior should be developed for the board in order to make the objectives of the board clear and operational; this is particularly important to establish an overall framework for ethical standards. Table 3 suggests that Bangladesh is more responsive to this provision. Although the other two countries' governance code identified major board responsibilities, the Bangladeshi governance code/Guidelines went further in recommending that the responsibilities be codified with detailed guidelines on the directors' role which must be reviewed every year and agreed by the directors. All of the sample governance codes broadly implemented the OECD Principles 2004 regarding board's performance evaluation. The OECD Principles 2004 state that besides compliance requirements on internal control, companies should include and disclose the self-assessment by the board of their performance as well as the performance of the CEO/Chairman. The Bangladeshi governance code further recommends that the evaluation should be done collectively as a board and individually including the chairman. The Indian governance code highlighted the evaluation of committees' performance as well. However the Bangladeshi SEC Guidelines made no mention on board self-assessment in its updated version. In contrast, the Pakistani governance code makes it mandatory for the listed companies to develop mechanisms that evaluate the performance of the Board.

Table 3 also indicates that all of the sample governance codes are similar in recommending that companies engage in board training to meet their needs. The nature and extent of directors' training varies with each sample governance code. For instance, the Bangladeshi governance code recommends that companies should provide funding to support training and the need for new directors to familiarize themselves with corporate governance while the Indian governance code emphasizes the need for training on financial reporting. The Pakistani governance code goes much further in making it mandatory for directors of the listed companies to attend an approved director's training program. Table 3 concludes by comparing the recommendations relating to board committees. It shows that the governance codes, with the exception of the Bangladeshi SEC Guidelines, recommend that boards should have audit, remuneration and nomination sub-committees. The Bangladeshi SEC Guidelines elaborate the provisions relating to the Audit Committee, but it does not mention about any other sub-committees. However, all of the governance codes recommend the presence of an independent audit committee to provide monitoring and oversight of the internal audit functions and to ensure true and fair reflection of the reported financial statements. The sample governance codes support the OECD Principles in defining the composition of the audit committee and the qualification of the Chairman of the audit committee. Each of them specifies detailed provisions relating to the major tasks, independence and transparency of an audit committee.

Lack of ethics and corruption are two of the most cited barriers to good governance in emerging countries (Chen and Roberts 2010; Ehrgott et al. 2011; Rwegasira 2000; Wanyama et al. 2009). Even though all of these sample governance codes emphasize developing a code of ethics, none has recommended developing a sub-committee on ethics as suggested by the OECD Principles 2004.

3.3 The Code Provision Relating to Shareholders' Participation

The Bangladeshi governance code has some recommendations relating to cumulative voting as a possible alternative voting method so as to increase the chances of the minority shareholders being represented on the board. It also proposes to change the hand count of voting system to a ballot procedure to ensure free and fair voting. Moreover, it supports the OECD Principles 2004 by recommending detailed provisions about the meeting agenda and offering the opportunity to shareholders to include related agenda items before the meeting. However, it does not stipulate the formation of a nomination sub-committee nor the disclosure of a company's remuneration policy thus depriving the opportunity for the shareholders to participate in these key governance decisions, whereas the Pakistani governance code is more comprehensive in this regard. Although cumulative voting[7] would not guarantee that a minority group could elect a director, the Bangladeshi governance code recommends that an organized group of shareholders might be able to do so. Hence, in addition to this, the Bangladeshi governance code raised awareness among shareholders' about their rights and responsibilities.

Table 4 shows that while each of the corporate governance guidelines have emphasize the right of shareholders to be informed and require detailed disclosure of matters that may directly or indirectly affect the interest of shareholders, the Bangladeshi governance code goes further and recommends issuing a 'Shareholders Handbook'. It argues that disinterest among shareholders about their rights is a primary concern in Bangladesh; thus whilst emphasizing their rights it is the responsibility of companies to educate and inform shareholders. Table 4 also suggests that the Bangladeshi governance code is more detailed than the SEC

[7] Cumulative voting system is "a method of stock voting that permits shareholders to cast all votes for one candidate. A voting system that gives minority shareholders more power, by allowing them to cast all of their board of director votes for a single candidate, as opposed to regular or statutory voting, in which shareholders must vote for a different candidate for each available seat, or distribute their votes between a number of candidates" (www.corp-gov.org)

Table 4 Shareholders' rights

		Bangladesh		Other emerging countries	
Nature of shareholders' right	OECD principles	Code – Bangladesh	SEC guidelines	Code – India	Code – Pakistan
Right to be informed	Company general and material information and changes; Notice about AGM;	Yes (including share holders' handbook)	No specific provision	Yes	Yes
Participation in meetings and decision making process	Through attending AGMs, voting, participating in key CG decisions,	Yes (attending AGMs; voting; asking questions to the board)	No specific provision	No specific provision	Yes
Voting rights	Elect and remove board members; vote in person or in proxy; cumulative voting	Yes (voting in person and in proxy; proposed cumulative voting)	No specific provision	No specific provision	Yes (especially to elect board directors, audit sub-committee)
Annual general meeting	Date, time and location; Agenda	Yes (notice together with all pertinent information)	No specific provision	No specific provision	Yes (shareholders must receive the notice with all pertinent information)

Source: European Corporate Governance Institute (www.ecgi.org); Dhaka stock exchange (www.dsebd.org); Bangladesh Enterprise Institute (www.bei-bd.org)

Guidelines and the Pakistani governance code in protecting minority shareholders' rights. The Indian governance code explains that the minority shareholders' rights are already protected by its company laws. In addition, to further protect the rights, the Indian governance Code recommends that "for every agenda item at the Board meeting, there should be attached an "Impact Analysis on Minority Shareholders" proactively stating if the agenda item has any impact on the rights of minority shareholders. The Independent Directors should discuss such Impact Analysis and offer their comments which should be suitably recorded" (p. 17). However, there is no direction in the event where there is a lack of consensus about the potential impact amongst all the IDs nor any guidance as to whom the IDs should discuss it with.

3.4 The Code Provisions Relating to Financial Reporting, Auditing and Non-financial Disclosure Issues

Disclosure, transparency and financial reporting are major challenges for ensuring good governance in Bangladesh (BEI 2004). The Bangladeshi governance code states that improving the quality of disclosure and audit practice in Bangladesh must be carried out as a joint undertaking between the regulators, The Institute of Chartered Accountants of Bangladesh (ICAB) and organizations themselves; and has developed its provisions accordingly.

Table 5 indicates some of the major provisions relating to disclosure. It shows that following the OECD Principles, the Pakistani code and the Bangladeshi governance code and the latter's SEC Guidelines all recommend listed companies prepare their reports using International Financial Reporting Standards (IFRS). All of these sample Codes recommend provisions for better transparency and disclosure. For instance, they adopt the OECD Principles and suggest that companies should, in a timely way, disclose their financial statements, information about contingent liabilities, material events, related party transactions, and ownership structure. The Indian governance code makes no specific recommendations on financial disclosure, maybe because they have detailed provisions in their mandatory guidelines and in other regulatory provisions.[8]

Although the disclosure, accounting and auditing provisions are quite detailed in the Bangladeshi governance code and the SEC Guidelines, the audit review process was not addressed. Earlier studies (World Bank 2009; Mir and Rahaman 2005) have identified that in the absence of a formal audit review process, companies are skeptical about the quality of the audit carried out. Moreover, neither the Bangladeshi governance code nor the SEC Guidelines produced appropriate

[8] For example the 'Report of the Kumar Mangalam Birla Committee on Corporate Governance' develops code provisions in 2000 which are mandatory for the listed companies. This code on corporate governance outlines the accounting standards, and financial disclosure provisions in detail which are still valid for Indian companies.

Table 5 Disclosure issues

		Bangladesh		Developing countries	
	OECD principles	Code – Bangladesh	SEC guidelines	Code – India	Code – Pakistan
Accounting standard	High quality internationally recognized standards	Companies need to conform to all Bangladesh Standards for Auditing (BAS); and rules set by The Institute of Chartered Accountants of Bangladesh (ICAB)	International Accounting Standard (as applicable for Bangladesh)	No specific provision	International Accounting Standard as applicable for Pakistan
Statements of financial performance	Should be audited; To include: Financial statements; Information about contingent liabilities and off-balance sheet transactions; Special Purpose entities	Should be audited To include: Relevant financial statements both half-yearly and annually; Report on end use of fund; Statement assuring the 'going concern' issue	Should be audited To include: Relevant financial statements; Summary of key financial data for preceding 3 years; Statement assuring the 'going concern' issue	No specific provision	Should be audited To include: Relevant financial statements, statement of compliance to International accounting standards
Disseminating information	Timely; Cost-effective for users' access	Disclosure should be made available to shareholders and the general public	Should be accessible by shareholders	No specific provision	Disclosure should be made available to shareholders and the general public
Information about any material events	Requires immediate disclosure	Requires immediate disclosure	Requires immediate disclosure	No specific provision	Requires immediate disclosure

Source: European Corporate Governance Institute (www.ecgi.org); Dhaka stock exchange (www.dsebd.org); Bangladesh Enterprise Institute (www.bei-bd.org)

recommendations to ensure a secure environment for whistleblowers, which could be an important source of information about bad governance especially for countries like Bangladesh where people have less faith in audited reports and external auditors. On the other hand, the Indian governance code has separate provisions requiring companies to put in place procedures for employees to report concerns about unethical behavior, actual or suspected fraud, or violation of the company's Code of Conduct or its ethics policy. It also suggests that companies safeguard the whistleblowers against victimization, and allow direct access to the Chairperson of the Audit Committee in exceptional cases.

3.5 Summary of the Comparative Analysis

The overall discussion comparing the sample code provisions reveals a number of significant findings. First, in emerging market countries, governance codes are issued mainly by the government and stock market regulators. So, even though attracting foreign investment is one of the reasons behind the corporate governance reform in these countries, institutional investors do not actively participate in developing corporate governance standards in these three sample countries.

Second, emerging market countries emphasize both the mechanisms for code enforcement, voluntary and mandatory. Whilst stock markets are more inclined to make code compliance mandatory, a voluntary compliance is encouraged from private think-tanks and governments.

Third, the revision of the Codes in these three countries indicates that the awareness about improving corporate governance standards is increasing in emerging markets. However, the Code for Bangladesh was issued nearly 10 years ago and needs updating.

Fourth, none of these sample governance codes contain provisions to discipline non-compliant companies or incentives to encourage companies improve their compliance status in future.

Finally, the governance codes are broadly similar in tackling governance issues. However, the Indian governance code, which was introduced to augment its existing mandatory requirements and address governance reform in India, has addressed some areas (such as remuneration, independent directors, and whistleblowers) whereas the Bangladeshi governance code has ignored these issues, and this could be due to an outdated Bangladeshi governance code. Although its SEC guidelines have expanded to include matters such as independent directors, audit committee and provisions relating to the Directors' Report, it still falls short in some critical areas like board performance evaluation and directors' training.

Nevertheless, it is undeniable that as an initial step to governance reform, the relatively detailed provisions of the Bangladeshi governance code are laudable and have met international standards. However, whilst achieving compatibility with international standards is part of the spirit of code development, the rest depends on the extent to which its provisions meet local needs and solve governance issues; and for the Bangladesh governance code and the SEC Guidelines, more reform is needed. Whilst the sample governance codes in emerging countries are generally similar in nature, each one has addressed some additional important factors (like whistle blowing in India, and requiring formal evidence of directors' training in Pakistan) Such incremental governance reforms can serve as a source of learning for the other emerging nations.

4 Analysis of Companies' Corporate Governance Structures

This section analyzes the key corporate governance characteristics of companies in emerging markets. Hence, to elaborate on the analysis, the top three banks from each of our three emerging market countries were chosen as our case study companies. Banks were chosen because financial institutions play a major role in developing the corporate sector of emerging countries. We selected these top ranked banks in terms of their market size in their respective economies and also as the information required for this study was publicly available. An analysis of the key corporate governance features of these sample banks may uncover any significant disparity in corporate governance practice and priorities amongst financial companies in emerging markets.

Data from these sample banks was hand collected from their 2011 annual reports as well as from the respective banks' websites.

4.1 Institutional Framework

The analysis begins with a description of the institutional environment for corporate governance in Bangladesh and highlights areas where it varies or is similar with the other two emerging countries.

Bangladesh, like India and Pakistan, is a common law country. The legal system of Bangladesh has not grown overnight; rather the present legal and judicial system has its foundations built from 200 years of British rule (Panday and Mollah 2011). In describing the evolution of the judicial system in Bangladesh, Panday and Mollah (2011, p. 6) stated that it has "*passed through various stages and the process of evolution has been partly indigenous and partly foreign and the legal system of the present day emanates from a mixed system which has structure, legal principles and concepts modeled on both Indo-Mughal and English law*". However the legal system of Bangladesh is different to the absolute form of English law when viewed from the perspectives of socio-cultural values and religious guidelines.

Table 6 The institutional framework

Item	Bangladesh	India	Pakistan
Legal structure	Common law	Common law	Common law
Company law	Companies Act, 1994; Last major amendment, 1994	Companies Act, 1956; Last major amendment, 2011	Companies ordinance, 1984; Last major amendment, 2002
Stock exchange	Two: Dhaka stock exchange (1954) and Chittagong stock exchange (1995)	Two: Bombay stock exchange (1875) and National stock exchange (1992)	Three: Karachi stock exchange (1947), Lahore stock exchange (1970). Islamabad stock exchange (1989)
Regulator	Securities and exchange commission	Securities and exchange board of India	Securities and exchange commission of Pakistan
Market capitalization (% of GDP) in 2011	21 %	54.9 %	15.6 %
Ownership structure	Concentrated; mostly with founding families	Concentrated; mostly with founding families	Concentrated; mostly with founding families
Type of board	One tier	One tier	One tier
Type of directors	Executive, NED, independent director	Executive, NED, independent director	Executive, NED, independent director
Accounting and audit standards adopted	International Accounting Standards (IAS) and International Standards on Auditing (ISA)	International Accounting Standards (IAS) and International Standards on Auditing (ISA)	International Accounting Standards (IAS) and International Standards on Auditing (ISA)

Source: World Bank Data www.data.worldbank.org

Unlike countries like the U.S where the company law varies across different states (Narayanaswamy et al. 2012), as Table 6 indicates, companies in our three countries are governed by the central government law. These Companies Acts govern the relationship between shareholders and their companies, audit system, transparency, disclosure procedures and the jurisdiction of the courts in relation to companies (BEI 2004). Table 6 shows Companies Act reforms take time with the Companies Act in Bangladesh of 1994 yet to be amended.

Economic liberalization, the increase in foreign direct investment, and globalization has prompted the growth of stock markets in emerging market countries. Table 6 shows that India and Bangladesh have two national stock exchanges each while Pakistan has three; and according to the World Bank Data in 2011,[9] the market capitalization of listed companies (% of GDP) in India (54.9 %) was the highest among the three countries, followed by Bangladesh (21 %) and Pakistan

[9] Source: World Bank Data www.data.worldbank.org

(15.6 %). Companies listed on a stock exchange must comply with its securities regulations in addition to the Companies Act requirements.

Nevertheless, the growth of the capital markets in all countries was slowed down by financial crises happening there. In Bangladesh, its stock market collapsed twice. The stock market was still recovering from the collapse in 1996 when in 2011, the stock market again collapsed triggering the biggest share market turmoil ever, with the impact severely felt by the small investors.

However, the SEC was held responsible for this crisis, because as a regulator it was their responsibility to investigate these illegal activities and prosecute the perpetrators. The SEC promised to take action and created a unit in 2011 dedicated to monitoring corporate governance. It also suspended a number of regulatory members involved in this scandal. However, the major players implicated in this scam have yet to be prosecuted.

One of the biggest challenges in emerging market countries is the nature of their corporate ownership structure (Farooque et al. 2007; Imam and Malik 2007). Table 6 shows that even today, the majority of companies in these countries are closely held small and medium-sized firms where corporate boards are dominated by founding families and where there is the prevalence of kinship in the ownership structure. Farooque et al. (2007) claim that in the case of Bangladesh, the ownership structure has evolved to become the dominant mechanism of governance because under the Companies Act 1994, a maximum of 50 % of the total issued share capital can be retained by sponsor directors post listing. These controlling board members exercise extensive influence on the board decision-making process and adapt the governance mechanisms accordingly.

Table 6 also shows that, in general, corporate boards in emerging market countries are one-tiered without a supervisory board. In studying the board structure of Bangladeshi companies, Rashid et al. (2010) reported that both executive and non-executive directors perform duties together in a single board and CEO duality exists in some listed companies. Table 6 also shows that corporate boards in all three countries are expected to contain the three types of directors namely executive, non-executive and independent.

India's accounting profession was among the earliest to develop historically when the Indian Companies Act was enacted in the mid-1800s. Table 6 indicates that to ensure international compatibility and improve accounting and audit quality, the regulators there have emphasized implementing International Accounting Standards (IAS) and the International Standards on Auditing (ISA). Hence, the accounting and auditing standards in these countries comply with these international standards.

We analyze the corporate governance features found in our sample banks in the following sections.

Table 7 Board structure, composition and audit committee

Panel A: board structure and composition	Bangladesh	India	Pakistan
Board characteristics			
Average board size	16	13	9
Majority NED? ("0" for "No"; "1" for "Yes")	1	1	1
Average number of independent directors	1	4.33	2.67
Split chairman/CEO role ("0" for "No"; "1" for "Yes")	1	0.67	1
Panel A: audit committee	**Bangladesh**	**India**	**Pakistan**
Audit committee features			
Average number of members	4	5	4
Majority NED? ("0" for "No"; "1" for "Yes")	1	1	1
Whether the chairman or the members have professional qualification on accounting or finance? ("0" for "No"; "1" for "Yes")	1	1	1
Average number of meetings	15.33	6.67	3.33

4.2 Board Structure and Composition

Section 3 has identified that the corporate board plays a central role in ensuring good governance – thus many of the code provisions relate to board structure, composition and its practices. Therefore, three aspects of board structure are examined in our sample banks: size, independence and separation of chairman/ CEO roles.

4.2.1 Size

The average board size in our sample Pakistani banks is relatively small. Table 7 (Panel A) shows that, on average, the Pakistani board consists of nine directors. In contrast, our sample Bangladeshi bank board is relatively large and on average its board size is 16. In fact, the Bangladeshi SEC Guidelines states that the number of the board members of a company should not be less than 5 (five) nor more than 20 (twenty) with a view to enabling access to diverse expertise and meaningful discussion.

4.2.2 Non-executive Director and Board Independence

The governance codes in our emerging countries recommend that boards consists of a majority of NEDs, and in their revised version of the Codes, they have emphasized IDs more, and Table 7 (Panel A) indicates that our sample banks are compliant with this provision. However, the main difference in board composition among our sample banks lies in the number of independent directors. As illustrated in the table, whilst almost all of the banks studied include at least one independent director, Indian banks lead with more independent directors on their boards. Having more independent directors on the board is perhaps a reflection of their governance code. Section 3 identified that the Bangladeshi governance code places more emphasis on the presence of non-executive directors, while the Indian version places more emphasis on having independent directors, and the survey findings reflect their compliance.

4.2.3 Separation of the Roles of Chairman and CEO

Our sample shows that with the exception of an Indian bank, (as indicated in Panel A, Table 7), all other sample banks split the role of Chairman and Chief Executive Officer/Managing Director. The Indian bank which did not split the Chairman/CEO roles is one of the oldest and largest state-owned banks. Perhaps that is the reason why convincing companies of the rationale for ensuring internationally compatible corporate governance standards in emerging markets is difficult. When a company is experiencing growth and there is no apparent sign of bad governance, it is not very surprising that the entrepreneur does not agree to comply with some fundamental governance provisions which reduce authority and incur an additional cost.

4.3 Board Sub-committees

Our case study finds that the sample banks from the three emerging market countries have placed strong emphasis on the audit committee not surprisingly as having an audit committee on the board is a listing requirement. In general, in emerging market countries, the audit committee is formed with the aim to assist the Board of Directors in handling matters such as to review the company's internal financial controls, internal audit function and risk management systems and to create efficiency in these operations. To ensure the independence of the audit committee and the effectiveness of the internal audit, the governance codes and SEC Guidelines require that audit committees be comprised of mainly NEDs, and at least one member of the committee (especially the Chairman) is expected to be an accounting or financial expert. The findings from our sample support this recommendation. All of our sample banks' audit committees consist mainly of NEDs; and in the case of India, our sample banks' audit committees are mainly served by independent directors. Moreover, as the Table 7 Panel B indicates, all of the sample banks' audit committees have at least one member who is an expert on finance or accounting.

Table 7 (Panel B) also suggests that on average our sample Bangladeshi banks' audit committees meet more frequently than the other two countries' audit committees. Whilst two out of three of them meet on average 8 times in a year (the third bank's audit committee met 30 times); the other two countries' bank audit committees met less frequently. With increasing evidence of company failures and scandals, this study also supports the suggestion by Ow-Yong and Cheah (2000) that audit committees in emerging markets should consider increasing the frequency of their meetings to assist them in discharging their duties more effectively.

4.4 Analysis and Discussion

Overall the analysis reveals some important findings about the corporate governance features in emerging market economies. First, it reveals that, even today the corporate sectors are dominated by family owned companies and the stock market is comparatively vulnerable to financial scandals -indicating that the governance approach should be different to that of mature countries like the UK and the US. However, due to the similarities in the governance codes, emerging markets' corporate governance features reflect an Anglo-American model approach. Hence, an analysis of the impact of such an approach/model is needed to understand the efficiency of this approach and the codes in handling governance issues of emerging markets.

Second, although the Codes/Guidelines in these three emerging market countries are similar, they do differ in their practices. A plausible reason for such differences in practice arises from the type of issuer and enforcement mechanism (voluntary/mandatory) adopted by the codes. The Indian companies are found to be relatively more compliant and up-to-date with the best practice recommendations, even though their governance code is voluntary. However, the Indian governance code was issued by the Ministry of Corporate Affairs in the Indian Government. Thus it is not surprising to find that the Indian governance code carries more influence than the Bangladeshi voluntary Code which was introduced by a private think-tank.

The enforcement mechanism also matters because Bangladeshi companies seem to be following the SEC Guidelines and not the voluntary Code. In some instances (for instance the provisions relating to board sub-committees) it was found that the voluntary provisions which are not in line with the SEC Guidelines were not adopted by the companies. Moreover, Bangladesh and Pakistan have updated their SEC Guidelines and made the provisions even stricter for compliance – indicating the influence of regulators over governance standards.

Third, in comparison to the other two countries, Bangladeshi companies have relatively large boards (Rashid et al. 2010).There are arguments for and against a large board. Researchers such as Goodstein et al. (1994) find that a large board offers easier access to critical resources, ensures diversity and better quality advice, whilst its critics argue that due to the large board size, decision-making is delayed, there is less cohesion, and less participation (Zahra and Pearce 1989). Fourth, regarding the extent to which companies disclose more about their directors' profiles, detailed disclosure is important to ensure transparency of the directors appointment, their qualification and performance evaluation. It matters more for emerging countries where kinship is one of the biggest challenges for ensuring good governance.

Finally, Indian companies give more emphasis to independent directors. Their committees and boards have a significant number of independent directors, which is certainly a positive sign. Hence, it is time to consider the relevance of the argument of the Bangladeshi governance code that Bangladesh does not have a sufficiently qualified and experienced management pool to draw its independent directors from.

5 Policy Implications and Future Developments

The findings of this study have some important policy implications for emerging markets in general and Bangladesh in particular. The governance codes in emerging market countries recommend companies to consider the interest of stakeholders without defining which stakeholders to serve and how. Simply asking companies to be responsible for stakeholders does not make much sense unless there is proper guidance. The policy makers, if they decide to follow the stakeholder approach, need to be proactive and develop provisions relating to the stakeholders integration process (if this is a better alternative), identifying who the stakeholders are, and the rights and responsibilities of these stakeholders very specifically to avoid potential confusion.

The analysis of the governance codes provides an important insight for the policy makers of these emerging countries to develop or reform their codes. In particular, the findings indicate that the voluntary code of Bangladesh needs updating. Thus the overall finding of this comparative analysis is for countries to learn from each other's experience.

The SEC Guidelines in Bangladesh have been revised and updated. However, the comparative analysis and board practices in the emerging markets serves as a guide for the policy makers to consider good practice elsewhere. For instance, the provisions relating to whistle-blowing in the Indian governance code and directors' formally approved training in the case of the Pakistani governance code are two areas which Bangladesh might wish to consider.

Finally the policy makers should consider certain governance provisions which need adapting to emerging market countries. For instance, companies in Bangladesh are typically family owned, so evaluation of board performance and appointment of NEDs/IDs are the main concerns for the minority shareholders. Hence policies relating to these sensitive areas need to designed and implemented appropriately.

Based on these implications, the following are some recommendations for further research. Firstly, it would be interesting to investigate the perceptions of the various stakeholder groups about the existing governance codes which would help in reforming these codes.

Secondly, our study only focused on some aspects of corporate governance. An understanding of the overall aspects including the trend of disclosure, and comparison of reporting practices across different industries within the country would also help the policy makers to develop code provisions.

Finally, future research could examine the impact of board size on the level of compliance and also on business performance, especially to see if having independent director(s) on board has any impact, particularly in Bangladesh where almost no research has been conducted.

6 Concluding Comments

Corporate governance evolves over time and brings up new challenges, demands and new policies. Thus once developed, codes must be reviewed regularly to pinpoint the scope for improvement and for making it effective enough to face today's issues and tomorrow's challenges. Thus through a comparative analysis of the codes, this chapter intends to help the emerging countries like Bangladesh to adapt and reform their corporate governance codes.

For example, the comparative analysis of the codes indicates that the Code for Bangladesh needs updating; and the SEC Guidelines need to address some critical issues (e.g. independent directors, board sub-committees, directors training, whistle-blowing) more strategically as has been the case in India and Pakistan.

Using case studies, it suggests that the institutional framework for corporate governance is similar across the three countries – a good sign indicating that none is far behind from another to adopt each others' best practices. The overall analysis also indicates that the enforcement mechanism and the issuer of the governance code matters to ensure high compliance with these codes.

This study emphasizes that continuous effort should be placed on identifying and matching the governance code provisions with the needs of a particular emerging market. While some aspects of the Code should be enshrined by the Government through its Ministry of Commerce, the SEC and other regulators, the effectiveness of a governance code depends on the willingness of the companies concerned to accept and comply with it. Nevertheless, this study also recognizes that the benefit of compliance can be fully realized when companies accept the Code compliance as important for their business process and not as a mere compliance issue. Hence, along with the legal and regulatory pressure for compliance, strong emphasis should be placed on raising awareness of good corporate governance.

References

Adu-Amoah, A., Tsamenyi, M., & Onumah, J. M. (2008). The influence of social and political relations on corporate governance systems: The case of rural banks in Ghana. *Research in Accounting in Emerging Economies, 8*, 311–333.

Aggarwal, R. (2010). Independent directors: Time to introspect, suspect, respect – an Indian perspective. *Journal of Indian Business Research, 2*(2), 123–132.

Aguilera, R. V., & Cuervo-Cazurra, A. (2009). Codes of corporate governance. *Corporate Governance: An International Review, 17*(3), 376–387.

Akkermans, D., van Ees, H., Hermes, N., Hooghiemstra, R., Van de Laan, G., Postma, T., & van Witteloostuijn, A. (2007). Corporate governance in the Netherlands: An overview of the application of the Tabakslat Code in 2004. *Corporate Governance: An International Review, 15*(6), 1106–1118.

Bauwhede, H. V. (2009). On the relation between corporate governance complaince and operating performance. *Accounting and Business Research, 39*(5), 497–513.

BEI. (2004). *Code of corporate governance for Bangladesh*. Dhaka: Bangladesh Enterprise Institute.

Belal, A. R., & Owen, D. L. (2007). The views of corporate managers on the current state of, and future prospects for, social reporting in Bangladesh: An engagement based study. *Accounting, Auditing and Accountability Journal, 20*(3), 472–494.

Bhagat, S., & Black, B. S. (2002). The non-correlation between board independence and long-term firm performance. *Journal of Corporation Law, 27*, 1231–1273.

Chen, J. C., & Roberts, R. W. (2010). Toward a more coherent understanding of the organization–society relationship: A theoretical consideration for social and environmental accounting research. *Journal of Business Ethics, 97*, 651–665.

Claessens, S., & Yurtoglu, B. B. (2013). Corporate governance in emerging markets: A survey. *Emerging Markets Review, 15*, 1–33.

Conyon, M., & Mallin, C. A. (1997). A review of compliance with Cadbury. *Journal of General Management, 22*, 24–37.

Ehrgott, M., Reimann, F., Kaufmann, L., & Carter, C. R. (2011). Social sustainability in selecting emerging economy suppliers. *Journal of Business Ethics, 98*, 99–119.

Farooque, O. A., Zijl, T. V., Dunstan, K., & Karim, W. A. K. M. (2007). Ownership structure and corporate performance: Evidence from Bangladesh. *Asia-Pacific Journal of Accounting and Economics, 14*, 127–150.

Fernández-Rodríguez, E., Gómez-Ansón, S., & Cuervo-García, Á. (2004). The stock market reaction to the introduction of best practices codes by Spanish firms. *Corporate Governance: An International Review, 12*(1), 29.

Goodstein, J., Gautam, K., & Boeker, W. (1994). The effects of board size and diversity on strategic changes. *Strategic Management Journal, 15*(3), 241–250.

Igor, G., Joerg Richard, W., & Jochen, Z. (2006). Does compliance with the German corporate governance code have an impact on stock valuation? An empirical analysis. *Corporate Governance: An International Review, 14*(5), 432–445.

Imam, M. O., & Malik, M. (2007). Firm performance and corporate governance through ownership structure: Evidence from Bangladesh stock market. *International Review of Business Research Papers, 3*(4), 88–110.

Krambia-Kapardis, M., & Psaros, J. (2006). The implementation of corporate governance principles in an emerging economy: A critique of the situation in Cyprus. *Corporate Governance: An International Review, 14*(2), 126–139.

Letza, S., Sun, X., & Kirkbride, J. (2004). Shareholding versus stakeholding: A critical review of corporate governance. *Corporate Governance: An International Review, 12*(3), 242–262.

MacNeil, I., & Li, X. (2006). "Comply or Explain": Market discipline and non-compliance with the Combined Code. *Corporate Governance: An International Review, 14*, 486–496.

Mallin, C., & Ow-Yong, K. (2012). Factors influencing corporate governance disclosures: Evidence from Alternative Investment Market (AIM) Companies in the UK. *European Journal of Finance, 18*(5–6), 515–533.

Mir, M., & Rahaman, A. S. (2005). The aoption of international accounting standards in Bangladesh. *Accounting, Auditing and Accountability Journal, 18*(6), 816–841.

Narayanaswamy, R., Raghunandan, K., & Rama, D. V. (2012). Corporate governance in the Indian context. *American Accounting Association, 26*(3), 583–599.

OECD. (1999). *Principles of corporate governance*. Paris: OECD.

OECD. (2004). *Principles of corporate governance*. Paris: OECD.

Ow-Yong, K., & Cheah, K. G. (2000). Corporate Governance Codes: A comparison between Malaysia and the UK. *Corporate Governance: An International Review, 8*(2), 125–132.

Palit, S. K. (2006). The impact of socio-economic reforms on governance: the Bangladesh experience. *Journal of Administration and Governance, 1*(1), 68–83.

Panday, P. K., & Mollah, M. A. H. (2011). The judicial system of Bangladesh: An overview from historical viewpoint. *International Journal of Law and Management, 53*(1), 6–31.

Parsa, S., Chong, G., & Isimoya, E. (2007). Disclosure of governance information by small and medium-sized companies. *Corporate Governance, 7*(5), 635–648.

Rashid, A., Zoysa, A. D., Lodh, S., & Rudkin, K. (2010). Board composition and firm performance: Evidence from Bangladesh. *Australasian Accounting Business and Finance Journal, 4* (1), 76–95.

Rwegasira, K. (2000). Corporate governance in emerging capital markets: Whither Africa? *Corporate Governance: An International Review, 8*(3), 258–267.

Sarker, A. E. (2011). The political economy of public enterprise privatization: The case of Bangladesh. *International Journal of Management, 28*(3), 595–611.

Wanyama, S., Burton, B., & Hellier, C. (2009). Frameworks underpinning corporate governance: Evidence on Ugandan perceptions. *Corporate Governance: An International Review, 17*(2), 159–175.

World Bank. (2009). *Report on the Observance of Standards and Codes (ROSC): Corporate Governance contry assessment*. The World Bank: Bangladesh.

Zahra, S. A., & Pearce, J. A. (1989). Boards of directors and corporate financial performance: A review and integrative model. *Journal of Management, 15*(2), 291–334.

Zattoni, A., & Cuomo, F. (2008). Why adopt Codes of Corporate Governance? A comparison of institutional and efficiency perspectives. *Corporate Governance: An International Review, 16* (1), 1–15.

Part IV
Corporate Governance: Laws, Reforms, and Practical Issues

Corporate Governance as an Antidote to Corruption in Emerging Markets

Duane Windsor

Abstract This chapter assesses what is known about the likely role of corporate governance reforms and best practices as an antidote to commercial and political corruption in emerging markets. The purpose of the assessment is to marshal knowledge about the relationship between corporate governance and corruption and to help identify best practices with respect to anti-corruption efforts. The methodology combines literature review and identification of sources of information and data about corporate governance and anti-corruption measures. The scope of the chapter includes corporate governance norms promoted by international institutions, effects of foreign direct investment, and interactions among quality of government, quality of corporate governance, and corruption levels and forms. The vital issue is whether and if so how and to what extent corporate governance reforms and best practices will operate to reduce corruption in emerging markets. General findings are that corporate governance best practices are desirable for several reasons, and such best practices, in combination with business integrity and governmental anti-corruption efforts, should operate gradually against commercial and political corruption. Effectiveness of governance and anti-corruption measures depend on personal integrity of business directors and executives. Structural measures typically recommended in corporate governance codes are not well linked to anti-corruption effectiveness.

1 Introduction

Emerging markets involve special concerns for both corporate governance and anti-corruption reforms. Such economies are rapidly growing, attracting foreign direct investment (FDI), and weak in the institutional infrastructure for good governance

---

D. Windsor (✉)
Jones Graduate School of Business, Rice University, Houston, TX, USA
e-mail: odw@rice.edu

S. Boubaker and D.K. Nguyen (eds.), *Corporate Governance in Emerging Markets*, CSR, Sustainability, Ethics & Governance, DOI 10.1007/978-3-642-44955-0_17,

and low corruption. Contributions of this chapter include a review of three relevant literatures, and a summary of the governance and corruption reform status of emerging markets, with focus on the Financial Times Stock Exchange (FTSE) 22 list of such markets (FTSE 2010). The three literatures – on good governance, FDI and corruption, and specific country studies – are not well integrated as yet. Scholars and practitioners are aware that governance reform and anti-corruption measures are greatly needed in emerging markets; but this chapter is an early effort at addressing the gaps across the three literatures and to making findings concerning how well corporate governance is likely to affect corruption in such markets.

The term "emerging markets" (Kearney 2012) was introduced in the late 1980s (Cavusgil et al. 2013, p. 3) by van Agtmael (2007). The older term "newly industrialized countries" (NICs) suggested export-led industrialization, as a breakout from less developed toward more developed status. Breakout attracts significant foreign direct investment (FDI), a key criterion for emerging market status. This classification schema suggests sequential categories of developing, industrializing, emerging, and advanced economies. Energy and mining resources alone are not automatically a basis for sustainable development; and may be associated with high corruption levels.

Corporate governance reform and anti-corruption reform have become global movements (Givens 2013; Goyer 2010). The relationship between corporate governance reform and corruption reduction operates in different ways depending on the home and size (as well as industry) of the business and on the local conditions (Licht et al. 2007). Multinational enterprises (MNEs) are likely to be global large businesses domiciled in advanced countries (Hadjikhani et al. 2012). Joint ventures between foreign and domestic entities may be important. There is a phenomenon of multinationals domiciled in emerging markets operating abroad. Ramamurti and Singh (2009) include the four BRICs (Brazil, Russia, India, and China), Mexico (CEMEX is a leading instance), South Africa, and Israel (which will be classified here as an advanced country).

Corporate governance reform operates at both international and national (within-country) levels. The chapter will review and assess key international codes for corporate governance, with particular attention to OECD, UN, and World Bank/IMF/MIGA guidelines and the Prague Declaration. An important instance of national reform is the set of King Reports in South Africa. Aspects of governance reform and practice expected to have effects on corruption will be discussed.

The main results and main conclusions of this chapter are as follows. What is important in this reform process is the effective influence of external institutions and entities (reflected in international codes and FDI, respectively) on quality of government and quality of corporate governance, and thus on corruption levels and forms. General findings are that corporate governance best practices are desirable for several reasons, and such best practices, in combination with business integrity and governmental anti-corruption efforts, should operate gradually against commercial and political corruption. Effectiveness of governance and anti-corruption measures depend on personal integrity of business directors and executives.

Structural measures typically recommended in corporate governance codes are not well linked to anti-corruption effectiveness.

The remainder of this chapter is organized as follows. Section 2 explains a working definition for emerging markets of interest to this study. Section 3 is a literature review. Section 4 provides corporate governance and corruption information on the Financial Times Stock Exchange (FTSE) 22 emerging markets – the set of countries of greatest interest for this study. The concluding Sect. 5 summarizes the contribution of this chapter.

2 Defining Emerging Markets

Country composition changes somewhat over time, since the category concerns a stage of economic development and conditions for sustained growth. The underlying idea is that an emerging market is moving from developed to developed status (Cavusgil et al. 2013, p. 5). An emerging market typically has started economic reforms, achieved steady growth in gross national product (GNP) per capita, and exhibits increased integration with the global economy (Cavusgil et al. 2013, p. 5). Such markets involve manageable business risks, are technologically competitive, and reflect increasing consumer purchasing power, investment opportunities, and income growth higher than in developed countries (Cavusgil et al. 2013, p. 2).

Three basic characteristics of emerging markets can be identified in terms of stage of economic development, sufficient population size, and sustained economic growth.

First, an emerging market economy lies between the categories of developing economies and advanced economies. An emerging market has developed and is moving toward advanced. Advanced economies are typically members of the Organisation for Economic Co-operation and Development (OECD), which in 2012 comprises 34 countries including North America (with Mexico, an emerging market), Europe (including some emerging or arguably even still developing economies), Japan, Australia and New Zealand, and Chile, Israel, South Korea, and Turkey. For purposes of this study, Chile and Turkey are classified as emerging, while Israel (a small economy) and South Korea are classified as already more advanced. Korea is sometimes grouped with Brazil, Russia, and India in the BRIK (Black et al. 2012).

Second, an emerging market economy must be sufficiently large to matter for this study. While Estonia, the Slovak Republic, and Slovenia are OECD members, they are not emerging markets for this study – without addressing whether they should be regarded as advanced or developing economies. The Czech Republic, Hungary, and Poland will be classified as emerging. (Greece is an advanced economy, like Italy, Portugal, and Spain – although these four countries have been working through an economic crisis in recent years.)

Third, whether a developing or a transitional (i.e. formerly communist) economy historically, an emerging market is one receiving significant foreign direct investment (FDI) and enjoying rising per capita gross domestic product (GDP).

In May 2007, the OECD invited Chile, Estonia, Israel, Russia, and Slovenia to open membership discussions; all became OECD members in 2010 other than Russia (which is not yet a member). The OECD then also offered a program of "enhanced engagement" to Brazil, China, India, Indonesia, and South Africa. The OECD thus includes or works with BRIC (O'Neill 2001) and MIST (Aspray 2011) and Chile.

Typically, emerging markets have significant levels of corruption and something less than fully democratic government and independent judiciary. Corporate governance practices are commonly something less than expected by UK, U.S., and European Union (EU) norms. Some information on corruption and democracy is available in various sources (such as Transparency International and Freedom House).

3 Literature Review

This section discusses three relevant literatures. One literature concerns the relationship between governance and corruption. Improved corporate governance should work against corruption. A second literature concerns the relationship between FDI and corruption. Corruption deters and taxes FDI, but FDI works against corruption. A third literature concerns country studies of the relationship between governance and corruption.

3.1 Relationship Between Governance and Corruption

Improved corporate governance should work against corruption (Aidt et al. 2008; Caron et al. 2012; Wu 2005). The UK's Cadbury Committee (1992) report helped initiate a global movement for improvement of corporate governance practices. The U.S. Foreign Corrupt Practices Act (FCPA) of 1977 helped initiate a global movement for reduction of corruption by both government (and political) officials and corporations. Each country is a quasi-experiment in this process.

In theory and practice, corporate governance should be understood in broad terms. There are four levels of influences on corporate governance, from international consensus and institutions at the global level to individual conduct within boards of directors and among employees – linked together by national requirements and corporate policies. There are in parallel four levels of influences on corruption, defined analogously (international, national, corporate, and individual)– although operating through partly different (and partly overlapping) institutions and corporate policies.

In theory, governance and anti-corruption efforts should work together as follows. One can think of parallel international consensuses for corporate governance best practices and against corruption. At the national level, there would be legislation and regulation for best practices and against corruption. Corporations would adopt best governance and anti-corruption policies. At the individual level, corporate personnel (from directors and chief executive officer down) would implement best practices and avoid bribery or extortion in all forms.

3.1.1 International Governance Guidance

In general, corporate governance practices are stated as principles and recommendations: what businesses ought to do. Enforcement is through stock exchange listing requirements and national public policy legislation. Public policy concerns guidance as distinct from criminal law enforcement or civil law compensation (Wilson 1989). Violations of legal requirements (such as misstated financial information) are what involve criminal or civil enforcement actions, which characterize anti-corruption efforts.

Considerable attention has been focused in the literature on problems of corporate governance in emerging markets (Aguilera et al. 2012; Aguilera and Jackson 2003, 2010; Braga-Alves and Morey 2012; Ficici and Aybar 2012; Gibson 2003; Gregory 2000; Klapper and Love 2002; Millar et al. 2005; Young et al. 2008). Clifford Chance (2011) includes recent information on transitional economies in Eastern Europe (see Klapper et al. 2006). Studies exist on Latin America generally (Chong and López-de-Silanes 2007) and Chile in specific (Lefort and Urzua 2008).

There is a serious question concerning whether conventional structure measures of corporate governance (e.g. board characteristics, stock ownership, or anti-takeover provisions) even explain very much of cross-sectional variation in multiple measures of performance (Larcker and Tayan 2011). Board functioning depends greatly on director capability, experience, and integrity (Adams et al. 2010). A study of 296 financial firms across 30 countries reported that firms with more independent boards and higher institutional ownership experienced worse stock returns during the 2007–2008 financial crisis, because such firms took higher risk prior to the crisis and raised more equity capital during the crisis (Erkens et al. 2012). While commercial governance ratings appear positively and significantly associated with market value, governance rating agencies do not seem to create incremental value through converting public data into aggregated ratings (Hitz and Lehmann 2012). A study reports on experience of Korean firms in that country's financial crisis (Baek et al. 2004).

The leading statement of governance principles (Verhezen and Morse 2009) is issued by the OECD (2004, revised from 1999; 2006), which also has a statement on state-owned enterprises (OECD 2005). The OECD countries are home to most of the world's multinational enterprises (MNEs). Siems and Alvarez-Macotela (2013) address the OECD Guidelines in relationship to emerging markets. The International Corporate Governance Network (ICGN) issues a statement of governance principles (ICGN 1999, 2009a). ICGN (2009b) also issues a statement of anti-corruption principles.

The Financial Stability Board (FSB) was established as an international coordination body for national financial authorities and international standard setting bodies. The FSB undertakes to develop and promote effective financial sector policies. The FSB Secretariat is located at Basel, Switzerland, with the Bank for International Settlements (BIS).

3.1.2 International Anti-Corruption Consensus

Political corruption occurs between business and government personnel, including in practice contract agents and consultants of the former and political party personnel interacting with the latter. Commercial corruption occurs business to business.

The UN Global Compact (UNGC) comprises ten principles concerning human rights (two principles), labor (four principles), environment (three principles), and anti-corruption (the tenth principle). The human rights, labor, and environment principles are grounded in the UN Universal Declaration of Human Rights, the International Labour Organization (ILO) Declaration on Fundamental Principles and Rights at Work, and the Rio Declaration on Environment and Development. The anti-corruption principle is grounded in the UN Convention against Corruption (UNCAC) (entered into force 14 December 2005). This Convention calls for prevention, criminalization, international cooperation, and asset recovery mechanisms by the signatory countries. The UNGC anti-corruption principle (Principle 10) states: "Businesses should work against corruption in all its forms, including extortion and bribery." This anti-corruption principle was partly preceded by and implemented by a number of regional accords together with the U.S. Foreign Corrupt Practices Act (FCPA) of 1977 (amended) and the UK Bribery Act of 2010 and the activities of the Transparency International (TI) network of country affiliates. A list of international anti-corruption conventions, with links to full texts, is available through a Transparency International website (http://archive.transparency.org/global_priorities/international_conventions). In addition to the UNCAC, there are globally the United Nations Convention against Transnational Organized Crime (UNTOC), OECD Convention on the Bribery of Foreign Public Officials in International Business Transactions (OECD Convention), and Revised Recommendation of the Council of the OECD on Combating Bribery in International Business Transactions. In Africa, there are the African Union Convention on Preventing and Combating Corruption (AU Convention), the Southern African Development Community Protocol against Corruption (SADC Protocol), and the Economic Community of West African States Protocol on the Fight against Corruption (ECOWAS Protocol). The Inter-American Convention against Corruption (OAS Convention) and the Asian Development Bank (ADB)-OECD Action Plan for Asia-Pacific cover those regions, respectively. The Council of Europe has adopted a Criminal Law Convention, a Civil Convention, an Agreement Establishing the Group of States against Corruption (Resolution (99) 4 of the Committee of Ministers of the Council of Europe), Twenty Guiding Principles for the Fight against Corruption (Resolution (97) 24 of the Committee of Ministers of the Council of Europe). The European Union has adopted a Convention on the Protection of the Communities' Financial Interests and the Fight against Corruption and two related Protocols.

The Prague Declaration on Governance and Anti-Corruption provides a reasonable action plan for implementation of anti-corruption efforts (see also the Council of Europe's Twenty Guiding Principles for the Fight against Corruption). The Prague Declaration, issued on March 21, 2012 (Mann et al. 2012), provides ten action principles: (1) anti-bribery policy; (2) financial disclosure rules for politicians and government officials; (3) prosecution for official corruption; (4) open government; (5) corporate zero tolerance for and disclosure concerning corruption; (6) investor responsibilities; (7) transparent campaign and party finance; (8) lobbying rules; (9) protection for whistleblowers; and (10) protections for non-governmental organizations (NGOs) and media. The Prague Declaration represents the work of the first World Forum on Governance, convened in Prague, the Czech Republic, in November 2011, co-directed by members of the Brookings Institution, the American Enterprise Institute, the Millstein Center for Corporate Governance and Performance, Yale School of Management, and a member of the board of GMI.

3.1.3 Individual Integrity

The parallel interaction of corporate governance and anti-corruption depends on individuals, especially directors and senior executives. Corporate culture and personal integrity must be mutually reinforcing. Anything else is costly monitoring, detection, and prosecution. Bear Stearns, Enron, Lehman Brothers, Parmalat, Royal Ahold, Tyco, and WorldCom all illustrate Warren Buffett's famous comment that "In reality, ... earnings can be as pliable as putty when a charlatan heads the company reporting them. Eventually truth will surface, but in the meantime a lot of money can change hands" (1990 Berkshire Hathaway Annual Report Chairman's Letter). Codes–whether of governance or conduct–are necessary but far from sufficient (Webley and Werner 2008). Sonnenfeld (2001) emphasizes the human dynamics with a board of directors functioning as a social system.

Recently uncovered LIBOR and money laundering scandals in major global banks indicate bad cultures and bad leadership undermining corporate policy. Bad individuals, bad situations, and bad cultures are all likely at work (Kish-Gephart et al. 2010). There are serious difficulties and lags in monitoring misconduct, as illustrated over the years by rogue traders such as Adoboli, Kerviel, and Leeson. Kweku Adoboli received a sentence of 7 years in a UK court for losing some $2.3 billion at UBS in London; he allegedly booked fake trades to hide losses. He was arrested after confessing in an email. The chief executive officer resigned. The UK Financial Services Authority fined UBS for failure to supervise.

Although the concern of this chapter is with the effect of corporate governance practices on deterring corruption, there may be a reverse influence of corruption on undermining corporate governance practices particularly in emerging and developing economies (Caron et al. 2012). The national regulatory framework depends on the integrity of public officials, who are in various countries often quite corrupt. Mexico (7.5), Indonesia (7.5), China (6.7), and Russia (6.6) are the four worst of the 28 countries in the Transparency International (TI) (2011) bribe payers index (BPI). (The CPI is reported annually; the BPI is periodic.). On the BPI, 0 means a country's enterprises always bribe; while 10 means a country's enterprises never bribe.

There is an important distinction among direct corruption affecting policy decisions – in the forms of corporate bribery (offer of payment) and official extortion (demand for payment by explicit or implied threat), facilitating payments made to minor officials for expediting officially approved actions, and political lobbying and donations (bundling together these two activities). ICGN (2012) recently issued a statement on political lobbying and donations. Direct corruption is almost universally illegal by national legislation; and prohibited by consensual international conventions at the UN and regional levels. The OECD in 2009 issued a recommendation against facilitating payments – which while legal under the FCPA are illegal under the UK Bribery Act and often under national legislation. Thus corporations should prohibit or strongly counsel against facilitating payments; and some do already.

Kaufmann and Vicente (2011) distinguish between legal corruption and illegal corruption as channels for influencing government. What is legal corruption is a function of cross-country variation in legal framework. The authors use a survey of 8,279 firms in 104 countries to measure legal and illegal corruption. They propose a continuum of three categories. Illegal corruption persists because the country's political elite does not face binding incentives to attempt to limit corruption. Legal corruption occurs when the political elite incurs some cost to protect corruption through the legal framework. Zero corruption means the general population can effectively react against corruption such that the political elite is responsive.

Direct and indirect lobbying forms and bribery can be complements and/or substitutes for the exercise of political influence by businesses (Campos and Giovannoni 2007). A firm can comply with public policy, bribe officials against implementation of public policy, or lobby government to relax public policy (Harstad and Svensson 2011). Politically connected firms exercise profit-gaining influence (Chen et al. 2010).

Strategic philanthropy may aim at increasing political influence. The lower the level of a country's development, the more likely firms are to practice bribery; the higher the level of a country's development, the more likely firms are to practice lobbying (Harstad and Svensson 2011). Economic development and democratic government may evolve in parallel, in this regard. Emerging economies may lie at the switching point between these two approaches. Thus in Table 1, South Africa and Poland rank well on corporate governance and corruption measures relative to other emerging markets.

The World Bank's World Business Environment Survey (WBES) was conducted in 80 countries with at least 100 firms in each country during 1998–2000. The survey covers emerging and developing countries. The survey provides

Table 1 Corruption Perceptions Index (CPI) and corporate governance information for 22 FTSE emerging markets

1	2	3	4	5	6	7
		2012 rank order among 176 countries or territories (1–176)	2012 CPI (0–100)	2011 WGI control of corruption quartile at 90 % confidence (0–100 %)	2010 GMI corporate governance ranking (1–10)	OECD status
Country	Group or region	1 is best	100 is very clean	100 is best	10 is best (UK 7.60) (U.S. 7.16)	
Brazil+	BRIC	89	43	50–75	3.91	Engaged
Russia	BRIC	133	28	0–25	3.90	Engaged
India	BRIC	94	36	25–50	4.54	Engaged
China	BRIC	80	39	25–50	3.37	Engaged
Mexico* +	MIST	105	34	25–50	2.43	Member
Indonesia*	MIST	118	32	25–50	3.14	Engaged
S. Africa* +	MIST	69	43	50–75	6.09	Engaged
Turkey* +	MIST	54	49	50–75	3.62	Member
Czech Republic+	Europe	54	49	50–75	GMI	Member
Hungary+	Europe	46	55	50–75	GMI	Member
Poland+	Europe	41	58	50–75	5.11	Member
Chile*	Latin America	20	72	75–100	2.13	Member
Colombia	Latin America	94	36	25–50	GMI	
Peru*	Latin America	83	38	50–75	GMI	
Egypt*	Arab World	118	32	25–50	GMI	
Morocco	Arab World	88	37	50–75	GMI	
UAE	Arab World	27	68	75–100	Excluded from GMI	
Malaysia* +	Asia	54	49	50–75	4.21	
Pakistan*	Asia	139	27	0–25	Excluded from GMI	

(continued)

Table 1 (continued)

1	2	3	4	5	6	7
		2012 rank order among 176 countries or territories (1–176)	2012 CPI (0–100)	2011 WGI control of corruption quartile at 90 % confidence (0–100 %)	2010 GMI corporate governance ranking (1–10)	OECD status
Country	Group or region	1 is best	100 is very clean	100 is best	10 is best (UK 7.60) (U.S. 7.16)	
Philippines*	Asia	105	34	0–25	GMI	
Taiwan+	Asia	37	61	75–100	3.64	
Thailand* +	Asia	88	37	25–50	4.20	
Emerging markets					3.94	

Notes: In Column 1, the FTSE 22 list is adopted from Cavusgil et al. (2013), pp. 4–5. FTSE Advanced economies are indicated in the table with +; the other economies in the table are FTSE Secondary. Cavusgil et al. (2013, p. 5–6) analyzes data for the four BRIC and also 11 "New Frontier Economies" indicated in the table with an *. Column 2 indicates BRIC or MIST grouping or region. In Columns 3 and 4, Transparency International (TI) Corruption Perception Index (CPI) data indicate rank order and CPI estimate, respectively. In Column 5, Worldwide Governance Indicators (WGI) control of corruption estimates accessed on March 7, 2013. In Column 6, Governance Metrics International (GMI) corporate governance rankings are as of September 27, 2010. GMI Emerging Markets coverage is very close to the FTSE 22 but excludes UAE and includes South Korea, classified in this study as more advanced. GMI does not calculate country averages if the number of companies covered is less than ten. These countries are indicated in the table by GMI. Column 7 reports OECD status

information at the firm level concerning determinants and effects of political influence, perception of corruption, and prevalence of bribe paying. Reducing the survey set for absences of information (not all questions were asked in all countries), Bennedsen et al. (2011) conducted regression analyses on some 4,000–5,000 observations from 57 countries. They report that measures of political influence and corruption (i.e. bribes) are uncorrelated at the firm level. The findings may indicate that influence and bribery occur in different firms rather than operating as complementary approaches in the same firms. Firms with certain characteristics (such as larger, older, exporting, government-owned, widely held, and in less competitive industries) have more political influence and perceive corruption as less of a problem and pay bribes less often. More influential firms tend to bend laws and regulations, while less influential firms tend to pay bribes.

3.2 Relationship Between FDI and Corruption

A second literature concerns the relationship between FDI and corruption (Al-Sadig 2009; Egger and Winner 2006; Habib and Zurawicki 2002; Kwok and Tadesse 2006; Larrain and Tavares 2004). Bai et al. (2004) examined the relationship between corporate governance and market valuation in China. Corruption deters and taxes FDI (Wei 2000), but FDI works against corruption. Illicit money flows may be a stimulus for FDI, however (Perez et al. 2012).

A literature survey reports reasonable evidence that improved governance is positive for emerging market firms in providing greater access to financing, lower cost of capital, better financial performance, and better treatment of multiple stakeholders (Claessens and Yurtoglu 2013). This positive relationship depends on strength of the country's governance system. There is less evidence on social and environmental performance effects. Banks, family-owned, and state-owned firms involve special governance issues.

Corruption is functionally a tax that reduces FDI (Wei 2000). Using a unique firm-level data set, Javorcik and Wei (2009) examine the impact of corruption in emerging markets on mode of entry and volume of FDI. Corruption reduces the volume of FDI and shifts ownership structure. Corruption both increases the value of a local partner for navigating less transparent bureaucracy which functions as a tax on FDI, and decreases the value of a local partner because effective protection of FDI is reduced in event of a dispute with a domestic partner. Such a dispute will not be adjudicated fairly (so partner selection is a critical step). Technological sophistication reduces the likelihood of joint ventures.

For China, Luo (2011) found that MNE subunits decrease investment commitment and increase export market orientation as perceived corruption increases in a specific business segment. The perceived corruption of the segment affects market orientation, while longitudinal change in perceived corruption affects investment commitment. Ethical awareness strengthens and local dependence weakens the effect for MNE subunits.

The Multilateral Investment Guarantee Agency (MIGA) is part of the World Bank Group. MIGA provides political risk insurance for eligible investment or lending projects in developing member countries throughout the world. Insured losses can include: currency inconvertibility and transfer restriction; expropriation; war, terrorism, and civil disturbance; breach of contract; and non-honoring of sovereign financial obligations. MIGA issues reports on world investment and political risk (MIGA 2013).

The German firm Siemens allegedly engaged in systematic bribery around the world (Baron 2008). Corrupt payments through consultants (Siemens maintained more than 2,700 consultant agreements) included Argentina, Bangladesh, China, Greece, Iraq, Israel, Nigeria, Russia, and Venezuela. The resulting penalties amounted to about $1.6 billion in addition to over $1 billion internally. During 2001–2007, an estimated $1.4 billion in corrupt payments occurred, more than 57 % in telecommunications, where a German executive controlled an annual bribery budget. False records concealed this conduct.

3.3 Country Studies

A third literature concerns country studies of the relationship between governance and corruption (Desai and Moel 2008; Javaid 2010; Khan 2006). There is a large literature on corruption in general (Damania et al. 2004; Dreher et al. 2007; Fan et al. 2008; Treisman 2007). This literature focuses on causes, effects, and patterns. Considerable attention has been paid to corruption in emerging markets (Goldsmith 1999; Lameira and Bertrand 2008; Leblanc 2012; Loredo et al. 2012; Parkinson and Meredith 2012). There are studies of corruption in the transition countries of Eastern Europe (Chavis 2013; Wieneke and Gries 2011). There are some studies by industry; telecom, as illustrated by the Siemens scandal, appears particularly dirty (Berg et al. 2012).

A basic research issue is whether best governance practices are universal or dependent on country and firm (or industry) characteristics (Black et al. 2012). Those authors surveyed year-end 2004 governance practices of Brazilian firms constructed a governance index, with sub indices. They report that the index (together with ownership structure, board procedures, and minority shareholder rights) predicts better market value (Tobin's q). But greater board independence has a negative effect; and firm characteristics matter – governance index predicts market value for nonmanufacturing, small, and high growth firms (and not for manufacturing, large, and slow growth firms). Their comparison of Brazil with existing studies of India, Korea, and Brazil finds evidence of country characteristics being influential.

The most prominent instance in the emerging market countries is the set of King Reports (King I, II, III) in South Africa (Andreasson 2011), initiated by the Institute of Directors and developed under the chair of Mervyn E. King, a former judge of the Supreme Court of South Africa (see King 2006). Prior to the codification process, there was reliance on common law. The 1994 First King Report on Corporate Governance provided a formal code of corporate governance in the form of principles and guidelines intended to be comprehensive. The March 2002 Second King Report reviewed and expanded on the initial version. The September 2009 Third King Code and Report on Corporate Governance (effective 1 March 2010) followed the new Companies Act 71 of 2008. This act codifies directors' duties and defines "prescribed officers" as directors subject to the same duties and liabilities. A prescribed officer is a non-director who has general executive authority over various aspects of the business (such as finance). The King III Code provides governance principles; the King III report provides best practices for each principle. The Institute of Directors issues Practice Notes on code implementation. Whereas King I and II relied on "comply or explain" (i.e. a firm could opt not to comply with a principle with explanation), King III shifted to "apply or explain" (i.e. a firm could opt not to apply a suggested practice with explanation, while still complying with the broad principles of fairness, accountability, responsibility, and transparency). King III applies to all legal business entities, whether exchange listed or not, and independently of the legal form of business. Listing requirements of the Johannesburg Stock Exchange (JSE) mandated compliance with certain provisions on a rolling schedule from March 1, 2010 through April 1, 2011. A director participating in a share incentive or option scheme is not "independent" in listed companies from April 1, 2011.

In Table 1, South Africa has the highest GMI ranking reported for an emerging economy. At 6.09, South Africa is at 80 % of the UK 7.6 ranking (the highest issued by GMI). This 6.09 level is 1.55 times the average 3.94 GMI ranking for emerging economies. South Africa is not in the lowest quartile for CPI corruption information: it ranks 54 of 176, just within the top third of included countries; the CPI is 43 (on the 100 % scale); the WGI quartile is 50–75 %. Since it is not simple to test for temporal effects (i.e. reduction in corruption following improvement in governance), one possibility is that governance codification is strong in South Africa while corruption is not marked relative to most other emerging economies (Camerer 2001). The High Court of Lesotho concluded that the head of the Lesotho Highlands Development Agency (LHDA) had accepted at least $2 million in bribes from agents for 12 MNEs over a decade. The Lesotho Highlands Water Project (LHWP) was a combined water supply and hydropower project of the governments of Lesotho and South Africa. Investigations included MNEs from several countries (Canada, France, Germany, Italy, Switzerland and Sweden, and the UK) including South Africa.

One instance concerning effective expropriation of a U.S. investor by a local minority partner and the subsequent international pressure on the Czech government to repay the U.S. investor illustrates the role of political connections; the U.S. investor was a former U.S. ambassador (Desai and Moel 2008).

In 2005, Alcoa established Alcoa Russia to operate two plants. William O'Rourke, a senior staff officer with 30 years experience in various departments, was made CEO (Graham 2012; O'Rourke et al. 2011). He set two strategic initiatives: to lead with safety to improve plant performance; zero participation in corruption. Among other experiences, O'Rourke was robbed by local police at an ATM; and received a "casual death threat" from a government official for refusing to make a payoff. (The term "casual" means the official stated to the effect that, 5 years earlier, O'Rourke would have been dead.) Local police stopped transport trucks delivering a $25 million furnace and demanded $25,000 for a government official. The Russians working for Alcoa Russia argued they could negotiate down to $10,000. Some home company executives emphasized the need to get plant going. O'Rourke refused to pay. After 72 hours police released the trucks.

In 2012, news reports revealed Walmart had closed a first internal investigation and then failed to report (until learning of news revelations coming) to law enforcement officials alleged bribery by executives of its Mexico and Central America subsidiary (Foroohar 2012; Wunker 2012). Walmart then opened a new investigation. From 1991, Walmart, now the largest private employer in Mexico which now hosts about 20 % of Walmart stores, opened more than 2,100 locations in Mexico. The bribes largely concerned construction permits. Walmart allegedly had received 31 similar reports of violations in various countries during 2006 (Foroohar 2012). Mexico subsequently enacted new anti-corruption legislation.

4 Basic Information for the FTSE 22 Emerging Markets

This chapter uses the FTSE 22 emerging markets (FTSE 2010). An advantage is that FTSE separates stock market indices by level of development (Cavusgil et al. 2013, p. 3). FTSE distinguishes between 10 advanced and 12 secondary emerging markets, as shown in Table 1 (Column 1). Cavusgil et al. (2013, pp. 4–5) compares the composition of the FTSE 22, the MSCI Emerging Markets Index, S&P Emerging BMI, Goldman Sachs Emerging Markets Equity Fund (see Wilson and Stupnytska 2007), and Grant Thornton (2010). There is a reasonably close (but not perfect) overlap of the FTSE 22, the MSCI, and S&P. The latter two lists drop or add a few countries relative to the FTSE 22. Goldman Sachs is considerably more restrictive, but adds Bangladesh and Vietnam. Grant Thornton is the broadest list, although dropping the Czech Republic, Morocco, Taiwan, and UAE. (There is then some consensus outside the FTSE 22 for not including the UAE; but no consensus on what other countries to add or drop.) Grant Thornton adds Algeria, Argentina, Bangladesh, Iran, Nigeria, Romania, Ukraine, Vietnam, and Venezuela. There are arguments for and against inclusion or dropping of the countries listed here. Table 1 includes most countries of the so-called CIVETS category (including Colombia, Indonesia, Egypt, Turkey, and South Africa, but excluding Vietnam). Table 1 uses commercially issued lists. Other entities, such as the International Monetary Fund (IMF), also maintain emerging markets lists; but Table 1 captures the essential core membership of the category.

The FTSE 22 contains the four BRIC countries and the four MIST countries, contained at the top of Table 1 (Column 2), together with 14 other countries classified in the table by region (Europe, Latin America, Arab World, and Asia).

The table's structure (Column 7) thus matches OECD status in terms of engaged or membership (BRIC, MIST, and Europe, together with Chile).

This study does not include a formal statistical analysis. The consideration of corporate governance in relationship to corruption is therefore qualitative rather than quantitative. For corruption information, this chapter focuses on Transparency International's (TI) Corruption Perception Index (CPI). TI compiles this CPI annually from a number of studies conducted by various entities. Kaufmann and Vicente (2011) out that country-wide (i.e. average) indices of perceived corruption, such as reported by TI, are subject to problems of endogeneity, whereas the corporate survey they use permits micro-level analysis.

The 2012 CPI information concerns 176 countries or territories. Table 1 includes the 2012 rank order (Column 3) and the 2012 CPI estimate (Column 4). Among the 22 FTSE emerging markets, Chile and UAE rank relatively high at 20 and 27, respectively, with CPI's of 72 and 68 (or roughly the level of the U.S. at 73 and the UK and Japan at 74). The top 20 on the CPI are Western Europe, Australia, New Zealand, Singapore, and Hong Kong. The four BRICs, especially Russia ranked at 133 (CPI of 28), are relatively corrupt (ranking between 80 and 94), as are the four MISTs, especially Indonesia ranked at 118 (CPI of 32). Pakistan is most corrupt, in this set, at 139 (CPI of 27).

The TI information is supplemented with 2011 WGI control of corruption information, reported in Column 5 by quartile (at 90 % confidence). Chile and USE fall in the 75–100 % quartile, together with Taiwan (ranked 27 at CPI of 61). Russia falls in the 0–25 % quartile, with Colombia, Pakistan, the Philippines, and Thailand. Other countries fall in the 25–50 % or 50–75 % quartiles (notably Brazil, South Africa, Turkey, the Czech Republic, Hungary, Poland, Peru, Morocco, and Malaysia). Table 1 does not report whether a country ranks toward the lower or upper end of a quartile, but detailed information on each country is available from the WGI website.

It is more difficult to assemble consistent corporate governance ranking information for emerging markets. (Davis et al. 2012, provide a detailed assessment of governance indicators.) GMI provides an average ranking for its set of emerging markets, reported in Table 1 in the last row as 3.94, which is about 52 % of the UK's 7.6 ranking. (GMI has a scale from 1 to 10; the UK received GMI's highest ranking.) GMI does not report specific country rankings if there are fewer than ten covered companies in a country. There are GMI rankings for the BRICs and MISTs. South Africa has a relatively high ranking of 6.09 – reflecting in part the lengthy process of the King Commission recommendations in that country. Poland has the next highest reported ranking of 5.11 and also reasonably moderate corruption. Mexico received a 2.43 ranking, and Chile a 2.13 ranking.

The World Bank conducts an initiative labeled Reports on the Observance of Standards and Codes (ROSC) at invitation of national authorities. This initiative benchmarks the member country's corporate governance framework and also company practices against the OECD Principles for Corporate Governance. The purpose is to assist member countries with developing and implementing action plans for institutional strengthening and raise awareness of good practices among

Table 2 Corporate governance codes for FTSE 22 emerging markets (countries in alphabetical order)

Column 1	Column 2	Column 3
Country	Initial year included	Latest code(s) per ECGI website
Brazil	2002	Code of Best Practice of Corporate Governance (4th edition) September 2009
China	2001	Provisional Code of Corporate Governance for Securities Companies 15 January 2004
		The Code of Corporate Governance for Listed Companies in China 7 January 2001
Chile	*	not reported
Colombia	2007	Colombian Guide of Corporate Governance for Closed Societies and Family Firms September 2009
		Colombian Code of Best Corporate Practice 2007
Czech Republic	2001	Corporate Governance Code based on the OECD Principles (2004) June 2004
Egypt	2006	Code of Corporate Governance for Listed Companies 13 February 2011
		Code of Corporate Governance for Private Sector in Egypt October 2006
		Code of Corporate Governance for State Owned Enterprises in Egypt July 2006
Hungary	2002	Corporate Governance Recommendations 11 March 2008
India	1998	Corporate Governance Voluntary Guidelines 2009 24 December 2009
Indonesia	2000	Code of Good Corporate Governance 2006 January 2007
Malaysia	2000	Malaysian Code on Corporate Governance 2012 March 2012
Mexico	1999	Código de Mejores Prácticas Corporativas 2010
Morocco	2008	Code Marocain de Bonnes Pratiques de Gouvernance des Etablissements et Entreprises Publics (EEP) 2 February 2011
		Code spécifique de bonnes pratiques de gouvernance des PME et Entreprises familiales October 2008
		Moroccan Code of Good Corporate Governance Practices 17 March 2008
Pakistan	2002	Code of Corporate Governance 2012 10 April 2012
Peru	2001	Principios de Buen Gobierno para las Sociedades Peruanas July 2002
		Código de Buen Gobierno Corporativo para Empresas Emisoras de Valores November 2001
Philippines, The	2000	Revised Code of Corporate Governance 15 July 2009
Poland	2002	Code of Best Practice for WSE Listed Companies 21 November 2012
		Best Practices in Public Companies 2005 29 October 2004
Russia	2002	The Russian Code of Corporate Conduct 4 April 2002
South Africa	1994	Draft Code for Responsible Investing by Institutional Investors in South Africa 1 September 2010

(continued)

Table 2 (continued)

Column 1	Column 2	Column 3
Country	Initial year included	Latest code(s) per ECGI website
		King Code of Governance for South Africa 2009 (King III) 1 September 2009
		King Report on Corporate Governance for South Africa – 2002 (King II Report) March 2002
		King I Report 24 November 1994
Taiwan	2002	Corporate Governance Best-Practice Principles for TSE/GTSM Listed Companies December 2010
Thailand	1998	The Principles of Good Corporate Governance For Listed Companies 2006 March 2006
Turkey	2003	Corporate Governance Principles February 2005
UAE	2007	Corporate Governance Code for Small and Medium Enterprises Dubai September 2011
		Corporate Governance Code for Joint-Stock Companies 9 April 2007

Note: European Corporate Governance Institute (ECGI), http://www.ecgi.org/codes/all_codes.php
*See: OECD, Corporate Governance in Chile 2010, Paris, France: OECD Publishing, 18 January 2011.

stakeholders in public and private sectors. An ROSC report is available on each of the FTSE 22 countries (as well as some others and various developing countries), with the exception of Taiwan (which is not a member of the World Bank or the United Nations, due to disputed sovereignty between the Republic of China and the People's Republic of China). Also not located at the ROSC website were China, Russia, and the UAE, although Hong Kong was included. China, Hong Kong, Russia, Taiwan, and the UAE are included in the Worldwide Governance Indicators (WGI) website, where downloadable reports are available. The WGI six dimensions of "good governance" arguably lack construct validity (Thomas 2010) and basically all measure the same broad conception of governance (Langbein and Knack 2010).

Table 2 provides basic information on corporate governance codes in the FTSE 22. The information is maintained at the website of the European Corporate Governance Institute (ECGI). Column 2 of the table is the reported first year of adoption of a code in a country, according to that website. Column 3 updates the history of codes in each country.

5 Conclusion

This chapter addresses whether corporate governance reforms and best practices can operate effectively as an antidote to commercial and political corruption. General findings are that (1) corporate governance best practices are desirable for a number of reasons, and (2) such best practices, in combination with business integrity and governmental anti-corruption efforts, should tend to operate against commercial and political corruption over time. The effectiveness of governance and anti-corruption measures depend on the personal integrity of business directors and executives. Structural measures recommended in corporate governance codes are not well linked to anti-corruption effectiveness. Emerging markets involve special concerns for both corporate governance and anti-corruption reforms. Such economies are rapidly growing, attracting foreign direct investment (FDI), and weak in the institutional infrastructure for good governance and low corruption. Contributions of this chapter include a review of three relevant literatures, and a summary of the governance and corruption reform status of emerging markets, with focus on the FTSE 22.

References

Adams, R. B., Hermalin, B. E., & Weisbach, M. S. (2010). The role of boards of directors in corporate governance: A conceptual framework and survey. *Journal of Economic Literature, 48*(1), 58–107.

Aguilera, R. V., & Jackson, G. (2003). The cross-national diversity of corporate governance: Dimensions and determinants. *Academy of Management Review, 28*(3), 447–465.

Aguilera, R. V., & Jackson, G. (2010). Comparative and international corporate governance. *The Academy of Management Annals, 4*(1), 485–556.

Aguilera, R. V., de Castro, L. R. K., Lee, J. H., & You, J. (2012). Corporate governance in emerging markets. In G. Morgan & R. Whitley (Eds.), *Capitalisms and capitalism in the 21st century* (pp. 319–344). Oxford, UK: Oxford University Press.

Aidt, T., Dutta, J., & Sena, V. (2008). Governance regimes, corruption and growth: Theory and evidence. *Journal of Comparative Economics, 36*(2), 195–220.

Al-Sadig, A. (2009). The effects of corruption on FDI inflows. *Cato Journal, 29*(2), 267–294.

Andreasson, S. (2011). Understanding corporate governance reform in South Africa: Anglo-American divergence, the King Reports, and hybridization. *Business and Society, 50*(4), 647–673.

Aspray, T. (2011, February 4). *BRICs vs. MISTs: A technical view.* http://www.forbes.com/sites/tomaspray/2011/02/04/brics-vs-mists-a-technical-view/

Baek, J. S., Kang, J. K., & Park, K. S. (2004). Corporate governance and firm value: Evidence from the Korean financial crisis. *Journal of Financial Economics, 71*(2), 265–313.

Bai, C.-E., Liu, Q., Lu, J., Song, F. M., & Zhang, J. (2004). Corporate governance and market valuation in China. *Journal of Comparative Economics, 32*(4), 599–616.

Baron, D. P. (2008). *Siemens: Anatomy of Bribery.* Stanford: Stanford Graduate School of Business. Case P-68.

Bennedsen, M., Feldmann, S. E., & Lassen, D. D. (2011, June 28). *Lobbying and bribes – A survey-based analysis of the demand for influence and corruption.* CESifo Working Paper Series No. 3496. http://ssrn.com/abstract=1873891

Berg, S. V., Jiang, L., & Lin, C. (2012). Regulation and corporate corruption: New evidence from the telecom sector. *Journal of Comparative Economics, 40*(1), 22–43.

Black, B. S., De Carvalho, A. G., & Gorga, E. (2012). What matters and for which firms for corporate governance in emerging markets? Evidence from Brazil (and other BRIK Countries). *Journal of Corporate Finance, 18*(4), 934–952.

Braga-Alves, M. V., & Morey, M. (2012). Predicting corporate governance in emerging markets. *Journal of International Money and Finance, 31*(6), 1414–1439.
Cadbury Committee. (1992). *Report of the committee on the financial aspects of corporate governance*. London: Gee.
Camerer, L. (2001, September). *Corruption in South Africa: Results of an expert panel survey. Pretoria: Institute for Security Studies (ISS)* (Monograph No. 65). Research and publication of this monograph funded by the European Union, and USAID, the Ford Foundation and Standard Bank for the ISS's Criminal Justice Monitor. http://www.iss.co.za/Pubs/Monographs/No65/Contents.html, http://dspace.cigilibrary.org/jspui/bitstream/123456789/31491/1/Momo65.pdf?1
Campos, N. F., & Giovannoni, F. (2007). Lobbying, corruption and political influence. *Public Choice, 131*(1), 1–12.
Caron, M. I., Ficici, A., & Richter, C. L. (2012). The influence of corruption on corporate governance standards: Shared characteristics of rapidly developing economies. *Emerging Markets Journal, 2*(1), 21–37. doi:10.5195/emaj.2012.17.
Cavusgil, S. T., Ghauri, P. N., & Akcal, A. A. (2013). *Doing business in emerging markets* (2nd ed.). Thousand Oaks: Sage.
Chavis, L. (2013). Social networks and bribery: The case of entrepreneurs in Eastern Europe. *Journal of Comparative Economics, 41*(1), 279–293.
Chen, C. J. P., Ding, Y., & Kim, C. (2010). High-level politically connected firms, corruption, and analyst forecast accuracy around the world. *Journal of International Business Studies, 41*(9), 1505–1524.
Chong, A., & López-de-Silanes, F. (Eds.). (2007). *Investor protection and corporate governance: Firm-level evidence across Latin America*. Washington, DC: World Bank.
Claessens, S., & Yurtoglu, B. B. (2013). Corporate governance in emerging markets: A survey. *Emerging Markets Review, 15*, 1–33.
Clifford Chance. (2011, December). *Core corporate governance issues: A comparative overview*. Frankfurt am Main. http://www.ecgi.org/codes/documents/clifford_chance_overview_31may2012_en.pdf
Damania, R., Fredricksson, P. G., & Mani, M. (2004). The persistence of corruption and regulatory compliance failures: Theory and evidence. *Public Choice, 121*(3), 363–390.
Davis, K., Fisher, A., Kingsbury, B., & Merry, S. E. (Eds.). (2012). *Governance by indicators: Global power through classification and rankings*. Oxford, UK: Oxford University Press.
Desai, M. A., & Moel, A. (2008). Czech mate: Expropriation and investor protection in a converging world. *Review of Finance, 12*(1), 221–251.
Dreher, A., Kotsogiannis, C., & McCorriston, S. (2007). Corruption around the world: Evidence from a structural model. *Journal of Comparative Economics, 35*(3), 443–466.
Egger, P., & Winner, H. (2006). How corruption influences foreign direct investment: A panel data study. *Economic Development and Cultural Change, 54*(2), 459–486.
Erkens, D. H., Hung, M., & Matos, P. (2012). Corporate governance in the 2007–2008 financial crisis: Evidence from financial institutions worldwide. *Journal of Corporate Finance, 18*(2), 389–411.
Fan, J. P. H., Rui, O. M., & Zhao, M. (2008). Public governance and corporate finance: Evidence from corruption cases. *Journal of Comparative Economics, 36*(3), 343–364.
Ficici, A., & Aybar, C. B. (2012). Corporate governance and firm value in emerging markets: An empirical analysis of ADR issuing emerging market firms. *Emerging Markets Journal, 2*(1), 38–51. doi:10.5195/emaj.2012.18.
Foroohar, R. (2012). Walmart's discounted ethics: Its Mexican bribery scandal shows the perils of bowing to local "custom". *TIME, 179*(18), 19.
FTSE. (2010, September). *FTSE global equity index series country classification*. http://www.ftse.com/Indices/Country_Classification/Downloads/Sept%202010/FTSE_Country_Classification_Sept_2010_Update.pdf
Gibson, M. S. (2003). Is corporate governance ineffective in emerging markets? *Journal of Financial and Quantitative Analysis, 38*(1), 231–250.

Givens, D. (2013). Defining governance matters: A factor analytic assessment of governance institutions. *Journal of Comparative Economics, 41*(4), 1026–1053.
Goldsmith, A. A. (1999). Slapping the grasping hand: Correlates of political corruption in emerging markets. *American Journal of Economics and Sociology, 58*(4), 865–883.
Goyer, M. (2010). Corporate governance. In G. Morgan, J. Campbell, C. Crouch, O. Pedersen, & R. Whitley (Eds.), *The Oxford handbook of comparative institutional analysis* (pp. 423–452). Oxford, UK: Oxford University Press.
Graham, A. (2012). Thought leaders: An interview with William J. O'Rourke. *Strategy + business* (Booz & Co.), Issue 69, Winter. http://www.strategy-business.com/media/file/00149-Thought-Leader-William-ORourke.pdf
Grant Thornton. (2010). *Emerging markets: Leading the way to recovery*. International business report 2010. http://www.internationalbusinessreport.com/files/gti_ibr_emarkets_2010final.pdf
Gregory, H. J. (2000). *International comparison of corporate governance: Guidelines and codes of best practice: Developing and emerging markets*. New York: Weil, Gotshal & Manges LLP. http://www.ecgi.org/codes/documents/international_comparison_emerging_markets.pdf
Habib, M., & Zurawicki, L. (2002). Corruption and foreign direct investment. *Journal of International Business Studies, 33*(2), 291–307.
Hadjikhani, A., Elg, U., & Ghauri, P. (Eds.). (2012). *Multinationals in emerging markets*. Bingley: Emerald Group Publishing.
Harstad, B., & Svensson, J. (2011). Bribes, lobbying and development. *American Political Science Review, 105*(1), 46–63.
Hitz, J.-M., & Lehmann, N. (2012, October 31). *The usefulness of corporate governance ratings*. http://ssrn.com/abstract=2042019
International Corporate Governance Network (ICGN). (1999, July 9). *Statement on global corporate governance principles*. http://www.ecgi.org/codes/documents/icgn_principles.pdf
International Corporate Governance Network (ICGN). (2009a). *ICGN global corporate governance principles: Revised*. London: ICGN. https://www.icgn.org/images/ICGN/Best%20Practice%20Guidance%20PDFS/short_version_-_icgn_global_corporate_governance_principles-_revised_2009.pdf
International Corporate Governance Network (ICGN). (2009b). *ICGN statement and guidance on anti-corruption practices*. London: ICGN. https://www.icgn.org/files/icgn_main/pdfs/best_practice/guidance_on_anti-corruption_practices/2009_anti-corruption_practices_(march).pdf
International Corporate Governance Network (ICGN). (2012). *ICGN statement and guidance on political lobbying and donations*. London: ICGN. https://www.icgn.org/images/ICGN/Best%20Practice%20Guidance%20PDFS/icgn_pld_mar2012_short.pdf
Javaid, U. (2010). Corruption and its deep impact on good governance in Pakistan. *Pakistan Economic and Social Review, 48*(1), 123–134.
Javorcik, B., & Wei, S.-J. (2009). Corruption and cross-border investment in emerging markets: Firm-level evidence. *Journal of International Money and Finance, 28*(4), 605–624.
Kaufmann, D., & Vicente, P. C. (2011). Legal corruption. *Economics and Politics, 23*(2), 195–219.
Kearney, C. (2012). Emerging markets research: Trends, issues and future directions. *Emerging Markets Review, 13*(2), 159–183.
Khan, M. H. (2006). Corruption and governance. In Jomo K. S. (J. Kwame Sundaram) & B. Fine (Eds.), *The new development economics: After the Washington Consensus* (pp. 200–221). New Delhi/London: Tulika Press/Zed Press.
King, M. (2006). *The corporate citizen: Governance for all entities*. London: Penguin Books.
Kish-Gephart, J. J., Harrison, D. A., & Treviño, L. K. (2010). Bad apples, bad cases, and bad barrels: Meta-analytic evidence about sources of unethical decisions at work. *Journal of Applied Psychology, 95*(1), 1–31.
Klapper, L. F., & Love, I. (2002, April). *Corporate governance, investor protection, and performance in emerging markets*. Washington, DC: The World Bank, Development Research

Group, Finance. http://www-wds.worldbank.org/servlet/WDSContentServer/WDSP/IB/2002/05/03/000094946_02041804272577/Rendered/PDF/multi0page.pdf

Klapper, L., Laeven, L., & Love, I. (2006). Corporate governance provisions and firm ownership: Firm-level evidence from Eastern Europe. *Journal of International Money and Finance, 25*(3), 429–444.

Kwok, C. C. Y., & Tadesse, S. (2006). The MNC as an agent of change for host-country institutions: FDI and corruption. *Journal of International Business Studies, 37*(6), 767–785.

Lameira, V. De J., & Bertrand, H. (2008). Ethics, corruption, governance and emerging markets. *REAd – Edição, 59* 14(1) jan-abr. http://ssrn.com/abstract=2047417

Langbein, L., & Knack, S. (2010). The worldwide governance indicators: Six, one, or none? *Journal of Development Studies, 46*(2), 350–370.

Larcker, D., & Tayan, B. (2011). *Corporate governance matters: A closer look at organizational choices and their consequences*. Upper Saddle River: Pearson Prentice Hall.

Larrain, F., & Tavares, J. (2004). Does foreign direct investment decrease corruption? *Cuadernos de Economia – Latin American Journal of Economics, 41*(August), 217–230.

Leblanc, R. (2012, November 22). *How boards can deal with corruption in emerging markets: Canadian companies must be vigilant about preventing corrupt practices in their overseas operations*. http://www.canadianbusiness.com/economy/boards-emerging-markets-corruption/.

Lefort, F., & Urzua, F. (2008). Board independence, firm performance and ownership concentration: Evidence from Chile. *Journal of Business Research, 61*(6), 615–622.

Licht, A. N., Goldschmidt, C., & Schwartz, S. H. (2007). Culture rules: The foundations of the rule of law and other norms of governance. *Journal of Comparative Economics, 35*(4), 659–688.

Loredo, E. N., Stanley, K. D., & Greenberg, M. D. (2012). *Anti-corruption regulations in emerging and expeditionary markets: New markets, new challenges*. Santa Monica: RAND Corporation. http://www.rand.org/pubs/conf_proceedings/CF304

Luo, Y. (2011). Strategic responses to perceived corruption in an emerging market: Lessons from MNEs investing in China. *Business & Society, 50*(2), 350–387.

Mann, T. E., Davis, S. M., Minow, N., & Ornstein, N. (2012, March 21). *Prague declaration on governance and anti-corruption*. http://www.brookings.edu/research/reports/2012/03/21-prague-declaration-mann

Millar, C. C. J. M., Eldomiaty, T. I., Choi, C. J., & Hilton, B. J. (2005). Corporate governance and institutional transparency in emerging markets. *Journal of Business Ethics, 59*(1/2), 163–174.

Multilateral Investment Guarantee Agency (MIGA). (2013). *2012 world investment and political risk*. Washington, DC: International Bank for Reconstruction and Development (IBRD), The World Bank. http://www.miga.org/documents/WIPR12.pdf

O'Neill, J. (2001, November 30). *Building better global economic BRICs*. Goldman Sachs Global Economics Paper No. 66. http://www.goldmansachs.com/our-thinking/archive/archive-pdfs/build-better-brics.pdf

O'Rourke, W., Rosenthal, J., & Kennedy, J. T. (2011, June 21). *Confronting corruption in emerging markets*. http://www.policyinnovations.org/ideas/video/data/000375

Organisation for Economic Co-Operation and Development (OECD). (2004). *OECD principles of corporate governance* [revised, first issued May 1999]. Paris: OECD. http://www.oecd.org/daf/ca/corporategovernanceprinciples/31557724.pdf

Organisation for Economic Co-Operation and Development (OECD). (2005). *OECD guidelines on corporate governance of state-owned enterprises*. Paris: OECD. http://www.oecd.org/corporate/ca/corporategovernanceofstate-ownedenterprises/34803211.pdf

Organisation for Economic Co-Operation and Development (OECD). (2006). *Methodology for assessing the implementation of the OECD principles of corporate governance*. Paris: OECD. http://www.oecd.org/daf/ca/corporategovernanceprinciples/37776417.pdf

Parkinson, J., & Meredith, L. (2012). Corruption in emerging markets. In C. Lerner (Ed.), *The US private equity compliance companion* (pp. 71–78). London: Private Equity International (PEI).

Perez, M. F., Brada, J. C., & Drabek, Z. (2012). Illicit money flows as motives for FDI. *Journal of Comparative Economics, 40*(1), 108–126.

Ramamurti, R., & Singh, J. V. (Eds.). (2009). *Emerging multinationals in emerging markets.* Cambridge, UK: Cambridge University Press.
Siems, M. M., & Alvarez-Macotela, O. S. (2013). The OECD principles of corporate governance in emerging markets: A successful example of networked governance? In M. Fenwick, S. Van Uystel, S. Wrbka (Eds.), *Networked governance, transnational business and the law*. Berlin: Springer, forthcoming 2014. http://ssrn.com/abstract=2214828
Sonnenfeld, J. (2001). Good governance and the misleading myths of bad metrics. *Academy of Management Executive, 18*(1), 108–113.
Thomas, M. A. (2010). What do the worldwide governance indicators measure? *European Journal of Development Research, 22*(1), 31–54.
Transparency International (TI). (2011). *Bribe payers index 2011*. Berlin: Germany.
Treisman, D. (2007). What have we learned about the causes of corruption from ten years of cross-national empirical research? *Annual Review of Political Science, 10*, 211–244.
van Agtmael, A. (2007). *The emerging markets century: How a new breed of world-class companies is overtaking the world*. New York: Free Press.
Verhezen, P., & Morse, P. (2009). Consensus on global governance principles? *Journal of International Business Ethics, 2*(1), 84–101.
Webley, S., & Werner, A. (2008). Corporate codes of ethics: Necessary but not sufficient. *Business Ethics: A European Review, 17*(4), 405–416.
Wei, S.-J. (2000). How taxing is corruption on international investors? *Review of Economics and Statistics, 82*(1), 1–11.
Wieneke, A., & Gries, T. (2011). SME performance in transition economies: The financial regulation and firm-level corruption nexus. *Journal of Comparative Economics, 39*(2), 221–229.
Wilson, J. Q. (1989). Adam Smith on business ethics. *California Management Review, 32*(1), 59–72.
Wilson, D., & Stupnytska, A. (2007, March 28). *The N-11: More than an acronym*. Goldman Sachs Global Economics Paper No. 153. http://www.chicagobooth.edu/alumni/clubs/pakistan/docs/next11dream-march%20'07-goldmansachs.pdf
Wu, X. (2005). Corporate governance and corruption: A cross-country analysis. *Governance: An International Journal of Policy, Administration, and Institutions, 18*(2), 151–170.
Wunker, S. (2012, April 25). *Four lessons for Wal-Mart on corruption in emerging markets*. http://www.forbes.com/sites/stephenwunker/2012/04/25/four-lessons-for-wal-mart-on-corruption-in-emerging-markets/
Young, M. N., Peng, M. W., Ahlstrom, D., Bruton, G. D., & Jiang, Y. (2008). Corporate governance in emerging economies: A review of the principal-principal perspective. *Journal of Management Studies, 45*(1), 196–220.

The Regulatory Conundrum: Achieving Corporate Governance Reforms in Developing Countries

Javed Siddiqui and Chowdhury Saima Ferdous

Abstract Based on an extensive review of existing literature, the chapter attempts to identify some unique characteristics of the developing markets with a view to understanding whether such socio-political and cultural traits may actually act as deterrents to the ongoing globalisation efforts Bangladesh is used as an example to highlight the distinctive characteristics of socio-political environment existing in many developing economies. Overall analysis suggests that the developing countries are different than developed economies. The corporate governance infrastructure in countries like Bangladesh has elements of both shareholder and stakeholder perspective, but none of them alone could solve the unique governance issues prevailing in developing countries. Also, low audit fees appear to be major hindrance of quality audit.

1 Introduction

Although scholars (for example, Shleifer and Vishny 1997; Turnbull 1997; Solomon 2007; Mallin 2010) extensively stress on the significant impact of cultural, political, historical, religious and other contextual differences on governance practices, there have been consistent calls for harmonisation of corporate governance practices throughout the globe. In recent years, as the developing economies have begun to open up their markets as part of the globalisation process initiated by various international financial agencies, there have been significant developments in the regulatory environment guiding corporate governance in those countries. Reed (2002) observes that most of the emerging economies seem to have adopted

J. Siddiqui (✉)
Manchester Business School, University of Manchester, Manchester, UK
e-mail: Javed.Siddiqui@mbs.ac.uk

C.S. Ferdous
University of Dhaka, Dhaka, Bangladesh
e-mail: saimachy77@yahoo.com

S. Boubaker and D.K. Nguyen (eds.), *Corporate Governance in Emerging Markets*, CSR, Sustainability, Ethics & Governance, DOI 10.1007/978-3-642-44955-0_18,

the Anglo-Saxon model of corporate governance, although such model is based on premises that primarily hold in developed economies. As these models are not considered to be entirely suitable with the socio-economic characteristics of the developing countries, the motivation for such adoption has been questioned by a number of researchers. Finding a series of issues relating to the non-compliance with international standard of corporate governance practices across developing countries critics (Rwegasira 2000; Sejjaaka 2007; Adu-Amoah et al. 2008; Ogbechie et al. 2009; Ogbuozobe 2009; Silveira and Saito 2009; Black et al. 2010; Wanyama et al. 2009) argue that the theoretical propositions of the Anglo-American model are in conflict with the traditional cultures, values, corporate and legal infrastructures of developing countries. In investigating the answer behind such adoption, studies (For example, Reed 2002; West 2006; Siddiqui 2010 etc.) reveal that this wholesale adoption of the shareholder model is in fact a result of the past failures of indigenous economic and industrial polices, and dependence on overseas assistance.

Researchers, like (Haniffa and Hudaib 2007; Alawattage and Wickramasinghe 2008; Siddiqui 2010) further argue that the mechanisms of good governance, developed in the context of developed economies, will only work under assumptions of an efficient capital market, higher investor sophistication, and presence of effective second order institutions (such as efficient regulators, judiciary etc.) that will complement such governance schemes. Any reforms not considering such institutional factors will be largely symbolic. However, despite this, attempts to harmonize corporate governance models and best practice recommendations have continued, and such efforts have been supported by international donor agencies such as the World Bank and the IMF who have sometimes prescribed adoption of such standards in member states as a condition for receiving loans. This sets the context for this chapter.

Based on an extensive review of existing literature, the chapter attempts to identify some unique characteristics of the developing markets with a view to understanding whether such socio-political and cultural traits may actually act as deterrents to the ongoing globalisation attempts. For the purpose of this chapter, Bangladesh is used as an example to highlight the distinctive characteristics of socio-political environment existing in many developing economies. Like many other developing economies, Bangladesh is financially reliant on international donors or lending institutions such as the World Bank and the IMF, and instances of donor influence in government policy making have been documented (Sobhan 2003). Siddiqui (2010) reports that, like many other developing countries, donor agencies attached conditions of financial sector reforms for advancing loans to the Bangladesh government for various projects. Since the early 1990s Bangladesh has taken some major initiatives to reform its corporate governance policies, capital market and financial system. Prioritizing the global need of aligning corporate governance standards according to best practice recommendations, the first voluntary code, namely the Code of Corporate Governance for Bangladesh (hereafter "the Code") was developed in 2004. Later, in 2006, to institutionalize the corporate practice of corporate governance in Bangladesh, the Securities and Exchange

Commission (SEC) issued a notification on Corporate Governance Guidelines (hereafter "SEC Guidelines") for the publicly listed companies of Bangladesh, which has been revised in 2012. This Code is designed in light of the shareholder model and in particular reflects the OECD Principles 2004. However, concern remains, as Siddiqui (2010) reports institutional pressures for the adoption the apparently incompatible Anglo-American model of corporate governance in Bangladesh and supporting such claim. In a recent study, Ferdous (2013) provides empirical evidences of such incompatibilities in the Bangladeshi corporate structure.

Interestingly, the studies on the accounting and auditing standards in Bangladesh also reveal the same. As part of the financial sector reforms, Bangladesh adopted the international standards of accounting (ISA) and auditing (IAS), and was advised to embrace a western styled model of corporate governance. Mir and Rahaman (2005), investigating adoption of ISAs in Bangladesh concluded that such adoption may have been due to a number of institutional pressures rather than reasons of efficiency, as these standards do not appear to be entirely suitable for the socio-economic conditions prevailing in Bangladesh. This provides the context for this chapter.

Overall analysis suggests that the developing countries are different than developed economies. The corporate governance infrastructure in countries like Bangladesh has elements of both shareholder and stakeholder perspective, but none of them alone could solve the unique governance issues prevailing in developing countries. Also, low audit fees appear to be major hindrance of quality audit.

The remainder of this chapter is organised as follows: the next section discusses the ongoing global emphasis on compliance, spearheaded by agencies such as the World Bank and the IFAC. A subsequent section then presents some distinctive attributes of socio-political environment existing in many developing countries, using Bangladesh as a case. This is followed by a discussion and conclusion section that attempts to assess the potential effects of such characteristics on the globalisation efforts, and summarises the findings in line with the issues addressed in this chapter.

2 Global Emphasis on Compliance

Since 1996, institutions like the World Bank and the Organization for Economic Cooperation and Development (OECD) are also developing codes in response to the need of an international benchmark of good governance. (Aguilera and Cuervo-Cazurra 2009; Awotundun et al. 2011). Following that spirit the 'OECD Principles of Corporate Governance' were issued in 1999 (and amended in 2004), and eventually that has "become a widely accepted global benchmark that is adaptable to varying social, legal and economic contexts in individual countries" (Krambia-Kapardis and Psaros 2006, p. 127). Since its inception it has worked as a guide for much of the corporate governance reforms, especially in developing countries.

In fact, as stated in the study of Ferdous (2013), existing literature reveals that in the case of developed countries too, along with other external factors,[1] these best practice recommendations set by international organizations are one of the major reasons behind the similarities in code contents around the world (e.g. Aguilera and Jackson 2003; Aguilera and Cuervo-Cazurra 2009) hence it is not surprising to find that most of the literature on compliance is based on these best practice recommendations.

Although there is a vast literature relating to harmonisation of accounting standards, corporate social reporting, disclosure, harmonisation of auditing practices has received relatively little attention. The few studies that have looked at harmonisation of auditing standards have largely concentrated in the area of audit reports. Gangolly et al. (2002), investigating harmonisation of auditing reports state that such attempts have been relatively new and have mostly been spearheaded by the IFAC. Similar to the code development initiatives, these attempts have also been supported by the World Bank and the IMF, who, as part of their ROSC programme, have suggested adoption of a number of SMOs proposed by the IFAC in developing countries. This chapter will now discuss the World Bank and IFAC efforts to initiate and disseminate one global set of corporate governance and audit standards in further details.

2.1 World Bank and IMF Joint ROSC Programme

The ROSC (Reports on the Observance of Standards and Codes) programme was jointly launched by the World Bank and the IMF in 1999 with a view to 'promote greater financial stability, at both the domestic and international levels, through the development, dissemination, adoption, and implementation of international standards and codes' (IMF 2005, p. 5). ROSC covers a set of 12 internationally recognised 'modules' consisting of core standards and codes relevant to economic stability and private and financial sector development of member countries.[2]

At the national level, The OECD Principles as international standards provide a benchmark that can help identify vulnerabilities as well as guide policy reform. However countries have been advised to customize these principles according to the local context. To best serve these objectives, however, the scope and application of such standards needs to be assessed in the context of a country's overall development strategy and tailored to individual country circumstances.

[1] such as globalization, liberalization of market, demands of foreign investors.

[2] The twelve standards are data dissemination, fiscal transparency, transparency in monetary and financial policies, banking supervision, securities market regulation, insurance supervision, payments and settlements, anti-money laundering, corporate governance, accounting, auditing, and insolvency and creditor rights (World Bank 2004).

In preparing the ROSCs the IMF and the World Bank are undertaking a large number of summary assessments of the observance of selected standards relevant to private and financial sector development and stability. In particular, in this report emphasizes on: (i) corporate governance, (ii) accounting and auditing, and (iii) insolvency regimes and creditor rights. These assessments are being collected as "modules" in country binders constituting the "ROSCs." As mentioned in the World Bank website, "under this modular approach, the Fund takes the lead in preparing modules in the area of data dissemination and fiscal transparency. Modules for the financial sector (monetary and financial policy transparency, banking supervision, securities market regulation, payment systems, deposit insurance) are mostly derived as by-products from a parallel Bank-Fund Financial Sector Assessment Program (FSAP)".

For corporate governance standards the World Bank considers the OECD Principles. A 2004 report by the World Bank, presenting an overview of the ROSC accounting and auditing module mentions that the module had twofold objectives: first, to assess the comparability of national accounting and auditing standards with International Accounting Standards (IAS) and International Standards on Auditing (ISA) respectively; and the degree to which corporate entities comply with established accounting and auditing standards in the country; and second, to assist the country in developing and implementing a country action plan for improving the institutional framework, which underpins corporate financial reporting regime in the country (World Bank 2004, p. 2). Under the project, and evaluation exercise is conducted to compare the national auditing standards with the ISAs. Also, the current strengths and weaknesses of the accounting and auditing profession in a member-state are evaluated. The ultimate outcome of the ROSC programme is the production of a country action plan for each member-state, which, 'if requested by country authorities' can result in the design of loans to be financed by the world bank (World Bank 2003, p. 6).

2.2 Global Corporate Governance Forum and Capacity Building Programs

The Global Corporate Governance Forum (GCGF) is a part of IFC Corporate Governance group. It is a donor support facility which is co-founded in 1999 by the World Bank and the Organization for Economic Co-operation and Development (OECD).

GCGF supports corporate governance reforms in emerging markets and developing countries. Its aim is to address the knowledge gap in corporate governance, particularly in emerging markets. In light of the OECD Principles of Corporate Governance, it develops advanced knowledge and training tool kits for promoting good practices in corporate governance and facilitates capacity building of director training organizations engaged in implementing corporate governance reforms.

With an aim to build capacity for promoting good governance, GCGF works as the global knowledge platform to support access to international best practices in corporate governance. In order to encourage board level participation in corporate governance training programs GCGF organizes 'Training of Trainers' program which highlights on the board practices and board leadership strategies. It also organizes training programs to develop a monitoring and evaluation mechanism to support the global knowledge platform.

2.3 The IFAC Compliance Programme

The IFAC was established in 1977 and headquartered in New York with a view to issuing international standards covering the areas of ethics, auditing and assurance, education and public sector accounting (IFAC website). The objective of IFAC is to provide globally homogenous standards that would yield higher coordination in the international accounting profession by developing ISAs. IFAC was successful in gaining the global recognition as the standard setter for auditing and its position was further strengthened when the European Commission announced its intention to mandate all the countries included in the European Union to adopt the ISAs under the condition that the ISAs as well as the governance of the IFAC itself have to be promoting the public interest (Loft et al. 2006). At present, the number of IFAC members has reached 159 in 124 member-countries representing 2.5 million accountants worldwide.

In 2006, IFAC issued seven statements of membership obligations (SMOs) to assist 'high quality performance by professional accountants' (IFAC 2006). The member bodies of IFAC, which includes national accountancy bodies from most of the countries in the world, are required to make their best efforts to abide by the SMOs, and failure to do such without satisfactory explanations would result in suspension or removal of membership. The seven SMOs issued by the IFAC cover areas such as audit quality, audit education, code of ethics for professional auditors, disciplinary procedures to be adopted by national auditing bodies, adoption of ISAs and IFRS, and accountability and auditing in the public sector.

SMO 1 is concerned with ensuring that member bodies will be subjecting their audit firms to quality review programs. At least audit firms that undertake audit and assurance engagements of listed companies should be reviewed for quality purposes. The IAASB is the one responsible for developing standards concerning audit quality (IFAC 2004, revised 2006). SMO 2 dictates the education requirements that are supposed to be followed by IFAC member bodies. According to SMO 3, members of IFAC are required to comply with the standards that are issued in terms of quality control, auditing, and assurance. SMO 4 is concerned with the IFAC Code of Ethics for Professional Accountants and pronouncements by the International Ethics Standards Board for Accountants (IESBA). Public sector auditing and accountability is incorporated in SMO 5. SMO 6 is related to the investigations of cases of misconduct such as cases of breaching any codes or standards. The IFAC does recognize that each country has its own legal systems. Consequently, the IFAC has set minimum requirements which could enable member firms to comply with this obligation. SMO 7 related to the adoption of IFRS and ISAs in member countries. The IFRS are issued by IASB and this SMO relates to member bodies complying with this obligation.

This section presented a brief overview of the corporate governance standards harmonisation and globalisation attempts initiated by the IFAC and disseminated by donor agencies such as the World Bank and the IMF. The next section will now present a review of corporate governance models adopted by the developing nations.

3 Adoption of Corporate Governance Models in Developing Nations

Donaldson and Preston (1995) identifies two different theories of corporation. The shareholder theory emphasizes that corporations are actually extensions of their owners, and that the owners should be benefitting from it. Therefore, the corporation should be accountable only to the shareholders (Friedman 1962). On the other hand, the stakeholder theory acknowledges corporation as a social entity that has responsibility to a wider group of stakeholders including shareholders, creditors, management, employees, the government, and other interested groups (Freeman and Reed 1983). Subsequent models of corporate governance have been based on these two views of the corporation. Whereas the Anglo-Saxon models of corporate governance have been embedded on the shareholder theory, the European model has incorporated the stakeholder model.

Letza et al. (2004) compare the two theories. The shareholder model (or the principal agent model (Jensen and Meckling (1976)) views that the purpose of the corporation is to maximise shareholders' wealth. According to this model, the main problem of governance arises because of the agency relationship. Like the agency theory, the shareholder model of corporate governance is also a rational actor model, where human beings are expected to be maximising their own interest. As the model is based on assumptions of strong market efficiency, a voluntary code of corporate governance is deemed to be sufficient, as managers in a strong market would have enough incentives to install corporate governance mechanisms in their firms. The stakeholder model, on the other hand, rejects the agency relationship as the principal problem of corporate governance. Rather, absence of stakeholders' involvement is viewed as the main obstacle for ensuring efficient controls. Contrary to the shareholder model, this model emphasizes on trust-based long term relationship between firm and stakeholders, protection of the rights of different stakeholders, employee participation, and business ethics (Letza et al. 2004).

Reed (2002) investigates adoption of corporate governance models in emerging economies. The paper states that typically, emerging economies tend to adopt the

Anglo-Saxon (shareholder) model of corporate governance, despite the fact that such model is based on assumptions of efficient markets and equity financing. Reed (2002) identifies a number of reasons for such preference. Firstly, many of these emerging economies are former British colonies, and enjoy historical ties to the Anglo-Saxon model. For example, the company laws of these countries may be inspired by the British company law. The failure of domestic economic and industrial policies may also have contributed to the adoption of apparently successful Anglo-saxon models. Reed (2002) identifies dependence on external bodies (such as the World Bank and the IMF) as one of the major reasons for the dissemination of the shareholder model in emerging economies-

> As a condition of renegotiating loans, international finance bodies imposed structural adjustment programmes on developing countries. These programmes included a variety of features that induced a move to an Anglo-saxon model of governance (Reed 2002, p. 230)

This is supported by Arnold (2005) who mentions that IFAs such as the World Bank, the IMF, and the ADB could be regarded as 'the new colonising influences arising from globalisation of economic governance'. Influences of development agencies in accounting standard setting in emerging economies are also reported by a number studies (for example, Ashraf and Ghani (2005) in Pakistan, Akhtaruddin (2005) and Mir and Rahaman (2005) in Bangladesh, Uddin and Tsamenyi (2005) in Ghana etc.). Reed (2002) also points out that adoption of the Anglo-Saxon model also has a legitimisation role. By adopting this model, governments in developing countries may try to send signals to the public that the unpopular reforms (promoting globalisation and free markets) are guided by efficient corporate structures that will help generate condition for economic growth and development. This is consistent with Enrione et al. (2006) who suggest that late adopters of corporate governance codes tend to mimic established practices for the sake of gaining legitimacy. Example of adoption of the Anglo-Saxon model has been reported in countries like India (Reed 2002), South Africa (West 2006), South Korea (Reed 2002) etc.

4 Features of Developing Markets

The socio-economic environment in many developing countries are characterised by the presence of relatively small number of publicly traded companies, many of which are owned and managed by families, poor perception regarding skill and competence of auditors, and absence of appropriate monitoring. Prior literature has identified a number of socio-political characteristics of the environment within which corporate practices take place in Bangladesh, namely, ownership concentration and family domination in public limited companies (Farooque et al. 2007; Khan et al. 2011), weak legal structure, poor incentives for companies to go public (Sobhan and Werner 2003), poor perception regarding the skill and competence of auditors (World Bank 2003) Siddiqui (2010), and the absence of 'second order' institutions (Siddiqui 2010). These factors will now be discussed in detail.

4.1 *Ownership Concentration and Family Domination in the Corporate Sector*

Like many other developing countries, most companies in Bangladesh are either family owned or controlled by substantial shareholders (corporate group or government). Farooque et al. (2007) report that, on average, the top five stockholders hold more than 50 % of a firm's outstanding stocks. The paper states that managements in many companies are effectively just extensions of the dominant owners. They are closely held small and medium-sized firms where corporate boards are owner driven. Consequently, most of the companies have executive directors, CEO and chairman from the controlling family. A survey conducted by Sobhan and Werner (2003) found that an overwhelming majority (73 %) of the boards of non-bank listed companies were heavily dominated by sponsor shareholders 'who generally belong to a single family- the father as the chairman and the son as the managing director is the norm' (Sobhan and Werner 2003, p. 34). Imam and Malik (2007) analyse the ownership patterns of 219 companies from 12 different industries listed on the Dhaka Stock Exchange, the major stock exchange in the country. It is reported that, on average, 32.33 % of the shares are held by the top three shareholders, the results being even higher for real estate, fuel and power, engineering, textile and pharmaceutical sectors. In a recent paper, Muttakin et al. (2011) point out that unlike many developed economies, family firm is actually the most dominant form of publicly listed companies in Bangladesh.

4.2 *Weak Legal Infrastructure*

Bangladesh is a common law country. The present legal and judicial system has its foundation mainly to 200 years of British rule (Panday and Mollah 2011). However, while describing the legal structure of Bangladesh, Ferdous (2013) reports "that the legal system of Bangladesh is different to the absolute form of English law from the perspectives of socio-cultural values and religious guidelines. The companies are governed by the Companies Act 1994 which is based on the British Companies Act 1844. All domestic companies of Bangladesh are incorporated under this Act" This Company Act governs the relationship between shareholders and a company, audit system, transparency, disclosure procedure and the jurisdiction of the courts in relation to companies (BEI 2004). Panday and Mollah (2011) studied the judicial system of Bangladesh. Although they reported that the country has a well-organized court system in which is the replica of the system introduced by British rulers, finding that the executive branch of Government exerts an influence over the judiciary, the paper concluded with questioning the independence of the judiciary system of the country.

Unfortunately, the efficiency of the legal system has been questioned by some other studies on Bangladesh (e.g. Akhtaruddin 2005; Sobhani et al. 2009; Siddiqui 2010). In studying the role of the judiciary in ensuring legal accountability of government officials, Mollah (2010) found that justice in Bangladesh is not blind and not fair for all. Perhaps that is the more than 90 % of the respondents of the study of Ferdous (2013) strongly opined that the weak legal system is the major barrier of good governance in Bangladesh. Reflecting on the compatibility of the Anglo-American model of governance in the corporate infrastructure of Bangladesh, Ferdous (2013) further claimed that instead of ensuring good governance, the legal and regulatory bodies are working as an 'indirect catalyst' for bad corporate practices. The study also finds empirical evidences indicating the legal system is weak to ensure good governance in Bangladesh mainly due to four reasons: the increasing lack of legal professionals; inadequate legal provisions; the lack of implementation and monitoring; and finally the institutionalized corruption.

4.3 Lack of Skill, Competence and Independence of Professionals

It's not only in case of corporate governance, rather, as the studies (e.g. Alam 2009; Ferdous 2013) claim, any sort of development initiatives in Bangladesh is often resisted due to the lack of knowledge and competence amongst top executive, middle level managers and general workforce. For instance, taking the case of independent director, the study of Ferdous (2013) argue that the agency problem in Bangladesh could be resolved by appointing effective independent directors, and board efficiency could be improved by ensuring wider board diversity. However, as the study found, misconception and lack of knowledge and lack of awareness among board members create a fear of 'losing power/authority' which in turn resist them to appoint an effective and qualified independent or non-executive director. Although having at least one independent director on board is a listing requirement of the SEC of Bangladesh, the study of Ferdous (2013) found in many cases companies are appointing 'anyone' who is 'convenient' and who, instead of working at the best interest of the companies, will work for pursuing the interest board members.

Rashid et al. (2010) examined the influence of corporate board composition in the context of independent outside directors on firm economic performance in Bangladesh and found that the idea of the introduction of independent directors may have benefits for greater transparency, but the non-consideration of the underlying institutional and cultural differences in an emerging economy such as Bangladesh may not result in economic value added to the firm. Moreover studies of neighbouring countries (like Aggarwal 2010; Olatunji and Stephen 2011) also have similar findings and urged for a reformulation of the provisions according to the country context.

Lack of knowledge about corporate governance norms also resists splitting the roles of Chairman and CEO. Like many other developing economies, the corporate sector of Bangladesh is still dominated by family owned companies where the first generation is still running the business and many of these family businesses have become conglomerates, showing growth, and paying dividends (Ferdous 2013). At this point, if corporate governance mechanisms require the management to be separated from owners, non-compliance or mock compliance will be an obvious consequence (Ferdous 2013).

A number of studies have identified the shortage of skilled manpower as a potential problem for the development of capital markets in Bangladesh. Despite having a very large population, the number of auditors in Bangladesh is surprisingly low, even compared with its neighbours. World Bank (2003) suggests that the auditing profession does not attract the best quality students, and the job does not really differentiate between an MBA and a professional auditor. Karim and Moizer (1996) identified that audit fees in Bangladesh were significantly low. Sobhan and Werner (2003) conducted a survey on the state of corporate governance in Bangladesh. The study reported that that majority of respondents did not believe that audit reports reflected a true a fair view of the affairs of the company. There was also a perception that except very few reputed audit firms, the auditors generally did not understand or apply relevant auditing standards. Based on this, the study commented the dismal state of the auditing profession in Bangladesh-

> The auditing function would seem to represent a vicious circle; auditors are not perceived as independent, and do not provide quality audits, therefore, companies and shareholders are not willing to pay high fees for an audit. The low fee structure, in turn, does not provide an incentive to provide quality personnel and audits. (Sobhan and Werner 2003, p. 62)

Siddiqui (2010) also questions the independence, skill and competence of the auditors. The paper states that the level of accountancy education offered at the undergraduate and professional stages affect the skill and proficiency of auditors. Also, due to the absence of most of the Big four firms in Bangladesh, auditors are deprived of the training schemes offered by these reputed firms. The skill, competence and independence were also highlighted recently after the share market collapse of 2011, as the share market manipulation prove committee identified auditors as one of the major parties involved in the collusion that resulted in the market collapse.[3]

[3] The probe committee report mentioned that systematic failure had allowed massive manipulation of stock markets in Bangladesh in 2011, and identified the SEC, Dhaka Stock Exchange, the Investment Corporation of Bangladesh, issuers, valuers, and auditors as those who had colluded in 'turning the market volatile' (Yahoo News, April 7, 2011).

4.4 Poor Shareholder Activism

Theoretically, the basic rights of the shareholders are protected by law in Bangladesh. According to the Company Act 1994, shareholders can elect and remove directors and can demand a variety of information and have a right to participate in shareholders meetings either in person or by proxy (Sobhan and Werner 2003; World Bank 2009). Most importantly, companies need to ask for shareholders' approval before making any changes to the company's articles, dividends and in some major transactions.

Nevertheless, the reality does not reflect the same. Scholars and different reports (e.g. Sobhan and Werner 2003 ; Farooque et al. 2007; World Bank 2009) believe, minority shareholders' rights are largely ignored by the companies in Bangladesh. In practice, these studies indicate that shareholders do not have sufficient rights over related party transactions, the choice of board members or disclosure of control. Moreover, as reported by Ferdous (2013), the predominance of family ownership structure rarely allows the NEDs (if any) to safeguard the interests of minority shareholders.

In addition to these problems, World Bank (2009) reports some other deficiencies in shareholders' rights in Bangladesh, like inaccessibility of information, unclear process of electing directors, no rights on approving directors' remuneration, no restrictions on informing shareholders before any related party transactions happen etc.

In a nutshell, the minority shareholder base of Bangladesh is considered to be weak enough to create pressure on companies to practices good governance. The study of Ferdous (2013) indicates that there are three major reasons for behind this weakness, and these are: lack of education, lack of awareness about their rights and responsibilities, and short term vision. One of the interviewees of the study depicts the scenario very interestingly:

> Generally shareholders are ignorant about their rights and responsibilities, they rarely read annual reports before coming to the AGM, and they are least bothered about the company moves. If you go to our capital market, you will see there are people who may be completely illiterate, or can only write his name, they are coming and investing. Now this is not the entire picture, of course there are people who are educated, but I cannot guarantee that they are educated enough to understand their responsibilities as shareholders (Ferdous 2013, p. 260)

As a consequence, it is not surprising to find that the effectiveness of AGMs has remained as a question. Theoretically, AGM is considered as one of the core mechanisms of check and balance for shareholders (Letza et al. 2004). In the absence of pressure from powerful shareholders and legal monitoring, AGMs have become a mere formality (Ferdous 2013).

Two very interesting facts emerged from the study of Ferdous (2013). First, while reviewing the Companies Act 1994, the study found that the penalty provision for not appropriately organizing an AGM is old and ineffectual enough to consider it as a punishment. According to the provision,[4] a defaulting company may be fined up to 10,000 taka (equivalent to £80 GBP approx.). Hence Ferdous (2013) strongly criticized that this amount fails to outweigh the cost of organizing an AGM. The interviewees invariably responded that the shareholders are reluctant to attend the AGM because they do not find it worth in terms of their time and energy.

Second, this is even more interesting. As the study indicates, "there are some shareholders who are knowledgeable and expert enough to challenge the management, but even they do not participate due to the havoc created by rowdy groups who are hired by the companies to create chaos in the AGM and indirectly to support the decisions of the companies' boards. These hooligans are not the local terrors, not even those who are patronized by political parties, rather they are the people who purchase a minimum amount of shares of many different companies and are basically unemployed, and they are hired by the companies to create chaos during AGM". This is consistent with Sobhan and Werner (2003) who reported similar presence of hooligans, possible appointed by the management, to control the AGMs.

4.5 *Easy Access to Bank Credit*

The capital market in Bangladesh is still in primitive stage. The country has two stock exchanges: Dhaka Stock Exchange (DSE) and the Chittagong Stock Exchange (CSE). Although the Dhaka Stock Exchange was set up in the early 1950s, the capital market in Bangladesh has not flourished in comparison with its South Asian counterparts, and has already experienced two major collapses, one in 1996 and another very recently in 2011. Market capitalisation to GDP ratio for Bangladesh is only 7.5 %, which is significantly lower, compared to other South Asian countries. Sobhan and Werner (2003) reports that the capital market does not seem to offer adequate incentives for companies to go public-

> Bank financing is readily available as result of excess liquidity and extensive competition in the banking sector due to the fact that new private bank licenses had been issued mostly on a political basis; banks therefore are reluctant to enforce additional requirements or strict conditions in lending. This phenomenon is substantiated by our survey which revealed that equity requirement had been the prime motivator for only 10 % of the public companies interviewed – the remaining companies had cited reasons like tax advantages and legal compulsion, for going public.(Sobhan and Werner 2003)

[4] Companies Act 1994, Part (iv) 82. "Penalty for default in complying with Section 81 – If default is made in holding a meeting of the company in accordance with sub- section (1) of Section 81, or in complying with any directions of the Court under sub-section (2) thereof, the company and every officer of the company who is in default, shall be punishable with fine which may extend to ten thousand taka and in case of a continuing default, with a further fine which may extend to 250 taka for every day after the first day during which such default continues".

Siddiqui (2010) mentions that bank loans are easily available as result of excessive liquidity. Competition in the banking sector also has resulted in lenient conditions for credit. Sobhan (2003) reports that the banking sector and the capital market it heavily affected by the existence of a 'default culture' where a class of entrepreneurs find it more convenient to obtain credit from the bank, and then take the opportunity of weak bank regulations, ineffective law enforcement, and political patronage to resort to malpractices of not repaying the credit. Khan (2003) points out that the sponsors, promoters, and beneficiaries of this 'default culture' all belong to a particular class of the society with connections with the government, and subsequently protect each other.

Easy access to bank credit, together with the scope for adopting malpractices for not repaying bank loans through the exercise of political influence have contributed to the development of a culture where companies prefer debt financing more preferable to raising capital through the capital market. The ADB quarterly economic update on Bangladesh (ADB 2006) identifies poor quality of auditing and corporate governance, lack of quality shares and inadequate and irregular participation of the institutional shareholders as major reasons for the stagnant capital market.

4.6 Absence of 'Second Order' Institutions

Unlike many developed economies, second tier accountancy bodies (such as the ACCA) are absent in Bangladesh. This, along with the very small number of qualified chartered accountants, implies that a vast majority of accountants working in the corporate sector do not possess any accounting qualifications. In addition to this, the other second-order institutions, such as the regulatory bodies and the judiciary, suffer from lack of skills and proper training, especially in dealing with corporate cases (Sobhan and Werner 2003). Also, unlike developed economies, there is acute shortage of skilled and experienced financial analysts and advisors. The corporate environment is characterized by lack of availability of skilled professionals who could sit in the board as independent members. Bangladesh is a former British colony, and has inherited the common legal system. The Companies Act 1994 (revised after 81 years from Companies Act 1913, when Bangladesh was part of British India) defines the structure of the firms, including the composition of the board of directors, appointment of the CEO, appointment and remuneration of the auditors etc. However, the problem with the legal environment has always been its poor implementation (Sobhan and Werner 2003). Uddin and Hopper (2003), examining the success of privatisation of state-owned companies in Bangladesh, also identified the lack of legal enforcement as a major problem. A World Bank study on the state of financial accountability and governance in Bangladesh (World Bank 2003) identifies that the sharing of responsibility by a number of government agencies complicates enforceability of corporate regulations.

> Responsibility for enforcement is shared among the Registrar of Joint Stock Companies, the Securities and Exchange Commission, the professional accountancy bodies, and the judiciary. The involvement of several bodies in corporate accountability complicates enforcement and reduces overall effectiveness. (World Bank 2003, p. 83)

Siddiqui (2010) reports that market regulators, such as the securities and exchange commission of Bangladesh (SEC) and the Bangladesh Bank are also constrained with severe shortage of manpower, and are seldom blamed for their failure to stop share market manipulations. Association of SEC has been reported in successive share market enquiry reports, resulting in decline of investor confidence on market regulators.

5 Discussion

The chapter investigates the harmonisation efforts initiated by the World Bank IFAC in the context of the corporate governance in an LDC, namely Bangladesh. In particular, this chapter identifies the ownership structure and family dominance, weak legal system, lack of competence, lack of strong shareholders, easy access to bank credit, and the absence of second tier institutions supplementing the audit market as major obstacles for implementing the best practice recommendations. However, despite this, countries such as Bangladesh, under pressure from the donor agencies, have been keen to demonstrate compliance with the international standards of corporate governance and IFAC harmonisation efforts, ignoring the fact that the socio-economic characteristics prevailing in Bangladesh may not necessitate such wholesale adoption.

Overall analysis suggests that elements of both shareholder and stakeholder theory have relevance in the Bangladeshi perspective, but none of them could fully encapsulate the reality of the corporate governance issues prevailing in Bangladesh. For instance, the dominant shareholder model seems to appropriate in explaining the consequences of agency problems; however it has largely ignored the fact that emotion, culture and the lack of competent professional will not allow separation of management from owners, and not even the voluntary code will work in the absence of a strong legal system and a culture of compliance (Ferdous 2013). In addition, the shareholder model of governance also did not address the other major problems like political influences, lack of knowledge and a short-term perspective among people whose views are resisting corporate governance initiatives in Bangladesh. Even if the three-tier hierarchical governance structure (AGM, board and executive managers) of the shareholder perspective is considered, which is used as the solution to address poor governance, seems to have failed to protect shareholders' interests. Whilst, the effectiveness of an AGM in Bangladesh is considered to be hampered due to the weak shareholders, the unethical mindset of companies and strong legal system, the board and executive managers are been accused for incompetence. Thus, as explained in the study of Ferdous (2013, pp. 303–304) "in the absence of a robust legal system and resilient capital market, it would be too optimistic to think that a shareholder perspective of governance will be able to ensure good governance in the existing vulnerable status of Bangladesh".

On the other hand the stakeholder perspective also seems to be inappropriate considering the existing lack of strong, competent and ethical stakeholders to support the assumptions of the stakeholder model. In a country like Bangladesh where corruption is endemic, legislation is weak to guard the companies against stakeholders' abuse, it would be too optimistic to think that the companies will welcome such approach which recommends good governance to be established through stakeholders' participation in company decision making. Although studies (e.g. Belal 2004, 2001; Siddiqui 2010; Ferdous 2013) appreciated the social values of the stakeholder theory, the reality seems to be incompatible to support such appreciation. The recent studies (Sobhani et al. 2009; Ferdous 2013) thus fundamentally refused the idea of incorporating stakeholders' value maximization as companies' major objective and any kind of stakeholder integration in companies' decision making process.

This might have important implications for the IFAC initiative to globalise auditing practices. As mentioned before, the IFAC SMOs mainly concentrate on areas such as audit quality, audit education, skill and competence, code of ethics, self-regulation and other disciplinary procedures taken by national auditing bodies, adoption of international auditing standards, and public sector auditing. Each of these areas has the potential of being significantly affected, individually or collectively by the socio-political characteristics prevailing in Bangladesh as identified above. In a recent study, Khan et al. (2011) reported audit fees in Bangladesh to be significantly negatively correlated to ownership concentration in the corporate sector. Muttakin et al. (2011) concluded that family dominance in the corporate sector in Bangladesh has led to the development of a corporate culture where the role of auditing as a governance mechanism is not generally appreciated. The paper found that family dominated firms, comprising more than 60 % of the companies listed in the DSE, paid significantly lower amounts of audit fees and were less inclined to employ better quality auditors. Poor incentives for companies to be listed in the capital markets, together with easy access to bank credit, have resulted in the reluctance of companies to be enlisted in the capital market. As demand for audited financial statements for companies not listed with the stock exchanges tend to be low, audit fees in these companies have also suffered.

The World Bank, in a report on the observance of standards and codes in Bangladesh (ROSC), has identified poor levels of education and training as one of the major problems for the development of the auditing profession in Bangladesh (World Bank 2003). Sobhan and Werner (2003) report that investors in Bangladesh perceive auditors not to be sufficiently skilled. This negative image of the auditors in the minds of the investors would be reflected in the audit fees. Auditing literature has long identified audit fees premium as an indication of audit quality. It is argued that better quality auditors would charge significantly higher levels of audit fees as a premium for the quality of their services. This implies that audit quality has a cost. Therefore, it can be argued that due to the low levels of audit fees prevailing in Bangladesh, auditors cannot afford to provide quality audit services.

6 Conclusion

Hence, based on literature review, the overall analysis fundamentally rejects the static polarized conception of corporate governance. Rather it appears that considering the features the developing countries which are quite different than that of the developed nations, an appropriate model for developing markets would be the one that goes beyond the dichotomized view to take a static approach between shareholder and stakeholder model, and is tailored to the country specific needs, and also by recognizing the existing deficiencies.

The characteristics of the Bangladesh as identified in the chapter are not unique. Rather, in many other developing countries have demonstrated similar traits (e.g. Nigeria, Uganda, Pakistan and so on). However, due to the 'check-list' approach adopted by the donor agencies and international institutions, it may seem that the globalisation efforts are being largely successful, especially in developing countries, which, under pressure from the World Bank and the IMF, would attempt to demonstrate such compliance even though the ground realities of these countries may be completely different. Considering the overall facts emerged from the discussion, this study argues the effectiveness of compliance can be ensured when companies realizes the necessity of having, implementing and practicing good governance norms, i.e., starts recognizing the significance of codes of corporate governance. Hence, the regulators and policy makers need to pay attention to ensure that the code reflects the needs and addresses the local deficiencies. Once an appropriate code is developed strong emphasis needs to be placed on raising awareness of corporate governance, so that companies voluntarily step for ensuring compliance.

References

ADB. (2006). *Bangladesh quarterly economic update*. Dhaka: Asian Development Bank.

Adu-Amoah, A., Tsamenyi, M., & Onumah, J. M. (2008). The influence of social and political relations on corporate governance systems: The case of rural banks in Ghana. *Research in Accounting in Emerging Economies, 8*, 311–333.

Aggarwal, R. (2010). Independent directors: Time to introspect, suspect, respect – an Indian perspective. *Journal of Indian Business Research, 2*(2), 123–132.

Aguilera, R. V., & Cuervo-Cazurra, A. (2009). Codes of corporate governance. *Corporate Governance: An International Review, 17*(3), 376–387.

Aguilera, R. V., & Jackson, G. (2003). The cross-national diversity of corporate governance: Dimensions and determinants. *Academy of Management Review, 28*(3), 447–465.

Akhtaruddin, M. (2005). Corporate mandatory disclosure practices in Bangladesh. *International Journal of Accounting, 40*(4), 399–422.

Alam, G. M. (2009). The role of science and technology education at network age population for sustainable development of Bangladesh through human resource advancement. *Scientific Research and Essay, 4*(11), 1260–1270.

Alawattage, C., & Wickramasinghe, D. (2008). Appear ance of accounting in a political hegemony. *Critical Perspectives on Accounting, 19*, 293–339.

Arnold, P. J. (2005). Disciplining domestic regulation: The World Trade Organization and the market for professional services. *Accounting, Organizations and Society, 30*, 299–330.

Ashraf, J., & Ghani, W. I. (2005). Accounting development in Pakistan. *The International Journal of Accounting, 40*, 175–201.

Awotundun, D. A., Kehinde, J. S., & Somoye, R. O. C. (2011). Corporate governance and stakeholders interest: A case of Nigerian banks. *International Journal of Business and Management, 6*(10), 102–112.

BEI. (2004). *Code of corporate governance for Bangladesh*. Dhaka: Bangladesh Enterprise Institute.

Belal, A. R. (2001). A study of corporate social disclosures in Bangladesh. *Managerial Auditing Journal, 16*(5), 274–289.

Belal, A. R. (2004) The prospect for corporate social reporting (CSR) in Bangladesh. Ph.D. Sheffield University Management School.

Black, B. S., Carvalho, A. G. D., & Gorga, É. (2010). Corporate governance in Brazil. *Emerging Markets Review, 11*, 21–38.

Donaldson, T. E., & Preston, L. E. (1995). The stakeholder theory of corporation: Concepts, evidence, and implications. *Academy of Management Review, 20*(1), 68–91.

Enrione, A., Mazza, C., & Zerboni, F. (2006). Institutionalizing codes of governance. *American Behavioral Scientists, 49*(7), 961–973.

Farooque, O., Zijl, T., Dunstan, K., & Karim, A. K. M. W. (2007). Corporate governance in Bangladesh: Link between Board Ownership and Financial Performance. *Corporate Governance: An International Review, 6*, 1453–1468.

Ferdous, C.S. (2013). Compliance with codes of corporate governance in developing economies: The case of Bangladesh. Unpublished Ph.D. thesis, University of Birmingham.

Freeman, R. E., & Reed, D. L. (1983). Stockholders and stakeholders: A new perspective on corporate governance. *California Management Review, 25*(3), 88–106.

Friedman, M. (1962). *Capitalism and freedom*. Chicago: University of Chicago Press.

Gangolly, J., Hussein, M., Seow, G., & Tam, K. (2002). Harmonization of the auditor's report. *The International Journal of Accounting, 37*, 327–346.

Haniffa, R., & Hudaib, M. (2007). Locating audit expectations gap within a cultural context: The case of Saudi Arabia. *Journal of International Accounting, Auditing & Taxation, 16*, 179–206.

IFAC. (2004). *Statements of membership obligations 1–7*. New York: International Federation of Accountants.

IFAC. (2006). *Statements of membership obligations* (pp. 1–7). Washington DC: International Federation of Accountants.

IMF. (2005). *The standards and codes initiative: is it effective?* Washington: International Monetary Fund.

Imam, O., & Malik, M. (2007). Firm performance and CG through ownership structure: Evidence from Bangladesh stock market. *International Review of Business Research Papers, 3*(4), 88–110.

Jensen, M. C., & Meckling, W. (1976). Theory of the firm: Managerial behaviour, agency costs, and capital structure. *Journal of Financial Economics, 3*, 305–360.

Karim, A. K. M. W., & Moizer, P. (1996). Determinants of audit fees in Bangladesh. *The International Journal of Accounting, 31*(4), 497–509.

Khan, M. M. (2003). *State of governance in Bangladesh*. Routledge: The Round Table.

Khan, A., Hossain, D., & Siddiqui, J. (2011). Corporate ownership concentration and audit fees: The case of an emerging economy. *Advances in International Accounting, 27*(1), 125–131.

Krambia-Kapardis, M., & Psaros, J. (2006). The implementation of corporate governance principles in an emerging economy: A critique of the situation in Cyprus. *Corporate Governance: An International Review, 14*(2), 126–139.

Letza, S., Sun, X., & Kirkbride, J. (2004). Shareholding versus stakeholding: A critical review of CG. *CG An International Review, 12*(3), 242–262.

Loft, A., Humphrey, C., & Turley, S. (2006). In pursuit of global regulation: Changing governance and accountability structures at the International Federation of Accountants (IFAC). *Accounting, Auditing and Accountability Journal, 19*(3), 428–451.

Mallin, C. (2010). *Corporate governance* (3rd ed.). Oxford: Oxford University Press.

Mir, M. Z., & Rahaman, A. S. (2005). The adoption of international accounting standards in Bangladesh: An exploration of rationale and process. *Accounting, Auditing, Accountability Journal, 18*(6), 816–841.

Mollah, M. A. H. (2010). Does the judiciary matter for accountability of administration in Bangladesh? *International Journal of Law and Management, 52*(4), 309–331.

Muttakin, M. B., Khan, A. R., & Siddiqui, J. (2011). Audit fees and auditor choice in a family-firm dominated economy. Working paper, Australia: Deakin University

Ogbechie, C., Koufopoulos, D. N., & Argyropoulou, M. (2009). Board characteristics and involvement in strategic decision making: The Nigerian perspective. *Management Research News, 32*(2), 169–184.

Ogbuozobe, F. (2009). A consideration of the impact of the companies and Allied Matters Act (1990) and the Insurance Act (2003) on the board of insurance companies in Nigeria – part 2. *International Journal of Law and Management, 51*(6), 421–456.

Olatunji, O. R., & Stephen, O. (2011). The role of non-executive directors in the profitability of Banks: A study of universal banks in Nigeria. *International Journal of Business and Management, 6*(2), 248–257.

Panday, P. K., & Mollah, M. A. H. (2011). The judicial system of Bangladesh: An overview from historical viewpoint. *International Journal of Law and Management, 53*(1), 6–31.

Rashid, A., Zoysa, A. D., Lodh, S., et al. (2010). Board composition and firm performance: Evidence from bangladesh. *Australasian Accounting Business and Finance Journal, 4*(1), 76–95.

Reed, D. (2002). CG reforms in developing countries. *Journal of Business Ethics, 37*, 223–247.

Rwegasira, K. (2000). Corporate governance in emerging capital markets: Whither Africa? *Corporate Governance: An International Review, 8*(3), 258–267.

Sejjaaka, S. (2007). Corporate mandatory disclosure by financial institutions in Uganda. *Research in Accounting in Emerging Economies, 7*, 123–148.

Shleifer, A., & Vishny, R. W. (1997). A survey of corporate governance. *Journal of Finance, 52*, 737–783.

Siddiqui, J. (2010). Development of corporate governance regulations: The case of an emerging economy. *Journal of Business Ethics, 91*, 253–274.

Silveira, A. D. M. D., & Saito, R. (2009). Corporate governance in Brazil: Landmarks, codes of best practices, and main challenges. *The IUP Journal of Corporate Governance, VIII*(2), 20–39.

Sobhan, R. (2003). *Aid, governance, and policy ownership in Bangladesh*. Dhaka: Centre for Policy Dialogue.

Sobhan, F., & Werner, W. (2003). Diagnostic study of existing corporate governance scenario in Bangladesh. In F. Sobhan & W. Werner (Eds.), *A comparative analysis of corporate governance in South Asia*. Dhaka: Bangladesh Enterprise Institute.

Sobhani, F. A., Amran, A., & Zainuddin, Y. (2009). Revisiting the practices of corporate social and environmental disclosure in Bangladesh. *Corporate Social Responsibility and Environmental Management, 16*, 167–183.

Solomon, J. F. (2007). *Corporate governance and accountability* (2nd ed.). Chichester: Wiley.

Turnbull, S. (1997). Corporate governance: Its scope, concerns and theories. *Corporate Governance: An International Review, 5*(4), 180–205.

Uddin, S., & Hopper, T. (2003). Accounting for privatisation in Bangladesh: Testing World Bank claims. *Critical Perspectives on Accounting, 14*, 739–774.

Uddin, S., & Tsamenyi, M. (2005). Public sector reforms and the public interest. *Accounting, Auditing and Accountability Journal, 18*(5), 648–674.

Wanyama, S., Burton, B., & Helliar, C. (2009). Frameworks underpinning corporate governance: Evidence on Ugandan perceptions. *Corporate Governance: An International Review, 17*(2), 159–175.

West, A. (2006). Theorising corporate governance in South Africa. *Journal of Business Ethics, 68*, 233–248.

World Bank. (2003). *Bangladesh: Accounting and auditing. Report on the observance of standards and codes (ROSC)*. Washington DC: The World Bank.

World Bank. (2004). *Overview of the ROSC accounting and auditing programme*. Washington DC: The World Bank.

World Bank. (2009). Report on the Observance of Standards and Codes (ROSC): Corporate governance country assessment, Bangladesh. The World Bank. [online]. Available from. http://www.worldbank.org. Accessed 12 Mar 2010.

Limitations of Legal Transplants and Convergence to Corporate Governance Practices in Emerging Markets: The Brazilian Case

Angela Donaggio

Abstract Little is known about the outcomes of legal transplants carried out by emerging economies aiming to develop their securities markets. This chapter contributes to fill this gap by analyzing the effectiveness of investor protection rules of the Novo Mercado, a self-regulatory transplant created in 2000 in Brazil to distinguish companies committed to higher governance standards. Employing the institutional autopsy approach through an in-depth qualitative analysis of two controversial cases, I conclude that the legal transplantation generated mixed results. On the one hand, Brazil greatly developed its capital markets after the Novo Mercado's creation. On the other hand, the Novo Mercado did not work as expected regarding investor protection due to deficient enforcement and rule's interpretation. I argue that these problems may derive from conflicts of interests of the stock exchange, the formalistic interpretation of rules and a lack of adequate oversight structure. The Brazilian case demonstrates that cultural, political, economic, and institutional elements permeate entire markets and that the transplant did not alter the main agency problem between controlling and minority shareholders that still characterizes Brazilian companies, even those listed on the Novo Mercado. I believe that this result should be considered for any legal transplantation.

1 Introduction

The world seems to be undergoing a convergence in investor protection rules following EU harmonization aiming at positively influence the development of securities and capital markets. Such a convergence should especially aid

---

A. Donaggio (✉)
Sao Paulo Law School (DIREITO GV) and University of Sao Paulo (USP), Sao Paulo, Brazil
e-mail: angela.donaggio@fgv.br; angela.donaggio@usp.br

S. Boubaker and D.K. Nguyen (eds.), *Corporate Governance in Emerging Markets*, CSR, Sustainability, Ethics & Governance, DOI 10.1007/978-3-642-44955-0_19,

developing markets by adding certainty, predictability, and control for foreign investors.[1] The advocates of the convergence thesis argue that this phenomenon can take place through legal transplants, in which a single rule or even an entire legal system is borrowed from another country (Watson 1993), or by functional convergence, in which different rules or institutions generate the same result (Gilson 2001).

There is little consensus in the literature on legal transplants and much debate regarding their very existence (e.g., Santos 2006; Legrand 1997; Siems 2008), their definition and occurrence (e.g. Watson 1978; Kanda and Milhaupt 2003), and their potential outcomes and effectiveness (e.g., Bebchuk and Roe 1999; Coffee 2000; Gilson 2001; Berkowitz et al. 2003). Despites the debates about legal transplant theory, the adoption of one's state legislation, as well as self-regulations, by another is commonplace (Watson 1978). In this sense, the convergence of investor protection rules would take place through the spread of self-regulation, which could be more effective than the local rules, especially when a country's legislation is insufficient to protect investors (Coffee 2000). Coffee (2000, p. 55) describes the evolving relation between strong self-regulation and regulation after legal transplants as follows: "If strong self-regulation can first bring about the appearance of deeper, more liquid securities markets, such legislation will predictably follow."

The National Association of Securities Dealers Automated Quotations (NASDAQ), the world's first electronic stock market focused on technology companies, is a well-known example of self-regulation. European stock exchanges, aiming to stimulate capital market-driven listings of younger and smaller companies with high growth potential, have started to replicate the NASDAQ model by transplanting self-regulation rules to improve investor protection through high standards of transparency[2] (Rasch 1994; Bottazzi and Da Rin 2002). This chapter highlights Germany's Neuer Markt, a higher-quality market established through self-regulatory standards that were more stringent than required by German law (Coffee 2000).[3] The Neuer Markt inspired a self-regulatory legal transplant into the Brazilian stock market: In 2000, the BM&FBovespa, the Brazilian stock exchange, launched a listing segment called the Novo Mercado (New Market). This premium listing segment aimed to distinguish companies committed to higher governance standards. Besides being a case of self-regulation transplanted from a developed country to an emerging country, the Novo Mercado has an additional peculiarity that makes it unique to researchers and practitioners: It can be considered a

[1] Some authors affirm that this view is based on the assumption that, if a rule could be neutral and apolitical, then it could be transplantable. See Legrand (1997), Santos (2006) and Siems (2008).

[2] Examples of these special listing segments created since 1996 wishing to replicate the success of NASDAQ are EASDAQ (Brussels), Nouveau Marché (Paris), Ü AIM (London), Nieuwe Markt (Amsterdam), Neuer Markt (Frankfurt), Nuovo Mercato (Milan) and Mercado Nuevo (Madrid).

[3] Specifically about Neuer Markt, Coffee (1999, p. 50) says: "Particularly noteworthy has been the success of the German Neuer Markt, a new small company market, patterned after NASDAQ's small capitalization market, to attract listing by start-up companies."

second-order legal transplant, since the German Neuer Markt is already a legal transplant from the U.S. NASDAQ.

This chapter aims to investigate investor protection outcomes deriving from the legal transplant carried out for the BM&FBovespa's Novo Mercado. Specifically, I analyze the effectiveness of corporate governance practices adopted by companies listed on the Novo Mercado. In principle, the Novo Mercado Listing Rules (NMLR)[4] ensure the effective protection of investors in the companies listed in this segment. However, certain cases throughout the 2000s cast doubt on whether this goal was achieved. I provide an in-depth and qualitative analysis of two controversial cases to assess the effectiveness of the NMLR and the role of the institutions responsible for its enforcement. My methodology employs an institutional autopsy approach, developed by Milhaupt and Pistor (2008).

This Brazilian case study is important for several reasons. First, Brazil is one of the largest emerging countries and a member of the BRICs. Second, the Brazilian Novo Mercado has been considered a success abroad, as well as an inspiration to be copied by other markets. Third, although certain negative experiences in terms of investor protection have occurred with Novo Mercado companies, studies providing in-depth analyses of such cases are lacking. Fourth, this research makes a broad contribution to the literature, since there is a lack of qualitative studies about the effectiveness of legal transplants in emerging markets.

As the main result, I argue that the legal transplantation did not alter the main agency problem between controlling and minority shareholders that still characterizes Brazilian companies, even those listed on the Novo Mercado. Perhaps this is the result of any legal transplantation. Even though, Brazil greatly developed its capital markets after the Novo Mercado's creation and passed through significant legislative reforms to improve shareholder rights and disclosure to investors. On the other hand, the Novo Mercado did not work as expected regarding investor protection rights due to two main factors: the lack of enforcement of Novo Mercado listing rules and rule interpretation. The cases analysis showed that these factors are related, in turn, to conflicts of interests, the formalistic interpretation of rules and a lack of adequate oversight structure.

The chapter is organized as follows. Section 2 describes the global convergence of investor protection rules and the influence of the German Neuer Markt on the Brazilian Novo Mercado. Section 3 addresses the motivation behind BM&FBovespa's creation of the Novo Mercado. Section 4 presents the implementation and evolution of the Brazilian capital markets since the Novo Mercado's creation, analyzes two cases involving companies listed on this premium segment and assesses potential positive effects of Novo Mercado on Brazilian regulation. Section 5 concludes.

---

[4] All mentions to Novo Mercado Listing Rules ("NMLR") referred to the rules valid until 9th May of 2011, period that evolved the cases analyzed.

2 Global Convergence of Investor Protection Rules: The German Neuer Markt and Its Influence on the Brazilian Novo Mercado

The 1990s were a period of significant changes in the European capital markets, particularly due to deregulation, implementation of a single currency, demutualization, and stock exchange mergers (Rasch 1994; Bottazzi and Da Rin 2002). This time was also characterized by high-tech innovations. The German stock exchange could not include small and medium-sized innovative company issues at that time and German companies were then cross-listing in the NASDAQ (Burghof and Hunger 2004). In support of the emergence of these entrepreneurial companies, the Deutsche Börse, among other stock exchanges, created a self-regulated listing platform in 1997, the Neuer Markt, considered the most demanding in terms of disclosure and accountability (Bottazzi and Da Rin 2002).

The Neuer Markt was the most successful of the European new markets, with the largest number of listed companies (more than 330, with over €234 billion of capitalization). However, with the bursting of the dotcom bubble, the segment collapsed to just two companies in 2000, with €29 billion of market capitalization (Burghof and Hunger 2004). However, the bubble bursting was only one element of that crisis; there were also problems such as insider trading, audit firms manipulating reports, and biased prospectuses resulting from conflicts of interests with banks hired to carry out the IPOs of unprepared companies (Hess et al. 2001 *apud* Burghof and Hunger 2004). Some of these problems were due to failures of compliance and enforcement of Neuer Markt rules. Burghof and Hunger (2004) note that noncompliance with Neuer Markt rules was rarely punished. Given the lack of enforcement of its rules, the fraud and irregularities, and the dotcom bubble bursting, weakened investor credibility in the companies listed in this segment ultimately led to the termination of the Neuer Markt in 2003.

Nonetheless, as detailed in the following sections, the BM&FBovespa (then called Bovespa) created the Novo Mercado by emulating the Neuer Markt. The similarities between the two listing segments were so great that it can be argued that a legal transplant indeed occurred.[5] In addition to the great similarity in the listing requirements, there were similarities in the segments' implementation, involving public and private institutions willing to change the culture of the business community.[6] It is also interesting to note that the German and Brazilian stock markets had been diagnosed with similar problems: weak equity markets in relation to the

[5] See Donaggio (2012, p. 58) for a comparative table of the Neuer Markt and Novo Mercado requirements.

[6] One example is the intensification of OECD's support for Brazilian reforms to ensure funding sources linked the adoption of higher standards of corporate governance, mainly Novo Mercado listed companies.

gross domestic product, low liquidity, high concentrations of control, and little issuer interest in new public offerings.[7]

3 Motivation for the Creation of the Novo Mercado

The Brazilian stock market's prospects in the late 1990s appeared particularly grim. On the one hand, there was not a significant interest in new initial public offerings (IPOs) since the domestic market was small and illiquid and had a low savings rate.[8] On the other hand, large Brazilian companies were increasingly interested in cross-listing their shares in the U.S. market, attracted by stock exchanges that would provide them greater visibility and lower cost of capital. As a result, part of the already scarce liquidity in the Brazilian market moved to international stock exchanges, especially the New York Stock Exchange. The trading volume at the Brazilian stock exchange fell from US$191 billion in 1997 to US$65 billion in 2001. This drop was followed by a reduction in the number of listed companies, from 550 in 1996 to 440 in 2001.

In addition to the macroeconomic problems and several crises involving emerging economies (including Brazil) in the late 90s, most of the factors that undermined the attractiveness of Brazilian stock market were associated with a lack of fairness and inequality in the treatment of minority shareholders. These problems were partly due to the 1976 Corporate Law, which allowed the issuance of up to two-thirds of its share capital in preferred (non-voting) shares, which allowed full control of a company with a reduced percentage of its shares (Nenova 2006). Additionally, opaque disclosure enabled indiscriminate related party transactions (OECD 2003) and the prosecution of controlling shareholders was probably a slow and onerous process for minority shareholders in addition to the lack of expertise by Brazilian courts at that time.

In April 2000 Brazil held the First Latin American Corporate Governance Roundtable in Sao Paulo organized by the OECD. The event was co-organized by BM&FBovespa getting support from the CVM, the Brazilian Institute of Corporate Governance (IBGC) [9] and the International Finance Corporation (IFC). It

[7] According to Milhaupt and Pistor (2008, p. 31) "conscious of the signaling power of law and legal reform, political actors and members of the legal community may use foreign as opposed to home-grown Law to signal some desired quality of their governance". All those similarities can be understood as desired by BM&FBovespa due to the "signaling function" of legal transplant.

[8] The listing of just eight new companies from 1995 to 2000 illustrates the unattractiveness of Brazilian equity market at that time.

[9] The Brazilian Institute of Corporate Governance (IBGC) was founded in 1995 as a non-profit entity and since its inception, IBGC has been the central forum for the introduction and dissemination of the corporate governance concept in Brazil and it stands today as the main reference in Brazil that focuses on the development of best practices in corporate governance. IBGC is well known for preparing the "Code of Best Practices in Corporate Governance", originally released in 1999, now in its fourth edition of 2009.

produced a "Synthesis Note" and a "White Paper on Corporate Governance in Latin America" aimed at promoting the development of the region's countries capital markets. Based on the typical characteristics of these countries' corporate governance practices, the following reform priorities were defined: (i) the fair treatment of shareholders (in cases of control change or delisting), (ii) the encouragement of investor activism, (iii) the improved quality and integrity of financial reporting, (iv) the improved disclosure of related party transactions and conflicts of interests, (v) the development of effective boards and independent directors, (vi) improvement of the quality of the legal structure (through better enforcement), and (vii) the increased effectiveness of regulators and better corporate dispute resolution.

Based on the OECD's analysis and recommendations, the BM&FBovespa decided to increase the protection of minority investors through contractual mechanisms. As a result, it created two related mechanisms: the BM&FBovespa special listing segments in 2000 (Novo Mercado, Level 2 and Level 1)[10] and the Market Arbitration Panel in 2001 to ensure the effectiveness of self-regulation. The migration to the Novo Mercado listing segment required the exclusive issuance of ordinary (voting) shares, ensuring the adoption of the one share – one vote principle.

4 Implementation and Evolution of the Novo Mercado

Although the Novo Mercado was created in late 2000, it was only after 2004 that the number of companies listed on it significantly increased. The evolution of the number of companies listed and the volume traded suggests that the Novo Mercado project contributed to the takeoff of the Brazilian stock market, as Fig. 1 shows.

The Novo Mercado seems to have helped the BM&FBovespa achieve many of its objectives, such as improving the corporate governance practices of listed companies, raising the market's attractiveness for domestic and international investors, increasing its institutional relevance and regional leadership, broadening the base of domestic investors, and increasing the market's competitiveness and efficiency.

Most companies that went public between 2000 and 2010 opted to list on the Novo Mercado directly. In addition, during that time no IPOs occurred in standard level. As expected, foreign investors boosted the Novo Mercado, accounting for around 70 % of the IPO volume. This high acceptance indicates that the BM&FBovespa was able to establish trust among investors and issuers through the Novo Mercado.

[10] According to Santana et al. (2008), BM&FBovespa wanted to create only one special listing level (Novo Mercado), however, some "blue chips" companies resisted to migrate to Novo Mercado but, at the same time, wanted to be seen as more friendly to investors. In order to accommodate the interests of large companies already listed BM&FBovespa created two intermediate levels (Levels 2 and 1).

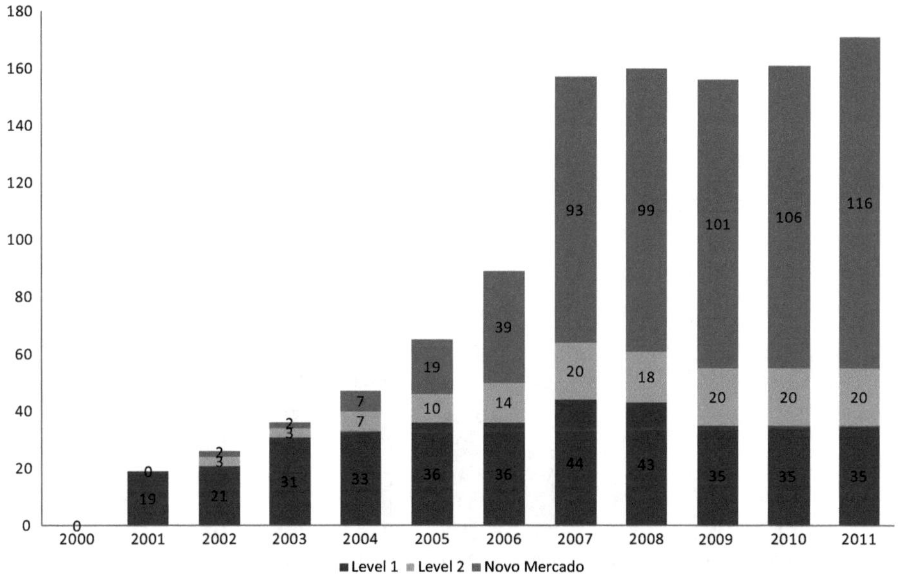

Fig. 1 Number of companies in the BM&FBovespa in special listing segments (Level 1, Level 2, and the Novo Mercado) from 2000 to 2011 (Source: BM&FBovespa)

An IPO wave occurred in Brazil from 2004 to 2007, with 113 IPOs during this period, about 20 times more than in the eight previous years. As a result, in early 2008 the Novo Mercado reached 100 listed companies. The growing interest of foreign investors, as well as the participation of domestic investors, substantially increased the volume traded and the liquidity of the shares, as Fig. 2 shows.

This growth brought complexity and a sense of euphoria to the market that led to the emergence of new problems, such as equity kicking, the issuance of Brazilian Depositary Receipts (BDRs) by Brazilian companies disguised as foreign companies, control acquisitions without mandatory tender offers or appraisal rights, and the implementation of new control-enhancing mechanisms like poison pills and pyramidal structures of control. Interestingly, some of these problems were also observed at the German Neuer Markt.

The emergence of controversial cases involving companies listed on the Novo Mercado have been criticized as violating the rights of minority investors. Considering the wide-ranging, negative publicity of certain cases, the BM&FBovespa would be expected to act in a way to verify if there was any violation of the NMLR.[11] As a result, the next two subsections analyze two cases of Novo Mercado-listed companies that potentially violated investor rights to verify if any

[11] According to item 12.1 of NMLR it is up to BM&FBovespa to send a written notice to the company, the senior managers and the controlling shareholder to preserve the compliance to NMLR whenever they are in breach of any obligations deriving from the NMLR.

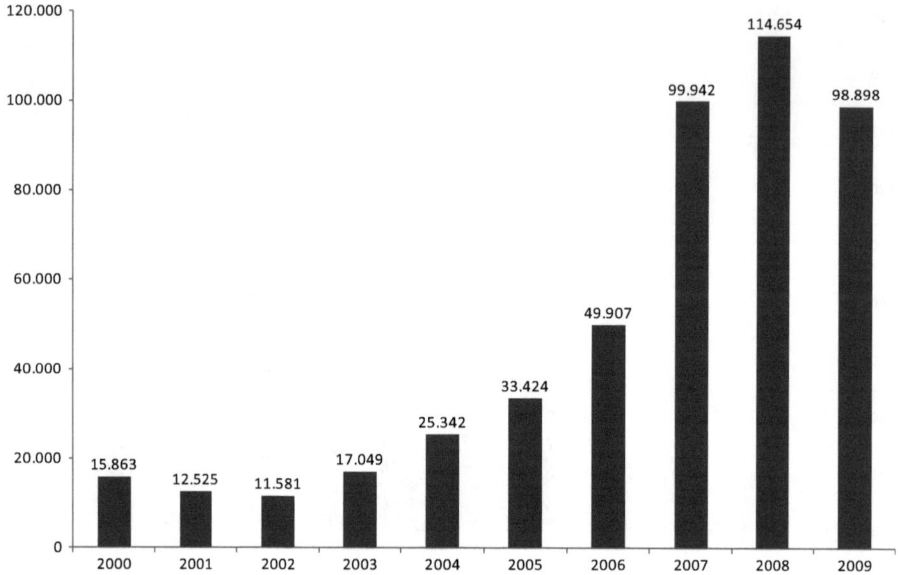

Fig. 2 Average monthly volume (millions of Brazilian reals) traded on the BM&FBovespa from 2000 to 2009 (Source: CVM Informative (through September 2009))

violation of the NMLR really occurred, as well as to compare the problems of the Novo Mercado today with those of the Neuer Markt before its collapse. Using Milhaupt and Pistor's (2008) approach, I analyze the two cases and their institutional responses, specifically regarding self-regulatory (BM&FBovespa) and regulatory (CVM) activities.

4.1 The Cosan Case

Cosan is one of the largest producers of sugar and ethanol worldwide. Founded in 1936, its revenues were R$6.3 million (around US$3.1 billion), with earnings before interest, taxes, depreciation, and amortization of R$718 million in 2009. In 2005, Cosan conducted its IPO directly on the Novo Mercado. Then, in 2007, the company announced a controversial reorganization plan: Its controlling shareholders, two firms controlled by Rubens Ometto Silveira Mello, decided to implement a complex change of Cosan's shareholding structure.

The restructuring plan consisted of a corporate reorganization comprising three stages. The first would involve a global offering of Cosan Ltd. at the New York Stock Exchange (NYSE) issuing American Depositary Receipts Level III. The second would be a corporate restructuring, with Cosan Ltd. becoming Cosan's new controlling shareholder. The last step would be the migration of shareholders from Cosan to Cosan Ltd., incorporated in Bermuda and listed on the NYSE. The second stage of the process was considered the most controversial for Cosan's minority shareholders because it required the conversion of Cosan's voting shares into two different classes of Cosan Ltd.: class A shares, each of which would be entitled to one vote, and class B shares, entitled to 10 votes each. This conversion was controversial because Brazilian Corporate Law (Article 110, Law 6.404/1976) forbids multiple voting shares. Additionally, class B shares would be exclusively held by Mr. Ometto and would automatically be converted into class A shares when sold. As a result, Ometto would control both Cosan Ltd. and Cosan with less than 10 % of the cash flow rights via a pyramidal structure (besides remaining as CEO and Chairman of the Board of both of them).

Unsurprisingly, investors did not welcome the proposed restructuring plan.[12] Ometto initially presented three options to minority shareholders: (i) to not exchange their shares, thus risking Cosan's delisting from the Novo Mercado (if Cosan's free float dropped below 25 %), (ii) to exchange Cosan shares for class A Cosan Ltd. shares traded on the NYSE, or (iii) to exchange Cosan shares for BDRs of Cosan Ltd. class A shares traded on the BM&FBovespa. Options (ii) and (iii) would submit the company and its investors to Bermuda's laws.

Due to the negative impact of the first proposal, a month later Ometto proposed another share class called B2. This new class of shares would also provide 10 votes per share but would not be traded on any stock exchange due to a 3 years lock-up period. After that, if negotiated for any purpose, it would be automatically converted into class A shares. In any case, Ometto would ultimately indirectly hold 51.6 % of the total capital and 91.1 % of the voting rights of Cosan Ltd. This plan seemed to not only harm minority shareholders' rights protected by the NMLR, such as the one share, one vote principle, but also violate the Brazilian legislation.

The first regulatory problem in this case deals with the request by Cosan Ltd. to CVM to be registered as a foreign company. Despite the fact that such a registration could set a precedent in unfair trade practices – since it involved a company subject to less stringent corporate rules than those for other companies (forbidden by Art. 4°, VII, Law 6.385/1976) – the Brazilian regulator granted the request. A second, related problem was the absence of an agreement between the CVM and the regulatory authority of Bermuda for monitoring and sharing information (or even a multilateral agreement).[13] The absence of monitoring is a relevant issue, since it could impede mechanisms presented in Art. 4°, Law 6.385/1976, which requires the CVM to protect investors and maintain the market's health.

Those two macro issues could have avoided violating Brazilian law if the CVM had not permitted an exception to a clear legal determination. There were two other

[12] According to Silveira and Dias (2010) there was a loss of R$840 million of Cosan's market value just 15 days around the announcement of the material fact and was not recovered until the last trading day of 2007.

[13] Even if the agreement had been signed, Cosan Ltd. would still be subject to corporate law more lenient than Brazilian Law.

regulatory problems. Cosan Ltd. requested an exemption from a legal device (Art. 33, CVM Instruction 361/2002) that prevents the offering of securities which are not admitted to negotiation in the Brazilian stock markets. Since Cosan Ltd. class A and B2 shares were not listed on a Brazilian organized market (and Cosan Ltd. was formally considered a foreign company), the company requested the CVM to let it adopt different procedures to register a voluntary tender offer (even when no onerous transfer of control would occur). Although the possibility exists for exceptional situations when listing shares (CVM Instruction 361/2002, Art. 34), it is clear that special circumstances are required, as well as the equitable treatment and adequate flow of information to shareholders. In response to the request, the CVM's technical department understood[14] that the exemption would be possible only for the exchange of class B2 shares and would not be legal or fair[15] for class A shares. Opposing its technical department, however, the CVM's board decided on January 8, 2008, to grant full exemption to Cosan Ltd. class A and B2 shares.

Finally, CVM exempted Cosan Ltd. from delivering an economic and financial feasibility study, a requirement for any company willing to launch its IPO when younger than 2 years (Art. 32, II, CVM Instruction 400/2003). The numerous subsequent investor complaints about compliance with corporate law reinforces this argument, with at least 23 formal complaints lodged directly with the CVM. Nonetheless, the CVM did not formally prevent the operation.[16] Thus, the CVM ultimately allowed a company governed by tax haven laws to exchange securities, which are forbidden in the Brazilian market, even without an agreement on cooperation and the exchange of information with the regulatory authority of the other country.

In addition to problems with the Brazilian regulation, there were problems with the enforcement of the Novo Mercado's self-regulation by the BM&FBovespa. The first was noncompliance with the NMLR, which requires BM&FBovespa to notify Cosan's controlling shareholders about potential noncompliance when it was clear that the outcome of the restructuring would be the delisting of Cosan from the Novo Mercado. The BM&FBovespa should have acted according to items 12.1 and 12.6.1 of the NMLR, by warning managers and controlling shareholders to ensure compliance with the NMLR. These rules also require that the BM&FBovespa disclose these warnings at its website, which it did not; nor did it provide notification of any exemption (possible under item 3.1.2 of the NMLR) to Cosan or its controlling shareholder.

---

[14] See Memorandum of SRE/GER-1 CVM 399/2007.

[15] Besides the two classes of shares, Cosan Ltd. provided a great disproportion between voting and economic rights, pyramidal structure and shark repellent with 15 % trigger.

[16] The unique attitude of the CVM regarding investor protection was an official letter to the controlling shareholder (Aug. 2007) regarding potential conflicts of interest between Cosan and Cosan Ltd. After that, Cosan Ltd. published a press release (Nov. 2007) about a commitment to offer commercial opportunities between Cosan Ltd., Cosan and Ometto.

According to reports from the specialized media, the second proposal (class B2 shares) was the outcome of a meeting between BM&FBovespa representatives and Ometto.[17] However, none of these supposed meetings (or notifications) were formally announced at the BM&FBovespa's website, as required by the NMLR. This suggests the noncompliance of the BM&FBovespa itself with its own NMLR.

The second problem regarding self-regulation was the lack of enforcement of the NMLR with respect to the proposed restructuring, which would ultimately have led to Cosan's delisting from the Novo Mercado. Since the listing level was created based on principles of investor protection, two related items dealing with mandatory tender offers (items 11.2 and 11.4 of the NMLR) could be applicable to the situation in order to avoid losses to minority shareholders, which did not happen. In addition, the BM&FBovespa could have used item 14.4, which allows its CEO to resolve cases not dealt with by the NMLR in the case of unforeseen events.

4.2 *The Tenda Case*

Tenda was a real estate company founded in 1994 by José Olavo Pinto (JO) and his son, Henrique Pinto (HP) that operated in affordable housing construction. The company went public in 2007, listing on the Novo Mercado. The controlling shareholder was HPJO Participações (HPJO), controlled by JO and his son. At its IPO, Tenda launched 47.7 % of its shares, reaching a price of R$9.00 per share. However, after the first quarterly report, shares devalued by 15 %. The company then presented reversed scenarios in 2008, dropping from a high of R$12.80/share (instead of an expected R$27.50/share) to R$3.75, its lowest value, by the end of August.[18]

On September 1st, 2008, JO and HP announced that they would incorporate a closed company, named Fit, a subsidiary of Gafisa (a real estate company also listed on the Novo Mercado). The transaction in fact resulted in Tenda's transfer of control from HPJO to Gafisa without a control premium. This unusual operation was curiously called an "original acquisition", since there was no previous controlling shareholder. As a result, Tenda shares were diluted by almost 60 %, with no

[17] According to news "Because he challenged the Stock Exchange" ("Por que ele desafiou a Bolsa") of Época Negócios Magazine (21 Nov. 2007), BM&FBovespa was among those most angered by Ometto because it had an additional concern–its own IPO–and did not like Cosan casting doubt on the credibility of the Novo Mercado.

[18] During 2008 first quarter, Brokers from Itau and Brascan Banks recommended shares with high expectation to reach R$27.50 by the end of 2008. On the contrary, shares reached their highest value (R$ 12.80, May 2008). From that period, shares dropped due to a set of facts: (i) the offering of 430,000 shares (R$ 4,643,000.00) holded by the controlling shareholders in a 7 day period and (ii) a leak of a criticizing e-mail of a Credit Suisse employee relating to quality of Tenda shares. Just 1 day after this email, Credit Suisse issued a report downgrading its recommendation (from buy to neutral) and reducing its price target (from R$21 to R$7). It is important to note that Credit Suisse have been one of the coordinators of the Tenda's IPO (with Itaú BBA S.A.).

appraisal rights for Tenda's minority shareholders. The announcement of the transaction led to an abnormal value destruction of around R$ 800 million for Tenda (Silveira and Dias 2010) and shares reached their lowest price (R$1.02) in late November 2008. A year later, Tenda and Gafisa announced the last stage of the complex incorporation of Tenda shares by Gafisa. In December of 2009, Tenda became 100 % part of Gafisa and was finally delisted from the Novo Mercado. These operations seem to have violated not only the rights of minority shareholders stated in the Novo Mercado's rules, but also the Brazilian legislation.

One can point out at least five major regulatory problems in the Tenda case. The first was the violation of the duties of diligence and loyalty by its controlling shareholder (Art. 153 and 155, Law 6.385/1976), since the negotiation benefited only Gafisa and not Tenda. These violations constituted an abuse of power since the controlling shareholders guided Tenda to favor another company to the detriment of its shareholders (Art. 117, Law 6.385/1976).

The second was that, despite the strong suspicion of the breach of the duties of diligence and loyalty and the nine formal claims filled by Brazilian and foreign minority shareholders, CVM did not investigate the operation or request any explanation from the controlling shareholders.

The third regulatory problem was the ratio of the stock prices used in the first transaction, the subject of another complaint made by foreign funds to the CVM. CVM Instruction 319/1999 forbids a company to set exchange ratios by using stock market prices unless its shares are part of broad stock market indices, such as Ibovespa. Although Tenda's shares never integrated any stock market indices, the company used its stock market prices as the exchange ratio, another abuse of power according to CVM Instruction 319/1999.

The fourth problem was a case of insider trading confessed by JO. The CVM investigated the case but instead of meting out any punishment, it accepted a commitment term with a fee paid by JO to settle the case.

Fifth, there was not a disclosure of a material fact by Tenda's director of investor relations after the unusual fluctuation of Tenda's shares. The CVM investigated the case in Administrative Process 3278/2010 and concluded that the material fact should have been mandatory. The Tenda's director of investor relations, JO, and HP then proposed another commitment term with a fee payment, also accepted by the CVM.

In addition to problems with the enforcement of Brazilian legislation, five other problems with the BM&FBovespa's enforcement of the Novo Mercado's self-regulation can be raised. The first self-regulatory problem was the non-application of items 8.4 and 8.6 of the NMLR by BM&FBovespa in potential disagreements relating to the transfer of control, which suggested the use of the Market Arbitration Panel to decide about controversial mandatory tender offers as well as issuing supplementary rules. On the contrary, the Stock Exchange ignored those items of NMLR, despite an unusual operation clearly planned to elude a tender offer rule designed to protect investors. That operation was constructed to avoid a tender offer,[19] turning shareholders into "prisoners," since the liquidity was extremely low after the operations' announcement.

The second problem was the violation of items 3.1, 3.1.1, and 3.1.2 of the NMLR, which determine that a company must maintain a minimum free float of 25 % while its securities are listed on the segment. Though there were exceptions to this free float percentage, they did not apply in Tenda's case. Therefore, there was a breach of the NMLR because Tenda had less than the minimum 25 % free float throughout 6 months and did not even ask the BM&FBovespa for an exception. If this exception had been requested and granted, the BM&FBovespa should have disclosed it on its website, according to item 3.1.2 of the NMLR.

The third problem was the violation of the lock-up period mandatory for controlling shareholders due to item 3.4 of the NMLR. The lock-up is 75 % in the first 6 months after a company's IPO, so JO and HP were obliged to hold a minimum of 15.15 % of Tenda's shares. Despite this, reports show that the percentage they held (12 %) was below this value, suggesting that they sold more shares than allowed in the period.

The fourth problem was that, after the operation involving Tenda and Fit, HP (its former CEO and controlling shareholder) was considered an independent director of Tenda, disregarding the concept of independent director established by item 2.1 of the NMLR.

The last issue was BM&FBovespa's lack of notification of Tenda's controlling shareholders about the breaches to the NMLR during the period analyzed. As mandated by item 12.1 of the NMLR, the stock exchange should have sent a written notice to Tenda to enforce the NMLR, but it did not. By not having used item 14.1 of the NMLR to decide on unforeseen events, the BM&FBovespa lost an opportunity to show its willingness to reduce problems caused by the operation.

4.3 Cases Results

The two cases analyzed demonstrate violations of investor protection rights established in the NMLR and Brazilian Corporate Law. Regarding the NMLR, both cases show at least five reasons why investor protection was not effective. The first concerns the relation between regulation and self-regulation in the Brazilian legal system, something crucial for effective investor protection. The second concerns the usual limitation of any rule: The NMLR's inherent incompleteness is a characteristic of objective rules, since it is impossible for a rule to embrace all situations yet to arise. The third is the BM&FBovespa's omission, once it could have interpreted the NMLR according to its founding principles when there were doubts about the fairness of the operations. The fourth reason highlight the need for

[19] The withdrawal or appraisal rights are established by Brazilian Corporate Law (Art. 109, V) and are considered an essential rights of shareholder that cannot be deprived by bylaws or general meetings.

additional specific procedures to apply the rules in accordance with the principles that guided the creation of the listing level segment. Finally, the fifth reason for the failure to ensure investor protection was the BM&FBovespa's lack of enforcement of the NMLR and the lack of punishment for its clear violations.

The BM&FBovespa's failure to perform its monitoring duty may have been due to conflicts of interest. While the stock exchange must ensure compliance with the NMLR, its listed companies contribute substantially to its revenue and any sanctions against them could negatively affect its financial outcome. Specifically, the BM&FBovespa could have acted as foreseen in items 12.1 and 12.6.1 of the NMLR. These rules do not need extensive interpretation or application; that is, they simply require that the BM&FBovespa notify companies and their controlling shareholders to guarantee compliance with the NMLR, as well as disclose the names of these companies on its website.

As the Cosan case shows, according to the specialized press, the stock exchange itself may have violated its own rules by not informing investors about a possible violation of the NMLR. As a consequence, if the BM&FBovespa (informally) tried to convince Ometto about changing his restructuring plan, it violated its own NMLR. In the Tenda case, however, the BM&FBovespa did not act at all, formally or informally (even after receiving two letters from foreign investment funds complaining about the operations), in violation of the mandatory free float, lock-up period, and concept of independent directors.

Thus, the lack of investor protection evidenced in both cases corroborates the argument that effective protection depend not only on a set of rules but, instead, on strict compliance through enforcement. In addition, since one could consider the NMLR a public self-regulation,[20] then there can be an intrinsic problem based on the reasons cited by Coffee (2001) of a self-regulator's weak incentives to enforce rules.

Regarding the role of the Brazilian regulator on Brazilian legislation, the evidence of both the Cosan and Tenda cases shows that the CVM's behavior was at least questionable. Among other duties, CVM should (i) promote the expansion and smooth and efficient functioning of the stock markets and encourage continued investments in the capital of publicly held enterprises; (ii) protect securities holders and market investors against irregular issues of securities and illegal acts of public corporations; and, (iii) ensure compliance with fair trade practices in the securities market.[21] However, in the Cosan case, the CVM allowed a company governed by tax haven laws whose shareholders and operations were all located in Brazil to

[20] It seems that Novo Mercado is a public self-regulation because is characterized by coercive submission of the participant and is subject to state sanction since there is an authorization of special listing segments granted by the CVM to the BM&FBovespa and every change in the segment rules must be submitted to the CVM's authorization (Art. 21, Law 6.385/1976 and CVM Instruction 312/1999). According to Van Waarden (1984) *apud* Moreira (1997), to identify the degree of autonomy of the self-regulation entity it is needed to verify (i) the degree of freedom of the self-regulatory body for modifications of its organization and operation and (ii) the need of the governmental authorization or ratification of decisions.

[21] According to Art. 4 of Law 6.385/1976.

exchange securities forbidden in the Brazilian market. Despite the CVM's technical department having decided that class A shares of Cosan Ltd. would not be permitted on Brazilian stock markets, the CVM's board opposed this decision and decided to make an exception for Cosan Ltd. The CVM then allowed the company to trade securities strictly forbidden by Brazilian legislation in the Brazilian market. The CVM also authorized the trading of depositary receipts of Cosan Ltd., which resulted in its lack of authority over the company since it was foreign based and without a prior agreement of cooperation or information exchange with its foreign regulator. The Brazilian regulator could have refused to accept the registration of a pseudo-foreign company established abroad only to avoid Brazilian laws.

In the Tenda case, the CVM favored the merger over a tender offer for economic reasons. However, this merger overrode the essential rights of minority shareholders, such as appraisal rights or a mandatory tender offer. The case also evidences breaches of CVM Instruction 319/1999, as in the exchange ratio of shares (Art. 11) and the CVM's own violation constitutes an abuse of control (Art. 15). In this sense, the letters of foreign investment funds to the CVM bore no results. The CVM also omitted about the second operation (taking place 1 year after the first) possibly being an illegal indirect transaction. The CVM only acted when the controlling shareholder confessed committing insider trading and when the atypical fluctuation of shares was obvious. These cases were concluded without a clear judgment due to a consent decree (which controlling shareholders simply paid a fine to settle).

The high number of formal complaints to the CVM in the two cases[22] and the wide dissemination of negative news by the specialized media[23] reinforce the view that both operations harmed investors. These cases show that investor protection depends on the regulator properly fulfilling its role (Kraakman et al. 2004) and suggest that the mere creation of a special listing segment is not sufficient to provide an institutional infrastructure or to ensure the enforcement of and compliance to its rules. In conclusion, analysis of these cases show that the typical Brazilian agency problem between controlling and minority shareholders may persist even for companies listed on the Novo Mercado.

4.4 Potential Positive Effects on Brazilian Regulation

Despite the CVM's lack of timely responses in both cases analyzed, it is important to note that the Brazilian legal framework developed substantially throughout the

[22] Cosan had at least 19 formal administrative proceedings related to operation with Cosan Ltd., whereas Tenda had at least nine formal administrative proceedings related to operation with Fit and Gafisa.

[23] An analysis of the news in the specialized media results in more than 30 negative news about Cosan (from Jun.25th to Dec.25th, 2007) and over 15 bad news associated with Tenda (from Sep.1st, 2008 to Dec.31, 2009).

2000s due to the enactment of new laws, as well as improvement of the CVM's activities regarding investor protection.

Regarding legal reforms, Brazil has faced major changes since 2000, with the enactment of Laws 10.303 of 2001, 10.411 of 2002, and 11.638 of 2007.[24] The CVM, in turn, has clearly increased its normative activity. For instance, it published 163 instructions between 2000 and 2010 regarding investor protection. In particular, CVM Instruction 480/2009 seems to have been an indirect response to the Cosan case, establishing new criteria for the registration of foreign companies.

One also observes a substantial increase in the number of consent decrees (with fines). While from 1997 to 2005 the average number of consent decrees was around 5 per year, this figure grew to around 60 per year from 2005 to 2009.

The CVM's activities have grown consistently with the increasing number of companies listed and trading volume. This evidence clearly indicates that, even if the Novo Mercado did not guarantee effective investor protection in the cases analyzed, the increased number of companies and complexity of the Brazilian market has improved the CVM's performance. In conclusion, it is clear that the Novo Mercado's transplant led to legislative and regulatory changes. The improvement of investor protection through more restrictive rules, along with other elements of the country's macroeconomic environment, resulted in a paradigm shift for Brazil's capital markets.

5 Conclusions

In this chapter I analyze the creation of the Novo Mercado, a self-regulated listing segment of the BM&FBovespa that was transplanted from the German Neuer Markt. I consider the context of the Novo Mercado's emergence, the details of its implementation, and its evolution during its first 10 years of operation. I also focus on two controversial cases involving companies listed on the Novo Mercado to analyze a regulator's responses, those of the CVM, and a self-regulator's responses, those of the BM&FBovespa.

The overall analysis indicates that the Brazilian legal transplant generated mixed results in terms of investor protection. On the one hand, the Brazilian capital markets developed significantly throughout the 2000s in terms of the number of newly listed companies, volume traded, investors and market intermediates. It is also clear that relevant legislative reforms have taken place since 2000 as well as CVM's regulatory activity, both aiming at improving shareholder rights and disclosure for investors. Even if the Novo Mercado did not ensure effective investor protection in the cases analyzed, one can affirm that development of a legal

[24] Law 10.303/2001 made many reforms towards greater protection of minority shareholders, Law 10.411/2002 granted greater autonomy to the CVM and established fixed terms to its directors and Law 11.638/2007 determined the mandatory elaboration of financial statements to large companies.

framework fostering better investor protection occurred in parallel with the development of the legal transplant.

On the other hand, the Novo Mercado did not work as expected at least on the controversial cases involving Cosan and Tenda analyzed in this chapter. They provide clear evidence of the violation of investor protection rights, the primary reason for the Novo Mercado's legal transplant. Two main factors appear to have led to investor losses in the two cases: the lack of enforcement by both the self-regulator (BM&FBovespa) and the regulator (CVM) and the interpretation of the rules. Several potential causes are associated with these factors.

The first one is conflict of interest. The BM&FBovespa must ensure that listed companies (including itself) comply with the NMLR but these same companies also contribute substantially to its own revenue. Any company sanction or even notification could negatively affect the BM&FBovespa's financial outcome.[25] This is not surprising, regarding the problems of self-regulation enforcement stated by Coffee (2000). The CVM's board, in addition, contradicted its own technical department in one of the cases analyzed. Although this would not be a problem per se, this decision allowed an exception to the enforcement of Brazilian corporate law when it was clear that it could potentially harm investors. Since the CVM's board consists of politically nominated directors and its technical department consists of only career officials, one could suppose this fact to be related to some kind of regulatory capture, an event that tends to occur more often in environments characterized by crony capitalism, something usually associated with Brazil.[26]

The second potential cause is a formalistic interpretation of the rules. The two cases analyzed provide evidence that both operations were thought to bypass the NMLR, as well as Brazilian legislation. The controlling shareholders used indirect operations that resulted in big losses for investors, in violation of their rights. The BM&FBovespa and the CVM did not interpret the self-regulatory and regulatory rules in their essence. Although Brazilian corporate law contains some of the same principles, the interpretation of rules is usually formalistic. Perhaps this is a clear example of a different outcome resulting from a legal transplant from a different legal environment. Thus, self-regulatory origins and traditions of a law's interpretation can have important impacts on its enforcement. In this sense, rules are not enough to guarantee a transplant's success, since its interpretation must adequately consider its legal environment.

The third is the lack of adequate oversight structure by the BM&FBovespa and the CVM. The rapid growth in the number of companies and in the complexity of the market probably was not matched by a corresponding increase in regulatory structure (e.g., in terms of budget and human and technical resources) to adequately

[25] To avoid this potential conflict of interest on monitoring and compliance of the NMLR – including its liability and punishments – the creation of an external structure to BM&FBovespa may be required.

[26] Lazzarini (2011) made several social network analysis' experiments with Brazilian companies and their connections. The author found a crony capitalism was even stronger (from 1996 to 2009) than before 1990s.

monitor the market. In the case of the BM&FBovespa, a strong monitoring structure requires a larger budget, which directly affects its profits. Since the BM&FBovespa is a publicly listed company, its ultimate goal is to maximize profits by minimizing costs. Therefore, the lack of oversight may have occurred due to the stock market inherent conflict of interest between maximizing profits, minimizing costs and monitoring its compliance with its own rules.

These three specific causes naturally fall within a broader context of intrinsically linked elements: the institutional, cultural, economic and political aspects. In any market, institutions can be more or less plastic (Coffee 1999), but they always attempt to reinforce themselves without major modifications (North 1990). Emerging markets such as Brazil have, at least in theory, less efficient institutions, possibly the result of lower economic development. These cultural, political, economic, and institutional elements permeate the entire market[27] and affect the existence of investor protection rules. These elements indicate that the conflict between controlling and minority shareholders, the key problem before the transplant, remained the same for companies in the Novo Mercado afterwards.

There are five potential lessons for emerging markets, based on the Brazilian experience. First, the legal transplantation and mere adoption of rules are not sufficient to protect investor rights, contradicting the massive literature on legal reforms from World Bank based on studies from La Porta et al. (1997, 1998) among others. Second, conflicts of interest from both the regulatory and self-regulatory spheres can hamper the enforcement of rules. Third, legal reforms aimed at increasing investor protection based on different law systems may have unexpected outcomes, since they are interpreted according to the context of the country in which they have been transplanted. Thus, legal transplants cannot ignore the context of the environment in which they are transplanted. On the contrary, typical agency problems pervade the entire legal system and derive from the ownership structure that generates the main conflict of interest in companies.[28] Fourth, although legal transplants can be quickly implemented at low cost and signal the adoption of better practices for investors (Milhaupt and Pistor 2008), it is necessary to develop an efficient structure to oversee company compliance of the rules as well as enforce investor protection rights. Therefore, the enforcement of the transplanted rules depend on the institutions involved and the way they interpret the rules within their context (Berkowitz et al. 2003; Milhaupt and Pistor 2008). Fifth, the legal transplant can have a direct impact on the growth of the legal framework aimed at protecting investors.

[27] Siems (2008, p. 3) states that "Legal rules must not be regarded in an isolated way, because the functioning of legal systems can only be understood as a whole."

[28] According to Kraakman et al. (2004, p. 215): "By necessity, corporate law in every jurisdiction must deal with three generic agency problems: the opportunism of managers vis-a-vis shareholders; the opportunism of controlling shareholders vis-a-vis minority shareholders; and the opportunism of the firm itself vis-a-vis other corporate constituencies, such as corporate creditors and employees. (...) the principal function of corporate law, as we conceive of it, is to respond to these three generic agency problems".

This chapter adds to the lines of research that investigate legal transplants, the enforcement of investor protection rules, the drivers of legislative and regulatory changes, and the unforeseen consequences (externalities) of legal transplants.

Acknowledgments The author is grateful to Professor Dr. Alexandre Di Miceli da Silveira for his detailed reading and valuable critique, to Professor Dr. Esdras Borges Costa (in memoriam) for his important review, and to Muriel Waksman for her careful research. All errors and omissions are the sole responsibility of the author.

References

Bebchuk, L. A., & Roe, M. J. (1999). A theory of path dependence in corporate ownership and governance. *Stanford Law Review, 52*, 127–170.

Berkowitz, D., Pistor, K., & Richard, J. F. (2003). Economic development, legality, and the transplant effect. *European Economic Review, 47*(1), 165–195.

Bottazzi, L., & Da Rin, M. (2002). Europe's "New" stock markets. EFA 2003 annual conference paper; IGIER Working Paper 218. Available at http://ssrn.com/abstract=319260.

Burghof, H., & Hunger, A. (2004). The Neuer Markt: An (overly) risky asset of Germany's financial system. *Emerald Group Publishing Limited, 10*, 295–327.

Coffee, J. (1999). The future as history: The prospects for global convergence in corporate governance and its implications. *Northwestern University Law Review, 93*(3), 641–673.

Coffee, J. (2000). Convergence and its critics: What are the preconditions to the separation of ownership and control? *Columbia Center for Law and Economies Working Paper, 179*, 1–56.

Coffee, J. (2001). The rise of dispersed ownership: The role of law in the separation of ownership and control. *The Yale Law Journal, 111*(1), 1–82.

Donaggio, A. R. F. (2012). *Governança Corporativa e Novo Mercado – Proteção ao Investidor e Falhas no Marco-Regulatório*. São Paulo: Saraiva.

Gilson, R. (2001). Globalizing corporate governance: Convergence of form or function. *The American Journal of Comparative Law, 49*(2), 329–357.

Hess, D., Lehmann, E., & Lüders, E. (2001). Vertrauenskrise am Neuen Markt?, In ZEW Finanzmarktreport, Jg. 10, Nr. 9.

Kanda, H., & Milhaupt, C. (2003). Re-examining legal transplants: The director's fiduciary duty in Japanese corporate law. *The American Journal of Comparative Law, 51*(4), 887–901.

Kraakman, R., Armour, J., Davies, P., & Enriques, L. (2004). *The anatomy of corporate law: A comparative and functional approach*. Oxford: Oxford University Press.

La Porta, R., Lopez-de-Silanes, F., Shleifer, A., & Vishny, R. W. (1997). Legal determinants of external finance. *Journal of Finance, 52*(3), 1131–1150.

La Porta, R., Lopez-de-Silanes, F., Shleifer, A., & Vishny, R. W. (1998). Law and finance. *Journal of Political Economy, 106*(6), 1131–1155.

Lazzarini, S. G. (2011). *Capitalismo de laços: Os donos do Brasil e suas conexões*. São Paulo: Campus.

Legrand, P. (1997). The impossibility of legal transplants. *Maastricht Journal of European and Comparative Law, 4*, 111–124. 112.

Milhaupt, C., & Pistor, K. (2008). *Law & capitalism: What corporate crises reveal about legal systems and economic development around the world*. Chicago: University of Chicago Press.

Moreira, V. (1997). *Autorregulação Profissional e Administração Pública*. Coimbra: Almedina.

Nenova, T. (2006). Control values and changes in corporate law in Brazil. *Latin American Business Review, 6*(3), 1–37.

North, D. C. (1990). *Institutions, institutional change, and economic performance*. Cambridge: Cambridge University Press.

OECD – Organisation for Economic Co-operation and Development. (2003). White paper on corporate governance in Latin America. Available at http://www.oecd.org/dataoecd/25/2/18976210.pdf.

Rasch, S. (1994). Special stock market segments for small company shares in Europe – what went wrong? Center for European economic research discussion paper. (pp. 93–13). Mannheim.

Santana, M.H., Ararat, M., Alexandru, P., Yurtoglu, B.B., & Cunha, M.R. (2008). Novo Mercado and its followers: Case studies in corporate governance reform, focus 5. Global Corporate Governance Forum/International Finance Corporation. Available at http://www.ifc.org/wps/wcm/connect/e1162a8048a7e69ea787e76060ad5911/Novo%2BMercado%2Btext%2Bscreen%2B4-21-08.pdf?MOD=AJPERES

Santos, A. (2006). The World Bank's uses of the 'rule of law' promise in economic development. In D. Trubek & A. Santos (Eds.), *The new law and economic development: A critical appraisal* (pp. 253–300). New York: Cambridge University Press.

Siems, M. (2008). What does not work in comparing securities laws: A critique on La Porta et al'.s methodology. *International Company and Commercial Law Review, 9*, 300–305.

Silveira, A. M., & Dias, A. (2010). What is the impact of bad governance practices in a concentrated ownership environment? *International Journal of Disclosure and Governance, 7*(1), 70–91.

Waarden, F. V. (1984). *Bureaucracy around the state: Varieties of collective self-regulation in the Dutch dairy industry*. Florence: European Univ. Inst.

Watson, A. (1978). Comparative law and legal change. Cambridge Law Journal, 37(2), 313–336.

Watson, A. (1993). *Legal transplants: An approach to comparative law* (2nd ed.). Athens: University of Georgia Press.

Do Pension Funds Improve the Governance of Investee Companies? Evidence from the Brazilian Market

Andre Carvalhal and Carlos Almeida

Abstract The role of pension funds in improving governance practices of investee companies has been vastly studied in developed countries, but there are only a few studies in emerging markets. This chapter examines the role of pension funds in the governance of investee companies in the Brazilian market. Brazil offers an interesting case study, because its governance environment is much weaker than the countries studied by most of the previous research. We use three variables to measure governance practices: a broad firm-level governance index, listing on the "New Market", a special stock exchange segment that requires high governance standards, and issue of ADRs in the U.S. To the best of our knowledge, such comprehensive governance metrics have not been related previously to pension fund's activism in emerging markets. Our analysis provides evidence that companies invested by pension funds have worse governance in Brazil. We use three econometric techniques to control for endogeneity, and show that there is a negative relation between pension funds and governance practices after controlling for different firm and industry characteristics. Our results are consistent with the literature that reports that institutional investors, especially pension funds, are ineffective as monitors to improve corporate governance.

A. Carvalhal (✉)
Pontifical Catholic University of Rio de Janeiro, Rio de Janeiro, Brazil
e-mail: andrec@coppead.ufrj.br

C. Almeida
Getulio Vargas Foundation, André Luiz Carvalhal da Silva, Rio de Janeiro, Brazil

S. Boubaker and D.K. Nguyen (eds.), *Corporate Governance in Emerging Markets*, CSR, Sustainability, Ethics & Governance, DOI 10.1007/978-3-642-44955-0_20,

1 Introduction

There is a vast literature on the efforts of pension funds (PFs henceforth) to improve corporate governance in developed countries. However, little evidence is available about the impact of PFs' investments on corporate governance structures in emerging markets.

This chapter examines the role of PFs in enhancing governance practices in Brazil, one of the largest emerging economies in the world. The Brazilian market offers interesting characteristics for this study, because its corporate governance environment – weak protection of minority shareholders, high ownership concentration, and predominance of family-controlled firms – is much different from most of the previous research on PF's activism.

The research on PFs' activism is not new. Since the late 1980s, shareholder activism has played a predominant role in efforts to reform corporate governance structures and improve firm performance. Smith (1996), Nesbitt (1994), and Barber (2007) analyze the activism of CALPERS, whereas Carleton et al. (1998) examine the role of TIAA-CREF. In more aggregated analyses, without specifically studying a particular institutional investor, Gillan and Starks (2003) show the positive effect of institutional investors in enhancing corporate governance practices in different countries.

Aggarwal et al. (2011) study the relation between institutional ownership and corporate governance in 23 countries during the period 2003–2008, and show that institutional investors promote good governance practices outside of the U.S., especially in countries with poor legal protection.

Hartzell and Starks (2003) show that institutional investors affect executive compensation, and Parrino et al. (2003) find a relation between CEO turnover and institutional ownership. Mergers and acquisitions, and anti-takeover amendments are also affected by the institutional activism (Chen et al. 2007; Brickley et al. 1988, respectively).

Brav et al. (2008), and Klein and Zur (2009) show the activism of PFs and hedge funds in order to improve the governance of investee companies. Ferreira and Matos (2008) show a positive relation between the presence of foreign institutional investors and firm value and performance. Del Guercio and Hawkins (1999) find that PFs are successful at monitoring and promoting changes in target firms.

There is also empirical evidence reporting that institutional investors are largely ineffective as monitors (Wahal 1996; Gillan and Starks 2000) and do not enhance shareholder value by monitoring firms (Karpoff et al. 1996). Woidtke (2002), Lipton and Rosenblum (1991), and Wohlstetter (1993) argue that institutional shareholders, especially PFs, do not have adequate monitoring skills to improve on managers' decisions and that their objectives may conflict with value maximization.

Recent research provides mixed results about the important role of institutional investors in corporate governance in emerging markets. Chhibber and Majumdar (1999) examine the relationship between foreign ownership and firm performance in India, and find that firms report superior performance only when foreigner investors control the company. On the other hand, Sarkar and Sarkar (2000) find no evidence that large institutional investors (typically mutual funds) are active in governance in India. Chen et al. (2012) analyze the role of venture capital funds in Taiwan and conclude that they create better corporate governance structures for new IPO firms.

In Brazil, Silveira (2011) examines the role of institutional investors in the governance of 239 Brazilian companies in the 2010–2011 period, and shows that the presence of PFs is associated with worse governance. The presence of mutual funds or private equity firms is positively associated with better governance practices.

This chapter contributes to the literature in three ways. First we analyze the role of PFs in enhancing governance practices in a country with weaker institutional environment when compared to most previous research on PF's activism. Second, our analysis of a broad time-series and cross-section of governance practices of Brazilian companies leads to new empirical evidence on the effect of PFs on the governance of investee companies. Finally, we use three variables to measure governance practices: a broad firm-level governance index, listing on the "New Market", a special stock exchange segment that requires high governance standards, and issue of ADRs in the U.S. To the best of our knowledge, such comprehensive governance metrics have not been related previously to PFs' activism in emerging markets.

We use three econometric techniques to control for endogeneity, and show that there is a negative relation between pension funds and governance practices after controlling for different firm and industry characteristics. Our results are consistent with the literature that reports that pension funds do not enhance shareholder value and are ineffective as monitors to improve corporate governance (Karpoff et al. 1996; Woidtke 2002; Lipton and Rosenblum 1991; Wohlstetter 1993).

The remainder of the chapter proceeds as follows. The next section shows the data and methodology, whereas Sect. 3 presents the empirical results on the relation between PFs and corporate governance. Section 4 presents the robustness analysis and Sect. 5 concludes the chapter.

2 Data and Methodology

At the end of 2011, there were 368 PFs in Brazil, with a total portfolio of US$ 306 billion, equivalent to 14.7 % of Brazilian GDP. Around 30 % of the portfolio was invested in equity or equity funds. There is a huge asset concentration in the hands of the largest pension funds: 22.8 % of the PFs (84 out of 368) are sponsored by State-owned companies, and they manage 64.8 % of total assets. The four largest PFs belong to State-owned companies and have 49 % of all PFs' assets.

Our sample consists of an unbalanced panel dataset of 323 Brazilian listed firms from 2002 to 2009, in which there are 95 firms invested by PFs. The final sample represents 80 % of the number of firms and 70 % of total market capitalization of the Sao Paulo stock exchange (BM&FBovespa) at the end of 2009.

Our objective is to assess if companies invested by PFs have better governance. We use three variables to measure governance practices. First we employ the firm-level governance index (CGI) developed by Leal and Carvalhal (2007), which has four attributes: disclosure and transparency, board of directors, ethics and conflict of interests and shareholder rights. To calculate CGI, each company receives a score for each attribute, and the total score represents the CGI. In this chapter, we normalize the CGI from 0 to 10 to facilitate visualization and interpretation.

Second, we check if the firm is listed on New Market, a special segment created by BM&FBovespa for companies that voluntarily decide to offer high standards of disclosure and governance practices. The main objective of the New Market is to provide investors with corporate governance rights beyond what is legally required, such as prohibition of non-voting shares, disclosure of a code of ethics, publication of financial statements in English, mandatory bid rule for voting and non-voting shares at 100 % of the control block price, and adoption of arbitration for resolution of corporate disputes.

The third governance metric was the listing of ADRs II or III on U.S. stock exchanges. Since the listing requirements in the U.S. are stricter than those in many emerging markets, the issue of ADRs is generally associated with the adoption of better governance practices by the companies.

We construct a database with information on CGI (firm-level governance index developed by Leal and Carvalhal 2007), NM (dummy variable equal to 1 if the company is listed on New Market), ADR (dummy variable equal to 1 if the company has ADRs II or III on U.S. stock exchanges), PF (dummy variable that equals 1 if a firm has pension funds as shareholders), LEV (leverage, measured by the ratio of total non-equity liabilities to total assets), ROA (return on assets, measured by the ratio of operating income to total assets), VOT (% of voting capital held by the controlling shareholder), GRO (average sales growth in the last 3 years), TANG (tangibility of assets, measured by the ratio of fixed assets and total assets), and DIV (dividend yield, measured by the ratio of annual dividends to the stock price at the beginning of the year).

The data come from the Economatica, a financial database that contains a wide coverage of Brazilian stock market data. The information on the shareholding structure and corporate charter provisions comes from the Brazilian Securities and Exchange Commission (CVM).

In order to evaluate if PFs improve corporate governance, we first divide the sample into two groups: those with and those without the participation of PFs. Difference tests are conducted to verify if firm characteristics vary between both groups.

Then we examine the effect of PFs on firm governance by modeling the latter as a function of firm characteristics. We define our measure of corporate governance (CGI) as:

$$CGI_{i,t} = \alpha_0 + \alpha_1 PF_{i,t} + \alpha_2 X_{i,t} + \varepsilon_{i,t} \quad (1)$$

where $PF_{i,t}$ is a dummy variable equal to 1 if pension funds are shareholders of the company *i* and 0 otherwise; $X_{i,t}$ is a set of exogenous observable characteristics of the firm, and $\varepsilon_{i,t}$ is the random error.

If the PF's decision to become a shareholder is correlated with corporate governance, $PF_{i,t}$ will be correlated with the error term in Eq. 1. The OLS estimate of α_1 will, therefore, be biased. We assumed that the PF's decision to become a shareholder is determined by:

$$\begin{aligned} PF^*{}_{i,t} &= \beta Z_{i,t} + \mu_{i,t} \\ PF_{i,t} &= 1 \text{ if } PF^*{}_{i,t} > 0 \\ PF_{i,t} &= 0 \text{ if } PF^*{}_{i,t} < 0 \end{aligned} \quad (2)$$

where $PF^*{}_{i,t}$ is an unobserved latent variable, $Z_{i,t}$ is a set of firm characteristics that affect the pension fund's decision to become a shareholder, and $\mu_{i,t}$ is an error term.

We follow Campa and Kedia (2002) and use three different techniques to control for the correlation between $PF_{i,t}$ and $\varepsilon_{i,t}$ in Eq. 1 and come up with an unbiased estimator of α_1. First, we control for unobservable firm characteristics that affect the PF's decision to become a shareholder by introducing fixed-firm effects. Second, we model the PF's decision to buy shares as a function of firm characteristics. We use the probability of the PF becoming a shareholder as an instrument in evaluating the effect of PFs on corporate governance. Last, we model an endogenous self-selection model and use Heckman's correction to control for the self-selection bias induced on account of PF's decision to acquire a stake in the company.

3 Corporate Governance and Pension Fund Ownership

Table 1 shows the descriptive statistics of the variables used in this chapter. On average, 22 % of the firms in our sample are owned by pension funds, 16 % are listed on New Market, and 10 % have ADRs in the U.S. On average, firms have poor governance practices (CGI of 4.79 out of 10), moderate profitability and leverage (ROA of 3.94 % and leverage of 60.23 %) and high sales growth (21.51 %).

Table 2 compares the economic and financial variables of companies segmented in accordance with the presence of PFs as shareholders. We perform statistical tests of differences (in mean and median) to verify if firm characteristics vary according to the presence or absence of PFs.

If PFs are active in improving the governance of investee companies they should be positively related to CGI, NM and ADR. This seems not to be the case in Brazil. The results indicate that companies with PFs do not have higher CGI. The average (median) CGI of companies with PFs is 4.70 (4.58), very close to the 4.81 (4.50) achieved by companies without PFs. The differences are not statistically significant.

Table 1 Descriptive statistics of firm characteristics

	Mean	Median	Minimum	1st Quartile	3rd Quartile	Maximum	Std. dev
CGI	4.79	4.50	0.75	3.50	6.00	9.50	1.69
NM	0.16	0.00	0.00	0.00	0.00	1.00	0.40
ADR	0.10	0.00	0.00	0.00	0.00	1.00	0.30
PF	0.22	0.00	0.00	0.00	0.00	1.00	0.20
VOT	61.33	59.65	0.00	39.15	88.50	100.00	27.44
ROA	3.94	3.30	−85.20	0.40	8.00	426.70	13.70
SIZE	6.03	6.08	0.48	5.48	8.85	6.56	0.91
LEV	60.23	61.80	0.00	45.50	78.70	99.90	23.10
GRO	21.51	13.85	−90.17	6.22	24.57	944.54	55.36
TANG	31.11	30.84	0.00	7.81	47.67	98.25	24.21
DIV	1.56	0.00	0.00	0.00	0.60	101.70	4.35

Note: descriptive statistics of firm characteristics. The definition of the variables can be found in Sect. 2

Table 2 Firm characteristics and pension fund ownership

	Firms without pension funds		Firms with pension funds		Tests for equality of means and medians (p-value)	
	Mean	Median	Mean	Median	Mean	Median
CGI	4.81	4.50	4.70	4.58	0.20	0.64
NM	0.16	0.00	0.14	0.00	0.15	0.36
ADR	0.08	0.00	0.16	0.00	0.00***	0.00***
VOT	63.04	61.65	54.82	53.10	0.00***	0.00***
ROA	3.81	3.10	4.50	4.20	0.30	0.00***
SIZE	5.94	6.00	6.38	6.39	0.00***	0.00***
LEV	59.76	61.60	62.17	62.40	0.03**	0.09*
GRO	21.51	13.87	21.50	13.76	0.99	0.90
TANG	29.81	28.44	36.40	37.49	0.00***	0.00***
DIV	1.37	0.00	2.98	0.70	0.00***	0.00***

Note: Characteristics of companies segmented into two groups (with and without pension funds). The definition of the variables can be found in Sect. 2. ***, ** and * indicate differences in mean and median (between companies with and without pension funds) statistically significant at 1 %, 5 % and 10 %, respectively

The proportion of firms listed on New Market is almost the same for both groups of companies. Approximately 14 % of the companies invested by PFs are listed on New Market, slightly below the 16 % found for companies without PFs (the difference in proportions is not statistically significant).

The results for ADRs are different from those obtained for CGI and NM. Companies invested by PFs tend to list more in the U.S. Around 16 % of companies invested by PFs have ADRs II or III, significantly higher than the 8 % for firms without PFs.

Regarding other firm characteristics (performance, size, leverage, dividend yield and tangibility of assets), firms with PFs are larger, more leveraged, have more fixed assets, lower capital concentration, and pay more dividends. There is no significant difference in performance (ROA and sales growth) between both groups of firms.

Table 3 shows the correlations between selected variables. The correlations of PF with CGI and ADR are positive and statistically different from zero. On the other hand, there is no significant correlation between PF and NM. These findings indicate mixed conclusions about the relation between PFs and governance.

There is a positive correlation between PF, SIZE, LEV, TANG and DIV, indicating that firms with PFs are larger, have more debt, fixed assets and distribute higher dividends. The negative correlation between PF and VOT suggests that the controlling shareholder has lower voting rights in firms with PFs. All results are consistent with those of Table 2.

Then, we estimate the relationship between the PF's presence and corporate governance through ordinary least squares (OLS), fixed effects, instrumental variables and self-selection models. Table 4 shows the results for CGI as dependent variable. Column 1 shows the OLS estimation results. The PF coefficient is negative and statistically significant at 1 %, indicating that corporate governance is negative related to the presence of PFs. This result is in line with the evidence that institutional investors are ineffective to improve governance (Wahal 1996; Gillan and Starks 2000; Karpoff et al. 1996; Woidtke 2002; Lipton and Rosenblum 1991; Wohlstetter 1993; Silveira 2011).

We introduce fixed effects to control for unobservable firm characteristics which affect the PF's decision to become shareholder. As seen in Column 2 of Table 4, the PF coefficient remains negative and significant at 5 %. The signs and significance of the coefficients of the other variables are essentially the same as the OLS estimation. Therefore, we conclude that the results for OLS and fixed effects show evidence that companies invested by PFs have worse governance.

Then we estimate the probability of PFs becoming a shareholder of a company. The results of this estimation is used in the instrumental variable estimation as well as in Heckman's self-selection model. The estimation of Eqs. 1 and 2 in a simultaneous equation framework is not easy because the natural instruments for *PF*, the observed firm characteristics, are already included in the corporate governance equation (Eq. 1). The characteristic of a good instrument for PF becoming a shareholder is such that it is not correlated with the error of Eq. 1 and that it is correlated with PF.

We have identified two valid instruments. The first consists of industry characteristics and the second is related to firm characteristics. Since PFs focused on the long term, its presence is stronger in industries that require long-term investments. Therefore, it is expected that industry characteristics influence the PF's decision to become a shareholder in a company. It is important to note that we add industry dummy variables in the OLS estimation, and the coefficients are not significant, suggesting that there is no evidence that economic sectors significantly affect governance in Brazil.

In addition to industrial factors, there are characteristics of companies that can affect the PF's decision to become a shareholder. As seen in Tables 2 and 3, companies invested by PF are larger, more leveraged, have more fixed assets,

Table 3 Correlation among selected variables

	PF	NM	ADR	CGI	ROA	SIZE	VOT	TANG	DIV	GRO	LEV
PF	1.00***										
	(0.00)										
NM	0.01	1.00***									
	(0.47)	(0.00)									
ADR	0.08***	−0.01	1.00***								
	(0.00)	(0.47)	(0.00)								
CGI	0.05***	0.65***	0.18***	1.00***							
	(0.00)	(0.00)	(0.00)	(0.00)							
ROA	0.07***	0.07***	−0.01	0.17***	1.00***						
	(0.00)	(0.00)	(0.47)	(0.00)	(0.00)						
SIZE	0.19***	0.14***	0.51***	0.40***	0.12***	1.00***					
	(0.00)	(0.00)	(0.00)	(0.00)	(0.00)	(0.00)					
VOT	−0.20***	−0.29***	−0.02	−0.30***	−0.03**	−0.04***	1.00***				
	(0.00)	(0.00)	(0.15)	(0.00)	(0.03)	(0.00)	(0.00)				
TANG	0.11***	0.03**	0.12***	−0.04***	−0.04***	0.15***	0.03**	1.00***			
	(0.00)	(0.03)	(0.00)	(0.00)	(0.00)	(0.00)	(0.03)	(0.00)			
DIV	0.12***	0.07***	0.04***	0.02	0.08***	0.16***	0.03**	0.00	1.00***		
	(0.00)	(0.00)	(0.00)	(0.15)	(0.00)	(0.00)	(0.03)	(0.99)	(0.00)		
GRO	0.00	0.08***	0.02	0.15***	0.00	0.01	−0.01	−0.09***	−0.05***	1.00***	
	(0.99)	(0.00)	(0.15)	(0.00)	(0.99)	(0.47)	(0.47)	(0.00)	(0.00)	(0.00)	
LEV	0.06***	−0.03**	0.01	−0.04***	−0.37***	0.20***	−0.03**	0.02	−0.05***	−0.02	1.00***
	(0.00)	(0.03)	(0.47)	(0.00)	(0.00)	(0.00)	(0.03)	(0.15)	(0.00)	(0.15)	(0.00)

Note: correlation among selected variables, with the corresponding p-values in parentheses. *** and ** indicate correlations statistically significant at 1 % and 5 %, respectively

Table 4 Corporate governance and pension fund ownership

	OLS	Fixed-effects	Instrumental variables	Self-selection
PF	−0.48***	−0.11**	−0.18**	−0.12**
	(0.00)	(0.04)	(0.04)	(0.05)
VOT	−0.02***	−0.01***	−0.02***	−0.02***
	(0.00)	(0.00)	(0.00)	(0.00)
ROA	0.00	0.00	0.01	0.01
	(0.50)	(0.13)	(0.17)	(0.22)
SIZE	1.09***	0.73***	1.04***	0.99***
	(0.00)	(0.00)	(0.00)	(0.00)
LEV	−0.01***	−0.01**	−0.01*	−0.01*
	(0.00)	(0.02)	(0.09)	(0.08)
Lambda				−0.17
				(0.76)
R^2 adj	0.25	0.85	0.83	0.85
# Obs	1,591	1,591	1,591	1,591

Note: ordinary least squares, fixed-effects, instrumental variable and self-selection models to estimate the relationship between the pension fund's presence as a shareholder and corporate governance. The dependent variable is CGI (governance index of Leal and Carvalhal 2007). The definition of each variable can be found in Sect. 2. The PF variable is a dummy that takes the value 1 when a pension fund is a shareholder of the company, and 0 otherwise. Standard errors are corrected for autocorrelation and heteroscedasticity, and the corresponding p-values are shown in parentheses. ***, ** and * indicate statistical significance at 1 %, 5 % and 10 %, respectively

lower capital concentration, and pay more dividends. The probit estimation includes all these characteristics of companies as potential determinants of the PF's decision to buy shares.

The maximum likelihood estimates of the probit coefficients are reported in Table 5. The data fit the model quite well. The model classifies 77 % of the observations correctly, and chi-squares testing whether the coefficient estimates are jointly zero are significant with p-values below 1 %. There is a positive and significant relationship between the PF's decision to become a shareholder and firm size, tangibility of assets, and dividend yield. This result indicates that PFs prefer to invest in large firms that pay higher dividends and have fixed assets. There is also a negative relationship between PF and VOT, suggesting that PFs tend to become shareholders of firms in which the controlling shareholder has less voting power.

We use the estimated probability of PF becoming a shareholder from the probit models as a generated instrument for the PF status. In the first stage, we use all the exogenous variables along with the probability of PF becoming a shareholder as explanatory variables in the PF's decision to buy shares, that is, *PF* variable. In the second stage, we use the fitted value from the first stage as an instrument for *PF*.

The coefficients of the instrumented *PF*, as reported in Table 4, is −0.18 (model 3) and is statistically significant at 5 %. This result indicates that companies invested by pension funds have worse governance.

Lastly, we report the results of a two-stage estimation of the endogenous self-selection model. The estimated parameters are reported in column 4 of Table 4. The

Table 5 Probit model for pension fund presence

Variables	Coefficient (p-value)
Intercept	−2.98***
	(0.00)
VOT	−0.01***
	(0.00)
ROA	0.00
	(0.18)
SIZE	0.39***
	(0.00)
LEV	0.00
	(0.20)
TANG	0.01**
	(0.02)
DIV	0.01*
	(0.10)
GRO	0.00
	(0.98)
Industry dummies	Yes
Year dummies	Yes
McFadden R^2	0.08
# Obs	1,792

Note: probit models to examine the determinants of the pension fund's decision to become a shareholder. The dependent variable takes the value 1 when a pension fund is a shareholder and 0 otherwise. The corresponding p-values are shown in parentheses. The definition of the variables can be found in Sect. 2. ***, ** and * indicate statistical significance at 1 %, 5 % and 10 %, respectively

estimated coefficient of *PF* is negative (−0.12) and is significant at 5 %. The coefficient of λ, the self-selection parameter, is not significant. This indicates the absence of self-selection and suggests that companies with better governance are not likely to receive PF's support.

In sum, there is no evidence of endogeneity with both the instrumental variables and self-selection models. After controlling for the potential endogeneity of the PF's decision to buy shares in a company, we provide evidence that the presence of PFs is negatively related to good governance.

4 Robustness Analysis

To check the robustness of our results, we use the four sub-indices of CGI as alternative measures of corporate governance. Table 6 shows the *PF* coefficients for various governance measures and model specifications. The *PF* variable is negative and statistically significant in two attributes (ethics and conflict of interests, and

Table 6 Alternative measures of governance and pension fund presence

	CGI	Disclosure and transparency	Board of directors	Ethics and conflict of interests	Shareholder rights
OLS	−0.48***	−0.13	−0.10	−0.51***	−1.20***
	(0.00)	(0.32)	(0.45)	(0.00)	(0.00)
Fixed-effects	−0.11**	−0.21	0.09	−0.13**	−0.21**
	(0.04)	(0.30)	(0.70)	(0.05)	(0.03)
Instrumental-variables	−0.18**	−0.18	0.10	−0.44**	−0.27**
	(0.04)	(0.61)	(0.83)	(0.03)	(0.04)
Self-selection	−0.12**	−0.13	0.08	−0.32**	−0.18**
	(0.05)	(0.60)	(0.79)	(0.03)	(0.04)

Note: ordinary least squares, fixed effects, instrumental variables and self-selection models to estimate the relationship between the PF's presence as a shareholder and corporate governance. The dependent variables are CGI (governance index of Leal and Carvalhal 2007), and its four sub-indices. The definition of each variable can be found in Sect. 2. This table shows the coefficients of the *PF* variable (dummy that takes the value 1 when a pension fund is shareholder of the company, and 0 otherwise) in each model. Standard errors are corrected for autocorrelation, and the corresponding p-values are shown in parentheses. The symbols *** and ** indicate statistical significance at 1 % and 5 %, respectively

shareholder rights). This result indicates that the companies invested by PFs have worse practices with regard to ethics and conflict of interest, and grant fewer rights to minority shareholders.

Finally, we analyze whether there is a relationship between PF presence and listing on New Market and in the U.S. through ADRs. Table 7 shows the results of probit models with NM and ADR as dependent variables. The *PF* coefficient is negative but is not statistically significant. So, we can conclude that firms invested by PFs are not likely to adopt better governance practices through listing on New Market and ADRs.

Overall our results indicate that PFs are not effective in improving governance in Brazil. This finding is consistent with Woidtke (2002), Lipton and Rosenblum (1991), and Wohlstetter (1993), who argue that institutional shareholders, especially PFs, do not have adequate monitoring skills to improve on managers' decisions and that their objectives may conflict with value maximization.

Moreover, since there is a huge asset concentration by State-sponsored pension funds in Brazil, our results are also consistent with the literature that argue that the managers of State companies have no incentive to improve their performance and, thus, exercise poor control of power (Ehrlich et al. 1994; Karpoff 2001).

Table 7 Probit model for listing on New Market and U.S. stock exchanges

	NM	ADR
PF	−0.09	−0.11
	(0.25)	(0.30)
VOT	−0.01***	−0.01
	(0.00)	(0.88)
ROA	−0.01*	−0.02**
	(0.07)	(0.02)
SIZE	0.80***	1.52***
	(0.00)	(0.00)
LEV	−0.01***	−0.02***
	(0.00)	(0.00)
McFadden R^2	0.24	0.40
# Obs	2,309	2,309

Note: probit models to examine the determinants of the firm's decision to list on New Market and in the U.S. through ADRs II and III. The dependent variables take the value 1 when the firm is listed on New Market or on U.S. stock exchanges (NM and ADR, respectively) and 0 otherwise. The definition of the variables can be found in Sect. 2. The corresponding p-values are shown in parentheses. ***, ** and * indicate statistical significance at 1 %, 5 % and 10 %, respectively

5 Conclusion

Several published studies show that companies in which there is greater activism by shareholders, especially institutional investors, have better governance. This study evaluates whether companies invested by pension funds have better governance in Brazil.

We measure the quality of governance through three variables: a broad firm-level governance index, the listing on "New Market", and the issue of ADRs on U.S. stock exchanges.

Our analysis of a broad sample of Brazilian companies from 2002 to 2009 indicates that firms with pension funds as shareholders have worse governance practices. The results are robust to different governance measures and econometric techniques. This finding is in line with the evidence that institutional investors, especially State-sponsored pension funds, are ineffective to improve governance.

References

Aggarwal, R., Erel, I., Ferreira, M., & Matos, P. (2011). Does governance travel around the world? Evidence from institutional investors. *Journal of Financial Economics, 100*, 154–181.

Barber, M. (2007). Monitoring the monitor: Evaluating CalPRES' activism. *Journal of Investing, 16*, 66–80.

Brav, A., Jiang, W., Partnoy, F., & Thomas, R. (2008). Hedge fund activism, corporate governance, and firm performance. *Journal of Finance, 63*, 1729–1775.

Brickley, J., Lease, R., & Smith, C., Jr. (1988). Ownership structure and voting on antitakeover amendments. *Journal of Financial Economics, 20*, 267–291.
Campa, J., & Kedia, S. (2002). Explaining the diversification discount. *Journal of Finance, 57*, 1731–1762.
Carleton, W., Nelson, J., & Weisbach, M. (1998). The influence of institutions on corporate governance through private negotiations: Evidence from TIAA-CREF. *Journal of Finance, 53*, 1335–1362.
Chen, X., Harford, J., & Li, K. (2007). Monitoring: Which institutions matter? *Journal of Financial Economics, 86*, 279–305.
Chen, J., Liao, W., & Lu, C. (2012). The effects of public venture capital investments on corporate governance: Evidence from IPO firms in emerging markets. *Abacus, 48*, 86–103.
Chhibber, P., & Majumdar, S. (1999). Foreign ownership and profitability: Property rights, control, and the performance of firms in Indian industry'. *Journal of Law and Finance, 42*, 209–239.
Del Guercio, D., & Hawkins, J. (1999). The motivation and impact of pension fund activism. *Journal of Financial Economics, 52*, 293–340.
Ehrlich, I., Gallais-Hamonno, G., Liu, Z., & Lutter, R. (1994). Productivity growth and firm ownership: An empirical investigation. *Journal of Political Economy, 102*, 1006–1038.
Ferreira, M., & Matos, P. (2008). The colors of investors' money: The role of institutional investors around the world. *Journal of Financial Economics, 88*, 499–533.
Gillan, S., & Starks, L. (2000). Corporate governance proposals and shareholder activism: The role of institutional investors. *Journal of Financial Economics, 57*, 275–305.
Gillan, S., & Starks, L. (2003). Corporate governance, corporate ownership, and the role of institutional investors: A global perspective. *Journal of Applied Finance, 13*, 16–17.
Hartzell, J., & Starks, L. (2003). Institutional investors and executive compensation. *Journal of Finance, 58*, 2351–2374.
Karpoff, J. (2001). The impact of shareholder activism on target companies: A survey of empirical findings. Available at SSRN: http://ssrn.com/abstract=885365. Retrieved on 30 May 2013.
Karpoff, J., Malatesta, P., & Walkling, R. (1996). Corporate governance and shareholder initiatives: Empirical evidence. *Journal of Financial Economics, 42*, 365–395.
Klein, A., & Zur, E. (2009). Entrepreneurial shareholder activism: Hedge funds and other private investors. *Journal of Finance, 64*, 187–229.
Leal, R., & Carvalhal, A. (2007). Corporate governance and value in Brazil (and in Chile). In A. Chong & F. Silanes (Eds.), *Investor protection and corporate governance: Firm-level evidence across Latin America* (pp. 213–288). Palo Alto: Stanford University Press.
Lipton, M., & Rosenblum, S. (1991). A new system of corporate governance: The quinquennial election of directors. *University of Chicago Law Review, 58*, 187–253.
Nesbitt, S. (1994). Long term rewards from shareholder activism: A study of the Calpers effect. *Journal of Applied Corporate Finance, 6*, 75–80.
Parrino, R., Sias, R., & Starks, L. (2003). Voting with their feet: Institutional ownership changes around forced CEO turnover. *Journal of Financial Economics, 68*, 3–46.
Sarkar, J., & Sarkar, S. (2000). Large shareholder activism in corporate governance in developing countries: Evidence from India. *International Review of Finance, 1*, 161–194.
Silveira, A. (2011). Institutional investors and corporate governance in Brazil. Available at http://ssrn.com/author=443083. Retrieved on 30 May 2013.
Smith, M. (1996). Shareholder activism by institutional investors: Evidence for Calpers. *Journal of Finance, 51*, 227–252.
Wahal, S. (1996). Pension fund activism and firm performance. *Journal of Financial and Quantitative Analysis, 31*, 1–23.
Wohlstetter, C. (1993). Pension fund socialism: Can bureaucrats run the blue chips? *Harvard Business Review, 71*, 78.
Woidtke, T. (2002). Agents watching agents? Evidence from pension fund ownership and firm value. *Journal of Financial Economics, 63*, 99–131.

Corporate Governance of Banks in Transition Countries

Gian Piero Cigna, David Risser, and Hind Sami

Abstract This paper contributes to our understanding of corporate governance in the banking sector by focusing on transition countries. We examine to what extent transitional countries have embraced the wave of new standards introduced by the Basel Committee, the Financial Stability Board or the European Banking Authority. Our analysis focuses on the main governance weaknesses targeted by the new regulatory and governance best practice framework. Questionnaires and interviews cover board composition and functioning, bank's strategy and risk appetite, risk governance, and incentives. The analysis is carried out in 16 countries in six regions. We show that governance practices of banks diverge within and across countries, shaped by different legislations, supervisory modes and governance frameworks. Responses to questionnaires indicate that board composition and functioning is the weakest governance part of the chain. Besides, board independence remains one of the biggest issues. In most cases, the board is also barely involved in setting and monitoring risk appetite. Finally, in most countries compensation is tied to short term business performance rather than to governance values and strategic goals. Overall, the large majority of surveyed banks present an embryonic risk culture and boards have a vast agenda ahead, beginning with strengthening risk management and changing incentives.

This paper is partially built upon the EBRD 2010–2012 Assessment on Corporate Governance of Banks.

G.P. Cigna
European Bank for Reconstruction and Development (EBRD), London, UK
e-mail: CignaG@ebrd.com

D. Risser
Nestor Advisors, London, UK
e-mail: drisser@nestoradvisors.com

H. Sami (✉)
University of Lyon – Lumière Lyon 2 University, Coactis E.A. 4161, Lyon, France
e-mail: hind.sami@univ-lyon2.fr

S. Boubaker and D.K. Nguyen (eds.), *Corporate Governance in Emerging Markets*, CSR, Sustainability, Ethics & Governance, DOI 10.1007/978-3-642-44955-0_21,

1 Introduction

Recent years in the world of finance have been dramatic and turbulent. The existence of the modern financial system appears to be in jeopardy. In August 2009, the International Monetary Fund (IMF) calculated that the total cost of the global financial crisis reached $11.9 trillion, including cash injections into banks, the cost of purchasing toxic assets, guarantees over debt and liquidity support from central banks. That was equivalent to one-fifth of the entire world's annual economic output. This estimate, only partially reflects the aggregate cost of the crisis and the painful effects that are being felt in the real economy. A substantial responsibility for the financial, then economic and now social and political crisis afflicting the world today comes from critical weaknesses in financial institutions and financial markets' governance (see e.g. Mehran et al. 2011).

The financial crisis was a crisis triggered by banks from developed countries. Transition countries were not directly involved and proved rather to be resilient – at least till the end of 2008 – and a source of liquidity and revenues for some international financial groups that would have been otherwise hit more severely. The response to the 2008–2009 financial crisis and the underlying events has been an avalanche of legislations and new corporate governance proposals. In 2010, the Basel Committee on banking supervision updated its principles for enhancing corporate governance to respond to governance failures, in particular to "an insufficient board oversight of senior management, inadequate risk management and unduly complex or opaque bank organisational structures and activities" and, in 2012 revised its core principles for effective banking supervision to include a principle specifically dedicated to corporate governance.

The present paper contributes to our understanding of corporate governance in the banking sector by further examining to what extent transitional countries have embraced this wave of new standards and follow what is now considered as bank governance best practice. Our analysis focuses on the main governance weaknesses targeted by the new regulatory and governance best practice framework. Therefore, the questionnaires typically cover board composition and functioning, board role in setting strategy and risk appetite, risk governance, and incentives. The analysis is carried out in 16 countries in six regions including Central Europe, South-Eastern Europe; Eastern Europe, Central Asia; Russia, and Turkey.

A large and well established literature has shown that governance mechanisms have an influence on banks' overall stability (e.g., Saunders et al. 1990; Gorton and Rosen 1995; Anderson and Fraser 2000; Caprio et al. 2007; Laeven and Levine 2009; Pathan 2009; Aggarwal et al. 2009). Other studies such as Bebchuk and Spamann (2010), DeYoung et al. (forthcoming), Fahlenbrach and Stulz (2011), and Bhattacharyya and Purnanandam (2012) focus on compensation structures in banks and risk taking behavior. Although these studies have clearly established a link between governance and bank stability, none of the studies investigates the influence certain governance characteristics might have on bank performance. In particular, lacking proper board involvement in strategy and risk appetite setting, insufficient board oversight over management, weak management of risks and inappropriate pay structures leading to excessive risk-taking and short-termism were named as significant weaknesses in the way financial institutions were run. This paper contributes to this corporate governance-related body of research by investigating each above mentioned governance aspect. Moreover, policy recommendations are provided where possible, although several issues have no clear answers.

Our analysis shows that governance practices of banks diverge within and across countries, shaped by different legislations, supervisory modes and governance frameworks, but also by widely varying ways of applying the governance framework. Responses to questionnaires and interviews indicate that board composition and functioning is the weakest governance part of the chain in transition countries. If boards are in general of adequate size, with directors considered being qualified enough, two-third of countries surveyed have a non-transparent and weak director nomination process. Also, director independence from management and controlling shareholders remains one of the biggest issues we found.

Overall, the board seems to serve mostly as an administrative and formalistic body. This in turn may partially explain why board's ability to review risk management ranks very low in our survey. The board is also barely involved in setting and monitoring risk appetite in two-third of the cases and in most cases, the board's approach to setting the risk appetite appears to consist solely of regulatory–driven credit. Turkey, Romania and Serbia are among the exceptions backed by a strict regulatory framework.

Regarding compensation, the current crisis has revealed that many banks organised incentives in a way that was inconsistent with their goals. In the majority of countries reviewed, chief risk officer and other senior managers compensation is tied to business performance. In addition, few banks demonstrate initiative and rather follow innovation of the regulatory framework.

The large majority of surveyed banks present an embryonic risk culture and boards have a vast agenda ahead, beginning with strengthening their risk management expertise, elevating the chief risk officer and changing her incentives.

The discussion of governance of banks in transitional countries begins with a look at the special case of banks and the consequences for the regulation and supervision of banks (Sect. 2). The paper then addresses board characteristics, which include the size of the board, the number of outside directors, the experience of the directors, and their other activities (Sect. 3). The next section explores the risk management function looking at the specific role of board in defining the banks' risk appetite and implementing the overall risk strategy (Sect. 4). The next topic -risk governance – explores the regulatory framework, looking at two specific inputs that permit efficient risk management (Sect. 5). Last, the paper focuses on compensation, including trends in compensation packages and recent evidence demonstrating how compensation practices may reduce excess risk (Sect. 6). The paper ends with a conclusion.

2 The Governance of Banks: Context and Methodology of the Study

Corporate governance in banks differs from the corporate governance of non-financial companies. This is due to the nature of the banking business (that is, dealing with money), the need for protection of the weakest party in the chain (that is, the depositor) and the systemic risks that a bank failure might cause.[1] Bank failure might also undermine one of the core elements of the market economy, people's confidence in banks. When depositor confidence is lost in a bank, its whole survival is put in jeopardy, and in turn, that of other interconnected banks as well. The potential externalities mean that the standards expected of corporate governance in a major life company should be in line with those for a major bank.[2]

Other substantial differences between banks and nonfinancial firms can be highlighted. First, the balance sheet of banks presents a much greater inherent opacity. This in turn makes it difficult for outsiders to evaluate the quality of the assets which a bank holds and, therefore, its true financial position (Freixas and Rochet 1998). Second, a bank serves several conflicting interests, from equity holders, to borrowers or depositors and good governance is important for balancing those interests (Bolton et al. 2007). Third, banks are very heavily leveraged, with a maturity mismatch between assets and liabilities. In addition, most of their liabilities are owed to a large number of atomized depositors who have the most to lose from abusive or negligent management. Finally, due to the potential negative externalities of bank failures banks are subject to strict regulation and supervision.

For this purpose, in 2007, jointly with the Organisation for Economic Co-operation and Development (OECD), the Legal Transition Team of the European Bank for Reconstruction and Development (EBRD) identified a number of key challenges affecting banks in *Eurasia* and proposed a set of recommendations to address them. Following the Eurasian experience, in 2009 the Legal Transition Team and the IFC-Global Corporate Governance Forum proposed a set of recommendations to implement sound corporate governance practices in banks *in South East Europe*. Under this background, the 2010–2012 assessment on corporate governance of banks aims at measuring the state of play[3] in the banking sector in the EBRD countries. The assessment examines key benchmarks to ascertain how the

[1] See Adams and Mehran (2003) and Adams (2012) for a discussion of differences between governance of banks in the United States and nonfinancial firms.

[2] A related body of research focuses on market competition and shows that competition is an important stability factor for banks (see e.g. Keeley 1990; Hellmann et al. 2003; Carletti and Hartmann 2003). Yet, we depart from this literature as our analysis follows the Basel approach that itself focuses on internal governance aspects. In addition, the transition countries we surveyed are characterized by relatively weak market competition. Indeed, the size of the top players usually reflects more an oligopolistic market.

[3] I.e., the status, level of approximation of local laws/regulations to international standards, effectiveness of implementation, future outlook, etc.

corporate governance practices in banks are laid down by laws and regulations and, most importantly, how they are implemented and how the overall system works.

More specifically, the assessment is based upon a checklist built on international best practice standards that identifies 43 key corporate governance challenges that banks face. The checklist includes bank-specific issues as well as general corporate governance issues addressed within eight corporate governance areas. These issues are derived from selected international best practice standards (Basel Committee on Banking Supervision 2006, 2010).[4] These issues were detailed in three separate but complementary questionnaires circulated to some among the largest banks in each jurisdiction, regulators, law firms and banking associations (see Exhibit 1.).

When analysing banks, we decided to follow the Basel Committee on Banking Supervision approach and focus on the internal governance aspects. Two main reasons explain this choice. First, the context and aim of this EBRD study, and second the oligopolistic nature of these markets, largely dominated by few top players.

The analysis, covering 60 banks, includes 16 countries in six regions:

- Croatia and Hungary in Central Europe;
- Albania, Bosnia and Herzegovina, Bulgaria, Former Yugoslav Republic (FYR) Macedonia, Romania, and Serbia in South-eastern Europe;
- Armenia, Azerbaijan, Georgia and Moldova in Eastern Europe and the Caucasus;
- Kazakhstan and Tajikistan in Central Asia;
- Russia, and
- Turkey.

In Azerbaijan, Georgia, Kazakhstan, Moldova, Romania, Russia, Serbia and Turkey responses to the questionnaires were complemented by face-to-face interviews where the EBRD assessment team met with bank representatives, lawyers and regulators.

Time constraints coupled with the amount of countries to be assessed limit the number of banks that could be reviewed and therefore banks covered were filtered based on the three criteria:

[4] Best practice sources are the Basel Committee on Banking Supervision (BCBS), and in particular "Enhancing corporate governance for banking organisation", 2006 and "Principles for enhancing corporate governance", 2010. Additional sources were the corporate governance codes of UK (Financial Reporting Council, 2010. The UK Corporate Governance Code), France (Association Française des Entreprises Privées/MEDEF, 2009. Corporate Governance Codes and Principles), Germany (The Government Commission on the German Corporate Governance Code, 2009. German Corporate Governance Code), The Netherlands (The Dutch Corporate Governance Code Monitoring Committee, 2008. and the Nederlandse Vereniging van Banken, 2009. The banking code), the European Bank for Reconstruction and Development; the Institute of International Finance; Organization for Economic Co-operation and Development; the Senior Supervisors Group and the European Commission.

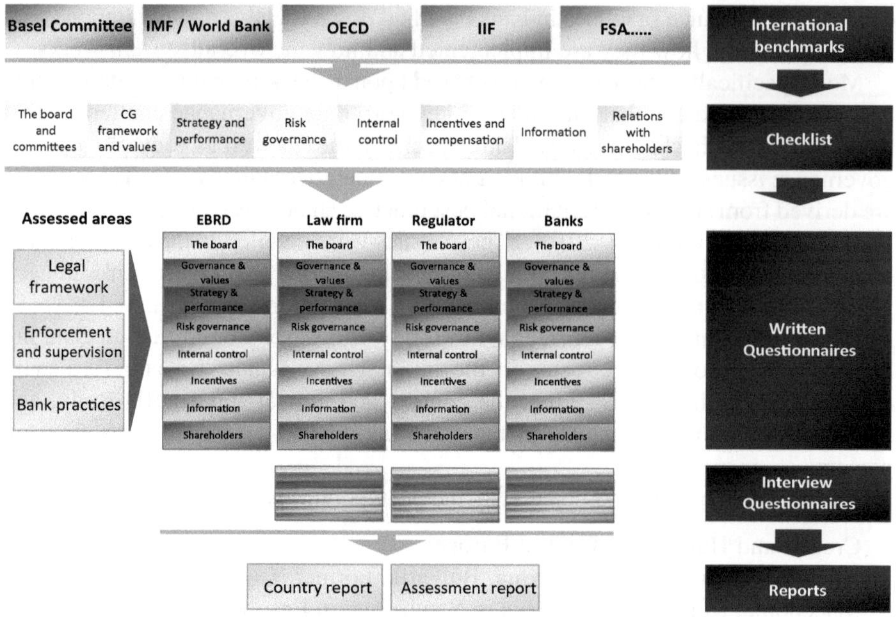

Exhibit 1 Assessment methodology

1. the selected local banks rank among the top five banks of the country, measured by the size of their assets.
2. among the top five banks, selected banks provide sufficient access to adequate information.
3. when possible, banks with EBRD equity participation were selected.

This sample of banks, encompassing both private and listed institutions, was therefore not built on a voluntary basis. The largest banks in each country were reviewed, regardless of their governance quality. This selection method may bias upward the overall results, given larger financial institutions are likely to be more sophisticated and present a better governance framework. We did not notice a major difference between listed and non-listed banks, but as further discussed, foreign-bank ownership is a discriminating factor. One should note that for this work, our analysis mostly reviewed individually the different governance characteristics.

3 Board Composition and Functioning

Numerous studies have focused on the board of directors as the main element that shapes the quality of corporate governance practices (see e.g. Hermalin and Weisbach 2003; Adams and Mehran 2003, 2012; Adams et al. 2010; and Adams 2012).

3.1 Board Structure

Banks – and in general all joint stock companies – can be organised either under a one-or a two-tier governance system. In the unitary system, a single management body (or a board), ideally made of both executive and non-executive directors, is in charge of management, direction and oversight.[5] In the dualistic system, the corporation is managed by a management body composed of executives who are supervised by non-executive directors sitting in the supervisory board. This entity is considered in our study as the board of directors.

Best practices suggest that the roles of chief executive officer and chairperson be separated or that other means be found to provide an appropriate counterbalance to the powers of the executive. In countries with two-tier boards, the roles should be separate by definition, since executives should not sit on supervisory boards. In countries where single-tier boards exist, there is continued discussion on whether the roles of chairperson and chief executive officer should be separated (see Junngmann 2006). The argument toward the one-tier board is that it provides a better understanding of the operational issues at board level and clearer direction. The arguments against are that it is hard for other board members to challenge a powerful chief executive officer who is also chairperson. As a result, the evaluation of board and executive performance might be biased. In the end, the discussion about the effectiveness of corporate governance in one-tier and two-tier board systems is related to the existence of conflicting incentives between the roles of monitor and executor.

The large majority of jurisdictions object of our analysis have a two-tier governance system but in some instances, substantial variations have been introduced.[6] Few countries are offering companies – and sometimes banks – the option to choose between the one-tier and the two-tier systems (see Exhibit 2).[7]

In an ideal two-tier structure, the general shareholders' meeting is in charge of appointing and removing the members of the supervisory board. In turn, the supervisory board should hold supervisory powers over senior management and should be in charge for appointing the management. This structure is followed in Armenia, in both entities in Bosnia Herzegovina, Bulgaria, Croatia, FYR Macedonia, Georgia, Kazakhstan, Romania, Serbia and Tajikistan (see Exhibit 3).

[5] This is the case for Turkey.

[6] For instance, in Russia and Kazakhstan, unlike in typical unitary board systems, boards are not given a broad mandate to manage their company coupled with the power to delegate responsibility as they see fit. Nor are boards just a supervisory body with all executive powers assigned to a management body.

[7] This is the case for Bulgaria and Romania. Here, banks may choose to mirror the corporate governance organization of their parent company and this can foster group coherence and consistency. The review indicates that especially in Romania banks make use of this option so to mirror the corporate governance framework and organization of their parent company.

Exhibit 2 Board structures of banks (Source: EBRD)

Albania	Two-tier (hybrid)
Armenia	Two-tier
Azerbaijan	Two-tier (hybrid)
Bosnia and Herzegovina	Two-tier
Bulgaria	Option one-tier or two-tier
Croatia	Two-tier
FYR Macedonia	Two-tier
Georgia	Two-tier
Hungary	Two-tier (hybrid)
Kazakhstan	Two-tier (hybrid)
Moldova	Two-tier (hybrid)
Romania	Option one-tier or two-tier
Russia	Two-tier (hybrid)
Serbia	Two-tier
Tajikistan	Two-tier
Turkey	One-tier

Instead in Albania, Azerbaijan, Hungary, Moldova and Russia, the default rule established by law is that the members of management board are directly appointed by the general shareholders meeting. This solution is of concern, especially because the jurisdictions under analysis are characterised by concentrated ownership and weak – if any- role of independent directors. Indeed, the question is whether the supervisory board can effectively monitor the management board without having any influence over its appointment and removal. In such cases, the controlling shareholder is in full control of the bank's activities, with little role for the board to provide some objective judgement on the bank's direction.

3.2 Board Size and Competence

A well-sized, trained, professional, and dedicated board is the most effective means to ensure sound bank governance. It is a key contributor to bank performance. Several empirical studies support the idea that large boards can be dysfunctional (Yermack 1996; Eisenberg et al. 1998). It is asserted that "*communication, coordination of tasks, and decision making effectiveness among a large group of people is harder and costlier that in smaller groups*". Further, it has been concluded that when boards get beyond a dozen people, they are also easier for the chief executive officer to control, unless there are powerful and effective board committees. Yermack (1996) provides empirical support for these arguments by showing a negative relation between board size and firm valuation. Contrary to largest banks in Western Europe, banks have relatively small boards. The large majority of boards have less than ten members.

Countries with two tier system	Body in charge of appointing the management
Albania	General Shareholders Meeting
Armenia	Board
Azerbaijan	General Shareholders Meeting
Bosnia and Herzegovina	Board
Bulgaria	Board
Croatia	Board
FYR Macedonia	Board
Georgia	Board
Hungary	General Shareholders Meeting
Kazakhstan	Board
Moldova	General Shareholders Meeting
Romania	Board
Russia	General Shareholders Meeting
Serbia	Board
Tajikistan	Board

Exhibit 3 Authority to appoint the board and management (Source: EBRD)

The next exhibit (Exhibit 4) shows that – on paper – boards are well sized for efficiently discharging their duties and allow adequate participation to all members.

Ideally, the board should also possess, both as individual board members and collectively, appropriate experience and competencies. These qualities should be in line with the bank's strategy, risk appetite and the board's oversight responsibilities.[8]

In all countries, banking regulation includes "fit and proper" requirements for members of the management (but much less for the board), and key officials in the bank. In most cases, the law tends to set forth rigorous qualification criteria for executives (i.e., management board members), while the criteria for non-executives (i.e., supervisory board members and board members committees) are limited. In addition, requirements towards supervisory board and committees' members may not be sufficient to ensure quality supervisory boards in all banks since the implementation of the codes' recommendations is generally voluntary and limited to listed entities (see Exhibit 5). The ultimate warrant for a "fit and proper" board should be the board and its nomination committee itself. However, the quasi-absence of such committees, perceived as barely needed given the ownership structure, limits banks in moving towards better equipped boards.

[8] The board's responsibilities might include finance, accounting, lending, bank operations and payment systems, strategic planning, communications, governance, risk management, internal controls, bank regulation, auditing and compliance.

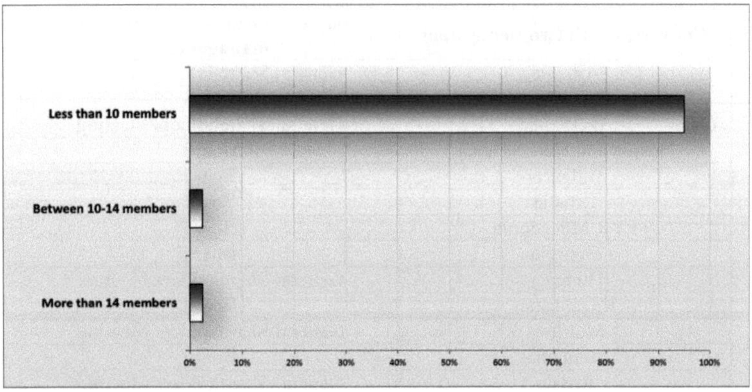

Exhibit 4 Board size (Note: question addressed to selected banks in 16 countries in the EBRD region. Source: EBRD)

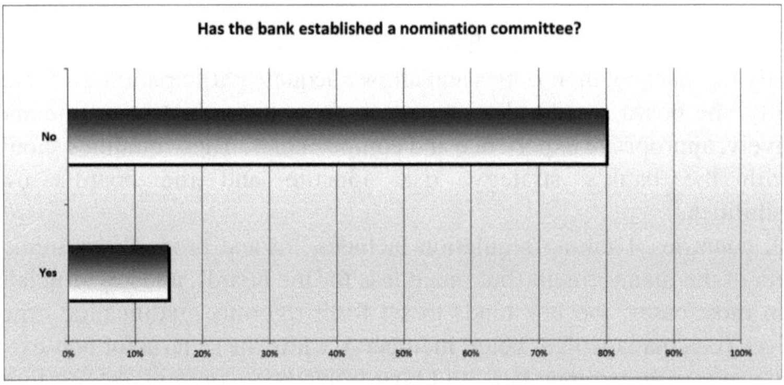

Exhibit 5 Presence of board nomination committees (Note: question addressed to selected banks in 16 countries in the EBRD region. Source: EBRD)

4 Independence

The shift in board composition away from insiders toward independent directors has been one of the most important empirical developments in international corporate governance over the past half century. The literature is filled with studies that show that an increase in the representation of outside directors should improve firm performance because they are more likely than insiders to be strong monitors. In particular, boards consisting of a majority of independent outside directors are more likely to replace poorly performing CEOs (Weisbach 1988), better performance (Rosenstein and Wyatt 1990), and better acquisitions (Byrd and Hickman 1992).

4.1 The Definition of Independent Directors

In practice, none of the banks reviewed reported having truly independent directors on their boards. In some cases, independent directors are confused with "non-executives" and in the majority of countries under analysis the independence is associated with having no ongoing relationship with the bank, not even being director.

In Hungary, due to conflicting legal provisions, the concept of independent directors does not seem to be well developed. The Company Act requires that the majority of members of supervisory board or board of directors (in one tier system) in public companies is independent. The definition of "independence" is fairly comprehensive and includes independence from the executives, as well as from the significant shareholders. The banking law instead only requires that members of the supervisory are not in employment with the bank (i.e. non-executive), except for employee representatives on the board. Further, the independence requirement applies only to public companies while out of eight largest banks in the country only two are public companies.

When looking at the information available online it seems that independence is sometimes confused with the fact that directors are non-executive. In Croatia, the banking law requires all banks to include at least one independent director on the board. However, the law does not provide guidance on its role on the board and on board committees. Now, having only one independent director on the board may not be sufficient in order to bring this "independent judgement" as it may be difficult for one director to speak up or have sufficient stature to convince other directors. The Croatian Corporate Governance Code provides a definition of "independent supervisory board member" but it is not clear whether unlisted banks apply the definition of independence provided by the Code. The Code also recommends that the majority of board members are independent and that board committees are made by a majority of independent board members, but the assessment revealed that these Code's recommendations are generally not complied with.

In Romania, there seems to be some confusion as to the mandatory nature of governance provisions included the company and banking framework. The Law on Commercial Companies requires the appointment of at least one independent non-executive director to all committees established by the board, including the audit committee. Instead, the banking regulation only requires fully non-executive audit committees as well as "independent judgement" from board directors. In practice, some banks had not appointed an independent director that met the independence criteria of company law despite the fact that the bank has established an audit committee.

Turkey, Kazakhstan, and FYR Macedonia appeared to be countries where banks have the most independent board among those revised. However, there are serious doubts about the real independence of boards. In Kazakhstan, the Law on Joint Stock Companies requires that one third of directors be independent and provides a definition of independence which includes independence from management and controlling shareholders. However, the role of independent directors on boards is not entirely clear. On 28 December 2011, the Joint Stock Company Law was deeply revised by the Law on Risk Minimisation which requires, among others, all joint stock companies to have a number of committees chaired by an independent director. This approach is questionable and might not provide the benefits that are hoped by the legislator. While these committees might be appropriate for systemically important banks, they are undoubtedly overburdening small joint stock companies. Moreover, the law still misses to regulate other aspects relating to the board committees (such as functions, reporting lines, etc.), which are key in making sure committees are working properly. As a result, there are many doubts that the law will provide substantial improvements in practice.

In FYR Macedonia, the law provides a definition of independence of board directors and establishes that at least ¼ of board members must be independent. Again, the framework does not stress sufficiently the value and role of independent directors and there is no requirement that independent directors sit on board committees. In Turkey, the corporate governance code issued by the capital markets board requires that one third of directors be independent and provides a definition of independence which includes independence from management and controlling shareholders. However, two of the four banks reviewed do not have independent directors that are both independent from management and majority shareholders. In the other two banks that have independent members, the independent directors account for no more than one third of the board. As in other jurisdictions, it seems that when respondents referred to their "independent" board members they referred in fact to non-executive directors as provided for by banking law and banking regulation.

4.2 *The Role of Independent Directors*

The EBRD survey has shown that regulators do not pose much attention on the role of independent directors and often this role is not fully understood.

In Moldova, the Law on Financial Institutions requires that the majority of the supervisory board is "non-affiliated" to the bank. The new regulation requires that members of the executive board may not be significant shareholders of the bank, nor affiliated to any such shareholder. Yet, the requirement to have independent directors usually applies to the supervisory board and not to the executive board. Executives should not be independent as they have the mandate to implement the strategy endorsed by shareholders.

In Tajikistan, Georgia, Bosnia and Herzegovina and Azerbaijan, there is no requirement for banks to appoint independent directors on the supervisory board.[9]

---

[9] Further, in Azerbaijan, it appeared that the Central Bank has no clear view on the role of independent directors.

In Republika Srpska, the Corporate Governance Standards recommend supervisory boards to include a majority of independent directors. However, listed banks do not publish any corporate governance compliance reports and unlisted banks are not subject to the Standards. In Albania, the law requires the presence of "non-affiliated" directors in the board (steering council), but there is no guidance on their role and no requirement that they should sit in committees.

In practice, while all banks reviewed have created audit committees – as required by law – these do not necessarily include the non-affiliated steering council members. In Bulgaria, the Public Offering of Securities Act requires that one third of the board is comprised of independent directors and gives a definition of non-independent directors. However, the Act applies only to publicly traded companies and most of the largest banks in the country are privately held.

In Armenia, the banking law requires that "all board members must be independent from the management" and the provision has been interpreted in the sense that directors should not be executives (or related to the bank's executives). Instead, the law does not tackle independence from controlling shareholders.

5 Board Role in Setting Strategy and Risk Appetite

5.1 Bank's Strategy

The board's role is to provide entrepreneurial leadership of the company within a framework of prudent and effective controls which enables risk to be assessed and managed. It is generally accepted that the "*job*" of the board is not to take – or to pretend to take – executive decisions, it is to set the overarching policies within which such decisions should be taken and to hold managers accountable for the use of the decision making powers that have been delegated to them (Ladipo et al. 2008).

In this context, the activities ranked at the board's top priorities are the (i) approval of the strategy, (ii) the definition of the budget for pursuing the strategy, (iii) the definition of the risks that the bank can face in attaining the strategy (so called "risk appetite"), and (iv) making sure the management decisions are taken in line with the strategy and within the risk appetite and budget outlined by the board. These key functions are clearly highlighted in the majority of the banks object of this analysis, but there are notable exceptions.

As outlined by the exhibit below, notwithstanding the clear recommendations by international standards that the board should be in charge for setting the strategy of the bank, this practice has not always been formalised in clear rules. This is especially the case for Azerbaijan, Bosnia and Herzegovina, Bulgaria, FYR Macedonia, Georgia, Hungary, Moldova, Romania and Serbia.

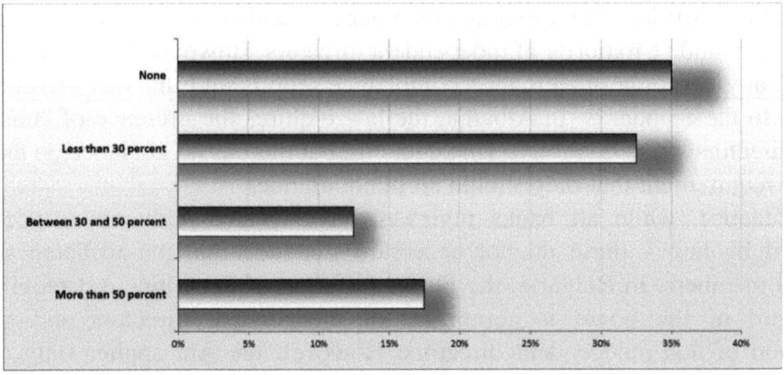

Exhibit 6 What percentage of the board is independent? (Note: question addressed to selected banks in 16 countries in the EBRD region. The definition of independence varies among jurisdictions. Corporate governance codes provide for definitions generally in line with best practices, but their implementation is limited, especially due to the high number of unlisted banks in the region. As illustrated by the chart below, about 35 % of the banks that participating in the EBRD survey declared to have no independent directors on their board. Source: EBRD)

Jurisdiction	Body in charge for approval of the strategy
Albania	Steering Council
Armenia	Supervisory Board
Azerbaijan	General Shareholders Meeting
Federation of Bosnia and Herzegovina	Undetermined
Republika Srpska	Supervisory Board
Bulgaria	One-tier: Board Two-tier: Undetermined
Croatia	Supervisory Board
FYR Macedonia	General shareholders Meeting
Georgia	Undetermined
Hungary	Board of directors
Kazakhstan	Supervisory Board
Moldova	General Shareholders Meeting
Romania	Strategy: Board Budget: General Shareholders Meeting
Russia	Board/General Shareholders Meeting
Serbia	General Shareholders Meeting
Tajikistan	Supervisory Board (undefined for state-owned banks)
Turkey	Board of Directors

Exhibit 7 Authority to approve the bank's strategy (Source: EBRD)

In Azerbaijan and Moldova, the default rule is that the general meeting of shareholders approves the strategy and the budget and, appoints senior management. Moreover, the law does not shed any light in defining the role of the strategic board in the governance structure of the bank. In Serbia, the major banks are all but one, subsidiaries of international banking groups whose boards seem to have a limited role in the development and approval of annual budgets. More specifically, targets are determined by the parent company and the budget is developed by senior executives of subsidiaries through a bottom-up process. In the Federation of Bosnia and Herzegovina, in FYR Macedonia and in Bulgaria[10] the law does not attribute the approval of the strategy and budget to the supervisory board. In contrast, the Republika Srpska has recently adopted a new company law explicitly delegates the approval of the strategy and budget to the supervisory board. This was already the case in Armenia, Hungary, Russia and Turkey. In these countries, boards are legally responsible for approving the strategy of the bank and for monitoring management performance.

Given that the business of banks consists in taking risk, strategy and risk are inextricably linked. While boards of financial institutions do not manage risks, they are expected to play a key role in ensuring that the appropriate systems of risk measures and mitigation are in place – and that they are actually functioning as intended. Bank boards also play a key role in defining their institutions' risk appetite and in balancing the different risk preferences of their various stakeholders; namely customers, employees, bondholders, shareholders and regulators. By defining its risk appetite, banks should arrive at an appropriate balance between uncontrolled innovation and excessive caution. It can guide management on the level of risk permitted and encourage consistency of approach across the bank.

5.2 Risk Appetite

The concept of risk appetite, as a forward looking, top-down process that guides risk taking in various areas of the bank activity is underdeveloped in the large majority of countries in the region.

Only few jurisdictions require banks to go the extra mile and make the effort to develop an autonomous and detailed forwarding looking assessment establishing the level of risk that the bank is prepared to accept. Bulgaria, Croatia and Hungary rank among the very few countries that have embraced the concept of risk appetite (see Exhibit 8).

This "acceptable level of risk" is generally embedded in the bank's strategy or derived from the group's risk appetite. Sometimes the law delegates the strategic decisions regarding risk management to the board, including approving the bank's risk management strategies and policies. In most jurisdictions, the board's approach to setting the risk appetite in their respective institution appears to consist solely of regulatory–driven credit and [sometimes] market risk limits. These limits often change upon management's request. A bottom-up risk appetite approach, driven by front office credit officers is mostly in place. This seems especially important in small economies with significant concentration of economic interests. Without top

[10] In Bulgaria, the banking law does not clearly assign the strategic role for approving the strategy, the budget and key policies to the supervisory board in two-tier system banks. Instead, these responsibilities appear to be delegated to the general meeting of shareholders or senior management.

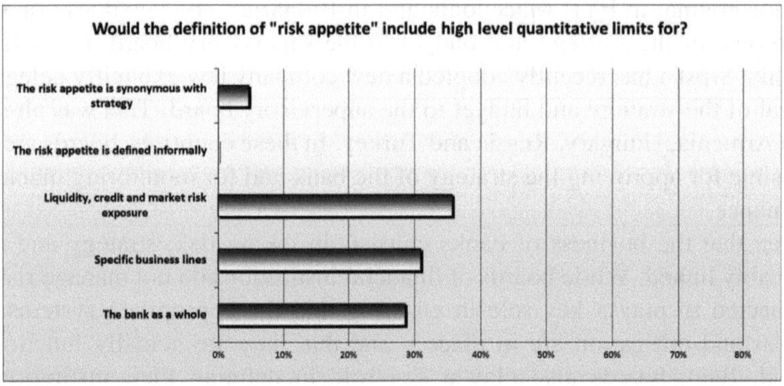

Exhibit 8 Risk appetite. (Note: question addressed to selected banks in 16 countries in the EBRD region. Source: EBRD)

down risk appetite boundaries to which the board is committed, credit will always be driven by the power of local economic interests over credit officers and committees.

In this respect, the assessment highlighted significant weaknesses especially in Azerbaijan, Tajikistan, Russia and Moldova. To be involved, a board needs to be adequately equipped. Too often, the composition of the boards does not include a sufficiently varied and mixed set of skills in order to be able to discuss issues related to risk taking and risk management. While approval of the risk appetite by the board should be part of the strategy and approved by the board, it is mostly prepared and discussed primarily by the management, with limited discussion and challenge at the board level.

The framing process of risk appetite, and more generally, risk governance, are at best addressed by guidelines released by central banks and so far poorly addressed by local banking regulation. This is for example the case of Russia, where the banking regulation does not address in much detail risk governance and risk management in banks. Boards are not explicitly responsible for approving the risk appetite and reviewing the risk profile of their banks. Also the Central Bank of Russia does not require the establishment of one or more management risk committee or the establishment of a risk committee at the level of the board.

6 Risk Governance

If the banks' business is the business of taking risks, then it is clear that risk governance is at the core of banks' good corporate governance. Risk governance is a relatively new term. The concept of "*risk governance*" is distinct from that of risk management. Risk management relates to how risks are identified, assessed and evaluated, controlled, communicated and monitored. Risk governance in turn, refers to an entity's risk culture and focuses on the roles, responsibilities, interactions of all actors that are in charge of ensuring an effective risk management. Risk governance ought to be aligned with the entity's risk appetite. It includes the skills, infrastructure (i.e., organization structure, controls and information systems), and culture deployed as directors exercise their oversight. Good risk governance provides clearly defined accountability, authority, and communication/reporting mechanisms. The Basel Committee recommends banks to have "an effective internal controls system and a risk management function (including a chief risk officer or equivalent) with sufficient authority, stature, independence, resources and access to the board". The importance of the chief risk officer (CRO) and the risk committee is examined in depth by Ellul and Yerramilli (2013).

6.1 Risk Regulatory Framework

Within the last 4 years, the large majority of countries object of our analysis have enacted regulations on risk management thereby offering guidance to banks in setting up their risk management function. As a result, boards are now tasked with the approval of policies and main internal rules for risk management and its governance (for example in Albania, Armenia, Azerbaijan, Bosnia and Herzegovina, Bulgaria, Croatia, FYR Macedonia, Hungary, Turkey). The board is required to monitor the bank's risk profile based on regular reports submitted by the senior management and to ensure that the bank has efficient risk management structure reporting both to the board and senior management.

In some countries such as Azerbaijan or Turkey, regulation sketches further the design of risk governance by requiring banks to set up an executive risk committee comprising members of the executive board and the head of the risk management function. On the contrary, in Tajikistan, there is no mandatory regulation setting the basic requirements on risk governance and risk management systems in banks. The National Bank has adopted a voluntary set of Guidelines on operational risk management in banks and it is assumed that banks follow such guidelines. However, it is not clear how these Guidelines are implemented in practice.

In most countries, the banking framework does not sufficiently highlight the need for the independence of the risk governance function and for the necessary checks and balances to ensure such independence. Ideally, the framework should provide guidance to banks regarding appointment of a chief risk officer (CRO) or equivalent senior executive function. The latter should be responsible for the risk management across the bank and should have direct access to the supervisory board. Instead, the law requires banks to appoint an independent chief risk officer with direct access to the board in few jurisdictions only such as Turkey, Romania or Croatia.

In most cases, there seems to be a perception that the risk function is not an integral part of the business but rather an additional "control". Croatia is an inspiring example as banks are now required to create independent risk management functions reporting to the management board on the bank's risk exposure. The regulation also requires banks to have clear lines of responsibility and communication so to ensure that senior executives have integrated and firm-wide perspective on risk. In Russia, instead the Central Bank does not explicitly require the appointment of a chief risk officer or the independence of the risk management function.

6.2 Risk Committees

It might be beneficial for financial institutions to establish a board-level committee focused on risk and the management of material business risks (as long as this committee does not take away from the board the overall responsibility for risk governance). The principal motivations for establishing such committee are as follows:

- the need to create a forum which is comfortable handling quite "specialised" discussions of risk;
- the need to ease the growing workload of the board and its audit committee; and
- the desire to sharpen the board's focus on longer-term risks.

We witnessed a sharp difference of opinion displayed as to the benefits and disadvantages of such committees. Two main explanations are often advanced against a dedicated risk committee. First, board members often believe that it would unnecessarily increase the workload borne by the non-executive directors due to "possible overlaps between the work done by an audit committee and the work done by a risk committee". Second, and more importantly, they are firmly of the belief that the board as a whole should carry out the kind of upstream risk analysis which is sometimes delegated to risk committees in other banks. We believe that it is hugely important for the board as a whole to retain this function.

On the management level, it is not a mandatory international practice to create senior risk committees. Yet, it is generally recommended that banks have a governance structure that has an integrated and firm-wide perspective on risk drawing on information available from all bank units. This ensures a more secure risk environment allowing a clearer picture of bank's risk profile. Otherwise, organisational "silos" can impede effective sharing of information across the bank and can result in decisions being made in isolation from the rest of the bank. Having a senior executive risk committee or a board committee focusing on risk issues may assist the bank in having a more adequate response to market challenges.

It is important for the effective implementation of enterprise risk management that there is effective high-level sponsorship of risk management. Non-executive directors should be well informed on the material risks facing their business and able to effectively challenge executive management. A specific board level risk committee would provide a clear message that risk management is not a "compliance exercise" within a particular institution.

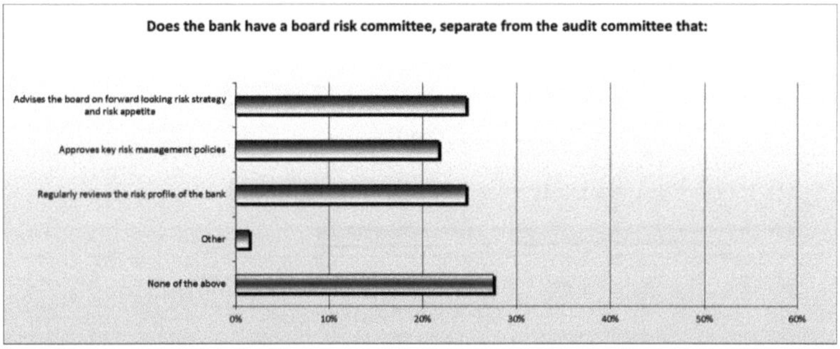

Exhibit 9 Risk committees (Note: question addressed to selected banks in 16 countries in the EBRD region. Source: EBRD)

In a majority of countries (for ex. Albania, Armenia, Azerbaijan, Bosnia and Herzegovina, Croatia, Tajikistan), the banking legislation does not expressly require banks to set up board or executive specific senior risk committees. In Hungary, the banking legislation does not expressly require banks to set up a risk committee at the board level. On the other hand, Recommendation 11/2006 provides that "large organizations may set up risk committees or compliance committees in order to increase efficiency". In Romania banking regulation allows banks to choose whether or not to establish risk committees, and whether to establish such committee at a board or management level.

Practices mirror the regulatory framework (see Exhibits 9 and 10). In Azerbaijan, for example, responses to questionnaires and interviews indicate that none of the three banks reviewed has established a risk committee at the supervisory board level responsible for regularly setting and reviewing the risk profile. This is not necessarily a bad thing in principle, given the small size of the boards. However, it must be noted that the risk management expertise of the board is generally low.

Fortunately, many financial institutions do not limit themselves to regulatory requirements and go beyond in adopting better practices. In Armenia for instance, the banking legislation does not expressly require banks to set up executive risk committees, but at least two banks reviewed have established senior executive risk committees which meet regularly and have an integrated view of all categories of risks and responsibility for the overall risk profile of the bank. We found similar examples in Bosnia and Herzegovina where three fourth of the banks reviewed have set up senior executive risk committees, having an integrated view of all categories of risks and responsibility for the overall risk profile of the bank. All banks have also established Assets and Liability Committees (ALCO) and Credit Committees and a few other executive committees. This is also the case in Croatia, Macedonia, Georgia, or Romania. The main driver for this extra mile step is related to the ownership structure of those banks that belong for many of them to international banking groups.

While boards should be allowed to determine the structure that best suits the needs of their banks, the establishment of a risk committee might ensure that there

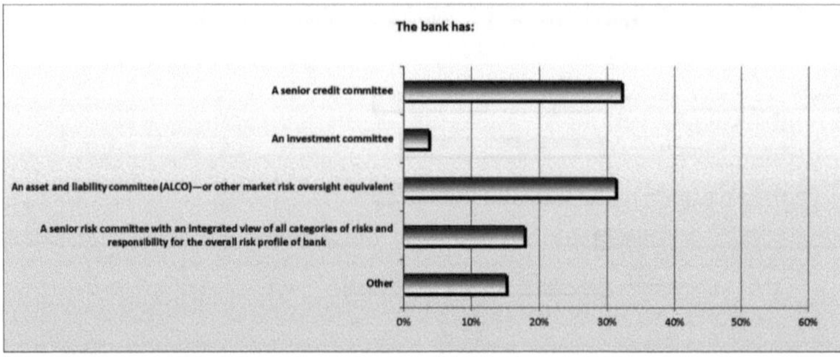

Exhibit 10 Risk committees (Note: question addressed to selected banks in 16 countries in the EBRD region. Source: EBRD)

is adequate focus at board level on risk exposure and future risk strategy, as well as focused accumulation of expertise.

6.3 *Chief Risk Officer*

There is a significant role to be played by senior risk professionals in financial institutions. Recent crises have demonstrated that an independent executive view of the risks facing an organisation is crucial to management taking a balanced view. Keys et al. (2010) find that larger relative power for the chief risk officer implies lower default rates on loans (mortgages and home equity loans) originated by the bank. Chief risk officers are executive managers and as such should report to either the chief executive officer and where appropriate to the chairman of the board. Their day-to-day role is to be adviser and counsellor to the chief executive officer and assist management in better understanding and addressing material risks. It should also be close enough to businesses to understand how they function and to equip operational managers with adequate tools that facilitate decision making.

In order to achieve a significant improvement in the management of risk across the financial services sector, the appropriate qualifications for chief risk officers must include a detailed understanding of the bank's different businesses, the enterprise wide risk management concepts as well as presenting strong quantitative skills. Chief risk officers need to be empowered where necessary to act as the ultimate 'whistle blower' bringing material risks to the attention to the board of directors. In order to have the authority, gravitas and reporting line to the board, chief risk officers should be able to report independently of management to the board.

In the countries under our review, regulation and practices tend to differ, and rather toward the right direction. Indeed, the presence of international banking groups that have themselves adopted good practices positively shape the practices of their subsidiaries.

In many countries such as Albania, Armenia, Croatia, FYR Macedonia, and Serbia, the law and banking regulations do not require banks to appoint a chief risk officer with direct access to the board. Although all banks reviewed reported that they appoint a chief risk officer, the chief risk officer's access to the board varies. In Azerbaijan, often the head of the senior risk committee is considered the bank's chief risk officer. In Bulgaria, the Guiding Principles on Risk Management require banks to appoint a chief risk officer with a bank-wide view of risk. In Turkey, the Regulation on the Internal Systems of Banks requires the establishment of independent risk management functions headed by a chief risk officer with a direct reporting line to the board.

Another important issue which might be affecting risk management objectivity and performance is the risk management function compensation. In particular, the variable payments for banks' executives and senior management should reflect long-term results of the bank, by for example, deferring at least part of such payment. Many banks reported that their chief risk officer is paid based on the same criteria as other senior management. This may jeopardise the objectivity of the chief risk officers in their views on risk management. Best practice recommends that for compliance and risk functions employees the compensation is aligned with the objectives of their functions.

7 Incentives

Compensation practices at large financial institutions are one of the factors that contributed to the financial crisis that began in 2007. High short-term profits led to generous bonus payments to employees and executives without adequate or no regard to the longer-term risks they imposed on their banks. These incentives amplified the excessive risk-taking and left banks with fewer resources to absorb losses as risks materialised. Recent research has investigated the link between banker pay structures and bank performance and risk taking (Fahlenbrach and Stulz 2011; DeYoung et al. forthcoming).

Few – if any – observers believe that compensation was the sole cause of the crisis, nor do they believe that changes limited to compensation practice will be enough to limit the chance of future systemic crises. However, absent such changes, other reforms are likely to be less effective. As a practical matter, most financial institutions have viewed compensation systems as being unrelated to risk management and risk governance. Compensation systems have been designed to incentivise employees to work hard in pursuit of profit and to attract and retain talented employees. Risk management systems have been designed to inform senior management about risk postures and to be an element of risk controls.

The current crisis has revealed that many firms took actions that were inconsistent with their own goals and internally determined risk appetite. Recent research has investigated the link between compensation structures and bank taking and a number of thoughtful reform of banker pay proposals have emerged (Bebchuk and

Spamann 2010; Becht et al. 2011). In April 2009 the Financial Stability Board (FSB) published nine principles for the achievement of sound compensation practices for financial institutions. This framework aims at ensuring effective governance of compensation practices, alignment of compensation with prudent risk taking and effective supervisory oversight and stakeholder engagement in compensation.

The principles also aim to redress deficiencies in compensation practices that contributed to the global financial crisis that began in 2007. Subsequently, in September 2009 the FSB introduced a set of standards that were designed to support the implementation of the principles. These were supplemented in January 2010 by an assessment methodology prepared by the Basel Committee to assist prudential supervisors in taking action.

7.1 Governance of Compensation

The firm's board of directors is called to actively oversee the compensation system's design and operation and ensure that the compensation system is not controlled by the chief executive officer and management team. In this respect, it is essential that board members have expertise in risk management and compensation and the objectivity to be able to exercise proper oversight. In addition, key staff engaged in financial and risk control must be independent, have appropriate authority, and be compensated in a manner that is independent of the business areas they oversee and commensurate with their key role in the firm.

To summarize, effective independence and appropriate authority of such staff are necessary to preserve the integrity of financial and risk management's influence on incentive compensation.

In the majority of countries object of this review,[11] it emerged that banks adopt the same compensation criteria for their chief risk officer as other senior management (see Exhibit 11).

In Bulgaria and Hungary instead banks use different compensation criteria for the chief risk officer or include some other measures to align such remuneration with prudent risk management.

In Hungary, the banking law was recently amended to include detailed rules on remuneration policies and procedures in banks. According to the regulation, the supervisory board is responsible for the oversight of the remuneration for the senior risk and compliance officers, which should be linked to their functions' objectives rather than the performance of the business lines. Accordingly, banks are required to have remuneration policies in line with their internal structure, nature, scope and complexity of their activities. Recommendation 1/2010 on the application of the remuneration policy points out that the control functions (such as risk control,

[11] Albania, Armenia, Azerbaijan, Bosnia, Croatia, FYR Macedonia, Georgia, Moldova, Tajikistan,

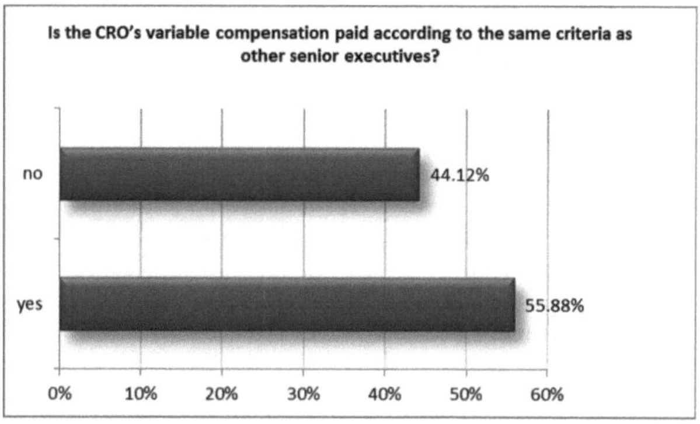

Exhibit 11 CRO compensation (Note: question addressed to selected banks in 16 countries in the EBRD region. Source: EBRD)

compliance and internal audit) should be compensated in accordance with their own objectives and not according to the performance of the business unities they oversee. The general shareholders meeting or supervisory board must approve such policies. The banks reviewed confirmed that their boards adopted bank wide compensation policies and establish the remuneration for the senior executives. Banks reviewed appointed remuneration committees comprising all or a majority of non-executive directors to assist their boards.

Some countries are requiring a distinct remuneration committee. In Bulgaria, in line with the newly adopted ordinance on the requirements for remunerations in banks, all banks have to set up remuneration committees. The remuneration is linked to individual and bank's performance. However, the board and its remuneration committees concentrate on the remuneration of the senior executives and do not design and approve the remuneration system across the bank.

On the other side of the spectrum one can find Russia. It is extremely weak on this matter, both in terms of framework and practices. Boards are not explicitly responsible for compensation practices and are not required to establish remuneration committees. In addition there are no requirements to link compensation to firm and individual performance or to link compensation to risk. Due to the ownership structure of the banks reviewed and their dual board structure, local management does not control its own compensation process which seems to be driven by the shareholders present on the board.

7.2 *Effective Alignment of Compensation with Prudent Risk Taking*

It is essential that compensation take account of the prospective risks and risk outcomes that are already realised on behalf of the firm. Profits and losses of different activities of a financial firm are realized over different periods of time. Variable compensation payments should be deferred accordingly. It is also essential that compensation payout schedules are sensitive to the time horizon of risks.

Exhibit 12 Alignment of compensation to prudent risk management (Note: Question addressed to regulators in 16 countries in the EBRD region. Countries that answered NO to the question are: Albania, Azerbaijan, Bulgaria, Hungary, Romania and Tajikistan. Source: EBRD)

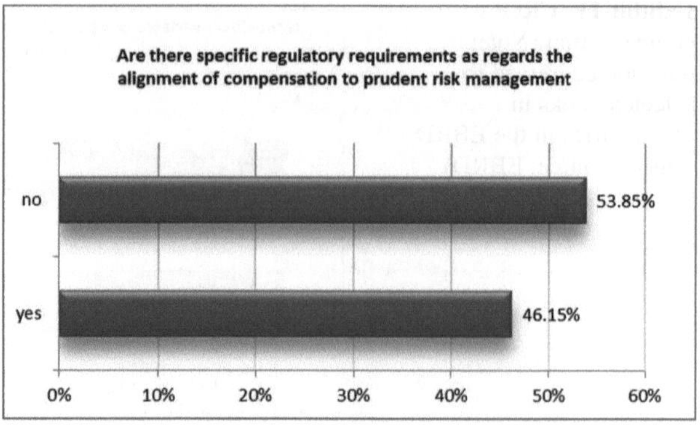

Payments should not be finalized over short periods where risks are realized over long periods. Further, compensation systems should link the variable part to the overall performance of the firm. Finally, the mix of cash, equity and other forms of compensation must be consistent with risk alignment (see Exhibit 12).

As a general matter, national legislations do not provide much guidance in relation to the principles of executive remuneration in banks and, in particular, the need to align compensation with prudent risk management. However, compensation practices do not encourage excessive short-term risk taking (see Exhibit 13).

A first group of countries present a low risk profile from this perspective with a limited variable part. In Albania, Armenia, Azerbaijan, Kazakhstan, Moldova and Tajikistan the variable part of the compensation is generally set at no more than 20–40 % of the annual salary. None of those countries do ask for deferred bonuses. Given the small amount of those bonuses, this point does not constitute an issue.

A second group of countries including countries such as Bulgaria, Croatia, FYR Macedonia, Georgia and Hungary, presents a slightly more risky profile with a variable part amounting to 40–70 % of senior executive's annual compensation. Practices regarding deferral differ. In Bulgaria, Georgia, some banks defer 50 % of such compensation for a couple of years while in Croatia, FYR Macedonia and Hungary there is no deferral at all.

Finally, in Russia, responses to questionnaires and interviews indicate that performance-based variable compensation represents more than 70 % of total compensation for senior executives in four of the banks reviewed. This makes the need for transparent remuneration process and clear link to individual performance and prudent risk management all the more important.

Exhibit 13 Variable compensation (Source: EBRD)

Country	% of the annual salary
Albania	20-40
Armenia	Varies widely
Azerbaijan	< 20
Bosnia and Herzegovina	>20
Bulgaria	Varies widely
Croatia	40-70
FYR Macedonia	40-70
Georgia	40-70
Hungary	70
Kazakhstan	20
Moldova	20-40
Romania	< 50
Russia	> 70
Serbia	n/a
Tajikistan	< 20
Turkey	< 50

7.3 *Effective Supervisory Oversight and Engagement by Stakeholders*

As with any other aspects of risk management and governance, supervisors should include compensation practices in their risk assessment. In turn, banks should disclose clear, comprehensive and timely information about the compensation policies and practices in place to facilitate constructive engagement by all stakeholders. Supervisors should have access to all information they need to evaluate the conformance of practice to prudent risk management. Regulatory framework considerably shapes local practices.

In Albania and Armenia, the law provides no guidance on remuneration practices in banks especially on the need to link compensation to prudent risk management. Here, the regulator does not seem to be entirely aware of banks' remuneration practices despite a monitoring of bank remuneration policies. In Armenia, the law further requires banks to disclose information about payments to the board members and executive management and banks generally comply with the aggregate remuneration paid to their governance bodies or to the entire staff. In Azerbaijan, the amount of remuneration paid out to their senior executives can be found in annual reports. Despite the fact that such reports do not itemise which part represents the variable part, this is a good step towards transparency. The Central Bank of Azerbaijan does not seem to monitor executive remuneration, but it is considering introducing new legislation to link compensation to prudent management and would start monitoring compensation arrangements.

In Bulgaria, banks are required to submit to the regulator their remuneration policies and information about remuneration to bank employees that exceeds certain thresholds established in the ordinance, which is border-line with excessive payment.

In Croatia, all banks reviewed disclose in their annual reports the aggregate amounts of remuneration paid to their governance bodies, but only one bank itemises the payments and indicates the amount of bonus paid, as well as other variables of the compensation. The Central Bank monitors bank remuneration policies and bank practices. In FYR Macedonia, as prescribed by law, banks disclose in their annual reports the aggregated amounts paid to management. The National Bank does not seem aware of banks' remuneration practices and does not regularly monitor the implementation of bank remuneration policies.

In Bosnia and Herzegovina although, not required by law, all banks reviewed disclose in their annual reports the aggregate amounts of remuneration paid to their governance bodies. In the same vein, in Georgia, at least two respondent banks have included in its financial statements the amount of equity based compensation to its top management and the total amounts paid to key management personnel. The National Bank does not monitor remuneration policies and does not seem to have a clear picture of the amount of variable compensation paid to executives. However, responses to interviews indicate that the regulator is currently considering the possibility of including new reporting requirements.

In Republica Srpska, the legal framework contains no guidance on the link between compensation and prudent risk management and responses to questionnaires indicate that the supervisory authority seems to have limited awareness of the banks' compensation practices. The same is in Kazakhstan, Moldova, Russia and Serbia, the regulator does not closely monitor or gather information on banks' remuneration practices. The link between compensation, performance and prudent risk management is not reviewed. Yet, supervisory authorities are also in the process of reviewing compliance with the regulation to ensure more transparency in this area.

In Tajikistan, the Corporate Governance Principles for banks recommend that banks should link their remuneration to corporate governance values, strategic goals and long-term results. However, it does not appear that the National Bank of Tajikistan encourages banks to develop remuneration policies that reflect the mentioned principles and does not closely monitor such policies. The new Commercial Code contains mandatory rules on executive remuneration and the requirement for all joint stock companies to disclose executive compensation. This should tackle the little transparency as regards executive remuneration, even to the supervisory authority. Responses to questionnaires and interviews indicate that boards' involvement in setting compensation policies and practices is not reviewed as part of the supervisory process. In addition it does not appear that remuneration reports are part of the information that is filed with the supervisory authority each year.

8 Conclusions

Banks, due to their specific nature are subject to strict regulation and supervision. Since the financial crisis, they are even under deeper international regulatory pressure. As a result, one would expect a relatively high level of convergence between governance practices of banks within and across countries. Such convergence should theoretically be re-enforced by the influence of international financial institutions that own many local banks. Unfortunately, this does not seem to be the case for a number of banks in transition countries. Indeed, our analysis shows that governance practices of banks diverge, shaped by different legislations, supervisory modes and governance frameworks, but also by widely varying ways of applying the governance framework.

A sound governance framework creates clear and strong lines of accountability. It is considered a good and common practice that management is accountable to the board that is in turn accountable to shareholders. This fundamental line of accountability is not applied the same way. In five countries, management is directly appointed by the general shareholders meeting. The board is not only considerably weakened, but management is de facto aligned with shareholders while, and particularly for banks, it should be aligned with the long term interest of the firm and of its key stakeholders. This feature therefore conditions the governance of financial institutions.

In countries where boards are empowered to play a strategic and governance role, boards are rather well engaged in discussing strategy and budget and in evaluating management performance. The board role in shaping the governance of the institution is more subject to discussion, but one can note the positive impact of foreign parent banks in transferring good practices. Three-fourth of countries with dominant foreign owners ranks in the top half.

Further, if boards tend to be engaged they unfortunately often lack of adequate tools. Indeed, board composition and functioning is the weakest governance part of the chain. If boards are in general of adequate size, with directors considered being qualified enough (mostly thanks to boards of banks belonging to international financial groups), two-third of countries surveyed have a non-transparent and weak director nomination process. As a result, directors are very close to shareholders and management. Director independence from management and controlling shareholders remains one of the biggest issues we found. The concept itself of independence is not fully understood both by banks and by regulators. In several instances, independent directors are confused with "non-executives" and in the majority of countries under analysis the independence is associated with having no ongoing relationship with the bank. It then does not come as a surprise that board contribution and constructive challenge ranks also among the lowest. The picture then provided is that of a board serving mostly as an administrative and formalistic body. The poor support provided by company secretaries not senior enough, the lack of director training and development and the limited board evaluations unfortunately support this view.

The above can partially explain why board's ability to review risk management ranks very low in our survey. Given bank's business, risk governance is core to good governance. Legislation in most countries focuses on the risk management function but not on risk governance aspects. Hence, if all banks claim to have a risk officer, in half of the countries surveyed, the function is not senior enough. The board is also barely involved in setting and monitoring risk appetite in two-third of the cases and in most cases, the board's approach to setting the risk appetite appears to consist solely of regulatory–driven credit and [sometimes] market risk limits. Turkey, Romania and Serbia are among the exceptions, backed by a strict regulatory framework. Board risk committees are far from being common, even for larger and more complex banks. The large majority of surveyed banks present an embryonic risk culture and boards have a vast agenda ahead, beginning with strengthening their risk management expertise, elevating the chief risk officer and changing her incentives.

Alignment is mostly done via compensation. The current crisis has revealed that many banks organised incentives in a way that was inconsistent with their goals. Alignment of compensation with prudent risk-taking is now considered as a good practice. The banks reviewed demonstrate only partial adherence to such good practices. In the majority of countries reviewed, chief risk officer compensation follows the same scheme as for other senior managers and is tied to business performance.

Limited guidance on compensation is provided in the reviewed countries and practices vary considerably. Half of the reviewed countries adopted a rather conservative approach with a variable compensation accounting for less than half of the annual salary. Our survey identified emerging positive practices with few countries that have adopted deferral bonuses. However, few banks demonstrate initiative and rather follow innovation of the regulatory framework.

Regulation drives most of bank disclosures and "Transparency to the market and regulators" is one of our highest ranked item. Most of banks are required to adopt IFRS and the regulator access to information is strong in almost all countries. Disclosure of governance, less subject to strict rules, is weaker, as expected.

With few exceptions, good governance practices are not driven yet by private initiatives and peer pressure but by the ownership of international groups and by voluntarist regulatory actions. Where there's a will there's a way.

References

Adams, B. R. (2012). Governance and the financial crisis. *International Review of Finance,* (special issue on Governance, Policy and the Crisis), *12*(1), 7–38.

Adams, B. R., & Mehran, H. (2003). Is corporate governance different for bank holding companies? *Economic Policy Review, 9*(1), 123–142.

Adams, B. R., & Mehran, H. (2012). Bank board structure and performance: Evidence for large bank holding companies. *Journal of Financial Intermediation, 21*, 243–267.

Adams, B. R., Hermalin, B., & Weisbach, M. (2010). The role of boards of directors in corporate governance: A conceptual framework and survey. *Journal of Economic Literature, 48*(1), 58–107.
Aggarwal, R., Erel, I., Stulz, R., & Williamson, R. (2009). Differences in governance practices between US and foreign firms: Measurement, causes, and consequences. *The Review of Financial Studies, 22*(8), 3131–3169.
Anderson, R. C., & Fraser, D. R. (2000). Corporate control, bank risk taking and the health of the banking industry. *Journal of Banking and Finance, 24*(8), 1383–1398.
Bebchuk, L., & Spamann, H. (2010). Regulating bankers' pay. *Georgetown Law Journal, 98*(2), 247–287.
Becht, M., Bolton, P., & Röell, A. (2011). Why bank governance is different. *Oxford Review of Economic Policy, 27*(3), 437–463.
Bhattacharyya, S., & Purnanandam, A. (2012). *Risk-taking by banks: What did we know and when did we know it?* WP. AFA 2012 Chicago Meetings Paper.
Bolton, P., Freixas, X., & Shapiro, J. (2007). Conflicts of interest, information provision, and competition in the financial services industry. *Journal of Financial Economics, 85*(2), 297–330.
Byrd, J. W., & Hickman, K. A. (1992). Do outside directors monitor managers? Evidence from tender offer bids. *Journal of Financial Economics, 32*, 195–221.
Caprio, G., Laeven, L., & Levine, R. (2007). Governance and bank valuation. *Journal of Financial Intermediation, 16*(4), 584–617.
Carletti, E., & Hartmann, P. (2003). Competition and financial stability: What's special about banking? In P. Mizen (Ed.), *Monetary history, exchange rates and financial markets: Essays in honour of Charles Goodhart* (Vol. 2). Cheltenham: Edward Elgar.
DeYoung, R., Peng, E., & Meng, Y. Executive Compensation and Business Policy Choices at U.S. Commercial Banks. *Journal of Financial and Quantitative Analysis*, forthcoming.
Eisenberg, T., Sundgren, S., & Wells, M. T. (1998). Larger board size and decreasing firm value in small firms. *Journal of Financial Economics, 48*, 35–54.
Ellul, A., & Yerramilli, V. (2013). Stronger risk controls, lower risk: Evidence from U.S. bank holding companies. *The Journal of Finance, 68*, 1757–1803.
Fahlenbrach, R., & Stulz, R. (2011). Bank CEO incentives and the credit crisis. *Journal of Financial Economics, 99*(1), 11–26.
Freixas, X., & Rochet, J.-C. (1998). Fair pricing of deposit insurance. Is it possible? Yes. Is it desirable? No. *Research in Economics, 52*(3), 217–232.
Gorton, G., & Rosen, R. (1995). Corporate control, portfolio choice, and the decline of banking. *The Journal of Finance, 50*(5), 1377–1420.
Hellman, J. S., Jones, G., & Kaufmann, D. (2003). Seize the state, seize the day: State capture and influence in transition economies. *Journal of Comparative Economics, 31*(4), 751–773.
Hermalin, B. E., & Weisbach, M. S. (2003). Boards of Directors as an Endogenously Determined Institution: A survey of the economic literature. *Economic Policy Review, 9*(1), 7–26.
Junngmann, C. (2006). The effectiveness of corporate governance in one-tier and two-tier board systems – Evidence from the UK and Germany. *European Company and Financial Law Review, 3*(4), 426–474.
Keeley, M. (1990). Deposit insurance, risk and market power in banking. *American Economic Review, 80*(5), 1183–1200.
Keys, B. J., Mukherjee, T., Seru, A., & Vig, V. (2010). Did securitization lead to lax screening? Evidence from subprime loans. *Quarterly Journal of Economics, 125*(1), 307–362.
Ladipo, D., Nestor, S., & Risser, D. (2008). *Board profile, structure and practice in large European Banks. A comparative governance study*. London: NestorAdvisors. 2008.
Laeven, L., & Levine, R. (2009). Bank governance, regulation and risk taking. *Journal of Financial Economics, 93*(2), 259–275.

Mehran, H., Morrison, A., & Shapiro, J. (2011). *Corporate governance and banks: What have we learned from the financial crisis*? Federal Reserve Bank of New York Staff Report No. 502, 1–42.
Pathan, S. (2009). Strong boards, CEO power and bank risk-taking. *Journal of Banking and Finance, 33*(7), 1340–1350.
Rosenstein, S., & Wyatt, J. G. (1990). Outside directors, board independence, and shareholder wealth. *Journal of Financial Economics, 26*, 175–191.
Saunders, A., Strock, E., & Travlos, N. (1990). Ownership structure, deregulation, and bank risk taking. *The Journal of Finance, 45*(2), 643–654.
Weisbach, M. S. (1988). Outside directors and CEO turnover. *Journal of Financial Economics, 20*, 431–460.
Yermack, D. (1996). Higher market valuation of companies with a small board of directors. *Journal of Financial Economics, 40*(2), 185–211.

Best Practice Sources

The Basel Committee on Banking Supervision (BCBS). (2006). *Enhancing corporate governance for banking organisation*. Bank for International Settlements, Basel, Switzerland.
The Basel Committee on Banking Supervision (BCBS). (2010). *Principles for enhancing corporate governance*. Bank for International Settlements, Basel, Switzerland.

Part V
Corporate Governance Matters: Lessons from Practitioners

Towards "Shareholder Spring" in the Middle East?

Alissa Amico

Abstract The events witnessed in the Middle East and North Africa (MENA) region over the past 3 years have resulted in a profound questioning of the economic and social pact in some countries of the region. And yet, the role of corporations as main actors of wealth generation and distribution has not been subject to much debate. As a result, corporate governance, as a field of research, has rarely found its place in the discussion on how to improve the productivity and integrity of MENA economies.

Good corporate governance is clearly a part of the solution to both immediate and longer-term challenges of the region. Examining some of the largest companies in the region – listed and state-owned – this chapter seeks to highlight key developments in their governance and demonstrate how these might have impacted their profitability, integrity and the maintenance of the "new pact" between governments and citizens in the region in the wake of the Arab Spring.

The key premise of this chapter is that unlike in other jurisdictions, developments in governance in the MENA region are driven almost entirely by regulation. Despite complaints against corruption, crony capitalism and other decisions taken against shareholders interest, the region has seen virtually no shareholder engagement. And yet, for corporate governance to serve the interest of companies and societies, it cannot be imposed through regulatory requirements only: shareholders, especially large institutional actors, also need to be part of the ongoing debate on the role of corporations in the future of the region.

The opinions expressed in this article do not reflect the official views of the OECD or its member countries.

A. Amico (✉)
Middle East and North Africa Manager, Corporate Affairs Division, OECD, Paris, France
e-mail: alissa.amico@oecd.org

S. Boubaker and D.K. Nguyen (eds.), *Corporate Governance in Emerging Markets*, CSR, Sustainability, Ethics & Governance, DOI 10.1007/978-3-642-44955-0_22,

1 Introduction

The analysis of the recent financial crisis has led to the now widely accepted conclusion that weak corporate governance practices, especially in the banking sector, exacerbated its extent (OECD 2010). One of the main concerns raised is that shareholders, including institutional actors, were at best insufficiently active in key decision-making processes or at worst absent. This observation has motivated a number of important corporate governance reforms in North America and Europe in particular, designed to provide shareholders with more say (e.g. Dodd Frank Act), as well as to encourage them to take advantage of their newly afforded powers. Say-on-pay provisions are now common in a number of countries, and proposals such as additional rights for long-term shareholders are now being seriously considered in several capitals.

While policymakers and corporations in the MENA region have been relatively slow to perceive good corporate governance as a policy priority, this has changed significantly in the new millennium, as countries have moved to introduce corporate governance codes and endow their securities regulators and stock exchanges with powers to enforce existing rules (Amico 2011). During the last few years, we have seen a growing emphasis on compliance with the newly imposed requirements and, in parallel, a further nuancing of laws or regulations where loopholes in companies' adoption of these requirements were noted. At the same time, and despite the demands voiced in the midst of the Arab Spring, shareholders have not been active in exercising their rights and demanding better governance of companies.

1.1 The Economic Face of the Arab Spring

The Arab Spring has now gone through a few seasons and has no end in sight as the conflict in Syria rages on and the situation in Bahrain, Yemen and Lebanon remains fragile. While much has been said about the desire of the Arab people for freedom of expression and political representation, not much – and certainly not enough – has been said about the economic roots of the events. And yet, if we look at the map of these revolts, it is clear that the frustrations on the streets of Tunis, Cairo and Damascus were as much linked to economic inequality and injustice as they were to political misrepresentation and repression of certain groups or ideologies. Many experts on Arab economies consider crony capitalism and a growing socio-economic divide among key sources of the events we have seen transpire.

At the heart of these frustrations is the debate about the role of the state and business elites in the concentration of economic power, be it through monopoly rents, fraudulent procurement procedures or sale of state assets below market prices. Be it state-owned enterprises, private local or foreign companies, no corporate form has escaped the wide-scale criticism of the citizens of Arab countries concerning their role in perpetuating the social divide. Corporations, as much as political groups, are therefore parties to the ongoing debate on the future of the Middle East and North Africa.

And yet, the corporate world has been largely left on the side of the road as popular debate continues to focus on political emancipation and representation, ethnic and religious balances and other issues tightly linked to preserving the delicate social balance in some of these countries. With the exception of Tunisia and Egypt, where companies controlled or suspected to be controlled by the former regime continue to be investigated,[1] the thrust of the efforts to combat corruption, address inequalities and improve the transparency of the decision-making has focused on the public, as opposed to the corporate sector.

Time has come to examine the role of corporations – in particular paying attention to how and in whose interest they are run – in the past and in the future of the Middle East, because as much as some might have been a part of the problem, they are clearly a part of the solution to both immediate and longer-term challenges. While the corporate world of all MENA countries is dominated by small to medium sized, family controlled companies, the focus of future debate in the region should arguably be on larger listed and state-owned enterprises, if not for any other reason than their size.

If investors perceive significant deficits in transparency or quality of reporting or opaque ownership arrangements in these large companies, their appetite for investing in the region would be reduced. The controlled nature of most companies and the low free float in most MENA markets, exacerbate the potential risk for investors in these markets. These concerns, taken into consideration in conjunction with existing investment restrictions for foreign investors in some markets, imply that the quality of governance in the region matters potentially more than in other markets and that consequently, companies with governance structures superior to the "baseline scenario" can potentially obtain significantly higher valuations (ISS 2012).

1.2 Corporate Governance: Evolving Interest in the Region

Corporate governance began seriously attracting the interest of policymakers in the region about a decade ago, and with the turn of the millennia a number of countries in the region, led by Oman and Egypt, have started to introduce corporate governance codes and regulations (Amico 2011). Today, securities regulators have been established in all but one MENA country (i.e. Yemen), and a number of them have dedicated corporate governance expertise or even departments to oversee the implementation of the local governance code and related requirements. For instance, the regulators in Saudi Arabia and Oman have specialised corporate

[1] For results of preliminary investigations carried out in Tunisia, please refer to 2011 Report by the Tunisian Anti-Corruption Commission.

governance departments and other regional regulators have expertise on corporate governance.

Initially, the attention to corporate governance was motivated by a broader interest of MENA governments to align with international standards, especially financial sector standards, in order to establish themselves as financial hubs in the region. As the race to become the region's financial hub between Bahrain, Dubai, Qatar, Saudi Arabia, Turkey and more recently Casablanca intensified, harmonisation of local standards and practices with international benchmarks (e.g. FSB and G20 standards) in financial reporting, governance and related areas was only natural.

Unlike Asia, where the 1997–1998 financial crisis has highlighted governance weaknesses and hence the need to review related standards and practices, the role of crises in underlying the need for better corporate governance in the MENA region has been relatively limited. The explosion of the market bubble in 2006, especially pronounced in the Gulf Cooperation Council (GCC) countries, has certainly reinforced the notion that governance is important. However, the sharp fall of GCC markets – where many households lost their savings[2] – is difficult to attribute to governance failures per se. As during the recent global financial crisis, the absence of effective risk management procedures and the failure to implement other good practices, have contributed to this stock market downturn, but were not a motivating factor.

The interest in corporate governance is increasingly related to the anti-corruption drive insofar as better governance arrangements are increasingly seen as relevant to reducing the opacity of ownership and managerial decision-making. In Egypt for instance, following the revolution, listed companies were required to disclose to the regulator and the exchange their beneficial owners to determine if the latter had any improper ties with political figures under investigation (Abdel Salam 2011). The Egyptian Financial Services Authority is estimated to have received approximately 400 complaints from the public in 2012. In Jordan, the securities regulator is also considering measures to introduce mandatory corporate governance requirements, above and beyond its comply-or-explain corporate governance code, in part with a view to target corruption in listed companies.

The corporate governance debate has over the years shifted from barely looking at the international good practices that would suit the local ownership landscape and customs to reflecting on how governance can actually serve the interests of individual companies and markets. In so doing, securities regulators are increasingly delving into technical issues, beyond governance structures such as the presence of certain board committees or the separation of CEO and Chairman posts. There appears to be a greater emphasis on governance behaviours that can mitigate key risks such as abusive related party transactions, tunneling of assets or

[2] Financial education and "know your customer" rules in these countries are developing and at the time of this crisis banks would not prevent unsophisticated investors from investing their entire savings into the capital market.

concentrated lending practices. Governance, anti-corruption and risk management are increasingly seen as part of the same equation.

Over the years, the interest in governance has shifted and with it, the idea that good governance is a "foreign concept" has dissipated, giving way to recognition that more rigorous governance requirements would address undesirable practices such as tunneling by controlling shareholders, excessive executive compensation or inefficient boards. The impetus to impose such requirements has come principally from securities regulators, stock exchanges and central banks, the latter being pioneers in introducing standards of governance in the region.[3] A number of surveys of governance arrangements of companies in the MENA region demonstrate that banks are on average better governed than other companies, including listed companies (IFC-Hawkamah 2008).

While the banking sector was historically the most regulated in terms of governance practices, policymakers have in recent years broadened their interest to include all types of privately owned (listed and unlisted companies) as well as state-owned enterprises. In a number of countries of the region, separate guidelines were created to address the peculiarities of different types of companies. For instance, Morocco has issued separate governance codes targeting listed companies, family owned companies and SMEs, credit establishments and SOEs. Egypt also has two separate governance codes for SOEs and for privately held companies and other countries of the region are increasingly looking to introduce further granularity in recommendations for different owners, sectors and economic contexts.

1.3 Better Governance of SOEs of Growing Interest

Policymakers across the region are starting to pay a particular attention to governance of state-owned enterprises (SOEs), an issue that only a few years ago was not a subject to a great level of interest. The Dubai debt crisis in 2008–2009 placed a spotlight on the difficulties of a number of high-profile real estate SOEs, prompting a better definition of what is and what is not a state-owned company. Only a few years ago, the term "government-related enterprise" was in common use and creditors of these companies assumed that in providing funding to them, they would benefit from a blanket state guarantee. In the past few years, governments have sought to more clearly define the scope of their ownership. For instance, in October 2012, the government of Abu Dhabi issued new decree requiring state-owned enterprises to apply for explicit sovereign guarantee before issuing debt.

[3] Considering the size of the banking sector in MENA countries and the implications of a potential banking crisis, this sector has historically been the most rigorously regulated, with "fit and proper" requirements for board members, mandated board structures and requirements for review of related party transactions.

There is also a growing interest to review the ownership arrangements for SOEs, considering that historically ownership has been decentralised, resulting in significant variance between standards imposed by different national entities (OECD 2012a). In parallel, concerns in Tunisia and Egypt that privatisations of SOEs were not conducted on an arm's length basis has prompted a re-evaluation of local institutional structures that would facilitate the most transparent and efficient oversight of SOEs. These types of concerns, coupled with pressures on governments to provide employment in the public sector (including through SOEs) have resulted in a significant slowdown in the privatisation drive in the region, with the possible exception of Tunisia and Iraq.

This implies that government ownership in the region is positioned to, at the minimum, stay at its current levels, and potentially even increase in the coming years. Increase in state ownership in the region could be motivated by a number of factors, not least the ongoing establishment of SOEs,[4] the growing orientation of sovereign wealth funds to local capital markets[5] and the fact that governments in the region are continuing to use SOEs key drivers of their industrial and developmental strategies.[6]

Indeed, a number of trends in the region point to a growing appetite for governments to ensure that SOEs are profitable, or if they are loss making, that they fulfill important social objectives.[7] The evidence of this shift in thinking is that in a growing number of jurisdictions, corporate governance guidelines recognise the particularities of SOE governance. A first clear sign of political will to bring state-owned companies to a higher governance standard emanated from Egypt, which introduced a code of corporate governance for SOEs already in 2006. This initiative was followed by similar guidelines in Morocco, followed by Lebanon, Bahrain and most recently the United Arab Emirates. Oversight of SOEs has also been strengthened by endowing state audit institutions with greater powers to conduct pre-audits and operational audits (as opposed to financial audits only).

The Abu Dhabi Accountability Authority, for instance, began in 2012 to provide reporting on its oversight of SOEs and the Moroccan state audit entity (Cour des Comptes) is planning to issue a report specifically dedicated to SOEs this year. This is in fact not a standalone phenomenon as indeed the anti-corruption agenda is gaining importance in SOEs as well. The interest in propriety of SOEs has grown in recent years as part of the general debate facilitated by the Arab Spring on

---

[4] In Morocco for instance, between 2001 and 2010, 350 additional SOEs were established (Semmar 2012).

[5] Although exact figures are unavailable, recent research and discussions with SWFs highlight that their capital allocations have in recent years been re-oriented towards domestic policy objectives, to some extent at the expense of international investments (Invesco 2012).

[6] Refer for example, to the UAE's federal and emirate-level competitiveness strategies.

[7] For instance, the state-owned cotton and weaving companies in Egypt are highly unprofitable, however they are situated in areas where they are the only source of employment and given the labour intensive nature of the industry, successive governments have been reluctant to restructure or privatise them despite their high cost to the public purse.

governance more generally, and more specifically on how and in whose interest state-owned companies are run.

As a result, the SOE anti-corruption agenda is now being addressed by both state audit bodies (SAIs) and national anti-corruption commissions. While state audit bodies in most countries – with notable exceptions of Morocco and Oman – a few years ago had no particular mandate or powers to oversee the efficiency and propriety in SOE operations, this is starting to change. As a general rule, the state audit bodies in the region have the right to review companies where the state has at least a 25 % stake. The anti-corruption commissions are also being vocal about SOE governance practices. Anti-corruption bodies in some countries such as Tunisia are also playing an important role in uncovering cases of corruption in SOEs and in facilitating prosecutions.[8]

1.4 Listed Companies as Ambassadors of "Corporate MENA"

Keeping with the objective to promote the development of local equity and debt markets, policymakers have in parallel continued their work on improving the governance of listed companies. While the motivations behind improving corporate governance in listed companies may have evolved in recent years along with the methods adopted by regulators, the focus on the listed sector has not waned, in part because governments have few mechanisms to impose governance requirements on privately held firms, and in part because listed companies, despite the recent decline in IPOs, continue to be the public face of the region's corporate world.

Over the past decade, the body of regulation for listed companies in the region has grown remarkably – albeit from a relatively low starting point – with the introduction of new corporate and securities laws, tightening of insider trading rules, the emergence of "comply-or-explain" corporate governance codes and the revision of listing requirements. Unlike their private and state-owned peers, listed firms are held to a higher and clear regulatory standard which makes an assessment of their ability to contribute to future development of MENA economies more objective.

Taken as a whole, over 1,400 companies are listed today on regional stock exchanges and already, a number of Gulf-based enterprises such as SABIC and Qatar National Bank feature in Financial Times' Global 500 list, highlighting that some regional champions are emerging on a global scale (Financial Times 2012). Indeed, the popularity of brands such as Emirates Airlines (a large non listed SOE) – are no longer confined to the perimeter of the region. Adding the non-listed hydrocarbon companies to those already part of the FT's list, the presence of the region in the global corporate space is not negligible.

[8] Refer, for instance, to the annual report of the Tunisian Anti-Corruption Commission (2011).

It is perfectly plausible to suggest that regional capital markets are positioned to grow in the next few years. While banks have historically been the primary source of capital for companies in the region, the role of capital markets is positioned to increase as high-growth enterprises find equity financing more attractive than debt. Corporate interest in capital markets might be also encouraged by the decline in the private equity industry in the region, from an estimated $6 billion USD in 2007 to $700 million in 2011 (MENA PE Association 2012). In addition, there is a growing concern that the banking sector may not be in position to satisfy the credit requirements of high growth, entrepreneurial enterprises.

Stock exchanges in the region have reacted to this observation by establishing special listing tiers or regimes for SMEs (Egypt, Dubai, Qatar), lowering free float requirements to address concerns of controlling shareholders, and providing other incentives for listing. So far, the impact of these initiatives has been limited, which is not inconsistent with the success of SME listing tiers globally. In addition, a number of stock exchanges (e.g. NASDAQ Dubai and Bahrain) have recently reviewed their listing requirements. These reviews are guided by exchanges' growing interest to attract small and medium, and family-owned companies through differentiated listing tiers.

Almost every major city in the region, from Dubai, to Amman to Casablanca is trying to establish itself as a financial center. Some markets such as the Casablanca Stock Exchange and the Saudi Tadawul are seeking to attract listings from abroad in order to establish themselves as centers of finance. In the case of the Casablanca Stock Exchange, its future growth model is predicated in a large part on being able to attract listings from other African countries with less developed market infrastructure.

From OECD's work with heads of MENA stock exchanges, it is clear that a number of the region's stock markets are looking for ways to re-invent and re-position themselves through internal governance changes. A number of stock exchanges such as the Kuwait Stock Exchange are looking to follow the path set out by most of the world's largest exchanges, in converting to private companies. Other markets such as the Casablanca Stock Exchange are demutualising in order to broaden its shareholding structure and add dynamism to the market. Boursa Istanbul has recently undergone significant structural changes that saw it established as a state-owned company as opposed to a governmental entity.

1.5 Yet Bourses Lack Dynamism

And yet, all these seemingly positive trends do not for the moment add up to vibrant MENA capital markets, temporarily putting on hold the hope that they might act as an effective mechanism of wealth redistribution in the region. A number of stock markets with potential to attract investment such as Lebanon principally act as a listing venue for government and bank bonds as opposed to a real alternative to corporate financing. Exchanges in countries such as Algeria and Syria are only at their very early stages of development, while certain larger, more liquid markets in the Gulf are restricted for non-GCC investors. Traditionally active markets such as Egypt have suffered from ongoing political instability. New listings are scarce and the turnover of these markets remains low.[9]

Given the family controlled nature of MENA companies, exchanges have faced enormous challenges convincing company owners to look beyond the regulatory requirements to better understand the value of listing to the growth prospects of their companies. Ownership structures are not the only obstacle to listing. The current regional geopolitical challenges, coupled with the global financial crisis, have created a difficult climate for MENA companies and stock markets. In 2012, 12 IPOs were conducted in the region, the vast majority of them in Saudi Arabia (MEED 2013). Although this is an improvement on the 2011 performance which has seen even fewer equity offerings, this lack of activity on the regions' stock exchanges is certainly a cause of concern.[10]

An arguably more alarming trend is that large MENA corporates are shying away from local markets and seeking their primary listings outside the region, primarily on the London Stock Exchange. While the issuance of depository receipts on the London Stock Exchange (LSE) was not uncommon for MENA companies seeking to tap into larger, more liquid pools of institutional capital, the primary listing of shares of Dubai Ports in 2011 on the LSE demonstrates the appetite for large MENA companies to list abroad. Clearly, at least some companies in the region are willing to accept higher governance requirements such as those imposed by the UK Combined Code in order to tap into the liquidity offered by the London Stock Exchange.[11]

Interestingly, this goes against the general trend in today's capital markets whereby companies domiciled in emerging markets raise capital domestically (OECD 2013). A significant part of the answer as to why local companies are listing on foreign stock exchanges is linked to low levels of liquidity in local markets and ineffective price discovery. A recent study demonstrated that indicators of price synchronicity are high by international comparison (World Bank 2011). The quality of price discovery is low especially in companies outside the main benchmark index. Only 12 % of MENA listed companies are currently followed by analysts (Elalfy 2013) and the level of trading in firms not followed is very low.[12]

[9] Overall, the turnover ratio of Arab stock markets stood at 64 % regionally or 17 % excluding Saudi Arabia in 2012 (Elalfy 2013).

[10] With the exception of the Tunis Stock Exchange, which has received a number of listing applications in 2012–2013, relative to the size of the exchange and the activity in neighbouring markets.

[11] Indeed, a recent study demonstrates that there was a reduction in the liquidity (measured by turnover) in MENA markets in the post crisis period and attributed it to poor corporate governance (Farooq et al. 2013).

[12] Some exchanges such as the Egyptian Stock Exchange have de-listed many illiquid firms which were initially lured to list by the fiscal incentives offered to listed firms.

And yet, unlike MENA companies, local investors have generally stayed loyal to local markets. Observing the fluctuations of most markets affected by recent political instability, it appears that beyond short periods of high volatility, capital flight from the stock exchanges in Egypt, Tunisia and other countries has not occurred on a major scale. A key explanation for this phenomenon is that MENA exchanges are characterised almost entirely by controlled companies, whose owners "understand" local circumstances, are less prone to panic and also have much at stake. Seen from this perspective, the relatively low level of foreign investment in the region can be argued to have been beneficial from the perspective of long-term stability of these markets.

1.6 Ownership Characteristics of MENA Markets

The controlled nature of MENA companies is by no means exceptional. Indeed, in markets all over the world (with the notable exception of the US, the UK and Australia) controlling ownership is prevalent and indeed is often said to mitigate key agent-principal problems. While the principal-agency problems are clearly different in controlled companies, a plethora of legal instruments such as the possibility for minority shareholders to approve related party transactions or to elect a director representing them have been developed.

Controlled ownership, somewhat contrary to some Anglo-Saxon corporate governance literature, does not necessarily give rise to governance failures.[13] The controlled nature of MENA companies has generally also meant that short-termist behaviors are less frequent than in jurisdictions with dispersed ownership. While the legal provisions designed to protect minority shareholder rights are perhaps not as developed as in Canada or Sweden where controlled ownership is also the norm, they arguably commensurate with the sophistication of local markets.

Taking away controlled stakes, the free float of MENA listed companies tends to be low, especially when the entire market – beyond a handful of most liquid companies – is considered. This free float tends to be dominated by retail investors: in Saudi Arabia for example, retail investors are estimated to account for approximately 90 % of market turnover, whereas in other markets such as Qatar or Egypt this figure stands at 60–80 % (World Bank 2011). This market structure obviously raises the question of whether MENA listed companies have adequate incentives to adopt good governance practices. In other words, what kind of corporate governance arrangements should they be adopting and in whose interest?

Although concentrated ownership and group structures are extremely common in the region, the possibility of minority shareholder abuse is limited by the fact that

[13] Refer to Hofstetter 2005 for a detailed explanation of benefits of controlled ownership structures.

one-share one-vote rule is the commonly accepted system in the region.[14] Furthermore, shareholder rights are protected via legal provisions enabling minority shareholders to table resolutions at annual shareholder meetings and vote on board appointments individually (not as a slate). More recently, a number of countries have reviewed their legal rules to enable shareholders to participate in company decisions virtually through electronic voting. Only last year, Saudi Arabia and Turkey moved to require all listed companies to enable electronic voting.

Despite these mechanisms, real shareholder engagement remains low, both due to regulatory barriers and to passive investor behavior. Shareholders in the region are not known to "vote with their feet" or to take on large blockholders by launching proxy fights. Only one shareholder-sponsored proposal was put forth in the region in 3 years ending 2012 despite the fact that the rate of negative recommendations by proxy advisors is not particularly low.[15] Inefficiencies in the judicial process effectively also present a barrier to proxy fights and other types of legal action by shareholders, an issue to which a number of regulators such as the Dubai Financial Services Authority (DFSA) and the Qatar Financial Center Regulatory Authority (QFCRA) have reacted to by establishing separate commercial courts.[16]

1.7 Obstacles to Effective Shareholder/Stakeholder Engagement

The absence of the relevant precedents, the lack of a litigation culture, and the lack of institutions such as shareholder associations all act as barriers' to effective exercise of shareholder rights. While shareholders are generally placid, conflicts between large shareholders are beginning to be treated in courts. In Kuwait for instance, the court of cassation has recently settled a long running board dispute in Kuwait's national telecom company, Zain. The court ruled against a member of the ruling family in the case of a board re-shuffle, effectively ending a long-standing dispute that prevented the company from making strategic acquisitions or divestments.[17]

These types of cases remain rare in the region, despite major revisions of legal frameworks regulating the composition of company boards, whereby a number of

[14] In several jurisdictions such as Egypt, Morocco and Tunisia multiple share classes exist, as do non-voting shares.

[15] For instance, according to the Institutional Shareholder Services, their rate of negative recommendations reached 19.8 % in Morocco and 22.2 % in Tunisia in 2012 (ISS 2012).

[16] Interestingly, in 2011, the jurisdiction of DIFC courts was expanded to cover commercial cases arising from disputes between companies not registered in DIFC provided they both agree to this in advance.

[17] In April 2012, the board member in question was voted off the board and was replaced by a Chairman of the Kharafi Group. Upon the request of the said board member, the board was dissolved by the lower court but on appeal, the court ruled that the discrimination lawsuit filed by the member of the royal family alleging an unfair board selection process was unfounded.

MENA jurisdictions have moved to require a percentage of the board to be composed of independent or at least non-executive directors.[18] Evidence from the region continues to point to the fact that practically, independent board members are not able to fulfill their duties due to the presence of powerful executive chairmen or instructions from controlling shareholders. Identifying and nominating independent board members in small jurisdictions such as Oman remains a challenge even conceptually, considering the tribal and social links in corporate circles. To address this issue, better definition of fiduciary and loyalty duties will be necessary in most jurisdictions.

Addressing the representation of key groups other than minority shareholders in the board is subject to an ongoing debate. Employees are generally not represented on boards of regional companies unlike for instance in Germany, and this has been a source of grievance in some countries. In Egypt, for example, employees of state-owned companies can elect some board members and the union representative has the right to attend board meetings. In Algerian companies, employees can sometimes participate in board deliberations and in Morocco, they are consulted on material matters affecting the company. These are, however, relatively isolated examples and given that unions are not permitted in all MENA countries, other mechanisms for fostering the participation of employees and stakeholders in company governance processes might be useful.

1.8 Tougher Enforcement Coming to Town

Improvements in company governance practices in the region can be seen as a by-product of increasingly rigorous corporate and securities laws and regulations, but also the result of a growing threat of enforcement by securities regulators. So far, the region has seen very few large enforcement cases, beyond relatively small penalties given by securities watchdogs or stock exchanges, usually as a result of late or inadequate disclosure. Exceptions to this rule include Egypt and to some extent also Kuwait, where a large number of companies were de-listed over the past few years for failure to disclose the required information (OECD 2012b).

A few high profile enforcement cases in the Gulf have recently raised public interest in securities market regulation. In Saudi Arabia, the legal battle of Algosaibi Group against the Saad Group has been ongoing for a number of years with lawsuits in Saudi Arabia, the United Kingdom, Cayman Islands, Bahrain, and the United States.[19] In the United Arab Emirates, the Damas case was perhaps the

[18] In Saudi Arabia for instance, a third of the board is required to be independent.

[19] It is alleged that Mr Al Sanea of the Saad Group has arranged unauthorised borrowing, provided by over 100 banks and amounting to over $9 billion USD, in the name of the Algosaibi Group. The outcome of the case remains unclear and the regulator has not officially issued any penalties, pending investigation of a committee constituted by the King of Saudi Arabia to look into this matter.

single most prolific enforcement example, where the regulator ordered the controlling shareholders of the famous jewelry and watch retailer to repay the sums embezzled from the company. While the $700,000 USD penalty imposed on the brothers in March 2010 was a first tough stance taken by the Dubai Financial Services Authority, it is relatively "soft" by international standards, especially considering that the application of most of this penalty was actually suspended.[20]

Such cases demonstrate that at least some regulators and stock exchanges in the region are "growing teeth". The Saudi Capital Market Authority is perhaps the most rigorous in the region in publishing its enforcement actions, which in 2011 exceeded 300 cases against listed companies, most of them related to corporate governance breaches, particularly the failure to disclose market-sensitive information. The Egyptian and Tunisian security regulators have also issued many penalties in recent years and the level of public scrutiny has grown.

A key question is whether this "regulatory compliance" approach to corporate governance is effectively sufficient to achieve the sought after corporate governance outcomes. With regulatory forbearance being the only threat, and in the absence of other real incentives, what can we realistically expect of companies? Often, the answer in the region, and indeed elsewhere, has been for companies to tick the boxes that the regulator has requested. With this approach, "governance on paper" has arrived, but "governance in spirit" is still missing in many, if not most firms of the region.

1.9 The Corporate Governance Equilibrium

The question of incentives for corporations to adopt better governance practices requires us to revisit the equilibrium theory. Transposing the concept of equilibrium to the corporate governance debate begs the question of incentives for better corporate governance. Theoretically, incentives that companies face to raise the standards of their governance can be generally categorized as supply-side incentives arising from regulatory requirements, and demand-side incentives arising from investor expectations. In the MENA region, the significant governance advances accomplished in the past 5 years have been driven almost exclusively by regulatory action.

The initially voluntary governance standards recommended were in a number of cases converted to comply-or-explain codes and some requirements were made mandatory with time. Egypt and Saudi Arabia are both examples of gradual regulatory tightening, resulting in growing awareness and sophistication of governance arrangements, especially among listed companies. The listing requirements in Egypt were tightened in recent years by virtue of the integration of key provisions

[20] On the other hand, the governance breaches that this penalty intended to address were severe. The Abdullah brothers used the accounts and goods of this company as their personal assets, despite the fact that the holding company under which it operated was listed.

of the corporate governance code in them. In Saudi Arabia, the Capital Market Authority has been revising corporate governance standards through regular circulars aiming to address issues of priority, in addition to those already covered by the code.

While the quality of regulation and supervision has had a visible impact on the quality of governance practices of firms, the investment and asset management community has not been a party to the corporate governance debate in the region. A number of explanations can be advanced to explain this phenomenon. First, the weight of investment funds in the region's capital markets is incomparable to their presence in European or North American markets. In the United States, institutional investors are estimated to hold over half of the total value of US public equities and 73 % of the equity of the 1,000 largest US corporations (Conference Board 2010). For the moment, MENA countries host less than 900 privately managed funds with approximately $67 billion USD of assets under management (World Bank 2010).

The development of insurance, pension and mutual funds in the region is expected to raise their weight in the capital markets, especially if regulations limiting their exposure to capital markets are revised. Likewise, foreign institutional investors typically do not allocate much of their portfolios to the region and hence have a limited impact on creating a corporate governance culture in the region. Going forward, domestic and foreign institutional investors are positioned to increase their participation in local stock markets and consequently, affect the governance debate.

1.10 Attracting Institutional Capital to the Region

With an increasing proportion of their assets allocated to emerging markets, MENA capital markets stand much to gain by positioning themselves competitively. If we consider only OECD-based institutional investors, with an estimated $65 trillion USD under management, they clearly could be important players in the region in the long term. Discussions with large institutional investors and asset managers demonstrate however, that the region does not receive the allocations that would be in line with its economic contribution to global GDP. This is attributable to the fact that MENA listed companies provide limited disclosure and most of them are not covered by analysts.

Given this limited understanding of MENA companies, large foreign investors tend to invest in the region through index products. Only Morocco and Egypt have been included in the emerging markets category by MSCI and other index providers, while other markets in the region are categorised as frontier markets and hence receive an even smaller portion of international investment portfolios that increasingly follow index-tracking strategies. Qatar and the UAE have been seeking an upgrade to the emerging markets category and the MSCI granted this request in

2013, however it is not clear whether the upgrade will have a significant effect on foreign capital inflows.[21]

As a mechanism to attract index investors, a number of markets in the region such as Abu Dhabi have launched exchange-traded funds (ETFs) to provide investors products which mirror the composition of local markets. The launch of ESG indices is another example of measures introduced to lure institutional investors to the region. The proliferation of indices that aggregate governance with other variables in order to select "best" performing companies has arguably not achieved its objectives and index providers no longer draw a positive relation between company performance and index selection criteria. It is questionable whether these products and strategies will bring greater institutional capital to the region.[22]

Until sufficient incentives are found to draw additional institutional capital to the region, retail investors will remain dominant shareholders in the region. McKinsey estimates that MENA households hold $2.7 trillion USD of assets, of which only 14 % are invested in fixed income and 18 % in equities (McKinsey 2011). While these figures illustrate the potential growth and influence of retail investors in MENA markets, they also highlight that unless savings of MENA households are channeled to capital markets through institutional funds, the levels of investor engagement might not increase given that retail investors (unless they possess sizeable stakes) can rarely influence governance processes in companies.

While small private investors can technically lodge complaints with regulatory bodies, regulators in the region are generally not empowered to launch derivative suits on behalf of investors or to support class actions.[23] Minority shareholders can also complain directly to companies which increasingly have investor relations departments and expertise to deal with the general public. However, and as elsewhere in the world, the real power of small retail investors to improve governance is insufficient in controlled companies. Indeed, their behavior might not be so dissimilar to banks engaging in "name lending" in that they might be tempted to "bet" on the success of the controlling shareholder based on family reputation or proximity to the elites. This strategy has proven financially lucrative in other markets

[21] A study conducted by the DIFC in 2012 shows that a change in market classification of the UAE and Qatar would not have much impact on capital flows to these markets (DIFC 2012). Other studies estimate that if Qatar and the UAE are upgraded, they can be expected to receive combined inflows of up to $5.4 billion out of the $380 billion USD invested in emerging markets funds (Healey 2011).

[22] Instead, academic studies suggest that institutional quality, investment restrictions and the level of bilateral trade are important variables to address in order to increase foreign portfolio investment (Abid and Bahloul 2011).

[23] That said, they have a number of alternative mechanisms for addressing shareholder rights infringements. For instance, the new Kuwait Companies Law issued in January 2013 allows the Ministry of Commerce and Industry, responsible for overseeing compliance with the Law, to appoint an external auditor or convene AGMs to repair any perceived weaknesses.

where political connections are shown to contribute to as much as 20 % of firm valuations.[24]

In summary, it is unclear whether MENA investors have either the incentive or the opportunity to engage with investee companies. Little information is available on investor behavior in the MENA region. This is unsurprising because unlike their counterparts in other countries, institutional investors in the region do not have a duty to disclose the nature of their voting policy or their voting results. It is plausible that large MENA investors, sovereign or private, do take into consideration governance characteristics of firms that they invest in. This would particularly be the case for private investors in state-owned firms, who would want to ensure adequate board representation and ability to affect key corporate decisions.

1.11 The Role of Large Investors

In the absence of developed mutual, pension and insurance fund industry, sovereign and private funds have a leadership role to play. Sovereign funds in the region already have large exposures to local capital markets and were estimated to have stakes in over 130 listed companies in GCC (Markaz 2008). This estimate can be revised upwards given the SWFs' domestic investment orientation in recent years (Invesco 2012). Private players such as the Saudi Kingdom Holding (with estimated $25 billion USD of assets under management) can also have enormous potential impact on the operation of MENA markets. Family offices is another category of investors with significant potential and a number of them already screen their investments according to governance criteria (e.g. SEDCO in Saudi Arabia).

These domestic investors, coupled with foreign institutional investors, collectively hold the power necessary to make MENA markets more attractive for themselves and for others. Although foreign investors currently hold small stakes in MENA companies, it is plausible to suggest that they can be convinced to increase the level of their investments, especially if greater disclosure was available beyond a handful of large listed companies in each of the markets. The development of electronic disclosure platforms such as the Tadawulaty platform in Saudi Arabia or the Public Disclosure Platform in Turkey will increase the availability and ease of access to key corporate information. At the same time, the introduction of Extensive Business Reporting Language (XBRL)[25] in United Arab Emirates and Saudi Arabia is also expected to facilitate analyst coverage of MENA companies.

[24] Refer, for example, to Fisman (2001) who demonstrates using the announcements concerning Suharto's health that in the period studied, over 20 % of the value of Indonesian firms was derived from political connections.

[25] XBRL allows the tagging of financial data and information reported by companies in order to allow comparisons between companies by analysts and potential investors. For additional information on the benefits of XBRL, please refer to: http://www.xbrl.org.

Fundamentally, these measures can only be as successful as the quality of the underlying corporate disclosure. While it has been improving, with the IFRS now being a common standard for listed companies (or banks and financial institutions at the minimum), some gaps remain particularly in the area of disclosure of related party transactions and beneficial ownership. For example, BATELCO, the national Bahraini telecom company, does not disclose its beneficial shareholders, indicating that 20 % of its equity is held by an owner in Cayman Islands. Obtaining information on beneficial owners of MENA companies remains a challenge and further policy measures are required to address this gap, beyond the existing standards requiring ownership disclosure for stakes exceeding 5 %.

These types of challenges need to be treated in dialogue between the investment management community on the one hand, and securities regulators and stock exchanges on the other. A precondition to the effectiveness of this dialogue is a robust discussion among large investors in the region and with their global counterparts. So far, a fundamental challenge to effective investor activism in the region is that it has no platform and therefore no coherent voice. And yet, experiences from investor collaboration experiments demonstrate clear benefits in terms of sharing costs of monitoring.

Investors in the region, whether local or foreign, could explore and leverage successful models of institutional investor coordination existing in the Netherlands (Eumedion), Australia (ACSI) or Switzerland (Ethos) to spread monitoring and engagement costs and to amplify their voice.[26] Likewise, launching investor associations might be effective in boosting levels of shareholder engagement. For the moment, no country in the region has a functioning shareholder association.

Another measure that could be complementary to such investor engagement is to require large institutional investors to disclose their voting record, or at least their voting policy, so as to ensure that they are indeed acting in the best interest of their ultimate beneficiaries. This is currently not required in the region whereas it is a common obligation in other countries. For example, in Chile, the sectoral regulator (i.e. the Pension Superintendence) can request information related to funds' position on issues such as board elections. In the United States, the Securities and Exchange Commission requires mutual funds adopt written policies on proxy voting.

Naturally, introducing such reporting requirements implies that institutional investors and their asset managers must have the capacity to monitor the governance of their investee companies. Further work on introducing such competencies in investment funds and their asset managers would be required. That said, placing further reporting requirements on institutional investors in MENA markets might be useful to understanding their position in the market and their role as change

[26] The risk of potential free riding is addressed by virtue of the structure of these organisations which help to keep the cost of engagement down while maximizing shareholder voice. It would still make sense for some large investors to do the necessary due diligence on some of their investee companies as it would give them a source of competitive advantage.

agents. Such requirements would enable a better understanding of investor experiences and would be useful in the context of a broader global debate on the role of large institutional investors in corporate governance.

A number of recent research studies point to the fact that institutional investors in developed markets such as UK and US have failed to live up to expectations of acting as stewards of assets they were entrusted with and that the incentives they have favour increasing size under management and asset churning as opposed as careful selection of companies based on their performance and risk profile (Gilson and Gordon 2013). Although these issues are not yet relevant in the MENA region, they are important to consider as the institutional investor industry develops in the region.

Requirements on local institutional investors to disclose their voting policy and their voting record in shareholder meetings will be increasingly beneficial when they become sufficiently large to make an impact in the market. In the interim, pilot projects aimed at introducing such disclosure requirements in government pension funds may demonstrate the potential impact of this measure. This piecemeal approach may be more realistic and hence preferential to initiatives that would seek to subscribe local funds – private or sovereign – to a set of single stewardship requirements such as the UK Stewardship Code. In particular, requiring large domestic institutional investors such as SWFs to disclose their voting policy would not be palatable.

While putting excessive hope in the hands of institutional investors may not be realistic in light of their recent behavior during the financial crisis (OECD 2012, 2013; Heineman and Davies 2011), it would be difficult to stimulate companies' interest to adopt better corporate governance practices exclusively via regulatory pressure. Market expectations need to play a role. If shares of badly governed companies were actually trading at a discount, and if large investors voted with their feet when they detected governance abuses, the "corporate governance equilibrium" in the region might become more balanced. A key question therefore is how can large private and sovereign investors be persuaded that considering governance in investment decisions is profitable.

1.12 Concluding Thoughts

The suggestions advanced in this paper are intended to address the demand-side of the corporate governance equilibrium. This equilibrium is important for a number of reasons. First, regulatory forbearance can only be as effective as the quality of enforcement and it might result in changes in governance form as opposed to culture. Companies might move to introduce audit committees and even populate them with independent directors but if all board members know that the Chairman makes the final decisions, the sought change in the governance behavior would not be achieved.

Engaging investors is necessary to target corporate behaviour as opposed to governance formalities. Today, it is unheard of for a general shareholder assembly of a MENA company to vote against a remuneration policy or to reject a board candidate. It is equally rare for investors to initiate proxy fights. As the complacency before the outbreak of the global financial crisis has aptly demonstrated, this is not necessarily an indication of the house being in order but more likely a sign that nobody is home to do anything about it. Greater shareholder activism and collaboration is necessary to address this vacuum and it is in the interest of existing local and foreign investors in MENA markets.

Regulators will have their side of the bargain to uphold by ensuring that at the minimum, companies do provide adequate level and quality of disclosure. Instances where large listed companies release their annual reports after the institutional investors' deadline need to be avoided. At the same time, regulators might wish to carefully consider the role of new products such as exchange traded funds and ESG indices that might look attractive but in the end might detract the focus away from corporate governance fundamentals at the company level. After all, it is important to recognise that investors may judge the overall market to be as strong as its weakest link.

But the buck cannot stop with the securities watchdogs, central banks and stock exchanges. They have already started to fulfill their side of the bargain. The ball is now in the court of large investors – sovereign wealth funds, family management offices, pension and insurance funds and their asset managers – to create a demand for better governed, transparent companies. This is a task hefty enough that its costs are prohibitive individually but profitable when undertaken collectively. When investor collaboration and engagement begins, other smaller investors might be tempted to "jump on the bandwagon" and shareholder spring might just blossom in the MENA region.

References

Abdel Salam, M. (2011). *Presentation to the taskforce of MENA stock exchanges for corporate governance*. 5 July 2011, Paris, France.

Abid, F., & Bahloul, S. (2011). Selected MENA countries' attractiveness to G7 investors. *Economic Modelling, 28*, 2197–2207.

Amico, A. (2011). *Second corporate governance wave in the Middle East and North Africa*. In OECD Financial Market Trends.

Conference Board. (2010). *Institutional investment report: Trends in asset allocation and portfolio composition*. New York: Conference Board.

DIFC (2012) From frontier to emerging: Does market reclassification matter? By Dr. Nasser Saidi, Aathira Prasad & Vineeth Naik. *Economic Note* No. 19.

Elalfy, A. H. (2013). *The regional market: Overview and priorities*. Presentation to the annual conference of the Arab federation of exchanges, Mubasher, Muscat, Oman, 4 Mar 2013.

Farooq, O., Derabi, M., & Naciri, M. (2013). Corporate governance and liquidity: Pre- and post-crisis analysis from the MENA region. *Review of Middle East Economics and Finance, 8*(3), 1–19.

Financial Times. (2012). FT global 500. Accessed http://www.ft.com/intl/companies/ft500, 15 Mar 2013.

Fisman, R. (2001). Estimating the value of political connections. *American Economic Review, 91*, 1095–1102.
Gilson, R. J., & Gordon, J. N. (2013). The agency costs of agency capitalism: Activist investors and revaluation of governance rights. *Columbia Law Review, 113*, 863–928.
Healey, R. (2011). *Trading in the Middle East: The road to Mecca.* Report by Tabb Group.
Heineman, B., & Davies, S. (2011). *Are institutional investors part of the problem or part of the solution?* Millstein Center for Corporate Governance and Performance. Washington.
Hofstetter, K. (2005). *One size does not fit all: Corporate governance for "controlled companies"*. Revised Draft, Harvard Law School.
Institutional Shareholder Services. (2012). *MENA region governance: Analysing the proxy.* Presented by Subodh Mishra, Vice President & Head of Governance Exchange on 22 June 2012.
International Finance Corporation-Hawkamah. (2008). *Corporate governance survey of listed companies and banks across the Middle East and North Africa.* Washington, DC: International Finance Corporation.
Invesco. (2012). Invesco Middle East asset management study. http://www.imeams.com/downloads/IMEAMS_2013_English.pdf
Markaz. (2008). *The golden portfolio: Reach of sovereign wealth funds in the GCC.* Kuwait Financial Centre.
McKinsey. (2011). *The emerging equity gap: Growth and stability in the new investor landscape.* http://www.mckinsey.com/insights/global_capital_markets/emerging_equity_gap
MEED. (2013). *Middle east floatations bounce back in 2012.* 10 Jan 2013.
MENA Private Equity Association. (2012). *Private equity and venture capital report annual report.* http://www.menapea.com/research-association.php
OECD. (2010). *Corporate governance and the financial crisis: Conclusions and emerging good practices to enhance the implementation of the principles.* Paris: OECD.
OECD. (2012). *The role of institutional investors in promoting good corporate governance.*
OECD. (2012a). *Towards new arrangements for state wnership in the Middle East and North Africa.* Paris: OECD.
OECD. (2012b). *The role of MENA stock exchanges in corporate governance.* Paris: OECD.
OECD. (2013). Institutional investors as owners: Who are they and what do they do? Working Paper. http://www.oecd-ilibrary.org/governance/institutional-investors-as-owners_5k3v1dvmfk42-en.
Semmar, A. (2012). Corporate governance of state-owned enterprises in Morocco: Evolution and perspectives. In *OECD, Towards New Arrangements for State Ownership in the Middle East and North Africa.* OECD Publishing.
Tunisian Anti-Corruption Commission. (2011). *Report of the National Investigation Commission on Corruption and Misappropriation.*
World Bank. (2010). *Investment funds in MENA. Chapter in the MENA financial flagship report.* Co-authored by Willam Mako, & Diego Sourrouille.
World Bank. (2011). *Financial access and stability: A roadmap for the Middle East and North Africa.* Washington, DC.

Challenges for Corporate Governance at Microfinance Institutions

Stephan Hartenstein

Abstract The chapter discusses corporate governance issues for microfinance institutions (MFIs). The importance of the topic lies in the fact that many MFIs have experienced huge difficulties because of gaps in their corporate governance systems. Since MFIs can play an important role in a country's economy, avoiding or overcoming these difficulties is not only important to them but also to the economies they are part of. The objectives of this chapter are to provide a well-structured basis for discussing governance issues at MFIs and to suggest guidelines for the establishment of corporate governance solutions in MFIs. The chapter is based on related case studies.

1 Introduction

MFIs are usually started as NGOs or small cooperatives by visionary individuals. Many attribute success to strong growth rates in business and staff; however, business development is not always adequately reflected and supported by the development of internal structures, processes and control measures. In quite a few MFIs, the lack of connection between business success and organisational strength has led to significant failures and losses. This chapter analyses corporate governance problems that have been observed and provides a new and enhanced structure for the development of appropriate solutions.

The above mentioned disconnect between business and organisational structure is avoidable. Research shows that strong boards can play a pivotal role in preventing such issues or turning around an MFI in distress[1] and regulators,

[1] See, for example Microfinance Banana Skins – 2012 The CSFI survey of microfinance risk, where Corporate Governance and related topics, like risk management, are presented as top risks

S. Hartenstein (✉)
NomoRisk GmbH, Frankfurt, Germany
e-mail: hartenstein@nomorisk.com

S. Boubaker and D.K. Nguyen (eds.), *Corporate Governance in Emerging Markets*, CSR, Sustainability, Ethics & Governance, DOI 10.1007/978-3-642-44955-0_23,

investors and other stakeholders are placing more and more emphasis on strengthening corporate governance at MFIs and provide support to develop and implement adequate solutions.

In particular, MFIs transitioning to licensed financial institutions are the target clients for the discussions presented here. These institutions often find themselves under severe pressure to manage a metamorphosis to more formalized institutions and face constant scrutiny from regulators and investors – who both insist on solid corporate governance structures.

The topic is still equally valid for many other MFIs. For example, MFIs facing competition, MFIs with difficulties to grow their business or those who have insufficient access to financings may find it useful to review and develop further their governance systems to overcome these challenges. By following the suggestions provided, these MFIs will be able to re-design their corporate governance system as necessary to deal with such challenges successfully or as part of a successful turn-around.

Many of the discussions in this chapter seem comparable to corporate governance discussions held for larger and mature financial institutions operating in developing economies. The reasons for this are that

- MFIs **are** financial institutions and therefore many of the organizational elements found in other financial institutions, like risk management or board supervision, provide useful and necessary support at MFI's, too;
- Regulators and investors take orientation at international standards in financial markets and therefore expectations are developed for MFIs, which come close to expectations related to other financial institutions;
- MFIs combine social, development and commercial objectives as part of a double-bottom-line. This does not make them immune to many of the risks faced by financial institutions.[2] In fact this expanded array of objectives can make governance at MFIs even more demanding than in financial institutions purely focused on profit.

All of the above calls for MFIs to develop governance solutions of the same standards as those needed for conventional financial institutions.

The approach taken in this chapter is to discuss the elements for an MFI's corporate governance system, which cover all aspects of corporate governance in a financial institution and which on top of that take the specific challenges and needs of MFIs and related stakeholders into consideration. Among the MFIs

to MFIs. Also: "Taking the good from the bad in Microfinance: Lessons learned from failed experiences in Latin America", Marulanda et al. (2010), "Microfinance – A Risky Business; A Time for Strong Leadership", Center for Financial Inclusion at Accion, May 2012, "Corporate Governance Success Stories", IFC 2010, "Weathering the Storm: Hazards, Beacons, and Life Rafts. Lessons in Microfinance Crisis Survival from Those Who Have Been There." Center for Financial Inclusion, 2011.

[2] Same Game, Different League: What Microfinance Institutions Can Learn from the Large Banks Corporate Government Debate, World Microfinance Forum Geneva, Oct 2010.

considering these discussions there will be very different needs and requirements. It is therefore important to scale and adjust the suggested solutions to match these needs and requirements and to develop solutions, which are adequate and appropriate for use at the MFI in question. The common denominator for all MFIs (and actually for any other type of company) is seen in the requirement to establish an efficient organization and, along with these, effective and adequate control structures – the two main pillars a corporate governance system is built on.

The challenge for an MFI is to find the most appropriate combination of the best practice corporate governance components, thereby developing the best possible corporate governance system for the MFI. This chapter provides a theoretical basis and some practical hints to achieve this target.

Another very important question to be addressed when starting to look at an MFI's corporate governance system is the question of responsibility. There is no doubt about the board of an MFI being responsible for the development and implementation of an adequate corporate governance system. This underlines the importance of the board for the institution: If the MFI's board is weak, the likelihood of a weak and / or dysfunctional corporate governance system is very high. If the board is not adequately composed, educated or engaged the MFI is prone to all the typical issues that have been observed, and which have caused material losses or which have even lead to a complete failure of the MFI. These issues are explored in more detail and suggested standards to avoid them are presented in the subsections below.

However, the fact that the board plays such a vital role in an MFI's corporate governance system does not mean that an MFI only needs to install a proper board (or equivalent organ) to fulfil the requirements related to an adequate corporate governance system. A proper board is the ideal starting point to develop the corporate governance system, but as such it is also just one of many elements, which make up a complete corporate governance system.

The outstanding role of the board also does not mean that MFIs, which at the moment cannot implement all suggestions related to the set-up of the board, could not find other ways to start building their corporate governance system by looking at other elements. This is still possible, provided other leaders can run such project for the MFI.

The chapter concludes that there are vital reasons for MFIs to review and develop further their corporate governance systems, especially with the objective to establish an adequate risk management function as a part of it. In this context, MFIs should not be seen as institutions totally different from conventional financial institutions, but should take orientation at the solutions developed there in the past decades.

The next sections will describe in further detail the "pros and cons" of the different elements of a corporate governance system, provide an overview on the difficulties MFIs encounter in establishing such systems to illustrate the argument and to provide impulses for MFIs and practitioners to find their own solutions.

2 Definition of Corporate Governance at MFIs: What and Why?

There are many definitions available on corporate governance in the market today. A good starting point may be one, which puts the focus on the relationship between the main organs of a company:

> Corporate governance can be defined as a set of relationships between a company's management, board, shareholders and other stakeholders. It encompasses the processes through which a company's objectives are set and achieved, and the structure through which stakeholders' interests are managed.[3]

However, it is evident that the 'good functioning' of the board of directors will not be enough to ensure an MFI achieves its targets and protects its assets. When discussing governance, it will therefore be necessary to broaden the discussion to include all stakeholders involved (employees, managers, elected officials, clients, donors, business partners, lenders, shareholders, regulators, etc.).[4]

The OECD fills the gap and suggests a definition, which is also referred to by the Basel Committee on Banking Supervision[5] (Bank for International Settlements 2010). Here, corporate governance is defined as involving "a set of **relationships between a company's management, its board, its shareholders, and other stakeholders**. Corporate governance also provides the **structure through which the objectives of the company are set**, and the **means of attaining those objectives** and **monitoring performance** are determined. Good corporate governance should provide **proper incentives** for the board and management to pursue objectives that are in the interests of the company and its shareholders and should facilitate **effective monitoring**. The presence of an effective corporate governance system, within an individual company or group and across an economy as a whole, **helps to provide** a degree of **confidence** that is necessary for the proper functioning of a market economy."[6]

This constitutes a very comprehensive view on corporate governance, and to help use it in practical terms, its components shall be structured and reviewed in more detail.

As the name suggests, corporate governance is about the governance of a corporation – in this case a Microfinance Institution. The overall question to be answered is: How should the MFI's governance be organized and how should it be run? And the simple answer is: In such a way that the MFI can efficiently and sustainably achieve its business and social objectives. An MFI's corporate

---

[3] Ibid.

[4] See: "Handbook for the analysis of the governance of microfinance institutions", C. Lapenu (CERISE), D. Pierret (IRAM), 2006, p. 10.

[5] "Principles for enhancing Corporate Governance", Basel Committee on Banking Supervision, October 2010, p. 1.

[6] OECD Principles of Corporate Governance, revised April 2004 (emphasis added).

governance structure can be judged as good (or efficient) if it generates long term returns on its objectives. To this end, the MFI needs to ensure smoothly running operations, compliance with regulations and external expectations (from clients and other stakeholders) and positive returns on its social, ecological and financial targets.

In order to establish such efficient governance structure, the different activities in the MFI must be organized, as all work exceeding a certain level of complexity should be organized for efficiency reasons.

This general aspect of **ORGANISATION** for efficient and effective execution includes

1. a clear definition of company objectives and profit distribution (if any);
2. implementation of an organisational structure for all business entities and functional entities (departments or processes) within;
3. a corresponding distribution of responsibilities for all staff on all levels – so from strategic and supervisory functions (e. g. board) over management to all employees.[7] Management responsibility needs to be clarified relating to business management, staff management, project management, change management and risk management;
4. the set-up of information flows including duties and rights to provide and receive information;
5. an incentive system to support the achievement of business targets;
6. proper documentation of all material aspects of the organization.

Besides the organisational aspects to ensure efficiency, appropriate **CONTROL** structures must be set up to ensure a well-balanced and sustainable business conduct and to provide an early-warning-system for relevant risks so these can be addressed quickly. Adequate control is necessary everywhere to compensate for the facts that mistakes will always happen and hidden incentives are not always guiding people to what is best for the MFI and its objectives. Indeed, "an institution's capacity to develop effective monitoring methodology with a rapid warning system in case of dysfunction is one of the fundamental elements of good governance".[8] The elements related with control tasks within the corporate governance system include:

1. The board
2. Reporting, disclosure and transparency standards to support external supervision and control

---

[7] This is especially interesting when thinking about the requirement to specialize work in such a way that complexity is reduced so that even less educated and skilled staff can execute at the required level of quality. This is another argument for the dependency of Corporate Governance solutions on the size of an MFI, with more specialization on certain functions (and therefore higher efficiency) possible and required (due to limitations of humans running and working in the MFI) with larger sized institutions.

[8] Handbook for the analysis of the governance of microfinance institutions, C. Lapenu (CERISE), D. Pierret (IRAM), 2006, p. 26.

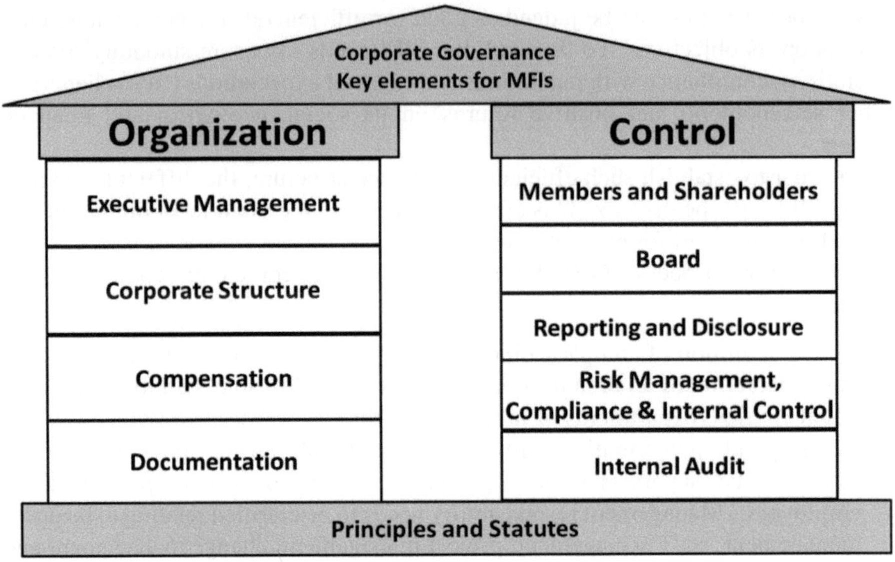

Fig. 1 Overview on elements of corporate governance

3. Risk management and internal control measures
4. Audit (internal and external).

On top, there is "control support" in form of **EXPECTATIONS OF VARIOUS STAKEHOLDERS** regarding the way the company is governed:

1. Shareholders or members,
2. Financial Regulators and their external auditors,
3. Legal requirements for the set up and maintenance of a company,
4. Investors, donors, refinancing partners (e.g. banks, guarantors),
5. Clients and customers,
6. Insurers,
7. Rating agencies,
8. Employees,
9. Public opinion/larger community.

Combining these elements to a system of governance, we can synthesize ten basic elements within an MFI, which would ensure the above listed requirements are met (Fig. 1).

These 10 elements of corporate governance should form the basis of an MFI's corporate governance system.[9]

[9] The author strongly believes that such structure of Corporate Governance provides a comprehensive view on all issues related to the topic. The enhanced view presented in this document completes most previous models to describe Corporate Governance Systems of MFIs, which were focused on the Board and Management.

As mentioned before, these elements of corporate governance will not be established equally in all MFIs, but there will be different specifications of these elements, which shall be combined in such a way to form the most adequate and efficient governance system for the MFI in question.

3 Objectives and Value Added of Corporate Governance at MFIs

There is evidence that organisations with a good corporate governance structure do perform better than those with inadequate corporate governance systems in place. This goes as far as stating that some MFIs had to close because of poor corporate governance. In this sense, the basic objective of those who advocate for improved corporate governance systems is the reduction of corporate governance risk. This is the risk of failure or hindrance of development of the MFI because of bad management and / or insufficient steering and oversight of the MFI. Given the possible impact, this is one of the most important risks that need to be considered when looking at an MFI.

The causal link between an MFI's performance and its corporate governance system may not always be 100 % clear. It could be that firms, which invest a lot in their corporate governance system do this, because they can afford it (they are good already) or it can be that improved performance is the result of increased activity in corporate governance matters – or there may be a bi-directional influence. Either way, the subsections below provide good arguments for why it is good for MFIs to invest in this area. The main arguments for setting up a good corporate governance structure can be categorized in five areas supported by good Corporate Governance:

1. On-going challenge of management,
2. Efficiency gains,
3. Profitability increase by reduction of financing cost,
4. Reduction of losses and inefficiencies by better control,
5. Economic gains for the country, which in turn lead to positive effects for the MFI.

3.1 On-Going Challenge of Management

When looking at those MFIs, which have failed over time, it shows that in many cases a better corporate governance system at the MFI would have helped avoid this failure.[10] This is plain to see for cases when MFIs had to close business because of

[10] The Rise and Fall of Corposol: Lessons Learned from the Challenges of Managing Growth, Accion 1998, or: "Taking the Good from the Bad in Microfinance: Lessons learned from failed experiences in Latin America", Calmeadow, June 2010.

- **Fraud**, which has been undetected for such a long time that the losses accumulated have exceeded the MFI's capital;
- **Uncontrolled growth,** whereby the MFI's management has focused purely on seizing business opportunities without taking into consideration the capacities to apply basic controls or to actually process all this new business, often because there was neither enough experienced staff available nor did the MFIs have a functioning MIS to allow management to see what was actually going on;
- **Loss of mission focus**, which occurs when top management is trying to follow just too many objectives at a time. For example, a well-meant diversification in other than core MFI activities will inevitably require additional management attention and capital. These resources are scarce, though, and when taken away from the MFI business, they may lead (and have led) to MFIs being deprived of what they needed to continue their core business. Sometimes the problem also lies in the fact that new business activities in new markets are started without the required preparations being finalized and tested – and then resulting in huge losses, simply because of the MFIs inability to execute such new business (such development could also fall under the category "uncontrolled growth").

What is in common with the above issues is that bad management decisions have been taken or management had been negligent about the risks the MFI was exposed to. Had the managers of these MFIs been challenged by an effective control system, which is one of the key elements of a good corporate governance system, negligence could have been avoided and apparently bad decisions about the development of the MFI's business could have been adjusted.

3.2 Efficiency Gains by Good Corporate Governance

The issues listed in the section above can lead to a complete failure of an MFI in extreme cases. But there are many more cases in which such deficiencies have led to unnecessary high costs, which could have been avoided by the implementation of corporate governance system elements like control, management reporting and relationship management with stakeholders like employees, investors and regulators.

- MFIs often have difficulties setting up a professional organizational and administrative structure to adequately support conduct of their business. With an appropriate corporate governance system solutions to both organizational and executive tasks can be implemented, which help the MFI conduct and grow its business in a well-balanced and risk-controlled way. Good corporate governance can then avoid inefficiency cost or losses and better control operational costs.
- Another positive element of corporate governance is the support of good relationships with all stakeholders. This also leads to better performance by providing motivation and by avoiding search and replacement cost. Stakeholders

(e. g. employees, lenders, ...) like to be treated responsibly, and are likely to leave if they feel they'd be treated better elsewhere.

- Improved Performance can also be expected through higher commitment from managers and employees, improved leadership processes and better information flows – which are all supported by a well-established corporate governance system. These elements will lead to better management decisions, a better allocation of resources and better work policies and processes.
- Higher performance is partly due to reduced capital costs as described in the following section, but also attributed to expected better future performance due to better management decisions.[11]

It is very difficult to quantify and measure the efficiency gains suggested above. To do this, the cost of inefficiencies in an MFI would need to be analysed by isolating and quantifying them before and after the implementation of corporate governance improvements – which is very difficult if not impossible. On one side, because no information exists on the amount of inefficiency costs caused by misallocation of resources, loss of client revenue caused by clients leaving the bank as a result of poor service, or the cost of wrong management decisions caused by lack of information, and on the other side, because it is totally unclear which cost has actually been saved once an improved corporate governance system is in place, which prevents such problems from happening in the first place.

Still, common sense supports this view and corporate governance projects, which have been implemented before, confirm this.[12]

3.3 *Profitability Increase by Reduction of Financing Cost*

The ability of an MFI to present a well-developed corporate governance system is often a pre-condition for getting access to capital. If the MFI can demonstrate they maintain a good corporate governance system trust and investor confidence are increased significantly. Alternatively, a missing or inadequate corporate governance system can break reputations by destroying confidence and losing goodwill and investor trust. Furthermore, investors value the risk-reducing effects of a good corporate governance system and are thus able to offer capital or loans at a reduced price. There are several examples which confirm that improvements of the Corporate Governance-system support the acquisition of capital and financing sources.[13]

The reason why MFIs should care about such access to external financing is the increased opportunities for maintaining and expanding their business and for

[11] Corporate Governance in Emerging Markets: A Survey by Stijn Claessens and Burcin Yurtoglu, 2012, p. 15.

[12] Corporate Governance Success Stories – IFC Advisory Services in the Middle East and North Africa, Cairo 2010.

[13] ibid.

establishing valuable contacts to possible sources of financing, which may be needed in times of distress (like, for example, during the recent financial crisis).

- Generally, a good corporate governance system reduces risks by continuous and professional identification and management of these. The corporate governance system thereby helps generate the trust needed for long term relationships initiated by lending or investment engagements. It was found that investors care about corporate governance as well-governed companies will tend to outperform their peers, they can safeguard and provide for higher returns on investment, better protect shareholder rights, and provide assurance that management acts in the best interest of the company and all shareholders and stakeholders.
- Depending on the details and maturity level of the corporate governance system, gradual improvements may materialize in form of reduced cost for capital or funding. Actually, the interest rate requested by investors is a direct representation of the investor's views on the risks at the MFI, just like many financial institutions apply risk based pricing to their loans. If the MFI can demonstrate that its corporate governance system does effectively reduce the level of risks, it may be able to negotiate better financing terms. "Nearly all companies rated the corporate governance impact on their ability to access finance as strong or substantial. They cited the impact that governance changes had on instilling market confidence and providing added assurance to investors, creditors or other debtors. The changes have reportedly helped these firms access significant financing the past 2 years, ranging from $2.5 million in one company to $1.5 billion in another".[14]
- As corporate governance also generates public trust, an MFI with a good reputation (which is created and maintained by its corporate governance system) will be more successful in attracting deposits, which usually are a cheap source of funding. Deposit rates may even be reduced in comparison to peer institutions with a less developed corporate governance system.

If investors appreciate the high quality of a corporate governance system in an MFI and therefore adjust their risk estimate / rating on the investment in such a way that finance costs reduce by 1 %, the saved amount can then be used to better achieve the MFI' business objectives. (Such downward adjustments of rates are often made annually under finance engagements with a term of more than 1 year.)

3.4 Reduction of Losses and Inefficiencies by Better Control

Firstly, business performance is improved by the power of risk management and control to avoid losses or other inefficiencies. Once professional and adequate risk

[14] Corporate Governance Success Stories – IFC Advisory Services in the Middle East and North Africa, Cairo 2010.

management and control systems are integrated in all areas of the MFI, they will help reduce issues of non-compliance or business errors and they will help deal with them effectively and efficiently. A special case can be made for fraud prevention by a good corporate governance system.

Looking at such a fraud prevention system from the bottom, the first component is a (Fraud) Risk Assessment, which is done to identify relevant scenarios of fraud risk before they actually happen. In case of fraud actually being committed, proper risk management processes and systems as a second component help identify them at an early stage, thereby reducing the overall damage. As a third component, a good risk management system will ensure that fraud events, which have actually happened, will be corrected adequately and that measures will be implemented to avoid recurrence. Overall, if board and Management have taken care to integrate measures to prevent fraud across the MFI, losses caused by fraud will be reduced.

Second, a wide-spread issue with management of companies is information asymmetries between managers and owners and shareholders. Once managers are hired to take care of running the MFI, they have much better insight and might use this information advantage for purposes different from the MFI's original objectives. They might also simply not deliver on all of their management obligations. An effective corporate governance system helps solve such principle-agent issues by reducing information asymmetries, setting clear rules for management, and by establishing a structure of incentives and independent controls to bring the organization's interests in line with the managers' interests. This helps ensure everybody at the MFI is doing what is expected to achieve the MFI's objectives, and this helps to ensure no one is doing something else, which would result in misallocation of the MFI's resources.

3.5 *Economic Gains for the Country and Regulation*

Even though not in focus for most investors and MFIs in their activities to develop corporate governance systems at the MFI, there is a welcome side-effect of good corporate governance, which comes as an overall support of economic development.

- From the economic and regulatory point of view, good corporate governance structures in financial institutions reduce the risk of financial crisis and other sorts of problems. Good corporate governance structures established in the financial industry of a country help build and protect good reputation – which will open the country to international markets and thus also attract foreign capital and investment. Good corporate governance thereby contributes to sustainable economic development by both the enhancement of the performance of the sector and by increasing its access to outside capital.
- Regulators apply the view that good corporate governance in the entities falling under their supervision helps them avoid problems. Consequently, they enforce

corresponding rules and regulations on MFIs. As regulators have the power to significantly influence the life of an MFI, it is necessary to comply with all such related regulations. For the MFI, this is the task of the Compliance function as an element of a corporate governance system. The key challenge here is to implement such regulatory requirements in a way that they correlate with the MFI's own organization and control objectives such that two birds can be killed with one stone. This may not always be possible, as sometimes external requirements are not driven by or even in contradiction to business needs of the MFI, but the majority of regulations actually are based on best practice in the industry, and hence bear the potential to support the MFI without being overly burdensome.

4 The MFI's Investment into Corporate Governance

The previously described benefits of good corporate governance do not come effortless or for free. In fact, many managers fear the cost associated with building certain elements of a corporate governance system (e. g. a well-funded Risk Management and Control system or the set-up of a professional and effective Supervisory board). Part of the difficulty is that investments in corporate governance are for a long-term horizon and often do not generate quick and tangible returns. Even worse, administrative formalization, documentation requirements and business controls, which to a certain extent come in with the development of corporate governance structures, are often perceived as the "natural enemy" of the revenue generating business activities.

While it is very difficult to do a precise cost-benefit-analysis for a corporate governance project, estimates can still be made on a qualitative basis. This section therefore discusses the main cost drivers of corporate governance systems and draws a qualitative comparison to the expected benefits.

1. Firstly, there are **direct overhead costs** caused by the implementation of additional supervisory and management layers, administrative elements, documentation and publication requirements and control structures like Internal Audit and Risk Management departments.
2. Second, there is **increased time to implementation** caused by administrative requirements and controls (for example by implementing a "New Product Approval Process") – an at least potential loss of efficiency for the MFI's main business objectives, as business processes might not be executed as quickly as before, and managers may feel restrained from pursuing their original business objectives.

However, a business cannot be run without organizing it, i.e. without coordinating each employee's or manager's activities. The simple truth is that no company can concentrate purely on its revenue generating activities alone, but must spend time and resources for control and documentation purposes to avoid lack of coordination, duplication of work, missing of objectives etc. While a certain level of cost must therefore be accounted for, the main question is about the ***adequate*** level of cost – which is equal to the question about the adequate set up and design of all elements of the MFI's corporate governance system.

What adds to the challenge is that many people have different views on what is adequate. While business executives tend to vote for less administration and less control in order to not "jeopardize" business performance and the ability to reach social and monetary business targets, risk and control experts like regulators, auditors, controllers and also risk managers sometimes tend to overweigh administration and control. This natural bias towards one's own expertise can be observed frequently and seems to be an unavoidable component of human behaviour.

Hence, the relative power of these seemingly contradicting forces often is the main determinant for the composition and the strengths of the corporate governance system in an MFI.

On the benefit side, the value added in the sections above must be considered. While it is impossible to exactly quantify the positive impact, the discussions given in the above sections may give an indication of what can be expected. This, in turn, may serve as an indication of the maximum allowable investment to take, so to provide evidence about the investment's positive returns.

5 Typical Corporate Governance Issues at MFIs and Suggested Solutions

This section holds a list of typical issues related to the corporate governance system of MFIs, as they are found in related publications and project experience. The issues listed describe by way of example what is meant by corporate governance Risk: The risk of material losses in the MFI due to shortcomings in any one (or more) of the elements of the MFI's corporate governance system. It becomes clear that for some of the issues the risk is very high indeed, and improper management of these risks may even result in complete failure of the MFI.

5.1 General Issues About Corporate Governance

- Some MFIs, especially at early stages of development or which have developed in a rather isolated manner, have not thought much about their Corporate Governance. In a way, it may be that the whole topic of corporate governance is not appropriately addressed and that necessary elements are set up rather spontaneously instead of being the result of proper analysis of business requirements. As a result, such MFIs may have a board, but its role and function is not clearly defined. They may have management reports, but these do not fully cover management needs. They may have an incentive system, but it was never well adapted with the MFI's product portfolio and its social and business objectives. The MFIs may also have policies and manuals, but they are not used and so they are outdated and lack practical relevance.

- In other cases it is found that the focus regarding corporate governance is put on formal aspects only, in order to establish a quick solution to a request from the regulator or an investor. However, this is done without the express intention to really adopt the actual corporate governance system and with lack of commitment to "live" the established rules. As an example, many MFIs follow the recommendation to implement Internal Audit and Risk Management departments, but they do so without giving these functions an appropriate mission and adequate resources. As a result, two more departments appear on the MFI's organisational chart, but they add little value and significant cost.
- MFIs who want to follow additional objectives besides the provision of financial services to the "un-served" often mix different activities within one legal entity and even one management team. This sometimes results in a combination of activities which are hard to coordinate and prioritize. Managers and staff then get overwhelmed with all the different responsibilities they have and lose their ability to perform. Resources, which should be used for MFI services are diverged for other activities like general development aid, financial literacy training or community development. A well planned corporate governance structure is required for such diverse organizations to bring in clarity and to allow for a clear allocation of resources, cost and also profits.

To address such cases, an assessment of the current corporate governance system should be done to make visible to the company (and to investors, if needed) which elements are put in practice how, and to identify room for improvement. Such assessment should come with a cost-benefit estimate on any suggested improvements identified.

5.2 Issues with the Board

The board of Directors is the top of the pyramid in an institutions hierarchy (unless an assembly of shareholders or members is held to decide on material aspects of the institution). "The board of directors, as the central mechanism for oversight and accountability in our corporate governance system, is charged with the direction of the corporation, including responsibility for deciding how the board itself should be organized, how it should function, and how it should order its priorities. The board's fiduciary objective is long-term value creation for the corporation; governance form and process should follow."[15] There are many possibilities to establish

[15] "National Association of Corporate Directors, Key Agreed Principles to Strengthen Corporate Governance for U.S. Publicly Traded Companies", Washington, 2008, p. 5.

structure and functioning of a board, and it is important to consider the following key risks:

- Responsibilities of board members are not sufficiently defined;
- Board members may not be adequately qualified (i.e.: lacking appropriate skills/know-how/experience in Microfinance, Finance and Accounting, Risk Management, Technology, International Network, Transformation, etc...);
- There is only an insufficient number of "independent" board members, while most board members are friends or family of the CEO or other members of executive management. Consequently, there is a lack of objectivity in the views expressed by the board members;
- Board members may not be adequately engaged. The challenge here is to find the right people who can fulfil on all expectations of all stakeholders. These people need to be experienced, qualified, engaged, courageous, they need to be able to dedicate sufficient time to their tasks and they should – at least partly – be "independent";
- Board members do not get the necessary information (due to weak reporting or MIS) or are even manipulated by a person or group in power (Chair or CEO) – so called "Management Capture". Similar issues can be expected if the board is not strong enough (in terms of power, seniority and leadership) to take decisions, which may be directed against management. Especially with family-owned MFIs, intra-familial disagreements may come up, or succession disputes and the like;
- Board members take a far too active role in managing the MFI ("board Capture"). Thereby they undermine the authority of Management and the fundamental idea of the board being an organ to provide independent control of Management activities;
- The board is unable to quickly identify issues of mission drift or a neglected double or double bottom line;
- The board has not established the appropriate committees to support its work;
- The board is not equipped appropriately to lead the MFI through the phase of transformation into a regulated entity;
- In many MFIs, mixed CEO and President/Chair of the board roles are observed, which may lead to an excessive concentration of power and responsibility in one person, reducing the ability to detect issues or react on them quickly, especially when generated by this person. This situation generally comes with high key person dependency for the MFI;
- There is inadequate performance monitoring of the board and its members, often in combination with inadequate remuneration and incentives.

In order to contain the above described or similar issues fundamental measures at board level need to be taken. These span from the selection of the "right" members of the board to agreed organizational and working standards of the board and all of its committees and members.

5.3 *Issues with Management*

Management is designated to manage the institution in line with the strategic outlines resolved by the board. Normally, ownership of the MFI and management are separate and so by design, there may be principle-agent problems arising. Furthermore, managers may be lured into activities not in line with business objectives.

- An MFI may have general principle-agent problems in a way that managers, who are by nature closer to business realities do not fully share all necessary information with the board in order to be able to pursue other than the MFI's agreed objectives;
- Another issue may be that managers avoid being controlled and therefore do not involve the board appropriately when preparing or already executing new business or material changes in business activities. Avoidance of control is often observed with mixed CEO and President roles, with one person having control of executive management and the board. (This issue is strongly linked with the issues on the set-up of appropriate risk management and control structures below and the issues related to the composition of the board above);
- Managers sometimes have insufficient oversight and therefore reduced abilities to manage the business due to lack of necessary information on business development, financials and risks. Root cause here is often the inability at MFIs to produce comprehensive MIS reporting for technical or organizational reasons;
- There may be motives or even incentives leading to mission drift and neglected double bottom lines caused by management. As an example, managers may get focused on profitability and expansion and then subordinate social objectives like provision of affordable loans and rewarding savings with adequate interest rates. The contrary may also happen in the form of an overly concentrated focus on an MFI's social mission, which may undermine its economic sustainability;
- Good business know how of managers may not always be complemented with their ability to manage projects, to manage change, to manage risks or to manage staff.

The issues listed must be addressed by appropriate control / oversight of management by the board and by business controls independent from managers responsible for business execution. Other elements should be looked at by way of clear documentation of staff management rules, project management standards, comprehensive reporting processes, and a well-balanced incentive system to support all managers' focus on business (and mission) objectives.

5.4 Issues with the Set-Up of Appropriate Risk Management and Control Structures

The top of the pyramid for risk management and control in the MFI is the board. Obviously, the board cannot engage at processing level of risk management and control, and therefore needs appropriate support throughout the MFI. This support should be given in the form of well-coordinated Audit, Risk Management, Compliance and other Control functions, which are equipped adequately to provide the services needed by the business. It is also necessary to clarify the board's responsibility with regards to risk management and control: the board must have oversight and provide general and strategic guidance. Management and Audit must execute the risk management and control functions.

Related issues often observed at MFIs are the following:

- The importance and usefulness of controls and risk management is not fully considered at top management and board level. The board does not execute its control rights properly, and senior management does not value and develop the risk management function. This often leads to inadequate risk management and control structures being set up, which still cost money, but do not generate appropriate value.
- Controls are often implemented spontaneously rather than as a result of a comprehensive risk assessment. As a result, controls are incomplete and insufficient, not protecting the MFI appropriately against all relevant risks.
- Another effect often observed is the implementation of functions charged with "control" in the widest sense (e. g. Internal Audit, Risk Management, Internal Control, Compliance, Information Security, Quality Assurance, ...) without appropriate coordination to form an efficient and comprehensive internal control system.
- The set-up of an expert Internal Audit (or Risk Management) function is often seen as a sufficient solution to all requirements relating to internal control. This neglects the responsibility for and the development of risk management and control expertise within the business.
- Control functions are not set up with an adequate level of independency from managers following the objective to generate business. Segregation of duties or the 4-eyes principle, however, are an important quality for controls functions to work effectively. As an example, the Internal Audit function should report directly to the board, but not to management, such that issues can be raised more freely.

Understandably, many MFIs focus on business development in the early years and consider risk management and control a luxury, which can only be afforded by mature and wealthy organizations. In contrast to this view, it is proposed to start setting the basics for an appropriate Internal Control System at early stages of development. Many extremely useful risk and control elements can be implemented at low cost and will lay the basis of a well-integrated internal control environment right from the start. The clear view is that all MFIs should be equipped with an Internal Audit function and a Risk Management and Control function. These should be set up to work independently from business responsibilities and should be promoted by top management and the board. Obviously, formal set up alone is not sufficient, but an effective integration into the business is required. All this must be supported by comprehensive and easy-to-understand reporting to management and board.

5.5 Investor, Shareholder or Member Related Issues

The general issue with a group of different shareholders (or members in the case of many non-profit MFIs) is that they probably do not always agree on how the MFI should be run and developed. Among old and new investors there may be short or medium term objectives on financial returns, while other shareholders or the board or management are looking for someone to support their long term objectives on social responsibility. Additional possibilities for conflicts come up in family-owned (and often family-run) MFIs, where family politics need to be reconciled with the objectives of the MFI. What is often observed is:

- Inadequate power of minority shareholders or members – this may be the case when too much power is given to founders holding a relative small portion of total shares or when rights for minority shareholders are neglected or simply ignored by majority shareholders.
- There may be conflicts of interests with investors who seek a profitable investment and do not actively support an MFI's social mission. As with comparable issues at the management level, the MFI's social objectives may fall behind business objectives (or vice versa).
- Important positions at the MFI may be filled with family and friends, thereby neglecting the requirement to ensure necessary skills and potentially ending up with a team of "leaders" who do not critically reflect what they are doing (excessive mutual loyalty and "group think").
- When expanding the number of shareholders or members the old balance of powers changes – often to the disadvantage of existing shareholders. It may also be possible that a true and fair valuation of shares is required, which may not be agreed upon by all shareholders easily.

The appropriate way to address such issues is to ensure the principles of the MFI are clearly formulated and fixed in its statutes or articles of association. The board needs to be aware of the possibility of the issues listed and must actively seek clarification on the objectives of investors before accepting new money, for example. Reporting needs to include both social and profit targets so that the MFI's performance can be monitored related to either objective.

Another important question to be asked in this context is why the actual leaders of some MFIs refuse to reform and improve their corporate governance systems, despite of obvious issues among shareholders, board members and management. Here are three reasons, which should be considered in such situations:

- Leaders are afraid of change and possible unexpected outcome and follow the rule to "never touch a running system". They are unwilling to invest in change;
- The current system ensures values and rents to current leaders, which these are afraid to lose. The more concentrated powers are, the higher will be feared losses and hence resistance against change;
- Current leaders fear they lose power when know-how is shared more widely in more transparent work environments.

Either of these situations would be a material hindrance to the development and well-being of an MFI and needs to be addressed quickly and with determination.

6 Regulations Related to Corporate Governance at MFIs

Law and legal enforcement also have a certain impact on an MFI's corporate governance system, as they define how different elements of the corporate governance systems must be set up and maintained formally. Related items are not only found in MFI regulations, but also in laws on taxation, consumer protection, bankruptcy, incorporation, corporation etc. In many countries codes on corporate governance established by industry associations provide additional recommendations. Such "local regulation can complement, rather than substitute for firm-level governance practice."[16] Hence, an MFI must comply with all local regulations, but where regulations are silent on certain elements of Corporate Governance, the MFI should close this gap itself – for the reasons and benefits explained above.

The risks regulators seek to address by issuing MFI related regulations are the risks of inappropriate lending or over-indebtedness, risks to retail deposits, the risks to the Microfinance sector of the country, corporate governance risk (as defined above), and liquidity risk. Typical components one finds addressed by regulations on MFIs, and which also relate to Corporate Governance, are requirements on:

- Corporate form and registration
- Management and staff capacities and required qualifications or even official registration and certification
- List of permitted business activities
- Operating regulations (e. g. interest rate caps and floors)
- Minimum capital levels and capital adequacy ratios
- Provisioning schedules
- Liquidity ratios
- Deposit insurance and other required coverage

[16] Corporate Governance in Emerging Markets: A Survey by Stijn Claessens and Burcin Yurtoglu, 2012, p. 22.

- Concentration risk limits
- Annual review by supervision body
- Reporting requirements.[17]

It may be a challenge for newly established MFIs to cope with these regulatory requirements, especially when the MFI was not in regulatory focus before. The MFI's corporate governance system must be developed further to deal with these requirements, which is typically the task of a comprehensive Compliance function. Another challenge to be aware of is the one of dealing with regulations in less transparent jurisdictions, where formal requirements are complemented or replaced by informal constraints. It is often found that in such markets political connections are necessary to run and develop an MFI and to increase its value and profit – and to increase the chances of being bailed out in case of trouble. However, when systems change and legal restrictions on political connectivity are enforced, such MFIs, which have gotten used to working under these informal constraints, are confronted with additional challenge to adopt to the changed environment.[18]

7 Conclusions

The Challenges for corporate governance at Microfinance Institutions are multisided and complex. This chapter provides an overview of the discussion rather than detailed solutions for MFIs to take home and implement. However, as so often, the first and most important step in solving a problem is to ask the right questions (at the right time) to get focused. Thanks to the financial crisis, the level of attention to corporate governance at Microfinance Institutions has increased recently, even though this interest developed too late for some MFIs or their supporters – especially those which were operating in unregulated and overheated markets, where demand and requirement for proper governance structures were too low.

Apparently, as long as business is going well, "second tier" business functions like Risk Management and Control, and other elements of Corporate Governance, are at best seen as a "nice to have". The true value of these functions only comes to surface at times of trouble, when it is exactly the level of quality of the corporate governance system, which decides on how well the institution can deal with problems and survive crisis. Those MFIs, which have survived or the ones which have not been affected materially should not lean back and hope that everything will be fine. Instead, they should prepare now to be ready to deal with the next crisis ahead – and they should do so by following the discussion outlined above, they should critically review the level of maturity of their own corporate governance system and apply improvements where necessary and appropriate. Even young and

[17] "Microfinance Regulation in Developing Countries – A comparative review of current practice", IRIS Center Maryland, 2002.

[18] ibid. p. 28.

small MFIs, which may think it is too early for them now to start such a project, should consider seriously where they are going and how their corporate governance will need to develop with expected business development. They would not need to fully address each of the elements mentioned in this chapter right away, but they should make sure they take them into account while moving ahead.

Besides this self-referring argument for support for continuous success there is an additional reason for why all MFIs need to get ready for Corporate Governance. National regulators increase demands for corporate governance systems and elements thereof. These requirements affect MFIs at different stages of development and those who start investing in this area today will not be surprised and overwhelmed by corresponding regulatory requirements in the future – when there will be other challenges to be addressed, too.

These investments into elements of corporate governance which are appropriate to the MFI's state of development may not show immediate return, but they will ensure the MFI will develop in a sustainable way. Even though no standard tool box is available today, which could be used as a blueprint for MFIs to develop their own solutions, local and regional associations have the networking potential to provide for the necessary exchange of information about best market practice to all of their members.

Next to the MFIs themselves, investors, regulators and other stakeholders should insist on the MFIs they work with to develop their corporate governance system along the above discussion and provide support in the form of technical assistance as needed. Indeed it should be considered negligent to invest in an MFI which does not fully commit to fundamental principles of Corporate Governance. Again, the discussion presented in this chapter can provide a guideline to ask the right questions in order to find out how well an MFI is managed and controlled. After all, this is what everybody wants to see: a smoothly and sustainably developing Microfinance industry, generating returns on economic and social objectives.

References

Bank for International Settlements. (2010). *Principles for enhancing corporate governance*. Basel: Basel Committee on Banking Supervision.

Claessens, S., & Yurtoglu, B. (2012). Corporate governance in emerging markets: A survey. http://ssrn.com/abstract=1988880

IFC. (2010). *Corporate governance success stories*. Cairo: IFC Advisory Services in the Middle East and North Africa.

Lapenu, C. (CERISE), & Pierret, D. (IRAM), (2006). *Handbook for the analysis of the governance of microfinance institutions*. Rome: International Fund for Agricultural Development (IFAD).

Lascelles, D. (2012). *Microfinance – A risky business. A time for strong leadership* (Center for Financial Inclusion Publication No. 11). Charleston: Accion International.

Marulanda, B., Fajury, L., Paredes, M., & Gomez, F. (2010). *Failures in microfinance: Lessons learned*. San José: Calmeadow.

Meagher, P. (2002). *Microfinance regulation in developing countries – A comparative review of current practice*. Washington, DC: IRIS Center, University of Maryland, USA.

National Association of Corporate Directors. (2008). *Key agreed principles to strengthen corporate governance for U.S. publicly traded companies*. Washington, DC.
OECD. (2004). *Principles of corporate governance*. Paris: OECD.
Pugliese, M. G. (2010). Same game, different league: What microfinance institutions can learn from the large banks. In: P. Sparreboom (Ed.), *Geneva papers on inclusiveness no 11*. Switzerland: World Microfinance Forum Geneva.
Rozas, D. (2011). *Weathering the storm* (Center for financial inclusion publication no. 11). Charleston: Accion International.
Steege, J. (1998). *The rise and fall of corposol: Lessons learned from the challenges of managing growth*. Charleston: Accion.

Convergence in Corporate Governance Practices: Evidence from Listed-Companies in Morocco

Lamia El Bouanani

Abstract This chapter takes an in-depth look at the recommendations of the Moroccan code of good practices of corporate governance, inspired by the Organization for Economic Cooperation and Development (OECD) Principles, against the findings of a recent survey, conducted in listed companies in 2012, by the Institute of Moroccan Directors (IMA). It illustrates how the country has elaborated its own corporate governance codes in a consultative way, involving all key stakeholders – companies, civil society, and government – and shows similarly, how listed companies implement those recommendations. It appears that there is a strong need to further build common understanding of governance principles; given that the Code's recommendations were more consistently implemented, when regulators were enforcing them as legal rules. IMA advocates for a pragmatic approach to help enforce the Codes' recommendations, through education, based on a better understanding of firms' profiles and markets' constraints; or risk that there remain merely symbolic, at the expenses of substantive reforms, to raise boards' practices.

1 Introduction

The latest Moroccan code of good governance for state-owned companies, issued in March 2012 requires that boards include at least 25 % of independent directors. Compliance with this recommendation is slowly taking shape in state companies' boardrooms; and a new project bill on banking sector is set to include a mandatory provision, relating to independent directors' appointment. But substantive reforms are still needed to translate recommendations into legal rules; as the survey on

L. El Bouanani (✉)
Moroccan Institute (IMA) of Directors, Rabat, Morocco
e-mail: ELBOUANANI@cdg.ma

S. Boubaker and D.K. Nguyen (eds.), *Corporate Governance in Emerging Markets*, CSR, Sustainability, Ethics & Governance, DOI 10.1007/978-3-642-44955-0_24,

governance practices of listed companies, conducted by the Moroccan Institute of Directors (IMA) showed.

Investors and regulators generally agree that "good governance practices" are critical to ensure effective monitoring of managers, and long-term viability of the firm. The objective is to better protect shareholders and minority shareholders in particular, in emerging markets, where ownership is usually more concentrated.

However, academic research on the topic doesn't provide for conclusive links between corporate governance and firms' performance. There are telling examples of massive frauds, occurring undetected by outside directors. And despite recent turmoil over fraud involving board members at a top Japanese firm, regulators found it hard to change rules in a country where insularity is shaping business culture and practices. National idiosyncrasies do matter in corporate governance.[1]

That leads us to ponder the following question, which is critical in Morocco: if implementation of corporate governance standards doesn't only depend on strict regulatory coercion: how could the various Moroccan Codes' recommendations find their way in the boardrooms, in the first place? In addition to regulatory efforts, a consistent and systematic reflection needs to be conducted on country's capitalism, its ownership patterns, corporate structures, power distribution within society, and culture, to find out the most effective means to enforce governance standards. This reflection should involve various constituencies, to build a common understanding of the rules.

With this respect, Morocco is a compelling case of a country where corporate governance codes stemmed from a long and truly consultative process, including private and public companies, and business associations. The main finding of the survey conducted by the Institute of Moroccan Directors on governance practices of listed companies; reported in the second section of this chapter; is that the Code's recommendations were consistently implemented whenever the regulators translate them into mandatory rules. When there is no legal obligation, companies have different understandings of governance concepts and different priorities. The challenge is two-pronged: building a common understanding of governance principles and translate those principles into dynamic and suitable practices, which are not mere transplants of foreign practices, or formal compliance with the law. This is the question we address in Sect. 3 of this chapter, to discuss the role of the Moroccan Institute of Directors.

[1] See Nestor and Thomson (2000).

2 Convergence in Governance Practices

2.1 The "Convergence Debate": Literature Survey

Globalization and competition for cheap sources of capital favored a harmonization in international legal standards, as one can observe in the wide adoption of corporate governance codes across the world.

Financial market and product market integration in the last two decades resulted in a convergence towards the Anglo-Saxon model[2]; with firms in emerging countries adopting international accounting rules, or getting through the tough listing and disclosure standards of the New York Stock Exchange, to signal their "good governance practices".

Academics (Gilson 2000) have made a distinction between convergence *in form* and convergence *in function*. The latter refers to governance institutions that can adapt to change, without amending their rules. The former refers to an entire adaptation of the legal framework. A third form of convergence mentioned in literature (Gilson 2000) is *contractual* convergence, when firms respond to change contractually, but lack the flexibility to formally change because of political barriers. Khanna et al. (2006)[3] differentiate between *de jure and* de facto convergence; using the telling example of the prevalence of rules against bribery and corruption, across many countries and the diverse levels of enforcement of such rules. The literature mainly "examines convergence in terms of adoption of the Anglo-American or US governance system and practices".[4]

Researchers have singled out the integration of financial markets[5]; product and market integration; diffusion of codes of good governance, and harmonization of accounting rules as the main drivers of convergence. The main argument is that competition for capital, and markets' shares lead to convergence and adoption of the more efficient elements of corporate governance systems.

However, there is limited evidence that convergence in corporate governance is occurring.

The "path dependency thesis"[6] postulates that "institutions evolve along path dependent trajectories", which are heavily shaped by institutions, legal, social and political conditions. In simple words, it means that corporate governance systems in a given country are the results of specific historical, political and institutional events. The structure of capitalism in Morocco still relies on informal institutions: relational connections,[7] and family ties, which result in specific corporate

[2] See Nestor and Thompson (2000).

[3] Cited in Yoshikawa and Rasheed (2009).

[4] See Yoshikawa and Rasheed (2009).

[5] See Yoshikawa and Rasheed (2009).

[6] See Coffee (1999) and Bebchuk and Roe (1999).

[7] See Rajan and Zingales (1995).

governance structures, in a market dominated by small and medium size companies, and concentrated ownership's patterns. With this respect, differences in property rights regimes are pointed out as "the principal source of diversity among national governance systems".[8]

Much of the convergence is occurring in form, rather than in substance, as the IMA study on Moroccan listed companies show. Those companies are devising their own governance mechanisms, which is away from the core assumption of the Anglo-American model of a clear separation between management and ownership.

More recently, research undertaken in emerging markets[9] is suggesting that over-regulation and stubborn implementation of Anglo-Saxon approach to corporate governance, can lead to negative business impacts. Emphasis should be put instead, on the way legal systems function within a specific country, to ensure enforcement and adaptation of legal reforms.

A recent paper has taken stock of the research made on the success of OECD principles' implementation in emerging markets[10], and pointed out that "practical effectiveness may be hindered by the lack of well-functioning local institutions". There are above all, the results of a "networked form of governance", dominated by various actors (law makers, firms, business associations...). Therefore, it is critical to understand the local context, as we will do in the following sections to put the governance practices of listed firms, into the broader context of reforms' dynamics and power bargaining, that led to the adoption of the Moroccan Code.

2.2 *Morocco Reform Dynamics*

Morocco has embarked since the 1990s, in a string of economic liberalization reforms and has pledged to strengthen its institutional, regulatory and legal frameworks. These efforts were awarded in 2011, when the country was raised to the investment grade category, and confirmed by rating agencies in 2012.

The state is still playing a prominent role in the Moroccan economy, as an investor in state-owned enterprises (SOEs) which represented in 2010 the equivalent of 30.3 % of gross fixed capital formation.[11] The divestment of publicly owned-shares, ranging from telecom to finance and infrastructure sectors, have also generated a great source of income and contributed to reduce the government's external debt. Between 1993 and 2011, total revenues from the divestment of state-owned enterprise shares, and the granting of telecom licenses, amounted to around US$12 billion (MAD 107 billion[12]). Privatization has also taken other forms,

---

[8] See See Yoshikawa and Rasheed (2009) p. 393.

[9] See Armour et al. (2008).

[10] See Siems and Alvarez-Macotela (2013).

[11] See Semmar (2012).

[12] See Semmar (2012).

through state companies transformed into joint-stock companies: while the state remains as an owner, the management of the company becomes closer to private commercial companies, resulting in changes in corporate governance.

Privatization has fostered the development of capital markets, since privatized SOEs still account for a significant share of the Casablanca Stock Exchange. Those reforms truly laid the ground for substantial corporate governance reforms.

One of the less acknowledged factors that played a vital role in bringing substantial changes in corporate governance mechanisms is the enactment of the joint stock company law 17–95 in 2001.[13] This law introduced a major change by providing for a clear separation between management and control, through a "board of directors and a president or a board of directors and a board of trustees"; compared to the previous legal regime in which the frontiers were blurred between executive and control functions of board members. The law raised the standards of transparency, and mitigates conflicts of interest: "under the former law, a director was able to make contracts with the company, to borrow money from the company and to guarantee his or her own debts by the company, all without the shareholders being informed of these actions." While the 17–95 law requires such "contracts to be submitted to prior authorization by the board of directors; to be the subject of an auditor's report and to be approved by the next ordinary general meeting". Moreover, the law introduced key reforms to minority shareholders' and third parties' rights. While the previous law was silent on minority's rights, the new law grants to individuals or shareholders, holding 10 % of the capital, the right to convene an ordinary general assembly meeting. Third parties are protected against limitations to the director's capacities; the law applies what is known in common-law countries as "the indoor management rule".[14]

Moroccan law allows firms to be incorporated as joint stock companies, limited liability companies and partnerships. There are approximately 1,500 registered joint stock companies (of which 76 are publicly traded). The State is holding direct equity shares in 239 state-owned enterprises; of which 42 are converted in joint stock companies. Participations in subsidiaries of public holdings (CDG, OCP, BCP[15]) amount to 190 majority shares and 244 minority shares.[16] The 69–00 law on State Financial Control of Public Enterprises (2003) introduced a classification of state-owned enterprises into three categories: (i) "state companies in which public bodies hold all the equity; (ii) public subsidiaries of which public bodies hold more than half the equity; and (iii) semi-public companies of which public bodies hold more than half of the equity".[17]

[13] See Quinn (2009).

[14] See Quinn (2009).

[15] CDG : Caisse de Dépôt et de Gestion is a public financial institution entrusted with the mission of transforming long-term savings into long-term investments with 133 subsidiaries as of 2011.

OCP: Office Chérifien des Phosphates is a Moroccan global leader in phosphate extraction and BCP (Groupe banque populaire) is the second biggest lender by market value in Morocco.

[16] See Semmar (2012).

[17] See Semmar (2012).

Harmonization of legal framework with international standards is in line with broader governments' efforts to attract foreign investors, and ensure that Moroccan companies can live up to challenges, arising from free-trade agreements and international competition.

Against this background of institutional reforms to increase firms' efficiency and competitiveness, one must bear in mind that Small and Medium Enterprises (SMEs) and micro-enterprises are marking up the bulk of the Moroccan economy, and that ownership remains concentrated in most companies.

There are no regular official statistics on SMEs, but latest data compiled in 2009 by Inforisk, a private consultancy, found 57,754 SMEs with annual turnover below US$ 8 million; of which 96 % with an annual turnover below US$ 350,000.

Listed companies are in majority owned by families and by domestic institutional investors. The largest three shareholders hold controlling stakes of 75 % on average (World Bank 2010). As of 2012, investors holding more than 50 % of listed equity shares represented 66 %.[18] The free float of the Casablanca Stock exchange is between 15 % and 20 % of the total market capitalization.

The financial market authority: CDVM (conseil déontologique des valeurs mobilières) currently chaired by the Minister of Finance, is about to become a fully independent body, endowed with its own budget, under the law 53.08 adopted in 2011. The supervisory role of CDVM was enlarged in 2008 to include oversight of the Casablanca Stock Exchange, the central depositor and all securities market intermediaries, and to ensure enforcement of disclosure rules of information to the public, among other regulations.

The Central bank of Morocco (BAM, Bank Al Maghrib) is a key actor that operates independently to supervise the banking system, in compliance with 21 out of the 25 Basel Core Principles (World Bank 2010). The project bill amending the banking law 34–03, which was open to public consultation in October 2012, will make mandatory, the nomination of independent board members. The regulator has translated most of the Codes' recommendations into requirements on banks' governance that the legal framework doesn't provide for all companies; such as the establishment of a risk management and an independent internal audit functions; and the establishment of an audit committee and compliance function.

Finally, the new Constitution passed by referendum in 2011 as an important institutional reform, sets a new distribution of power between legislative and executive branches. The consecration of accountability, transparency, and the right to information principles won't be without an impact, over the long term, on the governance of Moroccan corporations. Recent moves of large non-listed companies to introduce independent directors; parliamentary hearings of top executives of state-owned companies; regular annual press conferences, held by non-listed large companies; corporate social responsibility's media campaigns: those are all

[18] Source: Calculations provided by CDVM for the IMA survey "Corporate governance practices of listed firms in Morocco" (April 2013)

N.B: CDVM was part of the scientific committee reviewing the survey.

telling (if yet anecdotal) evidence of a visible shift in Moroccan corporate culture, over the past decade. Companies are wary to respond to an increasing demand of accountability and transparency, and multiply outreach initiatives to their stakeholders.

These institutional and legal reforms have laid the ground for the issuance of corporate governance codes between 2008 and 2012.

2.3 *Corporate Governance as a Consultative Process*

The issuance of general and specialized codes of corporate governance was the result of a subtle balance of powers and bargaining. The General Confederation of Moroccan Enterprises (CGEM) took the lead since 2003 and established an Ethics and Governance Commission. The then president of the Commission R. Belkahia testifies to the difficulties the initiative encountered: "I remember when meetings were convened at CGEM; we always used to invite representatives of the Ministry of Finance who used to sit in the meeting room, with the overt objective of undermining our work!" A new team and a clear political agenda had finally helped to enlist the support of both the Ministry of Finance and the Ministry of General Affairs and Governance. The National Commission on corporate Governance was eventually created in 2007 by the CGEM and the Ministry of General Affairs, bringing together the Ministry of Finance, the Ministry of Justice, CDG, CDVM, the Casablanca Stock Exchange, the Morocco Central Bank, the professional association of accountants (OEC[19]); the association of young corporate leaders (CJD[20]), the national agency of SMEs (ANPME) and the professional association of Morocco banks (GPBM[21]).

The first code to be published in March 2008, has emerged as the result of a complex and successful bargaining process between public, private and civil society actors. The National Commission was supported by the OECD and the Global Corporate Governance Forum (a joint initiative between OECD and the International Finance Corporation, IFC). Two Specific codes on SMEs and family-owned enterprises; and on banks were respectively issued in the form of annexes to the first general Code, in 2009 and 2010. In March 2012, the Code of governance of state-owned enterprises was published. In June 2009, the Institute of Moroccan Directors was created in a public-private partnership, sponsored by 13 institutions and companies, of which CDG (institutional investor), the Ministry of General

[19] Ordre des experts comptables.

[20] Centre des jeunes dirigeants.

[21] Groupement professionel des banques du Maroc.

Table 1 Classification of 2008 Codes' recommendations on board of directors

Description	Definition	Morocco 2008 code
Separation of Chairman and CEO	Strong: separation between Chairman and CEO, in case of CEO duality appointment of a lead independent director or public disclosure of the reasons behind the choice Semi-strong: separation between Chairman's and CEO's roles Weak: not objective and quantitative rigid rules but only general recommendations about the relationship between Chairman and CEO	Semi-strong: the separation is recommended but firms are given the choice to motivate its implementation
Board composition and independence	Strong: the majority of board members should be independent non-executive directors Semi-strong: less than half, but at least one-third of board members should be independent non-executive directors Weak: less than one-third of board members should be non-executive directors and not all of them should be independent; not objective and quantitative rigid rules but only general recommendations	Weak: independence is not precisely defined: the code highlights the role of non-executive members in strengthening the independence and effectiveness of the board
Evaluating board performance strong	Strong: self-evaluation at least once a year Semi-strong: self-evaluation less than once a year Weak: not objective and quantitative rigid rules, but only general recommendations	Strong recommendations of self-evaluation at least once a year and independent evaluations every 3 years
Remuneration and nomination committee	Strong: all members should be independent non-executive directors Semi-strong: all members should be non-executive directors, and the majority of them should be independent; less than the majority of its members should be independent non-executive directors, and separation between the chairman of the committee and the chairman of the board Weak: not independence recommendations, not objective and quantitative rigid rules but only general recommendations (i.e. the board should establish a nomination/remuneration committee)	Weak: recommendation to establish the nomination and remuneration committee including at least, one non-executive member

(continued)

Table 1 (continued)

Description	Definition	Morocco 2008 code
Audit committee	Strong: at least the majority of members and the chairman should be independent non-executive directors Semi-strong: all members should be non-executive directors, and the majority of them should be independent Weak: less than the majority of its members should be independent non-executive directors, not objective and quantitative rigid rules but only general recommendations (i.e. the board should establish an audit committee)	Weak: recommendation of a majority of non-executive directors

Source: Zanotti and Cuomo (2008) and adaptation from the author

Affairs and Governance, the private holding SNI (*Société Nationale d'Investissement*) and CGEM.[22]

The 2008 Code in its scope and recommendations is inspired from the OECD principles of corporate governance. The code comprises four chapters on (1) responsibilities of the board; (2) shareholders' rights and their equitable treatment; (3) transparency and disclosure of financial information; and (4) the role of stakeholders and their equitable treatment.

The Code provides for flexibility; calling on the companies to adopt a "comply or explain" approach and encouraging them to explain their motives in the case of non-compliance, in their annual reports.

To what extent did the Code's recommendations influence practices of Moroccan firms so far? The Institute of Moroccan Directors just completed a report on "governance practices of listed companies in 2012" (Table 1).

3 Governance of Moroccan Listed Companies: Findings Form a Recent Survey

The Financial Market Authority (CDVM) has mandated IMA to conduct on a 3-year basis, an independent survey on governance practices of listed companies; the first one having being launched by CDVM in 2010.

[22] The 13 founding members of IMA are: Caisse de Dépôt et de Gestion, the Ministry of General Affairs and Governance, SNI, OCP, RAM, BMCE, BCP, Casablanca Stock Exchange, CGEM, GPBM, CJD, the Accountants' association: Ordre des Experts Comptables and the Moroccan Federation of commerce industry and services chambers.

The survey was conducted via an online questionnaire, between October and December 2012, and was supplemented with a workshop discussion with respondents in March 2013. Listed companies were asked to state their board practices, following the Moroccan Code recommendations.

Forty two (42) out of the 76 listed companies participated in this voluntary survey; representing 45 % of the Casablanca stock exchange capitalization. Total market capitalization as of 2011 amounted to US$ 60 billion. As of 2012, the average market capitalization of the respondents amounted to US$ 588 million and the median market capitalization amounted to US$ 82 million. In 2011, the average annual turnover of the respondents amounted to US$ 387 million; and the median amounted to US$ 88 million.

The survey provides for insightful information on how the Code's recommendations are implemented, and how governance mechanisms are understood. IMA was particularly cautious in not pinpointing as "good" or "bad", governance practices adopted by listed companies, but simply acknowledging the choices and explaining the core governance principles that must be respected, regardless of the shareholders' structure, the size or the business of the company.

There is a fundamental progress to highlight: 71 % of the respondents against 57 % in 2010 refer to the 2008 Code. Four years after its publication, the wide endorsement of the Code is encouraging, and testifies to the right inclusive approach that was adopted, prior to its publication.

That said, there are limits to the Code's achievements. We will briefly report in the next section, on some of the main governance practices, demonstrating that companies are implementing the code at their own pace, and rightly tailoring it to their needs. But there is still a lack of formalization of boardrooms' procedures and functioning.

3.1 Board Responsibilities and Governance Tools

Moroccan listed companies are legally bound to be organized under the joint-stock company law 17–95, which provides for a one-tiered or two-tiered board. 90 % of listed companies are one-tiered board and 41 % are separating the functions of chairman of the board and general manager. It is significant to notice that 50 % of the companies who choose to separate the executive and control functions are family-owned; of which 20 % are held by a majority foreign shareholder.[23] The Moroccan Code recommends a two-tier board and a separation between chairman and executive officer. However, evidence shows that (besides foreign-held companies), listed companies which choose to separate the functions, do it to ensure better succession planning or when the founder/the major shareholder doesn't have a strong expertise, and needs the support of an experienced manager.

[23] IMA calculations based on information of the Casablanca Stock Exchange : www.casablanca-bourse.com

In line with the Code's recommendations, 70–80 % of respondents rated at the highest rank, the role of the board in management oversight, in the five core areas, spelled out by the Code: strategy guiding, strategy monitoring; approval of the annual budget and program of activities; risks' monitoring and the control of the main investments and divestments decisions. However, answers provided by respondents across sectors vary: while the most capitalistic (mines, oil and gas; industry) and regulated companies (banking and insurance companies) stated that their boards were fully undertaking their roles in management's oversight; other sectors (real estate, transport, technology and electronic firms) were more reserved on certain areas, related to strategy guiding and monitoring, and risks' control.

If the boards' role and functioning are well-defined and properly carried out, there is a need to formalize its procedures and policies. A surprising majority of respondents stated for instance, that there were no formal procedures to check the mandates of sitting directors in other companies; while there are wary to manage conflicts of interest. No formal board evaluation is undertaken, while the Code recommends an annual self-evaluation and an independent evaluation every 3 years. Along the same lines, the Code encourages induction and ongoing professional training for board members. In practice, less than half of respondents declared to offer an "induction program", to the newly elected board members, and 90 % do not identify their training needs.

3.2 Committees

The Moroccan Code recommends the creation of two committees: an audit committee and nomination and remuneration committee. The survey shows an outstanding progress with 69 % of listed companies endowed with an audit committee and 53 % with a remuneration and nomination committee; compared respectively to 50 % and 28 % in 2010. The role and scope of the audit committee, with respect to internal audit functions, and with respect to the selection of external auditors must be further researched in a next survey. The Code doesn't provide much guidance on internal audit. While banks are strictly required to establish an independent internal audit function; discussions held with respondents from other sectors, clearly showed that the audit committee was not standing, as the referee of internal auditors, who often exclusively report to their executives. Conversely, the independence of the external auditor is efficiently guaranteed by the legal framework, which imposes its approval by the general assembly, upon the board proposition.

Unsurprisingly, we also found that the company capitalization' size is positively correlated with higher compliance with code recommendations. One should bear in mind that listed companies composed of three to five board members, might not see benefits in setting up formal audit or nomination and remuneration committees. Indeed, joint-stock companies' boards are legally required to have at least three and no more than 15 board members (if the firm is public): the average size among respondents is 7.

3.3 Board Independence

The survey shows a consistent composition of 89 % of non-executive directors, compared to 85 % in 2010. The Moroccan Code doesn't provide for a clear-cut definition of independence: it recommends that board be composed of non-executive or external directors who can "ensure board efficiency (...) and display an independent and objective judgment". Consistently, "the capacity to defend independent views" was ranked by respondents in second position, among the four skills required from an independent board member. The lack of material relationships (family ties) with the listed company" was not deemed as equally important (See Table 2). One explanation of this paradox might lie in the lack of regulatory and legal definition of independence and directors' duties. Given the concentration of ownership, most directors are non-executive, but not necessarily independent.

Among the respondents, 15 % reported no independent board member (see Table 3) and the median, set at five independent directors, was reported by 5 % of companies. The two listed companies which stand out with five (fully) independent directors on board are family-owned and entrepreneurs-owned companies. The founders proposed the nomination of independent directors, as part of their efforts to bring in fresh perspectives, in the face of a growing global competition, and to ensure proper succession planning. One of the two companies, which is successfully exporting abroad, recruited two independent directors, from Europe and North America to help it strengthen its remit in these markets.

This anecdotal evidence helps us draw some assumptions: the majority of directors deemed to be "independent" by listed companies are in reality non-executive board members appointed by institutional investors' shareholders; but economic rationales are likely to push listed companies to slowly integrate full independent board members, in order to prepare smooth succession and to strengthen firm's competitiveness, by exposing it to challenging views. It's worth noting that none of the listed companies disclosing information about their board members defines criteria of independence. The top three criteria prevailing over the selection of board members are according to the survey's respondents: experience, credentials and ethics (see Table 4).

Independent directors are often regarded as a key element of the governance system to control management behavior; it has its theoretical background in the dominant agency theory, with the assumption that the firm will perform better if principal-agent conflicts are kept under check. But in a country where ownership is heavy-handedly concentrated, the challenge would rather lie in what academics identified as a "principal-principal" conflict[24] in emerging markets; where conflicts arise between controlling and minority shareholders. Indeed, minority shareholders are poorly organized in Morocco, and if they started to make headway and voice their concerns in the media, against some dramatic falls in stock prices since 2011;

---

[24] See Young et al. (2008).

Table 2 Qualities of independent directors

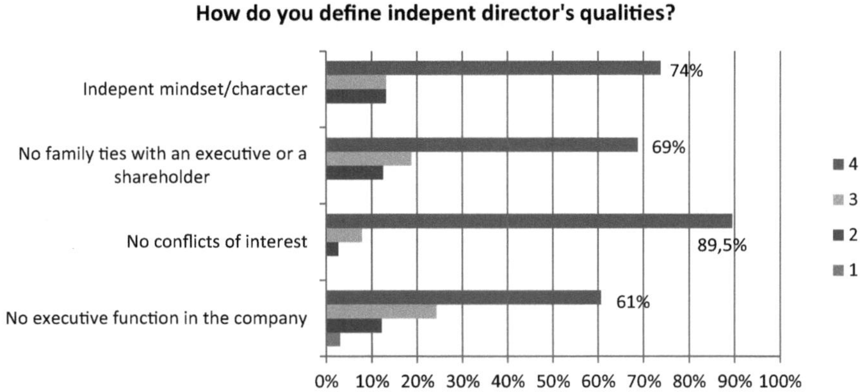

Source: IMA survey (2013) – *4*: the highest rank of satisfaction and *1*: the lowest rank of satisfaction

Table 3 Independent directors in listed companies

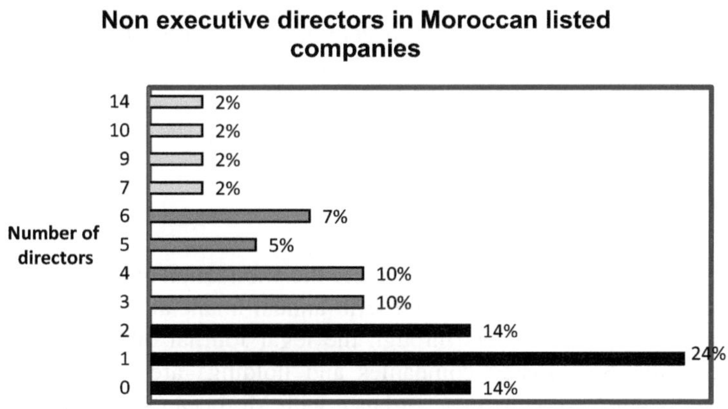

Source: IMA survey (2013)

there are not organized into powerful associations, like their western counterparts and are not actively participating in general assemblies.

Minority shareholders have better chances to be protected when the company is supervised by a regulator. With this respect, the nomination of banks' board members is closely monitored by the Moroccan Central Bank. More generally, compared to other sectors, in the survey, banks, insurance companies and financial institutions stand out as the "best in class" when reporting on their governance practices. For instance, the central bank reviews criteria and monitors banks' board members and senior executives. The amended project bill 34–03 on banking

Table 4 Prevalent criteria of board directors' selection

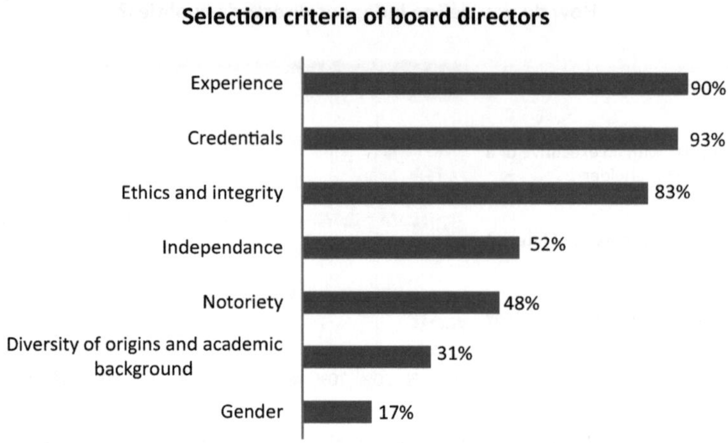

Source: IMA survey (2013)

institutions proposes to include in its article 33, a mandatory nomination of independent board members, in audit committees.

3.4 *Disclosure and Transparency*

The market regulator CDVM doesn't require the publication of an annual report but imposes the publication of annual and semi-annual financial statements which are made available to shareholders through the legal Journal of Finance and at the companies' premises. Listed companies and holdings are required to provide consolidated annual accounts in accordance with Moroccan Accounting Standards or International Financial Reporting Standards (IFRS).

Access of shareholders to financial information and regulated agreements were assessed to be effective and relevant. There is room for improvements in the disclosure of board directors and key executives' pay; non-financial information as well as control structures: -internal audit and risk management process- and ownership structures. In practice, ownership structures are publicly available but only direct ownership is disclosed. Few listed companies disclose information on the remuneration of their board members.

Listed companies fall short on a proper disclosure on corporate governance structures and policies; only 60 % deemed the access of shareholders to this information, to be efficient.

3.5 Shareholders' Rights

In general, the basic shareholders' rights are respected, in accordance with legal provisions and the Moroccan Code recommendations, related to vote and participation in general assemblies, the election and removal of directors; access to information; registration and transfer of shares. Minority shareholders are being more vocal in the media and holding managers accountable on shares' volatility as it was recently demonstrated by a heavy-handed media campaign against the chemical listed-company SNEP.[25] On the other hand, they are not formally organized in associations and don't have much weight in the nomination and election process of board members, even if they formally elect them. Majority shareholders still retain the power over this process.

* * *

Progress has been made, but the self-regulatory approach is facing some limits: listed companies tend to be more disciplined, when recommendations are translated into stringent legal requirements or when the market authority issues prescriptive requirements. This is probably due to the lack of strong external monitoring mechanisms of corporate governance practices, usually played by liquid capital markets and rating agencies, in more developed and market-oriented economies.

It would be also difficult to draw any conclusive results, on the way the code has influenced corporate governance practices and boards' behaviors in listed companies. But as the CDVM is set to improve in 2013, public disclosure requirements on corporate governance structures and policies of listed-companies; the Institute of Moroccan Directors should be able to monitor progress over time, by conducting more regular and in-depth surveys. That said, it ponders the question about the role of institute of directors, in advancing corporate governance practices.

4 Advocacy for a Pragmatic Approach to Enforce Governance Standards

It might seem too obvious to advocate for education to spread good governance practices, but it is a popular approach that is proving effective in many countries, where institutes of directors devise targeted training programs for board directors and financial market authorities require that board members undertake governance training. Training will not alone transform boardrooms, but it is an invaluable tool to help directors reflect on their own practices and to provide them with leadership skills.

[25] "SNEP: Les petits actionnaires menacent d'ester en justice", L'Economiste, June 5, 2012.

The Institute of Moroccan Directors (IMA) was created in June 2009, as the natural institutional outcome of the National Commission for Corporate Governance. The Commission enlisted the support of the Caisse de Dépôt et de Destion (CDG) to host IMA, incorporated under the 1958 Law on non-profit association. IMA is operating independently in its own premises since 2011, and CDG as a long-term institutional investor, continues to play a leading role in supporting the association's activities and human resources. CDG director general was reelected as IMA chairman in January 2013, and the 12 other founding members[26] were also reelected for a 3-year term.

IMA mission is to contribute to the professionalization of board directors through training and expertise. The Institute has already organized training governance workshops for 150 executives and board directors, over the past 3 years. In February 2013, it has launched its own certificate training program for board directors, in partnership with the International University of Rabat, the International Finance Corporation (IFC) and the Canadian Laval University-Collège des administrateurs de sociétés. The certificate is a pioneering initiative in Morocco. IMA has crafted an original curriculum, adapted to the Moroccan peculiarities of corporate law and governance systems. It is based on IFC and Laval University training methodologies that strongly rely on interactive learning and combine theoretical background with practical expertise, delivered by practitioners. Like its Canadian counterpart, the IMA-UIR certificate comprises five modules -spearheaded by academic and practitioner coordinators-, in the following areas: the role and responsibilities of the board; strategy and risk management; finance, audit and control; human resources, communication and values. In the fifth and final module, participants have the opportunity to role play in mock board and committees' meetings, to put their learning into practice. The certificate is issued upon the successful completion of a final written exam. The experience has yet to develop and position itself in the market to gain legitimacy and effectiveness, but the 34 executives and board directors, currently enrolled in the program might be an excellent market-trust test.

Education is an important component of IMA overall efforts to advance corporate governance; it has enlisted the support of key international partners such as Nestor Advisors, the governance consultancy, audit firms (Deloitte, PWC) and law firm (Clifford Chance), whose experts have already delivered training sessions in the certificate program. Memberships' development is critical to IMA's sustainability and is also meant to provide the market with a steady flow of certified and potentially independent directors. Network opportunities among peers' directors participating in IMA's activities (annual and quarterly conferences) are also a good avenue to encourage the dialogue between board directors, executives, regulatory bodies, audit firms. No matter how modest these initiatives are, there are genuine efforts to reflect on the practices and realities on the ground. It is critical to focus on the dynamics of the firms; to investigate their choices and their understanding of

[26] See note 19 above.

governance principles, in order to properly capture their priorities and difficulties, and help them make the right governance choices for their firms' sustainability.

IMA has also convened in April 2013, a national conference on "women on Moroccan boards", bringing for the first time to the public stage, the debate about women participation in corporate boards; where they are still poorly represented: 10 % at the national level; against 10 % in Moroccan listed companies and 5 % in state-owned enterprises.[27]

All Moroccan Codes are clearly promoting gender diversity. But as in many civil law countries, the codes fall short of strong enforcement mechanisms and there is a real risk that they remain symbolic. The survey initiative undertaken by IMA in partnership with CDVM, -of which we reported the results in this chapter- is an important step towards systematic monitoring of governance practices. Taking stock of progress is a first step to scale the ladder of high governance standards.

* * *

5 Conclusion

This chapter tempted to show how corporate governance is an iterative process. Morocco has embarked in a string of liberalization reforms and issued since 2008, four codes of corporate governance. However, there are limits to what a code and even hard law can achieve: regulatory coercion has already demonstrated its limits in more advanced and market-oriented economies. Even though listed companies appear to be more responsive to regulation than to recommendations; there should be emphasis on training efforts, and innovative venues should be explored to enforce the governance codes. The Moroccan Institute of Directors is taking important steps to engage the dialogue among board directors and encourage them to reflect on their practices, and to view public communication on governance, as an effective tool to strengthen investors' confidence in their companies. Reforming boards' practices does not only depend on institutions' reforms, but also on a continuing effort on the part of every actor, from the regulator to the banker and the family owner, to endorse basic governance and ethics principles.

[27] The study sponsored by UN-Women was carried out by a private consultancy, between November 2012 and January 2013 among 76 listed-companies, 37 commercial state-owned enterprises and 145 large companies. This study was commissioned by the IMA Working group on Women and Governance presided by the Ministry of General Affairs and Governance and gathering IMA, the Club of Women Directors, CGEM and individual men and women advocating for gender equality in the boardrooms.

References

Journal articles/working papers

Armour, J., Deakin, S., Sarkar, P., Siems, M. M., & Singh, A. (2008). *Shareholder protection and stock market development: An empirical test of the legal origins hypothesis*. CBR Working Paper ECGI – Law Working Paper No. 108/2008. University of Cambridge, Cambridge, UK.

Bebchuk, L., & Roe, M. J. (1999). *A theory of path dependence in corporate governance and ownership*. The Center for Law and Economics Studies, Columbia law school, New York, USA.

Coffee, J. C. (1999). The future as history: The prospects for global convergence in corporate governance and its significance. *Northwestern University Law Review, 93*(3), 641–708.

Gilson, R. J. (2000). *Globalizing corporate governance: Convergence of form or function*. Columbia Law School The Center for Law and Economic Studies, Working Paper No. 174; Stanford Law School, John M. Olin Program in Law and Economics, Working Paper No. 192.

Nestor, S., & Thompson, J. K. (2000). Corporate governance patterns in OECD economies: Is convergence under way? OECD. http://www.oecd.org/dataoecd/7/10/1931460.pdf

Quinn, S. (2009). *Moroccan company law reform and manufacturing firms' access to bank credit: A before/after panel evaluation*. University of Oxford, Oxford, UK.

Rajan, R., & Zingales, L. (1995). Insider ownership and the decision to go public. *Review of Economic Studies, 62*(3), 425–448.

Siems, M. M., & Alvarez-Macotela, O. (2013). *The OECD principles of corporate governance in emerging markets: A successful example of networked governance?* Paper for 8th annual Kyushu University Law Conference, 10–11 Feb 2013, Fukuoka, Japan.

Yoshikawa, T., & Rasheed, A. (2009). Convergence of corporate governance: Critical review and future directions. *Corporate Governance: An International Review, 17*(3), 388–404.

Young, M. N., Peng, M. W., Ahlstrom, D., Bruton, G. D., & Jiang, Y. (2008). Corporate governance in emerging economies: A review of the principal-principal perspective. *Journal of Management Studies, 45*(1), 196–220.

Zanotti, A., & Cuomo, F. (2008). Why adopt codes of good governance? A comparison of institutional and efficiency perspectives. *Corporate Governance, An International Review, 16*(1), 1–15.

Book

Moroccan codes of good corporate governance practices.. World Bank, Washington DC.

World Bank. (2010). *Corporate governance Morocco report on the observance of standards and codes*. World Bank, Washington DC.

Book chapter

Semmar, A. (2012). Corporate governance of state-owned enterprises in Morocco. In: *Towards new arrangements for state ownership in Middle East and North Africa*. OECD, Paris.

Guidance for Practical Corporate Governance: PhICS Model

Igor Belikov, Vladimir Verbitsky, and Ekaterina Nikitchanova

Abstract The international corporate governance best practices (CGBP) built up over the last decades present all-embracing set of recommendations covering all aspects of companies' corporate governance practices. Based on experience of publicly traded companies, CGBP recommendations are posed, in fact, as universal goal for all companies. Most of corporate governance rating, scoring and evaluation methods presume that the more CGBP recommendations are installed in a company the higher level of corporate governance practice it has. Lack of some components prescribed by CGBP recommendations or their more simple forms as compared with elaborated recommendations are considered as shortcomings to be corrected. In our view, PhICS model of corporate governance provides more effective and reasonable basis for improving corporate governance practices of most companies (primarily non-public). PhICS model is an evolving set of CGBP recommendations whose selection for a particular company is determined by key development factors whose specific combination usually stays relevant for this for the period of 3–5 years or even longer. These key development factors are: phase (stage) of corporate life cycle (Ph); predominant forms of investments (I) company primarily relies on; level of control the company's major owners want to have over the company, a leader style they exercise and their vision of company in their personal investment strategy (C); the company's strategy (S). Relevant model of corporate governance practice for a particular company (PhICS model) is a specific set of CGBP recommendations whose selection is determined by the above factors. Although PhICS model looks "imperfect" as compared to the "ideal corporate governance" model,

This article is based on years-long reflections of the authors as they studied how standards of corporate governance were being embedded in the Russian companies, and after they consulted with many large and midsized Russian companies about evaluation and synthesis of their corporate governance frameworks. It also relies on the authors' personal experience in the boards of Russian companies

I. Belikov (✉) • V. Verbitsky • E. Nikitchanova
Russian Institute of Directors (RID), Moscow, Russia
e-mail: belikov@rid.ru

S. Boubaker and D.K. Nguyen (eds.), *Corporate Governance in Emerging Markets*, CSR, Sustainability, Ethics & Governance, DOI 10.1007/978-3-642-44955-0_25,

in terms of the number of recommendations and degree of their elaboration, it provides more effective framework for successful and sustainable company development for a certain period of its; life cycle. Yet, it is important for each company's owners to timely readjust specific parameters of its PhICS model to significant changes in key development factors. It is only at a very advanced stage of its development and life cycle the company's corporate governance model may take on many or even most of CGBP recommendations.

1 Introduction

Multinational organizations, financial institutions, professional associations, rating agencies, consulting firms and think tanks have over the past two decades drafted a set of recommendations about what companies should do to mitigate their risks related to violations of shareholder rights and to business failures due to decisions that had been taken by their governance and control bodies without due preparation and prudence. A wealth of these recommendations has not translated into statutory regulations but companies are urged to adopt them. Collectively, these recommendations are known as *corporate governance best practices (CGBP)*.

Indeed, the first systemic step in this direction was a report of a commission chaired by Adrian Cadbury, *Financial Aspects of Corporate Governance* (1992) that set recommendations about arrangement of company boards to ensure reliability of corporate financial reporting. This document was followed by many others that contained general recommendations as well as special-focus advice on various components of corporate governance practices, such as the composition of the board of directors, its procedures, criteria for treating board members as independent directors and their role in the boardroom, composition of the board committees, their authority and procedures, composition of financial and nonfinancial information that companies should disclose, independence criteria for the company's external auditor and many other recommendations.[1] Overall, descriptions of the existing CGBP recommendations take up thousands of pages, and their volume is increasing. One can be sure to foresee that the ongoing discussions of lessons learnt from the global financial crisis that began in 2008 will result in new recommendations about governance practices in companies and particularly in banks and financial institutions (one example is a 2,400-page Dodd-Frank Law on financial reforms that was passed in the USA in 2010).

[1] See, for example, OECD Principles of Corporate Governance. 2005; Report of the High-level Group of Company Law-Experts on a Modern Regulatory Framework for Company Law in Europe, 2002; Report of the High-level Group of Company Law-Experts on Issued Related to Takeover Bids, 2002; Combined Code on Corporate Governance 2003; Review of the role and effectiveness of non-executive directors. Derek Higgs, January 2003; Combined Code Guidance: report and proposed guidance by an FCR-appointed group chaired by Sir Robert Smith, 2003; Modernizing Company Law and Enhancing Corporate Governance in the European Union: a Plan to Move Forward, 2003;

A review of recommendations that were offered since CGBP was first introduced highlights several important problems that are worthy of discussion, in our view.

The development of corporate governance best practices in a company is typically understood as a linear and continuously bottom-up process of introducing the largest possible number of CGBP components (such as bodies, policies and procedures). The more components are in place and the larger their scope, the higher is evaluation of a company's governance practices by experts of various entities (multilateral organizations, financial companies, rating agencies, etc.).

The absence of any given component in a company's governance practice is explicitly treated as a weakness – as is the existence of this component in a simpler form than what is advised by extensive and detailed recommendations that have been drafted by experts and are in place in large public companies with heavily dispersed ownership (these recommendations were the basis for building an "ideal model" of corporate governance). Thus, it turns out that an ideal company in terms of proper governance is a company which has all components of international best practices, and each of these components has been introduced to the highest possible extent. This is not an official standpoint but this conclusion would be logically suggested if we look at the general focus of OECD recommendations or carefully read analytical reports and studies, as well as rating agencies' reports about levels of corporate governance in companies. Indeed, the highest corporate governance rating means the highest consistency with the corporate model of a certain "ideal" company. This ideal model effectively applies to any company regardless of the stage of its development and specific features of its ownership. In our view, one example of such approach was Standard & Poor's Corporate Governance Scoring that had been assigned from late 1990s until late 2000s to companies from Russia and some other emerging markets. It used a scale where "1" was the lowest level and "10" was the highest or, in fact, corresponded to the "ideal model."[2]

All academic and practical publications on corporate governance practices in Russia, appeared since mid-1990s, have been entirely focused on such issues as importance of corporate governance, impact of corporate governance on companies' market capitalization/valuation and correlation between corporate governance and market capitalization/valuation, protection of minority investors rights and forms of violation of their rights, various aspects of corporate governance regulations under the Russian law and Russian best corporate governance recommendations (Code of Corporate Governance).[3] We have failed to find publications

---

[2] See: Standard and Poor's Corporate Governance Scores. Criteria, Methodology and Definitions. July 2002; Standard and Poor's Governance Services Launches New GAMMA Score. Press release, April 2008; Marathon takes crown in Energy Intelligence Governance survey. – International Oil Daily. January 15 2004; Jane Kim. Free web-link offers corporate-governance scores. – Wall Street Journal. May 10, 2005

[3] See, for instance: Andrei Vernikov. Does corporate governance really predict firms' market values in emerging markets? The case of Russian banks. – SSRN Working Papers Series, No

dedicated to analysis of how CGBP recommendations should be applied to Russian companies, which factors determine and succession, scope the pace of this process.

We believe that the most adequate approach to the development of corporate government practices would be their evolution within a PhICS model of corporate governance. This model is based on a combination of components of corporate governance best practices (CGBP) that are consistent with objective needs of a company's successful progress. These objective needs, in turn, are determined by key development factors which are phase (stage) of corporate life cycle (Ph); predominant forms of investments (I) company primarily relies on; level of control the company's major owners want to have over the company, a leader style they exercise and their vision of company in their personal investment strategy (C); the company's strategy (S). These factors usually last for medium term (3–5 years) or even for a longer term (from 5 to 12–15 years). Sustainable and successful development of every company requires its specifically tailored PhICS model of corporate governance. We believe that PhICS model have may relevance for improving corporate governance in other emerging markets.

2 "Ideal model" of Corporate Governance

We cannot say that conventional CGBP approach pays no attention at all to the quality of implementing these components. There is understanding that this factor is important. But the quantitative approach to a set of components that constitute the best practices, and to their content in companies, obviously prevails. For example, one key indication of this abstract ideal is a board of directors where the majority (preferably all) members are independent regardless of such factors as the structure of the company's equity, the role of major founding shareholders in the governance process, their plans with respect to their role, share of minority shareholders in the company, time span of their interest, etc.

It should be noted that several recent publications challenge this "ideal model" which has been construed on the basis of CGBR recommendations. Martin Lipton, a well-known governance expert and a managing partner in Wachtell, Lipton, Rosen & Katz, writes, "A board need not, and should not, simply accede to every list of corporate governance "best practices" promulgated each year by governance

2274282. July 2013; Wei-Xuan Li, Clara Chia Sheng-Chen, Joseph J. French. The relationship between liquidity, corporate governance and firm valuation; evidence from Russia. – Emerging Markets Review 13 (2012);. Corporate Governance in Russia: An Investor Perspective. The Institute of International Finance, 2004; Entrepreneurial Ethics and Corporate Governance in Russia: Interviews with Western Executives Working in Russia. Expert Publication. Moscow 2004; Pajuste A. Do Good Governance Provisions Shelter Investors from Contagion? Evidence from the Russian Crisis. – Beyond Transition. October/November/December 2004, vo. 15, No 1; Guriev S. Lazareva O. Rachinsky A. Tsukhlo S. Corporate Governance in Russian Industry. Moscow 2003; Black B. The Corporate Governance Behavior and Market Valuation of Russian Firms. – Emerging Markets Review, 2001, vol. 2.

activists and proxy advisory firms. That said, a board should proactively consider how best to organize itself and its committees to meet the increasing demands and responsibilities being placed on the board."[4]

The question whether – and to what extent – the "ideal model" of corporate governance which has been build over the past two decades is universal and applicable to all companies (even non-listed ones), and to what extent it ensures effectiveness and viability of companies, deserves a thorough discussion in itself. But in this article we do not want to analyze the "ideal model" or corporate governance as the target for the development of governance practices for all companies. Our focus is on the process of introducing CGBP recommendations. This process is long and its nature is evolutionary, which makes it very important for ensuring steady and successful development of companies.

In our view, regardless of the type of this "ideal model" which real companies should seek to achieve, the approach stating that the "ideal model" of corporate governance framework should be the ultimate goal for companies (without very close attention to the *process* of putting governance standards in place) does underestimate very important qualitative differences in fundamental characteristics of companies and their operational environment. An approach to the development of a company's governance practices which is based on a simple direct comparison with the "ideal model" precludes a correct assessment of the existing governance practices in real companies and their consistency with a company's specific features. Its recommendations inadequately reflect the companies' objectives, give inadequate targets for improvement of their actual governance practices and do not factor in the evolutionary nature of implementation of governance standards.

3 PhICS Model of Corporate Governance

In our view, it would be more appropriate to use an approach based on a "*PhICS model of corporate governance*" for evaluation and development of governance practices in companies and for drafting recommendations on how to improve these practices.

A PhICS model of corporate governance (M cg) is a set of components of international corporate governance best practices (CGBP). The scope of this set is sufficiently consistent with objective medium-term needs of successful development of a given company that are driven by the key development factors.[5] In our view, a company's key development factors (KDF) include:

[4] Martin Lipton. Some thoughts for board of directors in 2013. http://blogs.law.harvard.edu/corpgov/2012/12/31/some-thoughts-for-boards-of-directors-in-2013/

[5] We assume that all companies unconditionally comply with all corporate governance requirements that are described in applicable laws and regulations.

- The stage/phase of the company's development (life cycle) – **Ph** (phase);
- Forms of financing the company's development – **I** – (investments);
- The required level of control by its major owners and the company's role in their investment interests, as well as their management/leadership style – **C** (control);
- Development strategy – **S** (strategy).

With a certain degree of conventionality this functional dependence can be described by the following equation (we assume that this equation describes qualitative dependence):

$$_{\mathbf{cg}} = f(\mathbf{Ph}, \mathbf{I}, \mathbf{C}, \mathbf{S})$$

Let us now take a quick look on how these factors affect governance practices in a company.

*Stage/phase in a company's development **(Ph)**.* A generally accepted theory states that owners are at the same time top managers of a company just at earlier stages of its development. However, even in the developed economies there are many decades-old companies where the controlling shareholder is the top executive. This model is typical for most companies in the emerging markets – not only for private businesses but also for companies where some shares have domestic and global listings. This is particularly common for Russia. Every leading non-state Russian company (including those with domestic or global listings) de facto has the controlling shareholder or a small group of closely-related shareholders that effectively control the company. There is not a single Russian company where ownership is dispersed to such an extent that the controlling shareholder has disappeared, i.e. was "diluted." In November 2011, 57 % of 150 leading Russian companies had the controlling shareholder who is also the CEO, and in 43 % of companies he was chairman of the board with a high level of involvement in management.

A key recommendation of OECD is for the board (with a majority of seats held by independent directors) to exercise actual full-fledged oversight over the company's operations, particularly in such aspects as approval of strategy and evaluation of its outcomes. The board should also have a decisive impact on how internal control framework is built and operates. But in this environment these recommendations are scarcely feasible, to put it mildly. The controlling shareholders are heavily involved in management, and this encourages most of them to treat their boards as advisory, expertise-offering or negotiating bodies but not as overseeing bodies. No less important is the fact that nomination and election of most candidates to the board depend on the controlling shareholders in companies with high ownership concentration. The controlling shareholder can certainly nominate people who are not employed in the company or have business interests with it. But even in this case such board members clearly understand that their membership and reelection fully depend on the majority shareholder's position and his evaluation of their behavior in the boardroom. And, as facts show, in many or even most cases this becomes the decisive factor for the board members' behavior and their position toward problems in corporate development. Interestingly enough, there is high concentration of equity among minority shareholders, too. This is why their votes most often do not elect the "classical" independent directors who are equally distanced from all shareholders. They elect employees of an investment company who are tacitly required to represent interests of the company and those minority shareholders that had backed them with their votes. The work of these board members differs from "classical canons" and is very often controversial. On the one hand, in many cases they raised the timely alert when managers tried to strip assets and made deals that were obviously related-party transactions but were not officially recognized as such and exposed companies to possible damages. On the other hand, they are often interested in substantial improvement of the company's short-term performance that directly affects the value of their shares, so that holders of large minority stakes could sell them at a high profit. Meanwhile, pushing up for such short-term gains might be at variance with the company's long-term interests and strategy. The position of these directors poses an objective risk that they will use insider information in the interests of investment companies that they represent in the first place.

Recommendations to elect external board members who might prospectively have a strong influence on the process of taking strategic decisions and control will be objectively feasible only if and when major owners gradually disinvolve themselves from management. In this situation majority owners have an *objective* economic need to use some CGBP components while maintaining control over the company and its key managers as they themselves change the form of participation in the management process. A change of stage in the company's life cycle (its "prime" as Adizes put it) leads to a more complicated management framework including a corporate governance system. This is an objective basis for delegation of authority within the management hierarchy, building of the board as a body of real strategic governance and control, and for bringing in members who are expected to provide highly independent judgments/assessments and ready to defend them. Evolution toward more mature stages ("stability," "aristocracy" and "bureaucracy") would objectively require a more accomplished and complex system of corporate governance (including the necessary process and procedures of corporate governance as well as additional governance bodies, such as board committees, internal audit and risk management). Mismatch between the level of development and complexity of the corporate governance framework and the level of corporate maturity is in itself a major governance risk, says Adizes.[6]

Forms of financing the development of a company (investments) **(I)** make probably the strongest impact on its governance practices.

These forms might be arranged in the following order in terms of their impact:

- Self-financing by internally generated revenues;
- Project investment financing by banks;
- Private placements among private equity funds and other financial institutions;
- Financing via public debt (bonds);
- Financing via public equity (IPOs and subsequent share placements).

[6] Ichak K. Adizes. Corporate Life Cycles. Prentice Hall Press. 1990.

We would like to note that even when IPO is used as a form of financing (in this case a company must comply with the strongest requirements to governance practices) there are marked differences among listing rules that apply to governance practices, e.g., at LSE and NYSE, and among listing levels at one exchange (the main and alternative markets at LSE; "old" and "new" markets at São Paulo Stock Exchange; A1, A2, and B at MICEX). These differences might obviously be the basis for a company to develop its governance practices in a stage-by-stage way and match each stage with the requirements to these practices in the listing rules of a given exchange. While doing so, the company should measure costs and gains of entering the equity markets through a particular exchange and one or other of its listings.

Another factor that objectively makes a substantial impact on a company's needs in terms of its governance framework is the *required level of control over companies by their major owners (controlling shareholders), role of companies in their investment interests, and their management/leadership style* **(C).** This factor plays a particularly important role in companies with highly concentrated ownership; most Russian companies fall in this group, as do most companies on the emerging markets. Clearly, different plans of majority owners with respect to the level of control over a company, and differences in their leadership styles make a substantial impact on how governance frameworks are built in companies.

We can see at least two types of models that major shareholders use to control a company, a "hard" model and a "soft" one. The "hard" model means that a company is controlled by one owner or a small group of very closely related owners; the company is the major business, a "darling child" for all of them, and they believe it necessary to be actively involved in taking all important decisions. In terms of managerial/leadership style, this model is used by the controlling owners of charismatic (R. House) or entrepreneurial and production (I. Adizes) nature. The "soft" model means that a company is controlled by a group of owners that have a more or less equal standing and equal rights. The company is not the main business for all (or most) of them. It is administered by hired managers on the basis of a compromise between its main owners and through "involvement" of hired managers in corporate governance and award to them of a minority stake in the existing or planned business. In terms of the managerial/leadership style, this model is used by the controlling owners of transforming (J. Burns) or integrator (I. Adizes) nature.[7] Obviously, differences in these approaches to the model which is used for managing the company as a whole and in the views on the company's role in the business strategy of its owners are an objective basis for differences in how they build a corporate governance framework, stages of its development, and in how quickly the company will move from one stage to the next.

[7] see, Adizes I. Leading the leaders. Adizes 2004a; Adizes I. Management/mismanagement styles. Adizes 2004b; Burns J. Leadership. 1975.

Development strategy (S) is extremely important for understanding a company's basic needs in terms of its governance practices. Companies can always implement one of several strategic scenarios. Accordingly, there is a set of governance practices for each scenario – they give the best effect for development and differ from practices that correspond to other strategic scenarios. For example, the choice between selling a company and its further development as an autonomous entity (at least in the medium term) will be decisive for medium-sized companies in terms of their strategies. Clearly, the content and scope of work related to implementation of corporate governance practices in any given company will vary greatly, depending on which of these two strategic choices will be made by its major owners.

Sale of the company implies that it will be fairly quickly "equipped" in conformity with corporate governance standards that are tailored to a particular buyer in line with his preferences. Buyers (new owners) might vary greatly even due to their nature, i.e. whether the buyer is a strategic investor in the form of a public or private company, private equity fund, individual financial investor, etc.

Retention of control over the company by its existing owners will be the basis for a rather long and stage-by-stage evolution of corporate governance that would be owner-tailored.

A company's governance practices are influenced by such a strategic aspect as acquisition of businesses in the form of public companies in countries with different (usually better) practices of corporate governance. In our view, one reason why some Russian companies made unsuccessful attempts to buy such businesses in Europe was underestimation of the need to improve their own governance. One can expect that an analysis of these lessons will urge the controlling owners of large Russian companies that cherish the plans to expand into Europe or North America to raise governance standards in their own companies. There is a risk, however, that they will put in place some formal attributes. Key in this case is what strategy will be the basis for new acquisitions abroad: whether the Russian buyer will turn into a true public company with no controlling stake; be a "quasi-public company" (with a controlling shareholder and some free float); or choose the strategy of a private company.

In terms of governance practices in a company with a sole shareholder who is largely disinvolved in management, there is an objective need to put in place more elements of the governance framework that are recommended by CGBP. But the toolkit of these components will be limited, and they will be "non-classical" in terms of consistency with the CGBP requirements. In particular, the focus of such owner on the medium-term development of the company as an autonomous business requires looking for sound business ideas, competitive advantages and more sound managerial decisions. The owner might benefit from inviting a few external members to the board (but they may take a half the board seats, and certainly not all). Thanks to their competencies, experiences, expertise and clout these external members should be able to make a real tangible contribution to the development of the company in such aspects that are key for it (finance, marketing, strategic development, motivation, etc.). Furthermore, they should be motivated to defend their position (if their incentives are linked to the corporate performance). The more complicated and competitive a company's business is, the larger will be the objective gains from inviting such board members. We mean external board members, i.e. people who are not employed by the company, but not "independent members" that meet certain formal criteria of independence. In this situation the consistency with the independence criteria that are set in the global best practices does not make any sense. It is the ability to contribute to the development of the company that makes such members valuable for the company owner. The fact that they are dependent on the owner who can replace them at any time is of minor importance. The key factor in this case is their understanding of their value for the owner as a source of additional experience, view on the situation, and possibilities for corporate development. We believe it would be reasonable to invite professionals advising the company on its development strategy to sit on the board, so that they would implement this strategy "from inside" for a sufficiently long time.

Organization of the boardroom work which is based on the abovementioned changes in the key factors requires a more detailed and technical description of the board's authority. In particular, there is a need to outline issues that are the sole authority of the board. In the new conditions internal audit should report to the board instead of to CEO, and this is an objective need. At the same time the absence of board committees in such companies does not necessarily mean that governance practices are obviously weak. A small size of the board and a limited size of the company's business, as well as its relative simplicity, might make board committees unnecessary. CGBP recommendations about corporate information policy, information transparency and dividend policy look unreasonable for such companies. A high level of external information transparency does not give any advantages to mid-sized Russian businesses that focus on autonomous development in the medium term. Moreover, it is fraught with high risks. These risks are related to very poor legal protection of business in Russia and widespread raider takeovers. But there is also a risk of objective weakening of competitiveness if information is disclosed about intended new products, sources of inputs, parts and their prices, new orders, new customers, sales channels, unit costs, etc., which is typical for any markets. These risks should also be taken into account in evaluation of governance practices in such companies. What is important for the sole owner is not the formal independence of external auditor from the company but the auditor's qualification and understanding that his main customer is the owner who will decide how long the company will retain this auditor.

As the company moves to the sale stage, it should take certain relevant steps, e.g. make detailed financial and economic reports (not necessarily under IFRS in the Russian environment: good management reporting is far more important. Regular historical audits by an independent auditor are not particularly important either); conduct preliminary legal due diligence of the key managerial decisions that had been taken earlier (such as establishment of the company, issue of shares, changes among shareholders and executives); check whether the company legally owns its core assets, patents, trademarks, etc. The way of selling the business and the type of its buyer (strategic owner, private equity fund, or IPO) will certainly be

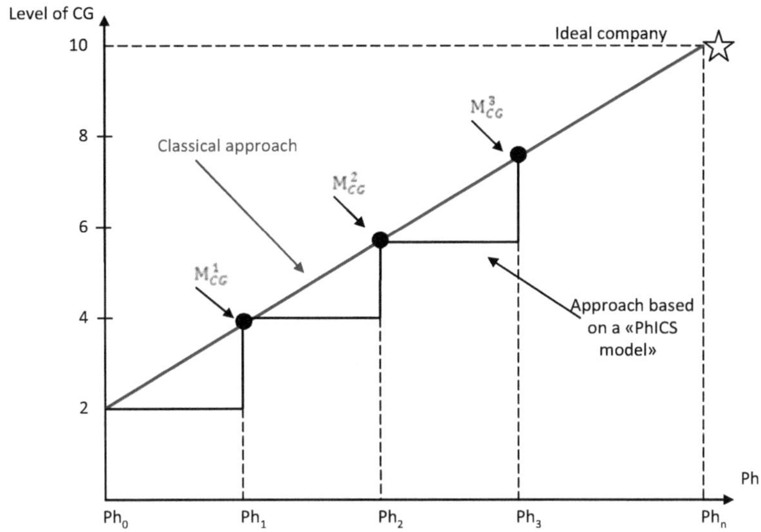

Fig. 1 The path of corporate governance development in companies

an important aspect of the further development of corporate governance in the company.

Thus, the path of an evolutionary progress of a company's governance practices in the process of shaping and furtherance of its PhICS model is not, in our view, a linear process where increasingly more features of an "ideal governance model" are put in place. It is a complicated path of moving within coordinates that are set by the factors described above. The focus of this movement is on the general effectiveness of a company's performance which is driven by the need to improve continuously. This process might be shown as follows in Fig. 1 (with a degree of conditionality).

In the above figure we showed the path of our proposed approach in the form of a step curve with inflection points (i.e. such points where the corporate governance model of a company changes fundamentally). M_{CG} are local PhICS models of a company's corporate governance that correspond to a certain set of the abovementioned variables of the key development factors.

We believe that a specific local PhICS model corresponds to each particular set of factors, and major changes in the set of CGBP recommendations are inappropriate from the economic standpoint within this model. Only a major change in one of the development factors can be an objective basis for substantial alterations in a company's governance practices, i.e. when a company effectively moves to a new local PhICS model. Therefore, we think it would not be constructive to criticize any given company for an "insufficiently high" current level of its corporate governance (for example, Level 4 corresponds to model M^1_{CG} on the rating scale) as compared to the highest possible level in the "ideal model" or to the governance level in another company (for example, a company with model M^3_{CG} that corresponds to Level 6). This would be the same as to criticize a Grade 3 pupil for not knowing

Fig. 2 PhICS model of corporate governance in a company

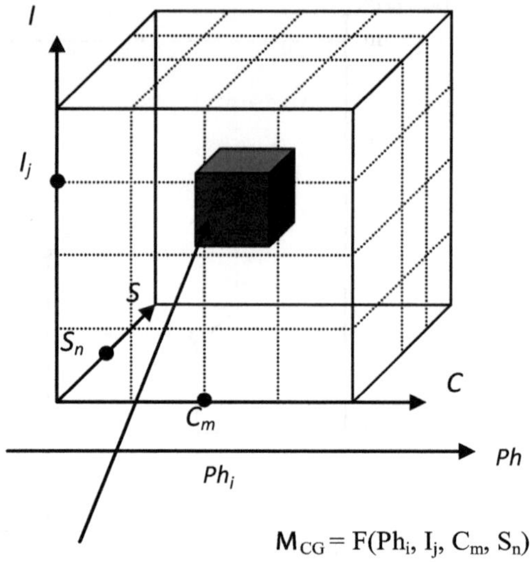

trigonometry (which he/she will study in Grade 9). Furthermore, we believe that a desire to achieve the absolute level of development for a company's corporate governance (grade "10" on the rating scale) would be contrary to the logic of development of companies that already have very definite sets of key development factors. This ambition will mean, at best, window-dressing for such companies. But this is exactly what often happens in companies globally, as was best demonstrated during the crisis of 2008.

In Fig. 2 we showed the full set of variants that are theoretically possible for local PhICS models of a company's corporate governance throughout its life cycle. We also showed the place of a particular local PhICS model with established variable values of its key development factors (**Ph_i, I_j, C_m, S_n**).

In theory, there are a certain number of possible local PhICS models of a company's corporate governance. This number is a product of the number of stages in a lifecycle of a company (i), number of forms of financing its development (j), number of levels of control/leadership styles (m) and the number of its possible development strategies (n). The actual PhICS model would be derived when we set the values of each variable factor of development (it is shown as a black cube in Fig. 2).

If the time axis of life-cycle stages is shown as a well-known Adizes curve, we will have a very nice and more illustrative picture, in our view (Fig. 3)

As a company moves along the curve, the cube sides will change along with changes in measurements of other development factors.

By way of summing up, we believe that the most adequate approach to the development of corporate government practices would be their evolution within a PhICS model of corporate governance. This model is based on a combination of components of corporate governance best practices (CGBP) that are consistent with objective needs of a company's successful progress. These objective needs, in turn,

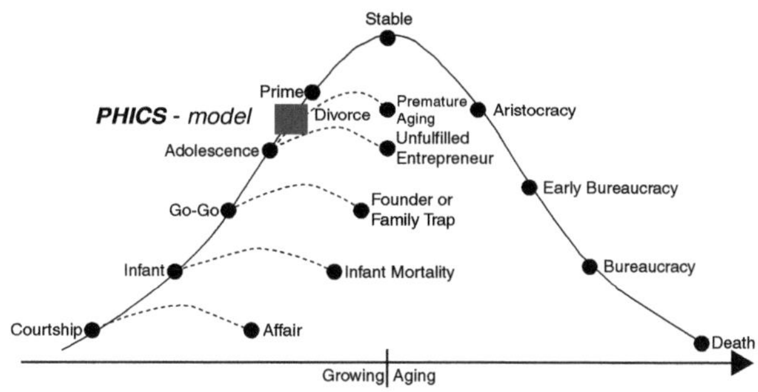

Fig. 3 PhICS model of corporate governance on the Adizes Curve

are determined by the key development factors for medium term (3–5 years) or for a longer term (from 5 to 12–15 years). Sustainable and successful development of every company requires its specifically tailored PhICS model of corporate governance. On the other hand, models of companies where development is based on similar key factors might be very much alike.

The design and evolution of a PhICS model requires a systemic and comprehensive approach from its key participants – owners and managers. Besides, they should regularly evaluate the efficiency of the selected combination of governance components in the company in terms of successful development of its current and future business (which is not a simple synonym of growth and/or higher market capitalization), and make necessary adjustments.

A PhICS model has an economic meaning: a pre-selected set of components of international CGBP should be used to implement shareholder rights and interests. Its other objectives are to help achieve the targets of better sustainability and successful development of the company (not only in terms of a successful IPO); match costs with the development goals; and avoid excessive costs and risks. The following comparison will be appropriate in this case. It is important for all companies to make good management reporting, improve quality and timely delivery of information which executives receive about its performance, analyze this information regularly and use it in decision-making. But not all companies, regardless of their size and specifics of operations, need to buy and implement the most complicated, expensive and newest models of ERP systems, Business Intelligence and other management technologies for meeting this target. Such management products might be an unaffordable financial burden for many midsized companies operating in narrow niches, and complicate their management process instead of simplifying it. A more effective practice for them would be to collect and process management information in simpler forms. The use of more sophisticated management technologies would be more appropriate for them as their business expands in scope and complexity. An approach to the development of a company's governance practices on the basis of building and advancing its PhICS model reflects a principle which has been repeatedly confirmed by the general management practice: a simpler system with higher efficiency of each component would work better than a more complicated system with lower efficiency of every link.

In our view, the use of a PhICS model toolkit reflects such needs and trends as comprehensiveness in taking key management decisions; focus on internal resources and sources of efficiency; and individualization of development strategies that ensure success and sustainability. The tighter the company's competitive environment, the more obvious is the need for this approach.

4 Conclusion

Implementation of the best corporate governance in the Russian environment is a part of implementation of modern management methods in general. We will give just one example to make our point. Studies show that if the quality of management improves by one score (on a five-score scale) this will drive labor productivity up by 65 % and is equivalent to an increase of capital by 65 %.[8] Labor productivity in Russia is 4–6 times below the level of developed economies and slightly less so as compared to the leading emerging markets.[9] This is why implementation of efficient management technologies becomes the key point for the Russian economy in general and for every company. Accordingly, the improvement of corporate governance should be focused not just on better protection of minority shareholders but on achievement of higher corporate performance. "Higher investment attractiveness" and "protection of investor rights" will lack their fundamental basis if corporate governance and strategic management at large do not improve significantly. They will become extremely narrow concepts and turn into a promise of formal legal and additional procedural protection just from embezzlement with respect to a company's assets.

We believe that the use of "PhICS model of corporate governance" offers some advantages as compared to the traditional approach which is based on an "ideal model" of corporate governance. Firstly, it will make the company's governance development efforts a more focused and effective work. Secondly, it will make evaluations of governance practices by experts more meaningful and link them better with the companies' objective development challenges. The analytical and instrumental value of comparing the companies in terms of their respective governance practices and comparing them with a universal ideal model does increasingly resemble efforts to compare technical characteristics of a horse and a tank. Thirdly, the use of this concept will give better benchmarks to regulators in terms of what sets of requirements should be offered to different companies as far as their levels of corporate governance.

---

[8] Vedomosti. 16.02.2010.

[9] McKinsey. Effective Russia. April 2009.

References

Adizes, I. (1990). *Corporate life cycles. How and why corporations grow and die and what to do about it.* Prentice Hall Press, 283 p.
Adizes, I. (2004a). *Leading the leaders.* The Adizes Institute Publishing, 311 p.
Adizes, I. (2004b). *Managemment/mismanagement styles. How to identify a style and what to do about it.* The Adizes Institute Publishing, 233 p.
Audit Committees Combined Code Guidance. (2003) A report and proposed guidance by an FRC-appointed group chaired by Sir Robert Smith. Submitted to the Financial Reporting Council in December 2002 and published in January 2003, 48 p.
Black, B. (2001). The corporate governance behavior and market valuation of Russian firms. *Emerging Markets Review, 2*, 89–108.
Burns, J. (1975). *Leadership.* Harper Torchbooks, 532 p.
Combined Code on Corporate Governance. (2003, July). 82 p.
Corporate Governance in Russia: An Investor Perspective. (2004). The Institute of International Finance, 26 p.
Entrepreneurial Ethics and Corporate Governance in Russia: Interviews with Western Executives Working in Russia. (2004). Moscow: Expert Publication, 27 p.
Guriev, S., Lazareva, O., Rachinsky, A., Tsukhlo, S. (2003). *Corporate governance in Russian industry.* Moscow, 57 p.
Jane, K. (2005). Free web-link offers corporate-governance scores. *Wall Street Journal.* 10 May 2005.
Marathon takes crown in Energy Intelligence Governance survey. *International oil daily.* 15 Jan 2004.
Martin, L. *Some thoughts for board of directors in 2013.* http://blogs.law.harvard.edu/corpgov/2012/12/31/some-thoughts-for-boards-of-directors-in-2013. 10 Apr 2013.
McKinsey. (2009, April). *Effective Russia.* 11 p.
Modernizing Company Law and Enhancing Corporate Governance in the European Union: a Plan to Move Forward. Brussels, 21 May 2003, 29 p.
OECD Principles of Corporate Governance. (2005). 40 p.
Pajuste, A. (2004, October/November/December). Do good governance provisions shelter investors from contagion? Evidence from the Russian crisis. *Beyond transition, 15*(1), 10–11.
Report of the High-level Group of Company Law-Experts on a Modern Regulatory Framework for Company Law in Europe. Brussels, 4 Nov 2002, 161 p.
Report of the High-level Group of Company Law-Experts on Issued Related to Takeover Bids. Brussels, 10 Jan 2002, 96 p.
Review of the role and effectiveness of non-executive directors. Derek Higgs, Jan 2003, 120 p.
Standard & Poor's Corporate Governance Scores. Criteria, Methodology and Definitions. July 2002, 16 p.
Standard & Poor's Governance Services Launches New GAMMA Score. Press release, Apr 2008, 10 p.
Wei-Xuan, L., Clara Chia, S.-C., & French, J. J. (2012). The relationship between liquidity, corporate governance and firm valuation; Evidence from Russia. *Emergin Markets Review, 13*, 465–477.

Index

S. Boubaker and D.K. Nguyen (eds.), *Corporate Governance in Emerging Markets*, CSR, Sustainability, Ethics & Governance, DOI 10.1007/978-3-642-44955-0,

MIX
Papier aus verantwortungsvollen Quellen
Paper from responsible sources
FSC® C105338

If you have any concerns about our products,
you can contact us on
ProductSafety@springernature.com

In case Publisher is established outside the EU,
the EU authorized representative is:
Springer Nature Customer Service Center GmbH
Europaplatz 3, 69115 Heidelberg, Germany

Printed by Libri Plureos GmbH
in Hamburg, Germany